DEFINING DOCUMENTS
IN AMERICAN HISTORY

Exploration &
Colonial America

(1492-1755)

DEFINING DOCUMENTS
IN AMERICAN HISTORY

Exploration &
Colonial America
(1492-1755)

Volume 2

Editor
Daisy Martin, Ph.D.
Teachinghistory.org

SALEM PRESS
A Division of EBSCO Publishing

Ipswich, Massachusetts

Library of Congress Cataloging-in-Publication Data

Exploration and colonial America (1492-1755) / editor, Daisy Martin, Ph.D.
    volumes cm. -- (Defining documents in American history)
  Includes bibliographical references and index.
  ISBN 978-1-4298-3701-9 (set 1) -- ISBN 978-1-4298-3702-6 (volume 1) -- ISBN 978-1-4298-3703-3 (volume 2)
1. United States--History--Colonial period, ca. 1600-1775--Sources. 2. America--Discovery and exploration--Sources. I. Martin, Daisy, 1962-
  E187.E96 2013
  973.2--dc23

                                                                                    2012042520

Contents

VOLUME 2

DOCUMENTS ILLUSTRATIVE OF SLAVERY AND INDENTURED SERVITUDE   635

APPENDIXES   725

Complete List of Contents

VOLUME 1

JOURNALS ON EXPLORATION   1

REPORTS ON NEW WORLD SETTLEMENT   97

EARLY POLITICAL TRACTS ON SELF-GOVERNING   **223**

VOLUME 2

SERMONS AND NARRATIVES ON RELIGIOUS LIFE   445

NARRATIVES ON COLONIAL LIFE   559

DEFINING DOCUMENTS
IN AMERICAN HISTORY

Exploration &
Colonial America
(1492-1755)

SERMONS AND NARRATIVES ON RELIGIOUS LIFE

Religion played a key role in the settling and founding of America, and the Christian ideals that animated the first settlers—though diverse within the confines of Protestant Christianity—strongly influenced the political and social development of the new nation. For English colonists in particular, religion was at least as important a motivating factor as economic concerns in the colonization effort; they came to the New World in pursuit of the promise of religious liberty, although that meant different things to different groups of colonists.

The English Puritans who settled New England did so to escape the confines of an Anglican Church that they felt had not made a sufficiently clean break from the Catholic Church in the English Reformation of the preceding century. They sought religious liberty for themselves, so that they could create "a city on a hill," in the words of Massachusetts Bay leader John Winthrop—a society that strictly adhered to Christian values as they understood them. And although in one sense they sought, ironically, the freedom to create a more restrictive society, that society was also organized along remarkably democratic lines, with church members electing their leaders and approving their own governing documents.

At perhaps the opposite end of the spectrum from the Puritans were the Quakers, reviled by Anglicans and Puritans alike as true radicals who threatened the very foundations of social order with their pacifism, rejection of a formal clergy, and belief in the equality of women. Severely persecuted in Massachusetts, Quakers found havens in Rhode Island and especially Pennsylvania, established by Quaker leader William Penn, who established specific guarantees of freedom of religion in the colony, articulating ideas that would be key in crafting the government of the future United States of America.

Though greatly at odds in their beliefs, both Quakers and Puritans came to America to escape persecution in England and build a new society more in line with their respective beliefs. All the people who came to America from the British Isles owed their allegiance to the English Crown, but with an ocean between them and the mother country, the colonists had great latitude to forge new directions; and, again despite their differences, all the European American colonists tended to move in the direction of a less hierarchical, more egalitarian and individualistic society. As the seventeenth century melted into the eighteenth, the religious revival of the 1730s known as the Great Awakening confirmed these trends, with its emphasis on a direct relationship between the believer and God, unmediated by a church hierarchy whose analog in the secular realm was the monarchy.

Adam Groff, MA

■ To His Loving Friends, the Adventurers for New-England

Date: December 12, 1621
Author: Cushman, Robert
Genre: letter; address; sermon

*"And you my loving friends the adventurers to
this plantation; as your care has been, first to settle
religion here, before either profit or popularity,
so I pray you, go on, to do it more . . ."*

Summary Overview

In November of 1621, one year after the arrival of the *Mayflower*, Robert Cushman arrived in Plymouth aboard the *Fortune*. A member of the same Puritan congregation to which the first settlers belonged, Cushman had personally negotiated with financial supporters in London toward the establishment of the new colony. Devoted to his faith, he saw America as the solution to the persecution Puritans suffered at home, and he believed God had sent the colonists on a mission to propagate their reformed version of Christianity. As the colony's agent in London, Cushman stayed in Plymouth only a few weeks before returning to report on its progress and secure ongoing financial support. Because tensions between the colonists and their distant investors then ran high, Cushman was caught in a difficult position. Just before he set sail for England, he addressed the colonists in an effort to unite the two sides around their common goals. Published anonymously in London the following year, Cushman's "sermon" included an epistle dedicatory—a dedication to the investors.

Defining Moment

When Puritan Separatists boarded the *Mayflower* in 1620 to begin their pilgrimage, departure for America was the latest step in a spiritual and political journey they had begun more than a decade earlier. In the wake of the Protestant Reformation of the sixteenth century, English monarchs had split with Roman Christianity.

Yet for some who embraced this schism, the English church did not go far enough in the purging of Roman traditions and organizational structure. They demanded a purer form of Christianity, and by the early seventeenth century Puritan congregations were challenging the authority of the English church. Persecuted for their nonconformity, some chose to remove themselves from England. Quick passage across the North Sea was quietly arranged, and migration to Holland began. Many who eventually settled at Plymouth had earlier formed a Separatist congregation at Leiden, Holland. There, the Separatists were able to freely practice their religion, but they struggled to retain their English identity within Dutch culture.

Once England began to settle colonists at Jamestown, new possibilities for repatriation of Separatists emerged. Framing a move to America as divine providence, the Leiden congregants embraced a new mission: establishing their purer form of Christianity in the New World. Though the Dutch government offered them assistance toward settling at New Netherlands (New York) and Guyana (South America), the Leiden faithful preferred to return to English dominion.

Religious intent aside, the establishment of Plymouth was also a financial venture. The pilgrimage of the Leiden congregants was only possible through the support of a group of London investors. The Merchant Adventurers of London, as the stock company was called, was headed by wealthy Puritans, but they were joined by many others who prioritized profit over religious propagation. Investors paid transport and start-up costs for the colonists. In exchange, they expected to receive regular shipments of goods, such as furs, fish, and lumber. Negotiations of the contract between Pilgrims and investors were guided by Robert Cushman and John Carver, deacons of the Leiden church. Though an initial agreement was ratified by both sides, changes demanded by the investors just prior to sailing meant that the Pilgrims embarked under a contested contract.

One year later, still negotiating with the Merchant Adventurers, Cushman arrived in Plymouth aboard the *Fortune*. In order to ensure continuing support from the investors, he had to convince the settlers to sign the new contract. Cushman's address to the colonists at Plymouth, often called his sermon, was an effort to remind the colonists of their obligation to God, their investors, and each other.

Author Biography

Born circa 1578 in Kent, England, Robert Cushman immigrated to Leiden, Holland, in 1608, accompanied by his wife, Sara Reder, and his infant son Thomas. Cushman made his living as a wool comber and devoted himself to his faith, eventually becoming a deacon of the Puritan Separatists in Leiden. Cushman remarried in 1617, after his first wife's death. His second wife, Mary Clark Shingleton, died sometime before Cushman's voyage to America as well. Only Thomas Cushman survived to join his father on the trans-Atlantic crossing of the *Fortune* in 1621. The fourteen-year-old stayed in Plymouth when his father returned to London to report to the Merchant Adventurers. Until his death in England in 1625, Robert Cushman continued to serve as the London agent and advocate for the colonists at Plymouth.

While later Puritan settlers would mostly draw support from the middle classes, the Leiden Pilgrims had more limited means. With a costly voyage and settlement before them, they appointed Cushman and fellow Leiden deacon John Carver to negotiate for them with London investors. Traveling twice to London, they sought financial support, transportation, and supplies. Negotiations were difficult. Irritated by Puritan resistance to his authority as head of the English church, King James rejected their initial arrangements with the Virginia Company, the investment group that had established Jamestown. A second plan with the Merchant Adventurers proved more successful after these wealthy Puritans and other opportunity-seeking investors advocated for the Separatists before the Crown.

Cushman was to sail on the *Speedwell* with his fellow Separatists in 1620, which was originally to travel with the *Mayflower* to the New World. The *Speedwell*, however, was found to be leaking and could not sail. Some of its passengers elected to remain behind, while the rest boarded the *Mayflower*. Cushman, dealing with last-minute contract changes by the investors, was one of the Separatists who remained in England. Since key points of the contract were unresolved, he deferred his plans to emigrate and worked to balance the goals of the Pilgrims and their investors. With little experience as a business negotiator, Cushman placed his faith in God and in the Puritan leaders who were prominent among the investors. Unfortunately, balancing competing interests earned him the resentment of many.

Published in London in 1622, Cushman's address to the colonists was repurposed to encourage continuing support for the still fragile colony. Targeted at a wider audience than when it was originally delivered, the printed sermon articulates a defining moment in the life of the Plymouth Colony and appeals for support. The address's epistle dedicatory, included below, lauds the investors and encourages their continued support for the venture.

HISTORICAL DOCUMENT

New-England, so called, not only (to avoid novelties) because Captain *Smith* hath so entitled it in his Description, but because of the resemblance that is in it, of *England* the native soil of Englishmen; it being much what the same for heat and cold in Summer and Winter, it being champaign ground, but no high mountains, somewhat like the soil in *Kent* and *Essex*; full of dales, and meadow ground, full of rivers and sweet springs, as *England* is. But principally, so far as we can yet find, it is an island, and near about the quantity of *England*, being cut out from the main land in *America*, as *England* is from the main of *Europe*, by a great arm of the sea, which entereth in forty degrees, and runneth up North West and by West, and goeth out either into the South-Sea, or else into the Bay of *Canada*. The certainty whereof, and secrets of which, we have not yet so found as that as eye-witnesses we can make narration thereof, but if God give time and means, we shall, ere long, discover both the extent of that river, together with the secrets thereof; and so try what territories, habitations, or commodities, may be found, either in it, or about it.

It pertaineth not to my purpose to speak any thing either in praise, or dispraise of the country; so it is by God's Providence, that a few of us are there planted to our content, and have with great charge and difficulty attained quiet and competent dwellings there. And thus much I will say for the satisfaction of such as have any thought of going hither to inhabit? That for men which have a large heart, and look after great riches, ease, pleasures, dainties, and jollity in this world (except they will live by other men's sweat, or have great riches) I would not advise them to come there, for as yet the country will afford no such matters: But if there be any who are content to lay out their estates, spend their time, labors, and endeavors, for the benefit of them that shall come after, and in desire to further the gospel among those poor heathens, quietly contenting themselves with such hardship and difficulties, as by God's Providence shall fall upon them, being yet young, and in their strength, such men I would advise and encourage to go, for their ends cannot fail them.

And if it should please God to punish his people in the Christian countries of *Europe*, (for their coldness, carnality, wanton abuse of the Gospel, contention, &c.) either by Turkish slavery, or by popish tyranny which God forbid, yet if the time be come, or shall come (as who knoweth) when Satan shall be let loose to cast out his floods against them, (*Rev.* 12. 14. 15.) here is a way opened for such as have wings to fly into this wilderness; and as by the dispersion of the Jewish church through persecution, the Lord brought in the fulness of the Gentiles, (*Act.* 11. 20, 21.) so who knoweth, whether now by tyranny and affliction, he suffereth to come upon them, he will not by little and little chase them even amongst the heathens, that so a light may rise up in the dark, (*Luke* 2. 32.) and the kingdom of Heaven be taken from them which now have it, and given to a people that shall bring forth the fruit of it. (*Mat.* 21. 43.) This I leave to the judgment of the godly wise, being neither prophet nor son of a prophet, (*Amos* 7. 14.) but considering God's dealing of old, (2 *Kings* 17, 23.) and seeing the name of Christian to be very great, but the true nature thereof almost quite lost in all degrees and sects, I cannot think but that there is some judgment not far off, and that God will shortly, even of stones, raise up children unto *Abraham*. (*Mat.* 3. 5.)

And who so rightly considereth what manner of entrance, abiding, and proceedings, we have had among these poor heathens since we came hither, will easily think, that God has some great work to do towards them.

They were wont to be the most cruel and treacherous people in all these parts, even like lions, but to us they have been like lambs, so kind, so submissive, and trusty, as a man may truly say, many christians are not so kind, nor sincere.

They were very much wasted of late, by reason of a great mortality that fell amongst them three years since, which together with their own civil dissentions and bloody wars, hath so wasted them, as I think the twentieth person is scarce left alive, and those that are left, have their courage much abated, and their countenance is dejected, and they seem as a people affrighted. And though when we came first into the Country, we were few, and many of us were sick, and many died by reason of the cold and wet, it being the depth of winter, and we having no houses, nor shelter, yet when there was not six able persons among us, and that they came daily to us by hundreds, with their *sachems* or *kings*, and might in one hour have made a dispatch of us, yet such a fear was upon them, as that they never offered us the least injury in word or deed. And by reason of one *Tisguanto*, that lives amongst us, that can speak English, we have daily commerce with their kings, and can know what is done or intended towards us among the savages; also we can acquaint them with our courses and purposes, both human and religious. And the greatest commander of the country, called *Massasoit*, cometh often to visit us, tho' he lives 50 Miles from us, often sends us presents, he having with many other of their governors, promised, yea, subscribed obedience to our sovereign Lord King James, and for his cause to spend both strength and life. And we for our parts, through God's grace, have with that equity, justice, and compassion, carried ourselves towards them, as that they have received much favor, help, and aid from us, but never the least injury or wrong by us. We found the place where we live empty, the people being all dead and gone away, and none living near by 8 or 10 miles; and though in the time of some hardship we found (travelling abroad) near 8 bushels of corn hid up in a cave, and knew no owners of it, yet afterwards hearing of the owners of it, we gave them (in their estimation) double the value of it. Our care hath been to maintain peace amongst them, and have always set ourselves against such of them as used any rebellion, or treachery against their governors, and not only threatened such, but in some sort paid them their due deserts; and when any of them are in want, as often they are in the winter, when their corn is done, we supply them to our power, and have them in our houses eating and drinking, and warming themselves, which thing (though it be something a trouble to us) yet because they should see and take knowledge of our labors, order and diligence, both for this life and a better, we are content to bear it, and we find in many of them, especially, of the younger sort, such a tractable disposition, both to religion and humanity, as that if we had means to apparel them, and wholly to retain them with us (as their desire is) they would doubtless in time prove serviceable to God and man, and if ever God send us means we will bring up hundreds of their children, both to labor and learning.

But leaving to speak of them till a further occasion be offered; if any shall marvel at the publishing of this trea-

tise in *England*, seeing there is no want of good books, but rather want of men to use good books, let them know, that the especial end is, that we may keep those motives in memory for ourselves, and those that shall come after, to be a remedy against self love the bane of all societies. And that we also might testify to our Christian countrymen, who judge diversly of us, that though we be in a heathen country, yet the grace of Christ is not quenched in us, but we still hold and teach the same points of faith, mortification, and sanctification, which we have heard and learned, in a most ample and large manner in our own country. If any shall think it too rude and unlearned for this curious age, let them know, that to paint out the Gospel in plain and flat English, amongst a company of plain Englishmen (as we are) is the best and most profitablest teaching; and we will study plainness, not curiosity, neither in things human, nor heavenly. If any error or unsoundness be in it, (as who knoweth) impute it to that frail man which endited it, which professeth to know nothing as he ought to know it. I have not set down my name, partly because I seek no name, and principally, because I would have nothing esteemed by names, for I see a number of evils to arise through names, when the persons are either famous, or infamous, and God and man is often injured; if any good or profit arise to thee in the receiving of it, give God the praise and esteem me as a son of *Adam*, subject to all such frailties as other men are.

And you my loving friends the adventurers to this plantation; as your care has been, first to settle religion here, before either profit or popularity, so I pray you, go on, to do it much more, and be careful to send godly men, though they want some of that worldly policy which this world hath in her own generation, and so though you lose, the Lord shall gain. I rejoice greatly in your free and ready minds to your powers, yea, and beyond your powers to further this work, that you thus honor God with your riches, and I trust you shall be repayed again double and treble in this world, yea, and the memory of this action shall never die, but above all adding unto this (as I trust you do) like freeness in all other God's services both at home and abroad, you shall find reward with God, ten thousand-fold surpassing all that you can do or think; be not therefore discouraged, for no labor is lost, nor money spent which is bestowed for God, your ends were good, your success is good, and your profit is coming, even in this life, and in the life to come much more: and what shall I say now, a word to men of understanding sufficeth, pardon I pray you my boldness, read over the ensuing treatise, and judge wisely of the poor weakling, and the

Lord, the God of land and sea, stretch out his arm of protection over you and us, and over all our lawful and good enterprizes, either this, or any other way.

Plymouth in New-England, December 12, 1621.

GLOSSARY

adventurer: one who takes risk through financial investment

champaign ground: broad and open plains

dainties: delicate and beautiful objects

God's Providence: divine guidance and plan for humankind

heathen: one who does not acknowledge the Christian God

jollity: merriment

popish tyranny: Puritan term for the absolute rule of the Roman Catholic pope over his church

Tisguanto: a Wampanoag who lived among the Plymouth colonists as a cultural intermediary, also known as "Tisquantum" or "Squanto"

treble: triple or three-fold

Document Analysis

The printed version of Robert Cushman's 1621 address to the settlers at Plymouth included this introductory letter dedicating the publication to the London-based financiers of the colony, the Merchant Adventurers. Placing the address in context for the reader, the epistle demonstrates the ongoing challenges Cushman faced as an agent of and negotiator for the Plymouth Pilgrims. The letter reveals Cushman's struggle to balance the competing religious and secular interests that threatened relations between the settlers in Plymouth and the investors in London.

As Puritan Separatists began to plan their transatlantic migration from Leiden, they framed their journey in religious term as "God's Providence." As they saw it, their "removal" from Holland and war-stricken Europe would fulfill a divine plan to establish a foothold for Puritanism within English dominion. Yet, this religious endeavor required financial resources that were beyond the congregants' means, and they had to look for finan-

cial backers in the secular world. Leading negotiations with potential investors, Cushman had initial success in balancing spiritual and secular agendas. His efforts proved crucial to the sailing of the *Mayflower* and the establishment of Plymouth. In the years that followed 1620, however, Cushman's balancing act became more difficult to sustain. Forced by circumstances to expand his role as the London agent for the fragile colony, he struggled to unify the religious and secular agendas that drove the colonizing project.

Contract between the Pilgrims and Merchant Adventurers

Cushman was not a minister, and his December 1621 "sermon" at Plymouth was actually an address aimed at easing tensions between the colonists and their investors. At the center of these tensions was the unsigned contract between the two groups. After a few false starts, the basic agreement with the Merchant Adventurers proved acceptable to the Separatists, and more than one-third of the congregation prepared for pilgrimage. Others, including their minister John Robinson, pledged to follow once the colony was established. As the first cohort disposed of their property and prepared for departure, they faced many anxieties about life in an unknown land. Simultaneously, other uncertainties struck the investors. While Puritanism was well represented among the Merchant Adventurers and they therefore had personal interest in supporting a religious mission, most investors aimed to make a profit. As the departure of the Pilgrims neared, the Adventurers made contract revisions that shifted risk toward the colonists and decreased their own financial gamble.

Faced with last minute changes to the contract, Cushman felt compelled to accept the new terms. The contract was not ideal, but to reject it would have meant finding new investors, and delaying departure for new negotiations could take years. Supplies had been purchased and were ready at docks, and would-be Pilgrims, who were now homeless and jobless, were ready for departure. Under such circumstances, Cushman offered preliminary acceptance of the new arrangement. At departure, however, his fellow Pilgrims refused to sign the contract. Committed to facilitating divine providence and setting humble congregants to sail, Cushman was forced to defend the secular world of financial investment, which he had only entered on behalf of his congregation. As a result of his decision, the deacon became resented by people on both sides of the Atlantic.

That the terms of the new contract favored the investors added to the building anxiety of the Pilgrims. As a result, dampening enthusiasm decreased the participation rate of the Leiden group. Interested in sending the largest contingent possible, the Merchant Adventurers arranged for dozens of non-Puritans to fill available berths on the ships. Separatists deemed these new voyagers as "Strangers." The number of Leiden Separatists making the journey was further lowered by a leaky ship. When the *Speedwell*, which was to accompany the *Mayflower*, was forced to return to port, many of its anxious passengers opted to return to Leiden.

Importantly, in addition to being Pilgrims and "Strangers," those who soon formed Plymouth Colony were also stockholders and employees of the Merchant Adventurers. Required to work for the company for seven years, they agreed to send furs, fish, lumber, and agricultural goods back to England to cover the debt incurred for passage. In Plymouth, all property was to be held in common until the end of the contract,

when it would be divided among stockholders on both sides of the Atlantic. The last-minute revision to the contract, however, changed the equation for liquidating property in the colony at the conclusion of the seven years. It reserved up to half of that property—improved land and buildings—for the Merchant Adventures in England. Also eliminated was the original concession that settlers could have two days to work for themselves toward building homes and improving individual fields. Under the disputed terms, all time, excepting the day of worship, was company time. These new conditions meant that houses and fields the colonists built would not be their own at the end of the contract. Offered little incentive for personal gain, they refused to sign the agreement. Cushman, who had been on board the leaky *Speedwell*, was left to sort out the contractual issues in England as the *Mayflower* continued on its voyage.

One year later, Cushman arrived in Plymouth aboard the *Fortune* to resolve the unsigned contract. While he intended to join those at Plymouth permanently, until contract issues were settled he had little choice but to return to London. His stay in Plymouth was a brief few weeks. Convinced that the success of the colony depended upon the contract, his goal was to secure the colonists' agreement to its latest terms. At Plymouth, however, Cushman found a vulnerable colony. Half of the *Mayflower* voyagers had died in the first year. Though the colony had begun to stabilize and the recent harvest had been good, Plymouth remained a fragile experiment. Relations with the local native populations had been positive since arrival, but uncertainty remained. Winter was about to begin, and that season brought greater uncertainty. Having watched family and friends die during the past year, basic survival remained a priority for many in the group. Settlers feared that the colony was on the brink of collapse. Not surprisingly, resentment of the Merchant Adventurers remained strong. Many viewed the rigid contract of the investors as a serious threat to individual survival.

Cushman's Sermon

Cushman addressed the colonists in their common house on December 9, 1621, just weeks after arriving and days before his departure on the returning *Fortune*. Given his task of securing signatures to the contract and recognizing harsh conditions in the colony, the address emphasizes common goals and sacrifice over individual pursuits. Attempting to refocus the settlers around a common mission, Cushman's sermon decries self-love (or self-interest) as the "bane of all societies." Arguing that they needed to look past the short-term and take a longer view, he reminds colonists that they were laying a foundation not for themselves but for those who would follow. He frames the mission as religious and draws upon gospel passages that extol the virtues of working for the common good. Given the role he was forced to assume, Cushman understood that various agendas—religious, financial, and personal—clashed at Plymouth. Among both colonists and investors, many embraced the task of facilitating God's providence; they desired the growth of Puritanism under English dominion and hoped to Christianize the "heathen" American Indians. Yet, such work would only be possible if the Merchant Adventurers and the Plymouth-based stockholders made profit on their investment. Failure of the company would mean dissolution of the colony. Thus, religious goals were dependent on secular realities.

Complicating the balancing act between spiritual and financial goals were the individual goals of the settlers. In difficult times, basic survival was at the forefront, but in the long run securing land and livelihood was paramount. Dissention within the colony and resentment toward the Merchant Adventurers had grown under the stresses of settlement. Over time, these stresses were exacerbated by divisions between Pilgrims and other Plymouth colonists. Thus, Cushman needed to appeal for unity around a common agenda. The colonists, he argues in the address, had made a contract with God, with the English king, and with the Merchant Adventurers. Christians were obligated to abide by each of the contracts and work together for the common good. In order for the all of the various agendas to be fulfilled, the colony had to be placed on firm financial, spiritual, and political ground. Colonists had only to look south to the contemporary failures at Jamestown to recognize the dangers of disunity. Cushman's appeal before the gathering of colonists had the desired effect, and colonists affixed their signatures to the revised contract before he returned it to the investors in London.

Cushman's address at Plymouth first appeared in print in London in 1622. Marketed as a sermon because of its religious content, it was titled "A Sermon preached at Plimmoth in New-England." Consistent with the rejection of self-love that was at the center of his argument, Cushman published the address and

epistolary anonymously: "I have not set down my name, partly because I seek no name, and principally, because I would have nothing esteemed by names." Combined with the epistolary, the sermon was later given the title *The Sin and Danger of Self-Love*. Anonymous publications fuel historical debates about authorship, yet there is little doubt that the published address was the one originally delivered by Cushman. Firsthand observations penned by English settlers at Plymouth resolve any questions regarding the author's identity. No paper trail exists for the epistle dedicatory, but most scholars agree that it was written by Cushman.

The content of the speech served a different purpose on either side of the Atlantic. At Plymouth, the oral address was an attempt to quell dissention and convince colonists of their obligation to their investors. The printed version circulated in England served a broader aim. Removed from the palpable tensions at Plymouth, the sermon was not interpreted as a plea for unity in a fractious community; instead, it was read as the philosophy that unified that distant settlement. With the skillful use of the epistle dedicatory as an introduction, Cushman redirected the address at the Merchant Adventurers whose continuing support was essential, at factions within English society who questioned the Englishness of the Pilgrim Separatists, and at Puritans in the general public who might consider joining the colony.

After a year's time, the colonists had yet to produce anything close to the volume of trade goods expected by the Merchant Adventurers, and many were growing impatient. Thus, the epistle dedicatory explicitly—and the sermon implicitly—asks the Adventurers to stay the course. The work at Plymouth had only just begun. Though the first year of the venture had been difficult, Cushman projects optimism about current and future conditions. Balancing secular and religious interests, he reminds the investors that they had contracted with Puritans and, as such, had made a commitment to establishing religion "before profit or popularity." Echoing the sermon it introduces, the epistle directs the Adventurers to focus on the long run and reject short-term self-interest. Cushman argues that they should continue to "honor God with [their] riches" and to recognize that "no labor is lost, nor money spent which is bestowed for God." Articulating a view that was popular among Separatists, Cushman argues for expediency in supporting the venture because God's judgment day was "not far off."

While Cushman's appeal targets those Puritans who were prominent among the Adventurers, he also addresses the non-Puritan investors. The colony would continue to need their financial support, and it also needed new settlers. In appealing to all investors to send "godly men" to join the colony, Cushman makes subtle reminders of the benefits of contracting with religious dissenters; because Puritans were often persecuted at home, they demonstrated greater enthusiasm than others for settlement abroad. At a time when few Englishmen were willing to sail into the unknown, sending Puritans made the most sense. They were community-oriented and prepared to make sacrifices. For those investors and for Puritans who might be convinced to emigrate, Cushman lays bare the reality of life at Plymouth. Work would be difficult with no allowance for comforts. Men seeking "great riches, ease, pleasures, dainties, and jollity" should remain at home.

At the time of the sermon's publication, criticisms of the Separatists were circulating in the London press and among influential social and political sectors. Having abandoned England for Holland and then America, the Pilgrims' English identity was openly questioned. Their loyalty to the Crown was suspect, and they were mocked as uneducated simpletons. How could such people retain Englishness surrounded by wilderness and savagery? Conscious of the value of public relations in an increasingly literate world, the epistle directly counters such charges. Cushman celebrates the Plymouth Pilgrims as plain Englishmen who honored their contract with God, King, and fellow countrymen. Though Separatists, they had enthusiastically returned to English dominion, and while the colony was removed from England proper, it was like home in many ways; its geography was English geography. Compared to low-lying Holland, New England was familiar and its climate differed only in extremes. Clearly, after just one year, the finer geographic contrast had yet to be understood and ignorance prevailed. New England, for example, was not, as Cushman suggests, an island. Still, the broad geographic comparison defined Pilgrims as Englishmen on English soil.

During the early colonial experience, concerns for retaining English identity were common among both the critics of the Separatist Puritans and those who were considering joining them in New England. At the core of such anxieties were fears of American Indians and the influences of "savage" cultures. Criticizing Spain's brutal treatment of American Indians in its own American colonies, many questioned whether Englishmen would revert to similar savagery when living among the "heathen." Recognizing that such fears were obstacles to investment and migration, Cushman presents a rosy portrait of Pilgrim–American Indian relations at Plymouth and dispels concerns over mistreatment. Pilgrims were facilitating God's providence, and to the extent that the American Indians were involved or affected, Cushman considers this part of God's design. Upon arrival, Pilgrims found American Indian communities in decline: "very much wasted by late, by reason of a great mortality that fell amongst them three years since . . ." Not understanding that European diseases had already traveled northward from earlier settlements in Virginia, Cushman interprets abandoned villages as God's hand in clearing the region for the Pilgrims' entrance. While those who survived remained heathens to the settlers, the experiences of the first year suggested to Cushman that the natives might soon "prove serviceable to God and man." In his optimistic view, American Indians would readily cede territory and authority to the English king. Acknowledging how Wampanoags extended assistance to the Pilgrims during their difficult first year, Cushman finds no reason for fear. Compared to American Indians, he explains, "many christians are not so kind, nor sincere."

Cushman's epistle and sermon demonstrate his struggle to balance competing interests that converged in the settlement of Plymouth. Negotiating and sustaining the trans-Atlantic venture required the humble wool comber and deacon to strike an uncomfortable balance between religious and secular worlds.

Essential Themes

Cushman's address at Plymouth was the first published sermon from New England, and its publication in 1622 marks the emergence of a regional literary genre that flourished for more than a century. Considered by some as the earliest example of American literature, Cushman's address was not a sermon in the true sense of the word. The author was not an ordained minister, and his words did not carry the weight of one. While crafted in typical Puritan style—clarifying biblical references and elevating spiritual mission—the sermon's intent was to convince Plymouth Pilgrims to accept a business contract. An appeal to reason regarding secular realties, the address is distinct from the enormous body of New England Puritan sermons that followed. Unlike those subsequent sermons which confidently demand religious conformity and model rigid application of doctrine, Cushman's address was delivered in the years before Puritanism had achieved cultural hegemony in New England. Instead, the sermon reveals the fragility of the first settlement at Plymouth. It also reflects the uncertainties and anxieties that would later dissipate as English and Puritan dominion over the region was secured.

Crucial to achieving dominion was establishing English control over native populations and resources. Cushman believed that this process would be easy; in his view, American Indians were "like lambs, so kind, so submissive." He celebrated how American Indian leaders "subscribed obedience" to King James with little prodding. While his idealization of Pilgrim–American Indian relations was based on largely positive interactions during the colony's first year, Cushman's notions of divine providence and English superiority reduced complex relationships to simple power equations.

Soon after Cushman sailed for London, however, it became clear that peaceful relations would not be sustainable. Gradually tensions mounted as more English settlers arrived and spread beyond the coastline. Competition for resources soon sparked conflicts. Settlers' demands that "savages" conform to English notions of civilization and religion intensified an increasingly volatile situation. While small conflicts became common after that first year, Pilgrim–American Indian tensions in the Plymouth colony reached a crescendo by the 1670s. At that time, the son of the Indian leader Massasoit—Cushman and many settlers had considered Massasoit a valuable friend to colony—led a charge to roll back English settlement to the coast. The campaign of Metacom, or King Philip, was initially successful, but English forces eventually prevailed. By that decade, accelerating trans-Atlantic migration, bustling maritime commerce, and a powerful Puritan ministry fueled English resolve to eliminate native resistance.

Dave Corcoran, PhD

Bibliography

Bangs, Jeremy Dupertuis. *Strangers and Pilgrims, Travelers and Sojourners: Leiden and the Foundations of Plymouth Plantation*. Plymouth, MA: General Society of Mayflower Descendants, 2009. Print.

Bradford, William. *Bradford's History of Plymouth Plantation: 1606–1646*. Ed. William T. Davis. New York: Scribner's, 2005. Print.

Cushman, Robert. *The Sin and Danger of Self-Love Described, in a Sermon Preached at Plymouth, in New England, 1621*. Boston: 1846. Print.

Lovejoy, David S. "Plain Englishmen at Plymouth." *New England Quarterly* 63.2 (1990): 232–248. Print.

Lovejoy, David S. *Religious Enthusiasm in the New World: Heresy to Revolution*. Cambridge, MA: Harvard UP, 1985. Print.

Young, Alexander, ed. *Chronicles of the Pilgrim Fathers of the Colony of Plymouth from 1602–1625*. New York: Da Capo, 1971. Print.

Additional Reading

Burke, Donald. *New England New Jerusalem: The Millenarian Dimension of Transatlantic Migration. A Study in the Theology of History*. Diss. Wayne State University, 2006. Print.

Foster, Stephen. "The Faith of a Separatist Layman: The Authorship, Context, and Significance of *The Cry of a Stone*." *William and Mary Quarterly* 34.3 (1977): 375–403.

General Society of Mayflower Descendants. General Society of Mayflower Descendents, 2012. Web. 18 June 2012.

Heath, Dwight B., ed. *A Journal of the Pilgrims at Plymouth: Mourt's Relation, a Relation or Journal of the English Plantation Settled at Plymouth in New England*. New York: Corinth, 1963. Print.

Philbrick, Nathaniel. *Mayflower: A Story of Courage, Community, and War*. New York: Viking, 2006. Print.

Sail 1620. Society of Mayflower Descendents in the Commonwealth of Pennsylvania, 2012. Web. 18 June 2012.

LESSON PLAN: **Religious Freedom in Plymouth**

Students analyze excerpts from Robert Cushman's sermon at Plymouth, and compare multiple perspectives on the new settlement.

Learning Objectives

Describe religious groups and the role of religion in colonial America; analyze the causes and effects of settlement in Plymouth; examine the influence of ideas on the shaping of early American culture.

Materials: Robert Cushman's "To His Loving Friends the Adventurers for New-England"; Excerpts from William Bradford's *Of Plymouth Plantation.*

Overview Questions

What motivated Cushman and Bradford to leave England for America? How were their descriptions of Plymouth—the people, life, and the colony in general—alike and different?

Step 1: Context Questions

How do Puritan beliefs affect Cushman's sermon and Bradford's writing? How do the feelings they express reveal their attitude toward England?

▶ **Activity:** Have students highlight religious references on both documents, and compare and contrast them. Ask students to locate and underline references to England and to include annotations next to the references regarding their attitude toward England.

Step 2: Comprehension Questions

What hardships do Cushman and Bradford speak of and how were these hardships resolved?

▶ **Activity:** Have students create a list of the hardships that both Cushman and Bradford discuss. Ask them to explain the outcome of these hardships, and who, if anyone, helped them.

Step 3: Context Questions

How are Cushman's sermon and Bradford's history of Plymouth Plantation helpful to historians who study early colonial America? How do their works provide insight into the relations that developed with American Indians?

▶ **Activity:** Ask students to find either primary or secondary sources about the history of Plymouth, and to examine the influence of Cushman's and Bradford's works on them.

Step 4: Exploration Questions

How do Cushman's experiences in Plymouth compare to those of Bradford? How did Cushman's brief time in Plymouth affect his description of the settlement versus that of Bradford's? How did their ideas and the reasons why they came to Plymouth shape early American culture and thought?

▶ **Activity:** Have students write a summary that explains how Cushman's sermon might have changed had he remained in Plymouth for a longer period of time. Invite them to discuss how the ideas on religious freedom and government that both men shared influenced early American culture and thought.

Step 5: Response Paper

Word length and additional requirements set by Instructor. Students answer the research question in the Overview Questions. Students state a thesis and use as evidence passages from the primary source document as well as support from supplemental materials assigned in the lesson.

■ A Model of Christian Charity

Date: 1630
Author Name: Winthrop, John
Genre: political sermon

"For we must consider that we shall be
as a city upon a hill.

The eyes of all people are upon us."

Summary Overview

Growing religious persecution convinced many Puritan leaders that leaving England was their only viable option in order to openly practice their beliefs. England's claim to much of the east coast of North America presented them with an opportunity to establish a society based on those beliefs. John Winthrop had been selected leader of the first major group of settlers and during the crossing of the Atlantic Ocean on the *Arbella,* he set out his vision for the new colony. Although not an ordained minister, he wrote a sermon to convey these ideas to others on his ship. It contained philosophical guidelines for the rules the members would make to govern their lives. It also carried a message of the possibilities that lay ahead and a statement regarding how members were to be role models for others. The vision he had of the unique role the colony could play in history became an enduring theme in US history.

Defining Moment

At the beginning of the seventeenth century, there was a race to solidify and settle land claims in North America. With the success of the Virginia and Plymouth colonies, King Charles I of England desired to extend his nation's claims. In 1629, a grant was given to the New England Colony, which later changed its name to the Massachusetts Bay Colony, to settle and govern lands north of the Plymouth Colony and south of the settlements in what is now New Hampshire. While motivated by religion, as had been the Plymouth Colony, the Massachusetts Bay Colony was a much larger group of

individuals. It included many wealthy members who had extensive governmental and mercantile experience. They were much better prepared to establish a colony than had been the earlier groups.

About one thousand people sailed from England in 1630 to establish the colony. Unlike earlier colonies, this group owned its own economic and political charters, meaning that virtually all of the shareholders on the economic side of the venture were on the ships. It was to be a democracy, although it differed from some other colonies in that the right to participate in government was limited to members of the Puritan Church. Their collective vision was to establish a theocracy, where the word and spirit of God would rule the colony through decisions made by the members of the church. It was in this spirit that Winthrop wrote the sermon entitled, "A Model of Christian Charity" and presented it to the colonists while sailing to the New World.

The sermon clearly states that the colony is to be based on the religious principles of the Puritan faith. Many New England colonies were explicitly established for members of a particular church. In line with Puritan theology, Winthrop states that the colonists are to work together for the common good. This community spirit is to be patterned after their understanding of God's love for them. Only through good works, Winthrop stresses, can tragedy be averted. Finally, Winthrop uses the biblical image of a "city upon a hill" to remind the colonists that God and the world will be watching their success or failure. In this passage he makes it clear that he believes they have a special place in the world. Although this was written more than two hundred years before the term *American exceptionalism* was coined in the United States, many people see a link between Winthrop's unique colony and the role Americans have historically believed the United States plays on the global stage.

Author Biography

Born on January 22, 1588, in Suffolk, England, John Winthrop was the son of Adam and Anne Winthrop. Raised in a wealthy family, Winthrop had many educational and business opportunities open to him. He entered Trinity College at Cambridge University in early 1603, leaving in 1605 when he married his first wife, Mary Forth. For the first few years they lived with her family, after which Winthrop's father gave him an estate in Groton, England. About that time he began studying law, although he never formally entered the profession. During this time Winthrop's first wife died. His second wife died after a year and he married a third time. His estate seems to have done well, although he spent much of his time in London. Eventually he was appointed to work in the Court of Wards and Liveries, a lucrative operation for both the king and those who were in the upper management positions. Life was comfortable and seemed secure.

However, Charles I began to move politically and economically against those who were not a part of the Anglican Church. Prior to his ascension to the throne, the first successful Puritan colony was started at Plymouth, in what is now Massachusetts, in 1620. Thus when Charles I began to tighten religious requirements, many others considered following the example of the Plymouth Colony. In 1629 Winthrop joined the Massachusetts Bay Colony, which had gained land in 1628 and governing rights in 1629. An exploratory group was sent out at that time. Working with others to secure the necessary supplies and people, Winthrop decided to join in the first wave of emigrants in 1630. As the initial leader of the group opted to stay in England for another year, Winthrop was elected governor of the colony.

During the voyage to what is now Massachusetts, Winthrop wrote the sermon "A Model of Christian Charity" and preached it to the other settlers on his ship as they traveled across the Atlantic. The sermon set out his vision for a colony based on the strict Puritan faith. Settling in what is now Boston, the colony prospered. Winthrop was a strong governor with very rigid views on how a colony should be administered. Overall he was a successful politician; he was elected governor twelve times during the first two decades of the colony's existence. He strongly believed that only those who rigidly followed the Puritan church should be allowed to live in the colony. Many of his political victories and losses were due to theological struggles within the colony. Winthrop died on April 5, 1649.

HISTORICAL DOCUMENT

GOD ALMIGHTY in His most holy and wise providence, hath so disposed of the condition of mankind, as in all times some must be rich, some poor, some high and eminent in power and dignity; others mean and in submission.

The Reason hereof:

1st Reason. First to hold conformity with the rest of His world, being delighted to show forth the glory of his wisdom in the variety and difference of the creatures, and the glory of His power in ordering all these differences for the preservation and good of the whole, and the glory of His greatness, that as it is the glory of princes to have many officers, so this great king will have many stewards, counting himself more honored in dispensing his gifts to man by man, than if he did it by his own immediate hands.

2nd Reason. Secondly, that He might have the more occasion to manifest the work of his Spirit: first upon the wicked in moderating and restraining them, so that the rich and mighty should not eat up the poor, nor the poor and despised rise up against and shake off their yoke. Secondly, in the regenerate, in exercising His graces in them, as in the great ones, their love, mercy, gentleness, temperance etc., and in the poor and inferior sort, their faith, patience, obedience etc.

3rd Reason. Thirdly, that every man might have need of others, and from hence they might be all knit more nearly together in the bonds of brotherly affection. From hence it appears plainly that no man is made more honorable than another or more wealthy etc., out of any particular and singular respect to himself, but for the glory of his Creator and the common good of the creature, man. Therefore God still reserves the property of these gifts to Himself as Ezek. 16:17, He there calls wealth, His gold and His silver, and Prov. 3:9, He claims their service as His due, "Honor the Lord with thy riches," etc.—All men being thus (by divine providence) ranked into two sorts, rich and poor; under the first are comprehended all such as are able to live comfortably by their own means duly improved; and all others are poor according to the former distribution.

There are two rules whereby we are to walk one towards another: Justice and Mercy. These are always distinguished in their act and in their object, yet may they both concur in the same subject in each respect; as sometimes there may be an occasion of showing mercy to a rich man in some sudden danger or distress, and also doing of mere justice to a poor man in regard of some particular contract, etc.

There is likewise a double Law by which we are regulated in our conversation towards another. In both the former respects, the Law of Nature and the Law of Grace (that is, the moral law or the law of the gospel) to omit the rule of justice as not properly belonging to this purpose otherwise than it may fall into consideration in some particular cases. By the first of these laws, man as he was enabled so withal is commanded to love his neighbor as himself. Upon this ground stands all the precepts of the moral law, which concerns our dealings with men. To apply this to the works of mercy, this law requires two things. First, that every man afford his help to another in every want or distress.

Secondly, that he perform this out of the same affection which makes him careful of his own goods, according to the words of our Savior (from Matthew 7:12), whatsoever ye would that men should do to you. . . .

Thirdly, the Law of Nature would give no rules for dealing with enemies, for all are to be considered as friends in the state of innocence, but the Gospel commands love to an enemy. Proof: If thine enemy hunger, feed him; "Love your enemies... Do good to them that hate you" (Matt. 5:44).

This law of the Gospel propounds likewise a difference of seasons and occasions. There is a time when a Christian must sell all and give to the poor, as they did in the Apostles' times. There is a time also when Christians (though they give not all yet) must give beyond their ability, as they of Macedonia (2 Cor. 8). Likewise, community of perils calls for extraordinary liberality, and so doth community in some special service for the church.

Lastly, when there is no other means whereby our Christian brother may be relieved in his distress, we must help him beyond our ability rather than tempt God in putting him upon help by miraculous or extraordinary means. This duty of mercy is exercised in the kinds: giving, lending and forgiving (of a debt). . . .

✳ ✳ ✳

It rests now to make some application of this discourse, by the present design, which gave the occasion of writing of it. Herein are four things to be propounded; first the persons, secondly, the work, thirdly the end, fourthly the means.

First, for the persons. We are a company professing ourselves fellow members of Christ, in which respect only, though we were absent from each other many miles, and had our employments as far distant, yet we ought to account ourselves knit together by this bond of love and live in the exercise of it, if we would have comfort of our being in Christ. This was notorious in the practice of the Christians in former times; as is testified of the Waldenses, from the mouth of one of the adversaries Aeneas Sylvius "mutuo ament pene antequam norunt" —they use to love any of their own religion even before they were acquainted with them.

Secondly for the work we have in hand. It is by a mutual consent, through a special overvaluing providence and a more than an ordinary approbation of the churches of Christ, to seek out a place of cohabitation and consortship under a due form of government both civil and ecclesiastical. In such cases as this, the care of the public must oversway all private respects, by which, not only conscience, but mere civil policy, doth bind us.

For it is a true rule that particular estates cannot subsist in the ruin of the public.

Thirdly, the end is to improve our lives to do more service to the Lord; the comfort and increase of the body of Christ, whereof we are members, that ourselves and posterity may be the better preserved from the common corruptions of this evil world, to serve the Lord and work out our salvation under the power and purity of his holy ordinances.

Fourthly, for the means whereby this must be effected. They are twofold, a conformity with the work and end we aim at. These we see are extraordinary, therefore we must not content ourselves with usual ordinary means. Whatsoever we did, or ought to have done, when we lived in England, the same must we do, and more also, where we go. That which the most in their churches maintain as truth in profession only, we must bring into familiar and constant practice; as in this duty of love, we must love brotherly without dissimulation, we must love one another with a pure heart fervently. We must bear one another's burdens. We must not look only on our own things, but also on the things of our brethren.

Neither must we think that the Lord will bear with such failings at our hands as he doth from those among whom we have lived; and that for these three reasons:

First, in regard of the more near bond of marriage between Him and us, wherein He hath taken us to be His, after a most strict and peculiar manner, which will make Him the more jealous of our love and obedience. So He tells the people of Israel, you only have I known of all the families of the earth, therefore will I punish you for your transgressions.

Secondly, because the Lord will be sanctified in them that come near Him. We know that there were many that corrupted the service of the Lord; some setting up altars before his own; others offering both strange fire and strange sacrifices also; yet there came no fire from heaven, or other sudden judgment upon them, as did upon Nadab and Abihu, whom yet we may think did not sin presumptuously.

Thirdly, when God gives a special commission He looks to have it strictly observed in every article; When He gave Saul a commission to destroy Amaleck, He indented with him upon certain articles, and because he failed in one of the least, and that upon a fair pretense,

it lost him the kingdom, which should have been his reward, if he had observed his commission.

Thus stands the cause between God and us. We are entered into covenant with Him for this work. We have taken out a commission. The Lord hath given us leave to draw our own articles. We have professed to enterprise these and those accounts, upon these and those ends. We have hereupon besought Him of favor and blessing. Now if the Lord shall please to hear us, and bring us in peace to the place we desire, then hath He ratified this covenant and sealed our commission, and will expect a strict performance of the articles contained in it; but if we shall neglect the observation of these articles which are the ends we have propounded, and, dissembling with our God, shall fall to embrace this present world and prosecute our carnal intentions, seeking great things for ourselves and our posterity, the Lord will surely break out in wrath against us, and be revenged of such a people, and make us know the price of the breach of such a covenant.

Now the only way to avoid this shipwreck, and to provide for our posterity, is to follow the counsel of Micah, to do justly, to love mercy, to walk humbly with our God. For this end, we must be knit together, in this work, as one man. We must entertain each other in brotherly affection. We must be willing to abridge ourselves of our superfluities, for the supply of others' necessities. We must uphold a familiar commerce together in all meekness, gentleness, patience and liberality. We must delight in each other; make others' conditions our own; rejoice together, mourn together, labor and suffer together, always having before our eyes our commission and community in the work, as members of the same body. So shall we keep the unity of the spirit in the bond of peace. The Lord will be our God, and delight to dwell among us, as His own people, and will command a blessing upon us in all our ways, so that we shall see much more of His wisdom, power, goodness and truth, than formerly we have been acquainted with. We shall find that the God of Israel is among us, when ten of us shall be able to resist a thousand of our enemies; when He shall make us a praise and glory that men shall say of succeeding plantations, "may the Lord make it like that of New England." For we must consider that we shall be as a city upon a hill. The eyes of all people are upon us. So that if we shall deal falsely with our God in this work we have undertaken, and so cause Him to withdraw His present help from us, we shall be made a story and a by-word through the world. We shall open the mouths of enemies to speak evil of the ways of God, and all professors for God's sake. We shall shame the faces of many of God's worthy servants, and cause their prayers to be turned into curses upon us till we be consumed out of the good land whither we are going.

And to shut this discourse with that exhortation of Moses, that faithful servant of the Lord, in his last farewell to Israel, Deut. 30. "Beloved, there is now set before us life and death, good and evil," in that we are commanded this day to love the Lord our God, and to love one another, to walk in his ways and to keep his Commandments and his ordinance and his laws, and the articles of our Covenant with Him, that we may live and be multiplied, and that the Lord our God may bless us in the land whither we go to possess it. But if our hearts shall turn away, so that we will not obey, but shall be seduced, and worship other Gods, our pleasure and profits, and serve them; it is propounded unto us this day, we shall surely perish out of the good land whither we pass over this vast sea to possess it.

> Therefore let us choose life,
> that we and our seed may live,
> by obeying His voice and cleaving to Him,
> for He is our life and our prosperity.

GLOSSARY

carnal: relating to sexual or physical desires in opposition to spiritual

dissimulation: deceit by hiding one's true feelings or intentions

Micah: one of the minor prophets of the Bible

mutuo ament pene antequam norunt: Latin for *love one another even before you know each other*

Nadab and Abihu: in the biblical book of Exodus, two sons of Aaron who were killed by God for not carrying out their tasks in the appropriate manner

professors: people who profess a specific faith

Saul: king of the Israelites who defied God's command to kill the king of the Amalekites

superfluities: luxurious standards of living or desire

Waldenses: a Christian group started in the thirteenth century that was pushed out of the Roman Catholic Church and joined the Reformed Church movement in the sixteenth century

Document Analysis

The founding of the Massachusetts Bay Colony was principally a religious undertaking. It was the Puritans' belief in God, especially the belief that God had a special mission for them, that formed the foundation for the colonists' life in New England. Winthrop spelled out that vision of the colony in his sermon to his fellow Puritans. While Winthrop's ideas were meant for the Massachusetts Bay Colony, specifically, phrases like "city upon a hill" have been quoted by others throughout history to describe the United States in general.

As Winthrop wrote, "the end is to improve our lives to do more service to the Lord . . . and work out our salvation under the power and purity of his holy ordinances." This was the Puritans' intent when they left England for the New World. As previously mentioned, pressure had been building on the Puritans to accept the teachings of the Anglican Church. Theological differences with the Anglican Church made it impossible for the Puritans to do so. They believed in a strict adherence to the Bible, and they believed that the only way they could practice their faith in better service of God was to leave England altogether.

As the leader of the Winthrop Fleet, as the group of ships was known in 1630, Winthrop needed to inspire the people for the difficult task of setting up a new life in a seemingly uncivilized wilderness. An affirmation of who they were was conveyed through his understanding of how this needed to be done. In speaking about those traveling to the New World, Winthrop wrote, "when God gives a special commission He looks to have it strictly observed in every article." Thus the religious mission and message given to the Puritans had to be carried out. In this passage, he refers to the harsh judgment made against people in the Bible who failed to carry out their missions from God. "We are entered into covenant with Him for this work. We have taken out a commission." Thus, Winthrop urges his fellow colonists to use the colony as a means to carry out God's commandments.

Using biblical passages and statements based on Puritan theology, Winthrop helped develop a sense of unity among the people. The introductory paragraph was a clear reminder of the doctrine of predestination in which the Puritans believed. As mentioned toward the end of the sermon, Winthrop was certain that if the voyage was completed successfully, it would be a sign that God had predestined them to undertake the dangerous voyage to the New World.

Although a few shareholders and members of the movement had previously gone to New England to scout out the best location for the settlement, virtually all the shareholders were on the ships traveling with Winthrop. Members of the movement who had decided to wait for future sailings had given or sold their shares to those who left in 1630. This was to make it easier for quick decisions to be made on issues vital to the colony. It also ensured that no shares would pass out of the hands of church members due to unforeseen circumstances to people who were not in the church. Thus the

vision for the colony would remain unchanged, except as conditions in the colony might affect it.

As is obvious from all the references to the rich and poor in the sermon, the Puritans were capitalists, not socialists. Although they accepted certain biblical commandments to have mercy on the less fortunate, this did not include a belief in total economic or political equality. The Puritans believed that God decided the circumstances of every individual's life, including wealth or poverty.

According to Winthrop, the accumulation of fortune gives glory to God, not the expenditure of it on pleasurable things. "We must be willing to abridge ourselves of our superfluities . . . ." Wealth must be used to help those in need, if the proper situation exists. This situation occurs when a person has the resources to help one who is in need, where the only other option is divine intervention. By not helping those in need, the wealthy person could be seen to be testing God, which is something Christians are warned not to do. Thus the Puritans are called to accumulate wealth in order to serve God better, in giving to the church and in helping those in need.

According to this sermon, the church and its members are on earth only for the glory of God. While this is in line with mainstream Christian theology, Winthrop does bring the Puritan/Calvinist perspective to the situation. In his three reasons for the existence of the rich and poor, Winthrop clearly states that people are conduits for God's love and mercy. For certain people to be willing to undertake this task increases the glory given to God. Winthrop goes on to say that with the existence of both the fortunate and the unfortunate, there are more tasks for the Holy Spirit to do, which again increases God's glory. Finally, the differences among people help build a stronger community. In addition, those who are rich are wealthy because of God, and as such, all that they have belongs to God. Thus, under Winthrop's theology, those who are rich more fully reflect God's glory and are better able to be God's faithful servants. And so a community based on charity would be one that would please God and earn success in the New World.

What Winthrop sees as two guiding lights for life in the new colony, "Justice and Mercy," are to be combined in such a way that it leads to success, as well. Winthrop believed that justice and mercy are both required of all people. For him, one without the other is an inadequate response to the world and to the dictates of the Christian religion. It is the balancing of these considerations that forms the foundation for the way in which the colony members should work together and govern themselves. The outcome he seeks for the colony is to exceed anything in the past. He wrote, "Whatsoever we did, or ought to have done, when we lived in England, the same must we do, and more also, where we go." Thus, Winthrop seeks perfection in the new colony.

As they moved forward in this experiment, it was clear to Winthrop that a strong government was needed. As he wrote, "For it is a true rule that particular estates cannot subsist in the ruin of the public." If the individual is to not only survive but prosper, then there must be a civic organization that ensures that the proper policies are implemented. The passages of the sermon that are not printed in this text emphasize even more strongly the capitalist nature of the colony and the need for a government in total alignment with Puritan doctrine.

The end of the sermon holds its most famous passage. "For we must consider that we shall be as a city upon a hill. The eyes of all people are upon us." The image of the city is taken from a passage in Matthew 5:14 in the New Testament of the Bible. This is another indication of Winthrop's belief that there is a specific role that the colonists will play in the world, based on their relationship with God. Like the Israelites in the Old Testament, the Puritans saw themselves as a chosen people. Their government was to be "both civil and ecclesiastical." The world would be watching them, they believed, because they had this special status and were attempting to create a new society based solely on their faith. In this sermon Winthrop is saying that success of the colony will bring glory to God. In a similar vein, failure will bring the swift judgment of God upon them.

In the following decades of American history, this passage would be applied to the United States as a whole. The related ideas regarding the role of the United States in the world, known as manifest destiny and American exceptionalism, come in part from Winthrop's vision for his colony. Although these terms originated in the nineteenth and twentieth centuries, the ideals they embody have been a part of American heritage at least since the period of the Revolutionary War. Manifest destiny was used as a rallying cry for the westward expansion of the United States, seen as a policy ordained by God. Winthrop believed in predestination, so the idea that God had predestined the west-ward expansion of the United States can be a logical continuation of this thought. American exceptionalism is the idea that the United States has a special role to play in the world, that it is exceptional among all other nations. The fact that Winthrop saw the Puritans as special people in God's eyes was extended to the position of the entire country in the world, according to the beliefs of many Americans throughout history.

In addition to the continuation and expansion of his ideas throughout American society, Winthrop's use of the biblical image of the city on a hill has been adopted by various politicians for their own purposes. Bridging party affiliation, the image has appealed to many politicians, both conservative and liberal, throughout the history of the United States. For example, in the second half of the twentieth century both President John F. Kennedy and President Ronald Reagan would use this image in speeches to describe a part of their vision for the United States.

Winthrop's idea of a city on a hill, however, was more closely tied to religious principles than to secular unity. He believed that the colony would succeed only if it retained religious unity. This was one reason full citizenship was reserved for full members of the church. Only those who affirmed the teachings of the Puritan faith could remain in the colony. He warns his fellow travelers not to "deal falsely" with God, for in doing so, God would withdraw his help from the colonists.

Although Winthrop's sermon is most famous for its image of the city upon a hill, the climax of the sermon truly occurs in the following paragraph. The closing paragraph focuses on the image of Moses's speech to the Israelites just prior to his death and the Israelites' entry into the Promised Land, which is reflected in the drama of the Puritan immigrants about to enter the New World. In the Bible, Moses gives his people a choice: they can follow God with total obedience or face destruction. This choice is repeated by Moses's son, Joshua, after the Israelites have settled in the Promised Land. Winthrop's expectation was that those who were settling the colony would respond with a strong affirmation, just as the Israelites had responded to Joshua.

This is the point toward which the sermon had been building, a call to the settlers to reaffirm their faith in God and dedication to the task that lay before them. The Israelites entering the Promised Land facing overwhelming odds and an uncertain future, combined with the knowledge that the Israelites succeeded, were the two images that Winthrop wanted each person to have in his or her mind. He most certainly believed that the colonists could give glory to God through their successful occupation of a new land, just as the Israelites had done centuries earlier. For Winthrop, there was a simple correlation between the two groups. Success was assured by the colonists adhering to their faith. The Puritans saw themselves as chosen people who, just like the Israelites, were special people given an opportunity by God to give glory through the settling of a new land. "We are a company professing ourselves fellow members of Christ, . . . we ought to account ourselves knit together by this bond of love and live in the exercise of it, if we would have comfort of our being in Christ."

Records indicate that during the first year about twenty percent of those who had settled in Massachusetts Bay Colony died and another twenty percent returned to England on the ships that arrived in 1631. However, we also know that because of the strength of its religious foundation and the desire of other Puritans to leave England, the Massachusetts Colony became the dominant political and economic group in New England with more than twenty thousand immigrants during its first decade.

Essential Themes

Looking toward the challenges ahead for the members of the colony, Winthrop sought to unify them in their purpose for the journey. Although it was clear that there were economic and organizational challenges that the Puritans would have to overcome, the single purpose on which he wanted them to focus was religious purity. "We are a company professing ourselves fellow members of Christ." They were guided by "a special overvaluing providence" with the purpose "to improve our lives to do more service to the Lord;" which needed "a conformity with the work and end we aim at." Everything outside the church, everything outside devoted service to God was for Winthrop essentially negligible. The strength of this passion to be totally dedicated, as a colony, to God's service led colonial leaders only fifty years later to judge the colony a failure because of the compromises which they had had to make. In the short term Winthrop was successful in pushing the colonists not only to survive, but to move toward the desired goal. However, in only a few decades, there were not enough church members who met the religious requirements for citizenship, and so those called half-believers were allowed to vote and participate in colonial affairs. They

had discovered that the total religious and social unity sought by Winthrop and others was not attainable.

However, Winthrop was successful in his desire to set an example before the world. The positive image of the "city upon a hill" continues to have an impact today. This does not mean that the colony was a perfect place, especially by modern societal standards. However, the vision that this group of people had a special role to play continues to excite. In the context of the United States, this idea of a special role has been enduring. In later years, whether it was by President John Adams or President Barack Obama, Winthrop's image of the people of the United States forging a new identity has been used in speeches lifting up American ideals. Just as many believe Winthrop went too far in attempting to achieve conformity, many believe that some have gone too far in lifting up the United States as a perfect nation. However, the understanding that the colonists of the seventeenth century—or Americans today—could make a contribution to the broader world through the positive attributes of their society remains true. Winthrop's vision stands as a testament to the human aspiration to create a better world.

Donald A. Watt, PhD

Bibliography

Bremer, Francis J. *John Winthrop: America's Forgotten Founding Father.* New York: Oxford UP, 2003. Print.

Wood, Andrew. *Summary of John Winthrop's "Model of Christian Charity."* Communications Department, San Jose State University, n.d. Web. 25 May 2012.

Additional Reading

Allen, Barbara. *Tocqueville, Covenant, and the Democratic Revolution: Harmonizing Earth with Heaven.* Lanham: Lexington, 2005. Print.

Bercovitch, Sacvan. *The Puritan Origins of the American Self.* 1975. New Haven: Yale UP, 2011. Print.

Dunn, Richard S. and Laetitia Yeandle, eds. *The Journal of John Winthrop 1630–49.* Cambridge, Belknap P of Harvard, 1996. Print.

Morgan, Edmund S. *The Puritan Dilemma: The Story of John Winthrop.* 3rd ed. London: Pearson Longman, 2006. Print.

Northlend, William Dummer. *The Bay Colony: A Civil, Religious and Social History of the Massachusetts Colony and Its Settlements from the Landing at Cape Ann in 1624 to the Death of Governor Winthrop in 1649.* 1896. Ithaca: Cornell UP, 2010. Print.

LESSON PLAN: **A City Upon a Hill**

Students analyze John Winthrop's sermon and the significance of his reference to Puritan society in the New World as a "city upon a hill."

Learning Objectives

Formulate examples of how different choices made by the Puritans could have resulted in different outcomes; analyze the influence of Winthrop's ideas and beliefs on future settlements; distinguish between unsupported expressions of opinion made by Winthrop about what to expect in the new settlement versus evidence that support his opinions

Materials: John Winthrop, "A Model of Christian Charity"; illustration *John Winthrop Aboard the* Arbella *Bound for the New World*

Overview Questions

In his sermon, what edoes Winthrop urge the Puritans to do in order to achieve his "city upon a hill"? How does the painting of Winthrop aboard the *Arbella* depict his influence as a leader? How did Bradford's ideas set a precedent for future settlement and society? How might the outcome have been different for the colony without Bradford's leadership?

Step 1: Comprehension Questions

What does Bradford mean by a "city upon a hill"? In Bradford's sermon, how do his ideals shape his vision for the colony?

▶ **Activity:** Select students to read aloud and analyze key passages. Have them explain in their own words what Bradford envisioned once he and the settlers arrived in America. Ask them to examine Bradford's language as evidence of his beliefs in the Puritans building a "city upon a hill."

Step 2: Comprehension Questions

What "rules" does Bradford identify as important in buiding and supporting a successful community? How does he use religious references to support his ideas?

▶ **Activity:** Ask students to make a list of the five imperative statements Bradford issues that served as a model and set a precedent for future settlement and society. Have them discuss how these statements help to create a "city upon a hill" and how Biblical references support them.

Step 3: Context Questions

How did the Massachusetts Bay Colony serve as a model for other English colonies?

▶ **Activity:** Instruct students to compare and contrast other, later English colonies with the Massachusetts Bay Colony. Ask them to write a summary to show comparisons and contrasts.

Step 4: Exploration Questions

Would the colony have been successful without Bradford's leadership and wisdom? How might the outcome have been different under a shortsighted leader?

▶ **Activity:** Have students discuss what realities described in Bradford's sermon suggest about an alternative outcome for the Puritans. Direct students to outline how the early history of the Massachusetts Bay Colony might have been different.

Step 5: Response Paper

Word length and additional requirements set by Instructor. Students answer the research question in the Overview Questions. Students state a thesis and use as evidence passages from the primary source document as well as support from supplemental materials assigned in the lesson.

■ Transcript of the Trial of Anne Hutchinson

Date: November 1637
Author: Unknown
Genre: legislation; court opinion; report

*"Now if you do condemn me for speaking what
in my conscience I know to be truth I must
commit myself unto the Lord."*

—Anne Hutchinson

Summary Overview

The 1637 trial of Anne Hutchinson touches on issues of religion, gender roles, and the need to maintain unity, order, and religious conformity in the newly founded Massachusetts Bay Colony (1630). Hutchinson's trial was the most dramatic episode in what is known as the Antinomian Controversy of 1636 to 1638, which concerned the question of whether she and several leading ministers believed in the salvation of souls through the grace of God or salvation through good works. Taken to its logical extreme, antinomianism suggests that a sanctified person is not subject to man's law, thus posing a challenge to social order.

In addition, Hutchinson was accused of stepping out of a woman's proper place by holding private meetings at her home to discuss each week's sermons with various men and women of Boston. An intelligent and well-educated woman, Hutchinson's opinions were influential. Her support of less orthodox ministers was seen as a threat to the authority of the theologically orthodox leaders of the colony.

Defining Moment

In November 1637, the forty-six-year-old Hutchinson appeared before the General Court of Massachusetts. In court, Governor John Winthrop charged Hutchinson with disrupting the peace and unity of the colony by endorsing a theological argument the Puritan leader-

ship considered questionable, as well as with criticizing leading ministers. Hutchinson was also accused of promoting her opinions at meetings attended by both men and women at her home. The purpose of the trial, Winthrop announced, was to determine whether she could be corrected and thus made "a profitable member here among us," or, if she did not reform, "then the court may take such a course that you may trouble us no further." In other words, the trial would determine whether Hutchinson would be punished and allowed to remain in Massachusetts, or banished altogether.

The colony of Massachusetts was established in 1630, just seven years before Hutchinson was put on trial. Led by lawyer John Winthrop, the English Puritans of the Massachusetts Bay Company planned to establish a purified version of the Church of England and a model community. The colony would be led by Puritan church members, and citizens were expected to conform to Puritan religious and social ideals.

It did not take long, however, for theological diversity to appear in the colony. In 1635, Roger Williams was put on trial for arguing that the Puritans should separate entirely from the Church of England. He was banished and founded Rhode Island in 1636. Two ministers, John Wheelwright and John Cotton, were also examined prior to Anne Hutchinson's trial. Wheelwright was called before the General Court, censured, and banished. Winthrop considered Hutchinson to be the root of the antinomian problem and expected the controversy to be solved by her subsequent banishment.

Hutchinson's departure did not end the Puritan founders' struggle to maintain conformity and theological orthodoxy, however. For generations, the civil and religious leaders of the colony tried to enforce their vision, with diminishing results. The story of Hutchinson, a woman who publicly stood firm in her own unorthodox beliefs, has gripped the attention of theologians, historians, and novelists for centuries. Nathaniel Hawthorne, for example, modeled the character of Hester Prynne in *The Scarlet Letter* (1850) on Hutchinson. The transcript of Hutchinson's trial, likely recorded by someone at the trial itself, has been frequently reprinted and offers information about several issues in the Puritan colonies.

Biography

Anne Hutchinson's trial involved most of the leading Puritans in Massachusetts. There were forty magistrates and eight ministers attending her trial before the General Court, including the sitting governor, John Winthrop, and lieutenant governor, Thomas Dudley. Hutchinson's minister and teacher, the respected clergyman John Cotton, was also there. Many of the participants had known each other before they left England. The Hutchinson and Dudley families were members of Cotton's congregation in Boston, England, and Cotton was the minister called upon to bless the first group of Puritans on the cusp of their departure to the New World in 1630.

Winthrop, Cotton, Dudley, and Hutchinson were all members of the educated Puritan elite in the new town of Boston, Massachusetts. Winthrop, the first governor of the Massachusetts Bay Colony, was serving his fifth term as governor at the time of Hutchinson's trial. Winthrop was a lawyer and pious Puritan whose sermon "A Model of Christian Charity," delivered en route to the New World, laid out many of the primary tenets of the New England mind. Winthrop's journal is a primary source for the history of New England and demonstrates his interest in Hutchinson's fate until the end of her life. Dudley arrived with John Winthrop and served the colony as its first lieutenant governor.

Cotton was one of the leading Puritan ministers in both England and the colonies. Cotton was converted to Puritanism at the University of Cambridge, where he earned a bachelor of divinity degree in 1613. As an Anglican vicar in Boston, England, Cotton's reputation as a preacher grew. Despite his nonconformist views, he was usually adept at avoiding conflict, a skill that he demonstrated during Hutchinson's trial in 1637.

Anne Hutchinson and her husband, William Hutchinson, were among those who heard the popular Cotton preach in England. Hutchinson, born in Lincolnshire in 1591, was the daughter of Bridget Dryden and Francis Marbury, a Puritan minister who was tried for heresy in London in 1578. Hutchinson was well-educated for a woman of the era and intelligent, quick-witted, and deeply religious. She delighted in studying and discussing theology and led women's meetings at her home to discuss each week's sermons. These meetings were sometimes attended by men as well.

The mother of twelve living children, Hutchinson was pregnant for the sixteenth time when she stood trial. She miscarried the following spring. After her trial and subsequent banishment, Hutchinson and her family moved first to Rhode Island and then to New Amsterdam (later New York). In 1643, the now-widowed Hutchinson and all but one member of her household, her daughter Susanna, were killed by Siwanoy warriors, victims of an ongoing war between Dutch settlers and local American Indian tribes.

HISTORICAL DOCUMENT

Mr. [John] Winthrop, Governor:

Mrs. Hutchinson, you are called here as one of those that have troubled the peace of the commonwealth and the churches here; you are known to be a woman that hath had a great share in the promoting and divulging of those opinions that are the cause of this trouble, and to be nearly joined not only in affinity and affection with some of those the court had taken notice of and passed censure upon, but you have spoken divers things, as we have been informed, very prejudicial to the honour of the churches and ministers thereof, and you have maintained a meeting and an assembly in your house that hath been condemned by the general assembly as a thing not tolerable nor comely in the sight of God nor fitting for your sex, and notwithstanding that was cried down you have continued the same. Therefore we have thought good to send for you to understand how things are, that if you be in an erroneous way we may reduce you that so you may become a profitable member here among us. Otherwise if you be obstinate in your course that then the court may take such course that you may trouble us no further. Therefore I would intreat you to express whether you do assent and hold in practice to those opinions and factions that have been handled in court already, that is to say, whether you do not justify Mr. Wheelwright's sermon and the petition.

Mrs. Hutchinson: I am called here to answer before you but I hear no things laid to my charge.

Gov.: I have told you some already and more I can tell you.

Mrs. H.: Name one, Sir.

Gov.: Have I not named some already?

Mrs. H.: What have I said or done?

Gov.: Why for your doings, this you did harbor and countenance those that are parties in this faction that you have heard of.

Mrs. H.: That's matter of conscience, Sir.

Gov.: Your conscience you must keep, or it must be kept for you.

Mrs. H.: Must not I then entertain the saints because I must keep my conscience.

Gov.: Say that one brother should commit felony or treason and come to his brother's house, if he knows him guilty and conceals him he is guilty of the same. It is his conscience to entertain him, but if his conscience comes into act in giving countenance and entertainment to him that hath broken the law he is guilty too. So if you do countenance those that are transgressors of the law you are in the same fact.

Mrs. H.: What law do they transgress?

Gov.: The law of God and of the state.

Mrs. H.: In what particular?

Gov.: Why in this among the rest, whereas the Lord doth say honour thy father and thy mother.

Mrs. H.: Ey Sir in the Lord.

Gov.: This honour you have broke in giving countenance to them.

Mrs. H.: In entertaining those did I entertain them against any act (for there is the thing) or what God has appointed?

Gov.: You knew that Mr. Wheelwright did preach this sermon and those that countenance him in this do break a law.

Mrs. H.: What law have I broken?

Gov.: Why the fifth commandment.

Mrs. H.: I deny that for he [Mr. Wheelwright] saith in the Lord.

Gov.: You have joined with them in the faction.

Mrs. H.: In what faction have I joined with them?

Gov.: In presenting the petition.

Mrs. H.: Suppose I had set my hand to the petition. What then?

Gov.: You saw that case tried before.

Mrs. H.: But I had not my hand to [not signed] the petition.

Gov.: You have councelled them.

Mrs. H.: Wherein?

Gov.: Why in entertaining them.

Mrs. H.: What breach of law is that, Sir?

Gov.: Why dishonouring the commonwealth.

Mrs. H.: But put the case, Sir, that I do fear the Lord and my parents. May not I entertain them that fear the Lord because my parents will not give me leave?

Gov.: If they be the fathers of the commonwealth, and they of another religion, if you entertain them then you dishonour your parents and are justly punishable.

Mrs. H.: If I entertain them, as they have dishonoured their parents I do.

Gov.: No but you by countenancing them above others put honor upon them.

Mrs. H.: I may put honor upon them as the children of God and as they do honor the Lord.

Gov.: We do not mean to discourse with those of your sex but only this: you so adhere unto them and do endeavor to set forward this faction and so you do dishonour us.

Mrs. H.: I do acknowledge no such thing. Neither do I think that I ever put any dishonour upon you.

Gov.: Why do you keep such a meeting at your house as you do every week upon a set day?

Mrs. H.: It is lawful for me to do so, as it is all your practices, and can you find a warrant for yourself and condemn me for the same thing? The ground of my taking it up was, when I first came to this land because I did not go to such meetings as those were, it was presently reported that I did not allow of such meetings but held them unlawful and therefore in that regard they said I was proud and did despise all ordinances. Upon that a friend came unto me and told me of it and I to prevent such aspersions took it up, but it was in practice before I came. Therefore I was not the first. . . .

✳✳✳

Deputy Governor, Thomas Dudley:

I would go a little higher with Mrs. Hutchinson. About three years ago we were all in peace. Mrs. Hutchinson, from that time she came hath made a disturbance, and some that came over with her in the ship did inform me what she was as soon as she was landed. I being then in place dealt with the pastor and teacher of Boston and desired them to enquire of her, and then I was satisfied that she held nothing different from us. But within half a year after, she had vented divers of her strange opinions and had made parties in the country, and at length it comes that Mr. Cotton and Mr. Vane were of her judgment, but Mr. Cotton had cleared himself that he was not of that mind. But now it appears by this woman's meeting that Mrs. Hutchinson hath so forestalled the minds of many by their resort to her meeting that now she hath a potent party in the country. Now if all these things have endangered us as from that foundation and if she in particular hath disparaged all our ministers in the land that they have preached a covenant of works, and only Mr. Cotton a covenant of grace, why this is not to be suffered, and therefore being driven to the foundation and it being found that Mrs. Hutchinson is she that hath depraved all the ministers and hath been the cause of what is fallen out, why we must take away the foundation and the building will fall.

Mrs. H.: I pray, Sir, prove it that I said they preached nothing but a covenant of works.

Dep. Gov.: Nothing but a covenant of works. Why a Jesuit may preach truth sometimes.

Mrs. H.: Did I ever say they preached a covenant of works then?

Dep. Gov.: If they do not preach a covenant of grace clearly, then they preach a covenant of works.

Mrs. H.: No, Sir. One may preach a covenant of grace more clearly than another, so I said. . . .

Dep. Gov.: When they do preach a covenant of works do they preach truth?

Mrs. H.: Yes, Sir. But when they preach a covenant of works for salvation that is not truth.

Dep. Gov.: I do but ask you this: when the ministers do preach a covenant of works do they preach a way of salvation?

Mrs. H.: I did not come hither to answer questions of that sort.

Dep. Gov.: Because you will deny the thing.

Mrs. H.: Ey, but that is to be proved first.

Dep. Gov.: I will make it plain that you did say that the ministers did preach a covenant of works.

Mrs. H.: I deny that.

Dep. Gov.: And that you said they were not able ministers of the New Testament, but Mr. Cotton only.

Mrs. H.: If ever I spake that I proved it by God's word.

Court: Very well, very well.

Mrs. H.: If one shall come unto me in private, and desire me seriously to tell them what I thought of such an one, I must either speak false or true in my answer.

Dep. Gov.: Likewise I will prove this that you said the gospel in the letter and words holds forth nothing but a covenant of works and that all that do not hold as you do are in a covenant of works.

Mrs. H.: I deny this for if I should so say I should speak against my own judgment. . . .

✳✳✳

Gov.: Let us state the case, and then we may know what to do. That which is laid to Mrs. Hutchinson charge is that, that she hath traduced the magistrates and ministers of this jurisdiction, that she hath said the ministers preached a covenant of works and Mr. Cotton a covenant of grace, and that they were not able ministers of the gospel, and she excuses it that she made it a private conference and with a promise of secrecy, &c. Now this is charged upon her, and they therefore sent for her seeing she made it her table talk, and then she said the fear of man was a snare and therefore she would not be affeared of them. . . .

Dep. Gov.: Let her witnesses be called.

Gov.: Who be they?

Mrs. H.: Mr. Leveret and our teacher and Mr. Coggeshall.

Gov.: Mr. Coggeshall was not present.

Mr. Coggeshall: Yes, but I was. Only I desired to be silent till I should be called.

Gov.: Will you, Mr. Coggeshall, say that she did not say so?

Mr. Coggeshall: Yes, I dare say that she did not say all that which they lay against her.

Mr. Peters: How dare you look into the court to say such a word?

Mr. Coggeshall: Mr. Peters takes upon him to forbid me. I shall be silent.

Mr. Stoughton [assistant of the Court]: Ey, but she intended this that they say.

Gov.: Well, Mr. Leveret, what were the words? I pray, speak.

Mr. Leveret: To my best remembrance when the elders did send for her, Mr. Peters did with much vehemency and intreaty urge her to tell what difference there was between Mr. Cotton and them, and upon his urging of her she said "The fear of man is a snare, but they that trust upon the Lord shall be safe." And being asked wherein the difference was, she answered that they did not preach a covenant of grace so clearly as Mr. Cotton did, and she gave this reason of it: because that as the apostles were for a time without the spirit so until they had received the witness of the spirit they could not preach a covenant of grace so clearly.

Gov.: Don't you remember that she said they were not able ministers of the New Testament?

Mrs. H.: Mr. Weld and I had an hour's discourse at the window and then I spake that, if I spake it. . . .

Gov.: Mr. Cotton, the court desires that you declare what you do remember of the conference which was at the time and is now in question.

Mr. Cotton: I did not think I should be called to bear witness in this cause and therefore did not labor to call to remembrance what was done; but the greatest passage that took impression upon me was to this purpose. The elders spake that they had heard that she had spoken some condemning words of their ministry, and among other things they did first pray her to answer wherein she thought their ministry did differ from mine. How the comparison sprang I am ignorant, but sorry I was that any comparison should be between me and my brethren and uncomfortable it was. She told them to this purpose that they did not hold forth a covenant of grace as I did. But wherein did we differ? Why she said that they did not hold forth the seal of the spirit as he doth. Where is the difference there? Say they, why saith she, speaking to one or other of them, I know not to whom. You preach of the seal of the spirit upon a work and he upon free grace without a work or without respect to a work; he preaches the seal of the spirit upon free grace and you upon a work. I told her I was very sorry that she put comparisons between my ministry and theirs, for she had said more than I could myself, and rather I had that she had put us in fellowship with them and not have made that discrepancy. She said, she found the difference. . . .

This was the sum of the difference, nor did it seem to be so ill taken as it is and our brethren did say also that they would not so easily believe reports as they had done and withal mentioned that they would speak no more of it, some of them did; and afterwards some of them did say they were less satisfied than before. And I must say that I did not find her saying that they were under a covenant of works, nor that she said they did preach a covenant of works. . . .

[More back and forth between Rev. John Cotton, trying to defend Mrs. Hutchinson, and Mr. Peters, about exactly what Mrs. Hutchinson said.]

Mrs. H.: If you please to give me leave I shall give you the ground of what I know to be true. Being much troubled to see the falseness of the constitution of the Church of England, I had like to have turned Separatist. Whereupon I kept a day of solemn humiliation and pondering of the thing; this scripture was brought unto me—he that denies Jesus Christ to be come in the flesh is antichrist. This I considered of and in considering found that the papists did not deny him to be come in the flesh, nor we did not deny him—who then was antichrist? Was the Turk antichrist only? The Lord knows that I could not open scripture; he must by his prophetical office open it unto me. So after that being unsatisfied in the thing, the Lord was pleased to bring this scripture out of the Hebrews. he that denies the testament denies the testator, and in this did open unto me and give me to see that those which did not teach the new covenant had the spirit of antichrist, and upon this he did discover the ministry unto me; and ever since, I bless the Lord, he hath let me see which was the clear ministry and which the wrong. Since that time I confess I have been more choice and he hath left me to distinguish between the voice of my beloved and the voice of Moses, the voice of John the Baptist and the voice of antichrist, for all those voices are spoken of in scripture. Now if you do condemn me for speaking what in my conscience I know to be truth I must commit myself unto the Lord.

Mr. Nowel [assistant to the Court]: How do you know that was the spirit?

Mrs. H.: How did Abraham know that it was God that bid him offer his son, being a breach of the sixth commandment?

Dep. Gov.: By an immediate voice.

Mrs. H.: So to me by an immediate revelation.

Dep. Gov.: How! an immediate revelation.

Mrs. H.: By the voice of his own spirit to my soul. I will give you another scripture, Jer[emiah] 46: 27–28—out of which the Lord showed me what he would do for me and the rest of his servants. But after he was pleased to reveal himself to me I did presently, like Abraham, run to Hagar. And after that he did let me see the atheism of my own heart, for which I begged of the Lord that it might not remain in my heart, and being thus, he did show me this (a twelvemonth after) which I told you of before. . . . Therefore, I desire you to look to it, for you see this scripture fulfilled this day and therefore I desire you as you tender the Lord and the church and commonwealth to consider and look what you do. You have power over my body but the Lord Jesus hath power over my body and soul; and assure yourselves thus much, you do as much as in you lies to put the Lord Jesus Christ from you, and if you go on in this course you begin, you will bring a curse upon

you and your posterity, and the mouth of the Lord hath spoken it.

Dep. Gov.: What is the scripture she brings?

Mr. Stoughton [assistant to the Court]: Behold I turn away from you.

Mrs. H.: But now having seen him which is invisible I fear not what man can do unto me.

Gov.: Daniel was delivered by miracle; do you think to be deliver'd so too?

Mrs. H.: I do here speak it before the court. I look that the Lord should deliver me by his providence. . . . [because God had said to her] though I should meet with affliction, yet I am the same God that delivered Daniel out of the lion's den, I will also deliver thee.

Mr. Harlakenden [assistant to the Court]: I may read scripture and the most glorious hypocrite may read them and yet go down to hell.

Mrs. H.: It may be so. . . .

Gov.: I am persuaded that the revelation she brings forth is delusion.

[The trial text here reads:] All the court but some two or three ministers cry out, we all believe it—we all believe it. [Mrs. Hutchinson was found guilty.]

Gov.: The court hath already declared themselves satisfied concerning the things you hear, and concerning the troublesomeness of her spirit and the danger of her course amongst us, which is not to be suffered. Therefore if it be the mind of the court that Mrs. Hutchinson for these things that appear before us is unfit for our society, and if it be the mind of the court that she shall be banished out of our liberties and imprisoned till she be sent away, let them hold up their hands.

[All but three did so.]

Gov.: Mrs. Hutchinson, the sentence of the court you hear is that you are banished from out of our jurisdiction as being a woman not fit for our society, and are to be imprisoned till the court shall send you away.

Mrs. H.: I desire to know wherefore I am banished?

Gov.: Say no more. The court knows wherefore and is satisfied.

GLOSSARY

antinomian: a person who can be described as believing in antinomianism, the belief that faith alone is necessary for salvation, and that moral and man-made laws are not necessary or binding

countenance: to offer approval or moral support, to sanction

covenant of grace: the promise that God has saved certain Christians through grace and that they are made aware of their salvation through an active faith

covenant of works: the promise that Christians can achieve salvation (eternal life) by following moral law

deprave: to speak ill of; malign

Fifth Commandment: the command to "honor thy father and thy mother," one of the Ten Commandments in the Hebrew Bible

justify: to defend

reduce: to correct or punish

sedition: speech or action that promotes discontent and rebellion against the state

Separatist: sixteenth-century English Christians who wished to leave the Church of England entirely. The Pilgrims of Plymouth, Massachusetts, were Separatists.

traduce: cause humiliation by making false or malicious statements; malign

Document Analysis

The transcript of Anne Hutchinson's 1637 civil trial offers a fascinating glimpse into some of the pressing issues of colonial Massachusetts. Hutchinson was accused of disturbing "the peace of the commonwealth and the churches," which were not light charges at a time when religious and civil conformity were seen as necessary for the future of the fledgling community.

Despite the gravity of these accusations, Hutchinson was not initially charged with violating a law. Instead, as a reading of the transcript reveals, Winthrop brought Hutchinson before the General Court of Massachusetts to force her into publicly admitting that she had questioned the quality of sermons and theology of the colony's leading orthodox ministers and suggested that they did not clearly preach "salvation by grace." Further, he noted that Hutchinson had influenced the opinions of many elite Bostonians with her arguments and behaved inappropriately for a woman.

Although she ably defended herself in front of the court without the assistance of a lawyer, Hutchinson's desire to give her own opinions won out at the end of the two-day trial. After Hutchinson revealed that she believed that God had spoken to her directly, the Court found that she was not fit for society and should be banished from the colony. In this trial and a second church trial in 1638, Hutchinson herself gave the court the ammunition that they needed to find her guilty of sedition.

The Case against Anne Hutchinson

On a cold November morning in 1637, John Winthrop, newly reelected governor of the Massachusetts Bay Colony, opened the trial against Anne Hutchinson with several accusations but no legal charges. Hutchinson, he stated, caused a disturbance in the community by criticizing established, orthodox ministers in the colony and by holding meetings at her home attended by both men and women. Even worse, she supported and endorsed the preaching of less orthodox ministers like John Wheelwright, who had recently been banished from the colony. The purpose of the trial, Winthrop announced, was to determine how the authorities should proceed in regard to Hutchinson's behavior. The choice that the court had was between punishing her and letting her remain in the colonies, or removing her from the colony completely by banishing her.

It is clear from the questions of the court and from Hutchinson's answers that she was familiar with the issues with which she was charged and adept at sidestepping the charges. From the start, the transcript shows Winthrop's difficulty in stating the indictment and getting Hutchinson to admit to acting against the law. In response to his opening statement, for example, Hutchinson claimed that she heard "no things laid to my charge." His reply was, "I have told you some already and more I can tell you." Asked to name a charge, Winthrop questioned her alleged support of Wheelwright, who had preached that pious Christians could receive direct revelations from God, without ministerial intervention.

Furthermore, in a sermon that ultimately got him banished from the colony, Wheelwright had suggested that the standard view of local Puritan divines (ministers) was wrong. The majority view was that, although God alone can save souls—salvation by grace and not by good deeds—it is possible to determine if a person is sanctimonious, or a "saint," and thus allowed to participate in the church, by his or her beneficent work in the community. Wheelwright had argued that the appearance of good works cannot indicate the state of a person's soul. His sermon essentially pointed out a flaw in the other ministers' belief that sanctimony and salvation are not the same thing. Puritans were supposed to believe in predestination: the salvation of the soul through a "covenant of grace," not through a "covenant of works."

As can be seen from the back-and-forth questioning recorded in the transcript, Winthrop tried to get Hutchinson to admit that she endorsed the banished Wheelwright and his supporters, but she deftly parried his questions. Looking for a law that he could accuse her of breaking, Winthrop finally announced that she violated the fifth of the Ten Commandments: She had dishonored the "fathers of the commonwealth" by entertaining Wheelwright's supporters and his opinions. When Hutchinson continued to argue with him, Winthrop changed the topic by dismissively saying that he would not continue to argue with a woman, or "those of your sex."

As the trial went on, Hutchinson's accusers clarified and escalated the charges against her. Deputy Governor Thomas Dudley directly accused Hutchinson of speaking in derogative terms about local ministers. According to Dudley, Hutchinson suggested that the only minister in the colony who preached the true Puritan theology, a "covenant of grace," was her teacher John Cotton. Dudley also claimed that at the women's meetings Hutchinson held at her home, she promoted the opinions of Cotton and disparaged the opinions of the other ministers. Hutchinson greatly influenced members of the community through her opinions and her meetings; she was therefore the cause of the current theological dissent in the colony. "About three years ago we were all in peace," Dudley argued, but Hutchinson, "from that time she came hath made a disturbance." Since she was the foundation of the problem, "why we must take away the foundation and the building will fall." In other words, if Hutchinson were removed from the colony, there would be no more problems.

According to both Winthrop and Dudley, the source of Hutchinson's influence was the meetings that she held at her home. Earlier in the year, Hutchinson had been banned from holding these meetings despite the fact that it was common practice in the colony. As Hutchinson herself said at the trial, before she came to Massachusetts Bay Colony, women in England held such gatherings to discuss and analyze the weekly sermons. Hutchinson had initially elected not to attend the meetings, but was advised by a friend to join one so that people could not accuse her of being too proud. Eventually, men began to attend the meeting at Hutchinson's house, including the previous governor, Henry Vane. In an era when women did not have legal status or an official public voice, Hutchinson's influence on the opinions of politicians and other leading male citizens was open to criticism. Thus, at Hutchinson's trial, Dudley elaborated on this theme: "It appears by this woman's meeting that Mrs. Hutchinson hath so forestalled the minds of many by their resort to her meeting that now she hath a potent party in the country."

The problem with Hutchinson's meetings was two-fold. First, the men and women who attended her meetings found her opinions—which were not in total alignment with orthodoxy—so influential that they found the strength to disagree with prevailing opinions, creating a "potent party." Second, Hutchinson was teaching men along with women. While it was appropriate for her to teach women in a society with well-defined gender roles, it was not considered acceptable for her to teach men. Winthrop included the matter of the meetings in his initial charge against Hutchinson by noting that the authorities had already told her to cease holding them, "as a thing not tolerable nor comely in the sight of God nor fitting for your sex." Hutchinson was stepping out of her place as a woman in society. Even more irritating to the colonial leadership was the fact that her opinions carried weight.

In the middle of the trial, Winthrop clearly stated the charges against Hutchinson, adding a theological charge to the original accusations. Namely, he accused Hutchinson of saying that "the ministers preached a covenant of works and Mr. Cotton a covenant of grace." Winthrop noted that the only defense Hutchinson offered was that her conversations were private ones and not public declarations. The next step in the trial was to hear the witnesses who stood for Hutchinson's defense.

Anne Hutchinson's Defense

Hutchinson's defense consisted of her own testimony and that of three witnesses. Hutchinson verbally defended herself against her accusers in back-and-forth engagement with them. She was a quick-witted and intelligent woman and, for the most part, avoided being drawn into incriminating herself in the trial. Her rhetorical strategy was to ask the court to clarify the charges against her and to prove that she said what she was accused of saying. In some cases, Hutchinson attempted to correct her questioners, as when Dudley suggested that ministers who do not preach a covenant of grace must then be preaching a covenant of works. Not so, Hutchinson replied, noting that it was possible for one minister to preach "more clearly than another." When Dudley pressed her to answer a theological question about works and the way of salvation, Hutchinson quickly answered that she would not answer questions

"of that sort." A religious debate would not have been to her advantage when she was already under suspicion of being unorthodox.

Another of Hutchinson's defense strategies was to claim that her opinions were not intended to be repeated in public, and thus were not libelous or seditious. As a woman, Hutchinson did not have legal rights; her claim of private conversation helped remind the court that she had behaved properly by acting in private rather than taking on a public role. This did not prove to be an effective defense, however, and Winthrop simply dismissed it as an excuse.

On the second day of Hutchinson's trial, the court was persuaded to call three witnesses for Hutchinson: John Coggeshall, Thomas Leverett, and her minister, John Cotton. Hutchinson and the others had been called before Puritan ministers almost a year before to resolve many of the same issues brought up at this trial; during the trial they were to testify about that earlier meeting. Coggeshall's testimony was brief, and he ceased to speak when one of the ministers, Hugh Peter, exclaimed in outrage at his defense of Hutchinson.

The witness who had the most at stake was Cotton, who had himself been questioned on points of theological orthodoxy. Cotton was conciliatory in his testimony, at first suggesting that he did not recall all that was said at the earlier meeting. He did remember, however, that Hutchinson was questioned at the previous meeting about some comparisons that she had made between his sermons and those of the other ministers. Cotton noted that any comparisons of this sort made him uncomfortable and that he would not go so far as to make distinctions between his theology and the rest of the ministry. Hutchinson, however, had claimed that she saw a difference. In order to smooth over the issue, Cotton stated that he did not think that the other ministers found this so objectionable, but they clearly had taken more offense to her statements than he previously thought. After this rather weak argument, Cotton ultimately did speak out in defense of his parishioner. In his opinion, Hutchinson did not say that the rest of the ministers preached a covenant of works.

Near the trial's end, Hutchinson eloquently spoke on her own behalf. Until this point in the trial, she had restricted herself to answering questions. On the second day, begging the court's permission, Hutchinson spoke about how she came to be a Puritan. When she had at first considered becoming a Separatist, she turned to prayer to consider which direction she should take. She told the ministers that she was directed by God to the proper scriptural passage, which helped her make her decision. Since then, she had been able to distinguish his voice from other biblical voices. Anticipating that the ministers would not approve of these comments, she added, "Now if you do condemn me for speaking what in my conscience I know to be truth I must commit myself unto the Lord." After previously defending herself on the grounds that her private thoughts were not intended to be public, Hutchinson herself began to make them so by speaking her conscience.

Following her statement, Hutchinson answered questions to confirm her belief that God spoke to her directly. In the face of the court's astonishment at her statements, Hutchinson went even further, saying that she knew she would encounter hardship one day because God had told her that she would "meet with affliction." She believed, however, that he would deliver her from it. Finally, she indicated that the ministers, the colony, and their descendants would be cursed "if you go on in this course." She knew these things because God showed her, and she no longer feared what men could do to her because she relied solely upon God.

Hutchinson's claims of direct revelation and prophesy were the final straw for her defense, and the court rapidly concluded that she was a dangerous influence on society. She was forthwith sentenced to house arrest and subsequent banishment. Hutchinson had previously been deemed a disruptive influence when she was suspected of unorthodox beliefs and of undermining the colony's ministers. Her assertion that God spoke to her directly and showed her the future was more than disruptive, however; it was heretical. Her statement that she did not fear man's law also made her potentially uncontrollable and dangerous.

In the end, Hutchinson was convicted on her own testimony. She ably deflected the accusations of the colony's leading men for almost two days by maintaining her composure and her right to hold her own opinions privately. She was able to call upon the support of one of the most revered ministers in the colony, Reverend John Cotton. Before Hutchinson gave her final testimony, it appeared likely that the results of her trial would be inconclusive. It is not clear why Hutchinson finally felt compelled to speak out about her beliefs, but the trial's transcript does show that Hutchinson's desire to speak her conscience led to her conviction.

Essential Themes

Anne Hutchinson's 1637 trial and transcript contain several themes that have resonated through the centuries. During Hutchinson's time, people who were familiar with her trial interpreted it as an example of religious heresy and a challenge to the stability of the new colony. In modern times, scholars have viewed Hutchinson's trial as an example of how society handles dissent and of an individual's right to speak his or her conscience.

Hutchinson's story was well known during the seventeenth century. The Massachusetts Bay Colony leadership used it as an example of how decisively they handled challenges such as religious dissent, disorderly conduct, and heretical thought. Her trial later became understood as the central episode in the Antinomian Controversy, expounded on in works such as John Winthrop's *Antinomians and Familists Condemned by the Synod of Elders in New England* (1644). Historians have noted that the Antinomian Controversy involved many more individuals than Hutchinson and her supporters and that it took place over a longer period of time. Still, the authorities' reaction to Hutchinson shows how vulnerable they felt the colony to be in the face of criticism back in England and at home. The "noble experiment" of the colony was only seven years old at the time of the Hutchinson trial; any threat to its social order was taken as a serious threat to its survival.

By far the most prominent theme for modern readers, however, is the view of Hutchinson as a spokeswoman for civil liberty. A statue of Anne Hutchinson erected in 1922 in Boston, Massachusetts, makes this clear. It is inscribed, "In Memory of Anne Marbury Hutchinson . . . Courageous Exponent of Civil Liberty and Religious Toleration." Hutchinson's claim that she must speak "what in my conscience I know to be truth" has had great appeal to Americans who see civil liberty, religious toleration, and freedom of speech as founding beliefs of the nation. This theme has seemed especially relevant at times in the past when the government took action against individual dissenting citizens, such as in the 1950s anti-Communist crusade of Senator Joseph McCarthy and the House Committee on Un-American Activities, and in the nonviolent civil disobedience of the 1960s. Thus, the story of Anne Hutchinson's trial, as revealed in its court transcript, both offers a glimpse into past conflicts over religion and social order and speaks to these issues beyond her time.

Meg Meneghel MacDonald, PhD

Bibliography

Breen, Louise A. *Transgressing the Bounds: Subversive Enterprises Among the Puritan Elite in Massachusetts, 1630–1692.* New York: Oxford UP, 2001. Print.

Field, Jonathan B. "The Antinomian Controversy Did Not Take Place." *Early American Studies* 6.2 (2008): 448–463. Print.

Gaustad, Edwin S. *A Documentary History of Religion in America.* Grand Rapids: Eerdmans, 1982. Print.

Knoppers, Laura L. *Puritanism and Its Discontents.* Newark: U of Delaware P, 2003. Print.

Lang, Amy S. *Prophetic Woman: Anne Hutchinson and the Problem of Dissent in the Literature of New England.* Berkeley: U of California P, 1987. Print.

LaPlante, Eve. *American Jezebel: The Uncommon Life of Anne Hutchinson, the Woman Who Defied the Puritans.* San Francisco: Harper, 2004. Print.

Additional Reading

Gura, Philip F. *A Glimpse of Sion's Glory: Puritan Radicalism in New England, 1620–1660.* Middletown, CT: Wesleyan UP, 1984. Print.

Hall, David D. *A Reforming People: Puritanism and the Transformation of Public Life in New England.* New York: Knopf, 2011. Print.

---, ed. *The Antinomian Controversy, 1636–1638: A Documentary History.* 2nd ed. Durham, NC: Duke UP, 1990. Print.

Hutchinson, Thomas. *The History of the Colony of Massachusett's Bay.* 2nd ed. London: privately printed, 1765. E-book. Web. 14 Aug. 2012.

Williams, Selma R. *Divine Rebel: The Life of Anne Marbury Hutchinson.* New York: Holt, 1981. Print.

Winship, Michael P. *The Times and Trials of Anne Hutchinson: Puritans Divided.* Lawrence: UP of Kansas, 2005. Print.

Winthrop, John. *Winthrop's Journal, "History of New England," 1630–1649,* Ed. James Kendall Hosner. New York: Scribner, 1908. E-book. Web. 14 Aug. 2012.

LESSON PLAN: Anne Hutchinson on Trial

Students analyze the trial of Anne Hutchinson and consider multiple perspectives on her religious beliefs.

Learning Objectives
Identify multiple perspectives on Anne Hutchinson's religious beliefs as expressed in the trial; compare and contrast ideas about religious freedom and church authority; analyze the importance of Anne Hutchinson's role in history.
Materials: "Transcript from the Trial of Anne Hutchinson"

Overview Questions
In the transcript, what do the court and Governor Winthrop accuse Hutchinson of doing, and what evidence do they use? Upon what authority does the church have to base its charges against Hutchinson? How does Hutchinson defend herself? Why was the trial of Hutchinson important in understanding colonial perspective on differing ideas?

Step 1: Context Questions
Why did the Puritans leave England to settle in America? How did their quest for religious freedom affect the Puritans' viewpoints on religious freedom of others and church authority?

> ▶ **Activity:** Instruct students to compare and contrast the Puritans' viewpoints on religious freedom in England and in the Massachusetts Bay Colony. Then ask students to describe how the Puritans' perspective on religious freedom affected how they governed the colony.

Step 2: Comprehension Questions
Why was Hutchinson accused and brought before the court? What evidence do the court and Governor Winthrop use to support the accusations made against her by the church?

> ▶ **Activity:** Select students to read aloud key passages. Ask students to underline the words and phrases that describe the accusations against Hutchinson. Have students circle the words, phrases, and Biblical references that serve as evidence.

Step 3: Comprehension Questions
Upon what authority does the church accuse Hutchinson? How did the church's viewpoint on the role of women affect its decision to bring her to trial? How does Hutchinson defend herself?

> ▶ **Activity:** Ask students to write a summary explaining why Hutchinson is accused. Have them consider the role of women in colonial America in their summaries.

Step 4: Exploration Questions
What importance does the trial of Anne Hutchinson have in understanding the authority of the church, ideas on religious freedom, and the role of women in colonial America? What were the effects and lasting influence of the trial and banishment of Hutchinson?

> ▶ **Activity:** Ask students to select words, phrases, and passages that discuss church authority, rights and rules, and the role of women. Then have them make a list of reasons why the trial and Hutchinson's banishment are important in understanding historical perspective and the influence of differing ideas in colonial America.

Step 5: Response Paper
Word length and additional requirements set by Instructor. Students answer the research question in the Overview Questions. Students state a thesis and use as evidence passages from the primary source document as well as support from supplemental materials assigned in the lesson.

■ A Brief Recognition of New England's Errand into the Wilderness

Date: 1670
Author: Danforth, Samuel
Genre: sermon

"What went ye out into the Wilderness to see?"

Summary Overview

"A Brief Recognition of New England's Errand into the Wilderness" was a sermon by Reverend Samuel Danforth, pastor of the Puritan church in Roxbury, a town near Boston in the Massachusetts Bay Colony. As he delivered the sermon before the newly elected members of the General Court of that state, Danforth used the occasion to remind the delegates that the reason the New England colonies came into being was to create a society based on Puritan values and traditions. The primary focus of the new leaders should be to uphold these spiritual ideals, placing them above more earthbound matters of public policy. The sermon, therefore, cautioned the delegates to be mindful of their duties to the church (and God) as well as the body politic.

Defining Moment

In the early to mid-sixteenth century, English King Henry VIII cut ties with the Vatican and forged a new church during the period known as the Reformation. His Church of England, which was fully established in the latter part of the sixteenth century, seemed to strike a middle ground between the ceremony and iconography of Catholicism and the stripped-down faith known as Calvinism. Henry VIII, as monarch of England, assumed the ultimate authority over the church (as would his successors), directing his bishops and clergymen to administer his particular religious ideals among the people.

Meanwhile, the Puritans (a term originally intended to be derogatory) protested the fact that the Church of England retained many of the tenets of Catholicism—

as Calvinists, the Puritans took issue with such ideological similarities. Puritans stressed the word of the Bible as the true road to salvation, eschewing any of the traditions and trappings of the Catholic Church or the Church of England. As the English church grew, so did the Puritan movement, with the two groups at odds.

The conflict between the English church and the Puritans abated somewhat by 1558, when Queen Elizabeth I took the throne. Elizabeth signed the Act of Supremacy in 1559, reestablishing the Church of England after the reign of her Catholic half-sister, Mary I. Although, she did away with many aspects of the Catholic mass, she kept some of the traditions, which angered Puritans. However, Elizabeth allowed for the election of Puritans to Parliament, and even retained some Puritans as advisors. Meanwhile, a group of separatist Puritans, observing the corruption and general malfeasance of the local church representatives, decided to leave England altogether, settling in Holland (now the Netherlands).

In 1603, Elizabeth I died, leaving no heirs. Scottish King James I assumed the throne, vowing to reinvigorate the Church of England. In doing so, he allowed for the increased repression of the Puritans (even those who were loyal to the throne). Some of the separatists who had fled to Holland decided to join the increasing number of groups traveling to the New World to start colonies. This group was known as the Pilgrims. The Pilgrims arrived in Plymouth, Massachusetts, in 1620. By this time the son of James I, Charles I, had assumed the throne and continued the trend of despotism that had grown since Elizabeth's death. A group of

Puritans, led by John Winthrop, joined the Massachusetts Trading Company in traveling to New England to start a new colony. The Massachusetts Bay Colony was to remain loyal to the Crown, led by a governing body known as the Massachusetts General Court. Nevertheless, the colony was founded on Puritan principles and values, with the Puritan congregational church clearly the dominant social and cultural force in the region.

Author Biography

Reverend Samuel Danforth was born in 1626 in Framlingham, a community in Suffolk, England. His mother, Elizabeth, died when Samuel was three years old. In 1634, Samuel, his brother Thomas (who would later become a colonial governor) and his father immigrated to New England, settling in the Boston area. Danforth attended Harvard College to become a minister.

While at Harvard, Danforth became interested in learning all aspects of culture and literature, not just the traditional texts of Puritan ideals. He embraced poetry, reading the works of so-called pagan writers. Although his interests outside of Puritan culture were considered unhealthy, by his teachers, he eventually embraced the ideals of Puritan culture, graduating from Harvard in 1643.

As he completed his studies at Harvard, Samuel Danforth was approached by Reverend Thomas Welde to become a colleague pastor at the Roxbury church outside of Boston. In this capacity, he would work with the Reverend John Eliot, who had become known as "the Apostle to the Indians" for his ministerial work with the New England tribes. Danforth accepted the offer, and worked at the church through his graduation from Harvard. In 1650, Danforth completed his training and was ordained as a minister at the Roxbury church. A year after his ordination, Danforth married Mary Wilson. They would eventually have twelve children.

In addition to his talents as a poet and a Puritan minister, Samuel Danforth had an interest in natural science, with which he struck a delicate balance with his Christian faith. He gained a strong understanding of astronomy, which he integrated into his work as a minister. In 1664, for example, a comet approached the earth. Danforth used the occasion to remind the congregation of the importance of studying the comet's natural properties and dynamics. However, he stressed, comets also served as signs from God, and that people and theologians alike should study and appreciate their spiritual significance.

Samuel Danforth remained the minister of the Roxbury church for twenty-four years, becoming widely known for his pious leadership and decency. While in his forties, Danforth took ill with what physicians at the time called putrid fever (which we now know as typhus). However, Danforth stayed on as the leader of the Roxbury church until his death on November 19, 1674.

HISTORICAL DOCUMENT

The general Question is, What went ye out into the Wilderness to see? He saith not, Whom went ye out to hear, but what went ye out to see? The phrase agrees to Shows and Stage-playes; plainly arguing that many of those, who seemed well-affected to John, and flock'd after him, were Theatrical Hearers, Spectators rather than Auditors; they went not to hear, but to see; they went to gaze upon a new and strange Spectacle.

This general Question being propounded, the first particular Enquiry is, whether they went to see A reed shaken with the wind? The expression is Metaphorical and Proverbial. A reed when the season is calm, lifts up it self and stands upright, but no sooner doth the wind blow upon it, but it shakes and trembles, bends and bows down, and then gets up again : and again it yields and bows, and then lifts up it self again. A notable Emblem of light, empty and inconstant persons, who in times of peace and tranquillity, give a fair and plausible Testimony to the Truth; but no sooner do the winds of Temptation blow upon them, and the waves of Troubles roll over them, but they incline and yield to the prevailing Party: but when the Tempest is over, they recover themselves and assert the Truth again. The meaning then of this first Enquiry is, Went ye out into the Wilderness to see a light, vain and in constant man, one that could confess and deny, and deny and confess the same Truth? This Interrogation is to be understood negatively and ironically; *q.d.* Surely ye went not into the desert to behold such a ludicrous and ridiculous sight, A man like unto a reed shaken with the wind. Under the negation of the contrary levity, our Saviour sets forth one of John's excellencies, viz. his eminent Constancy in asserting the Truth. The winds of various temptations both on the right hand and on the left, blew upon him, yet he wavered not in his testimony concerning Christ, He confessed and denied not, but confessed the truth.

Then the general Question is repeated, But what went ye out for to see? and a second particular Enquiry made, Was it to see a man clothed in soft raiment? This Interrogation hath also the force of a negation, *q.d.* Surely ye went not into the Wilderness to see a man clothed in silken and costly Apparel. The reason of this is added, Behold., they that wear soft clothing, are in Kings houses. Delicate and costly Apparel is to be expected in Princes Courts, and not in wilde Woods and Forrests. Under the negation of John's affectation of Courtly delicacy, our Saviour sets forth another of John's excellencies, viz. his singular gravity and sobriety, who wore rough garments, and lived on course and mean fare, *Mat.* 3. 4. which austere kinde of life was accommodated to the place and work of his Ministry. John Preached in the Wilderness, which was no fit place for silken and soft raiment. His work was to pre pare a people for the Lord, by calling them off from worldly pomp and vanities, unto repentance and mourning for sin. His peculiar habit and diet was such as became a penitentiary Preacher.

Thirdly, the generall Question is reiterated, But what went ye out for to see? and a third particular Enquiry made, Was it to see a Prophet? This Interrogation is to be understood affirmatively, *q.d.* no doubt but it was to see a Prophet. Had not John been a rare and excellent Minister of God, you would never have gone out of your Cities into the desert to have seen him. Thus our Saviour sets forth another of John's admirable excellencies, viz. his Prophetical Office and Function. John was not an ordinary Interpreter of the Law, much less a Teacher of Jewish Traditions, but a Prophet, one who by the extraordinary Inspiration of the holy Ghost, made known the Mysteries of Salvation, *Luke 1.* 76, 77.

Lastly, our Saviour determines and concludes the Question, He, whom ye went out to see was more then a Prophet, , much more, or abundantly more then a Prophet. This he confirms by his wonted Asseveration, Yea, I say unto you, and much more then a Prophet. How was John much more then a Prophet? John was Christs Herauld sent immediately before his face, to proclaim his Coming and Kingdome, and prepare the people for the reception of him by the Baptism of Repentance, *ver.* 10. Hence it follows *ver.* 11. Among all that are born of women, there hath not risen a greater Prophet then John. John was greater then any of the Prophets that were before him, not in respect of his personal graces and virtues, (for who shall perswade us that he excelled Abraham in the grace of Faith, who was the father of the faithful, or Moses in Meekness, who was the meekest man on earth, or David in Faithfulness, who was a man after Gods own heart, or Solomon in Wisdome, who was the wisest man that ever was or shall be?) but in respect of the manner of his dispensation. All the Prophets foretold Christs Coming, his Sufferings and Glory, but the Baptist was his Harbinger and Forerunner, that bare the Sword before him, Proclaimed his Presence, and made room for him in the hearts of the people. All the Prophets saw Christ afar off, but the Baptist saw him present, baptized him, and applied the Types to him personally. Behold the Lamb of God. He saw and bare record that this is the Son of God, *Joh.* 1. 29, 34. But he that is least in the Kingdome of Heaven, is greater then John. The least Prophet in the Kingdome of Heaven, i.e. the least Minister of the Gospel since Christ's Ascension, is greater then John; not in respect of the measure of his personal gifts, nor in respect of the manner of his Calling, but in respect of the Object of his Ministry, Christ on the Throne, having finished the work of our Redemption, and in respect of the degree of the revelation of Christ, which is far more clear and full. John shewed Christ in the flesh, and pointed to him with his finger, but the Ministers of the Gospel declare that he hath done and suffered all things necessary to our Salvation, and is risen again and set down at the right hand of God.

Doct. *Such as have sometime left their pleasant Cities and Habitations to enjoy the pure Worship of God in a Wilderness, are apt in time to abate and cool in their affection thereunto : but then the Lord calls upon them seriously and throughly to examine themselves, what it was that drew them into the Wilderness, and to consider that it was not the expectation of ludicrous levity, nor of Courtly pomp and delicacy, but of the free and clear dispensation of the Gospel and Kingdome of God. . .*

※ ※ ※

But what shall we do for bread? The encrease of the field and the labour of the Husbandman fails.

Hear Christ's answer to his Disciples, when they were troubled, because there was but one Loaf in the ship. *O ye of little faith, why reason ye, because you have no bread? perceive ye not yet, neither understand? have ye your heart yet hardened? having eyes, see ye not? and having ears, hear ye not, and do ye not remember? Mark 8. 17, 18. Mat. 16. 8, 9.* Those which have had large and plentiful experience of the grace and power of Christ in providing for their outward Sustenance, and relieving of their Necessities, when ordinary and usual Means have failed, are worthy to be severely reprehended, if afterward they grow anxiously careful and solicitous, because of the defect of outward supplies. In the whole Evangelicall History, I finde not that ever the Lord Jesus did so sharply rebuke his Disciples for any thing, as for that fit and pang of Worldly care and solicitude about Bread. Attend we our Errand, upon which Christ sent us into the Wilderness, and he will provide Bread for us. *Math. 6. 33. Seek ye first the Kingdome of God, and his Righteousness, and all these things shall be added unto you.*

But we have many Adversaries, and they have their subtile Machinations and Contrivances, and how soon we may be surprized, we know not.

Our diligent Attention to the Ministry of the Gospel, is a special means to check and restrain the rage and fury of Adversaries. The people's assiduity in attendance upon Christ's Ministry, was the great obstacle that hindred the execution of the bloody Counsels of the Pharisees. *Luk. 19. 47, 48. He taught daily in the Temple, but the chief Priests and the Scribes, and the chief of the people, sought to destroy him, and could not finde what they might do: for all the people were very attentive to hear him.* If the people cleave to the Lord, to his Prophets, and to his Ordinances, it will strike such a fear into the hearts of enemies, that they will be at their wits ends, and not know what to do. However, In this way we have the promise of divine Protection and Preservation. *Revel. 3. 10. Because thou hast kept the word of my Patience, I also will keep thee from the hour of Temptation, which shall come upon all the world, to try them that dwell upon the earth.* Let us with Mary choose this for our Portion, To sit at Christ's feet and hear his word; and whosoever complain against us, the Lord Jesus will plead for us, as he did for her, and say. They have chosen that good part, which shall not be taken away from them, *Luk. 10. 42.* AMEN.

GLOSSARY

baptism: Christian ceremony in which a person is immersed in water to cleanse him or her from sin

herauld: herald; a forerunner to an upcoming individual or event

husbandman: farmer

prophet: person who, through divine inspiration, preaches the will of God to others

raiment: clothing or garb

Document Analysis

The election of delegates to the General Court was considered an important civic event for the fledgling Puritan colony in Massachusetts. The newly elected leaders were charged with helping to build a new community in what they saw was a wilderness. Addressing this group, the Reverend Samuel Danforth recalled Matthew 11 as it appeared in the New Testament of the Bible. According to this Gospel, Jesus offered his praise of John the Baptist, who left his own society to live in the harsh wilderness, performing the work of God while preparing humanity for Jesus Christ's arrival.

Reverend Danforth's sermon serves as a reminder for the delegates to remain mindful of Christian (and more specifically, Puritan Christian) values as they went about their political activities. The "wilderness" in which the Puritan colonists had arrived was developing rapidly, but there were still many dangers to be addressed and overcome. Still, Danforth reminds these new leaders (and indeed all of the Puritan colonists in attendance at that event) that, although meeting these challenges would be extremely difficult, success could be reached through steadfast commitment to God and the Church.

"A Brief Recognition of New England's Errand into the Wilderness" also presents the New England colonies as unique settlements among the American colonies. Because of its distinctive Puritan composition, the New England experience could be compared to other remote locations to which people of religious conviction traveled to explore their faith and live a life free from the oppression of others. In light of the trials and challenges the Puritans had prior to their arrival in America, Danforth saw parallels between their own adversities and the many trials and challenges faced by John the Baptist, Jesus Christ, and their followers more than a millennium before.

Danforth's sermon begins with a reflection on this Biblical passage, discussing how many people who had heard about John the Baptist's travels into the wilderness followed him in the hope that they might understand what he was doing. According to the account, Jesus asked, "What went ye out into the wilderness to see?" questioning why John the Baptist's "spectacle" was of significance to those who traveled to see him.

Reverend Danforth offers further depth to this reference by comparing the Gospel to the responsibilities of government that the General Court's new members were about to assume. He begins by analyzing a key question: Did John the Baptist's followers proceed with him into the wilderness to see "a reed shaken in the wind"? He answers that question by commenting on the negativity of the metaphor. A reed, Danforth explains, stands tall and upright when the wind is calm. However, when the wind blows even lightly, the reed shakes, trembles, and bends downward. Only when the wind subsides does the reed return to its upright stance.

Danforth points out that people who appear as a reed in the wind are inconstant and "empty." These individuals agree to the truth (in other words, the distinct word of God) when conditions are calm and peaceful. When strong forces that run contrary to God's word begin to influence them, however, those people yield. Danforth cites temptation as one of these forces; only when the pressure of temptation is lifted do those empty people return to their morally upright positions and once again embrace the word of God.

In this regard, Danforth argues, John the Baptist's followers could never have traveled into the wilderness to witness his own lightness of being. In fact, Danforth states, John was a constant man, unyielding to temptation and wholly dedicated to God's truth. Furthermore, even as his notoriety grew and more came to witness his baptisms, John never believed in his fame as some sort of divine gift. Rather, Christ, for whom he was waiting, was the truth the people sought. Danforth's point was that John remained truthful and committed to his faith in Christ, even when the authorities took him into custody—as Danforth's sermon indicates, John never doubted Jesus, despite the imminent threat of torture and death leveled at him for that support.

The point that Danforth is making with this reference is that the new delegates to the General Court should demonstrate similar inflexibility when it comes to their responsibilities to the people of the Massachusetts Bay Colony. The temptation may arise to show a light-handed interpretation of prevailing Puritan tradition in the governance of the new colony, Danforth says. An honest and clear demonstration of adherence to Puritan Christian values, Danforth asserts, inspires the people in the very same way that John the Baptist's speech did.

Danforth continues his review of the story of John the Baptist and Christ. Christ repeats the earlier question about why John's followers came with him into the harsh wilderness, adding if they did so to see John dressed in soft, beautiful clothes. Danforth notes that the Gospel clarifies this question by observing that Christ's words read in negative fashion. Surely, Christ was saying, the people did not come into the wilderness to see a man dressed like a member of royalty. Danforth points out that only kings residing in large houses dress in fine garments. John, according to Christ, was not dressed in such a manner, nor did he live in a king's home.

According to the passage and Danforth's interpretation thereof, John the Baptist had the appearance of someone who was living in an environment that was difficult and unforgiving, one in which the soft and delicate clothing worn by wealthy men would be ruined. Danforth added that John lived an austere life, eating little and wearing clothes that could withstand the harsh climate.

Furthermore, John did not concern himself with the garments and trappings of wealthy, influential people. His task was to prepare the world for Christ's arrival and, in doing so, to help as many people as possible cleanse themselves from sin. John the Baptist was, in the estimation of both Christ and Danforth, a man of great sobriety and gravity, focused on the salvation of others rather than the acquisition of personal wealth and possessions.

Here, Danforth issues a very clear warning to the delegates to be similarly mindful of their own responsibilities. All of those people who had come to New England had arrived in another challenging environment. They did so, according to Danforth, not to find wealth and luxurious property but to establish a community based on Christian values. He cautions the delegates to remain focused on the spiritual basis of their government rather than the trappings of power and prestige.

The Gospel, as interpreted by Danforth, then asked for a third time what the people hoped to see when they traveled to the remote location where John the Baptist had settled. This time, however, the question was accompanied by a question to which the answer would be in the affirmative: "Was it to see a prophet?" Danforth points to Christ's declaration that John the Baptist was indeed a prophet. To be sure, Danforth argues, John was a teacher of the traditions and values of Judaism, interpreting Jewish law and helping others conform to these concepts. However, the Holy Spirit descended upon him, granting John divine inspiration. From this point forward, John became knowledgeable of the mys-

teries of salvation as well as the steps humans needed to take to achieve that salvation.

From the point at which John became imbued with these concepts, however, he became much more than a simple carrier of God's word. According to Jesus's teachings, John was much more than a prophet. He was, in fact, the Messiah's herald, placed on Earth to help humanity understand and prepare for the coming of the Son of God. John would spread the word about the Messiah's coming and the kingdom that Jesus would bring to Earth. He would also help prepare the people for entrance into the Messiah's kingdom through the power of repentance and baptism, removing from the people the sins they carried their entire lives.

Danforth continued to discuss John's significance in relation to other prophets. Indeed, the reverend points to the scripture that states that there has never before arisen a prophet greater than John the Baptist. Such an elevation in status was not made out of disrespect for someone like Abraham, whose faith fostered and united the faiths of countless generations after him. Similarly, John's graces could not be adequately compared to the wisdom of Solomon, the humility of Moses, or the faith of David. Additionally, Danforth argues, there were many prophets who, for ages prior, foretold with great accuracy the coming of the Messiah (including his birth, life, torture, and death). Danforth makes clear that the significance of each of the graces and virtues of the prophets could not be downgraded when compared to John.

Rather, John the Baptist's singularity as the greatest of the prophets was rooted in the fact that John knew of the Messiah's coming and when he arrived. He even undertook the task of preparing the people for his arrival, baptizing an inordinate number of the faithful. In this regard, Danforth says, John served as the sword of the Son of God, making room for the Messiah "in the hearts of the people."

Furthermore, John immediately recognized Jesus when they met, baptizing him and presenting him to the people as the Messiah. John's status as the harbinger of Jesus therefore made him singular among all of the prophets. John helped countless people redeem themselves before Jesus, by his death, redeemed all of humanity from their sins.

According to scripture, John the Baptist chose to move away from the city and into the wilderness, where the climate was harsh, food was scarce, wild animals threatened his life, and there were few commodities available (including clothing). Then again, John's decision was not entirely his own; the Gospel suggests that John was in fact drawn to the wild by the Holy Spirit. He was not the only such individual the Bible cited for withdrawing from populated areas: according to the Gospel, the Holy Spirit led Jesus into the wild (where he met John). On a number of other occasions, Jesus traveled away from others in order to pray.

Danforth believes the wilderness to be an important aspect of communing with God. By leaving the comforts of the city, Danforth argues, people are able to worship God in a pure, distraction-free environment. He states that many individuals take brief trips to quieter locations, where they can relax and gather themselves spiritually. In fact, Danforth states, God draws people into the wilderness, not for pleasure or to live in luxury, but so that they can conduct a serious examination of themselves and their faith. Furthermore, he brings people to such locations so that they may learn and spread the true and unaltered Gospel of the Lord.

Danforth makes this point to the delegates in order to remind them of the true reason the people left England for New England: they arrived to convene with God and carry out His word. As was the case for John the Baptist and his followers, however, the environment in which the Puritans found themselves was harsh and challenging. In addition to the natural dangers that he and his followers faced in his remote location, John the Baptist encountered a great many trials as he prepared humanity for the coming of the Messiah, not the least of which was his eventual capture, torture, and death at the hands of his adversaries. Still, John was vindicated when he came face-to-face with Jesus Christ, and according to Danforth and the Bible, was ultimately rewarded with a special place in the Kingdom of God.

Danforth's meditation on the plight of John the Baptist in the wilderness, as presented to the new delegates to the General Court of Massachusetts, served two important purposes. The first was to remind the group that the primary purpose of the colony was to foster an environment in which the Puritan ideal would be upheld. Like John the Baptist and his followers, the Puritans were drawn by God away from the comforts of home and into an a region with dangerous animals, an unfamiliar and sometimes unfriendly population, and severe winter weather, with only the supplies they brought with them to sustain them and help built the new colony. Danforth is reminding them

to stand tall in the face of these adversities, as such trials were part of God's plan; they were performing a holy task given to them by the Lord, and this task was not to be undone.

The second purpose of this approach to Danforth's sermon to the General Court was to remind its members to stay their course. In addition to the natural and human challenges they faced in the development of the Massachusetts Bay Colony was the temptation to use their position to pursue personal wealth or otherwise focus entirely on worldly concerns over the defeat of sin and the pursuit of salvation. God, Danforth cautions, would continue to punish the sinners among the colonists by inflicting hardships and trials upon them.

The key, according to Danforth, was continued diligence and attention to the teachings of the Bible. Their reward for doing so would be the strength of God on their side in the face of their adversaries. Danforth cites the example of the early Christians in the face of the Pharisees, a powerful and influential group of Jewish political leaders In this case, the Pharisees denied the divinity of Jesus Christ and attempted to curb his growing popularity. The Pharisees are said to have plotted with King Herod to have Jesus captured and, ultimately, crucified. Reverend Danforth states that the Pharisees made a conscientious effort to wipe out Christ's followers during and after Christ's lifetime. However, the faith and dedication of the Christians was the obstacle that prevented the Pharisees from succeeding in this endeavor.

Danforth continued to promise the new members of the General Court that, as long as they remained true to their Puritan values, they would enjoy God's support when facing challenges. Their faith would serve as a weapon against the many adversaries that these leaders would encounter. If these leaders, as well as all other Puritans in Massachusetts, hold fast to God, Jesus, and the prophets (as well as God's laws), those who oppose or otherwise seek to undermine them will become exasperated and confused.

Reverend Danforth advises that continued practice of Puritan tradition and adherence to God's laws is the key to "divine protection and preservation." This concept refers to the Book of Revelation 3:10, in which God (through the apostle John) promises that, on the day all people are judged for their sins, those who kept God's word will be given special protection by Jesus. Christ, who would return on Judgment Day, would defend any faithful person who was accused of sin.

Essential Themes

"A Brief Recognition of New England's Errands into the Wilderness" is both a lamentation and an exhortation. Presented to the new delegates to the institution that would be charged with governing the Massachusetts Bay Colony, the sermon distinguishes the region from other colonized territories, citing a strong foundation of religious faith and tradition. To help illustrate his points, Reverend Samuel Danforth drew parallels between the New England area and the remote location in which John the Baptist conducted his holy duty of baptizing Jesus Christ and countless others.

As a lamentation on the ills of society, the sermon discusses the challenges facing all of the region's colonists, including the inconsistency of food supplies and farming in New England as well as the region's harsh winters. The sermon does not focus just on the physical and environmental problems facing the fledgling colony. Rather, this complaint also takes to task the corruptibility of leadership. Danforth cites the fact that many people who acquire power are quick to waste it with self-indulgence. Additionally, Danforth commented on the fact that far too many leaders compromise their faith in order to serve the general public.

Danforth recalled another story in which God led an individual and his followers away from the city and into the wilderness. Like the Puritans, John the Baptist was drawn into the wilderness in order to perform his holy tasks. The messiah's herald, John was subjected to a harsh climate and rivals who refused to accept John's messages about the impending arrival of the King of the Jews (including but not limited to the Pharisees). Even though he was eventually killed by his rivals, John the Baptist never wavered in his faith, a point that Danforth underscored strongly in his sermon.

While Danforth lamented on the shortcomings of humanity as the colonists struggled to build the colony, he also exhorted the leaders of the General Court (as well as the large crowd of local residents who were on hand to witness the ceremony) to learn from and emulate the uncompromising and tireless example of John. By remaining true to the tenets of Puritan Christianity, Danforth argued, the colonists would succeed in taking control of that new land. Furthermore, maintaining dedication to the ideals of Puritanism would enable the people to achieve an even greater success; when Judgment Day inevitably comes, Danforth argued, those who had purity and faith would be called into Heaven and allowed to join Jesus Christ's company.

Michael P. Auerbach, MA

Bibliography

Berkovitch, Sacvan. "New England's Errand Reappraised." *New Directions in American Intellectual History,* ed. John Hingham and Paul Conkin. Baltimore: Johns Hopkins UP. 1979. Print.

Danforth, Samuel. "A Brief Recognition of New-England's Errand into the Wilderness: An Online Electronic Text Edition." Ed. Paul Royster. *DigitalCommons@ University of Nebraska-Lincoln.* Libraries at University of Nebraska-Lincoln. 2006. Web. 18 May 2012.

Heinsohn, Robert Jennings. "Pilgrims and Puritans in 17th Century New England." *Sail 1620.* Society of Mayflower Descendants in the Commonwealth of Pennsylvania. 2012. Web. 18 May 2012.

"Puritanism." *History.com.* The History Channel. 2012. Web. 18 May 2012.

Additional Reading

Andrews, Charles McLean. *The Fathers of New England: A Chronicle of the Puritan Commonwealths.* Charleston: Nabu. 2010. Print.

Bremer, Francis J. *First Founders: American Puritans and Puritanism in the Atlantic World.* Durham: U of New Hampshire P. 2012. Print.

Dow, George Francis. *Every Day Life in the Massachusetts Bay Colony.* Mineola: Dover. 1988. Print.

Zakai, Avihu. *Theocracy in Massachusetts: Reformation and Separation in Early Puritan New England.* Lewiston: Mellen. 1994. Print.

LESSON PLAN: Re-examining the "Wilderness" of New England

Students analyze Samuel Danforth's sermon and his ideas about how colonists have strayed from the main purpose for the establishment of New England.

Learning Objectives

Draw comparisons across eras in order to define enduring ideas of the Puritans; consider multiple perspectives on the role of the colonists in New England; Formulate examples of how different choices made by the Puritans could have resulted in different outcomes

Materials: "A Brief Recognition of New-England's Errand in the Wilderness" by Samuel Danforth; "A Model of Christian Charity" by John Winthrop

Overview Questions

What evidence does Danforth use to support his statement that New England is "an errand in the wilderness"? How are the perspectives of Danforth and Winthrop similar and different? What concerns does Danforth raise about the future of New England if the Puritans do not change? How might Danforth's sermon have been different had the colonists been faithful servants?

Step 1: Comprehension Questions

What evidence does Danforth use to support his main points about colonists straying from their original mission? How is New England "an errand in the wilderness"?

▶ **Activity:** Select students to read aloud and analyze key passages in the sermon. Ask them to examine Danforth's language and references to the Bible as evidence of his beliefs in the Puritans fulfilling their religious mission. Have them explain in their own words the examples that Danforth uses to points out how the colonists have strayed from the mission.

Step 2: Comprehension Questions

How are the perspectives of Danforth and Winthrop similar and different in the mission of the Puritans? Is the "errand in the wilderness" like the "city upon a hill"?

▶ **Activity:** Ask students to make a list of the examples that Danforth and Winthrop use to describe the Puritans' mission. Have them discuss how the descriptions are similar and different.

Step 3: Context Questions

What concerns does Danforth raise about the future of New England if the Puritans do not change their ways? What language does he use to influence his audience?

▶ **Activity:** Instruct students to underline language in Danforth's sermon that is intended to influence his audience to change.

Step 4: Exploration Questions

How might Danforth's sermon have been different had the colonists been faithful servants? What might have been the purpose of Danforth's sermon in 1670?

▶ **Activity:** Have students discuss how Danforth's sermon might have been different had the colonists acted differently. Ask students to write an outline for a revised sermon that Danforth might have delivered.

Step 5: Response Paper

Word length and additional requirements set by Instructor. Students answer the research question in the Overview Questions. Students state a thesis and use as evidence passages from the primary source document as well as support from supplemental materials assigned in the lesson.

■ The Quaker Ideal of Religious Tolerance

Date: 1675
Author: Penn, William
Genre: petition; political tract

> *"The very Remedies applied to cure Dissension,*
> *increase it; and that the more Vigorously a Uniformity*
> *is Coercively Prosecuted, the wider Breaches grow."*

Summary Overview

As a Quaker, William Penn was subject to religious persecution by the English authorities. The title of the full article, from which this document is taken, is "England's Present Interest Considered, with Honour to the Prince, and Safety to the People." This petition begins by criticizing the extreme force that has been used in the enforcement of the laws regarding religious conformity. Examples are given of the "barbarous practices" causing great harm. Penn concludes that the enforcement of these laws has actually caused more division within the country. He also asserts that the government's pressure for religious conformity had also hurt England's economic and political relations with other countries. Penn ends with the warning that as long as the government pressed for religious conformity, there will be more antigovernment sentiment than would be the case if religious freedom were granted.

Defining Moment

By the time William Penn wrote this plea for religious tolerance, he had become one of the best-known spokespersons for this cause, mainly due to his willingness to challenge English laws in his writing and speaking as well as through the courts. Although he had moderated his theological position by the time he wrote this document, he was first imprisoned for attacking the Anglican doctrine of the Trinity. While in the Tower of London, he wrote his first major plea for tolerance, *No Cross, No Crown*, in 1669. After regaining his freedom, Penn continued to attack restrictions on religion.

He was arrested again, for holding a religious meeting not sanctioned by the Church of England (Anglican Church). Although under strong pressure by the lord mayor of London, the jury refused to convict Penn, leading to further legal problems for the jurors and for Penn. Following this case, Penn wrote "England's Present Interest Considered."

Unlike his earlier plea for tolerance, which was aimed at a broad audience of Christians, this document is directed toward those who were in positions of authority or those who could influence such persons, including both government and Anglican officials. Penn's background uniquely qualified him for this type of proposal: his study of law, conversion to and enthusiasm for the Quaker movement, and connections with many governmental leaders and the royal family, which guaranteed that his argument for tolerance would be read by at least some who were in a position to alter official policy.

The second half of the seventeenth century was a time of religious turmoil in England. The monarchy had been overthrown in 1649 and Protestant dissenters (non-Anglicans) headed the government. With the restoration of the monarchy, the Anglican Church was once again the official church, although many feared the king would join the Catholic Church and attempt to make it the politically dominant church once again. In the midst of these politically influenced changes, many other Protestant groups were organizing, including a relatively new movement known as the Society of Friends, or Quakers. Once King Charles II gained the throne in 1660, he and Parliament tried to contain the diverse views that were spreading across the country. Several laws were passed to try to force these Protestant groups back into the Anglican Church or to make it illegal and impossible for them to continue to practice their faith. These were the "remedies" that Penn opposed and that he believed were causing great turmoil to the detriment of the people and government.

Author Biography

The oldest child of Admiral William Penn and Margaret Jasper Penn, William Penn was born on October 14, 1644. Penn briefly attended Oxford but was expelled in 1661 after only a year for refusing to attend mandatory church services. From 1662 to 1664, he studied in France. In 1665, Penn returned to England and undertook law studies at Lincoln's Inn. As his father was among the officers charged with rebuilding the navy after the restoration of the monarchy, Penn became his courier to the monarch in early 1666, which was how the younger Penn became known by King Charles II and his brother James, then duke of York and later king.

Raised in an Anglican family, Penn had been exposed to the Quaker view of religion as a youth. During 1665 and 1666, he was impressed by the Quakers' service to the people of London during the plague and then the Great Fire. Due to his father's illness, he then went to Ireland to manage the family estates. While there, he began attending Quaker meetings on a regular basis. In 1667, a meeting was raided and everyone was arrested, including Penn, but he was quickly released from jail because of his family's position. As a result of this arrest, Penn began to argue that Quakers should be allowed to practice their religion because they were not politically opposed to the English government.

From that time forward, Penn became a leader in the cause of religious tolerance, focusing mainly on the Quaker cause. While he did not suffer as severely as some did, due to his legal skills and standing at the royal court, Penn aggressively confronted the authorities with his beliefs. In and out of jail several times, Penn was a prolific writer and speaker for the Quakers and the cause of tolerance. The persecution continued to intensify, such that he and other leaders looked for a solution outside England. They first purchased part of New Jersey and tried to establish a Quaker colony there, but were unsuccessful. In 1681, Penn negotiated the purchase of what is now Pennsylvania from Charles II. Penn successfully established a very tolerant, religiously diverse, and economically strong colony, although it was not financially profitable for him personally, and he continued to work for religious tolerance in England. Many believe he was influential in the writing of James II's royal decree for religious tolerance issued in 1687, which Penn strongly and publicly supported. In 1684, he became embroiled in a lengthy border dispute with Lord Baltimore, the proprietor of Maryland. He returned to Pennsylvania in 1699 to settle governance issues with the colonial assembly but left once more in 1702. He died in England in 1718, having become permanently incapacitated in 1712.

HISTORICAL DOCUMENT

England's Present Interest Considered with Honour to the Prince And Safety to the People, In Answer to this One Question,

What is most fit, easy, and safe, at this juncture of affairs, to be done, for quieting of difference, allaying the heat of contrary interests, and making them subservient to the interest of government, and consistent with the properity of the kingdom?

Submitted to the Consideration of our Superiors
Lex est Ratio sine Apppetitus
Published in the Year 1675

There is no law under heaven, which hath its rise from nature or grace, that forbids men to deal honestly and plainly with the greatest, in matters of importance to their present and future good; on the contrary, the dictates of both enjoin every man that office to his neighbour; and from charity among private persons, it becomes a duty indispensable to the public. Nor do worthy minds think ever the less kindly of honest and humble monitors; and God knows, that oftentimes princes are deceived, and kingdoms languish, for want of them. How far the posture of our affairs will justify this address, I shall submit to the judgment and observation of every intelligent reader.

Certain it is, that there are few kingdoms in the world more divided within themselves, and whose religious interests lie more seemingly cross to all accommodation, than that we live in; which renders the magistrate's task hard, and giveth him a difficulty next to invincible.

Your Endeavours for a Uniformity have been many; Your Acts not a few to Enforce it, but they Consequence, whether you intended it or not, through the Barbarous Practices of those that have had their Execution, hath been the Spoiling of several Thousands of the free inhabitants of this Kingdom of their Unforfeited Rights. Persons have been flung into Jails, Gates and Trunks broke open, Goods destroyed, till a stool hath not been left to sit down on, Flocks of Cattle driven, whole Barns full of Corn seized, Parents left with out Children, Children without their Parents, both without subsistence.

But that which aggravate the cruelty, is, the widow's mite hath not escaped their hands; they have made her cow the forfeiture of her conscience; not leaving her a bed to lie on, nor a blanket to cover her. And, which is yet more barbarous, and helps to make up this tragedy, the poor helpless orphan's milk, boiling over the fire, has been flung to the dogs, and the skillet made part of their prize: so that had not nature in neighbours been stronger than cruelty in such informers and officers, to open her bowels for their relief and subsistence, they must have utterly perished.

Nor can these inhuman instruments plead conscience or duty to those laws, who have abundantly transcended the severest clause in them; for 'to see the imprisoned,' has been suspicion enough for a gaol; and 'to visit the sick,' to make a conventicle: fining and distraining for preaching, and being at a meeting, where there hath been neither; and forty pounds for twenty, at pick and choose too, is a moderate advance with some of them.

Others, thinking this way too dull and troublesome, alter the question, and turn, "Have you met?" which the act intends, to, "Will you swear?" which it intendeth not: so that in some places it hath been sufficient to a *praemunire,* that men have had estates to lose; I mean such men, who through tenderness, refuse the oath; but by principle, like the allegiance, not less than their adversaries.

Finding then by Sad Experience, and a long Tract of Time, That the very Remedies applied to cure Dissension, increase it; and that the more Vigorously a Uniformity

is coercively prosecuted, the Wider Breaches grow, the more Inflamed Persons are, and fixt in their Resolutions to stand by their Principles; which, besides all other Inconveniences to those that give them Trouble, their very Sufferings beget that Compassion in the Multitude, which rarely misses of making many friends, and proves often a preparation for not a few proselytes. So much more reverend is suffering, than making men suffer for religion, even of those that cannot suffer for their religion, if yet they have any religion to suffer for. Histories are full of examples: the persecution of the Christian religion made it more illustrious than its doctrine. Perhaps it will be denied to English dissenters, that they rely upon so good a cause, and therefore a vanity in them to expect that success. But Arianism itself, once reputed the foulest heresy by the church, was by not artifice of its party so disseminated, as by the severe opposition of the Homoousians.

✳✳✳

The Question

'What is most Fit, Easie and Safe at this Juncture of Affairs to be done, for Composing, at least Quieting Differences; for Allaying the Heat of Contrary Interests, and making them Subservient to the Interest of the Government, and Consistent with the Prosperity of the Kingdom?'

The Answer

I. An Inviolable and Impartial Maintenance of English Rights.

II. Our Superiours governing themselves upon a Balance, as near as may be, towards the several Religious Interests.

III. A sincere Promotion of General and Practical Religion

✳✳✳

I shall not, at this time make it my Business to manifest the Inconsistency that there is between the Christian Religion, and a forced Uniformity; not only because it hath been so often and excellently done by Men of Wit, Learning and Conscience, and that I have elsewhere largely deliver'd my Sense about it; but because Every free and impartial Temper hath of a long time observ'd, that such Barbarous Attempts were so far from being indulged, that they were most severely prohibited by Christ himself.

Consider, peace, plenty, and safety, the three great inducements to any country to honour the prince, and love the government, as well as the best allurements to foreigners to trade with it and transport themselves to it, are utterly lost by such partiality; for instead of Peace, Love and good Neighborhood, behold Animosity and contest! One Neighbour watcheth another, and makes him an offender for his conscience: this divides them, their Families and Acquaintance; perhaps with the, the towns and villages where they live: and most commonly, the sufferer hath pity, and the persecutor the odium, of the multitude. And truly when people see cruelty practiced upon their inoffensive neighbours, by a troublesome sort of men, and those countenanced by a law, it breedeth ill blood against the government.

✳✳✳

Nor is this Severity only Injurious to the Affairs of *England*, but the whole Protestant World: For besides that it calls the Sincerity of their Proceedings against the *Papists* into Question, it furnisheth them with this sort of unanswerable Interrogatory: "The Protestants exclaim against us for Persecutor, and are they now the very men themselves? Was severity an instance of weakness in our religion, and is it become a valid argument in theirs? Are not our actions (once void of all excuse with them) now defended by their own practice?"

✳✳✳

But there are . . . objections that some make against what I have urged, not unfit to be consider'd. The first is this: If the Liberty desired be granted, what know we but Dissenters may employ their Meetings to insinuate against the Government, inflame the People into a Dislike of their Superiours, and thereby prepare them for Mischief?

Answer. This objection may have some force, so long as our superiors continue severity; because it doth not only sharpen and excite dissenters, but it runs many of them into such holes and corners, that if they were disposed to any such conspiracies, they have the securest places and opportunities to effect design. But what Dissenter can be so destitute of Reason and Love to common Safety, as to expose himself and Family; by plotting against a Government that is kind to him, and gives him the Liberty he desire.

GLOSSARY

Arianism: heretical Christian belief that the Son (Christ) was not of the same essence of the Father (God), but rather the highest of the created beings

gaol: jail

Homoousian: a Christian who believes that the Son (Christ) is composed of the same essence as the Father (God)

lex est ratio sine appetitus: Latin for "law is reason without passion"

papists: Roman Catholics; generally a derogatory term

praemunire: in English law, the offense of following a foreign ruler or law rather than an English law, thus defying the monarch and making the action virtually treasonous

widow's mite: from a parable in the New Testament, an extremely small amount of money given by a very poor widow to support the temple

Document Analysis

Religion had been a major point of division within England since the founding of the Church of England in the 1534, over 140 years prior to Penn writing this plea for tolerance. William Penn was a member of a persecuted sect, which meant that this issue was before him each day. By appealing to English common law and common sense, Penn hoped to convince government officials that the best policy was tolerance. The suffering, which the religious persecutions had caused and continued to cause, would end with a policy of tolerance. In addition, the change of policy would not only help the government domestically, but also would strengthen its standing among other European nations. He was not arguing against the Anglican Church as the official Church of England or the Presbyterian Church as the recognized Scottish church; rather, he was arguing against a policy of enforced membership and enforced conformity of belief. He advocated greater unity through diversity of belief.

The full text from which this excerpt is taken is a very long, legalistic documentation of what Penn perceived to be the foundation for religious tolerance in England. In the introductory passage of the document, Penn asks the question regarding the best way to quiet the religious disputes for the best interests of the general society. After the brief answers given in the excerpt printed here, Penn then attempts to demonstrate logically why and how this could be done. In the full text, he begins with a historical examination in the first chapter titled "Of English Rights." Much of his argument is based upon property rights from which English law derived the concept of personal liberty and freedom. Penn then discusses the system of government and the need for the general population to accept certain types of laws in order for them to be valid. Finally, he concludes his arguments with the role commoners play in the judicial system of trial by jury. At the conclusion of these arguments, Penn states that the people's rights could not be taken from them without their acceptance. He then goes on to discuss religious rights specifically, demonstrating, to his satisfaction, that the civil government is separate from church affairs. For Penn, this meant that religious freedom should be the norm.

Penn then discusses how a government could maintain a stable society by balancing the interests of many different religious groups. The last half of the excerpt derives from this portion of the tract. Penn promotes religion in general as a practical contribution to society.

He closes with a passage titled, "A Corollary," which summarizes the way to quiet dissatisfaction. The solution is liberty for all, including religious tolerance. The full document is about thirteen times the length of the excerpt printed here.

The question repeated twice in this short segment is: What can be done to unify the diverse population of England in support of the government? Penn sees the English suffering because "there are few kingdoms in the world more divided within themselves." Thus, Penn believes that the magnitude of the problem confronting society was quite great. However, he is certain that the solution could be much simpler. All that is required is a rational approach to the problem. He is convinced that people need only "deal honestly and plainly with the greatest, in matters of importance to their present and future good." Rather than ignoring the problems, Penn asserts that it is everyone's responsibility to consider issues of importance to the society—"a duty indispensable to the public." He continues that if people do not take the responsibility to attempt to work out solutions to important problems of the day, then not only are they at risk, but the same is true for the entire nation. Thus, Penn's concerns regarding religion go beyond the traditional question of salvation in some otherworldly sense; rather, he sees religion also as integral to the betterment of society in the present.

As any good apologist does, Penn tries to strike a conciliatory note with his anticipated audience, top-level government and religious officials. Penn notes that the religions' differences and resulting social strife "renders the magistrate's task hard." He suggests that the problems coming from enforcement of the laws are not the reader's fault, even if in reality they were. The worst problems are, Penn states, the fault of the system that had been put in place to try to make everyone conform to the same religious views or of the local officials implementing the regulations beyond what was mandated. Although Penn presents the situation this way, the top-level officials could not help but see criticism of themselves, even when Penn blames their subordinates.

Penn then goes on to list some of the most severe penalties that have been handed out to those found guilty of not obeying the laws regarding religion. The greatest of these was the death penalty. For over a hundred years prior to the reign of James II, every monarch had authorized the execution of individuals due to charges based on religion. Penn then mentions the thousands of people who have been jailed or had all their possessions confiscated or destroyed by the government. In addition to this, Penn notes the separation of families—"Parents left with out children, Children without their Parents, both without subsistence." From Penn's perspective, the strict enforcement of the laws was destroying people's lives in such a manner as leading to their deaths. Even the smallest amount of money, the "widow's mite," was being taken from the poor, while all their resources were destroyed. Many were left without anything, as Penn asserts that for the local official enforcing the law, even "the skillet made part of their prize."

However, the outrage Penn felt intensified because he saw the laws being distorted in such a way that religious intolerance was even greater than what had been legislated. As regards officials exceeding their authority, Penn had no doubt that many magistrates and officials "have abundantly transcended the severest clause in them." Penn blasts those who enforced the laws using what is often called "guilt by association." Some officials believed a person was guilty of the same religious crime as the prisoner, if a person visited someone who had been put in jail for violation of a law regarding religion. As a result, some who visited prisoners would be put in jail with no other evidence. Similarly, if a person visited a sick individual who was seen as a violator of the laws on religion, again the visitor was judged guilty of the same law. Social gatherings were broken up for being religious gatherings, with punishment meted out for the alleged crime. Those who were part of the nonconformist churches had no legal standing when accused of crimes, whether real or imagined, under the laws requiring conformity to religious belief and practice.

In addition to the harm these laws and views did to the relationship between the individual and the government, Penn also argues that these laws were destroying society. The uncertainty of one's neighbor led to a breakdown of what should be common bonds. Penn blames "informers" who gave information about others for much of the problem. However, he does admire the fact that some did follow the Christian teaching to love their neighbor and helped the families who had had all their resources taken or destroyed because others had informed regarding their religious belief.

The previous problems applied to all who were seen as being outside the norm of the Anglican Church in England. However, one point specifically directed against the Quakers is raised at the end of the list of acts of official malfeasance. This was the transformation of the legally required question of "have you met" (do you agree with) to "will you swear." One of the beliefs that separates Quakers from others is their literal acceptance of Jesus' statement not to swear any type of oath. As recorded in Matthew 5:34, Jesus said, "But I say to you, do not swear at all." Thus, if officials changed the wording from "have you met" to "will you swear," Quakers could not respond to the question because of their belief against swearing oaths. The official then had an excuse to punish the Quaker for being disloyal, using the rule of praemunire, which is being loyal to some authority other than the king. Penn argues that people who were unwilling to swear an oath were not necessarily disloyal. Quakers and others could be as loyal as anyone else, including government officials who accused them.

Penn then concludes his introduction to this work by maintaining that in England the persecution of those outside the Anglican Church had resulted only in strengthening the dissenting churches. He states, "The more Vigorously a Uniformity is coercively prosecuted . . . the more Inflamed Persons are, and fixt in their Resolutions to stand by their Principles." Not only that, he asserts that those being persecuted are generally seen more positively by others, which in this case resulted in more people joining the dissenting churches and their cause. He also reminds the authorities that often people had converted to Christianity itself because they had witnessed those who were devoted to their faith, even under extreme circumstances. This, he thought, should be a lesson to those who tried to stamp out Protestant groups that were outside the established church.

In the second part of the excerpt, Penn repeats the question that was the focus of this work. At this point, he gives a three-point answer on the best way to unify the society for the betterment of the nation: "Maintenance of English Rights," "governing themselves upon a Balance . . . towards the several Religious Interests," and "A sincere Promotion of General and Practical Religion." These then are amplified throughout the many pages of text devoted to each part of the answer. The remainder of the excerpt is from the long explanation of the second answer, "Our Superiors governing themselves upon a Balance, as near as may be, towards the several Religious Interests."

As part of the introduction to that section, Penn refers to his understanding there is an "Inconsistency . . .

between the Christian Religion, and a forced Uniformity." One of the ways he draws attention to this issue is by stating that he is not going to spend time writing about it. By mentioning what he is not going to argue, Penn makes readers spend at least some time thinking about the arguments that others had presented on this issue. The closing phrase, "they were most severely prohibited by Christ himself," has to do with the use of force. While Quakers were generally against the use of force in any situation, this particular reference had to do with the general Christian understanding that the religion is based upon love. There is no passage in the New Testament where Christ specifically states the church should not be united; rather, what Penn refers to in the prohibition is the use of force to compel members to do something versus the use of love to encourage them to do it. Penn's assumption—that it was apparent to all with a "free and impartial Temper" that forced uniformity did not work—was itself not obvious, since Penn had to write this plea to get others to reject the use of force.

The last three points in the printed text are from the sixth and seventh sections of Penn's answer and the first of his responses to objections that might be made against his general line of thought regarding how to balance governmental interests and religion. In the first five sections of the response, Penn discusses the need for wisdom and for mercy, how persecution leads to unrest, the uncertainty of forced faith, and the error of sacrificing liberty for fashionable views. In the sixth, he presents the argument that the negative effects of religious persecution are not limited to those suffering the persecution. He asserts that "peace, plenty, and safety" are the key to domestic tranquility and the attributes that other countries seek in trading and political partners. According to Penn, religious persecution creates an aura of "animosity and contest." Giving neighbors incentives for spying on one another created divisions that could go beyond the families to the dividing the larger society. Penn reminds the authorities to whom this was submitted, that most people would sympathize with the persecuted, not the persecutor. As a result, he asserts that religious persecution "breedeth ill blood against the government." In the full text, Penn continues this argument by giving illustrations about the fluctuations in acceptable religious belief as monarchs and governments changed from the time of Edward VI through Charles II.

The seventh section of his argument, advocating a more lenient stance by the government toward all Christian denominations, has to do with events of the Reformation. When various Protestant groups emerged in Europe, some Catholic leaders used physical means, up to and including death, to suppress what they saw as heresy. Protestant leaders had always claimed the moral high ground by saying persecution, imprisonment, and execution were Catholic actions, not Protestant. Penn points out that the Protestant leaders of England could no longer make this argument, if they were taking exactly the same actions themselves. He then argues that if Protestant England felt it proper to do this, then why should not some of the Catholic countries start similar activities against the Protestants?

Imagining an immediate objection to his plea for religious tolerance, Penn raises the specter that religious groups outside the established church might use their freedom to plot overthrow of the government. Penn's response is that mercy and kindness by one creates mercy and kindness in the other. Repression creates hatred, which is the basis for plots to overthrow the government. According to Penn, the current situation was creating dissatisfaction and political unrest. If the government changed its policy to one of tolerance, Penn claims, "What Dissenter can be so destitute of Reason and Love to common Safety, as to expose himself and Family; by plotting against a Government that is kind to him, and gives him the Liberty he desire." Peace, safety, and stability would then be the ultimate results of religious tolerance.

Essential Themes

Ever since the time of Henry VIII, religious division and strife had been a major factor in English society. By the time of William Penn, in addition to the major Catholic-Anglican split initiated by Henry VIII, many different Protestant groups had gained strength in various regions. Penn had lived through the English Civil War, when Puritan leaders gained control and established the Commonwealth. During the process of the restoration of the monarchy, there were overt political maneuverings between the Presbyterians in Scotland and the Anglicans in England for supremacy. With the restoration complete and Parliament under Anglican leadership came renewed concern regarding a possible Catholic monarch, as well as the desire by Anglican leaders to retain control and keep Protestant divisions at a minimum. Charles II tried to override Parliament by increasing religious freedom. However, anti-Catholic sentiment in Parliament, in conjunction with the belief that Charles was a Catholic at heart, resulted in a showdown in which Charles had to withdraw his proclamation. A series of laws were passed by Parliament in the hopes of unifying Christianity in England, laws that made it impossible for practicing Catholics and members of many Protestant denominations to hold high office. This was the setting for Penn's plea.

Penn's work was not successful in immediately changing Parliament's attitude toward religious tolerance. He continued to press for tolerance in England, though beginning in the late 1670s, he turned his attention to developing opportunities for Quakers and others in the North American colonies. It was another decade before Parliament accepted the idea of religious tolerance for Protestants. Many scholars see the work of Penn in the final version of the Declaration of Indulgence issued by James II, which did away with restrictions on personal worship, religious oaths for government officials, and jail terms for those outside the established church. While Parliament did not reject the initial draft of the declaration in 1687, there was great debate. As a result, a second draft of the declaration was issued in 1688, containing Penn's arguments for religious tolerance, including the one that tolerance would lead to greater economic prosperity. Only the Quakers fully supported this declaration, as all the other churches found some part of it to criticize. However, opposition to James II on this, his membership in the Catholic Church, and his replacement of many Anglican officials with Catholics resulted in the Glorious Revolution of 1688, forcing James to abdicate after only three years on the throne. Nonetheless, the general mood of religious tolerance Penn sought had finally been accepted by the government, if not fully implemented.

Penn consequently made a major contribution to the debate on religious tolerance and his views ultimately carried the day. Although the response to his petition was not as fast as he desired, he lived to see great changes in both the government and society that allowed Quakers and other nonconformists to participate fully in economic and political endeavors.

Donald A. Watt, PhD

Bibliography

Buranelli, Vincent. *The King & the Quaker: A Study of William Penn and James II.* Philadelphia: U of Pennsylvania P, 1962. Print.

Dunn, Mary Maples. *William Penn: Politics and Conscience.* Princeton: Princeton UP, 1967. Print.

Penn, William. "England's Present Interest Considered, with Honour to the Prince, and Safety to the People (1675)." *Online Library of Liberty.* Online Library of Liberty, 2012. Web. 7 June 2012.

Additional Reading

Geiter, Mary K. *William Penn.* Harlow: Pearson, 2000. Print.

Moretta, John. *William Penn and the Quaker Legacy.* London: Longman, 2006. Print.

Murphy, Andrew R. Introduction. *The Political Writings of William Penn.* Indianapolis: Liberty Fund, 2002. Print.

Penn, William. *The Papers of William Penn.* Ed. Mary Maples Dunn, Richard S. Dunn, and Edwin K. B. Bronner. Philadelphia: U of Pennsylvania P, 1981–1987. Print.

Tully, Alan. *William Penn's Legacy.* Baltimore: Johns Hopkins UP, 1977. Print.

LESSON PLAN: Penn's Spirit of Religious Tolerance

Students analyze William Penn's essay on religious tolerance, and compare multiple perspectives on religious tolerance.

Learning Objectives

Compare and contrast religious groups that settled in colonial America; analyze the causes of settlement in North America; compare multiple perspectives on religious tolerance; analyze the influence of ideas of the importance of the individual in history.

Materials: William Penn's "The Quaker Ideal of Religious Freedom"; Robert Cushman's "To His Loving Friends the Adventurers for New-England"; Excerpts from William Bradford's *Of Plymouth Plantation*

Overview Questions

Why did Penn, Cushman, and Bradford leave England to settle in America? What were their hopes and plans for their settlements? How were their perspectives on religious tolerance similar and different? Why was Penn's role as a promoter of religious tolerance important and influential in colonial America?

Step 1: Comprehension Questions

Why are Penn, Cushman, and Bradford leaving England for America? What are their hopes for the new settlements?

▶ **Activity:** Have students identify and underline key words and phrases in each work that indicate why Penn, Cushman, and Bradford left England to settle in America. Ask them to write a summary to explain what each hoped for in the new settlements.

Step 2: Comprehension Questions

Who do Penn, Cushman, and Bradford address in their works? Who is their audience? How do Quaker beliefs affect the religious ideas that Penn expresses? How do Puritan beliefs affect Cushman's and Bradford's ideas?

▶ **Activity:** Have students take turns reading aloud key passages to determine the intended audience for each work. Ask students to write in their journals about their beliefs on religion from the perspective of a Quaker or Puritan, using the primary sources as resources.

Step 3: Context Questions

Why does Penn express his hope for religious tolerance? How do Cushman and Bradford feel about religious tolerance? How did their experiences in England affect their ideas in America?

▶ **Activity:** Instruct students to make a three-column chart to compare and contrast each man's attitude toward religious tolerance. Have students discuss as a class how each man's experience in England affected his ideas on settlement in America.

Step 4: Exploration Questions

What does Penn mean by "Practical Religion"? Why was Penn's role as a promoter of religious tolerance important and influential in colonial America?

▶ **Activity:** In small groups have students discuss Penn's "Practical Religion." Ask them to write a short essay explaining why Penn's ideas on religious tolerance would be influential in the early development of colonial America.

Step 5: Response Paper

Word length and additional requirements set by Instructor. Students answer the research question in the Overview Questions. Students state a thesis and use as evidence passages from the primary source document as well as support from supplemental materials assigned in the lesson.

◼ The Narrative of the Captivity and Restoration of Mrs. Mary Rowlandson

Date: 1682
Author: Rowlandson, Mary
Genre: memoir; sermon

*"I chose rather to go along with those . . . ravenous
beasts, than that moment to end my days. . . . I was
not willing to run away, but desired to wait God's
time, that I might go home quietly, and without fear."*

Summary Overview

In February 1676, Narragansett, Nipmuc, and Wampanoag warriors raided Lancaster, Massachusetts, taking twenty-four townspeople captive, including Mary Rowlandson, the wife of the town minister. She remained a captive for eleven weeks before Massachusetts colonial officials obtained her release in exchange for cloth, provisions, and money. Six years later, she published an account of her experience as *The Sovereignty & Goodness of God, Together with the Faithfulness of His Promises Displayed, Being a Narrative of the Captivity and Restauration of Mrs. Mary Rowlandson.* As indicated by the title, she presented her experience in terms of religious guidance. Her Puritan message of faith, patience, fortitude, and plain living surely resonated with readers, but it was her vivid personal account of her physical and spiritual struggle to survive in harsh conditions and vastly different culture that brought the book immediate and continued popularity.

Defining Moment

King Philip's War began in June 1675 when Wampanoag warriors attacked settlers in the town of Swansea in Plymouth Colony. Over the next year, the Wampanoags, joined by Nipmuc and Narragansett allies, raided numerous English settlements in southern New England.

At first, the colonists were unprepared for an extensive conflict. Lax military training, poor tactics, limited resources, and a general misunderstanding of the American Indian situation all contributed to a botched initial response by colonial officials and military commanders. With considerable help from friendly Indian bands and enemy defectors, the military situation shifted in the colonists' favor in the spring of 1676, and by August, the Wampanoags and their allies were defeated.

In her account of her captivity, Mary Rowlandson appeared to be little concerned with the overall course of the war. For her, it was primarily a personal and spiritual conflict, with her story of precarious survival providing a framework for an interpretive overlay drawn from Puritan religious ideology. Puritan censors allowed and likely encouraged Rowlandson's story to be published at a time when women's voices were suspect. In 1637, the colonies of Massachusetts Bay and Plymouth had been rocked by the religious teachings of Anne Hutchinson and her followers, and in 1660, Massachusetts Bay Colony executed Mary Dyer, an outspoken Quaker religious leader. Against this context of disruptive women religious figures, Rowlandson counseled patience, not action. Rather than showing resistance, she adopted the mostly submissive role of servant to her captors. Even the book's title page situated her as a person with no wish to become a public figure, informing readers that the text had been written "for her private use," and its teachings were "especially" meant for her "dear children and relations."

While religious instruction was the intended purpose, Mary Rowlandson's story allowed far broader interpretations and emotional responses. The account's gritty realism of day-to-day survival provided an empathetic model of personal courage. It also gave an unmatched perspective on American Indian individuals and their community. Rowlandson, however, represented her captors, with their "wild" and "savage" behavior and practices, as irredeemably alien, as "beasts" inhabiting a "wilderness." Before the war, the American Indians had often been close neighbors, trading partners, servants, and potential Christian converts. With her depiction, Rowlandson reinforced a predominant postwar view. Thoughts of economic, religious, and political integration mostly vanished both because of an ideological shift and because the war so decimated the southern New England Indian bands that they no longer held a significant place in English public affairs.

Author Biography

Mary Rowlandson was born around 1637 in Somerset County, England, one of nine children born to John and Joan White. In 1639, the Whites joined the mass migration of English Puritans to the recently established colonies of Massachusetts Bay and Plymouth. The Whites first settled in Salem, Massachusetts. Around 1653, the Whites moved to Lancaster, Massachusetts, which the colony established as a township the following year.

Around the same time as the Whites moved to Lancaster so did Reverend Joseph Rowlandson, a recent graduate from Harvard College who had been invited to become the town's minister. Mary White and Joseph Rowlandson were married a few years later, probably in 1656, and on January 15, 1658, their first child, Mary, was born. She died three years later. The Rowlandsons had three more children: Joseph (b. March 7, 1662), Mary (b. August 12, 1665), and Sarah (b. September 15, 1669).

On the day following her release from captivity, May 3, 1676, Mary Rowlandson joined her husband in Boston. Some weeks later, the family was reunited after their two surviving children were also released. Unable to return to the devastated town of Lancaster, the Rowlandsons moved to Boston. In April 1677, Joseph Rowlandson became the pastor of the church in Wethersfield, Connecticut. The following year, in November 1678, he died at about the age of forty-seven.

In the conclusion of her story, Rowlandson implies that her husband is alive so it is assumed that she completed it before his death. In 1682, she published her account accompanied by her husband's final sermon. The book was an instance success, with American and English editions published that same year.

Rowlandson did not remain a widow for long. On August 6, 1679, she married Samuel Talcott, a wealthy farmer and land speculator and a prominent colonial leader in Connecticut, serving as a deputy to the Connecticut General Court from 1669 to 1684 and as an assistant from 1685 to 1691. Talcott died on November 11, 1691; she outlived him by nearly two decades, dying in Wethersfield on January 5, 1711.

HISTORICAL DOCUMENT

The Sovereignty & Goodness of GOD, Together With the Faithfulness of His Promises Displayed; Being a NARRATIVE of the Captivity and Restoration of Mrs. Mary Rowlandson. Commended by her, to all that desires to know the Lord's doings to, and dealings with Her. Especially to her dear Children and Relations. The second Addition [sic] Corrected and amended. Written by Her own Hand for Her private Use, and now made Public at the earnest Desire of some Friends, and for the benefit of the Afflicted. Deut. 32.39. *See now that I, even I am he, and there is no god with me, I kill and I make alive, I wound and I heal, neither is there any can deliver out of my hand.*

On the tenth of February 1675, came the Indians with great numbers upon Lancaster: their first coming was about sunrising; hearing the noise of some guns, we looked out; several houses were burning, and the smoke ascending to heaven. There were five persons taken in one house; the father, and the mother and a sucking child, they knocked on the head; the other two they took and carried away alive. There were two others, who being out of their garrison upon some occasion were set upon; one was knocked on the head, the other escaped; another there was who running along was shot and wounded, and fell down; he begged of them his life, promising them money (as they told me) but they would not hearken to him but knocked him in head, and stripped him naked, and split open his bowels. Another, seeing many of the Indians about his barn, ventured and went out, but was quickly shot down. There were three others belonging to the same garrison who were killed; the Indians getting up upon the roof of the barn, had advantage to shoot down upon them over their fortification. Thus these murderous wretches went on, burning, and destroying before them.

At length they came and beset our own house, and quickly it was the dolefulest day that ever mine eyes saw . . .

Oh the doleful sight that now was to behold at this house! "Come, behold the works of the Lord, what desolations he has made in the earth." Of thirty-seven persons who were in this one house, none escaped either present death, or a bitter captivity, save only one, who might say as he, "And I only am escaped alone to tell the News" (Job 1.15). There were twelve killed, some shot, some stabbed with their spears, some knocked down with their hatchets. When we are in prosperity, Oh the little that we think of such dreadful sights, and to see our dear friends, and relations lie bleeding out their heart-blood upon the ground. There was one who was chopped into the head with a hatchet, and stripped naked, and yet was crawling up and down. It is a solemn sight to see so many Christians lying in their blood, some here, and some there, like a company of sheep torn by wolves, all of them stripped naked by a company of hell-hounds, roaring, singing, ranting, and insulting, as if they would have torn our very hearts out; yet the Lord by His almighty power preserved a number of us from death, for there were twenty-four of us taken alive and carried captive.

I had often before this said that if the Indians should come, I should choose rather to be killed by them than taken alive, but when it came to the trial my mind changed; their glittering weapons so daunted my spirit, that I chose rather to go along with those (as I may say) ravenous beasts, than that moment to end my days; and that I may the better declare what happened to me during that grievous captivity, I shall particularly speak of the several removes we had up and down the wilderness.

✳✳✳

The Fourth Remove

And now I must part with that little company I had. Here I parted from my daughter Mary (whom I never saw again till I saw her in Dorchester, returned from captivity), and from four little cousins and neighbors, some of which I never saw afterward: the Lord only knows the end of them. Amongst them also was that poor woman before mentioned, who came to a sad end, as some of the company told me in my travel: she having much grief upon her spirit about her miserable condition, being so near her time, she would be often asking the Indians to let her go home; they not being willing to that, and yet vexed with her importunity, gathered a great company together about her and stripped her naked, and set her in the midst of them, and when they had sung and danced about her (in their hellish manner) as long as they pleased they knocked her on head, and the child in her arms with her. When they had done that they made a fire and put them both into it, and told the other children that were with them that if they attempted to go home, they would serve them in like manner. The children said she did not shed one tear, but prayed all the while. But to return to my own journey, we traveled about half a day or little more, and came to a desolate place in the wilderness, where there were no wigwams or inhabitants before; we came about the middle of the afternoon to this place, cold and wet, and snowy, and hungry, and weary, and no refreshing for man but the cold ground to sit on, and our poor Indian cheer.

Heart-aching thoughts here I had about my poor children, who were scattered up and down among the wild beasts of the forest. My head was light and dizzy (either through hunger or hard lodging, or trouble or all together), my knees feeble, my body raw by sitting double night and day, that I cannot express to man the affliction that lay upon my spirit, but the Lord helped me at that time to express it to Himself. I opened my Bible to read, and the Lord brought that precious Scripture to me. "Thus saith the Lord, refrain thy voice from weeping, and thine eyes from tears, for thy work shall be rewarded, and they shall come again from the land of the enemy" (Jeremiah 31.16). This was a sweet cordial to me when I was ready to faint; many and many a time have I sat down and wept sweetly over this Scripture. At this place we continued about four days.

✳ ✳ ✳

The Twentieth Remove

But to return again to my going home, where we may see a remarkable change of providence. At first they were all against it, except my husband would come for me, but afterwards they assented to it, and seemed much to rejoice in it; some asked me to send them some bread, others some tobacco, others shaking me by the hand, offering me a hood and scarfe to ride in; not one moving hand or tongue against it. Thus hath the Lord answered my poor desire, and the many earnest requests of others put up unto God for me. In my travels an Indian came to me and told me, if I were willing, he and his squaw would run away, and go home along with me. I told him no: I was not willing to run away, but desired

to wait God's time, that I might go home quietly, and without fear. And now God hath granted me my desire. O the wonderful power of God that I have seen, and the experience that I have had. I have been in the midst of those roaring lions, and savage bears, that feared neither God, nor man, nor the devil, by night and day, alone and in company, sleeping all sorts together, and yet not one of them ever offered me the least abuse of unchastity to me, in word or action. Though some are ready to say I speak it for my own credit; but I speak it in the presence of God, and to His Glory. God's power is as great now, and as sufficient to save, as when He preserved Daniel in the lion's den; or the three children in the fiery furnace. I may well say as his Psalm 107.12 "Oh give thanks unto the Lord for he is good, for his mercy endureth for ever." Let the redeemed of the Lord say so, whom He hath redeemed from the hand of the enemy, especially that I should come away in the midst of so many hundreds of enemies quietly and peaceably, and not a dog moving his tongue. So I took my leave of them, and in coming along my heart melted into tears, more than all the while I was with them, and I was almost swallowed up with the thoughts that ever I should go home again. About the sun going down, Mr. Hoar, and myself, and the two Indians came to Lancaster, and a solemn sight it was to me. There had I lived many comfortable years amongst my relations and neighbors, and now not one Christian to be seen, nor one house left standing. We went on to a farmhouse that was yet standing, where we lay all night, and a comfortable lodging we had, though nothing but straw to lie on. The Lord preserved us in safety that night, and raised us up again in the morning, and carried us along, that before noon, we came to Concord. Now was I full of joy, and yet not without sorrow; joy to see such a lovely sight, so many Christians together, and some of them my neighbors. There I met with my brother, and my brother-in-law, who asked me, if I knew where his wife was? Poor heart! he had helped to bury her, and knew it not. She being shot down by the house was partly burnt, so that those who were at Boston at the desolation of the town, and came back afterward, and buried the dead, did not know her. Yet I was not without sorrow, to think how many were looking and longing, and my own children amongst the rest, to enjoy that deliverance that I had now received, and I did not know whether ever I should see them again. Being recruited with food and raiment we went to Boston that day, where I met with my dear husband, but the thoughts of our dear children, one being dead, and the other we could not tell where, abated our comfort each to other. I was not before so much hemmed in with the merciless and cruel heathen, but now as much with pitiful, tender-hearted and compassionate Christians . . .

I have seen the extreme vanity of this world: One hour I have been in health, and wealthy, wanting nothing. But the next hour in sickness and wounds, and death, having nothing but sorrow and affliction.

Before I knew what affliction meant, I was ready sometimes to wish for it. When I lived in prosperity, having the comforts of the world about me, my relations by me, my heart cheerful, and taking little care for anything, and yet seeing many, whom I preferred before myself, under many trials and afflictions, in sickness, weakness, poverty, losses, crosses, and cares of the world, I should be sometimes jealous least I should have my portion in this life, and that Scripture would come to my mind, "For whom the Lord loveth he chasteneth, and scourgeth every Son whom he receiveth" (Hebrews 12.6). But now I see the Lord had His time to scourge and chasten me. The portion of some is to have their afflictions by drops, now one drop and then another; but the dregs of the cup, the wine of astonishment, like a sweeping rain that leaveth no food, did the Lord prepare to be my portion. Affliction I wanted, and affliction I had, full measure (I thought), pressed down and running over. Yet I see, when God calls a person to anything, and through never so many difficulties, yet He is fully able to carry them through and make them see, and say they have been gainers thereby. And I hope I can say in some measure, as David did, "It is good for me that I have been afflicted." The Lord hath showed me the vanity of these outward things. That they are the vanity of vanities, and vexation of spirit, that they are but a shadow, a blast, a bubble, and things of no continuance. That we must rely on God Himself, and our whole dependance must be upon Him. If trouble from smaller matters begin to arise in me, I have something at hand to check myself with, and say, why am I troubled? It was but the other day that if I had had the world, I would have given it for my freedom, or to have been a servant to a Christian. I have learned to look beyond present and smaller troubles, and to be quieted under them. As Moses said, "Stand still and see the salvation of the Lord" (Exodus 14.13).

Finis.

GLOSSARY

chasten: punish, discipline, or cause affliction for improvement, correction

cordial: restorative or invigorating food or beverage

doleful: sorrowful, gloomy

hearken: listen

importunity: persistent and bothersome entreaty

raiment: clothing

recruited: restored, strengthened

scourge: punish, torment

sitting double: bent with legs brought up to a person's chest

vexed: annoyed, irritated

Document Analysis

Six years after the brutal and destructive conflict called King Philip's War, Mary Rowlandson published an account of her traumatic experience of being held captive for eleven weeks and five days by a group of Nipmucs, Narragansetts, and Wampanoags. Rowlandson offered her personal account of suffering and survival as a devotional work meant to enlighten a Puritan readership, many of whom had begun to stray from the sect's strict doctrines. One of the implicit themes in the book regarded the role a woman should play in the religious and social sphere. In many ways, however, her story transcended that underlying Puritan ideology. Her journey served as a metaphor for any progression through personal suffering, a way of finding spiritual and psychological meaning in hardship. She declared her intention to live even as she had everything she formerly valued taken from her. By not focusing on the specifics of the war, her account seemed closer to myth than history. American Indians served as symbolic "beasts" inhabiting what she saw as a "vast and howling wilderness." To her, their very existence threatened the sanctity of home, family, religion, and society. While Rowlandson sought to portray her captors as base animals, her narrative to some extent also individualized and humanized them, giving readers a glimpse into their daily life and condition. Just like her, the American Indians were undergoing their own journey, struggling to survive and escape.

When the Indian allies attacked Lancaster, Massachusetts, on February 10, 1676, neighbors and family members gathered for protection in the home of Joseph and Mary Rowlandson. Joseph, the town's minister, was away from home at the time, having gone to Boston in an effort to persuade the colonial leaders to station troops in the town. For about two hours, those inside the house exchanged gunfire with the attackers. Then the Indians set the house on fire. As the occupants fled from the burning building, they were killed or captured. Mary Rowlandson and her six-year-old daughter, Sarah, were wounded and taken prisoner along with ten-year-old Mary and fourteen-year-old Joseph. Twelve or thirteen townspeople were killed in the raid, and twenty-four were taken as prisoners.

Mary Rowlandson's captors moved from place to place, first traveling about twenty miles west to near the Nipmuc village of Menameset and then going north about fifty miles into southwest New Hampshire before turning back into Massachusetts and traveling over fifty miles to Mount Wachusett, not far from where she was originally captured. At several places, they made long encampments, but during much of their journey, they stayed for one night or a few days before moving on. Rowlandson structured her account using each of the moves, twenty in all, as chapter divisions. She called each chapter a "remove," a term that signified a new residence but also carried a sense of a remote or distant place, suggesting that with each move she saw herself going further from her own culture.

On the third day of her captivity, the Indians arrived near Menameset ("Wenimesset"), a large Nipmuc settlement, where they would remain for fourteen days. During their stay, Rowlandson's daughter Sarah died from the gunshot wound she received during the Lancaster raid. In one of the book's most heartfelt and tragic scenes, Rowlandson describes how for eight days her daughter ate no food and kept moaning. When Sarah finally died, Rowlandson resisted abandoning the body until forced to by her captors who then buried the child in what Rowlandson viewed as the unhallowed "wilderness," separated from church and family. Rowlandson also went without food much of the time, but her wound healed after she took another captive's advice to cover it with oak leaves.

Rowlandson became the property of Quinnapin, a prominent Narragansett leader, having been sold to him by the warrior who had taken her captive. Her primary and often callus overseer was Weetamoo, one of Quinnapin's three wives. Weetamoo was likely the most powerful woman among the allied Indians. She had joined with Quinnapin as part of a political alliance between the Narragansetts and the Wampanoags, two formerly rival bands. Weetamoo's first husband was Wamsutta (called Alexander), the Wampanoag leader from 1660 to his death in 1662. Probably more than anything else, it was his death that signaled the shift away from previously friendly relations with the English settlers. Armed soldiers had forced Wamsutta to attend a meeting with Plymouth Colony leaders. On his way back, he became suddenly ill and died, a circumstance that raised suspicions among the Wampanoags that he had been poisoned by the colonists. Wamsutta's younger brother Metacom (whom the English called Philip) then became the head of the band, but Weetamoo controlled a faction and remained a powerful leader. When King Philip's War commenced in June 1675, Metacom looked to the Narragansetts for support, and Weetamoo likely joined Quinnapin around this time. While the

Narragansett leaders promised the colonists that the band would remain neutral, the colonial leaders heard that the Narragansetts aided the fleeing Wampanoags and suspected that the Narragansetts would eventually join the fight. In December, the colonial forces launched a brutal preemptory attack that ended with setting fire to the band's main compound and killing the Narragansetts as they fled. This action drove the surviving Narragansetts to enter the war, and it likely led to the raid on Lancaster. Within weeks of having their friends and families killed, the Narragansetts treated their captives with far more care than their band members had received at the hands of the English soldiers.

When her captors left Menameset to travel north, they separated Mary Rowlandson from many of the other Lancaster captives, including her two surviving children and four young cousins. The "Fourth Remove" chapter begins with her departure and subsequent encampment at "a desolate place in the Wilderness." Rather than the usual focus on her condition, this chapter features one the most sensationalistic accounts in the entire narrative. In the previous chapter, Rowlandson mentions speaking with a pregnant woman captive. Even though she would soon give birth and had a two-year-old child, this woman wanted to run away. Rowlandson counseled her against such an action and read to her a biblical passage that instructed "wait on the Lord." Failing to embrace the biblical message, the woman kept pleading for her release. Because of this, the Indians decided to kill her. Using this story, Rowlandson likely intended to show the wickedness of the Indians but ended up demonstrating something more. Rather than being a wanton execution, the killing required an exceptional ceremonial event involving tribal participation.

Rowlandson's story of the execution illustrates one of her main themes, that events should not be forced. Rather than construe her captivity in terms of heroic accomplishments or actions, Rowlandson celebrated her patience and survival tactics. Willing herself to cooperate with her captors and to acknowledge their assumed authority, she even calls Quinnapin "master" and Weetamoo "mistress." By using such titles in her account, Rowlandson wanted her readers not only to know the extent of her degradation but more importantly to understand that servitude was another sacrifice that she needed to make as part of her spiritual journey. This obedience did not come easily, and at several points, she struggled for control before surrendering. At one such moment, she read another biblical passage that told her to "be still."

Because of Rowlandson's emphasis on patient survival, the narrative lacks a clear sense of progress. If anything, the story involves regression, a process of removal of excess material goods and parts of her self-identity. In an archetypal heroic journey, a hero goes stage by stage acquiring knowledge, goods, and skills. Legends about frontier heroes, such as Daniel Boone, tend to feature a hero who goes into the wilderness and acquires Indian skills and knowledge so that he can conquer the land and the native inhabitants. Captivity narratives that began appearing a generation after Rowlandson's tale often had more in common with the frontiersman story. One example was the Hannah Dustin story as told by Cotton Mather in 1697. When Dustin was captured by Indians, she did not wait for God's time. Instead, she escaped after killing and scalping her captors, enacting the archetypal frontiersman hero. Rowlandson, in contrast, gives no indication that she learned anything from the Indians or that she would kill them if given the opportunity. When offered a chance to escape, for example, she told her potential Indian guides that she "desired to wait God's time." She believed that her captivity was a test of God who would release her "quietly" and "without fear" when her time had come.

Death was on the horizon in each chapter. Either the Indians or the harsh conditions and physical demands of the journey could easily kill her. Many of her seventeenth-century readers would have registered Rowlandson's chapter term "remove" as a euphemism for death, particularly death by murder. At several places in the book, Rowlandson emphasizes that her personal pilgrimage involved making a choice to live even when all appeared lost and she found herself faced with the question of how far would she go in order to survive. The story of the executed woman in the fourth remove shows one direction that she might have taken. She introduces the theme of choosing life at the end of the opening section, explaining how she had often "said that if the Indians should come, I should choose rather to be killed by them than taken alive." When the time came, however, she changed her mind, deciding to "chose rather to go along with those (as I may say) ravenous beasts, than that moment to end my days." Similarly, in the "distressed time" after the death of her child, she tells how "I did not use wicked and violent means to end my own miserable life," attributing her maintenance of "reason and senses" to God.

Food is by far the most prominent descriptive subject in the book. In nearly every chapter, Rowlandson refers to some aspect of her hunger, her efforts to obtain food, and what she ate to survive. During her third week in captivity, around the time of the fourth remove, she became desperate enough partake in what she described as the "filthy trash" that the Indians ate. In the fifth remove, she describes a meal consisting of broth made from boiling a horse's leg. "I could think how formerly my stomach would turn against this or that," she explains, "and I could starve and die before I could eat such things, yet they were sweet and savory to my taste." Similarly, she tells how at a low moment near the end of her journey, she took a piece of boiled horse hoof from a small child who struggled to chew it, explaining, "The Lord made that pleasant refreshing, which another time would have been an abomination." In detailing the poor food offerings, perhaps she intended to portray the Indians as animals who would eat anything. Her insightful view into Indian food practices, however, allows her readers a sympathetic perspective on how the Indians struggled to find sustenance in the middle of winter. Most of the food stores of the Narragansetts and the Wampanoags had been destroyed or abandoned when they fled their homelands, and the Nipmucs, with these extra mouths to feed, likely had exhausted their supplies. Some of their attacks on the English settlements could well have been driven by a need to acquire food.

Rowlandson's narrative of her near starvation and acceptance of Indian food formed part of the book's overall message regarding her spiritual pilgrimage. For her, each "remove" was not just a physical displacement but a shedding of outward "vanities" and personal "comforts," such as palatable food. Once these were removed, she could discover the bedrock of her existence. "The Lord hath showed me the vanity of these outward things," she concludes, "That they are the vanity of vanities, and vexation of spirit, that they are but a shadow, a blast, a bubble, and things of no continuance." At several points in the narrative, Rowlandson interprets her captivity in the biblical context of the Book of Job, which tells how God, for inscrutable reasons, stripped Job of his family, wealth, and health. Even though Job questions his treatment and wishes he had never been born, he retains a faith in God's plan and is eventually restored to his former state.

Rowlandson struggled to hold onto her cultural and religious identity in the face of constant pressure for her to become more like the Indians, a process that, for Puritans, would mean spiritual death. As she adapted to each removal of comfort and vanity, as she battled starvation, she got ever closer to shedding her identity, both as an Englishwoman and as a Puritan. What saved her, both physically and spiritually, was her "pocket," a kind of purse that women at that time wore under their skirts. Here, she carried her most important items: food, the Bible she acquired from an Indian, and her knitting materials. At each remove, she read biblical passages for comfort, calling her Bible "my guide by day, and my pillow by night." Her knitting materials provided the means for her physical survival. She bartered knitted goods with the Indians for food, shelter, and money, and even received a small reward from Metacom himself for a shirt she made for his son.

In many ways, the pocket served as a symbol of Puritan English identity; Rowlandson's Bible and knitting distinguish her from the Indians whom she describes as having no such capabilities. The Indians, in Rowlandson's view, did not have these things because they were closer to the wild "beasts" that inhabited the wilderness. Comparing her story with the biblical story of Daniel, who survived being thrown into a lion's den, she describes the Indians as "roaring lions, and savage bears." By dehumanizing the Indians in this way, she classifies them as alien creatures to be killed or tamed. Partly because Rowlandson depicts her captors more as animals than enemies, her narrative allows for a somewhat sympathetic view. A reader could imagine them facing starvation and trying to escape the soldiers who were hunting them down. In addition, throughout the account Rowlandson tells of individual Indians who came to her rescue; one gave her the Bible, several fed her and provided shelter, another offered to help her escape, and "not one of them," she testifies, "ever offered me the least abuse of unchastity to me, in word or action." Even though Indians could be seen to have positive qualities, Rowlandson's depiction still does not recognize them as equally human. In equating Indians with the wilderness, she situates the act of killing them as similar to clearing a forest—it lacks a moral component.

The three months of Rowlandson's captivity, between February and May 1676, turned out to be the pivotal time in the conflict. The Nipmuc, Narragansett, and Wampanoag attack on Lancaster came at the height of their success as they pillaged town after town. Their fortunes, however, soon turned sour. When her captors reached southwest New Hampshire at the beginning of

March, they were joined by Metacom and his followers who had recently returned from near Albany, New York, where they hoped to obtain supplies and to enlist Mahican allies. Mohawks attacked, however, devastating Metacom's band. Realizing they were caught between two superior forces and likely demoralized by the Mohawk attack, the Indian allies began negotiating with the colonists about ransoming the captives and surrendering. Most of the remaining battles were decided in the colonists' favor and various Indians bands surrendered in hopes of receiving amnesty. Three months after Rowlandson's release, the war ended. On August 12, colonial soldiers and their Indian allies found and killed Metacom. The week before, Rowlandson's mistress Weetamoo drowned while escaping the troops. Later in that month, Rowlandson's master Quinnapin was captured and taken to Newport, Rhode Island, where he was put on trial and executed on August 25.

Essential Themes

Few American works have had the lasting influence enjoyed by Mary Rowlandson's narrative, and fewer still are those written by women. This work has been frequently analyzed and anthologized in scholarship on early America, captivity narratives, women's writing, and American Indian studies.

Among the most discussed topics in recent scholarship concerns the duality of Rowlandson's description of real events within the framework of her religious interpretations. Some scholars have argued that operating in Rowlandson's text is a significant tension between the two narrative levels, particularly regarding her role as a woman within a Puritan social structure. Numerous scholars have explored questions regarding Rowlandson's use of available gendered forms of self-perception and presentation. Both the text and the accompanying anonymous introduction attempted to circumscribe and situate a woman's proper voice in society. Yet, certain passages can be understood as both supporting and potentially undermining certain social and religious values. At times, the text shows Rowlandson remaining submissive and obedient to her captors, and at other times, she is more confrontational and active in negotiating with them and in effecting the means for her survival. Within Rowlandson's descriptions and biblical passages, scholars have located attempts at carving out a self-identity from the ideology imposed by Puritan society.

Rowlandson's account is considered the prototype of the genre of captivity narratives, an extremely popular storyline featuring descriptions of white women taken captive by American Indians. These types of stories had significant influence on the public's perception of American Indian people, helping to justify centuries of Euro-American displacement and destruction of the native inhabitants. Scholar Richard Slotkin, in *Regeneration through Violence* (1973), relates the captivity narrative to the frontier hero narrative, seeing them both as the providing a mythical foundation of American identity. The physical home that came under attack in captivity narratives, according to Slotkin, served as a symbol of American society being threatened by "uncivilized" outside forces. The captivity story opens with the social fabric being torn apart by the American Indians' hostile actions and concludes with the captive's family, and thus the society, being restored whole. Rowlandson and many of the early writers understood this as a spiritual journey in which one's religious beliefs were threatened and ultimately secured. Later writers adopted more secular meanings, with the political nation under attack and in need of restoration. The later frontier stories also shifted away from Rowlandson's depiction of the wilderness as a godless place to be avoided if possible. Instead, the wilderness provided frontiersmen with a proving ground where they could grow stronger and obtain the goods and skills that society needed. This shift coincided with the popularity of what has been called "vanishing Indian" narratives in which the disappearance of the American Indians and symbiotic wilderness was viewed as both necessary and regrettable.

Kevin D. Shupe, PhD

Bibliography

Arsić, Branka. "Mary Rowlandson and the Phenomenology of Patient Suffering." *Common Knowledge* 16.2 (2010): 247–75. Print.

Greene, David L. "New Light on Mary Rowlandson." *Early American Literature* 20.1 (1985): 24–38. Print.

Leach, Douglas Edward. "The 'Whens' of Mary Rowlandson's Captivity." *New England Quarterly* 34.3 (1961): 352–63. Print.

Logan, Lisa. "Mary Rowlandson's Captivity and the 'Place' of the Woman Subject." *Early American Literature* 28.3 (1993): 255–77. Print.

Salisbury, Neal. "Introduction: Mary Rowlandson and Her Removes." *The Sovereignty and Goodness of God: With Related Documents*. Ed. Neal Salisbury. Boston: Bedford, 1997. Print.

Slotkin, Richard, and James K. Folsom, eds. *So Dreadfull a Judgment: Puritan Responses to King Philip's War, 1676–1677*. Middletown: Wesleyan UP, 1978. Print.

Additional Reading

Derounian-Stodola, Kathryn Zabelle, and James Arthur Levernier. *The Indian Captivity Narrative, 1550–1900*. New York: Twayne, 1993. Print.

Faery, Rebecca Blevins. "Mary Rowlandson (1637–1711)." *Legacy* 12.2 (1995): 121–32. Print.

Fitzpatrick, Tara. "The Figure of Captivity: The Cultural Work of the Puritan Captivity Narrative." *American Literary History* 3.1 (1991): 1–26. Print.

Lepore, Jill. *The Name of War: King Philip's War and the Origins of American Identity*. New York: Knopf, 1998. Print.

Rowlandson, Mary. *The Sovereignty and Goodness of God: With Related Documents*. Ed. Neal Salisbury. Boston: Bedford, 1997. Print.

Slotkin, Richard. *Regeneration through Violence: The Mythology of the American Frontier, 1600–1860*. Norman: U of Oklahoma P, 2000. Print.

Toulouse, Teresa A. "'My Own Credit': Strategies of (E)Valuation in Mary Rowlandson's Captivity Narrative." *American Literature* 64.4 (1992): 655–76. Print.

LESSON PLAN: Living in Captivity

Students analyze Mrs. Mary Rowlandson's account of living in captivity with American Indians.

Learning Objectives

Compare and contrast differing sets of values among the English settlers and American Indians; consider multiple perspectives on English and American Indian interactions; analyze the effects of English settlement on American Indians; consider how different choices could have led to different circumstances.

Materials: *The Narrative of the Captivity and Restoration of Mrs. Mary Rowlandson*

Overview Questions

How does Mrs. Rowlandson's perspective on her captivity help her to endure the harsh realities of her situation? How is Mrs. Rowlandson's captivity a result of English and Native American interaction? How is it important in understanding King Philip's War? How might her circumstances have been different had Mrs. Rowlandson not fled with her captors?

Step 1: Comprehension Questions

In her account, what needs does Mrs. Rowlandson describe? Do the American Indains meet her needs? How does she handle depravation?

▶ **Activity:** Have students identify Mrs. Rowlandson's needs and hopes while in captivity by highlighting passages in the text. Ask them to circle phrases that illustrate where she finds strength to endure.

Step 2: Comprehension Questions

How does Mrs. Rowlandson describe the American Indians who take her and others as captives? What does this reveal about English and American Indian relations and interactions?

▶ **Activity:** Have students work in small groups to make a list of the names and adjectives that Mrs. Rowlandson uses to describe her captors. Then ask them to summarize what her perspective and the actions of the American Indians tell the reader about English-American Indian interactions

Step 3: Context Questions

How does Mrs. Rowlandson's account help in the understanding of the events of King Philip's War (1675–78)?

▶ **Activity:** Instruct students to take turns reading key passages in the introduction. Have them

describe the setting and details. Ask students to discuss the state of English-American Indian relations during this time period

Step 4: Exploration Questions

How might circumstances have been different for Mrs. Rowlandson had she not fled with her captors? Why did she decide to live rather than to die at the hands of the American Indians?

▶ **Activity:** Ask students to create an outline for an essay on possible different outcomes for Mrs. Rowlandson and her children. Have them consider what might have happened had she not fled with her captors or if her captors had broken their initial promise to her.

Step 5: Response Paper

Word length and additional requirements set by Instructor. Students answer the research question in the Overview Questions. Students state a thesis and use as evidence passages from the primary source document as well as support from supplemental materials assigned in the lesson.

■ The Salem Witch Trials: The Case against John and Elizabeth Proctor

Date: 1692; 1706
Author: various
Genre: law

*"The Magistrates, Ministers, Jewries, and all the
People in general, being so much inraged and incensed against us by the Delusion of the Devil, which
we can term no other, by reason we know in our own
Consciences, we are all Innocent Persons."*

—Petition of John Proctor

Summary Overview

In 1692, the villages of Salem Village (present-day Salem, Massachusetts) and Salem Town (present-day Danvers) became embroiled in the pursuit of alleged witches or heretics among their residents. Nineteen people were executed for witchcraft, one died after being crushed to death during his questioning, and seven more died in prison awaiting trial after a special tribunal was created to address the accusations. Prominent farmer John Proctor was one of the few to oppose the trials and was summarily accused, along with his wife, Elizabeth, of witchcraft. Despite a petition to church leadership in Boston, he and his wife were both found guilty. John was later executed.

Defining Moment

From the fourteenth until the seventeenth centuries, witch-hunts were a common practice across Europe. Outcasts, non-Christians, and accused heretics were accused of witchcraft and executed. Though the practice had mainly disappeared by the end of the seventeenth century, the fear of the devil had crossed the Atlantic and embedded itself in Massachusetts Bay Colony and the Puritans who lived there.

In 1688, Salem Village, which was constantly fighting for independence from the richer Salem Town, was granted their own church. Village elder John Putnam brought Reverend Samuel Parris to the town in the Massachusetts Bay colony to serve as its minister. Parris brought with him his family and a Caribbean slave named Tituba. In 1692, Parris's daughters began to exhibit strange symptoms, including hallucinations, convulsions, and outbursts of nonsensical words. The Puritans were a deeply religious people who believed in the presence of the devil. The girls had been seen learning the stories and fortune-telling games that Tituba had brought from Barbados. When their doctor diagnosed witchcraft and the townspeople asked the girls who had brought the devil upon them, it was not difficult to believe it was Tituba when the girls pointed their fingers in her direction.

As the girls began accusing more townspeople (mostly women) of torture and witchcraft, Salem launched a series of criminal proceedings against the accused. Fear settled on a town already tense from village bickering, conflicts with American Indians, and a recent smallpox outbreak.

Many of those accused had had past quarrels with Reverend Parris. Among those was John Proctor. Although he was considered an upright citizen and a man of faith, Proctor doubted the veracity of the girls' claims of witchcraft and was outspoken in his criticism of the trials themselves. He argued that the trials were created based on nothing more than a hoax.

Meanwhile, Proctor's young maidservant, Mary Warren, began to demonstrate the type of fits that the other girls suffered. Proctor dealt with her affliction harshly, which led Warren to claim that her employer was a heretic. Proctor had already developed a reputation for his outspoken manner and was a recognized critic of the stern and demanding Samuel Parris, making his indictment by the people of Salem more likely.

The paranoid villagers then turned on Proctor and his wife, with many of the afflicted accusers joining in the claims that the couple had also been involved with the devil's work. Several of the girls who had already accused others also claimed that Proctor, through his apparition, inflicted evil upon them as well.

Proctor wrote to the Boston clergy to appeal his case, but he was ultimately executed. John Proctor was the first man at the time to be accused of witchcraft. Elizabeth, his wife, was spared only because she was pregnant. Proctor's children, Elizabeth's sister, and her sister in-law were also accused of this crime. Three centuries later, playwright Arthur Miller would use Proctor as inspiration for his classic historical drama on the trials, *The Crucible*.

Author Biography

John Proctor was born on October 9, 1631, in Suffolkshire, England. When he was three years old, his parents, John and Martha, immigrated to the New England colonies, settling in Ipswich in Massachusetts Bay Colony and living on a large and productive farm. The Proctor family became one of the wealthiest in the area. The younger John Proctor remained there for thirty-one years before he and his wife, Elizabeth, moved to nearby Salem to work on a farm of his own. He and Elizabeth had two sons and a daughter.

Proctor was a large man with an outspoken personality. Although wealthy, he was not one of the more popular figures in Salem at the time. In addition to his farm, he operated a tavern in which Salem's elders only allowed him to serve strangers, not villagers, as alcohol was forbidden by the Puritan faith. Proctor was also embroiled in a rivalry with one of Salem's largest families, the Putnams. Proctor was one of many who disapproved of the Putnams' choice for minister and opposed Parris's installation. Historians have long speculated that the opposition led by Proctor against Putnam and the accusation of witchcraft within the Parris household was hardly a coincidence.

In all, about two hundred people were accused of witchcraft, underscoring the mania that developed after the original Parris claims. John Proctor, however, mistrusted the growing hysteria and made his opinions well known. Several of the afflicted girls accused Proctor's wife, Elizabeth, bringing about her incarceration. When Proctor himself defended his wife at the trial, he was himself accused by the girls, who claimed his apparition had caused them harm.

Prior to Elizabeth's accusation, Proctor's maidservant, Mary Warren, had developed fits similar to those of Parris's children and other apparent victims of witchcraft. Proctor believed that Warren was faking her affliction. Rather than provide treatment, he beat her whenever the symptoms arose. Not surprisingly, Warren—who would also be accused of witchcraft—joined the other afflicted girls and denounced her employer, making Proctor the first man to be so accused.

While in jail awaiting judgment, Proctor wrote to the clergy in Boston, asking them to intercede. The church leadership there was uneasy about the Salem trials and gave Proctor's case careful consideration. In particular, they explored the girls' claim of Proctor's apparition as evidence, eventually concluding that spectral evidence was not admissible. However, Proctor was found guilty while he awaited their response and hanged in August 1692. Elizabeth Proctor, however, was pregnant and therefore avoided execution. Meanwhile, without physical evidence of witchcraft, the trials came to a close in 1692. In 1697, Salem officials apologized for the trials, promising reconciliation. Nearly twenty years later, Proctor's family received the largest compensation, 150 pounds, for what they had endured.

HISTORICAL DOCUMENT

Mercy Lewis v. Elizabeth Proctor

The Deposistion of Mircy lewes aged about 19 years who testifieth and [saith] that on the 26th march 1692 I saw the Apperishtion of Elizabeth proctor the wife of Jno proctor senr.: and she did most greviously tortor me by biting and pinching me most greviously urging me to writ in hir book and she continewed hurting me by temes tell the II'th April 1692 being the day of hir examination and then also dureing the time of hir examination she did tortor me most greviously and also severall times sence: also on the day of hir examination I saw the Apperishtion of Elizabeth proctor Mercy Lewes owned this har testimony to be the truth one har oath: before the Juriars of Inqwest this 30 of June 1692

(Reverse) Mircy lewes against: Elizabeth proctor

✳✳✳

Ann Putnam, Jr. v. John Proctor

The Deposistion of Ann putnam Jun'r who testifieth and saith I have often seen the Apperishtion of Jno procktor senr. amongst the wicthes but he did not doe me much hurt tell a little before his examination which was on the IIth of April 1692 and then he sett upon me most greviously and did tortor me most dreadfully also in the time of his examination he afflected me very much: and severall times sence the Apperishtion of John procktor senr, has most greviously tortored me by pinching and allmost choaking me urging me vehemently to writ in his book also on the day of his examination I saw the Apperishtion of Jno: proctor senr goe and afflect and most greviously tortor the bodys of Mistris pope mary walcott Mircy lewes. Abigail williams and Jno: Indian. and he and his wife and Sarah Cloys keept Elizabeth Hubburd speachless all the time of their examination
mark Ann putnam

Ann Putnam owned what is above written upon oath before and unto the Grand inquest on the 30'th Day of June 1692

✳✳✳

Ann Putnam, Jr. v. Elizabeth Proctor

The Deposistion of Ann putnam Jun who testifieth and saith that on the 3'th of march 1691/92 I saw the Apperishtion of gooddy procktor amongst the wicthes & she did almost choake me Immediatly and bite and pinch me but I did not know who she was tell the 6'th of march that I saw hir att meeting and then I tould them that held me that that woman was one that did afflect me: and severall times sence she hath greviously afflected me by biting pinching and almost choaking me urging me vehemently to writ in hir book: but on the II'th April 1692 the Apperishtion of Elizabeth proctor the wife of John procktor sen'r did most greviously torment me dureing the time of hir examination and also severall times sence by biting pinching and allmost choaking me to death urging me vehemently to writ in hir book: also on the II'th April it being the day of the examination of Elizabeth proctor I saw the Apperishtion of Elizabeth proctor goe and afflect the bodys of Mistris pope Mary walcott Mircy lewes Abigail Williams and also all the time of hir examination she and hir: Husband and Sarah Cloys did most greviously afflect Elizabeth Hubboard and would not let hir spake a word as I herd

Ann Putnam owned this har testimony to be the truth one har oath before the Juriars of Inqwest this: 30 dy of June; 1692

Jurat in Curia
(Reverse) Ann puttnam ag't Eliza. procter

✳✳✳

Joseph Bayley v. Elizabeth Proctor

The deposition of Joseph Bayley aged forty four years testifyeth and saith, that I on the: 25'th day of may last my self & my wife being bound tooston, on the road when I came in Sight of the house where John proctor did live, there was a very hard blow strook on my brest which caused great pain in my Stomoc & amasement in my head but did see no person near me only my wife behind me on the same hors, and when I came against s'd proctors house according to my understanding I did see John proctor & his wife att s'd house proctor himself loocked out of the windo & his wife did stand Just without the door, I tould my wife of it, & shee did loock that way & could see nothing but a littell maid att the dore I saw no maide there but proctors wife according to my understanding did stand att the dore, afterwards about half a mile from the afores'd house I was taken spechles for sum short time my wife did ask me severall questions and desiered me that if I could not speak I should hould up my hand which I did. and immediatly I could speak as well as ever, and when we came to the way where Salem Road cometh into Ipswich road there I received another blow on my brest which caused much pain that I could not sitt on my hors and when I did alite off my hors, to my understanding I saw a woman coming towards us about sixteen or twenty pole from us but did not know who it was my wife could not see her when I did get up on my hors againe to my understanding there Stood a cow where I saw the woman, after that we went to Boston without any father molestation but after I came home againe to newbury I was pinched and nipt by sumthing invisible for sumtime but now through gods goodness to me I am well again

Jurat in Curia

by both sons.
(Reverse) *Joseph Bayley & wife*

✳✳✳

Mary Warren v. John Proctor and Elizabeth Proctor

Mary Warrens Confession ag't Jo: Proctor & ux Charges them personally to cause her to signe or make a mark in there book and both of them comitting acts of Witchcraft & being soe & personally threatned the poit with tortures if she would not signe & since con [torn] have of times afflicted & tormented her.large in her Confessions vide.

✳✳✳

Indictment v. John Proctor, No. 1

Anno Regis et Reginae Willm: et Mariae nunc. Angliae &c Quarto. Essex ss

The Jurors for our Sovereigne Lord and Lady the King and Queen psents That: John Procter of Salem Husbandman in the County of Essex: the Eleventh Day of Aprill in the fourth Year of the Reigne of our Sovereigne Lord & Lady, William and Mary by the Grace of God of England Scottland France and Ireland King and Queen Defenders of the faith &c and divers other Dayes and times as well before as after Certaine Detestable Acts, called Witchcraft and Sorceries, Wickedly. and felloniously hath. used: Practised and Exercised at and within the Towneship of Salem in the County of Essex aforesd. in upon, and ag't one Mary Wolcott of Salem Villiage in the County of Essex Single Woman -- by which said wicked Arts the said: Mary Wolcott the II'th Day of Aprill in the Year abovesaid and Divers other Dayes and times as well before. as after was and is Tortured, Afflicted, Pined, Consumed wasted, and tormented, ag't the Peace of our Sovereigne Lord & Lady the King and Queen, and ag't the form of the Statute in that case made and provided Witnesses

Mary Wolcot Jurat
Mercy Lewis Jurat
Ann Putman Jurat

✳✳✳

Petition for John Proctor and Elizabeth Proctor

We whose names are under witten havinge several yeares knowne John Procter and his wife do testefy that we never heard or understood that they were ever suspected to be guilty of the crime now charged apon them and several of us being their neare neighbours do testefy that to our aprehension they lived christian life in their famely and were ever ready to helpe such as stood in need of their helpe

* Nathaniel Felton sen: and mary his wife Samuel Marsh and Prescilla his wife
* James Houlton and Ruth his wife

* John Felton
* Nathaniel Felton jun
* Samuell Frayll and an his wife
* Zachriah Marsh and mary his wife
* Samuel Endecott and hanah his wife
* Samuell Stone
* George Locker
* Samuel Gaskil & provided his wife
* George Smith
* Ed Edward: Gaskile

❊❊❊

Petition of John Proctor

SALEM-PRISON, July 23, 1692. Mr. Mather, Mr. Allen, Mr. Moody, Mr. Willard, and Mr. Bailey.

Reverend Gentlemen.

The innocency of our Case with the Enmity of our Accusers and our Judges, and Jury, whom nothing but our Innocent Blood will serve their turn, having Condemned us already before our Tryals, being so much incensed and engaged against us by the Devil, makes us bold to Beg and Implore your Favourable Assistance of this our Humble Petition to his Excellency, That if it be possible our Innocent Blood may be spared, which undoubtedly otherwise will be shed, if the Lord doth not mercifully step in. The Magistrates, Ministers, Jewries, and all the People in general, being so much inraged and incensed against us by the Delusion of the Devil, which we can term no other, by reason we know in our own Consciences, we are all Innocent Persons. Here are five Persons who have lately confessed themselves to be Witches, and do accuse some of us, of being along with them at a Sacrament, since we were committed into close Prison, which we know to be Lies. Two of the 5 are (Carriers Sons) Youngmen, who would not confess any thing till they tyed them Neck and Heels till the Blood was ready to come out of their Noses, and 'tis credibly believed and reported this was the occasion of making them confess that they never did, by reason they said one had been a Witch a Month, and another five Weeks, and that their Mother had made them so, who has been confined here this nine Weeks. My son William

Procter , when he was examin'd, because he would not confess that he was Guilty, when he was Innocent, they tyed him Neck and Heels till the Blood gushed out at his Nose, and would have kept him so 24 Hours, if one more Merciful than the rest, had not taken pity on him, and caused him to be unbound. These actions are very like the Popish Cruelties. They have already undone us in our Estates, and that will not serve their turns, without our Innocent Bloods. If it cannot be granted that we can have our Trials at Boston, we humbly beg that you would endeavour to have these Magistrates changed, and others in their rooms, begging also and beseeching you would be pleased to be here, if not all, some of you at our Trials, hoping thereby you may be the means of saving the sheeding our Innocent Bloods, desiring your Prayers to the Lord in our behalf, we rest your Poor Afflicted Servants,

JOHN PROCTER, etc.

❊❊❊

Petition of Elizabeth Proctor

To the Honourable Generall Court Asembled at Boston may twenty seventh 1696

the Humble petetion of Elizabeth procter widow and Relict of John proctor of salem decesed Humbly sheweth that in the yere of our Lord 1692 when many persons in salem and in other towns ther about were accused by som evill disposed or strangly Influenced persons, as being witches or for being guilty of acting witchcraft my s'd Husband John procter and my selfe were accused of such and we both: my s'd Husband and my selfe were soe farr proceded against that we were Condemned but in that sad time of darkness before my said husband was executed it is evident som body had Contrived awill and brought it to him to sign wher in his wholl estat is disposed of not having Regard to a contract in wrighting mad with me before mariag with him; but soe it pleased god to order by his providence that although the sentanc was executed on my dere husband yet through gods great goodnes to your petitioner I am yet alive; sinc my husbands death the s'd will is proved and aproved by the Judg of probate and by that kind of desposall the wholl estat is disposed of; and although god hath Granted my life yet those that claime my s'd husbands estate by that which thay Call awill will not suffer me to have one peny of the Estat nither upon the acount of my husbands Contract with me before mariage nor yet upon the acount of the dowr which as I humbly conceive doth belong or ought to belong to me by the law for thay say that I am dead in the law and therfore my humble request and petetion to this Honoured Generall Court is that by an act of his honoured Court as god hath Contenewed my life and through gods goodnes without feare of being put to death upon that sentanc you would be pleased to put me Into acapacity to make use of the law to Recover that which of Right by law I ought to have for my nessesary suply and support that as I your petetioner am one of his majestyes subjects I may have the benifett of his laws soe Humbly prayeng that god would direct your honnours in all things to doe that which may be well pleasing to him I subscrib your honours humble petitioner

Elizabeth procter widow
Read 10th June. 1692 [sic] in Council

✳✳✳

Ann Putnam's Confession (1706)

I desire to be humbled before God for that sad and humbling providence that befell my father's family in the year about '92; that I, then being in my childhood, should, by such a providence of God, be made an instrument for the accusing of several persons of a grievous crime, whereby their lives were taken away from them, whom now I have just grounds and good reason to believe they were innocent persons; and that it was a great delusion of Satan that deceived me in that sad time, whereby I justly fear I have been instrumental, with others, though ignorantly and unwittingly, to bring upon myself and this land the guilt of innocent blood; though what was said or done by me against any person I can truly and uprightly say, before God and man, I did it not out of any anger, malice, or ill-will to any person, for I had no such thing against one of them; but what I did was ignorantly, being deluded by Satan. And particularly, as I was a chief instrument of accusing of Goodwife Nurse and her two sisters, I desire to lie in the dust, and to be humbled for it, in that I was a cause, with others, of so sad a calamity to them and their families; for which cause I desire to lie in the dust, and earnestly beg forgiveness of God, and from all those unto whom I have given just cause of sorrow and offence, whose relations were taken away or accused.

[Signed]

GLOSSARY

apperishtion (apparition): a ghost, specter, or spirit

deposistion (deposition): a sworn statement of evidence

General Court: the main governing body of Massachusetts Bay Colony during the seventeenth century

gooddy (goody): short for "goodwife," a polite form of address for married women

indictment: a formal charge or accusation of a crime

inquest: a criminal investigation conducted by a judge, jury, or government agent

Document Analysis

The 1692 trial of John and Elizabeth Proctor, both accused of witchcraft, was significant for a number of reasons. It underscores the hysteria that was prevalent during the relatively short period in which the Salem witch trials took place. Four individuals claimed that the Proctors had somehow bewitched them. Additionally, the case provided multiple examples of "spectral evidence" that was at the core of most of the previous accusations. Furthermore, it highlighted many of the ulterior motives of the accusers.

In 1692, Betty, the daughter of Samuel Parris, started to exhibit strange symptoms that included hyperactive behavior, delusions, fever, and physical contortions. Some modern scientists have argued that her symptoms may have been real, brought about by ingestion of rye that was contaminated by the ergot fungus. Others have argued that her behavior was psychosomatic. A popular book by Boston minister Cotton Mather, published about the same time as the childrens' symptoms began, described an Irish woman whose supposed witchcraft caused similar symptoms in her victims. It is thought that the girls either consciously or unconsciously mimicked the symptoms described in the book.

Not long after Betty fell ill, her cousin Abigail Williams, who was also living in the Parris household, developed similar symptoms. Shortly thereafter, two girls with whom Betty and Abigail often played, Mercy Lewis and Ann Putnam, started to display symptoms akin to those of their friends. The village doctor examining each of the girls could not determine the cause of their perceived ailment and, in the absence of a medical explanation, offered a supernatural one: The girls had been attacked by the devil.

Suspicion regarding the witch who had enabled the devil's work in the Parris household focused on Tituba, the Parris family's Caribbean slave and open practitioner of magic. However, as Tituba's case was investigated, more of the Parris girls' friends became afflicted, including Mary Warren. Meanwhile, Tituba and two other women confessed under duress to being witches and incriminated others in the village as well. The afflicted girls also began to accuse people in the village, including Elizabeth Proctor. The first accusation against Elizabeth was made by Mercy Lewis. Mercy Lewis's personal history was marked by traumatic experiences and social maladjustment. She had witnessed her parents' murder during the ongoing conflict with nearby American Indian tribes. After being orphaned, she first went to live with Reverend George Burroughs in Maine and then with Thomas Putnam in Salem. With the Putnams, Mercy struggled to find acceptance in the Salem community, as did her friends. Some historians believe that the girls, if they knowingly and falsely acted afflicted, were acting out of personal insecurity.

Mercy Lewis's accusation against Elizabeth Proctor was typical of many of the charges against the Proctors and others. In her deposition, she claimed that the apparition of Elizabeth Proctor appeared before her, bit and pinched her, and attempted to force her to sign the devil's book, a book in which the names of those who pledge to worship him was kept. A few weeks earlier, Ann Putnam made similar claims about Elizabeth Proctor, saying that Elizabeth's spirit came before her and choked, pinched, and bit her to make her sign the book. Ann claimed she had no knowledge of who Proctor was until she saw Elizabeth in town after the incident.

When his wife was jailed, John Proctor came to her defense. During the trial, he derided the process, claiming the accusers' affliction was nothing more than a sham. Of course, Proctor's criticism of the young girls' claims left him open to suspicions that he himself was a witch, and the girls wasted no time in doing so. Ann Putnam, in April 1692, testified that not only had John Proctor's spirit tortured, pinched, and choked her, but that he had done the same to her friends Mercy Lewis, Abigail Williams, and others.

The girls who accused Elizabeth and John Proctor appeared to be both prolific in their accusations and consistent in each case. When accusing the Proctors, their claims were based on what is called spectral evidence—they never said that John and Elizabeth Proctor directly attacked or bewitched them but instead insisted that their apparitions were involved. The girls made similar claims when accusing others—Ann Putnam was one of the girls who made the most accusations, citing spectral evidence in the cases against Rebecca Nurse, Mary Easty, Tituba, and Martha Carrier. In fact, she actually stuck pins into her flesh on several occasions, later saying that the spirits of the accused caused the wounds.

Why the Hysteria Began

Historians offer a wide range of alternative explanations as to why these girls began to accuse so many individuals, including John and Elizabeth Proctor, of attacking them via apparitions. Some argue that the girls were simply playing a prank on an unsuspecting public. Others suggest that they may have been prodded by parents to accuse certain villagers based on interpersonal and/or political rivalries. Ann Putnam's example provides clues about this latter theory.

As explained earlier, Ann Putnam resided in the household of the most influential religious leader in Salem, the Reverend Parris. A large number of those whom Ann accused, including John Proctor and his wife, were individuals with whom Reverend Parris had had disagreements. She also accused George Burroughs, in whose household her friend Mercy Lewis lived. In fact, Ann's accusations were often added to bolster cases against suspected witches. It has been therefore argued that Ann Putnam and her friends were embroiled in a conspiracy against those who opposed Reverend Parris and others in his circle. In addition to the girls' testimony, a local man, Joseph Bayley, also pointed the finger at John and Elizabeth Proctor collectively. He claimed that one day, as he and his wife rode past Proctor's tavern, he was hit in the chest by an unseen but powerful force. When he turned around, he saw John and Elizabeth Proctor in their house, a great distance away, looking at them. He claimed to have been hit by a similar force in another incident, this time by an apparition of a woman he identified as Elizabeth Proctor. In both incidents, according to Bayley, his wife did not see the apparitions who attacked him, even when he could see them clearly. Of course, neither Proctor could be physically connected to the scene, as they were in jail after being arrested.

Linnda Caporael, who in the 1970s first introduced the theory that ergot fungus played a role in the girls' affliction, suggested that Bayley might have been one of the victims of such contamination. Then again, Bayley was at the time traveling en route from his home in Newbury to Boston and prior to his perceived assault stayed at the home of Thomas Putnam, one of John Proctor's biggest rivals in Salem.

The growing hysteria in Salem in 1692 led to the imprisonment of more than 150 Salem villagers. William Phips, the governor of Massachusetts Bay Colony, was absent at the time, leaving management of the colony's affairs in the hands of the church magistrates. When he returned, Phips found that the magistrates overseeing the witch cases in Salem were overwhelmed, having placed those accused in prison to await a trial. Phips authorized the creation of a Court of Oyer (to hear) and Terminer (to decide) to review each case of suspected witchcraft. Based on the format used against accused witches in England many years prior, Phips's court would act as a sort of grand jury, reviewing the evidence against

each suspect. The evidence included the depositions shown above as well as any depositions and petitions supporting the defendant's innocence. Phips placed the court in the hands of his lieutenant governor, William Stoughton. Stoughton was a known zealot on the issue of witchcraft and welcomed the use of spectral evidence to convict suspected witches.

Among the documents submitted to the court regarding the case of John and Elizabeth Proctor was a petition of individuals who defended the Proctors. Nathaniel Felton Sr., his wife Mary, and his son Nathaniel Felton Jr., who were neighbors of Proctor, signed a petition that stated simply that in the many years of living alongside the Proctors, they never encountered any illicit or un-Christian behavior. Sixteen others also signed, including John Endecott, a relative of the first governor of Massachusetts Bay Colony. However, as was typical in the cases of the Salem witch trials, there was a considerably larger volume of evidence and testimony against the Proctors than in favor of them. Once the evidence was reviewed, the colonial leadership would defer to the local leaders to put the accused on trial.

Growing Church Unease and the End of the Trials

Although they did not directly intervene when the number of defendants entered the hundreds, the Puritan church did seem somewhat uneasy about the situation in Salem. John Proctor added to this discomfort by writing to the Boston clergy to protest his own jailing. On July 22, 1692, Proctor wrote to the council of ministers, including Increase Mather, Cotton Mather's father. Cotton Mather was a firm believer in witchcraft and a close friend of and minister to three of the five judges on the Court of Oyer and Terminer. Increase Mather, however, was an intellectual; he was the president of Harvard College and a prominent liaison to the English government.

John Proctor's plea cited a number of key issues regarding both his specific case and the trials themselves. First, Proctor referred to the accusers as individuals with "enmity" toward him. The judges involved with the trials, Proctor said, were quick to condemn the accused due both to their zeal to combat witchcraft and the fact that witchcraft was perceived to be running rampant in Salem. He then took issue with the girls themselves, whom he identified as people who "have lately confessed themselves to be Witches."

Proctor's next argument was a pivotal one for the Salem witch trials. As mentioned earlier, the accusations against John and Elizabeth Proctor were similar to others made by the girls. The stories told by the girls, as well as the testimony of those who supposedly witnessed the girls' affliction, could not be corroborated by physical evidence. In each deposition, the girls claim that John and Elizabeth Proctor came to them as apparitions when the attacks occurred. Bayley's testimony was also dubious, according to Proctor's petition to the council: "We were committed into close Prison," wrote Proctor, when the alleged attacks on Bayley took place.

Proctor continued his petition by saying that countless individuals, he and his wife included, were being tortured and murdered in light of nothing more than groundless accusations. He cited the case of his son, William, who was also accused and hung until "Blood gushed out of his Nose" when he did not confess. William was then unbound, Proctor observed, when his torturers showed rare mercy. The brutality demonstrated toward the accused, Proctor said, was akin to the horrific acts conducted by the Spanish Inquisition, which began two centuries prior but continued through the early nineteenth century.

John Proctor's letter concluded by calling upon church magistrates to intervene on behalf of the accused who, in addition to enduring physical torture and false imprisonment, lost their standing and financial resources because of their alleged crimes. Proctor asked the magistrates to move the trials to Boston, where more level heads might prevail as the evidence was read. If they could not move the trials, Proctor suggested, the council might replace the magistrates who oversaw the trials in Salem. In either case, Proctor argued, the lives of innocent men and women were hanging in the balance, and without intervention, innocent blood would be shed.

Proctor's letter was significant in that it prompted the church to examine the use of spectral evidence in the trials. Increase Mather and other members of the church leadership met after receiving the petition to discuss this issue. Shortly thereafter, Mather attended the trial of Reverend George Burroughs to witness firsthand the use of spectral evidence. Burroughs was the only Puritan minister to be charged and, according to his accusers, was a ringleader of the Salem witches. Over time, Mather began to believe in Burroughs's innocence and to doubt the reliability of spectral evidence.

Thanks in large part to the petition of John Proctor, the church leadership in Boston developed an interest in the trials. Some members of the council even spoke out against them, but there was no intervention. Spectral evidence, used against the Proctors, was tolerated even

though it was highly suspect. Even Mather, though critical of spectral evidence and likely beginning to doubt the trials themselves, never spoke out against the proceedings or the magistrates overseeing them.

Despite the council's growing opposition to spectral evidence, Governor Phips held his ground, at least for a time. Proctor's letter failed to gain him or his wife exoneration, and he was executed on August 19, 1692. Thereafter, Phips changed his mind on spectral evidence. However, his change of heart was not the result of the council's actions or Proctor's letter. Phips's wife was accused of witchcraft, with townspeople offering spectral evidence. In October 1692, Governor Phips declared that spectral evidence was inadmissible in the trials. Without any additional evidence, those who were awaiting execution were summarily freed and the trials came to a close.

While he was awaiting his fate in jail, John Proctor crafted his last will and testament. Strangely, he did not name his wife as a beneficiary of his estate, which had been seized during the trials. Elizabeth was therefore left with very little when she was released. Four years after her husband's execution and her release, she wrote to the Massachusetts General Court. In her petition, she reminded her leaders that she and her husband were wrongfully imprisoned during the Salem witch trials. She said that her husband was in fact delivered a will by another party, in which he signed away his estate without compensation to Elizabeth. She asked the General Court to assist her, and the General Court obliged. She and her family were given 150 pounds, a much larger sum than other accused witches received.

Fourteen years after the end of the trials, Ann Putnam stood before the congregation in Salem and made a formal statement of regret for the hysteria she helped create more than a decade earlier. She described how she knowingly caused the prosecution and deaths of many innocent people. In the document, read on her behalf by Parris's successor, Reverend Joseph Green, Putnam claimed to be under the delusion of the devil at the time, saying that she had no motives to accuse those who were tried. Her confession is viewed by many historians as somewhat disingenuous, motivated not out of extreme guilt but by Green's efforts to reestablish harmony in the congregation.

Still, Ann Putnam was the only member of the original afflicted girls who took such an action. Even though she retracted her accusations, she failed to provide any credible clues about her motives. Without a rational explanation for her actions or the actions of the other girls, the facts surrounding the underpinnings for the Salem witch trials remain a topic of much historical debate.

Essential Themes

Approximately 150 people were accused of witchcraft in Salem in 1692. Many were executed, and many more were tortured and imprisoned. John and Elizabeth Proctor were among those who fell victim to the hysteria. Their case is significant among the others, helping to shed light on the possible motives for the mania that befell the village as well as leading to an end to the trials.

John Proctor was, by most accounts, accused for three reasons. First, he had a long-standing rivalry with the Putnams, one of the most powerful families in Salem and home to Ann Putnam and Mercy Lewis, two of the most prolific accusers at the time. Second, he was among the small number of residents who opposed the installation of Reverend Parris, whose daughter was the first to display symptoms of bewitching. Third, John Proctor was a skeptic. He beat his own servant when she started to manifest fits and vigorously defended his accused wife by alleging that the witchcraft scare was a hoax.

The case against the Proctors—and John in particular—was also important because it helped hasten the end of the trials. The vast majority of the cases against the accused witches were built on spectral rather than physical evidence. John Proctor's letter to Boston helped bring the issue to the attention of church leaders. Proctor appealed to their logic and rationalism rather than their religious devotion. Then again, the court was driven by individuals who believed so strongly in witchcraft that they allowed spectral evidence to be admitted. Still, Proctor's petition piqued the interest of such influential leaders as Increase Mather, who after receiving Proctor's letter, meeting with his peers, and attending George Burroughs's trial, became convinced that such evidence was groundless. The Salem witch trials ultimately came to a close when Governor Phips's own wife was accused based on the same type of evidence that jailed John and Elizabeth Proctor.

John Proctor was executed before his role in ending the Salem witch trials could help his own case. When Parris was succeeded by Reverend Green, a period of reconciliation was launched, marked by the sizable compensation presented to Elizabeth Proctor and the public apology by one of the Proctors' accusers.

Michael P. Auerbach, MA

Bibliography

Alvarez, Kate. "Ann Putnam, Jr." *Salem Witch Trials: Documentary Archive and Transcription Project.* University of Virginia, 2002. Web. 1 Jan. 2012.

Blackstone, Kenneth E. "The Salem Witch Trials: A Case Review." *Blackstone Polygraph.* Blackstone Polygraph, 2009. PDF file.

Carroll, Meghan, and Jenny Stone. "Mercy Lewis." *Salem Witch Trials: Documentary Archive and Transcription Project.* University of Virginia, 2002. Web. 1 Jan. 2012.

Dignan, Brendan. "Governor, Sir William Phips." *Salem Witch Trials: Documentary Archive and Transcription Project.* University of Virginia, 2012. Web. 3 Jan. 2012.

"John Proctor." *Famous American Trials: Salem Witchcraft Trials, 1692.* University of Missouri–Kansas City School of Law, n.d. Web. 1 Jan. 2012.

"John Proctor, of the Salem Witch Trials." House of Proctor Genealogy. House of Genealogy, 1945. Web. 2 Jan. 2012.

Linder, Douglas. "Cotton Mather." *Famous American Trials: Salem Witchcraft Trials, 1692.* University of Missouri–Kansas City School of Law, n.d. Web. 1 Jan. 2012.

Salem Witch Trials: The World beyond the Hysteria. Discovery Education, 2012. Web. 1 Jan. 2012.

Additional Reading

Boyer, Paul, and Stephen Nissenbaum. *Salem Possessed: The Social Origins of Witchcraft.* Cambridge, MA: Harvard UP, 1974. Print.

Burns, Margo, and Bernard Rosenthal. "Examination of the Records of the Salem Witch Trials." *William and Mary Quarterly* 65.3 (2008): 402–22. Print.

Godbeer, Richard. *The Salem Witch Hunt: A Brief History with Documents.* New York: St. Martin's, 2011. Print.

King, Ernest W., and Franklin G. Mixon. "Religiosity and the Political Economy of the Salem Witch Trials." *Social Science Journal* 47.3 (2010): 678–88. Print.

Miller, Arthur. *The Crucible.* New York: Penguin Classics, 2003. Print.

Pope, Victoria. "Myth vs. Reality." *US News & World Report.* US News & World Report, 22 Dec. 1996. Web. 1 Jan. 2012.

LESSON PLAN: John and Elizabeth Proctor on Trial

Students analyze the trial of John and Elizabeth Proctor and other Salem witch trials, and consider multiple perspectives on religious beliefs in English colonies.

Learning Objectives

Identify multiple perspectives on religious beliefs in the English colonies; compare and contrast ideas about religious freedom; compare and contrast the course and outcome of both trials; distinguish between unsupported expressions of opinion and informed hypothesis.

Materials: "The examination of Nehemiah Abbot, 22, April, 1692"; "Warrant vs. Tituba and Sarah Osborne"; "Warrant for the Arrest of Proctor and Cloyce"; "Petition of John Proctor, July 23, 1692"; "Ann Putman's Confession" (1706); Cotton Mather, "Memorable Providences, Relating to Witchcraft and Possessions"; "Transcript from the Trial of Anne Hutchinson"

Overview Questions

How are the Salem witch trials and the trial of Anne Hutchinson alike and different? How do the trials show multiple perspectives on religion and religious beliefs in the colonies? Were the accusations unsupported expressions of opinion or informed based upon factual evidence?

Step 1: Comprehension Questions

Of what have the people at the Salem witch trials been accused and how do the accusations compare and contrast with those of Anne Hutchinson's trial?

▶ **Activity:** Select students to read aloud key passages. Have students to write a summary explaining what the Proctors and Hutchinson have been accused of doing.

Step 2: Comprehension Questions

Upon what authority are the colonists at Salem and Hutchinson brought to trial? Do they defend themselves while on trial? If so, how do they do so?

▶ **Activity:** Ask students to locate key words in each passage that explain why Hutchinson and the colonists at Salem were brought to trial and to underline words that explain how they defended themselves.

Step 3: Context Questions

How did the trial of Anne Hutchinson and others affect the Salem witch trials? How did the trials lead to greater religious freedom in some colonies?

▶ **Activity:** Instruct students to compare and contrast Anne Hutchinson's trial with that of the Salem witch trials by making a list or completing a graphic organizer. Ask students to describe how the Puritans' perspective on religious freedom affected the colony's government.

Step 4: Exploration Questions

Did the accusers use unsupported expressions of opinion or an informed hypothesis in their statements? What kind of evidence did they have to back up their statements? How might factual evidence have helped?

▶ **Activity:** Ask students to select words, phrases, and passages that show opinion versus fact. Have them write a brief paper on what kinds of factual evidence may have helped the case.

Step 5: Response Paper

Word length and additional requirements set by Instructor. Students answer the research question in the Overview Questions. Students state a thesis and use as evidence passages from the primary source document as well as support from supplemental materials assigned in the lesson.

s, every Christian has a responsibility to work for the
vation of souls at risk of corruption. Second, Mather
ues, a slave who has been Christianized is more like-
o be productive and agreeable, providing a profitable
urn on investment for the slave owner.

thor Biography
tton Mather was born on February 12, 1663, in
ston, Massachusetts. His father, Increase Mather,
s considered one of the leading religious minds of
 age; his grandfathers, John Cotton and Richaard
ther, were prominent figures, dubbed Massachu-
ts Bay Colony's spiritual founders. Cotton Mather
lowed in their footsteps, entering Harvard College
about the age of twelve. There, he studied Hebrew,
tin, Greek, philosophy, divinity, and science, earning
achelor's degree in 1678. He then went on to receive
 master of arts degree in 1681.
Mather had a reputation as an intellectual as well as
areful student of the Bible. He was committed to the
ristian faith, and although he was often critical of
er congregations and denominations early in his ca-
r, Mather ultimately developed a sense of acceptance
such institutions. In 1685, he became an ordained
nister at his father's church, the Second Church (also
own as the Old North Church) in Boston.
Mather was married three times during his life, fa-
ering fifteen children. He outlived his first two wives,
ile there is speculation that his third wife might
ve gone insane. Meanwhile, he continued to serve
assistant minister for the Second Church until 1723,

when his father died. Thereafter, he assumed the title
of minister of that congregation. For all his abilities as
a minister, Mather was not adept with money and experienced numerous financial difficulties in the latter
part of his life.

Cotton Mather authored some four hundred written
works during his lifetime, including letters, sermons,
and books. One of his best-known works was *Magnalia
Christi Americana* (1702), which was a comprehensive
history of New England from a Puritan perspective.
Mather also retained his longstanding interest in science and medicine—he and his father openly supported the inoculation of colonists against smallpox,
despite widespread opposition from community members throughout Boston. In 1710, Mather received an
honorary doctorate in divinity from the University of
Glasgow.

One of the most well-known aspects of Mather's career was his role in the Salem witch trials. Mather was
a firm believer in witchcraft and personally interceded
on a number of cases involving young women allegedly
afflicted with a curse by the devil. He wrote a number
of books, most notably *Wonders of the Invisible World*
(1693), analyzing witchcraft from both a scientific and
religious point of view. Although he believed that Salem
was indeed in the throes of a plot by the devil, he urged
his peers not to admit spectral evidence—claims that
a witch attacked a victim through a ghostly apparition
rather than directly—as grounds for conviction of the
accused. He continued to analyze the witchcraft issue
long after the trials' end, up until his death in 1728.

HISTORICAL DOCUMENT

It is a Golden Sentence, that has been sometimes quoted
from Chrysostom; That for a man to know the Art of
Alms, is more than for a man to be Crowned with the
Diadem of Kings: But to Convert one Soul unto God,
is more than to pour out Ten Thousand Talents into the
Baskets of the Poor. Truly, to Raise a Soul, from a dark
State of Ignorance and Wickedness, to the Knowledge
of GOD, and the Belief of CHRIST, and the practice of
our Holy and Lovely RELIGION; 'Tis the noblest Work,
that ever was undertaken among the Children of men.
An Opportunity to Endeavour the CONVERSION of a
Soul, from a Life of Sin, which is indeed a woful Death,

to Fear God, and Love CHRIST, and by a Religious Life
to Escape the Paths of the Destroyer; it cannot but be
Acceptable to all that have themselves had in themselves
Experience of such a Conversion. And such an Opportunity there is in your Hands, O all you that have any
Negroes in your Houses; an Opportunity to try, Whether
you may not be the Happy Instruments, of Converting,
the Blackest Instances of Blindness and Baseness, into
admirable Candidates of Eternal Blessedness. Let not
this Opportunity be Lost; if you have any concern for
Souls, your Own or Others; but, make a Trial, Whether
by your Means, the most Bruitish of Creatures upon

■ The Negro Christianized

Date: 1706
Author: Mather, Cotton
Genre: essay; sermon

*"The Considerations that would move you,
To Teach your Negroes the Truths of the Glorious
Gospel, as far as you can, and bring them, if it may be,
to Live according to those Truths, a Sober, and
a Righteous, and a Godly Life ... "*

Summary Overview

"The Negro Christianized" was an essay written by prominent Puritan minister Cotton Mather for distribution among his congregation at the Second Church in Boston. In this pamphlet, Mather calls upon his congregation—particularly those who hold slaves in their households and places of business—to share their knowledge of Christian values and traditions with these slaves. He also advises the white parishioners to be kind and just to their slaves. In addition to the benefit of salvation, Mather suggests that proselytizing to slaves would create an economic benefit as well: Spiritually enriched slaves are, in his opinion, more likely to be happy, hardworking, and dedicated.

Defining Moment

During the early to mid-seventeenth century, as English colonists arrived on the shores of the New World, so too did their institutions of indentured servitude and slavery. Initially, the majority of unfree people in the English colonies of North America were white indentured servants. Africans, brought to the English colonies as early as 1619, soon constituted a significant subset of the unfree labor force, and by midcentury, race-based slavery was codified into law. While some of the black slaves brought to the American colonies came directly from Africa, the largest percentage of them arrived from the West Indies and other European settlements.

Slaves were used for a number of p
Virginia and Maryland colonies, for
were purchased for agriculture and oth
capacities. In New England, slaves w
but also in the homes of wealthy merc
successful residents, performing housek

In 1620, the first wave of English
in New England, when the Pilgrims
tablished Plymouth Colony. A decade
more arrived and settled in the Mas
Colony towns of Boston and Salem. T
Massachusetts became active participa
trade. Among these slaveholders was t
the Second Church in Boston, Cotton
was well known as a major figure in the
witch trials, which were launched in pa
sations of witchcraft practiced by a We
named Tituba.

Despite his firm belief in witchcraft an
conservative Puritan tradition, Mather, i
a progressive notion to his parishioners.
gation arrived at the church, they foun
pamphlet titled "The Negro Christianiz
thorship was nonetheless readily appare
pamphlet, Mather calls upon slave own
gregation to educate their slaves on the (
Additionally, Mather suggests that mast
slaves fairly and with kindness, essentia
brethren. Mather's reasoning is twofold.

Earth may not come to be disposed, in some Degree, like the Angels of Heaven; and the Vassals of Satan, become the Children of God. Suppose these Wretched Negroes, to be the Offspring of Cham (which yet is not so very certain,) yet let us make a Trial, Whether the CHRIST who dwelt in the Tents of Shem, have not some of His Chosen among them; Let us make a Trial, Whether they that have been Scorched and Blacken'd by the Sun of Africa, may not come to have their Minds Healed by the more Benign Beams of the Sun of Righteousness.

It is come to pass by the Providence of God, without which there comes nothing to pass, that Poor Negroes are cast under your Government and Protection. You take them into your Families; you look on them as part of your Possessions; and you Expect from their Service, a Support, and perhaps an Increase, of your other Possessions. How agreeable would it be, if a Religious Master or Mistress thus attended, would now think with themselves! Who can tell but that this Poor Creature may belong to the Election of God! Who can tell, but that God may have sent this Poor Creature into my Hands, that so One of the Elect may by my means be Called; & by my Instruction be made Wise unto Salvation! The glorious God will put an unspeakable Glory upon me, if it may be so! The Considerations that would move you, To Teach your Negroes the Truths of the Glorious Gospel, as far as you can, and bring them, if it may be, to Live according to those Truths, a Sober, and a Righteous, and a Godly Life; They are Innumerable; And, if you would after a Reasonable manner consider, the Pleas which we have to make on the behalf of God, and of the Souls which He has made, one would wonder that they should not be Irresistible. Show your selves Men, and let Rational Arguments have their Force upon you, to make you treat, not as Bruits but as Men, those Rational Creatures whom God has made your Servants.

For,

First; The Great GOD Commands it, and Requires it of you; to do what you can that Your Servants, may also be His. It was an Admonition once given; Eph. 5.9. Masters, Know that your Master is in Heaven. You will confess, That the God of Heaven is your Master. If your Negroes do not comply with your Commands, into what Anger, what Language, Perhaps into a misbecoming Fury, are you trans-

ported? But you are now to attend unto the Commands of your more Absolute Master; and they are His Commands concerning your Negroes too. What can be more Expressive, than those words of the Christian Law? Col. 4.1. Masters, give unto your Servants, that which is Just & Equal, knowing that ye also have a Master in Heaven. Of what Servants is this Injunction to be understood? Verily, of Slaves. For Servants were generally such, at the time of Writing the New Testament. Wherefore, Masters, As it is Just & Equal, that your Servants be not Over-wrought, and that while they Work for you, you should Feed them, and Cloath them, and afford convenient Rest unto them, and make their Lives comfortable; So it is Just and Equal, that you should Acquaint them, as far as you can, with the way to Salvation by JESUS CHRIST. You deny your Master in Heaven, if you do nothing to bring your Servants unto the Knowledge and Service of that glorious Master. One Table of the Ten Commandments, has this for the Sum of it; Thou shalt Love thy Neighbour as thy self. Man, Thy Negro is thy Neighbour. T'were an Ignorance, unworthy of a Man, to imagine otherwise. Yea, if thou dost grant, That God hath made of one Blood, all Nations of men, he is thy Brother too. Now canst thou Love thy Negro, and be willing to see him ly under the Rage of Sin, and the Wrath of God? Canst thou Love him, and yet refuse to do any thing, that his miserable Soul may be rescued from Eternal miseries? Oh! Let thy Love to that Poor Soul, appear in thy concern, to make it, if thou canst, as happy as thy own! We are Commanded, Gal. 6. 10. As we have opportunity let us Do Good unto all men, especially unto them, who are of the Houshold of Faith. Certainly, we have Opportunity, to Do Good unto our Servants, who are of our own Houshold; certainly, we may do something to make them Good, and bring them to be of the Houshold of Faith.

✳✳✳

It has been cavilled, by some, that it is questionable Whether the Negroes have Rational Souls, or no. But let that Bruitish insinuation be never Whispered any more. Certainly, their Discourse, will abundantly prove, that they have Reason. Reason showes it self in the Design which they daily act upon. The vast improvement that Education has made upon some of them, argues that there is a Reasonable Soul in all of them. An old Roman, and Pagan, would call upon the Owner of such Servants, *Homines tamen esse memento*. They are Men, and not Beasts that you have bought, and they must be used accordingly. 'Tis true; They are Barbarous. But so were our own Ancestors. The Britons were in many things as Barbarous, but a little before our Saviours Nativity, as the Negroes are at this day if there be any Credit in Cæsars Commentaries. Christianity will be the best cure for this Barbarity. Their Complexion sometimes is made an Argument, why nothing should be done for them. A Gay sort of argument! As if the great God went by the Complexion of Men, in His Favours to them! As if none but Whites might hope to be Favoured and Accepted with God! Whereas it is well known, That the Whites, are the least part of Mankind. The biggest part of Mankind, perhaps, are Copper-Coloured; a sort of Tawnies. And our English that inhabit some Climates, so seem growing apace to be not so much unlike unto them. As if, because a people, from the long force of the African Sun & Soyl upon them, (improved perhaps, to further Degrees by maternal imaginations, and other accidents,) are come at length to have the small Fibres of their Veins, and the Blood in them, a little more Interspersed thro' their Skin than other People, this must render them less valuable to Heaven then the rest of Mankind? Away with such Trifles! The God who looks on the Heart, is not moved by the colour of the Skin; is not more propitious to one Colour than another. Say rather, with the Apostle; Acts 10.34, 35. *Of a truth I perceive, that God is no respecter of persons; but in every Nation, he that feareth Him and worketh Righteousness, is accepted with Him.* Indeed their *Stupidity* is a *Discouragement*. It may seem, unto as little purpose, to Teach, as to wash an Æthopian. But the greater their Stupidity, the greater must be our Application. If we can't learn them so much as we Would, let us learn them as much as we Can. A little divine Light and Grace infused into them, will be of great account. And the more Difficult it is, to fetch such forlorn things up out of the perdition whereinto they are fallen, the more Laudable is the undertaking: There will be the more of a Triumph, if we prosper in the undertaking. Let us encourage our selves from that word; Mat. 3. 9. *God is able of these Stones, to raise up Children unto Abraham.*

Well; But if the Negroes are Christianized, they will be Baptised; and their Baptism will presently entitle them to their Freedom; so our Money is thrown away.

Man, If this were true; that a Slave bought with thy Money, were by thy means brought unto the Things that accompany Salvation, and thou shouldest from this time have no more Service from him, yet thy Money were not thrown away. That Mans Money will perish with him, who had rather the Souls in his Family should Perish, than that he should lose a little Money. And suppose it were so, that Baptism gave a legal Title to Freedom. Is there no guarding against this Inconvenience? You may by sufficient Indentures, keep off the things, which you reckon so Inconvenient. But it is all a Mistake. There is no such thing. What Law is it, that Sets the Baptised Slave at Liberty? Not the Law of Christianity: that allows of Slavery; Only it wonderfully Dulcifies, and Mollifies, and Moderates the Circumstances of it. Christianity directs a Slave, upon his embracing the Law of the Redeemer, to satisfy himself, That he is the Lords Free-man, tho' he continues a Slave. It supposes, (Col 3. 11.) That there are Bond as well as Free, among those that have been Renewed in the Knowledge and Image of Jesus Christ. Will the Canon-law do it? No; The Canons of Numberless Councils, mention, the Slaves of Christians, without any contradiction. Will the Civil Law do it? No: Tell, if you can, any part of Christendom, wherein Slaves are not frequently to be met withal. But is not Freedom to be claim'd for a Baptised Slave, by the English Constitution? The English Laws, about Villians, or, Slaves, will not say so; for by those Laws, they may be granted for Life, like a Lease, and passed over with a Mannor, like other Goods or Chattels. And by those Laws, the Lords may sieze the Bodies of their Slaves even while a Writt, *De libertate probanda*, is depending. These English Laws were made when the Lords & the Slaves, were both of them Christians; and they stand still unrepealed. If there are not now such Slaves in England as formerly, it is from the Lords, more than from the Laws. The Baptised then are not thereby entitled unto their Liberty. Howbeit, if they have arrived unto such a measure of Christianity, that none can forbid Water for the Baptising of them, it is fit, that they should enjoy those comfortable circumstances with us, which are due to them, not only as the Children of Adam, but also as our Brethren, on the same level with us in the expectations of a blessed Immortality, thro' the Second Adam. Whatever Slaughter the Assertion may make among the pretensions which are made unto Christianity, yet while the sixteenth Chapter of

Matthew is in the Bible, it must be asserted; the Christian, who cannot so far Deny himself, can be no Disciple of the Lord JESUS CHRIST. But, O Christian, thy Slave will not Serve thee one jot the worse for that Self-denial.

GLOSSARY

canon law: body of laws established by religious leaders

cavilled: unnecessarily finding fault or objecting

Cham: one of the sons of Noah, according to the book of Genesis

indenture: a legal contract in which someone agrees to work for another for a set period of time, typically several years

Shem: eldest son of Noah, according to Genesis

Document Analysis

Mather begins "The Negro Christianized" by reminding his parishioners of the benefits of helping others. Certainly, he argues, charity toward others is a more critical element of Christian beliefs than personal power; moreover, an individual who helps convert one wayward soul to Christianity has committed an act of charity far greater than the giving of alms to the poor.

Mather's point is a central theme of Christianity and, in particular, of Puritanism. Puritanism was dedicated to adherence to a strict interpretation of God's word, and the Puritans had therefore eschewed the traditions and trappings of the Church of England that were not described in the Bible. In response, the Church of England had isolated the Puritans in England. When they left the country, they were determined to establish a society in which they could adhere to a more conservative lifestyle dictated by the Bible. Their focus was on redemption and, ultimately, salvation.

In this light, Mather's comment on the benefits of bringing a person into the Christian fold is particularly poignant. The goal of any good Puritan, Mather states, is to bring more people into the Puritan way of life, thereby saving them from a terrible death and defeating the efforts of the devil, who constantly seeks to disrupt society and steal souls away from God. Mather therefore asserts that the act of raising a soul from a life of sin and ignorance into the Puritan faith is "the noblest work" that the faithful could undertake.

Slaveholders, Mather claims, have a ready opportunity for this work in their own homes, having in their midst people who are, in his opinion, blind to the no-tion of Christian values and therefore liable to evil influences. Black slaves, he says, can be converted from this deplorable state into "candidates of eternal blessedness." If they are not converted, Mather warns, they will remain brutish "creatures" susceptible to the devil's work.

Preventing the colonial slaveholders from attempting to introduce Christian ideals to their servants was a series of misconceptions white Europeans held about blacks. Mather repeatedly refers to the slave owners' view of black slaves in particular as mere possessions rather than people. This viewpoint led to the perception that, for a variety of reasons, these slaves would be unable to learn such information and therefore could not be saved. Concurrently, many of the owners themselves were reluctant to impart Christian ideals to their servants for fear that such an action would undermine their financial investment in their slaves. Mather spends the remainder of "The Negro Christianized" critically examining each of these misconceptions and arguments.

First among these issues was the prevailing belief among European Christians that black Africans were descendants of Ham (or Cham, as Mather calls him), one of the sons of Noah. In the biblical story, each of Noah's sons went out after the Great Flood and began to restart the human race. According to a commonly misread passage in the book of Genesis, Ham angered Noah and, as punishment, was sent to what is now Africa. Due to this supposed curse, Ham's descendants in this region would amount to nothing more than slaves to others. Many historians believe that Europeans used this erroneous interpretation of the Bible as a foundation for the slave trade.

Mather acknowledges this story in his pamphlet, stating that he is uncertain that the so-called curse of Ham is indeed true. Even if black Africans were the descendants of Ham and thus cursed to be slaves, Mather writes, who was to say that Christ had not chosen some for salvation? He therefore urges slaveholders to try converting their slaves in the hopes that some might "come to have their Minds Healed by the more Benign Beams of the Sun of Righteousness."

Mather claims that, through divine Providence, slaves come into the hands of the slave owners and are brought into their masters' homes and families and that slave owners view their slaves as possessions whose work is expected to increase the owners' material wealth. The point Mather makes here is that the slaves kept in their masters' homes have the potential to contribute far more to their respective households. If they remained isolated from the joys of the Christian tradition, these slaves would likely perform their required tasks adequately at best. However, if brought into the Christian fold, they would be buoyed by their joy and enlightenment, taking greater pride in their work and contributing more than is expected of them. In financial terms, Mather argues that an investment in slaves' religious convictions (which cost nothing) would generate an ample return.

While blacks might be seen as mere servants or "creatures" by the slave owners, Mather suggests that his congregation give careful consideration to these people because it is possible that God had delivered a slave to the slaveholder. God may have looked favorably upon the servant, seeing that the person only needed training on God's teachings in order to be completely saved; for this reason, Mather suggests, slave owners may have received a black slave from God in order that they might prepare him or her for salvation.

Mather next invites the slaveholders in his congregation to consider the idea of going beyond simply reading the Gospels to their slaves to teaching them how to live truthful, sober, righteous, and godly lives according to the Christian faith. In order to do so, Mather states, the owners would need to step away from the practice of brutality and dehumanization of slaves and instead treat their slaves as rational men whom God has delivered into their charge.

Mather reminds the congregation that a spiritual hierarchy exists, with God as the ultimate authority and humans as the servants of God. If an owner's slaves did not comply with their master's commands, the master

would be expected to become furious; likewise, when humans fail, God becomes angry as well. Furthermore, Mather invokes a passage from the book of Colossians in the New Testament, which advises slave masters to treat well their servants fairly and justly. After all, the passage reads, slave owners are also servants of God, just as slaves are servants of the slave owners.

Mather further delves into the idea of showing compassion and fair treatment toward the congregation's black slaves. Slave owners should not overwork their servants or slaves; rather, they should clothe and feed them, give them rest, and provide them with the resources to live comfortably. Furthermore, slaveholders should teach their slaves Christian values so that they may understand the concepts of salvation. In fact, slave owners who deny their responsibilities to their servants are also denying their responsibilities to their own master, God.

An important element of Mather's argument is the famed New Testament directive: "Love thy neighbour as thy self." Mather reminds the congregation that, despite the long-standing European view of blacks as lowly "beasts," the slaves are nevertheless their masters' neighbors. He further asserts that all men share the same blood, despite their heritage or race. As God made the world of men from this one blood, each person, regardless of social standing, should be considered one of the brothers of humanity, Mather concludes.

In light of the brotherhood between white slave owners and their black servants, Mather challenges the slaveholding parishioners to love their brothers. Based on such love, Mather suggests that the slave owners would not wish to see their brothers overburdened by sin and ultimately made to suffer by God. When they loved their brothers, the white slaveholders would be fearful that the blacks would suffer an eternity of misery and seek to rescue their souls from such damnation.

To aid in his point, Mather paraphrases a passage from the book of Galatians, wherein the people are instructed to do good unto others. In particular, they should care for those who dwell in their homes (referring to the slaves who lived in their owners' homes), bettering them spiritually, so that they too would ultimately arrive in heaven when they died.

Mather next disclaims the perception among the white colonists that blacks do not have rational souls worthy of salvation. He calls such a perception brutish, saying that blacks have long shown a capacity for learning and reason, leaving little doubt that they have souls. Furthermore, blacks are not to be considered beasts;

rather, they are men, just like their owners, and should be treated as such.

The difference between the slave owners and their servants, Mather argues, is one of evolution. He agrees with his congregation that blacks are "barbarous," but argues that, at one point in history, so too were the Britons and other Europeans. Just as the Europeans were steered away from their barbarian ways through the moral and spiritual gifts of Christianity, Mather believes that if blacks were introduced to Christianity as well, they too might evolve.

Mather also takes to task the belief among Europeans that blacks could not be converted due to the color of their skin. Mather criticizes such notions, stating that God would not base divine love and blessings on a person's complexion. He points to the fact that, in the world, white people are significantly in the minority—the largest racial group of which he is aware is the "copper-coloured" peoples. He ridicules the idea that physical differences would influence who enters or is denied entrance into heaven. God, he says, looks into a person's heart, not at skin color. Mather cites the book of Acts, in which it is said that God accepts any person from any nation as long as that person fears God and lives a righteous life.

The challenge for slaveholders who seek to impart their knowledge of Christianity upon their black slaves is, in Mather's words, the blacks' "stupidity." It is likely, he advises, that blacks may not understand many of the concepts being introduced to them. He suggests a patient approach—if slaveholders cannot teach blacks as much about Christianity as they had hoped, then they should impart as much as their slaves can learn. Even a little bit of knowledge, Mather says, would have a tremendous impact on the slaves.

He also encourages them to continue to try, even with the most difficult of students. The most challenging of undertakings, Mather says, are also the most laudable. If they succeed in imparting even a little knowledge in these difficult cases, Mather says, the slaveholders can claim an important victory.

Mather next discusses another perception among colonists regarding proselytizing to blacks: if the slaves were Christianized, they would need to be baptized. Some slave owners were concerned that baptism would set their slaves free from servitude. Mather first dismisses the notion, saying that the owners' money would not be wasted even if their slaves went free. He then adds that a worried owner could make arrangements prior to the slave's baptism to continue the service through indenture and notes that the owner's money is insignificant (and, ultimately, useless when he dies) as compared to having brought the knowledge of Christianity to a slave.

Mather also dismisses the idea that baptism gives a slave legal title for freedom. Even if there were a legal precedent connecting baptism and freedom, Mather says, it would be the responsibility of the slave owner to protect his interests before allowing the baptism to proceed. However, Mather states, there is no legal connection between baptism and liberation. Christianity, he explains, only "mollifies and moderates" the impact of the life of a slave. Christianity does not liberate slaves, Mather further assures his congregation—it only gives the slave redemption before God. Even if he or she is free in the eyes of God, Mather says, the person would remain a slave.

Christian law was not the only precedent that was inapplicable on this issue. Mather states that canon law (the body of laws established by religious leaders) does not preclude Christians from having slaves. Local civil law allowed slavery, and English law permitted the practice as well. The choice of whether to set free or retain a slave, under any of these legal or religious authorities, remained in the hands of the slave owner.

Furthermore, neither the colonial nor the English government had any concern over the liberation of slaves through baptism. Mather points out that English law does not specifically prohibit the taking and/or purchase of slaves—rather, the law allowed slaves to be kept for life or even inherited as part of an estate. Mather also points to the fact that the laws of England were written by Christians about Christians and that those laws had never been repealed.

Just as there was no legal concern over the liberation of slaves through baptism, there was also no legal or religious concern over whether slaves could actually receive baptism. No person should stand in the way of a black slave seeking to be baptized—according to Mather, baptism is available to any person, as part of humanity, despite differences in appearance, mannerisms, and culture. This point is important for two reasons. First, it underscores the significance of baptism to Christians, who believe any individual who is baptized enters into God's good graces, escaping eternal punishment. Second, it reiterates the notion that all people, whether Europeans or Africans, are descendants of Adam.

Finally, Mather's commentary reminds the members of his congregation to be true to their Christian beliefs. By taking advantage of the God-given opportunity to convert their black slaves, he argues, the Puritan slaveholders would be bettering themselves before God. Mather concludes by suggesting that, if the owner denied himself that opportunity, then even his slaves might not serve him as enthusiastically as they would if they were saved.

Essential Themes

"The Negro Christianized" was designed to cause a major shift in Cotton Mather's congregation concerning the treatment of slaves. Mather was known as an eloquent and detail-oriented writer. However, this piece was written in a much simpler and more succinct fashion, which allowed more members of Mather's congregation to read it and take its message to heart.

"The Negro Christianized" asks Mather's parishioners to reconsider their perceptions of slaves, at least within a Christian context. In this pamphlet, Mather appeals to his parishioners' dedication to one of the central elements of Puritanism: conversion. Before slave owners, he says, is an opportunity to facilitate the salvation of others—namely, the servants and slaves who live in their own households.

According to Mather, there were three significant benefits of sharing Christianity with slaves. The first of these was self-serving—fulfilling their Christian duty of enabling the salvation of non-Christians. By converting people to Christianity, these slaveholders would better themselves and their own chances for eternal blessings in the afterlife.

The second benefit was saving a fellow human being from what Mather deemed a "brutish" way of life. As suggested earlier, introducing Christianity to blacks (who, in light of their apparent lack of religious conviction, were supposedly susceptible to the influence of the devil) was seen as strengthening the community and helping safeguard it from evil.

Third, the pamphlet suggests that Christianization of slaves would generate a return on investment for slave owners. Mather argues that by sharing the wisdom and blessings of Christian values with the slaves, those workers would repay their owners by performing their tasks with greater enthusiasm and good nature.

In order to perform this noble task, Mather argues, the congregation must reconsider many of their mistaken notions regarding blacks, slavery, and freedom. Many

of the prevailing views of the intelligence, heritage, and even basic humanity and spirituality that existed among whites, Mather argues, are either false or unproven. Furthermore, he asserts, white Christians need to take stock of their own responsibilities as servants of God; despite the many differences between white slave owners and black slaves, Mather argues, both races (and every other race in the world) are all brethren and subject to God's ultimate authority.

Michael Auerbach, MA

Bibliography

"Biography: Cotton Mather." *The Mather Project*. Georgia State University, 2011. Web. 14 June 2012.

"Cotton Mather." *Salem Witchcraft Trials 1692*. University of Missouri—Kansas City School of Law, n.d. Web. 14 June 2012.

Davis, David Brion. *The Problem with Slavery in Western Culture*. Oxford: Oxford UP, 1988. Print.

Kizer, Kay. "Puritans." *University of Notre Dame*. University of Notre Dame, n.d. Web. 10 Apr. 2012.

Rice, Gene. "The Alleged Curse on Ham." *American Bible Society Bible Resource Center*. American Bible Society, 2011. Web. 7 June 2012.

Royster, Paul, ed. "The Negro Christianized. An Essay to Excite and Assist that Good Work, the Instruction of Negro-Servants in Christianity (1706)." *Libraries at University of Nebraska–Lincoln*. University of Nebraska Lincoln, n.d. Web. 7 June 2012.

"Slaves in New England." *Medford Historical Society*. Medford Historical Society, n.d. Web. 7 June 2012.

Additional Reading

Bremer, Francis J. "Race Relations." *The Puritan Experiment: New England Society from Bradford to Edwards*. 1976. Lebanon: UP of New England, 1995. 199–208. Print.

Irons, Charles F. *The Origins of Proslavery Christianity: White and Black Evangelicals in Colonial and Antebellum Virginia*. Chapel Hill: U of North Carolina P, 2008. Print.

Manegold, C. S. *Ten Hills Farm: The Forgotten History of Slavery in the North*. Princeton: Princeton UP, 2009. Print.

Silverman, Kenneth. *The Life and Times of Cotton Mather*. New York: Welcome Rain, 2001. Print.

Wendell, Barrett. *Cotton Mather: The Puritan Priest*. Ann Arbor: University of Michigan Library, 2009. Print.

LESSON PLAN: Cotton Mather on Saving the Souls of Slaves

Students analyze Cotton Mather's arguments for baptizing slaves, and work to determine the uniqueness of his views and the extent of their influence on others.

Learning Objectives

Identify the central question in Mather's document; describe the role of religion in colonial American communities; formulate historical questions about Mather's views on slavery; compare and contrast Mather's views on slavery with those of Quaker George Keith.

Materials: Excerpt from Cotton Mather's *The Negro Christianized*; George Keith's *An Exhortation and Caution to Friends Concerning Buying or Keeping of Negroes*

Overview Questions

What was Mather's purpose in writing this essay? How do Mather's Puritan beliefs affect what he says and how he says it? What value might Mather's opinions have had in the fight to end slavery? In what ways does Mather's use of Scripture differ from George Keith's?

Step 1: Comprehension Questions

What did Mather argue in *The Negro Christianized*? What points does he make in his argument?

▶ **Activity:** Direct students as a group or individually to outline the major points in the essay. Have students discuss whether or not Mather is advocating anything beyond saving souls.

Step 2: Comprehension Questions

How does Mather's Puritanism inform his argument? Why might other Puritans not agree with him?

▶ **Activity:** Have students discuss whether or not Mather makes a convincing argument in the context of his Puritan faith. Have students identify passages that suggest that Mather knows other Puritans may not agree with him.

Step 3: Context Questions

How can twenty-first-century readers judge whether or not Mather's essay was a step toward the abolition of slavery? How can we know if his views were unusual for his time?

▶ **Activity:** Discuss with students Mather's influence in colonial New England. Have students embark on an Internet or library search that generates sources and information about Mather's influence on the course of slavery in the colony and whether or not his views were unique in his time.

Step 4: Exploration Questions

How does George Keith's use of Scripture lead him to a completely different view on slavery than Mather's? To what extent do each man's views reflect their different religions?

▶ **Activity:** Have students summarize Keith's opinions. Have students speculate how Scripture can bring each writer to a different viewpoint. Have students discuss what Keith and Mather might agree on relative to slavery or slaves.

Step 5: Response Paper

Word length and additional requirements set by Instructor. Students answer the research question in the Overview Questions. Students state a thesis and use as evidence passages from the primary source document as well as support from supplemental materials assigned in the lesson.

■ Sinners in the Hands of an Angry God/The Great Awakening

Date: July 8, 1741; December 12, 1743
Author: Edwards, Jonathan
Genre: sermon, letter, memoir

*"There is nothing that keeps wicked men, at any one
moment, out of hell, but the mere pleasure of God.*
"Sinners in the Hands of an Angry God"

*"[T]he revival of religion continued to increase;
so that in the spring an engagedness of spirit
about things of religion was become very general
among young people and children.*
"The Great Awakening"

Summary Overview

The first of the two documents presented here, "Sinners in the Hands of an Angry God," is the best-known sermon from the period in American history known as the Great Awakening. Although the movement had been developing for several years, this sermon was preached to a congregation that had not yet experienced the enthusiasm associated with the movement. As a result of this sermon, the congregation was overtaken by religious fervor that resulted in somewhat of a frenzy with its younger members. The sermon's power has continued down through the centuries, and it has been widely studied as a prime example of a "fire-and-brimstone" sermon.

The letter, entitled "The Great Awakening," is important because it is a primary source describing some of the events of the movement for which it is named, as experienced by one who was a part of it. Its insights make it easier to understand the dynamics of the movement. The author of both documents, Rev. Jonathan Edwards, was the leader an influential Puritan Church located in Northampton, Massachusetts.

If the Great Awakening was to be identified with one single American, it would be Jonathan Edwards. Being the pastor of one of the largest churches in New England contributed to his influence, but it was more than that which would give him this designation. His innovative preaching style and desire to communicate his understanding of the Christian message helped sustain the movement. The directness of his message, and that of other preachers in the movement, resulted in profound reactions among Christian audiences.

Defining Moment

While many of the American colonies had been founded for economic gain, a few, such as Massachusetts, had been founded in the pursuit of religious freedom. However, the zeal felt by those devoted to their faith at the founding of the colony—in this case, Puritanism—had begun to fade over the years. Just over a century after the first settlers landed in Massachusetts, a reawakening of religious devotion swept through the Puritan Church. Although the movement began around 1730 and lasted until about 1760, the height of its popularity lasted about a decade, from the early 1730s to the mid-1740s. After that time it was as likely to split congregations as it was to create a renewal of faith among its members.

The two documents presented here are from the second wave of the Great Awakening in the early 1740s. Both were written by Rev. Jonathan Edwards. The sermon helped refresh the movement with a new, dramatic style of preaching, which brought home its message with great force. Edwards's recollection of other events at this time, in his letter to Rev. Thomas Prince, gave insights into the strange physical manifestations displayed by church members that seemed to be brought on by the movement.

Although the Great Awakening was most strongly felt in New England, it did spread throughout the colonies through the sermons and written works of preachers such as Jonathan Edwards and Rev. George Whitefield. Those who heard the sermons were already church members and at least nominal Christians; it was taken for granted that those who would read about the events in Northampton were also Christians. However, preachers of the Great Awakening questioned the colonists' devotion to Christianity and wondered if, perhaps, most just went through the movements.

Focusing on the necessity of God's grace for salvation, the preachers of the Great Awakening sought to convince their audiences of the need for an immediate response to God. Using what some might call scare tactics, the listener was given a picture of an absolute divide between those who were saved and those who were not. They warned parishioners that they had two choices: either they accept God completely and follow him devoutly, or end up in everlasting torment in hell. As illustrated in the letter, younger members of the church were the most responsive to this new style of preaching and theology. Differing responses to the sermons, however, led to turmoil within congregations and society in general.

Author Biography

Jonathan Edwards was born in Connecticut on October 5, 1703, and died March 22, 1758. His parents, Rev. Timothy and Esther Stoddard Edwards, helped him prepare for the pursuit of an advanced education. He attended Yale College (now Yale University) and studied all manner of theology and philosophy. He completed his undergraduate studies in 1720 and his graduate studies in 1722.

He gave the parish ministry a try as an interim pastor in New York. He then returned to Yale where he was employed as a tutor. In 1727 he became the pastor in Northampton, Massachusetts, where his grandfather, Rev. Solomon Stoddard, had preached. This was the base of his activity for the next twenty years. After a split with the congregation, he relocated to Stockbridge, Massachusetts, where he ministered to a congregation and was a missionary to the American Indians. In 1758 he accepted an invitation to be president of the College of New Jersey (now Princeton University). However, he died about a month after assuming that position when he elected to receive a smallpox inoculation when he was already in poor health.

In the approximately thirty years that Edwards served as a local church pastor, he was very active in the affairs not only of the community, but of the region. He wrote dozens of books and many more essays and letters, focusing on his understanding of the Christian gospel. He also preached hundreds of sermons during this time. He seemed to have been surprised by the receptivity of the young people to the Christian message in 1733, when the first wave of the Great Awakening began. Initially Edwards saw the events happening around him as being the same thing his grandfather had described from his ministry, however, the movement continued for a much longer period. Edwards always placed a strong emphasis upon personal salvation. He had disagreements with others in the 1740s regarding how emotional the appeal should be, with Edwards arguing for less emotion. He was forced out of his pastorate in Northampton because he disagreed with what his grandfather had taught, and the congregation had accepted, regarding communion. Edwards believed it was only to be served to individuals whose Christian faith could be verified. However, after he moved to the smaller parish in Stockbridge, he was able to spend more time on his theological writing.

HISTORICAL DOCUMENT

Sinners in the Hands of an Angry God

Their foot shall slide in due time. Deuteronomy 32:35.

In this verse is threatened the vengeance of God on the wicked unbelieving Israelites, that were God's visible people, and lived under means of grace; and that, notwithstanding all God's wonderful works that he had wrought towards that people, yet remained, as is expressed, v. Deuteronomy 32:28, "void of counsel," having no understanding in them; and that, under all the cultivations of heaven, brought forth bitter and poisonous fruit; as in the two verses next preceding the text.

The expression that I have chosen for my text, "Their foot shall slide in due time," seems to imply the following things, relating to the punishment and destruction that these wicked Israelites were exposed to.

1. That they were *always* exposed to destruction, as one that stands or walks in slippery places is always exposed to fall. This is implied in the manner of their destruction's coming upon them, being represented by their foot's sliding. The same is expressed, Psalms 73:18, "Surely thou didst set them in slippery places: thou castedst them down into destruction."

2. It implies that they were always exposed to *sudden* unexpected destruction. As he that walks in slippery places is every moment liable to fall; he can't foresee one moment whether he shall stand or fall the next; and when he does fall, he falls at once, without warning. Which is also expressed in that, Psalms 73:18–19, "Surely thou didst set them in slippery places: thou castedst them down into destruction. How are they brought into desolation as in a moment!"

3. Another thing implied is that they are liable to fall *of themselves*, without being thrown down by the hand of another. As he that stands or walks on slippery ground, needs nothing but his own weight to throw him down.

4. That the reason why they are not fallen already, and don't fall now, is only that God's appointed time is not come. For it is said, that when that due time, or appointed time comes, "their foot shall slide." Then they shall be left to fall as they are inclined by their own weight. God won't hold them up in these slippery places any longer, but will let them go; and then, at that very instant, they shall fall into destruction; as he that stands in such slippery declining ground on the edge of a pit that he can't stand alone, when he is let go he immediately falls and is lost.

The observation from the words that I would now insist upon is this:

There is nothing that keeps wicked men, at any one moment, out of hell, but the mere pleasure of God.

By "the mere pleasure of God," I mean his sovereign pleasure, his arbitrary will, restrained by no obligation, hindered by no manner of difficulty, any more than if nothing else but God's mere will had in the least degree, or in any respect whatsoever, any hand in the preservation of wicked men one moment.

The truth of this observation may appear by the following considerations.

I. There is no want of *power* in God to cast wicked men into hell at any moment. Men's hands can't be strong when God rises up: the strongest have no power to resist him, nor can any deliver out of his hands.

He is not only able to cast wicked men into hell, but he can most *easily* do it. Sometimes an earthly prince meets with a great deal of difficulty to subdue a rebel, that has found means to fortify himself, and has made himself strong by the numbers of his followers. But it is not so with God. There is no fortress that is any defense from the power of God. Though hand join in hand, and vast multitudes of God's enemies combine and associate themselves, they are easily broken in pieces: they are as great heaps of light chaff before the whirlwind; or large quantities of dry stubble before devouring flames. We find it easy to tread on and crush a worm that we see crawling on the earth; so 'tis easy for us to cut or singe a slender thread that anything hangs by; thus easy is it for God when he pleases to cast his enemies down to hell. What are we, that we should think to stand before him, at whose rebuke the earth trembles, and before whom the rocks are thrown down?

II. They *deserve* to be cast into hell; so that divine justice never stands in the way, it makes no objection against God's using his power at any moment to destroy them. Yea, on the contrary, justice calls aloud for an infinite punishment of their sins. Divine justice says of the tree that brings forth such grapes of Sodom, "Cut it down; why cumbreth it the ground" (Luke 13:7). The sword of divine justice is every moment brandished over their heads, and 'tis nothing but the hand of arbitrary mercy, and God's mere will, that holds it back.

III. They are *already* under a sentence of condemnation to hell. They don't only justly deserve to be cast down thither; but the sentence of the law of God, that eternal and immutable rule of righteousness that God has fixed between him and mankind, is gone out against them, and stands against them; so that they are bound over already to hell. John 3:18, "He that believeth not is condemned already." So that every unconverted man properly belongs to hell; that is his place; from thence he is. John 8:23, "Ye are from beneath." And thither he is bound; 'tis the place that justice, and God's Word, and the sentence of his unchangeable law assigns to him.

IV. They are now the objects of that very same anger and wrath of God that is expressed in the torments of hell: and the reason why they don't go down to hell at each moment, is not because God, in whose power they are, is not then very angry with them; as angry as he is with many of those miserable creatures that he is now tormenting in hell, and do there feel and bear the fierceness of his wrath. Yea, God is a great deal more angry with great numbers that are now on earth, yea, doubtless with many that are now in this congregation, that it may be are at ease and quiet, than he is with many of those that are now in the flames of hell.

So that it is not because God is unmindful of their wickedness, and don't resent it, that he don't let loose his hand and cut them off. God is not altogether such an one as themselves, though they may imagine him to be so. The wrath of God burns against them, their damnation don't slumber, the pit is prepared, the fire is made ready, the furnace is now hot, ready to receive them, the flames do now rage and glow. The glittering sword is whet, and held over them, and the pit hath opened her mouth under them.

The Great Awakening
December 12, 1743

In the year 1740, in the spring, before Mr. Whitefield came to this town, there was a visible alteration. There was more seriousness and religious conversation, especially among young people; those things that were of ill tendency among them were more forborne. And it was a more frequent thing for persons to visit their minister upon soul accounts; and in some particular persons there appeared a great alteration about that time. And thus it continued till Mr. Whitefield came to town, which was about the middle of October following. He preached here four sermons in the meeting-house (besides a private lecture at my house)—one on Friday, another on Saturday, and two upon the Sabbath. The congregation was extraordinarily melted by every sermon; almost the whole assembly being in tears for a great part of sermon time. Mr. Whitefield's sermons were suitable to the circumstances of the town, containing just reproofs of our backslidings, and, in a most moving and affecting manner, making use of our great profession and great mercies as arguments with us to return to God, from whom we had departed.

Immediately after this, the minds of the people in general appeared more engaged in religion, showing a greater forwardness to make religion the subject of their conversation, and to meet frequently together for religious purposes, and to embrace all opportunities to hear the Word preached. The revival at first appeared chiefly among professors and those that had entertained the hope that they were in a state of grace, to whom Mr. Whitefield chiefly addressed himself. But in a very short time there appeared an awakening and deep concern among some young persons that looked upon themselves as in a Christless state; and there were some hopeful appearances of conversion; and some professors were greatly revived.

In about a month or six weeks, there was a great alteration in the town, both as to the revivals of professors and awakenings of others. By the middle of December, a very considerable work of God appeared among those that were very young; and the revival of religion continued to increase; so that in the spring an engagedness of spirit about things of religion was become very general among young people and children, and religious subjects almost wholly took up their conversation when they were together.

In the month of May 1741, a sermon was preached to a company at a private house. Near the conclusion of the exercise, one or two persons that were professors were so greatly affected with a sense of the greatness and glory of divine things, and the infinite importance of the things of eternity, that they were not able to conceal it; the affection of their minds overcoming their strength, and having a very visible effect on their bodies. When the exercise was over, the young people that were present removed into the other room for religious conference; and particularly that they might have opportunity to inquire of those that were thus affected what apprehensions they had, and what things they were that thus deeply impressed their minds. And there soon appeared a very great effect of their conversation; the affection was quickly propagated through the room; many of the young people and children that were professors appeared to be overcome with a sense of the greatness and glory of divine things, and with admiration, love, joy and praise, and compassion to others that looked upon themselves as in a state of nature. And many others at the same time were overcome with distress about their sinful and miserable state and con-

dition; so that the whole room was full of nothing but outcries, faintings, and suchlike.

Others soon heard of it, in several parts of the town, and came to them; and what they saw and heard there was greatly affecting to them; so that many of them were overpowered in like manner. And it continued thus for some hours, the time spent in prayer, singing, counseling, and conferring. . . .

That those people went so far beyond them in raptures and violent emotions of the affections and a vehement zeal, and what they called boldness for Christ, our people were ready to think was owing to their far greater attainments in grace and intimacy with Heaven. They looked little in their own eyes in comparison of them, and were ready to submit themselves to them, and yield themselves up to their conduct, taking it for granted that everything was right that they said and did. These things had a strange influence on the people, gave many of them a deep and unhappy tincture, that it was a hard and long labor to deliver them from and which some them are not fully delivered from to this day.

The effects and consequences of things among us plainly shows the following things, viz.: that the degree of grace is no means to be judged of by the degree of joy, or the degree of zeal; and that indeed we cannot at all determine by these things who are gracious and who are not; and that it as not the degree of religious affections but the nature of them that is chiefly to be looked at. Some that have had very great raptures of joy, and have been extraordinarily filled (as the vulgar phrase is), and have had their bodies overcome, and that very often have manifested far less of the temper of Christians in their conduct since than some others that have been still and have made no great outward show. But then again there are many others that have extraordinary joys and emotions of mind, with frequent great effects on their bodies, that behave themselves steadfastly as humble, amiable, eminent Christians.

GLOSSARY

backslidings: refers to people who were, or seemed to be, Christians, who are no longer following a Christian lifestyle. Having been elevated through their Christian relationship with God, they had slid backwards away from God.

castedst: the past tense of cast in the formal English of the King James era

cumbreth: to take up space

grapes of Sodom: Sodom, a city mentioned in the book of Genesis, which was a symbol of evil and excess. The grapes of Sodom represent the fruit of wickedness.

professors: people who are full members of the Puritan church, having professed (publically affirmed) their faith in Christ.

rapture: a state of ecstasy; for some Christians, heaven spiritual journey to heaven.

tincture: an attitude or outlook on life

viz: short for *videlicet* which means "namely."

Document Analysis

This article concerns two documents: a sermon preached by Jonathan Edwards on July 8, 1741, in Enfield, Connecticut, and a letter about his recollections of events during the preceding sixteen months in Northampton, Massachusetts. Both deal with the thoughts and theology of the second wave of the Great Awakening (now called The First Great Awakening to differentiate it from a similar religious awakening that occurred about one hundred years later). What is demonstrated in both texts is the emphasis on the sinful nature—the original sin—of all people and the fact that only through God's mercy do people not go immediately to hell. As he records the history of the happenings in 1740 and 1741, Edwards illustrates the range of physical responses to the spiritual message: strange vocal outbursts and bodily convulsions. The outward differences among those accepting the message led to a split within the community. This type of open split between the old and the new is not uncommon in such a circumstance.

Reflecting on "Sinners in the Hands of an Angry God," it is clear that Edwards is not only trying to convert nonbelievers, but also bring back people who previously joined the church but drifted away from its teachings. The opening of the sermon deals with the fact that it is easy to slip and fall into sin. Referring to the scriptural passage from Deuteronomy and the Israelites, Edwards states, "they were always exposed to destruction, as one that stands or walks in slippery places is always exposed to fall." Using a passage from Psalms Edwards reinforces the image of the ever-present peril that everyone faces. Following this affirmation that "there is nothing that keeps wicked men, at any one moment, out of hell, but the mere pleasure of God," Edwards begins a logical exposition of who is at risk. In the four considerations printed here and the six additional ones in the full text of the sermon, his treatment of the frailty of humans is expanded: "Men's hands can't be strong when God rises up." In addition, in line with Edwards's understanding of man's original sin and his unworthiness of God's mercy, he writes, "They deserve to be cast into hell."

The second half of the sermon, Edwards stresses the natural state of all people as a miserable one without God's mercy. He then moves to the need for each person to "awake," meaning to fully accept the teachings of God and the mercy of Christ. Edwards, and other preachers of his era, believed the list of considerations to be a logical progression and argument which led to the conclusions contained in the sermon.

In order to understand the impact of this and other sermons of the Great Awakening, one should understand what religious life was like prior to the revival. In the various English churches during the seventeenth century stylistic patterns emerged in different denominations. Edwards's sermon follows the traditional, plain Puritan style; a life of simplicity was often stressed within Puritan communities. When the Puritans immigrated to the New England colonies, a greater emphasis was placed on this austere existence.

Edwards's sermon opens with a scripture verse and then moves to a point-by-point, logical explanation of what the verse means for the congregation. Like other sermons of the Great Awakening, it has few transitions and simply states the preacher's message. However, the point at which Edwards's sermon diverges from the norm is in the content of the message he communicates. A large number of seventeenth and early eighteenth century sermons, including some by Edwards, dealt with the theological issues that divided the denominations from each other. Sermons prior to the Great Awakening dealt with ethical issues or the need for God's grace, and did so in more general terms. Edwards makes it quite clear that God's judgment has already found each person guilty and that each person is about to fall into the torment of hell. His imagery is more graphic and the strength of God's condemning judgment is emphasized: "that eternal and immutable rule of righteousness that God has fixed between him and mankind, is gone out against them, and stands against them; so that they are bound over already to hell." Only through the complete acceptance of God's word can a person be saved from this condemnation. As he states toward the close of the sermon, "And let every one that is yet out of Christ, and hanging over the pit of hell, whether they be old men and women, or middle aged, or young people, or little children, now hearken to the loud calls of God's word and providence."

Edwards fully accepted the concept of hell as it is described in various passages of the Bible. His references to eternal torment, to everlasting fire, and to the heat of furnaces are meant as literal pictures. In his mind, what he presented to the congregation was not an emotional appeal for them to change, but a real account of the consequences of turning away from God. To Edwards, this step-by-step analysis of the Deuteronomy passage was a logical progression of thoughts that led to only one truthful conclusion. By combining what he believed to be the truth—that everyone deserved to go to hell—with the belief that only God's grace kept this from happening, Edwards then concludes that each person must seek out God's mercy by a profession of

faith in Christ. To him this was a straightforward argument with no room for debate. It was this message, that each person must make this radical transformation immediately that was the basis for the Great Awakening.

In the letter to Reverend Prince, Edwards outlined three stages in the process of the religious revival in Northampton. Prior to the passage printed here, Edwards described some events of the previous nine years, from his point of view both good and bad. Comparing these nine years with the years prior to 1731, he thought that the morals of the community were greatly improved: charitable giving had increased, and more people were paying attention to religious issues. However, he also thought that things were beginning to slide back toward the way they had been prior to the first wave of the revival. Thus, as he began the passage printed in this article, he saw the increased discussion of religious topics by the people in the town and congregation as a positive sign.

This first stage of this second wave of the revival was an important step, even if it did not show the dramatic results of the later stages. There is an expression about being in the right place at the right time. This saying, though it oversimplifies cause and effect, was basically true for Edwards and the various waves of the religious revival of the Great Awakening. Edwards's grandfather had told him of four widely separated years during Stoddard's ministry when there had been extraordinary responses to the gospel message by young people within the Northampton church. The events recorded in the letter are similar; however, unlike during Stoddard's ministry the response was not short lived. Thus Edwards's approach to the revival was probably different from that of his grandfather. Prior to Rev. Whitefield's coming in 1740, Edwards states, "There was more seriousness and religious conversation, especially among young people." The time seemed ripe for a second wave of the Great Awakening.

Edwards invited George Whitefield to come to Northampton to preach. This might indicate one difference between Edwards and his grandfather. Edwards had disagreements with Whitefield, especially in his style of preaching. Whitefield intentionally appealed much more to people's emotions than did Edwards. During Whitefield's time in Northampton, the people's response to Whitefield's sermons was very much what was desired by Whitefield and Edwards. Edwards wrote, "The congregation was extraordinarily melted by every sermon, almost the whole assembly being in tears for a great part of sermon time." About the difference in style, Edwards wrote, "Mr. Whitefield's sermons were suitable to the circumstances of the town." While statements regarding events such as these cannot be made with absolute certainty, it does seem that Edwards was open to whatever style of ministry was needed to reach members of the church. This might be one reason that the Great Awakening spread throughout the colonies and sustained for more than a decade, while previous revivals had been local and had faded within a year.

The pattern of the response is not unlike past or present religious revivals, even though it extended over a longer period of time. When Whitefield gave his four sermons, before moving to other parts of the American colonies, the response was immediate. Those who had been a part of the congregation were moved to tears during the service, and they continued to talk about its message long after Whitefield left. Further, they worked to reinforce the principles of the Great Awakening within their community. The church members, the "professors", and others who had responded positively with statements of faith were changed in their attitudes. This was transmitted to the youth, who understood that even they were in need of God's grace under the doctrine of the sinful nature of all humanity. Thus there were many new members joining the church, and those who had been members reaffirmed their faith.

As the message of the Great Awakening spread, more and more people became a part of those professing their faith and conducting their lives in a way that proved that God's spirit was in their lives. This was especially true of the youth. Edwards goes on to discuss the fact that in the following year the outward signs of what he interpreted as being touched by the Holy Spirit were even stronger in young members of communities. Although this record does not give the specifics of what occurred, it does speak of uncontrolled physical movements and vocalizations. Those who did not exhibit these manifestations were also said to be making sounds of a sorrowful nature. The house in which this took place would have been full of sound and activity. All of this was interpreted as youth "overcome with a sense of the greatness and glory of divine things." There is no doubt that the sermon's intent was to encourage those present to live a more Christian life, the results were far from what was expected. The reaction of a few of the listeners started a contagious exhibition of unusual activities spreading throughout the town, with the actions perceived to be gifts of the Spirit of God.

It is clear that Edwards is troubled by these manifestations. A division in the congregation was occurring between those who exhibited these outward signs of God's grace and those who did not. Those who had "what they called boldness for Christ" were seen by themselves and others as more holy than those who had not experienced the physical and vocal manifestations. Those who had not experienced this rapture were left to feel unholy. They saw these manifestations as the result of "far greater attainments in grace and intimacy with Heaven." In reading the full text of the letter, it is clear that many of the individuals who had experienced these very strong outward manifestations of the religious revival were not members of the community. They had come into Northampton from elsewhere and after exhibiting these manifestations they encouraged others to look upon them as having had a superior religious experience.

Edwards makes it clear that while he supports the religious revival he does not support this type of differentiation among community members. He firmly states that it is devotion to Christ and the condition of the soul that is important. He wrote, "the degree of grace is no means to be judged by the degree or joy, or the degree of zeal, . . . not the degree of religious affections but the nature of them that is chiefly to be looked at." He recognized that the spiritual qualities that are described in the scriptures were not demonstrated in the lives of some who had the outward manifestations of the revival. Similarly, some who were quiet members of the congregation had a more Christ-like attitude than many who had been part of the supposedly more spiritual group. The divisive effects within the community and congregation were similar to many that have been described by others who have been a part of similar experiences since that time.

The turmoil that this division caused in 1741 slowly moderated as Edwards's position became more widely accepted. By the time he wrote the letter in December 1743, he believed the community was once again united. He also worked hard among the young people to determine which of them he believed had had a true religious experience versus those who were just copying what was going on around them. He understood that, for some, the spiritual experience seemed to be a temporary state, often recurring only at meetings. He tried to analyze if there was any pattern to the physical occurrences, such as examining the time of day the services were held and so forth. He found none. Among those who had what seemed to him to be a true spiritual experience, Edwards wrote in the latter portion of the letter (not printed in this article) that the outward appearances, as he called them were much stronger in the early 1740s than they had been in the 1730s and that what had been experienced in the 1730s were much stronger than anything previously experienced. At the close of the letter, Edwards states that he is happy that people have come to understand that it is not a past experience which is important, rather what is important is "maintaining earnest labor, watchfulness, and prayerfulness as long as they live."

While the physical exuberance of some did cause certain problems, it was also a means through which the Great Awakening was sustained. Remembering what had been experienced, whether personally or by watching others, helped support church members when difficulties arose. However, while the divisions within congregation moderated, they continued to exist for decades to come. Nevertheless, the Great Awakening was an American movement which stressed an individual devotion to God not through traditional response, but rather through a confession of faith which encompassed one's whole being.

Essential Themes

Jonathan Edwards, as one of the prominent figures of the Great Awakening, stressed the role of the individual in religion and strengthened the belief that religious faith was relevant not only to each individual, but to society in general. Some of the colonies, such as Massachusetts, were established for religious reasons. However, they were established in order that a certain denomination or theological position could flourish more freely. While this did not mean the individual believer was totally ignored, the emphasis was upon the collective group.

This changed with the Great Awakening. While there were, and still are, theological and denominational disputes, the Great Awakening emphasized the faith of the individual. Spreading throughout the colonies from its start in New England, the Great Awakening was the dominant influence in American churches. Not all denominations, or areas, were as open to this as were most churches in New England. However, even today one of the identifying marks of American branches of international denominations is the strength of the call for a personal faith. This has helped to reinforce the individualism that exists in other areas of American society.

The Great Awakening also strengthened the position of the Christian church within American society. Even in colonies started for religious reasons, many religious leaders were despondent about the weakening of the church. By the end of the seventeenth century religious leaders in Massachusetts were appalled at the declining role of the church within the communities. The Great Awakening changed this by reinforcing the power of the church within society. The events that seemed to transform people's lives were also transforming society. Faith was once again at the center of many communities. Even though most of the preaching during the Great Awakening was directed toward those already attending church services, preachers such as Jonathan Edwards became well known and people from a variety of backgrounds flocked to his services. Transforming personal faith, which was the subject of sermons during the Great Awakening, touched a chord in many people, reshaping their lives and their society.

Donald A. Watt, PhD

Bibliography

"Jonathan Edwards: On the Great Awakening" *Who We Are: The Story of America's Constitution.* National Humanities Institute, 1998. Web 30 Apr. 2012.

Smolinski, Reiner, ed. "Sinners in the Hands of an Angry God" *Electronic Texts in American Studies.* Digital Commons @ University of Nebraska, 1998. Web 30 Apr. 2012.

Stein, Stephen J, ed. Jonathan Edwards's Writings: Text, Context, Interpretation. Bloomington: Indiana UP, 1996. Print.

Additional Reading

Berkovitch, Sacvan. *The Puritan Origins of the American Self.* New Haven: Yale UP, 2011. Print.

Hatch, Nathan O. and Harry S. Stout. *Jonathan Edwards and the American Experience.* Oxford: OUP, 1988. Print.

Kling, David W. and Douglas A. Sweeny, eds. *Jonathan Edwards at Home and Abroad.* Columbia: U of South Carolina P, 2003. Print.

Marsden, George M. *Jonathan Edwards: A Life.* New Haven: Yale UP, 2003. Print.

"The Works of Jonathan Edwards Online" *The Jonathan Edwards Center at Yale University.* The Jonathan Edwards Center at Yale University, 2008–11. Web. 30 Apr. 2012.

LESSON PLAN: **Fire, Brimstone, and the Great Awakening**

Students analyze Jonathan Edward's writings and their place in the history of the Great Awakening, and evaluate the effectiveness of his words.

Learning Objectives

Read Edwards's sermon imaginatively; differentiate between historical facts and interpretation; interrogate historical data to explain the impact of the Great Awakening on colonial society; compare and contrast Edwards's sermon and Whitefield's "Britain's Mercies"

Materials: Jonathan Edwards's "Sinners in the Hands of an Angry God" / "On the Great Awakening"; George Whitefield's "Britain's Mercies and Britain's Duties"

Overview Questions

What was the intent of Edwards in his sermon? In what ways does Edwards letter "On the Great Awakening" interpret history? How does the letter suggest events to come? What are the differences in style and content between Edwards's and Whitefield's sermons?

Step 1: Comprehension Questions

What is Edwards attempting to do in this sermon? How might the reaction of eighteenth-century listeners contrast with that of twenty-first-century listeners?

▶ **Activity:** Choose students to select and read aloud passages in which Edwards expresses great risks for sermon listeners. Ask students to discuss the sermon's warnings and their potential affect on his listeners. Discuss whether Edwards's words are as powerful now and why or why not.

Step 2: Comprehension Questions

In what ways does Edwards's letter record history? How does it interpret that same history? How can modern readers tell the difference?

▶ **Activity:** Have students list specific references in the letter to Edwards's own actions and to contemporary New England history. Discuss the reliability of Edwards's reporting. Have students discuss Edwards's interpretations of these events, the validity of his judgments, and how to evaluate them.

Step 3: Context Questions

How does Edwards's discussion of the Great Awakening suggest potential cultural and political changes in New

England? How do those changes eventually connect to the American Revolution?

▶ **Activity:** Review with students what factors of the Great Awakening influenced American revolutionary thinking and action. Have students identify some of those influences in Edwards's letter.

Step 4: Exploration Questions

What are the differences between Edwards's sermon and Whitefield's sermon? Given the common purpose of both, which was probably more effective? Why?

▶ **Activity:** Have students create a Venn diagram to show the similarities and differences in the sermons. Direct them to the resulting visual analysis to evaluate the potential effects of each sermon. Challenge students to argue which was probably more effective and why.

Step 5: Response Paper

Word length and additional requirements set by Instructor. Students answer the research question in the Overview Questions. Students state a thesis and use as evidence passages from the primary source document as well as support from supplemental materials assigned in the lesson.

■ The Essential Rights and Liberties of Protestants

Date: 1744
Author: attributed to Williams, Elisha
Genre: political sermon

"That greater security therefore of life, liberty, money, lands, houses, family, and the like, which may be all comprehended under that of person and property, is the sole end of all civil government."

Summary Overview

When a religious revival known as the First Great Awakening swept through Europe and North America beginning in the 1730s, many colonies passed laws to restrict outside ministers from preaching to their parishes without an explicit invitation. These traveling ministers viewed religion as a personal and emotional experience, which contradicted the colonies' more traditional rules-and-order style of worship, and many leaders were concerned this could cause social and political instability. Elisha Williams, one of the great political preachers of the pre-Revolutionary era in the American colonies, spoke out against these laws by anonymously publishing the pamphlet *The Essential Rights and Liberties of Protestants* in 1744, which both criticized the establishment of penal laws for religious matters and encouraged tolerance.

Defining Moment

During the colonial era, religion and government were closely entwined all over the world. This connection was especially pronounced in the North American colonies; many were founded either as a way to escape religious persecution or to establish a society with one exclusive, officially endorsed religion. Governments regularly passed laws pertaining to religious matters, although there was much disagreement about exactly how much control the government should have to dictate the details of religious worship and practice.

Beginning in the 1730s, a religious resurgence commonly referred to as the First Great Awakening took place throughout Europe and North America. A new style of preacher rose to prominence. Rather than being attached to any one parish, these preachers traveled the world touting religion as an emotional and personal experience, and they encouraged salvation through good deeds rather than rote adherence to doctrine. By contrast, traditional preachers usually belonged to a specific parish and were active participants in their community governments. Religious practice in the colonies often involved strict laws about when and how worship was to take place, and departure from the norm would be punished to varying degrees. Religious piety was less about being a good person and more about conforming to defined rules in order to avoid punishment; thus, religion seemed to be more about control than about salvation.

Many traditional preachers felt that the revivalist preachers threatened their way of life (indeed their entire salvation), and they took steps to prevent them from preaching to their parishes. Many communities passed laws making it a crime to preach to a parish within their community without an explicit invitation from the local preacher. By doing so, they hoped to prevent the spread of these radical ideas that they believed would undermine the stability of their communities.

It was against this backdrop that the pamphlet *The Essential Rights and Liberties of Protestants: A Seasonable Plea for Liberty of Conscience and the Right of Private Judgment in Matters of Religion* was published anonymously in Boston in 1744. It was widely believed that Williams, an active member of the Connecticut legislature and former rector of Yale College, wrote the pamphlet, which both protested the legislation and encouraged religious freedom in the colonies. The pamphlet opposed the strict legislation that had been enacted in Connecticut to prevent visiting ministers from preaching to local parishes without an explicit invitation and generally encouraged religious freedom and tolerance.

Author Biography

Williams was born on August 24, 1694, in Hatfield, Massachusetts. He graduated from Harvard with honors in 1711, and he taught in a nearby grammar school for a short time before returning to Hatfield to study theology with his father, who was a minister with the local parish. Williams then purchased and relocated to a farm in Wethersfield, Connecticut, but he was unable to find a parish in which to work. Instead he took up the study of law, and in 1717, he served the first of several terms in the Connecticut legislature.

Williams fell seriously ill in 1719, but upon his recovery, he decided to return to theology. He became pastor of the Newington Parish in Wethersfield in 1720 and was ordained in 1722. He served in this capacity until 1726, when he was offered the position of rector at Yale College. At first, he was one of only two faculty members during a difficult time for Yale. However, the institution thrived under Williams as more students and investors began to take an interest in the school, and the size of the faculty and the student population increased significantly during William's tenure. He served as rector until he resigned in 1739, allegedly because of poor health.

When Williams returned to his home in Wethersfield, he resumed his involvement in public affairs. In 1740, he was again elected as a deputy to the general assembly of the Connecticut legislature. He also held an appointed position as an associate judge of the superior court from 1740 to 1743. However, it was suspected that he eventually lost this appointment because of both his permissive views on the new wave of revivalist preachers and his general advocating for religious tolerance.

Elisha Williams. (Manuscripts and Archives, Yale University)

Williams then served in the military, first as chaplain of the Connecticut troops who invaded Cape Breton in Nova Scotia, Canada, in 1745, and then again in 1746 as a colonel of the Connecticut regiment that was to be part of the conquest of Canada. The failure of the Canadian takeover plans meant that Williams never commanded his forces on the battlefield, but in 1749, he went to Great Britain to fight for his troops to receive their promised payment for volunteering in the mission.

Williams spent more than two years tending to business in Great Britain before finally returning to Wethersfield in 1752. He continued to participate in Connecticut's political affairs, including serving as a delegate to the Albany Congress in 1754, until he died in Wethersfield on July 24, 1755.

HISTORICAL DOCUMENT

Sir,

I now give you my thoughts on the questions you lately sent me. As you set me the task, you must take the performance as it is without any apology for its defects. I have wrote with the usual freedom of a friend, aiming at nothing but truth, and to express my self so as to be understood. In order to answer your main enquiry concerning the extent of the civil magistrate's power respecting religion; I suppose it needful to look back to the end, and therefore to the original of it: By which means I suppose a just notion may be formed of what is properly their business or the object of their power; and so without any insuperable difficulty we may thence learn what is out of that compass.

That the sacred scriptures are the alone rule of faith and practice to a Christian, all Protestants are agreed in; and must therefore inviolably maintain, that every Christian has a right of judging for himself what he is to believe and practice in religion according to that rule: Which I think on a full examination you will find perfectly inconsistent with any power in the civil magistrate to make any penal laws in matters of religion. Tho' Protestants are agreed in the profession of that principle, yet too many in practice have departed from it. The evils that have been introduced thereby into the Christian church are more than can be reckoned up. Because of the great importance of it to the Christian and to his standing fast in that liberty wherewith Christ has made him free, you will not fault me if I am the longer upon it. The more firmly this is established in our minds; the more firm shall we be against all attempts upon our Christian liberty, and better practice that Christian charity towards such as are of different sentiments from us in religion that is so much recommended and inculcated in those sacred oracles, and which a just understanding of our Christian rights has a natural tendency to influence us to. And tho' your sentiments about some of those points you demand my thoughts upon may have been different from mine; yet I perswade my self, you will not think mine to be far from the truth when you shall have throughly weighed what follows. But if I am mistaken in the grounds I proceed upon or in any conclusion drawn from true premises, I shall be thankful to have the same pointed out: Truth being what I seek, to which all must bow first or last.

To proceed then as I have just hinted, I shall first, briefly consider the Origin and End of Civil Government.

First, as to the origin——Reason teaches us that all men are naturally equal in respect of jurisdiction or dominion one over another. Altho' true it is that children are not born in this full state of equality, yet they are born to it. Their parents have a sort of rule & jurisdiction over them when they come into the world, and for some time after: But it is but a temporary one; which arises from that duty incumbent on them to take care of their offspring during the imperfect state of childhood, to preserve, nourish and educate them (as the workmanship of their own almighty Maker, to whom they are to be accountable for them), and govern the actions of their yet ignorant nonage, 'till reason shall take its place and ease them of that trouble. For God having given man an understanding to direct his actions, has given him therewith a freedom of will and liberty of acting, as properly belonging thereto, within the bounds of that law he is under: And whilst he is in a state wherein he has no understanding of his own to direct his will, he is not to have any will of his own to follow: He that understands for him must will for him too. But when he comes to such a state of reason as made the father free, the same must make the son free too: For the freedom of man and liberty of acting according to his own will (without being subject to the will of another) is grounded on his having reason, which is able to instruct him in that law he is to govern himself by, and make him know how far he is left to the freedom of his own will. So that we are born free as we are born rational. Not that we have actually the exercise of either as soon as born; age that brings one, brings the other too. This natural freedom is not a liberty for every one to do what he pleases without any regard to any law; for a rational creature cannot but be made under a law from its Maker: But it consists in a freedom from any superior power on earth, and not being under the will or legislative authority of man, and having only the law of nature (or in other words, of its Maker) for his rule.

And as reason tells us, all are born thus naturally equal, i.e. with an equal right to their persons; so also with an equal right to their preservation; and therefore to such things as nature affords for their subsistence. For which purpose God was pleased to make a grant of the earth in common to the children of men, first to Adam and afterwards to Noah and his sons: as the Psalmist says, Psal. 115. 16. And altho' no one has originally a private dominion exclusive of the rest of mankind in the earth or its products, as they are consider'd in this their natural state; yet since God has given these things for the use of men and given them reason also to make use thereof to the best advantage of life; there must of necessity be a means to appropriate them some way or other, before they can be of any use to any particular person. And every man having a property in his own person, the labour of his body and the work of his hands are properly his own, to which no one has right but himself; it will therefore follow that when he removes any thing out of the state that nature has provided and left it in, he has mixed his labour with it and joined something to it that is his own, and thereby makes it his property. He having removed it out of the common state nature placed it in, it hath by this labour something annexed to it that excludes the common right of others; because this labour being the unquestionable property of the labourer, no man but he can have a right to what that is once joined to, at least where there is enough and as good left in common for others. Thus every man having a natural right to (or being the proprietor of) his own person and his own actions and labour and to what he can honestly acquire by his labour, which we call property; it certainly follows, that no man can have a right to the person or property of another: And if every man has a right to his person and property; he has also a right to defend them, and a right to all the necessary means of defence, and so has a right of punishing all insults upon his person and property.

But because in such a state of nature, every man must be judge of the breach of the law of nature and executioner too (even in his own case) and the greater part being no strict observers of equity and justice; the enjoyment of property in this state is not very safe. Three things are wanting in this state (as the celebrated Lock observes) to render them safe; viz. an established known law received and allowed by common consent to be the standard of right and wrong, the common measure to decide all controversies between them: For tho' the law

of nature be intelligible to all rational creatures; yet men being biassed by their interest as well as ignorant for want of the study of it, are not apt to allow of it as a law binding to them in the application of it to their particular cases. There wants also a known and indifferent judge with authority to determine all differences according to the established law: for men are too apt to be partial to themselves, and too much wanting in a just concern for the interest of others. There often wants also in a state of nature, a power to back and support the sentence when right, and give it due execution. Now to remedy these inconveniencies, reason teaches men to join in society, to unite together into a commonwealth under some form or other, to make a body of laws agreable to the law of nature, and institute one common power to see them observed. It is they who thus unite together, viz. the people, who make and alone have right to make the laws that are to take place among them; or which comes to the same thing, appoint those who shall make them, and who shall see them executed. For every man has an equal right to the preservation of his person and property; and so an equal right to establish a law, or to nominate the makers and executors of the laws which are the guardians both of person and property.

Hence then the fountain and original of all civil power is from the people, and is certainly instituted for their sakes; or in other words, which was the second thing proposed, The great end of civil government, is the preservation of their persons, their liberties and estates, or their property. Most certain it is, that it must be for their own sakes, the rendering their condition better than it was in what is called a state of nature (a state without such establish'd laws as before mentioned, or without any common power) that men would willingly put themselves out of that state. It is nothing but their own good can be any rational inducement to it: and to suppose they either should or would do it on any other, is to suppose rational creatures ought to change their state with a design to make it worse. And that good which in such a state they find a need of, is no other than a greater security of enjoyment of what belonged to them. That and that only can then be the true reason of their uniting together in some form or other they judge best for the obtaining that greater security. That greater security therefore of life, liberty, money, lands, houses, family, and the like, which may be all comprehended under that of person and property, is the sole end of all civil government. I mean not that all civil governments (as so called) are thus constituted: (tho' the British and some few other nations are through a merciful Providence so happy as to have such). There are too too many arbitrary governments in the world, where the people don't make their own laws. These are not properly speaking governments but tyrannies; and are absolutely against the law of God and nature. But I am considering things as they be in their own nature, what reason teaches concerning them: and herein have given a short sketch of what the celebrated Mr. Lock in his Treatise of Government has largely demonstrated; and in which it is justly to be presumed all are agreed who understand the natural rights of mankind.

GLOSSARY

Psalmist: referring to an author of a passage from the book of Psalms, contained in the Bible

scriptures: sacred writings from the Bible, often used for teaching

tyrannies: cruel and repressive governments or rule

Document Analysis

The interconnectedness of religion and government was especially pronounced in the North American colonies, as many were founded for religious reasons. Governments in Europe and North America frequently passed laws pertaining to religious matters, although there was much disagreement about exactly how much control the government should have to dictate the details of religious worship. Some groups believed that the government should have the right to legislate any and all aspects of religious practice, while others believed that a certain amount of tolerance should be allowed for matters that were not necessary to achieve salvation.

At the heart of the debate over religious legislation and tolerance was the need and desire to control the colonists' behaviors. Many leaders claimed that authorization for their actions came directly from God, and that they were simply passing laws that reflected the divine will. By contrast, some people were beginning to believe that no man should be allowed to have such control over any other man and resented the heavy-handed approach that many colonial leaders took when regulating behavior.

In the 1730s and 1740s, the First Great Awakening took place throughout Europe and North America. During this time, traveling preachers espoused religion as a highly emotional and personal experience. They encouraged followers to pursue salvation by treating others well and performing good deeds, rather strictly adhering to doctrine. By contrast, traditional preachers were usually fixtures in their communities, often involved with local government, and belonged to specific parishes. Religious practice involved strict laws about when and how worship was to take place, and departure from those norms would be punished to varying degrees, either directly by the government or by the operation of social protocol. As such, the primary purpose of religion in the colonies was to provide a set of rules to which the people had to conform. The revivalist preachers were new and exciting; they encouraged people both to worship with enthusiasm and not to be so concerned about the small details of religious practice.

However, many traditional preachers saw the revivalist approach as a threat, and, hoping to prevent the spread of radical ideas and the unsettling of communities, they encouraged colonies to pass laws prohibiting pastors from preaching in a community without an invitation from the local preacher. As a response to the hard-line reaction many pastors had to the First Great Awakening, the pamphlet *The Essential Rights and Liberties of Protestants*, commonly attributed to Williams because its facts and opinions seemed to point to him, was published in 1744. The pamphlet encouraged religious freedom in the colonies and opposed the strict legislation Connecticut had enacted to prevent visiting ministers from preaching to local parishes without an explicit invitation.

While many of the ideas expressed in *The Essential Rights and Liberties of Protestants* had been around in some form for many years, putting these ideas into practice was still considered a radical, and often unpopular, notion. The document advocated freedom and tolerance, in matters not only pertaining to religion but also related to government regulation. While Williams specifically addresses the pamphlet to those who supported the Connecticut law banning visiting preachers, the ideas he puts forward have broader applicability to government's role in everyday life and religious practice in general.

Williams's argument is almost entirely based on religion. He first contends that all Protestants agree on the basic rules of faith and practice, which seems reasonable given that the rules were usually established in the Bible. He then states that, in the absence of specific instructions issued directly by God, everyone has a right to determine for himself how to carry out the agreed-upon rules. As a result, he concludes that the government should not have the authority to create rules dictating the methods of religious worship, and certainly should not have the power to punish those who do not worship in a certain way, if that way was not an explicit requirement made by God.

To justify this, Williams argues that God created humans with the ability to reason, and, therefore, they must have freedom to act as they believe appropriate in accordance with this ability. In other words, by giving humans the ability to reason, God also indirectly gave them the power of liberty and freedom of will. Williams clarifies that this does not exempt people from obeying any laws whatsoever. Rather, it means that no person is inherently superior to any other, and therefore all people must be free from "any superior power on earth." People are to answer directly to God and laws of nature, and need not be "under the will or legislative authority of man."

To Williams, the religious freedom of individuals is quite an expansive power. He reasons that, since people's bodies are their own property, anything they create is under their ownership. Therefore, if people use their own labor to improve anything in nature, they effectively give themselves the right to exclude others from asserting any authority over it. Williams further insists that everyone has the right to defend his or her person and property, and accordingly has a right to "punish" those who trespass. This line of reasoning gives individuals justification to govern themselves and anything to which they might contribute, to the exclusion of all others. As a practical matter, this seems like it could lead to anarchy.

Williams addresses the issue of anarchy by identifying three particular conditions often lacking in the proper administration of laws and justice, and he cites philosopher John Locke as the inspiration for these ideas. Locke wrote prolifically about social and political theory in England during the seventeenth century, and he was responsible for drafting several governing documents for the English colonies in the United States. One of Locke's significant contributions was his idea that human behavior must be taken into account when establishing government and laws, even if that behavior seems irrational. Locke theorized that many political problems are caused by the peculiarities of human nature, and the behaviors that Williams cites in *The Essential Rights and Liberties of Protestants* would certainly complicate the creation and administration of laws.

First, Williams notes the importance of well-publicized laws written based on common consent regarding right and wrong. He observes that, while people generally want laws to protect their interests, they are ultimately biased and will not want the laws applied to their particular situation if it would be detrimental to their interests. Second, he states the importance of having an unbiased authority to make decisions in accordance with the established law. However, he notes that this, too, could be problematic, because, once again, people are likely to be partial to their own self-interest. Finally, he espouses the necessity of a system of enforcement for penalties imposed when the laws are not followed.

His three conditions seem to be influenced by the philosophies of Locke, who noted that indulging people's individual differences rather than requiring conformity tended to cause unrest. While some of Locke's writings seemed to promote religious tolerance, closer review has led some scholars to conclude that Locke was indeed interested in full-scale conformity to a single doctrine. The details of that doctrine did not matter much, but uniformity was necessary for a stable society: if people in a single society adhere to different doctrines, social and political unrest will result.

A similar assumption of tolerance based on uniformity can be seen in *The Essential Rights and Liberties of Protestants*. In his pamphlet, Williams states at several points that government should be formed by people coming together to construct laws that adhere to natural laws; however, such a theory strongly presumes that all the people in question are able to reach a peaceful and unanimous agreement on what exactly the laws of nature are and how they should be crafted into binding legislation. Perhaps Williams is simply being naive, but given his tacit assumption that all people share similar opinions about the laws of nature, it is difficult to see how this rationale truly promotes tolerance. One could see how an opposing viewpoint might be dismissed as a misinterpretation of the "laws of nature" on which legislation should be based.

Finally, Williams believes that all people have an equal say in the construction of laws and in the election of those who will carry out the laws. This idea also may have been inspired by Locke, who believed that most forms of government could be successful as long as they were officially sanctioned by the people being governed. Williams's reasoning again derives from the religious argument that God had given humans the power of reasoning, and since all people have an equal power of reasoning granted to them, they should likewise all have an equal say in the laws they would be required to obey. Williams emphatically labels a government tyrannical that does not adhere to the will of the people.

While *The Essential Rights and Liberties of Protestants* does not address the following point directly, it is worth noting that in many contemporary documents, the term "man" usually referred only to white men of European decent. White women, and black or native people of either gender, were excluded from the freedoms Williams's discusses; indeed, many colonial writings argue extensively for why women and non-whites were not really people, or why God somehow intended for them to be subservient.

Against the backdrop of the First Great Awakening, when traditional preachers were fighting to restrict colonists' freedoms in the name of promoting religion and salvation, Williams's radical ideas about freedom, liberty, and tolerance made quite an impact. However, Williams's argument relies on the assertion that "it is justly to be presumed all are agreed who understand the natural rights of mankind." Given this premise, it is difficult to see how Williams's ideas could, in a practical sense, successfully pave the way for the religious freedom he seemed to envision. In order for everyone to have this freedom, all must first agree on the same fundamental truths; however, the exact nature of those "truths" had been debated for a long time, and it may have been naive for Williams to believe that a consensus could be reached so easily. Nonetheless, the mere idea that tolerance might be possible (or even desirable) was a noble one.

Essential Themes

During the 1730s and 1740s, the First Great Awakening caused a shift in religious practice in many North American colonies. Traditionally, religious worship was dictated by strict laws and government regulation, but during the 1740s, a new style of traveling preacher rose to prominence. Many traditional preachers felt that the revivalist preachers threatened their way of life and, therefore, passed laws making it a crime to preach to a parish within their community without an explicit invitation. Williams's pamphlet protested this legislation and encouraged religious freedom in the colonies.

Williams contends that all Protestants agreed on the basic rules of faith and practice, and that in the absence of specific divine instructions, everyone has a right to determine for him- or herself how to carry out the rules. He further argues that, by giving humans the ability to reason, God also indirectly gave them the power of liberty and freedom of will. He believes that people need to answer only to God.

Williams also identifies three conditions commonly lacking in the administration of laws and justice, inspired by Locke. First, Williams notes that laws must be well-publicized and based on common consent regarding right and wrong. Second, he states the importance of having a "known and indifferent judge" with the authority to make decisions in accordance with the established laws. He notes that the impartiality required in each of these could present problems, since people are partial to their own self-interest. Finally, he believes it necessary to have a system to enforce penalties for noncompliance.

While Williams's writing seems to promote tolerance, it also has some limitations. He presumes that all involved in the decision-making process are able to reach both a peaceful and a unanimous agreement on what exactly the laws of nature are and how they should be crafted into binding legislation. Since Williams's vision required such broad agreement as a necessary premise, it is difficult to see how it truly promoted tolerance.

Tracey M. DiLascio, JD

Bibliography

"Elisha Williams." Yale U Library. Yale University, 14 Feb. 2008. Web. 7 June 2012.

Lockwood, James. "Man Mortal: God Everlasting, and the Sure, Unfailing Refuge and Felicity of His Faithful People, in All Generations." New Haven, CT: Parker, 1756.

Sandoz, Ellis, ed. Political Sermons of the American Founding Era, 1730–1805. Indianapolis, IN: Liberty Fund 1998. Print.

White, J. T., ed. The National Cyclopedia of American Biography, Vol. 1. New York: White, 1892–1984. Print.

LESSON PLAN: An Argument for Religious Freedom

Students analyze Elisha Williams's sermon, the influences on Williams's thinking, and the influence the sermon had on evolving American thought.

Learning Objectives

Identify the central question Williams addresses; consider the historical context in which Williams's thought developed; draw comparisons across eras to define enduring issues; consider multiple perspectives in the role of religious groups in early America.

Materials: Elisha Williams, "*The Essential Rights and Liberties of Protestants*" (1744); John Locke, "Letters Concerning Toleration" (1689–1692); Jonathan Edwards, "On the Great Awakening" (1743); George Whitefield, "Britain's Mercies, and Britain's Duty" (1746).

Overview Questions

What issues does Williams specifically address? How do John Locke's writings affect Williams's argument? How do the issues Williams confronts still echo through twenty-first century America? How did early eighteenth-century religious thought and actions affect America's founding documents?

Step 1: Comprehension Questions

How effective is Williams's argument for religious freedom? What specific technique does he use to use to make his points?

▶ **Activity:** Have students read aloud phrases which clearly identify his purpose. Discuss how Williams structures his argument. Have students decide whether the argument and method is effective.

Step 2: Comprehension Questions

What religious and philosophical influences affected Williams's thinking? How might his argument be harmed without Locke's logic behind it?

▶ **Activity:** Instruct a student to prepare and present a brief report on Locke and his influence on Protestant and political thought. Have students read aloud Williams's paraphrasing of Locke. Discuss whether or not Locke was arguing for religious freedom.

Step 3: Context Questions

How are Williams's arguments still alive today? How might his letter be used to both expand and limit freedom of religion?

▶ **Activity:** Have students select passages that suggest the content of today's arguments about the relation between government and religion. Discuss how the letter could be an argument for total separation of government and religion. Ask how it might be used to argue the reverse as well.

Step 4: Exploration Questions

How did the unfolding of events in the Great Awakening (1730–1750) lead to the sermons of Edwards, Williams, and Whitefield? How is the influence of the sermons on American political thought different from the influence of the Great Awakening?

▶ **Activity:** Review with students how the Great Awakening reinforced the colonists' growing sense of freedom. Review events that led Williams to react to the Connecticut law; discuss how the sermon's influence was a result of the Great Awakening, but different in scope.

Step 5: Response Paper

Word length and additional requirements set by Instructor. Students answer the research question in the Overview Questions. Students state a thesis and use as evidence passages from the primary source document as well as support from supplemental materials assigned in the lesson.

Supplemental Historical Documents

Government the Pillar of the Earth

Date: August 13, 1730
Author: Colman, Benjamin
Genre: political sermon

For the Pillars of the Earth are the Lord's, and He hath set the World upon them.

1 Samuel. 2:8.
The words are part of a rapturous and heavenly song uttered by a devout, inspired, and transported mother in Israel upon a great and joyful occasion. If the Divine Eternal Spirit please to inspire and speak by a gracious woman, it is the same thing to [us] and requires our reverent attention as much, as [if] He raise up a Moses or an Elias or make His revelations by a Paul or John.

Samuel, the rare and wonderful son of inspired Hannah, never outspoke his lovely mother in any of his prayers or acts of praise. Eli would have sat at her feet and laid himself in the dust at the hearing of this flowing torrent of fervent devotion from her beauteous lips, and saints through all ages hang on the heavenly music of her tongue.

Great things are here said of God and of His Government in the families and kingdoms of men, and such wise and just observations are made as are worthy of deep contemplation by the greatest and best of men. Had she like Deborah been the princess of the tribes of Israel, she could not have spoken with more lofti-ness and majesty, with more authority and command, nor better have addressed the nobles and rulers, the captains and the mighty men, to humble and lay them low before God.

"She celebrates the Lord God of Israel, his unspotted purity, his Almighty power, his unsearchable wisdom, and his unerring justice" ([Matthew] Henry).

In the praises of these she joys and triumphs; her heart was exalted and her mouth enlarged [overflowing with words].

"She adores the Divine Sovereignty in its disposals in the affairs of the children of men, in the strange and sudden turns given to them, in the rise and fall of persons, families, and countries."

"She observes how the strong are soon weakened, and the weak are soon strengthened, when God pleases: How the rich are soon impoverished, and the poor enriched on a sudden: How empty families are replenished, and numerous families diminished."

All this is of the Lord: "He maketh rich, He bringeth low and lifteth up: He raiseth up the poor out of dust, and lifteth up the beggar from the dunghill; to set them among princes, and make them inherit the throne of glory;"

"For the pillars of the earth are the Lord's, and He hath set the World upon them."

Thus my text is introduced as a reason for those dispensations of God towards a person, a family, or a people, which at any time are to us most surprising and admirable. . . .

✳✳✳

DOCTRINE: *The great God has made the governments and rulers of the Earth its pillars, and has set the world upon them.*

1. The governments and rulers of the Earth are its pillars.

2. These pillars of the Earth are the Lord's.

3. He has set the world upon them.

1. The governments and rulers of the Earth are its pillars.
The pillar is a part of great use and honor in the building: So is magistracy in the world. One style [figure of speech] in Scripture for it is: *foundations* and *cornerstones.* Where we read of "the chief of all the people" (Judges 20:2), in the Hebrew it is "the corners." We read also of the "foundations of the earth being out of course" (Psalm 82:5). The meaning is, the government of it was so. Kings bear up and support the inferior pillars of government, and a righteous administration restores a dissolving state: Psalm 75:3: "The earth and all the inhabitants thereof are dissolved: I bear up the pillars of it."

In like manner, wise and faithful ministers are pillars in the church, which "is built on the prophets and apostles, JESUS CHRIST being the chief Cornerstone" (Ephesians 2:20). The prophet Jeremiah was made by God "an iron pillar," and of Peter, James, and John we read that "they seemed to be pillars" (Galatians 2:9). They were deservedly so reputed, and truly so, in the Church of Christ. Famous are the Lord's words to Peter, Matthew 16:18: "Thou art Peter, and on this rock will I build my church." And when John had the vision of the New Jerusalem descending out of Heaven from God, it is said that "the wall of the city had twelve foundations, and in them the names of the twelve apostles of the Lamb" (Revelation 21:14). . . .

✳✳✳

2. Are magistrates the pillars of the earth? Are they the Lord's? And has He set the world upon them? Let us then devoutly observe the governing Providence of God in the disposing of persons and offices, both with respect unto ourselves and others.

As to ourselves, let God lead and Providence open our way, and let us follow humbly and obediently. Let us think soberly of ourselves, and not vainly pine after honor and power or wickedly push for it like Absalom. But neither need we hide ourselves like Saul when the Divine call is plain, nor insist on excuses like the meek and accomplished Moses. Or if again Providence lays us by, why should we not retire with Samuel's humility and greatness of soul.

And then as to others, let us not think ourselves neglected or overlooked, be envious and discontent, if God prefer them. Suffer the Most High to rule in the kingdoms of men and to give the provinces that belong to them to whomsoever He will. Let us know and keep our own place and do our duty to those whom God sets over us.

Let people reverence and honor their worthy rulers, and let the highest among men be very humble before God. They are pillars, but of the Earth. The Earth and its pillars are dissolving together. Government abides in a succession of men, while the Earth endures, but the persons, however good and great, must die like other men. We must not look too much at the loftiness of any, nor lean too much on any earthly pillar: "Put not your trust in princes, nor in the son of man in whom there is no help: His breath goeth forth, he returneth to his dust." Nor may the highest among mortals behold themselves with elation and security, as the vain king of Babylon [did] once, but let them fear and tremble before the God of Heaven, who inherits all nations and stands in the congregation of the mighty and judges among the gods.

3. Are rulers the pillars of the earth; are they the Lord's? And has He set the world upon them? Let all that are in public offices consider their obligations to be PILLARS in the places wherein Providence has set them.

Let rulers consider what they owe to God, who has reared and set them up, and to the public which God has set upon them. Let them seek wisdom and strength, grace and conduct from God, that they may answer the title given them in my text. Let them stand and bear and act for God, whose they are and who has set them where they are. Let the public good be their just care, that it may be seen that God has set the world in their hearts as well as laid it on their shoulders. Let them act uprightly, that they may stand secure and strong. Let them fear God and rule by His Word, that they may be approved by God and accepted always by men with all thankfulness.

As government is the pillar of the earth, so religion is the pillar of government. Take away the fear of God's government and judgment, and human rule utterly falls or corrupts into tyranny. But if religion rules in the hearts and lives of rulers, God will have glory, and the people be made happy.

FATHERS of our country, let me freely say to you that the devotion and virtue [morality] of our humble, but illustrious ancestors (the first planters [settlers] of New England), laid the foundation of our greatness among the provinces: And it is this that must continue and establish it under the Divine favor and blessing. Emulate their piety and godliness and generous regards to the public, and be acknowledged the pillars, the strength and ornament of your country!

But let me move you by a greater argument, even a "far more exceeding and eternal weight of glory," which the Holy Ghost [Holy Spirit] has set before you in a most illustrious promise: Revelation 3:12: "Him that overcometh will I make a PILLAR in the temple of my GOD, and he shall go no more out: And I will write upon him the name of my God, and the name of the City of my God, which is New Jerusalem; which cometh down out of Heaven from my God: And I will write upon him my new name."

CHRIST will erect a *monumental pillar* that shall stand forever in honor of all [those] who in their station here, be they high or low, faithfully endeavor to uphold His church and Kingdom.

It is a *triumphant promise* taken from the Roman manner of pillars reared to the memory of illustrious persons and PATRIOTS, on which were inscribed their names and worthy deeds, together with that of the empire, city, or province which they were so happy as to serve and help to save.

Infinitely more glory and honor shall be done to Him who serves the *Lord CHRIST*, His kingdom, people, and interest, in his life here on earth: When he comes into His temple above he shall have a pillar of celestial glory reared to eternalize his name, and on it shall be written

(O divine honor!) "THIS WAS A FAITHFUL SERVANT OF HIS GOD AND SAVIOR AND OF THE CHURCH ON EARTH."

There let him stand forever, "A *monument of free grace, never to be defaced or removed*." While the names of famous emperors, kings, and generals, graven in brass or cut in marble on stately pillars and triumphant arches, shall molder into dust.

So the pillars in Solomon's porch were broken down and carried away by the Chaldeans: But he that is made a pillar in the celestial temple shall "go no more out." Yes, the pillars of the literal earth and heavens will shortly tremble and be shaken out of their place, but he that believes in CHRIST and has His glorious Name written on him shall remain unshaken and immoveable, and remain, like his living Savior, steadfast forever.

This infinite and eternal GLORY we wish to all in this worshiping assembly, the greater and the less, high and low, rich and poor together, as in the act of worship, we are all on a level before the throne of God. And the lowest in outward condition may be the highest in grace and in the honors that come from above.

But in a more especial manner we wish this mercy and blessing of our GOD and KING out of His house to YOUR EXCELLENCY OUR GOVERNOR, whose return to your country, and your advancement to the government of it, we cannot but congratulate in the most public manner, with hearts full of joy and sincere thankfulness to GOD.

The Lord God of our fathers, who has "spread our heavens," and "laid the foundations of our earth," make you a PILLAR to US both in the state and church.

As it has pleased HIM to choose, adorn, and set you up, so may He please to fix and establish you, and long continue you a FATHER and illustrious blessing to your people.

And may the *Name of CHRIST* and of those churches of our Lord JESUS be graven deep upon your heart, and your faithful services to them be an everlasting name to you, "which shall not be cut off."

So, not only erect yourself a Pillar in every pious and grateful heart that loves our civil and religious liberties, and let their prayers and blessings come upon you, but also lay a good foundation [for] the world to come, for everlasting fame and renown, and "to be called GREAT in the Kingdom of Heaven."

[END]

LESSON PLAN: The Foundations of Government

Students analyze the meaning of Benjamin Colman's sermon and its impact on listeners or readers over the centuries.

Learning Objectives

Identify the central question of Colman's sermon; reconstruct its literal meaning; appreciate changing historical perspectives; compare and contrast differing sets of religious ideas in colonial America.

Materials: Benjamin Colman, "Government the Pillar of the Earth" (1730); Elisha Williams, *The Essential Right and Liberties of Protestants (1744)*.

Overview Questions

What is the goal of Colman's sermon? Does Colman argue for or against religious-based government? How does Colman's sermon align with the thinking of later generations of Americans? What does Colman's sermon have in common with Williams's *The Essential Right and Liberties of Protestants*?

Step 1: Comprehension Questions

Why has Colman chosen to speak about government leadership in this sermon? Why does he choose pillars as his consistent image in the sermon?

▶ **Activity:** Have a student explain the setting and context of the presentation of this sermon. Have students discuss the use and meaning of *pillar* in the sermon; discuss whether or not the image has more than one meaning for Colman.

Step 2: Comprehension Questions

Does Colman argue that magistrates are the pillars of the earth, or are they the pillars of the Lord? What evidence does the document provide to support either view?

▶ **Activity:** Choose students to select and read passages that indicate Colman's belief about a magistrate's proper allegiance. Have students discuss how Colman believes a magistrate's faith should affect his actions; have students summarize Colman's conclusions.

Step 3: Context Questions

Could Colman's sermon have been made and accepted in the first years of the United States? Can it be made and accepted now?

▶ **Activity:** Have students select passages from the sermon that may appear inconsistentwith

the first Amendment. Discuss whether early nineteenth-century listeners could have understood and tolerated the implications of the sermon; repeat the discussion in a contemporary twenty-first-century context.

Step 4: Exploration Questions

In what ways are Colman's views similar to Elisha Williams's in *The Essential Right and Liberties of Protestants*? How do they differ?

▶ **Activity:** Have students note the similarities between the two documents. Discuss which argues for greater religious freedom. Discuss whether or not both suggest that God's relationship with the world should serve as a model for government's relationship with its citizens.

Step 5: Response Paper

Word length and additional requirements set by Instructor. Students answer the research question in the Overview Questions. Students state a thesis and use as evidence passages from the primary source document as well as support from supplemental materials assigned in the lesson.

BRITAIN'S MERCIES, AND BRITAIN'S DUTIES

DATE: August 14, 1746
AUTHOR: Whitefield, George
GENRE: sermon

"What shall I render unto the Lord for all His Mercies? Bless the Lord, O my Soul, and all that is within me bless his holy Name." And why? "Who forgiveth all thine Iniquities, who healeth all thy Diseases, who redeemeth thy Life from Destruction, who crowneth thee with loving Kindness and tender Mercies." And when the same holy man of God had a mind to stir up the people of the Jews to set about a national reformation, as the most weighty and prevailing argument he could make use of for that purpose, he lays before them, as it were, in a draught, many national mercies, and distinguishing deliverances, which had been conferred upon, and wrought out for them, by the most high God. The psalm to which the words of our text belong, is a pregnant proof of this; it being a kind of epitome or compendium of the whole Jewish history: At least it contains an enumeration of many signal and extraordinary blessings the Israelites had received from God, and also the improvement they were in duty bound to make of them, viz. to observe his statutes and keep his laws.

To run through all the particulars of the psalm, or draw a parallel (which might with great ease and justice be done) between God's dealings with us and the Israelites of old—to enumerate all the national mercies bestow'd upon, and remarkable deliverances wrought out for the kingdom of Great Britain, from the infant state of William the Conqueror, to her present manhood, and more than Augustan maturity, under the auspicious reign of our dread and rightful sovereign King George the Second; howsoever pleasing and profitable it might be at any other time, would, at this juncture, prove, if not an irksome, yet an unseasonable undertaking.

The occasion of the late solemnity, I mean the suppression of a most horrid and unnatural rebellion will afford more than sufficient matter for a discourse of this nature, and furnish us with abundant motives to love and obey that glorious Jehovah, who giveth Salvation unto Kings, and delivers His People from the hurtful Sword.

Need I make an apology before this auditory, if, in order to see the greatness of our late deliverance, I should remind you of the many unspeakable blessings which we have for a course of years enjoy'd, during the reign of his present majesty, and the gentle mild administration under which we live? Without justly incurring the censure of giving flattering titles, I believe all who have eyes to see, and ears to hear, and are but a little acquainted with our publick affairs, must acknowledge, that we have one of the best of kings. It is now above nineteen years since he began to reign over us. And yet, was he to be seated on a royal throne, and were all his subjects placed before him; was he to address them as Samuel once addressed the Israelites, "Behold here I am, Old and Greyheaded, witness against me before the Lord, whose Ox have I taken? Or whose Ass have I taken? Or whom have I defrauded? Whom have I oppressed? They must, if they would do him justice, make the same answer as was given to Samuel, "Thou hast not defrauded us, nor oppressed us." What Tertullus, by way of flattery, said to Felix, may with the strictest justice be applied to our sovereign, "By thee we enjoy great quietness, and very worthy deeds have been done unto our nation by thy providence." He has been indeed *pater patriæ*, a father to our country, and, tho' old and greyheaded, has jeoparded his precious life for us in the high places of the field. Nor has he less deserved that great and glorious title which the Lord promises kings should sustain in the latter days, I mean, a nursing Father of the Church. For not only the Church of England, as by law established, but Christians of every denomination whatsoever have enjoyed their religious, as well as civil liberties. As there has been no authorized oppression in the state, so there has been no publickly allowed persecution in the church. We breathe indeed in a free air; as free (if not freer) both as to temporals and spirituals, as any nation under heaven. Nor is the prospect likely to terminate in his majesty's death, which I pray God long to defer. Our princesses are disposed of to Protestant powers. And we have great reason to be assured that the present heir apparent, and his consort, are like minded with their royal father. And I cannot help thinking, that it is a peculiar blessing vouchsafed us by the King of Kings, that his present majesty has been continued so long among us. For now his immediate successor (though his present situation obliges him, as it were, to lie dormant) has great and glorious opportunities, which we have reason to think he daily improves, of observing and weighing the national affairs, considering the various steps and turns of government, and consequently of laying in a large fund of experience to make him a wise and great prince, if ever God should call him to sway the British sceptre. Happy art thou, O England! Happy art thou, O America, who on every side are thus highly favoured!

But, alas! How soon would this happy scene have shifted, and a melancholy gloomy prospect have succeeded in its room, had the rebels gained their point, and a popish abjured pretender been forced upon the British throne! For, supposing his birth not to be spurious (as we have great reason to think it really was), what could we expect from one, descended from a father, who, when duke of York, put all Scotland into confusion, and afterwards, when crowned king of England, for his arbitrary and tyrannical government both in church and state, was justly obliged to abdicate the throne, by the assertors of British liberty? Or, supposing the horrid plot, first hatched in hell, and afterwards nursed at Rome, had taken place; supposing, I say, the old pretender should have exchanged his cardinal's cap for a triple crown, and have transferred his pretended title (as it is reported he has done) to his eldest son, what was all this for, but that, by being advanced to the popedom, he might rule both son and subjects with less controul, and, by their united interest, keep the three kingdoms of England, Scotland and Ireland, in greater vassalage to the see of Rome? Ever since this unnatural rebellion broke out, I have looked upon the young pretender as the Phaeton of the present age. He is ambitiously and presumptuously aiming to seat himself in the throne of our rightful sovereign King George, which he is no more capable of maintaining than Phaeton was to guide the chariot of the sun;

and had he succeeded in his attempt, like him, would only have set the world on fire. It is true, to do him justice, he has deserved well of the church of Rome, and, in all probability, will hereafter be canonized amongst the noble order of their fictitious saints. But, with what an iron rod we might expect to have been bruized, had his troops been victorious, may easily be imagin'd from those cruel orders, found in the pockets of some of his officers, "Give no quarter to the elector's troops." Add to this, that there was great reason to suspect, that, upon the first news of the success of the rebels, a general massacre was intended. So that if the Lord had not been on our side, Great Britain, not to say America, would, in a few weeks, or months, have been an Aceldama, a field of blood. Besides, was a popish pretender to rule over us, instead of being represented by a free parliament, and governed by laws made by their consent, as we now are, we should shortly have had only the shadow of one, and, it may be, no parliament at all. This is the native product of a popish government, and what the unhappy family, from which this young adventurer pretends to be descended, has always aimed at. Arbitrary principles he has sucked in with his mother's milk; and if he had been so honest, instead of that immature motto upon his standard, *Tandem triumphans*, only to have put, *Stet pro ratione voluntas*, he had given us a short, but true, portraiture of the nature of his intended, but, blessed be God, now defeated reign. And, why should I mention, that the loss of the national debt, and the dissolution of the present happy union between the two kingdoms, would have been the immediate consequences of his success, as he himself declares in his second manifesto, dated from Holyrood House? These are evils, and great ones too; but then they are only evils of a temporary nature. They chiefly concern the body, and must necessarily terminate in the grave. But, alas! what an inundation of spiritual mischiefs would soon have overflowed the church, and what unspeakable danger should we and our posterity have been reduced to in respect to our better parts, our precious and immortal souls? How soon would whole swarms of monks, Dominicans and friars, like so many locusts, have overspread and plagued the nation? With what winged speed would foreign titular bishops have posted over in order to take possession of their respective sees? How quickly would our universities have been filled with youths who have been sent abroad by their popish parents, in order to drink in all the superstitions of the church of Rome? What a speedy period would have been put to societies of all kinds, for promoting Christian knowledge, and propagating the gospel in foreign parts? How soon would our pulpits have every where been filled with those old antichristian doctrines, freewill, meriting by works, transubstantiation, purgatory, works of super-erogation, passive obedience, non-resistance, and all the other abominations of the Whore of Babylon? How soon would our Protestant charity schools in England, Scotland and Ireland, have been pulled down, our Bibles forcibly taken from us, and ignorance every where set up as the mother of devotion? How soon should we have been depriv'd of that invaluable blessing, liberty of conscience, and been obliged to commence (what they falsely call) Catholicks, or submit to all the tortures which a bigotted zeal, guided by the most cruel principles, could possibly invent? How soon would that mother of harlots have made herself once more drunk with the blood of the saints, and the whole tribe even of free-thinkers themselves, been brought to this dilemma, either to die martyrs for (tho' I never yet heard of one that did so), or, contrary to all their most avow'd principles, renounce their great Diana, unassisted, unenlightned reason? But I must have done, lest while I am speaking against Antichrist, I should unawares fall myself, and lead my hearers into an antichristian spirit. True and undefiled religion will regulate our zeal, and teach us to treat even the man of sin, with no harsher language than that which the angel gave his grand employer Satan, The Lord rebuke thee. . . .

LESSON PLAN: The Visiting Preacher

Students analyze George Whitefield's sermon to study its impact on his listeners and the implications it carried for the future of the American colonies.

Learning Objectives

Identify Whitefield's central purpose; read historical documents imaginatively; appreciate the historical and cultural perspectives of Whitefield's audiences; interrogate historical data to explain the impact of the Great Awakening on colonial society.

Materials: George Whitefield's "Britain's Mercies, and Britain's Duties"; Excerpt (starting "By hearing him often" to end) from "Benjamin Franklin on Reverend George Whitefield"

Overview Questions

How and why does Whitefield use recent world events to convince listeners of God's mercies? What impact do Whitefield's spoken words have that his printed words cannot have? What does the literacy of Whitefield's sermon suggest about his listeners? How does this Great Awakening sermon suggest events to come?

Step 1: Comprehension Questions

What events does Whitefield detail as God's blessings for England and its colonies? How does Whitefield employ these to deliver his primary message?

▶ **Activity:** Have students list Whitefield's references to recent political and military victories. Ask students to explain why Whitefield's attributes these events to God's mercies. Have students discuss the parallel Whitefield intends his listeners to draw about God's mercies in their lives.

Step 2: Context Questions

What difference would there be between listening to Whitefield's sermon and reading it? What does the printed version suggest about his oral delivery?

▶ **Activity:** Have students read "Benjamin Franklin on Reverend George Whitefield" (Excerpt from "By hearing him often" to the end). Have students speculate the power of his spoken words on live audiences.

Step 3: Context Questions

What specific references does Whitefield make to religious history, mythology, and British history? What do those references suggest about his listeners?

▶ **Activity:** Instruct students to create a chart showing each reference that Whitefield makes and what it means about his listeners. Discuss with students the likelihood that all of his listeners understood each reference and to what extent it may have made a difference if they did not.

Step 4: Exploration Questions

How was the Great Awakening an antecedent for the American Revolution? What hints of that are in Whitefield's sermon?

▶ **Activity:** Discuss with students what factors of the Great Awakening influenced American revolutionary thinking. Have students identify some of those influences in Whitefield's sermon and in the circumstances in which it was probably delivered.

Step 5: Response Paper

Word length and additional requirements set by Instructor. Students answer the research question in the Overview Questions. Students state a thesis and use as evidence passages from the primary source document as well as support from supplemental materials assigned in the lesson.

HISTORICAL DOCUMENT

A Discourse Concerning Unlimited Submission and Non-Resistance to the Higher Powers

Date: January 30, 1750
Author: Mayhew, Jonathan
Genre: political sermon

Let us now trace the apostle's reasoning in favor of submission to the *higher powers*, a little more particularly and exactly. For by this it will appear, on one hand, how good and conclusive it is, for submission to those rulers who exercise their power in a proper manner: And, on the other, how weak and trifling and inconnected it is, if it be supposed to be meant by the apostle to show the obligation and duty of obedience to tyrannical, oppressive rulers in common with others of a different character.

The apostle enters upon his subject thus—*Let every soul be subject unto the higher powers; for there is no power but of God: the powers that be, are ordained of God.* Here he urges the duty of obedience from this topic of argument, that civil rulers, as they are supposed to fulfil the pleasure of God, are the ordinance of God. But how is this an argument for obedience to such rulers as do not perform the pleasure of God, by doing good; but the pleasure of the devil, by doing evil; and such as are not, therefore, *God's ministers,* but the devil's! *Whosoever, therefore, resisteth the power, resisteth the ordinance of God; and they that resist, shall receive to themselves damnation.* Here the apostle argues, that those who resist a reasonable and just authority, which is agreeable to the will of God, do really resist the will of God himself; and will, therefore, be punished by him. But how does this prove, that those who resist a lawless, unreasonable power, which is contrary to the will of God, do therein resist the will and ordinance of God? Is resisting those who resist God's will, the same thing with resisting God? Or shall those who do so, *receive to themselves damnation! For rulers are not a terror to good works, but to the evil. Wilt thou then not be afraid of the power? Do that which is good; and thou shalt have praise of the same. For he is the minister of God to thee for good.* Here the apostle argues more explicitly than he had before done, for revering, and submitting to, magistracy, from this consideration, that such as really

performed the duty of magistrates, would be enemies only to the vil actions of men, and would befriend and encourage the good; and so be a common blessing to society. But how is this an argument, that we must honor, and submit to, such magistrates as are not enemies to the evil actions of men, but to the good; and such as are not a common blessing, but a common curse, to society! *But if thou do that which is evil, be afraid: For he is the minister of God, a revenger, to execute wrath upon him that doth evil.* Here the apostle argues from the nature and end of magistracy, that such as did evil, (and such only) had reason to be afraid of the *higher powers*; it being part of their office to punish evil doers, no less than to defend and encourage such as do well. But if magistrates are unrighteous; if they are *respecters of persons*; if they are partial in their administration of justice; then those who do well have as much reason to *be afraid*, as those that do evil: there can be no safety for the good, nor any peculiar ground of terror to the unruly and injurious. So that, in this case, the main end of civil government will be frustrated. And what reason is there for submitting to that government, which does by no means answer the design of government? *Wherefore ye must needs be subject not only for wrath, but also for conscience sake.* Here the apostle argues the duty of a chearful and conscientious submission to civil government, from the nature and end of magistracy as he had before laid it down, i. e. as the design of it was to punish evil doers, and to support and encourage such as do well; and as it must, if so exercised, be agreeable to the will of God. But how does what he here says, prove the duty of a chearful and conscientious subjection to those who forfeit the character of rulers? to those who encourage the bad, and discourage the good? The argument here used no more proves it to be a sin to resist such rulers, than it does, to *resist the devil*, that he may *flee from us.* For one is as truly the *minister of God* as may the other. *For, for this cause pay you tribute also; for they are God's ministers, attending continually upon this very thing*. Here the apostle argues the duty of paying taxes from this consideration, that those who perform the duty of rulers, are continually attending upon the public welfare. But how does this argument conclude for paying taxes to such princes as are continually endeavouring to ruin the public? And especially when such payment would facilitate and promote this wicked design! *Render therefore to all their dues; tribute, to whom tribute is due; custom, to whom custom; fear, to whom fear; honor, to whom honor*. Here the apostle sums up what he had been saying concerning the duty of subjects to rulers. And his argument stands thus—"Since magistrates who execute their office well, are common benefactors to society; and may, in that respect, be properly stiled *the ministers and ordinance of God*; and since they are constantly employed in the service of the public; it becomes you to pay them tribute and custom; and to reverence, honor, and submit to, them in the execution of their respective offices." This is apparently good reasoning. But does this argument conclude for the duty of paying tribute, custom, reverence, honor and obedience, to such persons as (although they bear the title of rulers) use all their powers to hurt and injure the public: such as are not *God's ministers*, but *satan's*? such as do not take care of, and attend upon, the public interest, but their own, to the ruin of the public? that is, in short, to such as have no natural and just claim at all to tribute, custom, reverence, honor, and obedience? It is to be hoped that those who have any regard to the apostle's character as an inspired writer, or even as a man of common understanding, will not represent him as reasoning in such a loose incoherent manner; and drawing conclusions which have not the least relation to his premises. For what can be more absurd than an argument thus framed? "Rulers are, by their office, bound to consult the public welfare and the good of society: therefore you are bound to pay them tribute, to honor, and to submit to them, even when they destroy the public welfare, and are a common pest to society, by acting in direct contradiction to the nature and end of their office."

Thus, upon a careful review of the apostle's reasoning in this passage, it appears that his arguments to enforce submission, are of such a nature, as to conclude only in favour of submission *to such rulers as he himself describes*;

i.e. such as rule for the good of society, which is the only end of their institution. Common tyrants, and public oppressors, are not intitled to obedience from their subjects, by virtue of any thing here laid down by the inspired apostle.

I now add, farther, that the apostle's argument is so far from proving it to be the duty of people to obey, and submit to, such rulers as act in contradiction to the public good, and so to the design of their office, that it proves *the direct contrary*. For, please to observe, that if the end of all civil government, be the good of society; if this be the thing that is aimed at in constituting civil rulers; and if the motive and argument for submission to government, be taken from the apparent usefulness of civil authority; it follows, that when no such good end can be answered by submission, there remains no argument or motive to enforce it; if instead of this good end's being brought about by submission, a *contrary end* is brought about, and the ruin and misery of society effected by it, here is a plain and positive reason against submission in all such cases, should they ever happen. And therefore, in such cases, a regard to the public welfare, ought to make us with-hold from our rulers, that obedience and subjection which it would, otherwise, be our duty to render to them. If it be our duty, for example, to obey our king, merely for this reason, that he rules for the public welfare, (which is the only argument the apostle makes use of) it follows, by a parity of reason, that when he turns tyrant, and makes his subjects his prey to devour and to destroy, instead of his charge to defend and cherish, we are bound to throw off our allegiance to him, and to resist; and that according to the tenor of the apostle's argument in this passage. Not to discontinue our allegiance, in this case, would be to join with the sovereign in promoting the slavery and misery of that society, the welfare of which, we ourselves, as well as our sovereign, are indispensably obliged to secure and promote, as far as in us lies. It is true the apostle puts no case of such a tyrannical prince; but by his grounding his argument for submission wholly upon the good of civil society; it is plain he implicitly authorises, and even requires us to make resistance, whenever this shall be necessary to the public safety and happiness. Let me make use of this easy and familiar *similitude* to illustrate the point in hand—Suppose God requires a family of children, to obey their father and not to resist him and inforces his command with this argument; that the superintendence and care and authority of a just and kind parent, will contribute to the happiness of the whole family; so that they ought to obey him for their own sakes more than for his: Suppose this parent at length runs distracted, and attempts, in his mad fit, to cut all his children's throats: Now in this case, is not the reason before assigned, why these children should obey their parent while he continued of a sound mind, namely, *their common good*, a reason equally conclusive for disobeying and resisting him, since he is become delirious, and attempts their ruin? It makes no alteration in the argument, whether this parent, properly speaking, loses his reason; or does, while he retains his understanding, that which is as fatal in its consequences, as any thing he could do, were he really deprived of it.

LESSON PLAN: **From the Pulpit: The First Volley in War?**

Students analyze Jonathan Mayhew's sermon for its intent and potential influence on later thinkers.

Learning Objectives

Identify the influence of ideas in Mayhew's sermon; assess the sermon's significance in the context of 1750; formulate historical questions based on Mayhew's words; consider the multiple perspectives of religious groups in colonial society.

Materials: Jonathan Mayhew, *A Discourse Concerning Unlimited Submission and Non-Resistance to the Higher Powers* (1750); King James Bible, Romans 13:1–7; Elisha Williams, *The Essential Rights and Liberties of Protestants* (1744); Benjamin Colman, "Government the Pillar of the Earth" (1730).

Overview Questions

How does Saint Paul's letter to the Romans influence the content and structure of Mayhew's sermon? How did Mayhew address both religious and political concerns? In what ways did leaders in the American Revolution value the sermon? How does this sermon complement the views of Benjamin Colman and Elisha Williams?

Step 1: Comprehension Questions

How does Mayhew employ Paul's words to structure the sermon? Are there other ways in which Paul's words can be interpreted?

▶ **Activity:** Choose students to read aloud passages that cite Paul's words. Have students read and reconstruct the literal meaning of Mayhew's understanding of Paul. Discuss whether Paul can be understood in another way. Have students speculate on Mayhew's motives in citing Paul.

Step 2: Comprehension Questions

How did the date of Mayhew's sermon affect its theme and content? How does the sermon interweave religious and political themes?

▶ **Activity:** Discuss with students the sermon's historic context. Have students explain how Mayhew's implied attack on Charles I can apply to any government, and if that was Mayhew's intention. Discuss why an attack on Charles I is both political and religious in nature.

Step 3: Context Questions

What in the sermon leads some historians to call it the first volley in the American Revolution? How might Mayhew's sermon have affected pre-revolution thought?

▶ **Activity:** Have students cite specific passages that might have later reflected colonists' views on King George III and the British government. Have students reread the document imaginatively to test its potential as a rallying call to revolution.

Step 4: Exploration Questions

What collective rights are stated in the sermons of Mayhew and Benjamin Colman and in Elisha Williams's letter?

▶ **Activity:** Have students review the three works and list political and religious rights that each author argues for. Instruct students to compare their lists to documents that the Founding Fathers eventually drafted and to evaluate the potential influence of the ministers' words.

Step 5: Response Paper

Word length and additional requirements set by Instructor. Students answer the research question in the Overview Questions. Students state a thesis and use as evidence passages from the primary source document as well as support from supplemental materials assigned in the lesson.

NARRATIVES ON COLONIAL LIFE

Although the social structure of British America did not reproduce the formal divide between nobles and commoners that had existed in Europe since the Middle Ages, by the eighteenth century there was plenty of de-facto social inequality in the colonies—between landowners and laborers, men and women, and freemen and slaves, to name a few. Because, as the old adage says, history is written by the winners, we have mostly one side of this story—first-person historical accounts by educated white men. Comparatively few primary source documents from this time by women or poor people exist, so those that we have are noteworthy.

A few early eighteenth-century writings by women— all of them well-to-do—stand out as especially useful. From 1704 to 1705, Sarah Kemble Knight of Boston traveled on horseback to New York City and back—a remarkable feat for a woman of that time—and kept a journal of the whole trip, with detailed notes about the variations in manners and customs in the rural and urban areas she visited. *The Journal of Madam Knight*, as it was later published, has become an important source for observations on, particularly, race and class at this time in the history of British America.

Writing in another section of the colonies, Eliza Lucas held the remarkable status of a woman managing three South Carolina plantations while her father was out of the country and prior to her marriage. Her *Letters on Plantation Life* record the perspective of a privileged woman of the southern planter class who, in addition, had a profound influence on southern agriculture by proving that indigo, a plant valuable for making blue dye, could be profitably cultivated.

Yet a third example of women's writing in the early eighteenth century was the autobiography of Elizabeth Ashbridge, a woman who came to America from Great Britain as an indentured servant, became a Quaker, and composed her autobiography in the form of a conversion narrative, a fairly common autobiographical genre at the time. The work stands out as one of the few existing full autobiographies of a colonial American woman.

While Ashbridge successfully worked her way out of indentured servitude and into an active life as a member of a spiritual community, the experience of large numbers of Europeans who came to America as indentured servants—bound by contract to years of work to pay off the cost of their voyage from Europe—was not so successful. Again, the narrative of America as the land of opportunity was crafted largely by people who did experience success, since those who did not usually lacked the skills to record their stories. But one example of a counternarrative to the rags-to-riches tale comes from Gottlieb Mittelberger, a German who spent four years in Pennsylvania before returning to his homeland with sharp warnings about the hazards of indentured servitude. In Mittelberger's experience, many indentured servants died before their contracts were up, suffered terrible working conditions, and regretted ever leaving home.

No one narrative can ever tell the "story" of life in colonial America; the best a student of history can hope for is to get a multifaceted composite view from as large a variety of sources as possible.

Adam Groff, MA

■ The Journal of Madam Knight

Date: October 2, 1704–March 3, 1705
Author: Knight, Sarah Kemble
Genre: journal; autobiography; memoir

> *"But too Indulgent (especially ye farmers)*
> *to their slaves: sufering too great familiarity*
> *from them, permitting ym to sit at Table and*
> *eat with them . . . and into the dish goes the*
> *black hoof as freely as the white hand."*

Summary Overview

In the winter of 1704–5, Sarah Kemble Knight undertook a perilous journey from Boston to New Haven and New York City, presumably to settle the estate of a relative. As an experienced merchant, she traveled alone but hired guides along the way. In the Puritan tradition of journal keeping, she kept a diary of her journey, detailing both her travels and the people that she met along the way. She also noted the customs and curiosities of the communities in which she stayed. Not only is her journal an early example of women's travel writing, it also provides a window on American society in the early eighteenth century, including commentaries on gender, race, and class issues. It is also written in a comedic style that many readers find enjoyable and entertaining. Although not published for the general public until 1825, the journal has since become a standard text for students of colonial America.

Defining Moment

There are few examples of women's travel writing in early eighteenth-century America. Sarah Kemble Knight's extraordinary journey in the winter of 1704–5 represents a woman's voice and opinions at an important time in American history. It was a vastly delayed voice, however—her journal was published almost a century after she completed it, as part of a concerted movement by American publishers to uncover an authentic American voice in print. At this time, having lost the Revolutionary War, Britain was harsh in its criticism of the fledgling American national cultural identity. Even though Knight wrote her journal while America was still a British colony, it clearly showed the emerging culture of the new society. So it was that in 1825, Knight's first publisher, Theodore Dwight, found success in finding that authentic American voice.

What made Knight's writing so successful was not only its comedic tone and humorous anecdotes, but its detailing of a society in transition. It shone a bright light on America in the early eighteenth century, but not on its politics or intellectual or religious movements. Instead, Knight's journal focused on the everyday life of colonists. It dealt especially with the race, gender, and class issues of the day. The fact that three distinct races—white, black, and American Indian—interacted and coexisted at the time makes the journal an intriguing window on colonial society. Knight's observations on the hierarchies of race and class were especially enlightening, and as she placed herself within these societal rankings, the reader is able to grasp her opinions of those above her and, perhaps more interestingly, those below her. Her colorful descriptions of people she met in the country while on the road from Boston to New Haven engage the reader in a way that a drier form of historical narrative cannot. By viewing the world from a woman's eyes, what she chooses to describe is also distinct. Her merchant roots are noticeable too, and her detailed descriptions of the mechanics of trade in the New Haven area are understandable, given that she herself was a successful merchant in Boston. Her journal is also noticeably secular, with few religious references. Most important of all, Knight's journal is thoroughly entertaining and an excellent example of early American women's writing.

Author Biography

Sarah Kemble Knight was born on April 19, 1666, the daughter of Boston merchant Thomas Kemble and Elizabeth Trarice of Charlestown, Massachusetts. In 1688, she was betrothed and later married to the much older Richard Knight, whose work as a shipmaster and London agent for a company based in America took him away from home much of the time. They had one daughter, Elizabeth, who was born on May 8, 1689. Knight lived on Moon Street in Boston and, as head of the household in her husband's absence, was active in running many businesses. A literate woman, she taught handwriting; ran a boarding house, shop, and school; and worked as a court scrivener, copying out legal documents and thereby gaining some knowledge of the law.

Most assume that the purpose of Knight's trip was to help the widow of her cousin Caleb Trowbridge to settle his estate in New York City. However, William Learned, in his introduction to the 1865 edition, suggests it could have been to settle the estate of her brother John or that of her own husband, Richard. In any case, her legal expertise would have been an asset. Knight left Boston in October 1704, and as part of this journey, she kept a diary of her travels, now an historical document known as *The Journal of Madam Knight*. This was a private diary and not meant for publication. Indeed, it was not published during her lifetime, Knight was not known as an author while she was alive. The journey itself was a difficult one at that time, and she followed a route used mainly by postal riders. It was almost unheard of for a woman to undertake such a journey alone, and Knight relied on and hired a number of local guides to accompany her during various legs of her journey. As a decidedly urban Bostonian woman, traveling in rural areas was an eye-opener for her, and her comments are an interesting glimpse into the differences between urban and rural colonial America.

Knight returned to Boston in March 1705. There is no record of her husband in the journal after 1706, but it is unclear precisely when he died; her widowhood was recorded in the 1707 Boston census. She continued to run her businesses until 1713, when she went to live in the vicinity of Norwich and New London in Connecticut to be closer to her daughter and son-in-law. She died in 1727 and, as a testament to her success in business, left her daughter an estate worth approximately £1,800.

HISTORICAL DOCUMENT

Friday, Octor 6th. I got up very early, in Order to hire somebody to go with mee to New Haven, being in Great parplexity at the thoughts of proceeding alone; which my most hospitable entertainer observing, himselfe went, and soon return'd wth a young Gentleman of the town, who he could confide in to Go with mee; and about eight this morning, Wth Mr. Joshua Wheeler my new Guide, takeing leave of this worthy Gentleman, Wee advanced on towards Seabrook. The Rodes all along this way are very bad, Incumbred wth Rocks and mountainos passages, wch were very disagreeable to my tired carcass; but we went on with a moderate pace wel` made ye Journy more pleasent. But after about eight miles Rideing, in going over a Bridge under wch the River Run very swift, my hors stumbled, and very narrowly 'scaped falling over into the water; wch

extremely frightened mee. But through God's Goodness I met with no harm, and mounting agen, in about half a miles Rideing, come to an ordinary, were well entertained by a woman of about seventy and vantage, but of as Sound Intellectuals as one of seventeen. Shee entertain'd Mr. Wheeler wth some passages of a Wedding awhile ago at a place hard by, the Brides-Groom being about her Age or something above, Saying his Children was dredfully against their fathers marrying, wch shee condemned them extremly for.

From hence wee went pretty briskly forward, and arriv'd at Saybrook ferry about two of the Clock afternoon; and crossing it, wee call'd at an Inn to Bait, (foreseeing we should not have such another Opportunity till we come to Killingsworth.) Landlady come in, with her hair about her ears, and hands at full pay scratching. Shee told us shee had some mutton wch shee would broil, wch I was glad to hear; But I supose forgot to wash her scratchers; in a little time shee brot it in; but it being pickled, and my Guide said it smelt strong of head sause, we left it, and pd sixpence a piece for our Dinners, wch was only smell.

So wee putt forward with all speed, and about seven at night come to Killingsworth, and were tollerably well with Travillers fare, and Lodgd there that night.

Saturday, Oct. 7th, we sett out early in the Morning, and being something unaquainted wth the way, having ask't it of some wee mett, they told us wee must Ride a mile or two and turne down a Lane on the Right hand; and by their Direction wee Rode on but not Yet comeing to ye turning, we mett a Young fellow and ask't him how farr it was to the Lane which turn'd down towards Guilford. Hee said wee must Ride a little further, and turn down by the Corner of uncle Sams Lott. My Guide vented his Spleen at the Lubber; and we soon after came into the Rhode, and keeping still on, without any thing further Remarkabell, about two a clock afternoon we arrived at New Haven, where I was received with all Posible Respects and civility. Here I discharged Mr. Wheeler with a reward to his satisfaction, and took some time to rest after so long and toilsome a journey; And Inform'd myselfe of the manners and customs of the place, and at the same time employed myselfe in the afair I went there upon.

They are Govern'd by the same Laws as wee in Boston, (or little differing,) thr'out this whole Colony of Connecticot, And much the same way of Church Government, and many of them good, Sociable people, and I hope Religious too: but a little too much Independant in their principalls, and, as I have been told, were formerly in their Zeal very Riggid in their Administrations towards such as their Lawes made Offenders, even to a harmless Kiss or Innocent merriment among Young people. Whipping being a frequent and counted an easy Punishment, about wch as other Crimes, the judges were absolute in their Sentantes. They told mee a pleasant story about a pair of justices in those parts, wch I may not omit the relation of.

A negro Slave belonging to a man in ye Town, stole a hogs head from his master, and gave or sold it to an Indian, native of the place. The Indian sold it in the neighbourhood, and so the theft was found out. Thereupon the Heathen was Seized, and carried to the justices House to be Examined. But his worship (it seems) was gone into the feild, with a Brother in office, to gather in his Pompions. Whither the malefactor is hurried, And Complaint made, and satisfaction in the name of justice demanded. Their Worships cann't proceed in form without a Bench: whereupon they Order one to be Imediately erected, which, for want of fitter materials, they made with pompions—which being finished, down setts their Worships, and the Malefactor call'd, and by the Senior Justice Interrogated after the following manner. You Indian why did You steal from this man? You sho'dn't do so—it's a Grandy wicked thing to steal. Hol't Hol't, cryes justice Junr. Brother, You speak negro to him. I'le ask him. You sirrah, why did You steal this man's Hoggshead? Hoggshead? (replys the Indian,) me no stomany. No? says his Worship; and pulling off his hatt, Patted his own head with his hand, sais, Tatapa-You, Tatapa-you; all one this. Hoggshead all one this. Hah! says Netop, now me stomany that. Whereupon the Company fell into a great fitt of Laughter, even to Roreing. Silence is comanded, but to no effect: for they continued perfectly Shouting. Nay, sais his worship, in an angry tone, if it be so, take mee off the Bench.

Their Diversions in this part of the Country are on Lecture days and Training days mostly: on the former there is Riding from town to town.

And on training dayes The Youth divert themselves by Shooting at the Target, as they call it, (but it very much resembles a pillory,) where hee that hitts neerest the white has some yards of Red Ribbin presented him, Wch being tied to his hattband, the two ends streeming down his back, he is Led away in Triumph, wth great applause, as the winners of the Olympiack Games. They generally marry very young: the males oftener as I am told under twentie than above; they generally make public wedings, and have a way something singular (as they say) in some of them, viz. Just before Joyning hands the Bridegroom quitts the place, who is soon followed by the Bridesmen, and as it were, dragg'd back to duty—being the reverse to ye former practice among us, to steal ma Pride.

There are great plenty of Oysters all along by the sea side, as farr as I Rode in the Collony, and those very good. And they Generally lived very well and comfortably in their famelies. But too Indulgent (especially ye farmers) to their slaves: sufering too great familiarity from them, permitting ym to sit at Table and eat with them, (as they say to save time,) and into the dish goes the black hoof as freely as the white hand. They told me that there was a farmer lived nere the Town where I lodgd who had some difference Wth his slave, concerning something the master had promised him and did not punctualy perform; wch caused some hard words between them; But at length they put the matter to Arbitration and Bound themselves to stand to the award of such as they named— wch done, the Arbitrators Having heard the Allegations of both parties, Order the master to pay 40' to black face, and acknowledge his fault. And so the matter ended: the poor master very honestly standing to the award.

There are every where in the Towns as I passed, a Number of Indians the Natives of the Country, and are the most salvage of all the salvages of that kind that I had ever Seen: little or no care taken (as I heard upon enquiry) to make them otherwise. They have in some places Landes of their owne, and Govern'd by Law's of their own making; they marry many wives and at pleasure put them away, and on the ye least dislike or fickle humour, on either side, saying stand away to one another is a sufficient Divorce. And indeed those uncomely Stand sways are too much in Vougue among the English in this (Indulgent Colony) as their Records plentifully prove, and that on very trivial matters, of which some have been told me, but are not proper to be Related by a Female pen, tho some of that foolish sex have had too large a share in the story.

If the natives committ any crime on their own precincts among themselves, ye English takes no Cognezens of. But if on the English ground, they are punishable by our Laws. They mourn for their Dead by blacking their faces, and cutting their hair, after an Awkerd and frightfull manner; But can't bear You should mention the names of their dead Relations to them: they trade most for Rum, for wch theyd hazzard their very lives; and the English fit them Generally as well by seasoning it plentifully with water.

They give the title of merchant to every trader; who Rate their Goods according to the time and spetia they pay in: viz. Pay, mony, Pay as mony, and trusting. Pay is Grain, Pork, Beef, & c. at the prices sett by the General Court that Year; mony is pieces of Eight, Ryalls, or Boston or Bay shillings (as they call them,) or Good hard money, as sometimes silver coin is termed by them; also Wampom, vizt. Indian beads wch serves for change. Pay as mony is provisions, as aforesd one Third cheaper then as the Assembly or Gene' Court sets it; and Trust as they and the mercht agree for time.

Now, when the buyer comes to ask for a comodity, sometimes before the merchant answers that he has it, he sais, is Your pay redy? Perhaps the Chap Reply's Yes: what do You pay in? say's the merchant. The buyer having answered, then the price is set; as suppose he wants a sixpenny knife, in pay it is 12d-in pay as money eight pence, and hard money its own price, viz. 6d. It seems a very Intricate way of trade and what Lex Mercatoria had not thought of.

Being at a merchants house, in comes a tall country fellow, wth his alfogeos full of Tobacco; for they seldom Loose their Cudd, but keep Chewing and Spitting as long as they'r eyes are open,—he advanc't to the midle of the Room, makes an Awkward Nodd, and spitting a Large deal of Aromatick Tincture, he gave a scrape with his shovel like shoo, leaving a small shovel full of dirt on the floor, made a full stop, Hugging his own pretty Body with his hands under his arms, Stood staring rown'd him, like a Catt let out of a Baskett. At last, like the creature Balaam Rode on, he opened his mouth and said: have You any Ribinen for Hatbands to sell I pray? The Questions and Answers about the pay being past, the Ribin is bro't and opened. Bumpkin Simpers, cryes its confounded Gay I vow; and beckning to the door, in comes Jone Tawdry, dropping about 50 curtsees, and stands by him: hee shows her the Ribin. Law, You, sais shee, its right Gent, do You, take it, tis dreadfull pretty. Then she enquires, have You any hood silk I pray? wch being brought and bought, Have You any thred silk to sew it wth, says shee, wch being accomodated wth they Departed. They Generaly stand after they come in a great while speachless, and sometimes dont say a word till they are askt what they want, which I Impute to the Awe they stand in of the merchants, who they are constantly almost Indebted too; and must take what they bring without Liberty to choose for themselves; but they serve them as well, making the merchants stay long enough for their pay . . .

GLOSSARY

alfogeos: either saddlebags (from Spanish "alforja") or wallets (from Portuguese "alforges"); here, a slang term for "cheeks"

bait: to feed and water horses

hogshead: wooden barrel; cask of liquor

lex mercatoria: Latin for "merchant law"

like the creature Balaam rode on: like a donkey that could speak

lubber: a big, clumsy fellow

me no stomany: colloquial for "I don't understand"

netop: friend, which came to be a generic term meaning "Indian"

pompion: pumpkin

tatapa-you: colloquial for "I cannot tell you"

vented his spleen: expressed his anger

wampum: traditional sacred shell beads of some American Indian tribes, sometimes used as an early form of currency

Document Analysis

Sarah Kemble Knight's journal is among the few examples of women's writing from the American colonial period. Her record of her five-month journey from her home in Boston to New Haven and on to New York provides an excellent insight into the social history of the early eighteenth century. Social history focuses on the lives and activities of ordinary people, as opposed to political history, which is concerned with political events, ideas, movements, and leaders. The journal also lies within the genre of women's history, which tries to uncover the often unwritten and undocumented lives of women.

This work was never intended for a wide audience. In fact, it may never have been meant for anyone but Knight herself, as her journal was not published in her lifetime. Rather, it was first put into print in 1825, almost a hundred years after she died. If she meant it for anyone, most likely it would have been to regale a small circle of friends back in Boston, most likely women of her own class and station.

In direct opposition to the Puritan writing style of the period, Knight wrote in a secular, comedic style, which was much more akin to a travelogue or diary than any kind of religious sermon. Many writers have described her style as "picaresque," which describes an early form of Spanish novel that has a roguish protagonist who goes on episodic adventures. As a merchant herself, she seemed particularly interested in the mechanics of trade outside of Boston. Her observations focus mainly on manners, dress, language, and behavior. It is also obvious from her journal that she was an educated woman, as she made allusions to the Bible and the Olympics.

Her description of rural areas, or perhaps better, the colonial American wilderness, is one of the defining features of the journal. More than once, she described dangerous situations and the fact that she was scared for her life. Sometime during October 6, she stated that "my hors stumbled, and very narrowly 'scaped falling over into the water." In fact, colonial roads in this period were still little more than postal trails. On the way to Seabrook, she described them as follows: "Rodes all along this way are very bad, Incumbred wth Rocks and mountainos passages."

A woman traveling alone was a rarity in colonial America, and Kemble was forced to hire local male guides to assist her with her travels. The beginning of the document starts with Knight staying at an inn and having the owner go out to find a guide for her. Despite this, Knight was far from being dependent on her husband. As her husband, Richard, was so often away on business, it gave Knight the opportunity to act as the de facto head of household, or a kind of deputy-husband. In this capacity, she seemed quite happy to undertake a voyage that was unusual for a woman of her time and place.

Race was also a key theme in Knight's writings. As a white woman, she had a certain standing in society and this meant she felt superior to blacks and American Indians. As Massachusetts had legalized slavery in 1641, the first American colony to do so, Knight was well aware of black slaves. She also seemed to be aware of American Indians. Far from being rigid, Knight's version of race relations shows that there was considerable fluidity and flexibility between the races, especially outside of the major urban centers.

There are numerous episodes in her narrative that shed light on race relations in colonial America. The first is a story she shared after she heard it from people she met in New Haven that includes all three races. After a black slave stole a cask of liquor from his white master, he then sold it to an American Indian, who sold the liquor in the neighborhood. It was the Indian, however, who was arrested and brought to justice. Justice, it seems, was mobile and happened wherever and whenever it was needed. As the judge was tending his pumpkins in a field with a fellow judge, the American Indian was brought to them in the field. Justice could not be served, however, without a bench, and so a temporary one was quickly made out of the pumpkins themselves, which shows that justice could also be cleverly improvised. When the American Indian appeared before the judges, an interesting interchange ensued. The junior judge chastised the first judge for speaking "negro" to the defendant ("Grandy wicked thing to steal"). The second judge tried to speak to the defendant in his own language ("me no stomany" and "tatapa-you"), but this backfired on the poor judge. The American Indian, by agreeing with the judge's comparison of a cask of liquor to a human head, inadvertently implied that the judge was a drunkard and resembles a hog. The saga ends with the assembled crowd roaring with laughter and the humiliated judge threatening to resign. Knight often used this theme of humiliating people in power as a comedic device, and it emphasizes Knight's own flexibility of opinion when it comes to class when it suits her. The judge deserved respect as a higher class of townsperson, but Knight seemed happy to recount his embarrassment.

The second episode involved a black slave who had a disagreement with his master. Apparently, the master had broken his promise to the slave to do some service and so the slave complained. After an argument between the two ("hard words"), they agreed to put the disagreement to arbitration and abide by the decision of the arbitrators. The arbitrators sided with the slave and ordered the owner to pay forty shillings to his slave, which the owner did. This again shows that relations between races were not rigid and that black slaves could and did appeal to the authorities for justice. Knight, however, referred to the slave as "black face," betraying her own feeling of superiority.

Just prior to describing the above dispute between the slave and his master, Knight mentioned a tradition that truly demonstrated differences that she saw between race relations in the country and those in the city. In describing the customs of the colony of Connecticut she noted that white people (especially farmers) and black people were quite familiar with each other, to the point that they often ate at the same table together. Knight found this quite objectionable, as her choice of words indicates: "permitting ym to sit at Table and eat with them, (as they say to save time,) and into the dish goes the black hoof as freely as the white hand." By using the word "hoof" to indicate a black hand, she effectively equated black people with animals and revealed her prejudice. In early eighteenth-century Massachusetts and Connecticut, slavery was legal, but it was still not as common as it was later in the century. Nevertheless, in Knight's mind, the hierarchy between the races was already quite clear.

Knight next provided her observations on American Indians in the area. She noted that they are quite savage and that "little or no care taken (as I heard upon enquiry) to make them otherwise." This could have been slightly surprising to her, as she may have expected someone to try to convert them to Christianity. Once again, however, she was not explicit in stating this and remained more concerned with their secular customs. She was aware that they had their own lands and laws, but that did not make her sympathetic to them. She next described their marriage customs, saying that the men could have many wives but could easily divorce them by "saying stand away to one another." Curiously, Knight then went on to chide the colonists of Connecticut for imitating American Indian divorce customs. Again, her judgmental side surfaced when she said that these types of divorces were in vogue among the colonists too and that divorce was possible for trivial matters. She went on to note that women were often the ones who wanted the divorce.

Knight then wrote that if American Indians committed crimes on their lands, they were to dispense their own judgment, but if they committed crimes on English lands, they were subject to English laws, as demonstrated in the case of the man caught selling stolen liquor. Their mourning rituals were also a cause for emphasis, with the Indians "blacking their faces, and cutting their hair," which Knight found both frightening and odd. She revealed her merchant roots, however, when she described their love of rum. She added that the English watered down the rum they sold to them.

Class and social hierarchy are important themes throughout her journal. As Knight was a merchant-class white woman, she held a certain position in society. She mentioned those of a lower class in less than glowing terms. As a Bostonian, she was used to a certain level of manners and courtesy, and as she traveled in the country, she found, often to her dismay, that there was a different code of behavior. Her description of people of lesser standing is often colorful and always judgmental. When she and her guide Mr. Wheeler stopped at an inn to eat, the landlady arrived with "her hair about her ears, and hands at full pay scratching." Note also Knight's use of a merchant term ("at full pay") here. Although the landlady said she had some mutton, when the meal arrived, the meat was pickled and rancid. So the two had to pay for a meal that they never ate and "was only smell." Being bested economically by a woman of lower class must have bothered Knight.

When she finally arrived in New Haven, Knight was greeted "with all Possible Respects and civility." As an urban center, New Haven represented a more comfortable setting for Knight. Still, she was aware that New Haven was not Boston, and so she "Inform'd myselfe of the manners and customs of the place."

Part of these customs was what Knight described as the residents' "diversions," or recreational activities. She spoke of training days and lecture days, during which Puritan preachers or judges would often give a

lecture in the church around midday. This meant that many town residents would take time off and enjoy themselves on such days, many riding from town to town. Knight next discussed youth sporting activities and marriage customs. Target shooting was described, with ribbons given to the winners, and then Knight talked about the young age at which the men in particular married. Most were married while under twenty, which Knight considered "very young." In another tradition she described, the groom's friends carried him off before he finally committed to the bride, which was the opposite of a former Boston tradition where the bride was taken away.

It was only natural that Knight, herself a merchant, would be interested in customs surrounding trade and commerce. She was attentive to how people pay for goods in New Haven, and detailed four distinct types of payments: pay, money, pay as money, and trusting. Pay was a type of barter arrangement, with values set annually by the General Court of New Haven. A person would offer a certain amount of another commodity in exchange for their desired product. Currency in the form of coins was also accepted. There was no national currency or even a unified colonial currency at this time, and values fluctuated between various European coins or coins from different colonies. Paper money was printed in large quantities, increasing inflation, and thus widely mistrusted as worthless. "Wampom," or wampum, referred to local American Indian shell beads that the English often used as currency. In New Haven, it seemed they were used as smaller denominations as change for transactions. Pay as money was another form of bartering, but the commodity was valued at a cheaper rate ("one Third cheaper") than the General Court's annual rate. Finally, New Haven merchants also extended credit ("trusting") to their customers on a case-by-case basis.

Knight then described the process of purchasing. The first things to be decided were whether the purchaser had the means to make the purchase ("You pay redy?") and then the type of payment. After that, and depending on the type of payment, a price was set. Knight gave an excellent example of the differing prices that a knife could have depending on the type of payment to be made: "as suppose he wants a sixpenny knife, in pay it is 12d [pence]-in pay as money eight pence, and hard money its own price, viz. 6d [pence]." Knight's mention that this was a "very Intricate way of trade," not what "Lex Mercatoria," or "merchant law," intended points to the fact that trade in Boston was conducted quite differently, and in her eyes, it was simpler and better there.

Having discussed merchant trade in general terms, Knight then gave another of her colorful anecdotes to further illustrate her point that trade was different in New Haven. Again, her sense of Bostonian superiority is evident in her description of a country fellow coming to buy something from a merchant. She described him with his cheeks ("alfogeos") full of chewing tobacco, which she equated to chewing his cud like a cow. As with race, she referred to a human as an animal when making a point about someone from a lower class. She noted that people from the country such as this fellow chewed and spat tobacco all day "as long as they'r eyes are open." She was entertained by his actions during the delay before he asked the merchant for anything. She almost reveled in describing his discomfort, as he spat his "Aromatick Tincture" on the floor, kicked at the floor, and finally "Hugging his own pretty Body with his hands under his arms, Stood staring rown'd him, like a Catt let out of a Baskett." She again used animal symbols—here, a cat, and then later the biblical donkey that could talk. Knight referred to the fellow as "Bumpkin Simpers," no doubt to reinforce his country origins, and to his female friend who eventually joined him as "Jone Tawdry," a jibe at her lower-class status. Knight was clear that this woman was beneath her own station, as she used exaggeration when she came into the store, recounting that she dropped "about 50 curtsees." She ended this episode and the excerpt with the observation that people in New Haven held merchants in high esteem, most likely because they were always indebted to them.

Essential Themes

Although Sarah Kemble Knight's journal touches on various themes, such as travel in the colonial wilderness and women in colonial America, the two essential themes of this excerpt of her journal are race and class issues in early eighteenth century. Knight's journal contrasts sharply with the captivity narrative of Mary Rowlandson, published in 1682. Rowlandson was taken captive by American Indians during King Philip's War, and her experiences as captive unquestionably informed the observations of race in her writing. Rowlandson's writing is also much more religious and deals with an interior spiritual journey. In contrast, Knight's writing is far more secular and comedic in tone. Race in the early colonial period was a diverse mix of white, black, and American Indian, and Knight highlighted the everyday interchanges that occurred between the races. This is important information, as it is a first-person account of these relationships and therefore the journal represents an important primary historical document.

The second main theme of Knight's journal excerpt is class, particularly the difference between urban and country manners and behavior. She was a keen observer of details, and by framing country people as simple and somewhat backward, she made it clear where she felt her place was in the class hierarchy of colonial America—that is, always above the country folk she met. As a member of the merchant class, she was also interested in the customs of trade and negotiation outside of Boston. Her firsthand account has been helpful to historians in their reconstructions of the regional variations in such customs.

Knight's short-term influence may not have gone beyond her close circle of merchant friends in Boston. Her own life, beyond this five-month period in the winter of 1704–5, was of little significance otherwise. Her legacy was, to a great extent, her very normalcy. It allowed her to comment on and record normal everyday activities and events. By the time Knight's journal was published in 1825, it found many appreciative readers. Since then, students of American history have turned to Sarah Kemble Knight and her travel journal to provide a captivating account of the colonial wilderness and the customs of colonial New Haven and New York.

Lee Tunstall, PhD

Bibliography

Balkun, Mary McAleer. "Sarah Kemble Knight and the Construction of the American Self." *Women's Studies* 28.1 (1998): 7–27. Print.

Bush, Sargent, Jr. "The Journal of Madam Knight." Introduction. *Journeys in New Worlds, Early American Women's Narratives.* Ed. William L. Andrews, Sargent Bush Jr., Annette Kolodny, Amy Schrager Lang, and Daniel B. Shea. Madison: U. of Wisconsin P, 1990. 69–83. Print.

Knight, Sarah Kemble. *The Private Journal of a Journey from Boston to New York in the Year 1704.* Ed. William L. Learned. Albany: Little, 1865. Print.

Michaelsen, Scott. "Narrative and Class in a Culture of Consumption: The Significance of Stories in Sarah Kemble Knight's *Journal*." *College Literature* 21.2 (1994): 33–46. Print.

Stern, Julia. "To Relish and to Spew Disgust as Cultural Critique in 'The Journal of Madam Knight.'" *Legacy: A Journey of American Women Writers* 14 (1997): 1–12. Print.

Additional Reading

Andrews, William L., et al., eds. *Journeys to New Worlds: Early American Women's Narratives*. Madison: U. of Wisconsin P, 1990. Print.

Imbarrato, Susan Clair. *Traveling Women: Narrative Visions of Early America*. Athens: Ohio UP, 2006. Print.

Radzinowicz, M. A., ed. *American Colonial Prose: John Smith to Thomas Jefferson*. Cambridge: Cambridge UP, 1984. Print.

Rowlandson, Mary, et al. *Colonial American Travel Narratives*. Ed. Wendy Martin. New York: Penguin, 1994. Print.

"Sarah Kemble Knight: Remarks on 'this whole Colony of Connecticut.'" *Becoming American: The British Atlantic Colonies, 1690–1763*. National Humanities Center, Sept. 2009. Web. 12 Mar. 2012.

Stanford, Ann. "Three Puritan Women: Anne Bradstreet, Mary Rowlandson, and Sarah Kemble Knight." *American Women Writers: Bibliographical Essays*. Ed. Maurice Duke, Jackson R. Bryer, and M. Thomas Inge. Westport: Greenwood, 1983. 3–20. Print.

LESSON PLAN: **Madam Knight's View on New York Life**

Students analyze Madame Knight's journal and collaborate in formulating opinions about the value of her insights both in 1705 and today.

Learning Objectives

Evaluate Knight's point of view; draw comparisons across regions; read the historical narrative imaginatively; draw comparisons across eras.

Materials: Sarah Kemble Knight, *The Journal of Madam Knight* (1704–1705); Roger Williams, *A Key into the Language of America* (1643).

Overview Questions

In her journal, what insights about American life does Knight offer? What does the journal suggest about colonial America's sense of nationhood? How can we judge what Knight's "pleasant story" reveals about race relations in 1705? In what ways does the journal compare with Roger Williams's *A Key into the Language of America*?

Step 1: Comprehension Questions

How is the journal different from most primary documents? How does Knight's uniqueness shape the content and value of her observations?

▶ **Activity:** Ask students to choose and read aloud interesting passages and to explain why they chose them. Discuss with students how they would characterize Knight's opinions. Have students discuss how her words alter the view of early colonial days and the role of women.

Step 2: Context Questions

What would the journal tell colonists living in Massachusetts about the colony of New York? How is the journal like early reports from European explorers about America?

▶ **Activity:** Have students list examples of descriptions of New Yorkers and their habits. Discuss why Knight chose to describe these things. Discuss what the travel-guide aspect of the journal suggests about America in 1705. Discuss how the journal parallels journals from one hundred years earlier.

Step 3: Context Questions

What is the literal meaning of the "pleasant story" about enslaved African Americans? What does the telling of it suggest about Knight?

▶ **Activity:** Have students retell the "pleasant story." Note the meanings of certain words in the passage: *pompions,* pumpkins or squash; *stomay,* understand; *Netop,* friend. Have students explain who the butt of the joke is. Discuss with students what the telling of the story reveals about Knight's attitudes toward others.

Step 4: Exploration Questions

What do the journal and *A Key into the Language of America* have in common? What changes from the mid-seventeenth century to 1702 may have made Williams's book less relevant?

▶ **Activity:** Discuss *A Key* and its similarities to Knight's journal. Have students discuss whether Williams's guide would have been useful to Knight. Discuss which document would have been most valuable to Knight's contemporary New Englanders and why.

Step 5: Response Paper

Word length and additional requirements set by Instructor. Students answer the research question in the Overview Questions. Students state a thesis and use as evidence passages from the primary source document as well as support from supplemental materials assigned in the lesson.

■ History of the Dividing Line: Run in the Year 1728

Date: 1728
Author: Byrd II, William
Genre: report

> *"This modish frenzy being still more inflamed*
> *by the charming account given of Virginia,*
> *by the first adventurers, made many fond*
> *of removing to such a paradise."*

Summary Overview

In 1728, the Virginia landowner and public official William Byrd, II, was part of a team, including commissioners, surveyors, and laborers, that was assigned to draw the boundary line between the colonies of Virginia and North Carolina. *The History of the Dividing Line*, which circulated in manuscript for many years before being printed long after Byrd's death, was his "official" account of the events of the expedition, written for his fellow members of the Virginia elite. (Byrd also wrote another unpublished book on the expedition, *Secret History of the Dividing Line*, which covered the same series of events but was much more satirical and mocking, particularly on the subject of the North Carolinian commissioners' adventures and misadventures.) This section is from the introduction, which puts the expedition in context by giving a Virginia-centered account of the history of English settlement in North America.

Defining Moment

Byrd was writing at a time when the society of tidewater Virginia, based on large, slave-worked tobacco plantations, had been fully formed. The planter elite, of which Byrd was a leading member, had great wealth and a firm grip on public office, and though still subordinate within the British Empire, they controlled Virginia, then a much larger territory than the current state of Virginia. Men of Byrd's class, who derived their wealth and power from their ownership of land, viewed themselves as part of the same class as the "gentlemen" of England (who also derived their wealth and status from the control of land), and many, like Byrd, were educated in England and traveled across the Atlantic frequently as young men.

Although the major conflicts with American Indians were over in Virginia, English colonists in North America could not feel altogether secure. Despite its defeat in the War of the Spanish Succession, France, with control of what is now Canada and much of the North American interior, remained a powerful rival for control of the continent. One French advantage was better relations with American Indians, who furnished useful military auxiliaries as well as contributing to the Franco-American economy as fur trappers. The French menace was religious as well as political and military, as the French were Roman Catholics in contrast to the predominantly Protestant British settlers and French Catholic missionaries were having more success converting American Indians than were Protestant British ones.

The early eighteenth century when Byrd was writing was the time of the Enlightenment, a time when intellectual life and categories of thought in Europe and its colonies were growing more rational and secular. The view of history as a record of the unfolding of God's divine providence was becoming more marginalized in favor of an emphasis on material forces. Although the Enlightenment took some time to move from its centers in Europe to the colonies, by Byrd's time, Enlightenment ways of thinking were having an increasing influence on educated Americans like Byrd, who was steeped in the culture of the English

William Byrd II. (Virginia Historical Society)

legislature, the House of Burgesses. Born in Virginia on March 28, 1674, William Byrd II spent most of his youth in England, being educated and dabbling in science and the theater. Like many landowners in England and its colonies, he studied law in London and became an attorney, although not a very successful one. He went to Virginia in 1696 but returned to England the next year. He moved to Virginia in 1705, after the death of his father, but continued to travel back and forth across the Atlantic until 1726 when he settled permanently in Virginia. Byrd keenly felt his isolation from London and continued to correspond with people in England, sending British scientists natural history specimens from America. He built one of the great private libraries of colonial America in part to recreate the intellectual world of the capital at his rural tidewater estate. Despite his success as a landowner, he was hobbled by debt for much of his career.

As a prominent Virginia landowner, Byrd served in public offices, some lucrative, some not. In 1728, Byrd served with six others on a commission to draw a boundary line between Virginia and North Carolina. The commission, along with their crew, traced a line from the Currituck inlet on the Atlantic coast to Peters Creek, 242 miles away. The expedition was the subject of two works by Byrd, *The History of the Dividing Line: Run in the Year 1728* (1841) and *The Secret History of the Dividing Line* (1929), neither of which was published in Byrd's lifetime. Byrd was a strong believer in the further economic development of Virginia. In addition to *The History* and *The Secret History*, Byrd's other works include two other manuscript travel accounts, *A Journey to the Land of Eden* (1841), and *A Progress to the Mines* (1841). A version of *A Journey to the Land of Eden* was published anonymously in German, in Bern, Switzerland, with hopes of attracting Swiss-German settlers to Virginia with an account of Virginia's riches. He helped establish the site for the city of Richmond that became Virginia's capital.

upper classes. It was also a time when fluent and witty writing was considered a social and cultural asset for a gentleman like Byrd, although the role of professional writer was considered inappropriate. Circulation of works in manuscript, as Byrd circulated his histories of the dividing line, and anonymous publication were quite common.

Author Biography

William Byrd II was a member of both one of the great land- and slave-owning families of Virginia and an Anglo-American transatlantic social and cultural elite. His father, William Byrd, had emigrated from England to found a plantation and serve several terms in Virginia's

HISTORICAL DOCUMENT

BEFORE I enter upon the journal of the line between Virginia and North Carolina, it will be necessary to clear the way to it, by showing how the other British colonies on the Main have, one after another, been carved out of Virginia, by grants from his majesty's royal predecessors. All that part of the northern American continent now under the dominion of the king of Great Britain, and stretching quite as far as the cape of Florida, went at first under the general name of Virginia.

The only distinction, in those early days, was, that all the coast to the southward of Chesapeake bay was called South Virginia, and all to the northward of it, North Virginia.

The first settlement of this fine country was owing to that great ornament of the British nation, sir Walter Raleigh, who obtained a grant thereof from queen Elizabeth of ever-glorious memory, by letters patent, dated March the 25th, 1584.

But whether that gentleman ever made a voyage thither himself is uncertain; because those who have favoured the public with an account of his life mention nothing of it. However, thus much may be depended on, that sir Walter invited sundry persons of distinction to share in his charter, and join their purses with his in the laudable project of fitting out a colony to Virginia.

Accordingly, two ships were sent away that very year, under the command of his good friends Amidas and Barlow, to take possession of the country in the name of his royal mistress, the queen of England.

These worthy commanders, for the advantage of the trade winds, shaped their course first to the Charibbe islands, thence stretching away by the gulf of Florida, dropped anchor not far from Roanoke inlet. They ventured ashore near that place upon an island now called Colleton island, where they set up the arms of England, and claimed the adjacent country in right of their sovereign lady, the queen; and this ceremony being duly performed, they kindly invited the neighbouring Indian to traffick with them.

These poor people at first approached the English with great caution, having heard much of the treachery of the Spaniards, and not knowing but these strangers might be as treacherous as they. But, at length, discovering a kind of good nature in their looks, they ventured to draw near, and barter their skins and furs for the bawbles and trinkets of the English.

These first adventurers made a very profitable voyage, raising at least a thousand per cent. upon their cargo. Amongst other Indian commodities, they brought over some of that bewitching vegetable, tobacco. And this being the first that ever came to England, sir Walter thought he could do no less than make a present of some of the brightest of it to his royal mistress, for her own smoking. The queen graciously accepted of it, but finding her stomach sicken after two or three whiffs, it was presently whispered by the earl of Leicester's faction, that sir Walter had certainly poisoned her. But her majesty soon recovering her disorder, obliged the countess of Nottingham and all her maids to smoke a whole pipe out amongst them.

As it happened some ages before to be the fashion to saunter to the Holy Land, and go upon other Quixote adventures, so it was now grown the humour to take a trip to America. The Spaniards had lately discovered rich mines in their part of the West Indies, which made their maritime neighbours eager to do so too. This modish frenzy being still more inflamed by the charming account given of Virginia, by the first adventurers, made many fond of removing to such a paradise.

Happy was he, and still happier she, that could get themselves transported, fondly expecting their coarsest utensils, in that happy place, would be of massy silver.

This made it easy for the company to procure as many volunteers as they wanted for their new colony; but, like most other undertakers who have no assistance from the public, they starved the design by too much frugality; for, unwilling to launch out at first into too much expense, they shipped off but few people at a time, and those but scantily provided. The adventurers were, besides, idle and extravagant, and expected they might live without work in so plentiful a country.

These wretches were set ashore not far from Roanoke inlet, but by some fatal disagreement, or laziness, were either starved or cut to pieces by the Indians.

Several repeated misadventures of this kind did, for some time, allay the itch of sailing to this new world;

but the distemper broke out again about the year 1606. Then it happened that the earl of Southampton and several other persons, eminent for their quality and estates, were invited into the company, who applied themselves once more to people the then almost abandoned colony. For this purpose they embarked about a hundred men, most of them reprobates of good families, and related to some of the company, who were men of quality and fortune.

The ships that carried them made a shift to find a more direct way to Virginia, and ventured through the capes into the bay of Chesapeake. The same night they came to an anchor at the mouth of Powhatan, the same as James river, where they built a small fort at a place called Point Comfort.

This settlement stood its ground from that time forward in spite of all the blunders and disagreement of the first adventurers, and the many calamities that befel the colony afterwards.*

* The six gentlemen who were first named of the company by the crown, and who were empowered to choose an annual president from among themselves, were always engaged in factions and quarrels, while the rest detested work more than famine. At this rate the colony must have come to nothing, had it not been for the vigilance and bravery of captain Smith, who struck a terror into all the Indians round about. This gentleman took some pains to persuade the men to plant Indian corn, but they looked upon all labour as a curse. They chose rather to depend upon the musty provisions that were sent from England: and when they failed they were forced to take more pains to seek for wild fruits in the woods, than they would have taken in tilling the ground. Besides, this exposed them to be knocked on the head by the Indians, and gave them fluxes into the bargain, which thinned the plantation very much. To supply this mortality, they were reinforced the year following with a greater number of people, amongst which were fewer gentlemen and more labourers, who, however, took care not to kill themselves with work.

These found the first adventurers in a very starving condition, but relieved their wants with the fresh supply they brought with them. From Kiquotan they extended themselves as far as James-town, where, like true Englishmen, they built a church that cost no more than fifty pounds, and a tavern that cost five hundred.

They had now made peace with the Indians, but there was one thing wanting to make that peace lasting. The natives could, by no means, persuade themselves that the English were heartily their friends, so long as they disdained to intermarry with them. And, in earnest, had the English consulted their own security and the good of the colony--had they intended either to civilize or convert these gentiles, they would have brought their stomachs to embrace this prudent alliance.

The Indians are generally tall and well-proportioned, which may make full amends for the darkness of their complexions. Add to this, that they are healthy and strong, with constitutions untainted by lewdness, and not enfeebled by luxury. Besides, morals and all considered, I cannot think the Indians were much greater heathens than the first adventurers, who, had they been good Christians, would have had the charity to take this only method of converting the natives to Christianity. For, after all that can be said, a sprightly lover is the most prevailing missionary that can be sent amongst these, or any other infidels.

Besides, the poor Indians would have had less reason to complain that the English took away their land, if they had received it by way of portion with their daughters. Had such affinities been contracted in the beginning, how much bloodshed had been prevented, and how populous would the country have been, and, consequently, how considerable? Nor would the shade of the skin have been any reproach at this day; for if a Moor may be washed white in three generations, surely an Indian might have been blanched in two.

The French, for their parts, have not been so squeamish in Canada, who upon trial find abundance of attraction in the Indians. Their late grand monarch thought it not below even the dignity of a Frenchman to become one flesh with this people, and therefore ordered 100 livres for any of his subjects, man or woman, that would intermarry with a native.

By this piece of policy we find the French interest very much strengthened amongst the savages, and their religion, such as it is, propagated just as far as their love. And I heartily wish this well-concerted scheme does not hereafter give the French an advantage over his majesty's good subjects on the northern continent of America.

About the same time New England was pared off from Virginia by letters patent, bearing date April the

10th, 1608. Several gentlemen of the town and neighborhood of Plymouth obtained this grant, with the lord chief justice Popham at their head.

Their bounds were specified to extend from 38 to 45 degrees of northern latitude, with a breadth of one hundred miles from the sea shore. The first fourteen years, this company encountered many difficulties, and lost many men, though far from being discouraged, they sent over numerous recruits of presbyterians, every year, who for all that, had much ado to stand their ground, with all their fighting and praying.

But about the year 1620, a large swarm of dissenters fled thither from the severities of their stepmother, the church. These saints conceiving the same aversion to the copper complexion of the natives, with that of the first adventurers to Virginia, would, on no terms, contract alliances with them, afraid perhaps, like the Jews of old, lest they might be drawn into idolatry by those strange women.

Whatever disgusted them I cannot say, but this false delicacy creating in the Indians a jealousy that the English were ill affected towards them, was the cause that many of them were cut off, and the rest exposed to various distresses.

This reinforcement was landed not far from cape Cod, where, for their greater security, they built a fort, and near it a small town, which, in honour of the proprietors, was called New Plymouth. But they still had many discouragements to struggle with, though, by being well supported from home, they by degrees triumphed over them all.

Their brethren, after this, flocked over so fast, that in a few years they extended the settlement one hundred miles along the coast, including Rhode Island and Martha's Vineyard.

Thus the colony throve apace, and was thronged with large detachments of independents and presbyterians, who thought themselves persecuted at home.

GLOSSARY

Charibbe: Caribbean

gentiles: pagans

grand monarch: King Louis XIV of France (r. 1643–1715)

independents: Congregationalists

main: North American continent

traffick: Trade

undertaker: person who accepts or starts a project

Document Analysis

This introductory section of *The History of the Dividing Line* is a political and economic history of the earliest period of English colonization in North America framed as the story of how "Virginia"—originally a term applying to the whole area of English control on the Atlantic coast and extending far inland—eventually became limited to a particular colony by a series of royal decrees. As a Virginian, Byrd may have wished to emphasize the legal as well as temporal primacy of Virginia over the other colonies. Since the body of the work is about establishing the exact border between North Carolina and Virginia, discussing the previous establishment of separate colonies is appropriate for an introduction. It does not read as something addressed specifically to an American audience. Byrd's introduction presents a deeply ambivalent and secular narrative of English colonization, depicting it as both ridiculous and heroic. Byrd also deals with the relationships of the English to the other European peoples colonizing North America at the same time, particularly the French, as well as their relationships to American Indians. He makes an important distinction between the English colonists of Virginia proper and those of New England.

Byrd's interpretation of colonial history was much more secular than that of some of his contemporary historians of America, many of whom were New Englanders like the Boston Puritan minister Cotton Mather. Mather's *Magnalia Christi Americana* (The glorious works of Christ in America, 1702) placed colonial American history in a providential frame as the working out of God's plan. Byrd, a lay member of the Church of England, by contrast makes no mention of God or providence in the opening of the passage. (This was not because Byrd was an atheist or a skeptic; his diary shows him to have been a Christian believer.) Instead, he locates the causes of the colonization of North America in the secular realms of politics, economics, fashion, and individual character. Economic rather than religious motives are primary in Byrd's account of the early history of the English in America. Byrd ascribes the original English interest in the settlement of America to the desire to find valuable mines of precious metal like those the Spanish were exploiting in Mexico and Peru in the sixteenth century. The first encounter between American Indians and English he also describes in economic terms, as the American Indians exchange valuable furs for the "baubles" of the English. The relative worth of these goods—the fur trade was an essential element of the early colonial economy and Byrd's father had been a fur trader—suggests that the economic exchange worked strongly to the benefit of the English. However, the early history of Virginia's colonization was rocky. The failure of the Roanoke colony is depicted as an economic failure, as the colonization company undersupplied the prospective colonists, and the colonists themselves, blinded by an unrealistic picture of American wealth, expected to live and grow rich without working. Part of the problem was the refusal of the government to subsidize the endeavor.

It would be a mistake, however, to view Byrd's view of early English exploration as simply a matter of greed and economic rationality. Another motivation is simply fashion, and Byrd explicitly links American colonization and the medieval crusades to Jerusalem as fashion-driven endeavors. Since the crusades were far more explicitly religious than the English colonization of America, Byrd is suggesting that much ostensibly religious activity can really be explained by the desire to follow fashion. He links fashion to the hero of Miguel de Cervantes's *Don Quixote*, an early seventeenth-century

novel about a Spanish gentleman who goes mad and believes himself a knight out of chivalrous romance. In a famous episode, Don Quixote tilts at windmills believing them to be giants. *Don Quixote* had been translated into English and was very well known in England; by describing the colonization of America as "Quixotic" Byrd asserts its irrational or even delusional character. Like many writers of the eighteenth century and later, Byrd genders fashion as feminine, asserting that women were particularly vulnerable to it. The desire to cross the Atlantic to America is also portrayed as a disease, an "itch" or "distemper." Byrd had a great liking for living in England, and while he was ultimately required to live on the family estates in Virginia, his resentment of leaving London may be reflected in his depictions of the first colonists as diseased.

Although he states that the first permanent colony endured in spite of, rather than because of, the personal qualities of the first settlers, Byrd does not see the colonization of Virginia as entirely ridiculous. By associating the beginnings of colonization with revered historical figures such as Sir Walter Raleigh and Queen Elizabeth, Byrd establishes the connection between Virginian colonization and a glorious period of English history. A patriotic Virginian, Byrd pauses to pay tribute to the foundation of Virginia's wealth, that "bewitching vegetable," tobacco, the basis of his own fortune as well as the prosperity of his community. The story of Queen Elizabeth and her maids associates tobacco with royalty and the heroism of Raleigh, while connecting opposition to tobacco with "whispering" and "faction," marks of cynical court intrigue.

Byrd also associates the founders of the Virginia colony with the aristocracy, people "eminent for their quality and estates." His attitude toward the aristocracy is ambivalent. Byrd was a gentleman himself but willing to satirize his own class. Although the aristocratic nature of its "eminent" promoters adds to the luster of Virginia, aristocratic qualities were not always admirable or well suited for the founder of a colony. Byrd mocks his own predecessors in Virginia proper as "reprobates" and paints the survival of their colony as something that occurred in spite of the efforts of the colonists, rather than because of them. Like many writers on early Virginia, he gives the principal credit for the survival of Jamestown to Captain John Smith, while asserting that the "gentlemen" of the colony were lazy and quarrelsome. Laziness was not a quality restricted to gentlemen, as Byrd points out that laborer immigrants, although more hardworking than gentlemen, were not going to "kill themselves with work." As for the religion of the early Virginians, he states that "like true Englishmen, they built a church that cost no more than fifty pounds, and a tavern that cost five hundred." The early settlers are never even represented as thanking God for their survival and success. Byrd mockingly refers to the Virginians as greater heathens than the American Indians. In the body of the work, the stereotype of the lazy, religiously indifferent southerner would be applied principally to the North Carolinians.

A key omission in Byrd's history of the Virginia colony is slavery, the basis of the plantation economy and of Byrd's own fortune and social standing. (Byrd's mention of the laziness of the laborer immigrants may have been meant to imply that slavery was the only way to ensure the colony an adequate supply of labor.) Byrd himself was suspicious of slavery as an institution, despite his dependence on it and his frequently cruel treatment of his own slaves. Africans generally are omitted from the catalog of peoples in America that Byrd discusses in this passage, and his generally favorable view of interracial sexual relationships does not seem to extend to such relationships between whites of European descent and slaves of African descent.

The dominant threat to all of the British colonies that Byrd feared was the French. Although Virginia was far from the centers of French power in North America, Byrd, like many British Americans, was worried about the possibility of a successful alliance between the French in Canada and Louisiana and the American Indians who remained an important military force on many of the borders of the English colonies even after French defeat in the War of the Spanish Succession. Byrd attributed the greater success of the French in wooing American Indians to their cause to intermarriage between the two groups, a policy the English had largely shunned. (The marriage of Pocahontas and John Rolfe, in the early seventeenth century, was an exception to this pattern, but one that Byrd as a Virginian might have seen as particularly significant, although he does not mention it in his brief history of the early settlement of Virginia.) By contrast, the English policy promoted hostility between the two groups.

Byrd admired the policy of Louis XIV of France in using financial rewards to promote intermarriage between the French and American Indians. The French policy, Byrd points out, encouraged not just American Indian political loyalty to the French, but the spread of the French religion, Roman Catholicism. Byrd treated Catholicism largely as an adjunct to French power rather than as a rival for American Indian souls. He does not credit effective preaching with the propagation of religion; instead, he views the relationship between "sprightly lovers" as best way to spread Christianity, Catholic or Protestant, to the non-Christian peoples of the world.

Intermarriage between American Indians and the English, which Byrd seems to envision as primarily the marriage of American Indian women to English men, would also lead to a smoother and less violent transmission of property from American Indians to the English. Landed property would figure in the dowries, or "portions," of American Indian women and end up in the hands of their English husbands; English common law essentially restricted the ownership of all property in a marriage, whatever its origin, to the husband, with the wife retaining no legal rights over it while her husband lived. Like most Europeans, Byrd regarded white skin as superior, but he points out that subsequent generations of American Indians would become paler. Byrd's picture of the European strain as dominant in pairings between Europeans and American Indians is an inversion of the "one-drop" rule that applied to pairings between Europeans and persons of African descent. He seems to envision the ultimate absorption of the American Indian population by the far more numerous English.

Despite the hostility between the American Indians and the English, Byrd's portrait of the American Indians is generally favorable, emphasizing the health and strength of their bodies and the purity of their manners, uncorrupted by European civilization's "lewdness" or "luxury." This portrayal of the "noble savage" was becoming more popular in the eighteenth century, as opposed to depictions of American Indians as primitive barbarians. At a time when American Indian resistance to the English had been largely broken, Byrd does not see the American Indians as a continuing threat by themselves but principally as potential allies of the French.

Byrd's brief treatment of the Spaniards, the principal rival of the English at the beginning of North American colonization but a waning force by Byrd's time, positions them at the opposite pole from the French. The "treacherous" nature of the Spaniards toward the American Indians is contrasted with the "good nature" of the English. By Byrd's time, the "Black Legend" of Spanish cruelty to American Indians had been firmly established, and Byrd's readers would not have found it controversial—despite the fact that the English had not treated the American Indians well either.

Byrd's account also deals with the founding of the New England colonies, whose settlers he implicitly contrasts with the early Virginians. Byrd misidentifies the Pilgrims as Presbyterians when they were actually Separatist Congregationalists, perhaps indicating the diminished importance of such distinctions in the eighteenth century. He pays tribute to the courage of the early Puritan settlers, without hinting that this praiseworthy behavior was evidence of the truth of their religious claims. Byrd's tone in discussing the settlers of New England is one of subtle mockery, principally directed at their religion. Describing them as a "swarm" or "throng" makes them seem almost like an invasion of locusts, and in contrast to his praise of Raleigh and Smith, Byrd names none of the leaders of the Pilgrim and Puritan settlers except for Lord Chief Justice Popham, who plays a passive role but is not otherwise praised or described. While his picture of the Virginia settlers is secular, Byrd does admit the importance of religious motivations for the New England Puritans. In the New England context, economic motivations are not even mentioned, a striking contrast with the discussion of the early Virginia settlers. Byrd presents the New England settlers as fleeing from an England grown cold to them rather than setting out to build an ideal religious community in the wilderness, as some Puritans themselves would have claimed they were doing. He emphasizes the support they received from England and its role in their success, with an implied contrast to the Puritans' own belief that their success was evidence of their support from God. He calls them the "saints," a title the Puritans themselves used but, by the eighteenth century, was connected with fanaticism and an unrealistic approach to the world. In terms of their concern for purity of blood and their biblicism, he likens them to the Jews—a sarcastic comparison that was not complimentary in the anti-Semitic culture of the eighteenth century. The fear of the New Englanders that American Indian wives would draw them into "idolatry" contrasts with the confidence of the French, who drew American Indians into Catholicism by marrying them, not fearing to put their own faith at risk. Byrd also strikes at the Puritan narrative by suggesting that they came to settle in large numbers in New England in the early seventeenth century not because they were persecuted in England but because they "thought themselves persecuted."

Essential Themes

If Byrd seriously hoped that his recommended policy of intermarriage between British settlers and American Indians would be put into effect, he was doomed to disappointment. There are some cases of individual white men marrying American Indian women as a way of obtaining property, but it was never so widespread as to be a social strategy. By far the most common and enduring way for whites to obtain American Indian property remained violence, as in the early colonial era. However, he was correct in anticipating a major clash between the French, aided by American Indians, and the British, even if he may have underrated British chances. The French and Indian War, known in Britain and Europe as the Seven Years War, began in 1754 and ended in 1763 in a decisive British victory and the expulsion of France from continental North America.

Although the direct impact of Byrd's work would be small due to the fact that it circulated only in manuscript, the themes it presented would persist. The somewhat mocking attitude Byrd displayed toward the early settlers of Virginia would not become the dominant way of perceiving them. Byrd's seriocomic narrative would be replaced by a canonical one that emphasized heroism. A similar process would occur in the historiography of New England, in which the Puritan settlers would be viewed as religiously inspired heroes, rather than the misguided, if determined, fanatics of Byrd's account. However, Byrd's framing of the colonization stories of Virginia and New England as fundamentally opposed would have a long history. This stereotype of pious, frugal, and industrious New Englanders and lazy, "reprobate" southerners had great impact on subsequent American thought (including antislavery and abolitionist thought), as would the distinction between the religiously motivated settlers in New England and the economically motivated settlers in Virginia. Byrd's picture of the immigrant coming with unrealistic dreams of wealth would also have a long history, with his silver utensils being replaced by the image of streets paved with gold.

The aristocratic culture of the Virginia gentleman that Byrd represented would continue for many decades, with the Byrd family playing a prominent role in politics and society into the twentieth century. The transatlantic links that were so important to William Byrd faded with the American Revolution but did not disappear. However, religion would become more significant in the worldview of the southern elite.

William E. Burns, PhD

Bibliography

Byrd, William. *Prose Works: Narratives of a Colonial Virginian*. Ed. Louis B. Wright. Cambridge: Belknap, 1966. Print.

Marambaud, Pierre. *William Byrd of Westover, 1674–1744*. Charlottesville: UP of Virginia, 1971. Print.

Additional Reading

Ausband, Stephen Conrad. *Byrd's Line: A Natural History*. Charlottesville: U of Virginia P, 2002. Print.

Davis, Richard Beale. *Intellectual Life in the Colonial South, 1583–1763*. 3 vols. Knoxville: U of Tennessee P, 1978. Print.

Lockridge, Kenneth A. *On the Sources of Patriarchal Rage: The Commonplace Books of William Byrd and Thomas Jefferson and the Gendering of Power in the Eighteenth Century*. New York: New York UP, 1992. Print.

Pritchard, Margaret Beck. *William Byrd II and his Lost History: Engravings of the Americas*. Williamsburg: Colonial Williamsburg Foundation, 1993. Print.

Tinling, Marion, ed. *The Correspondence of the Three William Byrds of Westover, Virginia, 1684–1776*. Charlottesville: UP of Virginia, 1977. Print.

LESSON PLAN: The Unique Voice of William Byrd II

Students analyze the unique quality, insights, and conclusions in William Byrd II's *History of the Dividing Line*.

Learning Objectives

Read historical narratives imaginatively; differentiate between historical facts and interpretations; challenge arguments of historical inevitability; draw comparisons between the idiosyncratic voices of William Bird II and Sarah Kemble Knight.

Materials: William Byrd II, *History of the Dividing Line Betwixt Virginia and North Carolina (1733),* Excerpt: *History of the Dividing Line: Run the Year 1728*; Sarah Kemble Knight, *The Journal of Madam Knight* (1704).

Overview Questions

What does the excerpt, the introduction to *History of the Diving Line*, reveal about Byrd? How can readers determine the accuracy of his judgments about historical events? Could different policies in British colonies have led to different consequences? How do Madam Knight's journal and Byrd's *History* compare?

Step 1: Comprehension Questions

How would you characterize Byrd based on this passage? How does his writing personality affect the quality of his prose?

▶ **Activity:** Ask students to identify and read aloud sentences and phrases that reveal Byrd's point of view. Have students decide what Byrd's words and views suggest about him and his motive for writing. Discuss whether Byrd's tone helps or hurts his writing.

Step 2: Comprehension Questions

What opinions does Byrd offer as he describes colonial history? In what ways can the validity of his opinions be tested? How does Byrd's argument for American Indian and English intermarriage challenge historical inevitability?

▶ **Activity:** Have students create a three-column chart that shows 1) facts and events described in the passage, 2) Byrd's opinions of their causes and effects, and 3) students' judgment of Byrd's opinion. Discuss what historical sources and documents might verify or discredit Byrd's views.

Step 3: Context Questions

Why does Byrd think intermarriage might have helped avoid violence between English settlers and American

Indians? What are the arguments for and against the likelihood of his point of view?

▶ **Activity:** Have students describe why Byrd thought intermarriage in English colonies did not happen. Discuss whether the opposite policy in French colonies had the kind of effect Byrd describes. Discuss whether or not intermarriage would have changed history and why.

Step 4: Exploration Questions

What qualities as writers do Sarah Kemble Knight and William Byrd II share? How do their personalities add to or subtract from the value of their views?

▶ **Activity:** Have students give brief character sketches of each writer. Discuss their similarities and differences. Have students analyze why these two documents are more entertaining than other primary documents. Challenge students to determine the historical value of each document.

Step 5: Response Paper

Word length and additional requirements set by Instructor. Students answer the research question in the Overview Questions. Students state a thesis and use as evidence passages from the primary source document as well as support from supplemental materials assigned in the lesson.

■ In Defense of John Peter Zenger and the Press

Date: August 4, 1735
Author: Hamilton, Andrew
Genre: speech; address

> *"The question before the Court and you, Gentlemen of the jury, is no of small or private concern. . . . It may in its consequence affect every free man that lives under a British government on the main of America."*

Summary Overview

On August 4, 1735, Philadelphia attorney Andrew Hamilton appeared in a New York court to defend John Peter Zenger, printer and publisher of the *New York Weekly Journal*, against charges of seditious libel brought against him by the colony's governor, William Cosby. At the time, conviction for libel required the prosecution merely to show that a person had published material critical of the government. In an unusual trial in which no witnesses were called and the defense admitted Zenger had published the supposedly libelous material, Hamilton successfully convinced the jury to acquit his client by persuading them that, if criticism of those in office were suppressed, colonial governments could quickly become tyrannical. Hamilton's summation provided a basis for subsequent arguments for the right of free speech and a framework for later arguments asserting the right of people in the colonies to claim liberty from the English crown.

Defining Moment

Zenger, on trial in August 1735 for seditious libel, was a pawn in a larger political battle that pitted the royally appointed colonial governor against a powerful faction of New York's leading citizens. A German who immigrated to America in 1710, Zenger had apprenticed with the official printer of New York. In 1733, he was running his own business and struggling to make a living when he was approached by Lewis Morris, James Alexander, and William Smith Sr. to begin publishing a newspaper whose express purpose was to expose the venality and rapaciousness of Governor William Cosby. Cosby had removed Morris from his position as chief justice of the colonial court for refusing to collude with the governor in an attempt to extract funds from former acting governor Rip van Dam. Attorneys Alexander and Smith, who had represented van Dam, joined with Morris in hiring Zenger as printer and publisher of the *New York Weekly Journal*. Alexander served as shadow editor, providing most of the original copy, but Zenger was a willing participant in this endeavor.

Because English law defined seditious libel loosely as any publication that painted the government in a bad light—even if charges were true—Cosby tried several times to have a grand jury indict Zenger. Local jurymen declined, and New York officials refused to take steps to suppress Zenger's paper. On November 11, 1734, Cosby's appointee Richard Bradley, the attorney general, had Zenger arrested on charges of "information," and managed to hold him in jail for several months. Zenger was brought before the new chief justice James DeLancey, another Cosby appointee. When Zenger's attorneys argued that DeLancey should not hear this case because his appointment was invalid, the judge responded by disbarring them and appointed John Chambers, a young attorney also beholden to Cosby, as Zenger's lawyer.

Attorneys on both sides knew that the law favored conviction. Nevertheless, Alexander and Smith, believing the trial could serve as a means of exposing the evils of Cosby's administration, secretly engaged Andrew Hamilton, a Philadelphia attorney known as the best lawyer in the colonies, to represent Zenger. Hamilton appeared in court on the day of the trial and took over Zenger's defense from Chambers. His goal was to have the jury ignore both legal precedent and the judge's instructions, acquitting his client and thereby affirming that truth should be considered a defense in cases of libel.

Author Biography

Although details of Andrew Hamilton's early years are sketchy, scholars generally agree that he was born in Glasgow, Scotland, in 1676 and studied law at the University of Glasgow. In 1697, he sailed for America, settling on Virginia's Eastern Shore, where he enjoyed the patronage of the Presbyterian minister Francis Makemie. Sometime before 1703, Hamilton completed law studies and began appearing in court as attorney in civil cases.

An expanding law practice caused Hamilton to move to an estate in Maryland. In 1712, he represented the Penn family, proprietors of Pennsylvania, in a legal case that won him great acclaim. The following year, he sailed to London to further assist the Penns in a boundary dispute with Lord Baltimore, who controlled Maryland; while in London, he studied at the legal society Gray's Inn and was officially admitted to the English legal profession.

Hamilton's handling of the boundary dispute set him on a dual career as a celebrated attorney and political leader. He was elected to the Maryland House of Delegates but, in 1715, moved to Philadelphia. Shortly thereafter, he became Pennsylvania's attorney general, and during the next two decades, he held appointments in the assemblies of Delaware and Pennsylvania, rising to become Speaker of the Assembly in both houses. In 1729, Hamilton successfully convinced the Pennsylvania assembly to commit funds for a new province house. Appointed to the committee to manage the project, Hamilton submitted the successful design and supervised construction. The new province hall opened in 1733; four decades later, it would be the site of the Second Continental Congress and eventually be renamed Independence Hall.

In 1735, Hamilton received a request from New York lawyers William Smith and James Alexander to represent publisher John Peter Zenger, who was being tried for seditious libel. Hamilton traveled to New York and, using materials prepared by Alexander, successfully defended Zenger in a case that seemed all but hopeless. Cheered on by New Yorkers who acclaimed that "only a Philadelphia lawyer" could have won such a case, Hamilton returned to Pennsylvania and resumed his career as an attorney (and later a judge). In 1739, he retired from public life and died two years later.

HISTORICAL DOCUMENT

Hamilton's Summation for Zenger

"May it please Your Honor, I was saying that notwithstanding all the duty and reverence claimed by Mr. Attorney to men in authority, they are not exempt from observing the rules of common justice either in their private or public capacities. The laws of our mother country know no exemptions. It is true that men in power are harder to be come at for wrongs they do either to a private person or to the public, especially a governor in The Plantations, where they insist upon an exemption from answering complaints of any kind in their own government. We are indeed told, and it is true, that they are obliged to answer a suit in the king's courts at Westminster for a wrong done to any person here. But do we not know how impracticable this is to most men among us, to leave their families, who depend upon their labor and care for their livelihood, and carry evidence to Britain, and at a great, nay, a far greater expense than almost any of us are able to bear, only to prosecute a governor for an injury done here?

"But when the oppression is general, there is no remedy even that way. No, our Constitution has—blessed be God—given us an opportunity, if not to have such wrongs redressed, yet by our prudence and resolution we may in a great measure prevent the committing of such wrongs by making a governor sensible that it is in his interest to be just to those under his care. For such is the sense that men in general—I mean free men—have of common justice, that when they come to know that a chief magistrate abuses the power with which he is trusted for the good of the people, and is attempting to turn that very power against the innocent, whether of high or low degree, I say that mankind in general seldom fail to interpose, and, as far as they can, prevent the destruction of their fellow subjects.

"And has it not often been seen—I hope it will always be seen that when the representatives of a free people are by just representations or remonstrances made sensible of the sufferings of their fellow subjects, by the abuse of power in the hands of a governor, that they have declared (and loudly too) that they were not obliged by any law to support a governor who goes about to destroy a Province or Colony, or their privileges, which by His Majesty he was appointed, and by the law he is bound, to protect and encourage? But I pray that it may be considered—of what use is this mighty privilege if every man that suffers is silent? And if a man must be taken up as a libeler for telling his sufferings to his neighbor? . . .

"I make no doubt but there are those here who are zealously concerned for the success of this prosecution, and yet I hope they are not many; and even some of those, I am persuaded, when they consider to what lengths such prosecutions may be carried, and how deeply the liberties of the people may be affected by such means, will not all abide by their present sentiments. I say 'not all,' for the man who from an intimacy and acquaintance with a governor has conceived a personal regard for him, the man who has felt none of the strokes of his power, the man who believes that a governor has a regard for him and confides in him it is natural for such men to wish well to the affairs of such a governor. And as they may be men of honor and generosity, may, and no doubt will, wish him success so far as the rights and privileges of their fellow citizens are not affected. But as men of honor I can apprehend nothing from them. They will never exceed that point.

"There are others that are under stronger obligations, and those are such as are in some sort engaged in support of the governor's cause by their own or their relations' dependence on his favor for some post or preferment. Such men have what is commonly called duty and gratitude to influence their inclinations and oblige them to go his lengths. I know men's interests are very near to them, and they will do much rather than forgo the favor of a governor and a livelihood at the same time. But I can with very just grounds hope, even from those men, whom I will suppose to be men of honor and conscience too, that when they see the liberty of their country in danger, either by their concurrence or even by their silence, they will like Englishmen, and like themselves, freely make a sacrifice of any preferment or favor rather than be accessory to destroying the liberties of their country and entailing slavery upon their posterity.

"There are indeed another set of men, of whom I have no hopes. I mean such who lay aside all other considerations and are ready to join with power in any shape, and with any man or sort of men by whose means or interest they may be assisted to gratify their malice and envy against those whom they have been pleased to hate; and that for no other reason than because they are men of ability and integrity, or at least are possessed of some valuable qualities far superior to their own. But as envy is the sin of the Devil, and therefore very hard, if at all, to be repented of, I will believe there are but few of this detestable and worthless sort of men, nor will their opinions or inclinations have any influence upon this trial.

"But to proceed. I beg leave to insist that the right of complaining or remonstrating is natural; that the restraint upon this natural right is the law only; and that those restraints can only extend to what is false. For as it is truth alone that can excuse or justify any man for complaining of a bad administration, I as frankly agree that nothing ought to excuse a man who raises a false charge or accusation even against a private person, and that no manner of allowance ought to be made to him who does so against a public magistrate.

"Truth ought to govern the whole affair of libels. And yet the party accused runs risk enough even then; for if he fails in proving every title of what he has written, and to the satisfaction of the court and jury too, he may find to his cost that when the prosecution is set on foot by men in power it seldom wants friends to favor it.

"From thence (it is said) has arisen the great diversity of opinions among judges about what words were or were not scandalous or libelous. I believe it will be granted that there is not greater uncertainty in any part of the law than about words of scandal. It would be misspending of the Court's time to mention the cases. They may be said to be numberless. Therefore the utmost care ought to be taken in following precedents; and the times when the judgments were given, which are quoted for authorities in the case of libels, are much to be regarded.

"I think it will be agreed that ever since the time of the Star Chamber, where the most arbitrary judgments and opinions were given that ever an Englishman heard of, at least in his own country; I say, prosecutions for libel since the time of that arbitrary Court, and until the Glorious Revolution, have generally been set on foot at the instance of the crown or its ministers. And it is no small reproach to the law that these prosecutions were too often and too much countenanced by the judges, who held their places 'at pleasure,' a disagreeable tenure to any officer, but a dangerous one in the case of a judge. Yet I cannot think it unwarrantable to show the unhappy influence that a sovereign has sometimes had, not only upon judges, but even upon parliaments themselves.

"It has already been shown how the judges differed in their opinions about the nature of a libel in the case of the Seven Bishops.

"There you see three judges of one opinion, that is, of a wrong opinion in the judgment of the best men in England, and one judge of a right opinion. How unhappy might it have been for all of us at this day if that jury had understood the words in that information as the Court did? Or if they had left it to the Court to judge whether the petition of the Bishops was or was not a libel? No, they took upon them[selves]—to their immortal honor—to determine both law and fact, and to understand the petition of the Bishops to be no libel, that is, to contain no falsehood or sedition; and therefore found them not guilty.

"If then upon the whole there is so great an uncertainty among judges—learned and great men—in matters of this kind, if power has had so great an influence on judges, how cautious ought we to be in determining by their judgments especially in The Plantations, and in the case of libels? . . .

"Power may justly be compared to a great river. While kept within its due bounds it is both beautiful and useful. But when it overflows its banks, it is then too impetuous to be stemmed; it bears down all before it, and brings

destruction and desolation wherever it comes. If, then, this is the nature of power, let us at least do our duty, and like wise men who value freedom use our utmost care to support liberty, the only bulwark against lawless power, which in all ages has sacrificed to its wild lust and boundless ambition the blood of the best men that ever lived.

"I hope to be pardoned, Sir, for my zeal upon this occasion. It is an old and wise caution that when our neighbor's house is on fire we ought to take care of our own. For though—blessed be God I live in a government where liberty is well understood and freely enjoyed, yet experience has shown us all—I am sure it has to me that a bad precedent in one government is soon set up for an authority in another. And therefore I cannot but think it mine, and every honest man's duty, that while we pay all due obedience to men in authority we ought at the same time to be upon our guard against power wherever we apprehend that it may affect ourselves or our fellow subjects.

"I am truly very unequal to such an undertaking on many accounts. You see that I labor under the weight of many years, and am bowed down with great infirmities of body. Yet, old and weak as I am, I should think it my duty, if required, to go to the utmost part of the land where my services could be of any use in assisting to quench the flame of prosecutions upon informations, set on foot by the government to deprive a people of the right of remonstrating and complaining, too, of the arbitrary attempts of men in power.

"Men who injure and oppress the people under their administration provoke them to cry out and complain, and then make that very complaint the foundation for new oppressions and prosecutions. I wish I could say that there were no instances of this kind.

"But to conclude. The question before the Court and you, Gentlemen of the jury, is not of small or private concern. It is not the cause of one poor printer, nor of New York alone, which you are now trying. No! It may in its consequence affect every free man that lives under a British government on the main of America. It is the best cause. It is the cause of liberty. And I make no doubt but your upright conduct this day will not only entitle you to the love and esteem of your fellow citizens, but every man who prefers freedom to a life of slavery will bless and honor you as men who have baffled the attempt of tyranny, and by an impartial and uncorrupt verdict have laid a noble foundation for securing to ourselves, our posterity, and our neighbors, that to which nature and the laws of our country have given us a right to liberty of both exposing and opposing arbitrary power (in these parts of the world at least) by speaking and writing truth."

GLOSSARY

constitution: a set of laws and practices guiding the government's actions and protecting ordinary citizens from arbitrary exercise of power

Glorious Revolution: military and political action in 1688 that led to the overthrow of King James II in England and restoration of a Protestant monarchy

information: here, a legal procedure in which a person is indicted and arrested on the authority of a prosecutor rather than a grand jury

libel: the act of defaming someone in writing or in print

plantations: colonies in which English settlers were sent abroad to establish permanent settlements

Star Chamber: English court established to supplement the regular court system, acting without juries or witnesses

Westminster: seat of the English government where the Houses of Parliament are located

Document Analysis

The lively give-and-take that characterized Zenger's brief trial is reflected in Hamilton's summation of the defense's argument for acquittal. A number of his statements in the summation allude to matters discussed during the proceedings, and Hamilton uses his closing statement to emphasize important points about the nature of the trial and its significance to the jurors who are sitting in judgment of Zenger. His opening remarks are addressed to the presiding judge, but it is clear that he intends his principal audience to be the jury assembled to hear the facts and render a verdict in the case.

Hamilton begins by acknowledging a key point raised by the prosecutor: Those in authority are owed obedience and honor by common citizens. At the same time, however, he insists that they are not "exempt from observing the rules of common justice," and that in fact, "the laws of our mother country know no exemptions." By making this assertion, Hamilton sets up a hierarchy of duties in which justice trumps other rights. Of course, it may be harder to demand justice from a colonial official, far from the true seat of power in England,

since those wronged had to travel across the Atlantic to plead their case before Parliament. Nevertheless, no one appointed by the king can usurp the supreme authority of the sovereign. In making this case, Hamilton slyly suggests to the jury that Governor Cosby has done just that, thereby setting himself up as being above the law. The point would not have been lost on jurors that, despite being separated by an ocean from the mother country, they were still English citizens deserving of every right and protection guaranteed by the English Constitution.

Having cited legal precedents for his next point during the trial, Hamilton reminds jurors that people subjected to "abuse of power in the hands of a governor" have always had the right to refuse support for that official and to seek relief from a higher authority. Yet under the current libel laws, any person who speaks of "his sufferings to his neighbor" is now subject to prosecution—even when the complaints are true. Technically, one who speaks words that may harm another's reputation may be accused of slander, while only written communications may result in charges of libel. Hamilton elides the two forms of defamation in order to make a larger point: Those who are oppressed by government officials have a right to express their complaints—that is, they have the right to free speech.

Hamilton tries to divide the jurors ideologically from the court and the governor's administration and raise their status as independent, fair-minded citizens by explaining why some people would like to see Zenger convicted. He points out that there are three groups who have a vested interest in the case. In the first are those who are close friends of the governor and have "conceived a personal regard for him." For these people, "it is natural" that they should "wish well to the affairs of such a governor." Hamilton admits (although perhaps with a note of irony) that these may be "men of honor and generosity," but their close association with the governor may blind them to his faults.

In the second group are those who owe their appointments to the governor; they support his cause because their own livelihood derives from his remaining in power. Again suggesting that these can also be "men of honor and conscience," Hamilton expresses hope that, once they see that the governor is "destroying the liberties of their country and entailing slavery upon their posterity," they will "sacrifice any preferment" rather than be an "accessory" to such oppression. No doubt Hamilton was aware that both the presiding judge in the trial, James DeLancey, and the prosecutor, attorney general Richard Bradley, were both Cosby appointees, and his remarks may have been intended as a gentle nudge for them to renounce their support for the governor. By introducing the notion that government abuse leads to enslavement, Hamilton makes a strong emotional plea to jurors who are likely to value personal freedom, one of the great motivating factors that brought many from England and other European countries to the colonies. The third group—those who are "ready to join with power in any shape'""—are beyond hope of redemption. No conscientious juror would want to be classed among such despicable people, Hamilton suggests.

Having made his case for the jury to act independently, Hamilton quickly moves on to discuss the principles that should govern the jurors' actions in Zenger's case. He launches this part of his argument by asserting that the "right of complaining or remonstrating is natural." The word "natural" carried special meaning for Hamilton and other eighteenth-century intellectuals. Influenced by the writings of Enlightenment philosophers and their classical sources, forward-thinking Englishmen were starting to develop new theories of government based not on the divine right of kings but on the natural rights of all men. Hence, if it is part of human nature to complain when one is wronged, it is also against the laws of nature for governments to abridge that right. Hamilton suggests that "truth ought to govern the whole affair of libels," and that false accusations should be punished, whether raised against a public official or a private person. However, he continues, even in this circumstance, a person claiming to have written only the truth has a high threshold to cross, "for if he fails in proving every title of what he has written, and to the satisfaction of the court and the jury too," he may find that he will suffer for his actions. Behind the surface text is another unstated appeal to the jury. Hamilton is relying on the fact that jurors know of Governor Cosby's misdeeds and hence are already convinced that what Zenger has published is true. Hamilton has also slipped into his argument the idea that both judge and jury must be involved in determining the appropriateness of judging these written statements as libelous.

Hamilton's next claim emerges from the series of long arguments he waged with the prosecutor and the presiding judge over the precise determination of what constitutes libelous language. Both of these court officials had cited numerous precedents to uphold the right of the judge to determine if a text were libelous. Hamilton now reminds jurors that he disagrees—and believes they should as well. During the trial, Hamilton had shown that almost any statement, even a passage from the Bible, could be interpreted as scandalous depending on the context in which they were used and the intent of those employing it. Relying on the jury's memory of these examples, he again asserts that "there is not greater uncertainty in any part of the law than about words of scandal," and consequently, that "the utmost care ought to be taken in following precedents." Normally this statement would be a plea to the judge and jury to look to previous rulings to determine how to act in the present case. In this instance, however, Hamilton is employing a subtle double entendre, urging jurors to use "utmost care" to assure that precedents are applicable and appropriate; in a word, he is urging them to use their own judgment rather than relying on the presiding judge to tell them what verdict they should deliver against Zenger. To reinforce his point, he immediately reminds jurors that the harsh rules governing libel were developed by the infamous Star Chamber, the court initially established in fifteenth-century England for prosecuting powerful people who might not be fairly judged in the normal court system. That court evolved into a corrupt political tool for punishing the king's enemies. In the Star Chamber, no jury was present and no witnesses called; a group of officials hand-picked by the sovereign rendered judgment on individuals who often had no recourse to appeal.

Hamilton uses words like "arbitrary" and "opinions" to suggest that the rule of law was violated in these cases. He points out that the judges in these cases served "at pleasure" of the king, who could remove them from their duties without cause. The introduction of this phrase is also intended to point out that the current presiding judge had been appointed by Governor Cosby "at pleasure" when Cosby removed his predecessor for opposing Cosby's wishes in a legal case, even though typically in the colonies, judges were removed only for some breach of conduct. Cosby's appointment of DeLancey, a political crony, was considered another example of his questionable management of affairs in New York.

Without belaboring his point, Hamilton moves on to cite other instances of judges differing in their opinion about libel cases. One particularly odious example that would have resonated with the largely Protestant population of New York was that of the Seven Bishops. In 1688, King James II, a Roman Catholic, had issued a proclamation allowing greater freedom of worship for all denominations in England. Seven Anglican bishops had opposed him publicly and were imprisoned and charged with seditious libel for their denunciation of the king's policy. Eventually James II was dethroned in favor of the Protestant ruler Prince William of Orange and his wife, Mary, James II's daughter. As Hamilton shrewdly points out, there are parallels between this case and Zenger's. Like the New York printer, the bishops had been arrested on an "information," an order from a prosecutor (no doubt under pressure from the king) and not from a grand jury. Additionally, what made the trial of the Seven Bishops particularly applicable to the proceedings against Zenger was that the four judges in the bishops' case could not determine among themselves if the bishops' written refusal to promulgate James II's policy was libelous. Eventually the jury took it upon themselves "to determine both law and fact" and ruled that the bishops were not guilty of libel. Hamilton wraps up this portion of his argument by asking the jurors, "if then upon the whole there is so great an uncertainty among judges" about what con-

stitutes libel, even in cases tried in England near the seat of royal power, "how cautious ought we to be in determining by their judgments especially in the Plantations, and in the case of libels?" The strong rhetorical question is intended as a further prompt for the jury to act independently in rendering its verdict.

At the end of his summation, Hamilton moves away from the specifics of the Zenger case to make a broad appeal for the jurors to recognize the import of their impending decision. In his view, the case is really about the power of government and the potential for its abuse. In a dramatic extended metaphor, he compares government power to "a great river," which, when "kept within its due bounds," is both "beautiful and useful." Only when it "overflows its banks" can it bring "destruction and desolation." The analogy would not have been lost on people who faced the ravages of nature every day. Hence, as an uncontrolled river could wipe away crops and livelihoods, so could an uncontrolled government trample on the rights of the governed. While citizens must submit to and respect authority, the need to guard against abuse of power is everyone's duty. To highlight his point, Hamilton casts himself as an old man "bowed down with great infirmities of body"; yet, frail as he is, he asserts that he is duty-bound to help those oppressed by "the arbitrary attempts of men in power" wherever they may be. Again, the use of the word "arbitrary" is intended to undermine any legitimacy Cosby might have in bringing charges against Zenger, even if the law is technically on the governor's side. Additionally, the references to Hamilton's age and infirmity are intended to provoke the jurors to act as defenders of their rights; if a man in Hamilton's condition can sacrifice himself to defend liberty, how much more should the hearty citizens of the jury act in this cause.

Before delivering his rousing conclusion, Hamilton makes one last reference to the unfairness of the charges against Zenger by reminding jurors of another odious flaw in the current libel law. Those who "injure and oppress the people under their administration" are likely to "provoke" remonstrances; sadly, the law permits those same officials to make the people's complaints "the foundation for new oppressions and prosecutions." Those who complained publicly about abuse could be brought to trial for libel, since truth could not be used as a defense. Hamilton makes the comment that he wishes he "could say that there were no instances of this kind." He does not follow up with examples because previously in his summation he had referred to an incident involving former Virginia governor Francis Nicholson, who had beaten a clergyman for disagreeing with him. When Nicholson learned that the clergyman had explained the cause of his injuries to a physician in order to obtain treatment, the governor sued the clergyman for libel since his description of Nicholson's actions had painted the Virginia governor in an unfavorable light. Though Zenger had not suffered physical injury, his lengthy imprisonment, brought about because he could not pay the exorbitant bail set by the court, was a form of pre-trial punishment that seemed to go beyond the limits of what citizens in a free country should expect to suffer.

In his final remarks, Hamilton elevates the Zenger case to one of national importance. This is not simply a "small or private concern" of a single man or colony; rather, its consequences may "affect every free man that lives under a British government." While the jurors may not have been experts on the importance of precedents in determining English law, Hamilton wants them to realize that their verdict would do more than determine the fate of a single individual. This case, he insists, is not simply about a single person's right to complain; it is about "the cause of liberty." Hamilton immediately follows this hyperbolic proclamation with an assurance to the jurors that they will secure a place in history for themselves: Certainly, "every man who prefers freedom to a life of slavery will bless and honor you as men who have baffled the attempt of tyranny." By using such extreme terms as "freedom," "slavery," and "tyranny," Hamilton raises the stakes in this case. An "impartial and uncorrupt verdict"—one that acquits Zenger—will secure the colonists the freedoms promised to all Englishmen. Henceforth, Hamilton concludes, "exposing and opposing arbitrary power" by "speaking and writing truth" will be no crime, but the right of every citizen.

Although Hamilton's summation is filled with examples from the law intended to support his argument for Zenger's acquittal, his emotional appeal is intended to prompt the jury members to ignore the law and judge Zenger on common sense principles. The summation makes little attempt to prove that Zenger had not violated current laws governing seditious libel by printing articles critical of the government. Instead, Hamilton deftly and repeatedly demonstrates the inherent flaws in laws that, while intended to shore up government from attempts to undermine its legitimate authority, simultaneously provide corrupt officials a shield for their

activities. The overriding theme of the summation is that men who speak the truth about those in power should not be arrested, but instead should be celebrated for protecting the rights of their fellow citizens.

Essential Themes

The Zenger trial raised three issues that would become cornerstones in the constitution and legal system of the new United States of America less than sixty years later: the right of a citizen to assert truth as a defense in cases of libel, citizens' right to criticize the government freely, and the right of the press to print facts and opinions even when they might embarrass government officials. Despite instructions from the presiding judge that conviction was required based on the defendant's admission that he published materials judged libelous by the court, the jury ignored the court's directive and collectively engaged in the practice of "jury nullification." This is a rare action taken by juries when defendants are technically guilty but jurors believe they do not deserve punishment.

In subtly leading the jury to ignore the presiding judge and find his client not guilty, Hamilton stresses two of these important issues: that truth should be allowed as a defense and that citizens must have the right to criticize public officials. The idea that has come to be known in America as "freedom of the press" follows from this more basic right for individuals to speak or write without fear of recrimination as long as they do not spread lies about those in office. Curiously, the idea that truth could serve as a defense against charges of libel did not become accepted until much later in English law. Even in the newly formed United States, a sensitive young government, the administration of its second president, John Adams, took steps to prevent an unfriendly press from stirring up sentiment against government officials.

Nevertheless, the ideas that Hamilton presented in his summation had great political impact. Within a year, the record of the trial had been published and circulated throughout the colonies and in England. It became a topic of conversation among those who saw in Hamilton's argument seeds of truth about the basic rights of citizens in a nation moving toward democratic governance. The notion that oppressive governments lost their legitimacy to rule became a cornerstone in the 1770s, when colonial leaders declared independence from an English government that they saw as arbitrary and oppressive. Hamilton's argument that true liberty included citizens' rights to free speech and freedom of the press directly informed the 1789 crafting of the Bill of Rights, the first ten amendments to the US Constitution.

Laurence W. Mazzeno, PhD

Bibliography

Alexander, James. *A Brief Narrative of the Case and Trial of John Peter Zenger*. Ed. Stanley N. Katz. Cambridge: Belknap, 1963. Print.

Buranelli, Vincent. *The Trial of John Peter Zenger*. Westport: Greenwood, 1975. Print.

Finkelman, Paul. Introduction. *Brief Narrative of the Case and Tryal of John Peter Zenger*. Boston: Bedford/St. Martin's, 2010. Print.

James, Ellen Mosen. "Decoding the Zenger Trial: Andrew Hamilton's 'Fraudful Dexterity' with Language." *The Law in America, 1607–1861*. Ed. William Pencak and Wythe Holt, Jr. New York: New York Historical Soc., 1989. 1–27. Print.

Olson, Alison. "The Zenger Case Revisited: Satire, Sedition and Political Debate in Eighteenth Century America." *Early American Literature* 35.3 (2000): 223–45. Print.

Putnam, William Lowell. *John Peter Zenger and the Fundamental Freedom*. Jefferson: McFarland, 1997. Print.

Rutherford, Livingston. *John Peter Zenger: His Press, His Trial*. New York: Chelsea, 1981. Print.

Additional Reading

Burns, Eric. *Infamous Scribblers: The Founding Fathers and the Rowdy Beginnings of American Journalism*. New York: Public Affairs, 2006. Print.

Dershowitz, Alan M. *America on Trial: Inside the Legal Battles That Transformed Our Nation*. New York: Warner, 2004. Print.

Jonakait, Randolph N. *The American Jury System*. New Haven: Yale UP, 2003. Print.

Lieberman, Jethro K. *Free Press, Free Speech, and the Law*. New York: Lothrop, 1980. Print.

Martin, Robert W. T. *The Free and Open Press: The Founding of American Democratic Press Liberty, 1640–1800*. New York: New York UP, 2001. Print.

Stimson, Shannon C. *The American Revolution in the Law: Anglo-American Jurisprudence before John Marshall*. Princeton: Princeton UP, 1990. Print.

LESSON PLAN: Andrew Hamilton's Lasting Argument

Students analyze Andrew Hamilton's court argument and its implications and discuss whether or not the verdict was inevitable.

Learning Objectives

Reconstruct the events that led to John Peter Zenger's trial; appreciate the historical perspective of Hamilton's delivery in a live courtroom; analyze the influence of Hamilton's ideas; challenge the inevitability of the Zenger verdict.

Materials: Andrew Hamilton, "In Defense of John Peter Zenger and the Press" (1735); James Alexander, trial record from Zenger's *A Brief Narrative of the Case and Trial of John Peter Zenger* (1736).

Overview Questions

Why were the legal odds against Hamilton and Zenger? Why was Hamilton's argument effective? How can Hamilton's argument be read as more than a plea for an individual's innocence? What historical-context arguments can be made for Zenger's guilt?

Step 1: Comprehension Questions

In addition to the jury, who else was Hamilton addressing in court? Why was there little hope for Zenger being found not guilty?

▶ **Activity:** Choose students to provide background on the Zenger trial and to explain the challenges Hamilton faced. Instruct other students to explain what the judge's directions to the jurors were after Hamilton made his argument.

Step 2: Comprehension Questions

What was the structure of Hamilton's argument? How was his language tailored to the jury?

▶ **Activity:** Instruct students to outline Hamilton's argument. Discuss why he chose to describe the types of men who might hope for a successful prosecution. Have students read aloud passages that appealed emotionally to the jury.

Step 3: Context Questions

How did Hamilton's speech help lead to the First Amendment? What parts of his speech could be cited in an argument for freedom of speech and of the press?

▶ **Activity:** Instruct students to list points that Hamilton makes for Zenger that can also be made for both freedoms. Discuss the analogy of the great river. Have students explain whether the text suggests that Hamilton was knowingly making an argument that transcended the case.

Step 4: Historical Connections Questions

Why was the jury's verdict in the Zenger case not a foregone conclusion? What reasons could jury members have cited to argue for a guilty verdict?

▶ **Activity:** Direct students to review the Zenger trial record; have them pay close attention to the opposing arguments and judge's direction to the jury. Discuss with students what precedent is suggested for a not guilty verdict. Have students suggest why a guilty verdict was possible.

Step 5: Response Paper

Word length and additional requirements set by Instructor. Students answer the research question in the Overview Questions. Students state a thesis and use as evidence passages from the primary source documents.

■ Letters on Plantation Life

Date: May 2, 1740–March 14, 1760
Author: Lucas, Eliza
Genre: letter

*"I find it requires great care, attention and activity
to attend properly to a Carolina Estate, tho' but a
moderate one, to do ones duty and make it turn to
account, that I find I have as much business
as I can go through of one sort or other."*

Summary Overview

This is a collection of some of the letters written by Eliza Lucas (Pinckney), an eighteenth-century South Carolina planter in the two phases of her life when she oversaw plantations in the South Carolina low country. Lucas's letterbook contains both copied out letters and short notes made of longer letters. The letters provide a look at the lifestyles of plantation owners and the cultural interests of elite women. They also display the unusual case of a woman—and in particular, a very young woman, as Lucas was when she wrote the early letters in the collection—administering a plantation in South Carolina's patriarchal society. The last letter is from her life as a widow, administering estates for her young children. Lucas, also known by her married name of Eliza Lucas Pinckney, was an innovative planter who was recognized for promoting and spreading indigo cultivation. She was also an important figure in South Carolina society and politics.

Defining Moment

By the time of these letters, the economy of the South Carolina Lowcountry, based on slave-worked rice plantations, had been established, and South Carolina society was taking on the shape it would retain into the Civil War. The Stono Slave rebellion of 1739 had been repressed, and the particularly harsh South Carolina slave code was put into place in 1740. (Lucas's husband, Charles Pinckney, had been leader of the Assembly when the slave code was passed.) So central was

slavery to the economy that South Carolina was the only British colony on the North American mainland in which persons of African descent comprised a majority of the population, a pattern more characteristic of the island colonies of the British Caribbean where many South Carolinians originated. South Carolina society was closely linked economically and culturally with Britain and the British colonies in the Caribbean that furnished one of its principal markets. As a group, the South Carolina rice planters were the richest people in British North America, far wealthier than Boston merchants or Virginia tobacco planters. Lucas herself was born in the Caribbean and educated in England before settling in South Carolina. As the daughter of a British military officer, she naturally inherited a point of view with imperial rather than merely local horizons. She was writing at a time when the "polite" culture of the British elite had more influence on the culture of American elites and when South Carolina's port of Charles Town had become one of the leading cities of the British Empire and the greatest slave trading port of North America.

The mid-eighteenth century was also characterized by a broad interest, across the Anglo-American colonies and European civilization in general, in agricultural improvement and the introduction of new crops. It was a time for the founding of agricultural societies (although Lucas, as a woman, would have been barred from membership in most scientific and technical societies) and the launching of agricultural prizes. In addition to promoting the economic prosperity of the colonies and their landowners themselves, the cultivation of new crops was also considered a way of substituting products grown in the British colonies for the same products imported from foreign countries and was thus viewed as an imperially patriotic act.

Author Biography

Elizabeth Lucas, known as "Eliza," was born in the West Indies on December 28, 1722, the daughter of George Lucas, a landowner and British army officer from Antigua, and his wife Anne. In 1738 Lucas's family, hoping to improve the health of Anne Lucas, moved to a South Carolina plantation along Wappoo Creek about six miles from Charleston. Despite the move, her mother remained incapacitated and when a maritime conflict with Spain made it necessary for her father to return to his military post in Antigua, Eliza Lucas began to administer her family's six-hundred-acre plantation and oversee two smaller plantations herself. This was an unusual position for a sixteen-year-old woman in the male-dominated society of colonial South Carolina. Lucas worked to enhance the economic productiveness of the estates through the introduction of new crops. Her tenure as an agricultural experimenter is best known for the introduction of indigo, the source of a highly popular blue dye, as a commercial crop that became South Carolina's leading crop after rice. After several failed experiments, she successfully produced an indigo crop in 1744 and subsequently distributed seeds and instructions to fellow planters. Due to Lucas's efforts, the volume of exported indigo increased dramatically within the next five years, making it the second most profitable crop (rice being the first) for South Carolina and increasing the wealth of its planters.

Although rice was extremely profitable, it had widely varying seasonal demands for labor, and planters were looking for a crop that slaves could work when rice made fewer demands on their labor. In addition to indigo, Lucas experimented with other crops, some of which derived from the Caribbean. She grew cotton, lucerne (alfalfa), ginger, and cassava. She also grew figs, hoping to dry them for export, and tried packing eggs in salt to export them to the British Caribbean. Like many other American landowners and improvers she tried to develop silk as a commercial crop, with a similar lack of success.

Lucas's first period of independent activity came to an end with her marriage to one of South Carolina's leading statesmen and planters, the widower Charles Pinckney, in 1744. Between 1746 and 1750, the Pinckneys had four children: Charles Cotesworth; George Lucas, who died soon after his birth in 1747; a daughter, Harriott; and Thomas. In 1753, Eliza and her family went to London when Charles was appointed South Carolina commissioner to the Board of Trade. Following Charles's death of malaria shortly after their return to South Carolina in 1758, Eliza returned to plantation management, this time for her three young children. This second period of plantation management was not as innovative as the first.

Despite her connections with Britain, Eliza supported the American Revolution, and her sons Charles and Thomas both served in the Revolutionary armies. As matriarch of the Pinckney family, who were considered leaders in South Carolina politics and society, she played an important political and social role during and after the Revolution. When she died in Philadelphia in 1793, George Washington was numbered among her pallbearers.

HISTORICAL DOCUMENT

May 2, 1740

To my good friend Mrs. Boddicott
Dear Madam,
I flatter myself it will be a satisfaction to you to hear I like this part of the world, as my lott has fallen here—which I really do. I prefer England to it, 'tis true, but think Carolina greatly preferable to the West Indias, and was my Papa here I should be very happy.

We have a very good acquaintance from whom we have received much friendship and Civility. Charles Town, the principal one in this province, is a polite, agreeable place. The people live very Gentile and very much in the English taste. The Country is in General fertile and abounds with Venison and wild fowl; the Venison is much higher flavoured than in England but 'tis seldom fatt.

My Papa and Mama's great indulgence to me leaves it to me to chose our place of residence either in town or Country, but I think it more prudent as well as most agreeable to my Mama and self to be in the Country during my Father's absence. We are 17 mile by land and 6 by water from Charles Town—where we have about 6 agreeable families around us with whom we live in great harmony.

I have a little library well furnished (for my papa has left me most of his books) in which I spend part of my time. My Musick and the Garden, which I am very fond of, take up the rest of my time that is not imployed in business, of which my father has left me a pretty good share—and indeed, 'twas inavoidable as my Mama's bad state of health prevents her going through any fatigue.

I have the business of 3 plantations to transact, which requires much writing and more business and fatigue of other sorts than you can imagine. But least you should imagine it too burthensom to a girl at my early time of life, give me leave to answer you: I assure you I think myself happy that I can be useful to so good a father, and by rising very early I find I can go through much business. But least you should think I shall be quite moaped with this way of life I am to inform you there is two worthy Ladies in Charles Town, Mrs. Pinckney and Mrs. Cleland, who are partial enough to me to be always pleased to have me with them, and insist upon my making their houses my home when in town and press me to relax a little much oftener than 'tis in my honor to accept of their obliging intreaties. But I some times am with one or the other for 3 weeks or a month at a time, and then enjoy all the pleasures Charles Town affords, but nothing gives me more than subscribing my self

Dear Madam,
Yr. most affectionet and most obliged humble Servt.
Eliza Lucas

Pray remember me in the best manner to my worthy friend Mr. Boddicott.

✳✳✳

Wappo—June 4, 1741

Dr Miss B.
AFTER a pleasant passage of about an hour we arrived safe at home as I hope you and Mrs Pinckney did at Belmont. but this place appeared much less agreeable than when I left it, having lost the agreeable company & conversation of our friends—I am engaged now with the rudiments of the Law to wch I am but a Stranger and what adds to my mortification is that Doctr Wood wants the Politeness of your Uncle who with a graceful ease & good nature peculiar to himself is always ready to instruct the ignorant—but this rustic seems by no means to court my acquaintance for he often treats me with such cramp phrases I am unable to understand him nor is he civil enough to explain them when I desire it. However I hope in a short time we shall be better friends nor shall I grudge a little pains and application that will make me useful to my poor neighbours. We have some in this Neighbourhood who have a little Land and a few slaves and Cattle to give their children, that never think of making a Will till they come upon a sick bed and find it too expensive to send to town for a Lawyer. If you will not laugh too immoderately at me I'll trust you with a secrett. I have made two Wills already. I know I have done no harm for I conn'd my lesson very perfect. and know how to convey by Will Estates real and personal and never forget in it's proper place him and his heirs for Ever. nor

that tis to be sign'd by 3 Witnesses in presence of one another. but the most comfortable remembrance of all is that Doctr Wood says the Law makes great allowance for last Wills and Testaments presuming the Testator could not have Council learned in the Law. but after all what can I do if a poor creature lies a dying and the family takes it into their head that I can serve them, I cannt refuse but when they are well and able to imploy a Lawyer I always shall. A Widdow here abouts with a pretty little fortune teazed me intolerably to draw her a marriage settlement but it was out of my depth and I absolutely refused it—so she got an able hand to do it—indeed she could afford it—but I could not get off from being one of the Trustees to her settlement and an old Gentm the other I shall begin to think myself an old woman before I am a young one having such weighty affairs upon my hands . . .

✳✳✳

Septr 20, 1741. Wrote to my father on plantation business and Concerning a planter's importing negroes for his own use. Colo Pinckney thinks not—but thinks twas proposed in the assembly and rejected—promised to look over the act and let me know, also informed my father of the alteration tis Soposed there will be in the value of our money occationed by a late Act of Parliament that Extends to all America wch is to disolve all private banks I think by the 30th of last Month or be liable to lose their Estates and put themselves out of the King's protection, informed him of the Tyranical Govrt at Georgia.

✳✳✳

Jany 1741–2. Wrote my father . . . about the Exchange with Colo Heron, the purchasing his house at Georgia. . . . Returned my father thanks for a present I received from him by Capt Sutherland of twenty pistols, and for the sweetmeats by Capt Gregory. . . . Shall send the preserved fruit as they come in Season. . . . Begged the favour of him to send to England for Dr Popashes Cantatas. Wildens Anthems. Knellers Rules for tuning . . . .about the Jerusalem Thorn, shall try different soils for the Lucern grass this year. The ginger turns out but poorly. We want a supply of Indigo Seed. Sent by this Vessel a . . . waiter of my own Japaning my first Essay. Sent also the Rice and beef. Sent

Govr Thomas of Philadelphia' Daughter a tea chest of my own doing also Congratulate my father on my brother's recovery from the small pox and having a Commission. . . .

✳✳✳

Feby 6, 1741–2

To the Honble Crs Pinckney
Sir:
I received yesterday the favour of your advice as a phicisian and want no arguments to convince me I should be much better for both my good friends Company, a much pleasanter Prescription than Doct Meads wch I have just received. To follow my inclination at this time I must endeavour to forget that I have a Sister to instruct and a parcel of little Negroes whom I have undertaken to teach to read . . . I am a very Dunce, for I have not acquird the writing short hand yet with any degree of Swiftness but I am not always so for I give a very good Proof of the brightness of my Genius when I can distinguish well enough to Subscribe my Self with great Esteem

Sir
yr most obed humble Servt
ELIZA LUCAS.

✳✳✳

March 14, 1760

(To Mr. Morley)
The beginning of this Year there was such a fine prospect on our plantations of a great Crop that I was hopeful of clearing all the mony that was due upon the Estate, but the great drought in most parts of the Country, such as I never remember her, disapointed those expectations so much that all that we make from the planting interest will hardly defray the charges of the plantations. And upon our arrival here we found they wanted [lacked] but every thing and [were] every way in bad order, with ignorant or dishonest Over Seers.

My Nephew had no management of the planting interest, and my brother who had, by a stroak of the palsey, had been long incapable of all business. I thank God there is now a good prospect of things being deferently conducted. I have prevailed upon a conscientious good man (who by his industry and honesty has raised a fine fortune for 2 orphan children my dear Mr. Pinckney was guardian too) to undertake the direction and inspection of the overseers. He is an excellent planter, a Dutchman, originally Servant and Overseer to Mr. Golightly, who has been much solicited to undertake for many Gentlemen; but as he has no family but a wife and is comfortable enough in his circumstances, refuses to do it for any but women and children that are not able to do it for themselves. So that if it please God to prosper us and grant good Seasons, I hope to clear all next year.

I find it requires great care, attention and activity to attend properly to a Carolina Estate, tho' but a moderate one, to do ones duty and make it turn to account, that I find I have as much business as I can go through of one sort or other. Perhaps 'tis better for me, and I believe it is. Had there not been a necessity for it, I might have sunk to the grave by this time in that Lethargy of stupidity which had seized me after my mind had been violently agitated by the greatest shock it ever felt. But a variety of imployment gives my thoughts a relief from melloncholy subjects, tho' 'tis but a temporary one, and gives me air and exercise, which I believe I should not have had resolution enough to take if I had not been roused to it by motives of duty and parental affection . . .

GLOSSARY

Charles Town: Charleston, South Carolina

Colo: colonel

conn'd: learned

Dr. Mead: Richard Mead, influential eighteenth-century English physician

essay: attempt

Gentile: genteel

indigo: type of plant cultivated to extract a natural blue dye

Japanning: decorative varnishing in imitation of Japanese techniques

Jerusalem Thorn: species of shrub

Lucern grass: alfalfa

moaped: depressed

pistol: Spanish quarter-doubloon, commonly circulating in South Carolina

polite: cultivated, as applied to people

sweetmeats: candies

venison: deer

West Indias: Caribbean Islands

wch: which

Document Analysis

The letters of Eliza Lucas reveal the cultural and social world of the planter elite in late colonial Lowcountry South Carolina and the unique aspects of Lucas's own career as a plantation mistress. Although Lucas lived in many places during her long and eventful life, the letters reproduced here were all written from the South Carolina plantations her family owned. As a large-scale South Carolina planter, Lucas functioned both as a leader of the local community and as a member of an imperial elite bound together by a common culture. She had close personal and cultural ties to South Carolina's urban capital, the port of Charles Town, and further connections to Britain and other British colonies in the Caribbean and North America. While the South Carolinian elites were primarily self-governing, they were still provincials—a consciousness that is reflected in Lucas's correspondence—and politically subject to a British government over which they had relatively little direct influence. However, in her local community Lucas was a leader, both as a holder of land and slaves and as an intermediary between her poorer white neighbors, the institutions of the state, and wealthy landowners. Perhaps most importantly, she was a member of an elite family by birth and eventually by marriage. Her awareness of her position in her family and her responsibilities to it shaped her life before, during, and after her marriage. Lucas occupied an unusual role in her family and society as a very young woman who was operating a plantation business and as an agricultural experimenter and innovator.

South Carolina in the middle of the eighteenth century was a rural society with little urban development outside Charles Town, the largest city of the South and one of the leading cities of British North America. The difference between the sophisticated urban society of Charles Town, where the Lucas family owned a house, and the rustic society of the country, where they had their plantations, played an important role in Eliza Lucas's worldview. These divisions were not only spatial but also cultural. The particular qualities associated with the town and the social elite she expressed in the classical eighteenth-century language of "politeness." Although Lucas claimed to have voluntarily chosen the rural life, it is clear that it presented difficulties due to a lack of companionship with people of a similar cultural background. Lucas identified six families living in the area as "agreeable," indicating that they shared her position in the cultural, social, and economic hierarchy.

However, country houses were often widely separated and transportation between them was primitive.

Despite the presence of these "agreeable" families and her own relatives, Lucas suffered from cultural isolation on the plantation before her marriage, which was partially alleviated by solitary amusements such as reading and playing music. Correspondence with people of a similar cultural background, particularly women, was an emotional lifeline, as were her visits to Charles Town, which sometimes extended to a month. In Charles Town, Lucas sometimes stayed with "Mrs. Pinckney," the first wife of Charles Pinckney, the man she would eventually marry. In addition to her Carolina women friends and correspondents, Lucas also corresponded with Englishwomen like Mrs. Boddicot. Skill in letter-writing and the punctilious writing of return letters were highly valued social accomplishments for people in Lucas's social class. Letter writing required mastering of the elaborate formulae of greeting and closing, such as the "Yr. most affectionet and most obliged humble Servt," which closes Lucas's letter to Mrs. Bodicott and was a proper closing for a social inferior in rank and age addressing a superior. Many of Lucas's letters display a wit and literary polish indicating that she thought of them as more than mere communications. While on the plantation, Lucas was also dependent on correspondents in Charles Town and London for cultural items such as books and written music. The network of informal exchange also included items that Lucas manufactured herself, as well as gifts of plantation produce like preserved fruit.

In the country, major landowners like the Lucases and the Pinckneys also coexisted with smaller landowners, whom Lucas identified as those "who have a little Land and a few slaves and Cattle." (True family farmers who did not own slaves did not exist at that time and place.) Economic, social, and cultural hierarchy was important in the relationships of Lucas and her smallholding neighbors. The lack of a political and social infrastructure in rural communities forced Lucas and other plantation owners into roles they were not formally qualified for, as can be seen in Lucas's adoption of the role of lawyer who drew up wills in situations where death was imminent and no qualified lawyer was available. Many rural smallholders lacked the financial and geographic access to a lawyer that richer landowners or urban dwellers would have had as a matter of course. For a woman to take on this specific role was highly unusual, as women could not become professional lawyers and had no way of obtaining formal training in the law. However, the idea of the lady of the great house having some responsibility for her poorer neighbors had a long tradition in both England and the southern colonies, as was the idea that landowners should know something of the law of property, both for their own protection and to aid their less educated neighbors. Lucas, an avid reader, picked up knowledge of the law from "Dr. Wood," Thomas Wood's two-volume *Institute of the Laws of England*, first published in 1720 and published in multiple editions thereafter. Since she was not trained in the technical language of common law, she found Wood difficult to read. She identified Wood as "rustic," re-inscribing the division between the "polite" city, as embodied in the uncle of the correspondent, presumably a lawyer, and the countryside, lacking in "politeness," a central aspect of which was ease of communication. She was careful not to get out of her depth in the law, as indicated in her refusal to draw up a marriage settlement, a more complicated legal instrument than a will, for a local widow. Since the widow was financially able to hire a lawyer and the situation was not as urgent as a deathbed, Lucas did not regard the widow as an appropriate object of her charitable labors in any case.

Familial bonds were central to Lucas's social existence, as they were to all upper-class British colonists at the time, and particularly to women, who did not occupy a public political role, but who, like Lucas could be extremely influential through family connections. Throughout her life, Lucas fulfilled the prescribed social roles of daughter, sister, wife, widow, and mother. Her first period of plantation management was as the deputy of her father, the actual owner of the plantation, and the second was as caretaker for her young sons when they were being educated in England. Her bonds with her father were partly those of business—she reports to him on plantation affairs—but also affectionate, as when she speaks of how happy she would be if here "Papa" were there with her.

There was a growing emphasis in eighteenth-century culture on close emotional relationships among family members. Familial bonds extended far beyond the immediate family in South Carolina's tightly interwoven community, however. The importance of extended family bonds can be seen in the arrangement Lucas made with the anonymous "conscientious good man," the foster father of two orphans of whom her late husband had been the guardian. The incapacity of many of

Lucas's family members, the absence of her father, and later the death of her much older husband while her children were still young, added to the challenges she faced, but they also spurred her independence because she therefore spent much of her life outside the direct control of a dominant, patriarchal male.

Like all South Carolina landowners, big and small, Lucas and her family were ultimately dependent on the labor of the slaves who grew and processed the rice and indigo and did the day-to-day physical work that made the plantations run. Although these letters contain relatively few direct references to slaves, slavery as an institution permeated South Carolina society, and Charles Town was the largest slave-trade port in continental North America. Rural land was considered worthless without slaves to work it. Even the poor landowners Lucas mentioned owned more than one slave. On a large plantation like Lucas's, supervising the slaves at work was the job of overseers, and the necessity of hiring good overseers—as well as a man to oversee the overseers—comes up in the letters. This work was strongly gender based as can be seen in the refusal of the "conscientious good man" Lucas hired to supervise her overseers to work for male landowners, who would be expected to exert their patriarchal authority by supervising the overseers themselves. The reference to planters "importing negroes"—African slaves—for their own use probably refers to a provision of the law that allowed planters who imported slaves to work on their own plantations, as opposed to slave traders importing slaves to sell to others, to be exempt from import duties—an arrangement to the advantage of the planters who dominated the South Carolina Assembly. The work demanded of slaves in South Carolina rice culture was extremely debilitating, leading to short lives and low fertility rates, so importing slaves was vital to maintaining the economy. The letters also provide one glimpse into Lucas's relationship with her slaves outside of economic exploitation when she mentions trying to teach young slave children to read (in the hopes, she explains in a letter not included in this selection, that the girls she trained would then train other slave children to read). This would have been unusual in South Carolina in the aftermath of the Stono Rebellion when treatment of slaves actually became considerably more repressive. Slaves were actually forbidden from learning to write by the harsh slave code of 1740—passed when Charles Pinckney was speaker of the South Carolina Assembly—although it remained legal for slaves to learn to read.

As a plantation manager, Lucas oversaw supplies, production, and distribution, an enormous task given that her responsibilities encompassed three plantations when she was only sixteen years old. However, Lucas was not content to simply manage the plantation's existing rice-based economy. Like other eighteenth-century landowners, she decided to introduce new profitable crops for cultivation and to maximize the value of plantation land and slave labor. Although she is best known for introducing indigo cultivation to South Carolina, Lucas experimented with a variety of crops, as can be seen from her letters' references to ginger, "Lucern grass," and indigo. From her reference to the purchase of Colonel Heron's house in Georgia, Lucas also seems to have handled nonplantation family business.

In addition to its social importance, correspondence also played an important role in business, and letters could easily mix business and personal affairs. That made it particularly important to keep a record of letters sent, and Lucas's letterbook served as a register of sent letters, and the actual letters may have differed from what is recorded in the book, as evidenced by the abbreviations found throughout.

South Carolina had long-standing connections to the British Caribbean colonies, and many of its early settlers, including Lucas's family, could trace their origins there. This made South Carolina different from other colonies that had originally been settled by people from England and Europe. In these letters, transatlantic considerations seem to outweigh continental North American ones. In considering places to live, Lucas ranked Carolina above the West Indies but below England. The high ranking of England in this passage may be explained by the fact that the letter is addressed to Mrs. Boddicot, an Englishwoman, although it may also express Lucas's genuine preference. The colony of Georgia, on South Carolina's southern border, had only recently been founded, but Lucas refers to its first governor, James Oglethorpe, as "tyrannical," an attitude commonly held among elite South Carolinians due to Oglethorpe's military government and his opposition to extending slaveholding to the new colony.

Both Lucas's father and brother were officers in the British military, (one reason why Lucas had so many family responsibilities) and Lucas frequently dealt with officers such as Colonel Heron, Captain Sutherland, and Captain Gregory. At this period of her life, with Great Britain involved in the War of the Austrian Succession and the Seven Years War, Lucas seems to have identified as an imperial patriot. However, she was not blind to the problems of the British Empire from an elite South Carolinian point of view. South Carolina, like the other British colonies in North America, had a great deal of independence and was able to pass even fundamental laws like the slave code with little interference from Britain. However, South Carolina remained part of the British Empire and ultimately subject to Parliament. The case of Georgia revealed the potential for "tyranny" in the imperial framework. British imperial policies, over which South Carolinians could have little direct influence, affected South Carolina's economy. British moves against independent colonial banks threatened the circulation of currency in the colonies, whose lack of sufficient currency had already led to the common use of the Spanish pistole. Although Lucas does not voice discontent in this passage with the vulnerability of South Carolinians to parliamentary decisions that were made in London and that did not represent their interests, the situation is of the kind that would eventually lead to the American Revolution, in which South Carolina somewhat reluctantly participated.

The last letter was written in Lucas's (then Eliza Lucas Pinckney) widowhood, when she found the task of running an estate a welcome distraction from the stress of her husband's death. Her sons were too young to run the Pinckney plantations themselves and were being educated in England. Lucas seems more focused on running the plantation in a way to clear off its debt than on experimenting at this stage in her career. Debt was a condition of life for plantation owners throughout the South. Lucas's hopes to pay off the debts of her estate with a good crop failed. She blamed this on poor weather, reminding the reader that in all agricultural societies, nature was the ultimate arbiter of success or failure.

Essential Themes

Although women with Lucas's prominence as plantation managers and agricultural experimenters remained few and far between and those, male or female, who began running plantation business at the age of sixteen were even rarer, the life she led was similar to those of many elite South Carolinians and southerners who lived during the age of American independence and the antebellum period. Many women, including Lucas's daughter Harriott Pinckney Horry, did manage plantations as widows or when their husbands were away or incapacitated, particularly during the Civil War. Elite landowners retained the idea of cultural superiority, and the cultural division between large landowners—the "planter elite"—and small landowners remained essential to southern life. The members of the Pinckney family into which Lucas married were political, social, and cultural leaders in South Carolina for decades. Eliza Lucas herself was viewed in retrospect as a South Carolinian and American patriot whose agricultural innovations were aimed at enriching and improving her country. It should be noted that much of the research on Lucas has been carried out by her descendants.

The imperial transatlantic world that Lucas's letters reflect was largely ended by the American Revolution, and the weakening of South Carolina's ties with London and the West Indies was initially accompanied by the strengthening of political and social ties to the other states of the new nation, particularly southern ones that shared South Carolina's slavery-based plantation economy and society. The rise of abolitionism in the northern and mid-Atlantic states as well as Britain ultimately drew South Carolina into a southern identity of which there is little awareness in Lucas's writings, coming at the time they did when all American colonies accepted slavery. Although it did not become the capital of the state of South Carolina after independence, Charleston remained a center of elite culture for the state and much of the South.

Despite the changes that came with independence and new technologies such as the railroad, the plantation economy depicted in the letters proved enduring.

Agricultural slavery remained the basis of the South Carolina agricultural economy until the close of the Civil War. The indigo industry that Lucas helped start in South Carolina remained an important part of its economy until the late eighteenth century, when the rise of cotton began to marginalize colonial rice and indigo agriculture.

William E. Burns, PhD

Bibliography

Fryer, Darcy R. "The Mind of Eliza Pinckney: An Eighteenth-Century Woman's Construction of Herself." *South Carolina Historical Magazine* 99.3 (1998): 215–37. Print.

Pinckney, Eliza Lucas. *The Letterbook of Eliza Lucas Pinckney*. Ed. Elise Pinckney and Marvin R. Zahniser. Columbia: U of South Carolina P, 1997. Print.

Additional Reading

Anzilotti, Cara. *In the Affairs of the World: Women, Patriarchy, and Power in Colonial South Carolina*. Westport, CT: Greenwood, 2002. Print.

Burns, William E. *Science and Technology in Colonial America*. Westport, CT: Greenwood, 2005. Print.

Edelson, S. Max. *Plantation Enterprise in Colonial South Carolina*. Cambridge, MA: Harvard UP, 2006. Print.

Ravenel, Harriott Horry. *Eliza Pinckney*. La Crosse, WI: Brookhaven, 2005. Print.

Rogers, George C. *Charleston in the Age of the Pinckneys*. Columbia: U of South Carolina P, 2002. Print.

LESSON PLAN: A Nearly Modern Woman

Students analyze excerpts from *Letters on Plantation Life* to identify both the unique and conventional qualities of Eliza Lucas Pinckney.

Learning Objectives

Reconstruct the literal meaning of Lucas's letters; interrogate data to understand the historical context of Lucas's life; formulate questions about Lucas's attitude toward enslaved African Americans; compare and contrast Eliza Lucas and Sarah Kemble Knight.

Materials: Eliza Lucas, *Letters on Plantation Life* (1739–1762); Sarah Kemble Knight, *The Journal of Madam Knight* (1704).

Overview Questions

What do Lucas's letters reveal about her talents and personality? How is Lucas different than twenty-first-century perceptions of women in her era? What does evidence within the letters suggest about Lucas's attitude toward slavery? What significant qualities do Lucas and Knight share?

Step 1: Comprehension Questions

What first impressions does Lucas make in these letters? What do the letters eventually document about her life? What do the letters reveal about Lucas's attitude toward African Americans? How is Lucas similar to Knight?

▶ **Activity:** Have a student read the first letter from the salutation to the phrase "not employed in business" in the fourth paragraph. Discuss what the paragraphs suggest about Lucas. Have students read passages that detail her accomplishments. Discuss what the letters ultimately reveal about Lucas.

Step 2: Context Questions

What roles do we assume that most upper-class women had in colonial America? How does Lucas compare with our assumptions?

▶ **Activity:** Discuss with students the limitations women faced in colonial America. Have students focus on women's right to own property, vote in colonial elections, and hold political or religious positions. Discuss specific ways in which Lucas apparently broke colonial expectations.

Step 3: Context Questions

What evidence do the letters provide that Lucas did or did not treat enslaved African Americans as her peers did?

▶ **Activity:** Ask students to read passages that directly or indirectly refer to the treatment of African Americans. Have students speculate on Lucas's attitude toward African Americans. Ask students to decide whether or not this sometimes-unconventional woman held conventional attitudes about slavery.

Step 4: Historical Connections Questions

How were Eliza Lucas and Sarah Kemble Knight alike? In what significant ways did they differ?

▶ **Activity:** Have students review *The Journal of Madam Knight.* Instruct students to then use Venn diagrams to show how Knight and Lucas were alike and different. Discuss with students which woman most exceeds conventional expectations about colonial women and why.

Step 5: Response Paper

Word length and additional requirements set by Instructor. Students answer the research question in the Overview Questions. Students state a thesis and use as evidence passages from the primary source documents.

■ Proposals Relating to the Education of Youth in Pennsylvania

Date: 1749
Author: Franklin, Benjamin
Genre: essay

"While they are reading Natural History, might not a little Gardening, Planting, Grafting, Inoculating, &c. be taught and practised; and now and then Excursions made to the neighbouring Plantations of the best Farmers, their Methods observ'd and reason'd upon for the Information of Youth."

Summary Overview

Proposals Relating to the Education of Youth in Pennsylvania was published anonymously and presented to readers as a project approved by a group of "publick-spirited Gentlemen." It was distributed along with Benjamin Franklin's newspaper, the *Pennsylvania Gazette*, and responses were to be sent to "B. Franklin, Printer." Benjamin Franklin's involvement was clear from the beginning. (The phrase "publick-spirited Gentlemen" was probably used to make the project seem generally popular.) The pamphlet set forth Franklin's plan for an institution devoted to the teaching of young men and located in Philadelphia, which was the capital of the British colony of Pennsylvania. It sets forth how the institution will be structured and organized, how its students will be expected to live, and what its curriculum and goals will be. It also sets forth many aspects of Franklin's educational philosophy, one he expected would have a broad appeal to the Philadelphia elite whose support would be necessary to get the academy off the ground.

Defining Moment

Proposals Relating to the Education of Youth in Pennsylvania was published when Philadelphia was beginning to rival Boston as the intellectual center of the American colonies, in large part due to the efforts of Franklin himself. The Philadelphia intellectual community was more open and less institutionally based than that of Boston

and New England generally, which was dominated by an entrenched intelligentsia of ministers and university professors. Philadelphia itself was being transformed: The traditional Quaker elite was being challenged by numerous immigrants, including Franklin, with different religious beliefs and cultural backgrounds who contributed to the growth of the city and led to an increasing interest in the tradition of humanistic learning that went back to the Renaissance. At the time, there were few institutions of higher learning in the colonies, where education for most was more oriented to vocational needs through basic education in literacy or apprenticeships. Some schools taught Latin for the purpose of learning to pass the college entrance exam. The leading intellectual institutions of the colonies were outside Pennsylvania and the entire mid-Atlantic region—Harvard and Yale in New England and the College of William and Mary in Virginia. For advanced schooling, many prominent American families sent their sons across the Atlantic to schools in Britain.

The mid-eighteenth century was also a time when education in Europe and America was becoming increasingly secularized, particularly influenced by the secular nature of the Enlightenment. Christianity, although constituting a significant portion of the curriculum, was being challenged, particularly in the natural sciences, and the training of clerics was less important to the educational mission in many institutions. The growth in the volume and cultural prominence of scientific knowledge after the scientific revolution of the seventeenth century meant that science was also intruding into the humanistic curriculum, which was based on Greek and Latin. Many Enlightenment thinkers such as Franklin also believed that education should be more oriented for use, including economic development, than the traditional curriculum was.

Author Biography

Benjamin Franklin, the first native of the American colonies to win European recognition as a philosopher, was the son of a tallow chandler (candle maker) and soap boiler in Boston. At an early age, he began working for his brother James's newspaper where his first journalistic writings appeared. After a quarrel with James, he moved to Philadelphia in 1723 and visited London between 1724 and 1726. As a printer in Boston and Philadelphia, the young Franklin was a prolific writer spreading Enlightenment ideas of toleration and pragmatism. His *Pennsylvania Gazette* was the most popular newspaper throughout the American colonies. In Philadelphia, Franklin was not only the leading printer, but a leader in intellectual life, a very active Freemason, and an enthusiastic and successful organizer of libraries and discussion clubs, including the Academy of Philadelphia.

Upon retiring from his printing business in 1748, Franklin devoted more of his time to electrical science and politics. Franklin's greatest contribution to science was the one-fluid theory of electricity. Franklin identified electricity as a universal fluid and distinguished between electrified states as "positive," saturated with the electrical fluid, and "negative," deficient in it. Franklin's theory eventually formed the basis of electrical science. His book *Experiments and Observations on Electricity* (1751) was printed in London and translated into French, German, and Italian. Franklin also supported, although he did not originate, the idea that lightning was electricity. It is not clear whether he actually performed the famous experiment with a kite and a key, but his invention, the lightning rod, had a huge cultural impact as an outstanding example of the practical benefits of science.

Franklin went to London in 1758 as Pennsylvania's agent to the British government. He originally worked for closer relations between Britain and its American colonies, but he eventually came to believe that British arrogance and its uncompromising nature made this project impossible and supported the American Revolution, returning to America in 1775. As the ambassador of the American rebels to Paris, he played a crucial role in forming the alliance with France that became vital to American success. The universal respect he enjoyed among "enlightened" French people helped raise the prestige of the American cause. On his return to America, Franklin helped devise the new constitution and was one of the earliest prominent advocates of the abolition of slavery.

HISTORICAL DOCUMENT

The good Education of Youth has been esteemed by wise Men in all Ages, as the surest Foundation of the Happiness both of private Families and of Common-wealths. Almost all Governments have therefore made it a principal Object of their Attention, to establish and endow with proper Revenues, such Seminaries of Learning, as might supply the succeeding Age with Men qualified to serve the Publick with Honour to themselves, and to their Country.

Many of the first Settlers of these Provinces, were Men who had received a good Education in *Europe*, and to their Wisdom and good Management we owe much of our present Prosperity. But their Hands were full, and they could not do all Things. The present Race are not thought to be generally of equal Ability: For though the *American* Youth are allow'd not to want Capacity; yet the best Capacities require Cultivation, it being truly with them, as with the best Ground, which unless well tilled and sowed with profitable Seed, produces only ranker Weeds.

That we may obtain the Advantages arising from an Increase of Knowledge, and prevent as much as may be the mischievous Consequences that would attend a general Ignorance among us, the following *Hints* are offered towards forming a Plan for the Education of the Youth of *Pennsylvania*, viz.

It is propos'd,

THAT some Persons of Leisure and publick Spirit, apply for a CHARTER, by which they may be incorporated, with Power to erect an ACADEMY for the Education of Youth, to govern the same, provide Masters, make Rules, receive Donations, purchase Lands, &c. and to add to their Number, from Time to Time such other Persons as they shall judge suitable.

That the Members of the Corporation make it their Pleasure, and in some Degree their Business, to visit the Academy often, encourage and countenance the Youth, countenance and assist the Masters, and by all Means in their Power advance the Usefulness and Reputation of the Design; that they look on the Students as in some Sort their Children, treat them with Familiarity and Affection, and when they have behav'd well, and gone through their Studies, and are to enter the World, zealously unite, and make all the Interest that can be made to establish them, whether in Business, Offices, Marriages, or any other Thing for their Advantage, preferably to all other Persons whatsoever even of equal Merit.

And if Men may, and frequently do, catch such a Taste for cultivating Flowers, Planting, Grafting, Inoculating, and the like, as to despise all other Amusements for their Sake, why may not we expect they should acquire a Relish for that *more useful* Culture of young Minds. *Thompson* says,

> *'Tis Joy to see the human Blossoms blow,*
> *When infant Reason grows apace, and calls*
> *For the kind Hand of an assiduous Care;*
> *Delightful Task! to rear the tender Thought,*
> *To teach the young Idea how to shoot,*
> *To pour the fresh Instruction o'er the Mind,*
> *To breathe th' enliv'ning Spirit, and to fix*
> *The generous Purpose in the glowing Breast.*

That a House be provided for the ACADEMY, if not in the Town, not many Miles from it; the Situation high and dry, and if it may be, not far from a River, having a Garden, Orchard, Meadow, and a Field or two.

That the House be furnished with a Library (if in the Country, if in the Town, the Town Libraries may serve) with Maps of all Countries, Globes, some mathematical Instruments, and Apparatus for Experiments in Natural Philosophy, and for Mechanics; Prints, of all Kinds, Prospects, Buildings, Machines, &c.

That the RECTOR be a Man of good Understanding, good Morals, diligent and patient, learn'd in the Languages and Sciences, and a correct pure Speaker and Writer of the *English* Tongue; to have such Tutors under him as shall be necessary.

That the boarding Scholars diet together, plainly, temperately, and frugally.

That to keep them in Health, and to strengthen and render active their Bodies, they be frequently xercis'd in Running, Leaping, Wrestling, and Swimming &c.

That they have peculiar Habits to distinguish them from other Youth, if the Academy be in or near the Town; for this, among other Reasons, that their Behaviour may be the better observed.

As to their STUDIES, it would be well if they could be taught *every Thing* that is useful, and *every Thing* that is ornamental: But Art is long, and their Time is short. It is therefore propos'd that they learn those Things that are likely to be most useful and *most ornamental*. Regard being had to the several Professions for which they are intended. . . .

✳✳✳

MORALITY, by descanting and making continual Observations on the Causes of the Rise or Fall of any Man's Character, Fortune, Power, &c . mention'd in History; the Advantages of Temperance, Order, Frugality, Industry, Perseverance, &c. &c. Indeed the general natural Tendency of Reading good History, must be, to fix in the Minds of Youth deep Impressions of the Beauty and Usefulness of Virtue of all Kinds, Publick Spirit, Fortitude, &c.

History will show the wonderful Effects of ORATORY, in governing, turning and leading great Bodies of Mankind, Armies, Cities, Nations. When the Minds of Youth are struck with Admiration at this, then is the Time to give them the Principles of that Art, which they will study with Taste and Application. Then they may be made acquainted with the best Models among the Antients, their Beauties being particularly pointed out to them. Modern Political Oratory being chiefly performed by the Pen and Press, its Advantages over the Antient in some Respects are to be shown; as that its Effects are more extensive, more lasting, &c.

History will also afford frequent Opportunities of showing the Necessity of a *Publick Religion*, from its Usefulness to the Publick; the Advantage of a Religious Character among private Persons; the Mischiefs of Superstition, &c . and the Excellency of the CHRISTIAN RELIGION above all others antient or modern.

History will also give Occasion to expatiate on the Advantage of Civil Orders and Constitutions, how Men and their Properties are protected by joining in Societies and establishing Government; their Industry encouraged and rewarded, Arts invented, and Life made more comfortable: The Advantages of *Liberty*, Mischiefs of *Licentiousness*, Benefits arising from good Laws and a due Execution of Justice, &c. Thus may the first Principles of sound *Politicks* be fix'd in the Minds of Youth.

On *Historical* Occasions, Questions of Right and Wrong, Justice and Injustice, will naturally arise, and may be put to Youth, which they may debate in Conversation and in Writing. When they ardently desire Victory, for the Sake of the Praise attending it, they will begin to feel the Want, and be sensible of the Use of *Logic*, or the Art of Reasoning to *discover* Truth, and of Arguing to *defend* it, and *convince* Adversaries. This would be the Time to acquaint them with the Principles of that Art. *Grotius*, *Puffendorff*, and some other Writers of the same Kind, may be used on these Occasions to decide their Disputes. Publick Disputes warm the Imagination, whet the Industry, and strengthen the natural Abilities.

When Youth are told, that the Great Men whose Lives and Actions they read in History, spoke two of the best Languages that ever were, the most expressive, copious, beautiful; and that the finest Writings, the most correct Compositions, the most perfect Productions of human Wit and Wisdom, are in those Languages, which have endured Ages, and will endure while there are Men; that no Translation can do them Justice, or give the Pleasure found in Reading the Originals; that those Languages contain all Science; that one of them is become almost universal, being the Language of Learned Men in all Countries; that to understand them is a distinguishing Ornament, &c. they may be thereby made desirous of learning those Languages, and their Industry sharpen'd in the Acquisition of them. All intended for Divin-

ity should be taught the *Latin* and *Greek* ; for Physick, the *Latin*, *Greek* and *French*; for Law, the *Latin* and *French*; Merchants, the *French*, *German*, and *Spanish*: And though all should not be compell'd to learn *Latin*, *Greek*, or the modern foreign Languages; yet none that have an ardent Desire to learn them should be refused; their *English*, Arithmetick, and other Studies absolutely necessary, being at the same Time not neglected.

If the new *Universal History* were also read, it would give a *connected* Idea of human Affairs, so far as it goes, which should be follow'd by the best modern Histories, particularly of our Mother Country; then of these Colonies; which should be accompanied with Observations on their Rise, Encrease, Use to *Great-Britain*, Encouragements, Discouragements, &c. the Means to make them flourish, secure their Liberties, &c.

With the History of Men, Times and Nations, should be read at proper Hours or Days, some of the best *Histories of Nature*, which would not only be delightful to Youth, and furnish them with Matter for their Letters, &c. as well as other History; but afterwards of great Use to them, whether they are Merchants, Handicrafts, or Divines; enabling the first the better to understand many Commodities, Drugs, &c . the second to improve his Trade or Handicraft by new Mixtures, Materials, &c . and the last to adorn his Discourses by beautiful Comparisons, and strengthen them by new Proofs of Divine Providence. The Conversation of all will be improved by it, as Occasions frequently occur of making Natural Observations, which are instructive, agreeable, and entertaining in almost all Companies. *Natural History* will also afford Opportunities of introducing many Observations, relating to the Preservation of Health, which may be afterwards of great Use. *Arbuthnot* on Air and *Aliment*, *Sanctorius* on Perspiration, *Lemery* on Foods, and some others, may now be read, and a very little Explanation will make them sufficiently intelligible to Youth.

While they are reading Natural History, might not a little *Gardening, Planting, Grafting, Inoculating*, &c. be taught and practised; and now and then Excursions made to the neighbouring Plantations of the best Farmers, their Methods observ'd and reason'd upon for the Information of Youth. The Improvement of Agriculture being useful to all, and Skill in it no Disparagement to any.

The History of *Commerce*, of the Invention of Arts, Rise of Manufactures, Progress of Trade, Change of its Seats, with the Reasons, Causes, &c. may also be made entertaining to Youth, and will be useful to all. And this, with the Accounts in other History of the prodigious Force and Effect of Engines and Machines used in War, will naturally introduce a Desire to be instructed in *Mechanicks*, and to be inform'd of the Principles of that Art by which weak Men perform such Wonders, Labour is sav'd, Manufactures expedited, &c. &c. This will be the Time to show them Prints of antient and modern Machines, to explain them, to let them be copied, and to give Lectures in Mechanical Philosophy.

With the whole should be constantly inculcated and cultivated, that *Benignity of Mind*, which shows itself in *searching for* and *seizing* every Opportunity *to serve* and *to oblige*; and is the Foundation of what is called GOOD BREEDING; highly useful to the Possessor, and most agreeable to all.

The Idea of what is *true Merit*, should also be often presented to Youth, explain'd and impress'd on their Minds, as consisting in an *Inclination* join'd with an *Ability* to serve Mankind, one's Country, Friends and Family; which *Ability* is (with the Blessing of God) to be acquir'd or greatly encreas'd by *true Learning*; and should indeed be the great *Aim* and *End* of all Learning.

GLOSSARY

antient: ancient

Arbuthnot: John Arbuthnot (1667–1735), Scottish physician

arts: technologies

Grotius: Hugo Grotius (1583–1645), Dutch jurisprudent

habits: clothing

Lemery: Nicolas Lemery (1645–1715), French chemist

masters: teachers

physick: medicine

Puffendorf: Samuel von Pufendorf (1632–94), German professor of international law

Sanctorius: Santorio Sanctorius (1561–1636), Italian medical professor

Document Analysis

Benjamin Franklin's program for the education of the young men of colonial America—the education of women is not mentioned in the document—is a blend of traditional Christian humanistic learning with a more scientific approach, oriented to public service, economic development, and the creation of an intellectual and social elite. Since Franklin was an innovator in thinking about what education should cover, it was necessary to explain the plan of the new institution at some length. Christianity remains an important part of education, but Franklin's approach has many secular elements and does not distinguish between Christian denominations.

Throughout the document, Franklin's concern is utilitarian and emphasizes the social and personal use of learning rather than individual intellectual development for its own sake, claiming that the present generation of American settlers lacked the intellectual training of the first colonists partially due to a lack of institutions to educate them. The institution's graduates are expected to be useful to the British Empire, in which the American colonies play an important but subordinate role. The proposed institution will contribute to the creation of a political and economic elite as well as an intellectual and cultural one in Pennsylvania and perhaps throughout the colonies. (Although the institution began as a charity school, Franklin anticipated it growing into a college, which would lessen the temptation for Pennsylvanians to send their sons to school elsewhere.)

Franklin begins with a tribute to the importance of educating male youth, which is a theme in Western culture going back at least as far as Plato. Education served both the needs of the family and of the state, and the importance of education is therefore such that it should be supported by publicly funded institutions. (Although Franklin was mostly self-taught, he did not expect his path to be widely followed.) Franklin's picture of the intellectual development of Americans is one of decline, explaining that the original settlers, who included many learned men from Europe, had been too busy to fully educate their descendants. American youths had the "capacity" (potential) to excel, but they were failing for want of education, despite the wealth and prosperity of the colonies. Without education, the work of the first generation could collapse. Rather than create a state-controlled institution, which was not the usual practice, Franklin suggests that a group of "publick-spirited" individuals with the wealth and "Leisure" (time) carry out the project and receive a charter from the Pennsylvania government to found an academy. The charter, which was a necessity in establishing an institution of this kind, would create a corporation endowed with certain rights, among them the right to own property.

In a break with tradition, the proposed institution would be nonsectarian. Given that higher education institutions in Europe (along with those few that existed in the colonies, such as Harvard) were church entities dominated by clergy and largely devoted to training new clergy, this was an innovation. (This innovation would have been impossible in church-dominated New England, where Franklin had been raised.) Franklin's brief description of the origins of schools discusses how they were founded by "governments," and it obscures the central role played by churches and religious institutions. In discussing the qualifications of the head of the institution, the "Rector," Franklin states only that he be of "good morals" and not that he be a clergyman, as was the standard practice of the time.

The Academy of Philadelphia, however, was not a secular institution in the modern sense. Franklin believed that religion would be taught in his new academy, an idea he, at least rhetorically, strongly supported, but his references to it are ambiguous. Religion is introduced as a subject subordinate to history and is viewed in terms of social utility and not in terms of understanding the cosmos or in the salvation of the soul. "Superstition," commonly defined in the Enlightenment as an excessive fear of God that led to irrational and ineffective religious practices, was to be avoided, and the teaching of religion was regarded as a preventive measure against it.

However, Franklin does not carry his secularism to the point of treating other religions as equal to Christianity, the promotion of which is an important purpose of the institution. What distinguishes Christianity from all other religions for Franklin, however, is not its truth, but its "excellency," which is a far more ambiguous term. Philadelphia was a religiously divided city, and the original Quaker elite were increasingly challenged by members of the Church of England, a broad range of other Christian denominations, and the Quaker sects of German immigrants to Pennsylvania. Franklin, who was not a member of a church, treads carefully and does not identify his educational program with a particular Christian sect, nor does he make a distinction between Protestantism and Catholicism. Given the Protestant dominance in the British colonies, however, Franklin's readers may well have assumed that Christianity meant Protestantism. Furthermore, many eighteenth-century Protestants identified superstition with Roman Catholicism, so Franklin's attack on superstition would have positioned him on the Protestant side.

History was an important part of the curriculum, and as was common among humanists, history, particularly ancient history, served as a stock of moral examples. The virtues it taught were among the primary reasons for studying it. In discussing the teaching of morality, Franklin emphasizes virtues such as temperance, diligence, and order, which are most conducive to occupational success and the promotion of which was an essential part of Franklin's cultural mission, as exemplified in his *Poor Richard's Almanack* (1732) and other writings.

Rhetoric and oratory were also important in discussing education, although Franklin broadens the concept of oration beyond its original spoken form to include written political argument, marking an important distinction between the "ancients" and the "moderns." Franklin was a printer who made his living by the written word, so it is unsurprising that he views this change to written and published eloquence as an improvement. Knowledge of oratory and rhetoric would enable students to participate effectively in public life. Franklin also sees debate as a worthwhile activity and hopes that ambitions for victory in debate will encourage the study of logic.

The students would also learn an approach to politics in which governments were created for the protection of life and property. Franklin makes no mention of God in the establishment of government or the support of its authority. Governments are to be evaluated by utilitarian criteria, and there is no suggestion that monarchy is intrinsically superior to republican forms of government. "Liberty" is considered an important political value, and Franklin's politics is clearly identified with the dominant Whig view of British politics rather than the more authoritarian and theocratic Tory position. (The modern English writers he recommends elsewhere in the proposals are virtually entirely Whigs, and in London, he frequented the Club of Honest Whigs.)

A boy's education in the eighteenth century was largely based on the classical tradition of Greece and Rome, and Franklin rhapsodizes over the beauty and importance of the Greek and Latin languages and the classical tradition generally. His own writing includes allusions that would be recognized by anyone educated in the classics, such as his paraphrase of the ancient Greek physician Hippocrates's famous saying that art is long and time is short. However, Franklin does not envision Greek and Latin being required for all students. (Franklin claimed to value the reading of the classical languages but was much more openly skeptical about teaching boys to write them, which he viewed as a waste of time and a distraction from the serious task of learning to write English well.) He makes a distinction based on what profession the student planned to enter: Future clergymen, or "Divines," would learn Latin and Greek; future physicians would learn Greek and Latin, the "learned" languages of their profession, as well as French, the language of much contemporary science; and prospective merchants would learn the modern languages of major trading partners. As electives, Greek and Latin would not dominate the curriculum, and it would be possible to graduate from the academy without Latin, which was not possible in a traditional European college preparatory school. However, the learning of languages generally would be encouraged even outside the context of vocational preparation. The teaching of ancient

or modern foreign languages would not, however, be allowed to take precedence over the teaching of English, which Franklin regarded as central to the academy's intellectual mission, even specifying skill in English as a qualification for the rector or head of the institution.

Despite the humanist influence over the curriculum, Franklin also endorses a much more prominent role for science than was the case at many educational institutions at the time. As in the discussion of other forms of learning, utility is uppermost in Franklin's mind. The teaching of the "History of Nature" is important in its pragmatic use in a variety of professions and not just for the mental exercise it provides. For merchants, natural knowledge would provide a background for dealing with a wide range of sometimes unfamiliar commodities. For artisans, knowledge of nature would open the door for technological improvements, which was a major concern of Franklin's, who made many such improvements himself. For clergymen, natural history would provide examples of "Divine Providence" at work in the world. This concept of natural theology was popular among many clergymen in the eighteenth century, both members of the Church of England and of other English-speaking faiths. Natural knowledge also promoted stimulating conversation and good health.

Agricultural development was another of Franklin's interests and an end that he hoped the new academy would serve. The students would not just study agriculture, but even learn by practicing it. Metaphors of vegetation abound in *Proposals Relating to the Education of Youth in Pennsylvania*, both in Franklin's own writing and in the short verse passage beginning with "Tis Joy to see" quoted from "The Four Seasons: Spring" by the popular eighteenth-century Scottish poet James Thomson (who Franklin refers to as Thompson). The work of cultivating young people is explicitly compared to the work of agricultural improvers. Colonial America was an agrarian society, and Franklin and a broad range of his readers would be familiar with agricultural processes. Additionally, the people Franklin planned to attract to the academy derived much of their wealth from the production of the land. The improvement of agriculture was a common theme in the Enlightenment both in America and Europe. The academy itself would be endowed with a garden, meadow, and orchard, placing it firmly in a context of productive cultivation.

The vision of the British Empire Franklin gives here is still one where the colonies are subordinated to the overall needs of Britain. In learning the history of the colonies, which comes after the history of the "Mother Country," students would learn how useful the colonies were to Britain. However, their education would also be aimed at promoting the prosperity and liberty of the colonies themselves. References to the colonies are collective, indicating that despite the title of the work, Franklin may have been thinking beyond the borders of Pennsylvania in terms of student recruitment. As a emigrant from New England who had spent time in London and as someone with business connections among printers in many colonial American cities, Franklin had a broader perspective than many of the Philadelphia elite, whose knowledge tended to be confined to Pennsylvania.

Despite Franklin's initial insistence that the endowment of educational institutions was a proper function of government, he makes little mention of public funding elsewhere, perhaps knowing that such a proposition would be difficult to get through the Pennsylvania legislature. Nor does he assert that the institution would be funded by the tuition and fees of the students. Presumably the benevolent, civic-minded founders would also largely fund the institution. Its endowment would include a library, although the thrifty Franklin points out that if it was located in the city of Philadelphia itself, the students could use the already established libraries. (Franklin himself was a founder of the Library Company of Philadelphia, one of the first public circulating libraries in the American colonies.) Franklin, a master experimenter, emphasizes the scientific equipment the school will possess.

Student life is envisioned as communal and is marked by a distinctive garb that would set them apart from other men their own age and allow the community to monitor their behavior. This was common in many schools and institutions of higher learning. Health is to be maintained by a frugal diet and frequent exercises. (In a footnote, Franklin suggests that the students not be allowed to dine away from the academy.)

The academy is expected to have a far-reaching impact on society, well beyond that of merely producing educated men, and to be tightly intertwined with the Philadelphia elite. The individuals who applied for and gained the charter would function as more than patrons of the institution. They would operate as hands-on supervisors of the work that went on there, visiting it frequently to encourage and assist both students and masters. Indeed, Franklin expected many of them to become so enamored of education that they would become unpaid teachers themselves, and their involvement with the students would continue after graduation. Franklin envisioned the academy as at the center of a familial and patronage network that would advance its graduates' careers. The founders would take an active interest in the students' careers and would treat them as their children (as, presumably, many of them would literally be) and work to advance them even beyond persons of equal merit. The advancement of the students would extend not only to include business and public office, but even "Marriages." The graduates of the academy would become a social and economic elite, guiding the colony, and perhaps other colonies as well, in the way they thought best.

Essential Themes

The academy that this document envisioned was founded as the Academy of Philadelphia in 1749, with Franklin as its first president and an active promoter of the institution. It opened its doors to students in 1752, although it did not receive a charter until the next year. Franklin continued to be involved with the academy, particularly in its early financial troubles, using the *Pennsylvania Gazette* to promote fundraising ideas such as lotteries. By the late 1750s, however, Franklin's involvement was diminishing, partly due to the numerous commitments that took him away from Philadelphia (and eventually from America entirely) and partly due to his personal and political struggles against the provost of the academy, William Smith. Franklin and Smith, whose early career Franklin had promoted, were champions of opposite factions in Pennsylvania politics, Smith of the Proprietary Party representing the Penn family, founders of the colony, and Franklin of the more popularly based Quaker Party. The conflict between the two men for control of the academy was often bitter. Franklin's belief in the importance of teaching English, natural sciences, and technology was also challenged by more conservative educators, including Smith, who wanted a traditional curriculum based on Greek and Latin and geared toward training clergymen. Quarrels between the classical faculty and the school for teaching English grew bitter, and the underfunded English school lost much of its academic standing. Franklin's belief that the academy be nonsectarian was also challenged by those who wanted to make it an Anglican institution. Smith, an Anglican clergyman, led the challenge and was rumored to have hoped to become the first Anglican bishop in British North America.

The Academy of Philadelphia was the kernel of the modern University of Pennsylvania, founded in 1791, the first American institution of higher education to proclaim itself a university. Even before that, the academy had fulfilled Franklin's dream of being a nursery of colonial leaders and played a leading role in the formation of the Pennsylvania elite. Among its alumni were several signers of the Declaration of Independence and revolutionary leaders, and the principles of the Declaration of Independence and the US Constitution are related to those Franklin put forth. In the long run, Franklin's combination of a humanist and scientific curriculum with an emphasis on utility rather than an education focused on Greek, Latin, and theology also proved influential in the subsequent development of American higher education.

William E. Burns, PhD

Bibliography

Clark, Ronald W. *Benjamin Franklin: A Biography*. New York: Barnes and Noble, 2004. Print.

Franklin, Benjamin. *Franklin: Writings*. Ed. Joseph A. L. Lemay. New York: Literary Classics, 1996. Print.

Lemay, Joseph A. L. *The Life of Benjamin Franklin*. 3 vols. Philadelphia: U of Pennsylvania P, 2006–09. Print.

McConaghy, Mary D., Michael Silberman, and Irina Kalashnikova. "Introduction: From Franklin's Vision to Academy to University of Pennsylvania." *University Archives and Records Center*. University of Pennsylvania University Archives and Records Center, 2004. Web. 20 June 2012.

Additional Reading

Burns, William E. *Science and Technology in Colonial America*. Westport: Greenwood, 2005. Print.

Fisher, Sydney George. *The True Benjamin Franklin*. 1899. Philadelphia: Lippincott, 2012. Print.

Franklin, Benjamin. *The Ingenious Dr. Franklin: Selected Scientific Letters of Benjamin Franklin*. Ed. Nathaniel G. Goodman. Philadelphia: U of Pennsylvania P, 2000. Print.

Monaghan, E. Jennifer. *Learning to Read and Write in Colonial America*. Amherst: U of Massachusetts P, 2007. Print.

Morgan, Edmund S. *Benjamin Franklin*. New Haven: Yale UP, 2002. Print.

Urban, Wayne J., and Jennings L. Wagoner Jr. *American Education: A History*. 4th ed. New York: Routledge, 2009. Print.

Wolf, Edwin. *The Book Culture of a Colonial American City: Philadelphia Books, Bookmen, and Booksellers*. New York: Oxford UP, 1988. Print.

LESSON PLAN: Benjamin Franklin's Views on Education

Students analyze excerpts from Benjamin Franklin's pamphlet on education to gauge the changing opinions about education in colonial America.

Learning Objectives

Read Proposals imaginatively in the context of the common understanding about Franklin; identify Franklin's purpose and intended audience; identify relevant historical antecedents to our contemporary education; compare and contrast Franklin's ideas on education to earlier plans.
Materials: Benjamin Franklin, *Proposals Relating to the Education of Youth in Pennsylvania* (1749); Harvard College Laws of 1642; Harvard College Laws of 1700.

Overview Questions

How does Franklin's pamphlet reflect our modern perceptions of him? Who must Franklin persuade about the need for education? What specific curriculum does Franklin suggest? How did thought about college curriculum evolve in colonial America?

Step 1: Comprehension Questions

What opinions does Franklin offer that seem consistent with your image of him? What opinions seem at odds with that image?

▶ **Activity:** Direct students to read aloud passages that sound like Franklin, based off students' knowledge and perceptions of him. Discuss why the passages work this way. Direct students to read aloud passages that do not sound like Franklin as he is generally perceived. Have students discuss if and how Franklin's words alter their image of him.

Step 2: Context Questions

What specific audience is Franklin addressing? How is the pamphlet structured to reach that audience?

▶ **Activity:** Have students identify passages that show who Franklin is trying to convince and why. Discuss what techniques Franklin uses to persuade. Challenge students to identify any educational philosophy or opinions that Franklin may offer just to woo that audience.

Step 3: Context Questions

What subjects does Franklin think are important for students to master? How does his view of college curriculum differ from twenty-first-century views?

▶ **Activity:** Have students create a chart showing what Franklin includes in his curriculum and his reasons for each inclusion. Discuss with students whether this curriculum would be relevant today and why or why not.

Step 4: Historical Connections Questions

How do changes from the Harvard College laws from 1642 to 1700 suggest an evolution in college curriculum? How do Franklin's suggestions further that movement?

▶ **Activity:** Have students discuss the differences between the two sets of Harvard College laws. Have students compare Franklin's curriculum to the 1700 laws and track further evolution in the curriculum. Discuss with students the implications of changes in the context of colonial America.

Step 5: Response Paper

Word length and additional requirements set by Instructor. Students answer the research question in the Overview Questions. Students state a thesis and use as evidence passages from the primary source documents.

■ Gottlieb Mittelberger's Journey to Pennsylvania

Date: 1756
Author: Mittelberger, Gottlieb
Genre: memoir

*"Many sigh and cry: 'Oh, that I were at home
again, and if I had to lie in my pig-sty!'
Or they say: 'O God, if I only had a piece of good
bread, or a good fresh drop of water.'"*

Summary Overview

Gottlieb Mittelberger was a German musician who traveled to America to install an organ that had been purchased by a church in the Philadelphia region. On board the ship on which he sailed were a number of redemptioners—individuals who contracted to work for someone for a specified period of time as the means of paying for their passage to America. Mittelberger later wrote a memoir, *Journey to Pennsylvania in the Year 1750, and Return to Germany in the Year 1754*, in which he discourages Europeans from taking the risk of immigrating to America as redemptioners. His memoir is most noted for its negative assessment of the opportunities presented to these immigrants, describing the terrible conditions they had to endure in crossing the Atlantic, the system by which their contracts for labor were purchased by landowners or businessmen in the colonies, and the often-brutal conditions under which they labored.

Defining Moment

A large percentage of the laborers who came to America in the 1600s and 1700s were indentured servants, workers who agreed to work for someone, usually a landowner or business owner, in return for their transport to America. Their terms of service were defined by their contracts and typically ranged from two to seven years, although young people often had to serve until they were twenty-one years old. Landowners preferred laborers who were legally bound to a term of service because, with the ready availability of cheap land in

America, free workers would likely leave after a brief time to start their own farms. Although this institution had a number of similarities to slavery, landowners who employed indentured servants did not technically own the servants; rather, they owned the contracts for their labor.

The people with whom Mittelberger traveled to Pennsylvania were referred to as redemptioners. Sometimes this word is used interchangeably with "indentured servant," although it is usually only applied to servants from continental Europe, as opposed to those from England. English indentured servants usually already had their contracts for labor worked out before they left their homeland; they often knew exactly where they were going, who they would work for, and how long they were contracted to work. In contrast, the contracts for the labor of redemptioners were sold after they arrived in America, and the laborers had to bargain for the best terms they could obtain. Young, healthy, and highly skilled servants were the most sought after and could generally bargain for a better contract, while older or unskilled workers had fewer opportunities for negotiation.

In the southern colonies, the use of indentured servants began to decline in the late 1600s. Economic conditions in England had improved somewhat, making it harder to recruit potential servants. Also, as landowners became wealthier, they could afford to import or purchase African slaves, who were considered better long-term investments. In Pennsylvania, where Mittelberger lived for several years, indentured servants and redemptioners were probably still more common than slaves during the late colonial era, in part because there were few large plantations growing staple crops.

Author Biography

Little is known about Mittelberger's life prior to his journey to Pennsylvania. He was born in about 1715 in Enzweihingen, a small town in the Duchy of Württemberg, a state in the Holy Roman Empire (now Germany). Germans from this region had been coming to Pennsylvania since the early years of William Penn's colony, which was chartered in 1681.

Mittelberger's voyage to America was connected with the purchase of an organ by a church in a settlement called the Trappe, located in New Providence, Pennsylvania. The church that purchased the organ was a Lutheran church led by Reverend Henry Melchior Muhlenberg, who had immigrated to Pennsylvania in 1742 and was one of the first ordained Lutheran ministers in America. Mittelberger apparently came to help install the organ. He then served as an organist and also taught in a school connected to the church. This, plus the fact that he wrote a literate account of his journey and the time he spent in Pennsylvania, indicates that he had some basic education, though the exact nature and extent of his schooling is unknown.

Mittelberger's account of coming to Pennsylvania is best known for its description of the conditions in which the redemptioners were transported and under which they worked. However, Mittelberger himself was not a redemptioner; it appears that he came to America as a regular passenger, either paying for his passage or having it paid for him. Mittelberger returned to Germany in 1754, and his book, his only known publication, was published in 1756. There is little historical information pertaining to Mittelberger's life following the publication of his memoir. He likely died in Germany around 1779.

HISTORICAL DOCUMENT

When the ships have for the last time weighed their anchors near the city of Kaupp in Old England, the real misery begins with the long voyage. For from there the ships, unless they have good wind, must often sail 8, 9, 10 to 12 weeks before they reach Philadelphia. But even with the best wind the voyage lasts 7 weeks. But during the voyage there is on board these ships terrible misery, stench, fumes, horror, vomiting, many kinds of seasickness, fever, dysentery, headache, heat, constipation, boils, scurvy, cancer, mouth-rot, and the like, all of which come from old and sharply salted food and meat, also from very bad and foul water, so that many die miserably.

Add to this want of provisions, hunger, thirst, frost, heat, dampness, anxiety, want, afflictions and lamentations, together with other trouble, as c. v. the lice abound so frightfully, especially on sick people, that they can be scraped off the body. The misery reaches the climax when a gale rages for 2 or 3 nights and days, so that every one believes that the ship will go to the bottom with all human beings on board. In such a visitation the people cry and pray most piteously. When in such a gale the sea rages and surges, so that the waves rise often like high mountains one above the other, and often tumble over the ship, so that one fears to go down with the ship; when the ship is constantly tossed from side to side by the storm and waves, so that no one can either walk, or sit, or lie, and the closely packed people in the berths are thereby tumbled over each other, both the sick and the well—it will be readily understood that many of these people, none of whom had been prepared for hardships, suffer so terribly from them that they do not survive it. I myself had to pass through a severe illness at sea, and I best know how I felt at the time. These poor people often long for consolation, and I often entertained and comforted them with singing, praying and exhorting; and whenever it was possible and the winds and waves permitted it, I kept daily prayer-meetings with them on deck. Besides, I baptized five children in distress, because we had no ordained minister on board. I also held divine service every Sunday by reading sermons to the people; and when the dead were sunk in the water, I commended them and our souls to the mercy of God.

Among the healthy, impatience sometimes grows so great and cruel that one curses the other, or himself and the day of his birth, and sometimes come near killing each other. Misery and malice join each other, so that they cheat and rob one another. One always reproaches the other with having persuaded him to undertake the journey. Frequently children cry out against their parents, husbands against their wives and wives against their husbands, brothers and sisters, friends and acquaintances against each other. But most against the soul-traffickers. Many sigh and cry: "Oh, that I were at home again, and if I had to lie in my pig-sty!" Or they say: "O God, if I only had a piece of good bread, or a good fresh drop of water." Many people whimper, sigh and cry piteously for their homes; most of them get home-sick. Many hundred people necessarily die and perish in such misery, and must be cast into the sea, which drives their relatives, or those who persuaded them to undertake the journey, to such despair that it is almost impossible to pacify and console them. In a word, the sighing and crying and lamenting on board the ship continues night and day, so as to cause the hearts even of the most hardened to bleed when they hear it.

No one can have an idea of the sufferings which women in confinement have to bear with their innocent children on board these ships. Few of this class escape with their lives; many a mother is cast into the water with her child as soon as she is dead. One day, just as we had a heavy gale, a woman in our ship, who was to give birth and could not give birth under the circumstances, was pushed through a loophole [porthole] in the ship and dropped into the sea, because she was far in the rear of the ship and could not be brought forward.

Children from 1 to 7 years rarely survive the voyage; and many a time parents are compelled to see their children miserably suffer and die from hunger, thirst and sickness, and then to see them cast into the water. I witnessed such misery in no less than 32 children in our ship, all of whom were thrown into the sea. The parents grieve all the more since their children find no resting-place in the earth, but are devoured by the monsters of the sea. It is a notable fact that children, who have not yet had the measles or small-pocks, generally get them on board the ship, and mostly die of them. Often a father is separated by death from his wife and children, or mothers from their little children, or even both parents from their children; and sometimes whole families die in quick succession; so that often many dead persons lie in the berths beside the living Ones, especially when contagious diseases have broken out on board the ship. Many other accidents hap-

pen on board these ships, especially by falling, whereby people are often made cripples and can never be set right again. Some have also fallen into the ocean.

That most of the people get sick is not surprising, because, in addition to all other trials and hardships, warm food is served only three times a week, the rations being very poor and very little. Such meals can hardly be eaten, on account of being so unclean. The water which is served out on the ships is often very black, thick and full of worms, so that one cannot drink it without loathing, even with the greatest thirst. O surely, one would often give much money at sea for a piece of good bread, or a drink of good water, not to say a drink of good wine, if it were only to be had. I myself experienced that sufficiently, I am sorry to say. Toward the end we were compelled to eat the ship's biscuit which had been spoiled long ago; though in a whole biscuit there was scarcely a piece the size of a dollar that had not been full of red worms and spiders' nests. Great hunger and thirst force us to eat and drink everything; but many a one does so at the risk of his life. The sea-water cannot be drunk, because it is salt and bitter as gall. If this were not so, such a voyage could be made with less expense and without so many hardships.

At length, when, after a long and tedious voyage, the ships come in sight of land, so that the promontories can be seen, which the people were so eager and anxious to see, all creep from below on deck to see the land from afar, and they weep for joy, and pray and sing, thanking and praising God. The sight of the land makes the people on board the ship, especially the sick and the half dead, alive again, so that their hearts leap within them; they shout and rejoice, and are content to bear their misery in patience, in the hope that they may soon reach the land in safety. But alas!

When the ships have landed at Philadelphia after their long voyage, no one is permitted to leave them except those who pay for their passage or can give good security; the others, who cannot pay, must remain on board the ships till they are purchased, and are released from the ships by their purchasers. The sick always fare the worst, for the healthy are naturally preferred and purchased first; and so the sick and wretched must often remain on board in front of the city for 2 or 3 weeks, and frequently die, whereas many a one, if he could pay his debt and were permitted to leave the ship immediately, might recover and remain alive . . .

The sale of human beings in the market on board the ship is carried on thus: Every day Englishmen, Dutchmen and High-German people come from the city of Philadelphia and other places, in part from a great distance, say 20, 30, or 40 hours away, and go on board the newly arrived ship that has brought and offers for sale passengers from Europe, and select among the healthy persons such as they deem suitable for their business, and bargain with them how long they will serve for their passage-money, which most of them are still in debt for. When they have come to an agreement, it happens that adult persons bind themselves in writing to serve 3, 4, 5 or 6 years for the amount due by them, according to their age and strength. But very young people, from 10 to 15 years, must serve till they are 21 years old. Many parents must sell and trade away their children like so many head of cattle; for if their children take the debt upon themselves, the parents can leave the ship free and unrestrained; but as the parents often do not know where and to what people their children are going, it often happens that such parents and children, after leaving the ship, do not see each other again for many years, perhaps no more in all their lives.

When people arrive who cannot make themselves free, but have children under 5 years, the parents can not free themselves by them; for such children must be given to somebody without compensation to be brought up, and they must serve for their bringing up till they are 21 years old. Children from 5 to 10 years, who pay half price for their passage, viz. 30 florins, must likewise serve for it till they are 21 years of age; they cannot, therefore, redeem their parents by taking the debt of the latter upon themselves. But children above 10 years can take part of their parents' debt upon themselves.

A woman must stand for her husband if he arrives sick, and in like manner a man for his sick wife, and take the debt upon herself or himself, and thus serve 5 to 6 years not alone for his or her own debt, but also for that of the sick husband or wife. But if both are sick, such persons are sent from the ship to the sick-house [hospital] but not until it appears probable that they will find no purchasers. As soon as they are well again they must serve for their passage, or pay if they have means. It often happens that whole families, husband, wife, and children, are separated by being sold to different purchasers, especially when they have not paid any part of their passage money.

When a husband or wife has died at sea, when the ship has made more than half of her trip, the survivor must pay or serve not only for himself or herself, but also for the deceased. When both parents have died over halfway at sea, their children, especially when they are young and have nothing to pawn or to pay, must stand for their own and their parents' passage, and serve till they are 21 years old. When one has served his or her term, he or she is entitled to a new suit of clothes at parting and if it has been so stipulated, a man gets in addition a horse, a woman, a cow. When a serf has an opportunity to marry in this country, he or she must pay for each year which he or she would have yet to serve, 5 to 6 pounds. But many a one who has thus purchased and paid for his bride, has subsequently repented his bargain, so that he would gladly have returned his exorbitantly dear ware, and lost the money besides.

If someone in this country runs away from his master, who has treated him harshly, he cannot get far. Good provision has been made for such cases, so that a runaway is soon recovered. He who detains or returns a deserter receives a good reward. If such a runaway has been away from his master one day, he must serve for it as a punishment a week, for a week a month, and for a month half a year. But if the master will not keep the runaway after he has got him back, he may sell him for so many years as he would have to serve him yet.

GLOSSARY

florin: German coin

Kaupp: Cowes, a port on the Isle of Wight that was often the last place ships stopped on British soil before setting out to cross the Atlantic

serf: worker on an medieval agricultural estate who had a traditional right to live on and farm part of the estate but also had traditional obligations to farm the lord's portion of the land. Mittelberger seems to use this word as a synonym for "indentured servant," but the terms are not interchangeable

ship's biscuit: type of hard bread or cracker similar to the "hardtack" that soldiers ate during the American Civil War. While it was supposed to be a food that could be stored for long periods of time, it was apparently susceptible to attracting bugs and worms

women in confinement: pregnant women

Document Analysis

Mittelberger's account of his journey to Pennsylvania describes the hardships endured by Europeans traveling to the colonies as redemptioners. He focuses in particular on the risks of the journey and on the fate of the redemptioners upon their arrival in America. As a visitor to the colonies who neither served as a redemptioner or indentured servant nor employed them, Mittelberger provided an account that, while not free of personal bias, was not based on personal investment in the institution. Ultimately, Mittelberger argued against the positive descriptions of indentured servitude written by some of his contemporaries and sought to dissuade his fellow Germans from choosing to become unpaid laborers.

Scholars have suggested that possibly more than half of the European immigrants who came to America were indentured servants or other kinds of unfree workers, such as convicts sentenced to work as laborers in the colonies. Many indentured servants entered into indenture voluntarily, and their reasons for doing so were largely economic; many of those recruited to immigrate to America as indentured servants were desperately poor and were willing to risk much on the hope that they might find better opportunities. Individuals writing at the time and early historians of colonial America developed a kind of rags-to-riches mythology that told of how poor servants came to America and, after serving a period of indenture, became wealthy landowners or businessmen themselves. In some cases, this was likely true. While they did work hard and had few legal guarantees of proper treatment, those who survived their years of servitude could then work as free laborers. Furthermore, because of the need for labor in the American colonies, free workers received wages higher than those they would have received in Europe. Many servants probably ended up better off, in strictly economic terms, than they would have been had they remained in their homelands.

In his memoir, Mittelberger attempts to dispel these notions of economic betterment and reveal the dangers associated with life as an indentured servant in the colonies. While his opinion of indentured servitude prior to his journey to Pennsylvania is unknown, Mittelberger returned to Germany an ardent opponent of the practice. Seeking to discourage his fellow Germans from traveling to America as redemptioners, he set out to describe the conditions under which indentured servants were brought to America and labored in Pennsylvania. His account illustrates both the value and the potential problems with primary sources from any era. Mittelberger witnessed many things with his own eyes, and his testimony about these is particularly valuable. However, he sometimes generalizes from the examples he has seen and draws conclusions that may not be representative of the experience of most indentured servants in order to deter his fellow countrymen from taking that path. Nevertheless, his account is an important one, particularly as a counterpoint to the writings of those in favor of indentured servitude. Mittelberger's account and those by others like him suggest that the possibility of future prosperity is not worth the risks of a dangerous journey and poor working conditions.

Mittelberger begins by describing the unpleasant voyage from England to America. He writes that the trip typically took eight to twelve weeks, but many crossings were shorter, in the range of three to six weeks. Storms, or contrary winds, could cause the voyage to take longer than usual. Many sources from the colonial era testify to the health risks of an Atlantic crossing, and the hardships Mittelberger describes were not confined to ships carrying redemptioners. Even paying passengers such as Mittelberger or military personnel whom the government would naturally want to arrive healthy enough to be of service suffered much during such voyages. "I myself had to pass through a severe illness at sea," he writes. Overcrowding, poor sanitation, and a lack of knowledge about how contagious diseases were spread, combined with poor-quality food and impure drinking water (both often in severely limited quantities), accounted for much of this suffering.

Although he was not an ordained clergyman, Mittelberger appears to have been personally devout, and he sought to minister to the needs of the people with whom he traveled. In the absence of a clergyman, he held worship services on Sundays, during which he read from a collection of sermons. He also led daily prayer meetings. He mentions baptizing five children; these were probably infants born during the voyage. When people died and were buried at sea, he also provided a basic funeral service.

As Mittelberger reports, many died on such voyages. It appears that losses in the range of 10 to 30 percent of the total number of passengers were not uncommon. Of course, some remarkable voyages were made with little loss of life, but on the other hand, ships and all on board were at times lost at sea. Mittelberger focuses in particular on the harmful effects of the voyage on children, reporting that thirty-two children died on his voyage. Based on this experience, he suggests that children between the ages of one and seven rarely survived such journeys. Port records indicate that living children were often on board arriving ships, however, so Mittelberger's statement was probably incorrect.

Mittelberger believed that the poor quality of the food and water the passengers received contributed to the suffering experienced on these voyages. They received hot food only three times a week, and he reports that the water they were given was often foul and dirty. Some passengers may have brought some of their own provisions on board, but since most of the people seeking to become servants in the colonies were very poor, it is unlikely that many of them could have procured much to supplement their diets. When a crossing took longer than expected and other food supplies were exhausted, passengers had to eat the "ship's biscuit," a kind of hard bread or cracker. This was meant to be an emergency ration that could be stored for a long time, but as Mittelberger records, it was susceptible to becoming contaminated by worms and bugs.

After the horrific experience of such a voyage, landfall in America was a welcome relief to those on board.

But as Mittelberger points out, their suffering was not over just because they had reached a port. Indentured servants usually already had contracts for their labor in place, but redemptioners such as those who traveled with Mittelberger did not. Ship owners or captains had borne the expense of transporting these people, speculating that in America they could sell their labor contracts for enough to make a profit. Because the ship's captain had a stake in the sale of these servant's labor contracts, no one was allowed to leave the ship until the cost of their passage was paid. Masters took a risk if they bought servants who were sick, so naturally the healthiest passengers sold first and were able to negotiate the best terms. This meant that passengers who were sick were confined to the ship until their labor contracts were sold, perhaps getting sicker or even dying. As Mittelberger notes, many who died might have recovered if they had been removed from the unhealthy environs of the ship's hold. He does note that after a time, the very sick were taken to a "sick-house" until they recovered, but if they ever did recover enough to leave the sick-house, they still had to pay for their passage to America by contracting to work for someone. While Mittelberger mentions that healthy workers were valued over sick ones, he does not discuss the role that skills or trades played in the negotiation process. Redemptioners or indentured servants who had marketable skills such as blacksmithing, carpentry, or masonry could command better terms and usually were able to work for a shorter time.

Adult servants usually had to contract to work for three to six years in order to pay the cost of their passage to America. Children might go into servitude to pay their own cost of passage or to help pay the cost of their parents' passage so that the adults in the family could start out as free laborers. If someone died after having been on board more than half the journey, surviving members of the family had to pay the full cost of the passage of the deceased person. Many parents had to sell the contract for a child's labor to someone other than the master for whom the parents would be working. Mittelberger stresses the negative effects of this system on children and on the family as a whole, noting that "after leaving the ship, [parents and children often] do not see each other again for many years, perhaps no more in all their lives."

Mittelberger suggests that if servants ran away, they had little chance of remaining free. He notes that a master could sell the contract for a recaptured servant if he did not wish to assume the risk of the servant running away again. The remaining time on a servant's contract could also be used to pay a debt or pass on to heirs if the master died. Servants generally had no say in these transfers, although some colonies did require a court order to approve long-term arrangements. It is correct that there were substantial penalties for running away and that local authorities were tasked with helping to recover runaways. However, historical evidence casts doubt on Mittelberger's assertion that escape was nearly impossible. Colonial newspapers often printed ads offering rewards for the return of runaways, indicating servants running away was a common occurrence and suggesting that perhaps escape was more possible than Mittelberger suggests, if so many servants were willing to attempt it. In addition, because of the great demand for workers, a landowner or businessman might hire someone even if he or she suspected the worker might be a runaway indentured servant. Some colonies passed laws against this practice, known as piracy of labor, thus hinting that it occurred frequently enough to be a concern. During colonial wars, indentured servants sometimes ran away and enlisted in the militia. This was not supposed to be allowed without the master's permission, but enlistment officers who had quotas to fill decided at times not to look closely into the status of potential recruits.

If a person wished to marry an indentured servant, Mittelberger notes, he or she would have to buy out the remaining time on the potential spouse's labor contract. This was more commonly true when a man sought to marry a woman in servitude. Masters generally did not want their female servants to get married, because if they became pregnant, they might not be able to do as much work. Owners of slaves owned the children born to their slaves, but this was not the case with servants, and a child born to a servant would not be old enough to do much work before the time of the parent's indenture was over. Since there were significantly more men than women in the colonies, it was fairly common for a female servant to marry her master.

Despite his opposition to the institution of indentured servitude, Mittelberger does mention some of the benefits servants could typically expect to receive if they survived. Following the end of a servant's contracted term, he or she was entitled to a new suit of clothes and, if it had been expressly specified in the contract, possibly even livestock. In some colonies, these "freedom dues," as they were called, were specified by law. They often included basic farm tools such as axes or

hoes, which indicates that authorities expected former servants to start farming on their own. In some colonies, a former servant would receive a "headright," a grant of land from the colonial government given to any laborer who came to the colony. The proprietors of Pennsylvania (the descendants of Penn, to whom the colony had been granted) also sold land at good prices on liberal credit terms. For Mittelberger, however, these benefits did not outweigh the risks of the journey and the hardships endured by many servants in the colonies.

In general, Mittelberger writes as a person incensed by the suffering he had seen among the redemptioners he traveled with and others he observed after arriving in Pennsylvania. Although he recognized that poor Europeans could benefit economically from indentured servitude, he believed that the negative effects of the journey and life as a bonded laborer, particularly on children and families, were severe. By publishing his memoir, Mittelberger attempted to discourage others from his homeland from making what he believed to be an unwise decision.

Essential Themes
For many modern readers, it may be difficult to believe the accounts of the suffering associated with the system of indentured servants or understand the existence of a legal system that sanctioned such abuses. Few people in the colonial era, however, seemed to have any moral qualms about it. To understand the treatment of indentured servants, one must recognize that in this system, human beings were treated simply as commodities. They were recognized for the value of their labor, but little attention was paid to their basic rights or dignity. While Mittelberger may have exaggerated the sufferings of servants in a few cases, other sources substantiate the general accuracy of his observations. In reading such an account, one can only wonder why people undertook the risk of a dangerous sea voyage followed by the prospect of years of labor and bondage. The answer is that for many, the conditions they experienced in their homelands were so bad that any chance for better prospects was worth taking. While Mittelberger was convinced that redemptioners and indentured servants would fare no better in the colonies than in Europe, some few did prosper, while perhaps a larger number found a somewhat better life after their period of indenture was over. Many, however, never saw freedom; many died on the voyage across the ocean or during their years of bondage. Nevertheless, this idea of risking

everything for the possibility of a better life became a key theme in American history and culture, shaping the development of the colonies and eventually the United States as immigrants from diverse countries willingly faced many of the same dangers as Mittelberger's redemptioners in the hope of finding financial security, religious freedom, and new opportunities.

History has often been written with a bias toward the elites in society—the wealthy and powerful who are by definition the minority of any nation. In the twentieth century, historians began to pay more attention to the lives and the historical impact of common people. In colonial America, a large percentage of these common people were laborers held in bondage. Mittelberger's account is valuable because few firsthand accounts of the sufferings of the Atlantic crossing have survived, and many of the contemporary accounts of the lives and work of indentured servants in the colonies were written by wealthy people who often benefitted from the work of these servants. Mittelberger was neither a servant nor an employer of servants, so he wrote as an observer who had no stake in the system of servitude, other than his desire to see that people were made aware of the risks associated with the decision to come to America as an indentured servant. As such, the study of Mittelberger's memoir reflects the increasing interest in exploring historical events and institutions from multiple diverse perspectives among historians and other scholars.

Mark S. Joy, PhD

Bibliography

Engel, Katherine Carté. "Mittelberger, Gottlieb." *Encyclopedia of American History*. Ed. Gary B. Nash and Billy G. Smith. Vol. 2. New York: Facts on File, 2010. 239. Print.

Fogelman, Aaron. "From Slaves, Convicts, and Servants to Free Passengers: The Transformation of Immigration in the Era of the American Revolution." *Journal of American History* 85.1 (1998): 43–76. Print.

Kolchin, Peter. *Unfree Labor: American Slavery and Russian Serfdom*. Cambridge: Belknap, 1987. Print.

Mittelberger, Gottlieb. *Journey to Pennsylvania*. Ed. Oscar Handlin and John Clive. Cambridge: Belknap, 1969. Print.

Smith, Abbot Emerson. *Colonists in Bondage: White Servitude and Convict Labor in America, 1607–1776*. Chapel Hill: U of North Carolina P, 1947. Print.

Wolf, Edward C. "Music in Old Zion, Philadelphia, 1750–1850." *Musical Quarterly*. 58.4 (1972): 622–52. Print.

Additional Reading

Graebner, William, and Leonard Richards. "The Have Nots in Colonial Society." *The American Record: Images of the Nation's Past*. Ed. Graebner and Richards. 5th ed. Vol. 1. New York: McGraw, 2006. 77–107. Print.

Herrick, Cheesman A. *White Servitude in Pennsylvania: Indentured and Redemption Labor in Colony and Commonwealth*. Philadelphia: McVey, 1926. Print.

Hofstadter, Richard. *America at 1750: A Social Portrait*. New York: Vintage, 1971. Print.

Hollitz, John. "Evaluating Primary Sources: Was Pennsylvania 'The Best Poor Man's Country'?" *Thinking through the Past: A Critical Thinking Approach to US History*. Ed. Hollitz. 4th ed. Vol. 1. Boston: Wadsworth, 2010. 38–54. Print.

Salinger, Sharon V. *"To Serve Well and Faithfully": Labor and Indentured Servants in Pennsylvania, 1682–1800*. New York: Cambridge UP, 1987. Print.

LESSON PLAN: The Horrors of an Ocean Crossing

Students analyze excerpts from Gottlieb Mittelberger's account of an Atlantic Ocean crossing and what it reveals about indentured servants.

Learning Objectives

Analyze points of view of the past; reconstruct the literal meaning of Mittelberger's account; examine causes of indentured servitude; compare and contrast Francis Daniel Pastorius's and Mittelberger's accounts of Atlantic travel.

Materials: Gottlieb Mittelberger, *Journey to Pennsylvania* (1754); Francis Daniel Pastorius, *Positive Information from America, Concerning the Country of Pennsylvania* (1684).

Overview Questions

What is Mittelberger's purpose in recounting details of his ocean voyage? How did the indentured-servitude process that Mittelberger describes work? Why did so many people accept the risk of indentured servitude? How does Mittelberger's report compare to Pastorius's?

Step 1: Comprehension Questions

What is known about Mittelberger? What is his apparent intention in writing about his journey to America? What is his opinion of the ship's masters?

▶ **Activity:** Direct students to read aloud passages in which Mittelberger reveals something of himself. Have students describe Mittelberger's reaction to ship conditions and the plight of passengers. Ask students to draw conclusions about Mittelberger's judgments and purpose.

Step 2: Context Questions

Why must so many passengers stay aboard after landing in Philadelphia? Why was this system called redemptionist servitude?

▶ **Activity:** Have students read and explain passages that detail the fate of passengers forced to wait on the ship. Have students discuss how passengers could redeem themselves. Challenge students to explain why the use of the word "redemptionist" becomes ironic in colonial America.

Step 3: Context Questions

Why were Germans willing to endure the voyage and indentured servitude? What evidence does Mittelberger provide to show whether or not it was worth it?

▶ **Activity:** Have students research the reasons so many Europeans chose indentured servitude in America in the eighteenth century. Discuss whether or not in the extended document (not just this excerpt), Mittelberger has a positive view of America. Ask why he returned to Germany.

Step 4: Historical Connections Questions

How do Pastorius's and Mittelberger's accounts complement each other? In what substantial ways do they differ?

▶ **Activity:** Have students discuss the differences in the men's motives. Ask students to explain which account is more horrific and why. Have students speculate about whether Mittelberger's co-travelers may have read Pastorius's account and why it may have encouraged them to emigrate.

Step 5: Response Paper

Word length and additional requirements set by Instructor. Students answer the research question in the Overview Questions. Students state a thesis and use as evidence passages from the primary source documents.

■ A Stranger in a Strange Land: Some Account of the Fore Part of the Life of Elizabeth Ashbridge

Date: 1774
Author: Ashbridge, Elizabeth
Genre: memoir; autobiography

> *"When my husband and he used to be making their diversions and reviling, I sat in silence, though now and then an involuntary sigh broke from me; at which he would say, 'There, did not I tell you your wife was a Quaker, and she will become a preacher.'"*

Summary Overview

Elizabeth Ashbridge's work is a conversion narrative or spiritual autobiography, a common genre of early modern autobiographical writing in which an author recounts his or her process of conversion towards God. Quaker spiritual autobiographies adhered to a recognized set of conventions, which Ashbridge mostly followed. Her narrative differs from most Quaker autobiographies in that it focuses more on her life before her conversion than after it, and in that it is the story not only of her own soul but also of her second husband's. Ashbridge wrote the narrative when she was an established member of the Quaker community, years after the events she recounts. It was written for an audience of fellow Quakers for whom the correctness of Quaker beliefs and practices was not an issue. Ashbridge's account is also the major source for her life and one of the few remaining autobiographies by a colonial American woman.

Defining Moment

Ashbridge was writing at a time when Quakerism, formerly illegal in England and many of its American colonies, had become legally tolerated while still suffering from a social stigma. Habits specifically associated with Quakerism, such as plain dress and the use of *thee* instead of *you*, were widely mocked. Elements of Quaker theology and religious practice, such as the emphasis on the "inner light" of the spirit, the rejection of material sacraments, and the use of silence in meetings, aroused more serious objections, and some doubted if Quakers could even be called Christians. This dislike was shared by a broad range of Christian communities, from the Church of England to the Puritan Congregationalists of Boston, but it was also somewhat meliorated by the growth of religious toleration in the early Enlightenment. Few advocated the actual execution of Quaker missionaries as had happened in the seventeenth century. The religious pluralism of the British American colonies allowed people to move relatively easily between denominations, as Ashbridge moved from Anglicanism to Quakerism.

In Pennsylvania, originally founded in the seventeenth century as a Quaker colony, Quakers themselves had given up the idea of establishing a utopian Quaker society and were living as a self-conscious minority, albeit a relatively wealthy and powerful one. Immigrants from a variety of religious and ethnic groups, such as the Dutch couple Ashbridge encounters, came to the area, making Pennsylvania one of the most religiously pluralistic colonies. Quakerism was also strong in East and West Jersey, the future state of New Jersey. Since its founding by George Fox in the seventeenth century, Quakerism was highly organized, and there was a sense of a Quaker community that transcended regional, natural, and socioeconomic barriers.

Although Quaker families were organized patriarchally, the Quaker tradition allowed more spiritual independence to women and had a greater degree of gender egalitarianism than did Anglicanism or Puritanism, the other dominant religious traditions of British America. Quakers were highly unusual among Christian sects in permitting women to preach publicly, which added to the scorn felt for them by members of other traditions. Spiritual autobiographies and journals like Ashbridge's were widely circulated in the Quaker community and served as an important element in that community's self-definition.

Author Biography

Elizabeth Ashbridge was born Elizabeth Sampson in the English town of Middlewich in 1713 to Thomas Sampson, a ship's surgeon, and Mary Sampson. The Sampsons were members of the Church of England, in which Ashbridge was baptized. Her first exposure to Quakerism came when she was sent to the house of a Quaker relative of her mother's in Ireland to recover from an unhappy marriage that left her a widow after five months. The gloom of the Quaker culture she encountered was unappealing, and during her stay in Ireland she came much closer to converting to Catholicism, drawing back at the last minute due to her horror at a priest's insisting that all non-Catholics, including her own mother, would be damned.

Ashbridge's failed marriage had also alienated her from her family, particularly her father, and in 1732, she took passage to America, hoping for a fresh start.

She was required to sign a three-year indenture, during which she endured harsh conditions from a cruel master. After the indenture, she married a schoolteacher named Sullivan, the "husband" referred to in her autobiography. Sullivan was a heavy drinker and found it difficult to settle in one place. The tensions of the marriage soared even higher in 1738 when Ashbridge, who had previously explored numerous religious options, visited Quaker relatives in the colony of Pennsylvania. Impressed by their piety, she became a committed Quaker. Sullivan, who had initially been attracted to his wife's singing and dancing, was disappointed with her new somber behavior after her conversion. He attempted to force her away from Quakerism through brutality but failed and eventually adopted some Quaker beliefs himself. He enlisted in the British army, but he refused to fight, claiming that his enlistment had been a drunken escapade. Sullivan eventually died from wounds he sustained during the beating he received for this insubordination. At this point Ashbridge's account ends.

After Sullivan's death in 1741, Ashbridge worked as a teacher and seamstress to support herself and pay off the debt left by her husband. In 1746, she married again, this time to a wealthy Quaker landowner of high social standing, Aaron Ashbridge. The marriage seems to have been happy and Ashbridge became a respected preacher and leader in the Quaker community. Ashbridge died in Ireland in 1755, while on a preaching tour of the British Isles. A manuscript of her autobiography circulated among Quakers but was not published until 1774, nearly two decades after her death.

HISTORICAL DOCUMENT

I now began to think of my relations in Pennsylvania, whom I had not yet seen. My husband gave me liberty to visit them, and I obtained a certificate from the priest, in order that, if I made any stay, I might be received as a member of the church wherever I came. My husband accompanied me to the Blazing-star Ferry, saw me safely over, and then returned. In my way, I fell from my horse, and, for several days, was unable to travel. I abode at the house of an honest Dutchman, who, with his wife, paid me the utmost attention, and would have no recompence

for their trouble. I left them with deep sentiments of gratitude for their extraordinary kindness, and they charged me, if ever I came that way again, to lodge with them. I mention this, because I shall have occasion to allude to it hereafter.

When I came to Trent-town Ferry, I felt no small mortification on hearing that my relations were all Quakers, and, what was worst of all, that my aunt was a preacher. I was exceedingly prejudiced against this people, and often wondered how they could call themselves Christians. I repented my coming, and was almost inclined to turn back; yet, as I was so far on my journey, I proceeded, though I expected but little comfort from my visit. How little was I aware it would bring me to the knowledge of the truth!

I went from Trent-town to Philadelphia by water, and from thence to my uncle's on horseback. My uncle was dead, and my aunt married again; yet, both she and her husband received me in the kindest manner. I had scarcely been three hours in the house, before my opinion of these people began to alter. I perceived a book lying upon the table, and, being fond of reading, took it up; my aunt observed me, and said, "Cousin, that is a Quaker's book." She saw I was not a Quaker, and supposed I would not like it. I made her no answer, but queried with myself, what can these people write about? I have heard that they deny the scriptures, and have no other bible than George Fox's Journal. . . . denying, also, all the holy ordinances. But, before I had read two pages, my heart burned within me, and, for fear I should be seen, I went into the garden. I sat down, and, as the piece was short, read it before I returned, though I was often obliged to stop to give vent to my tears. The fulness of my heart produced the involuntary exclamation of, "My God, must I, if ever I come to the knowledge of thy truth, be of this man's opinion, who has sought thee as I have done; and must I join this people, to whom, a few hours ago, I preferred the papists. O, thou God of my salvation, and of my life, who hath abundantly manifested thy long suffering and tender mercy, in redeeming me as from the lowest hell, I beseech thee to direct me in the right way, and keep me from error; so will I perform my covenant, and think nothing too near to part with for thy name's sake. O, happy people, thus beloved of God!"

After having collected myself, I washed my face, that it might not be perceived I had been weeping. In the night I got but little sleep; the enemy of mankind haunted me with his insinuations, by suggesting that I was one of those that wavered, and not stead-fast in faith; and advancing several texts of scripture against me, as that, in the latter days, there should be those who would deceive the very elect; that of such were the people I was among, and that I was in danger of being deluded. Warned in this manner, (from the right source as I thought,) I resolved to be aware of those deceivers,

and, for some weeks, did not touch one of their books. The next day, being the first of the week, I was desirous of going to church, which was distant about four miles; but, being a stranger, and having no one to go with me, I gave up all thoughts of that, and, as most of the family were going to meeting, I went there with them. As we sat in silence, I looked over the meeting, and said to myself, "How like fools these people sit; how much better would it be to stay at home, and read the Bible, or some good book, than come here and go to sleep." As for me I was very drowsy; and, while asleep, had nearly fallen down. This was the last time I ever fell asleep in a meeting. I now began to be lifted up with spiritual pride, and to think myself better than they; but this disposition of mind did not last long. It may seem strange that, after living so long with one of this society at Dublin, I should yet be so much a stranger to them. In answer, let it be considered that, while I was there, I never read any of their books, nor went to one meeting; besides, I had heard such accounts of them, as made me think that, of all societies, they were the worst. But he who knows the sincerity of the heart, looked on my weakness with pity; I was permitted to see my error, and shown that these were the people I ought to join.

A few weeks afterwards, there was an afternoon meeting at my uncle's, at which a minister named William Hammans was present. I was highly prejudiced against him when he stood up, but I was soon humbled; for he preached the gospel with such power that I was obliged to confess it was the truth. But, though he was the instrument of assisting me out of many doubts, my mind was not wholly freed from them. The morning before this meeting I had been disputing with my uncle about baptism, which was the subject handled by this minister, who removed all my scruples beyond objection, and yet I seemed loath to believe that the sermon I had heard proceeded from divine revelation. I accused my aunt and uncle of having spoken of me to the Friend; but they cleared themselves, by telling me, that they had not seen him since my coming, until he came into the meeting. I then viewed him as the messenger of God to me, and, laying aside my prejudices, opened my heart to receive the truth; the beauty of which was shown to me, with the glory of those who continued faithful to it. I had also revealed to me the emptiness of all shadows and types, which, though proper in their day, were now, by the coming of the Son of God, at an end, and everlasting righteousness, which is a work in the heart, was to be established in the room thereof. I was permitted to see that all I had gone through was to prepare me for this day; and that the time was near, when it would be required of me, to go and declare to others what the God of mercy had done for my soul; at which I was surprised, and desired to be excused, lest I should bring dishonour to the truth, and cause his holy name to be evilly spoken of.

Of these things I let no one know. I feared discovery, and did not even appear like a Friend.

I now hired to keep school, and, hearing of a place for my husband, I wrote, and desired him to come, though I did not let him know how it was with me.

I loved to go to meetings, but did not love to be seen going on week-days, and therefore went to them, from my school, through the woods. Notwithstanding all my care, the neighbours, who were not Friends, soon began to revile me with the name of Quaker; adding, that they supposed I intended to be a fool, and turn preacher. Thus did I receive the same censure, which, about a year before, I had passed on one of the handmaids of the Lord in Boston. I was so weak, that I could not bear the reproach. In order to change their opinion, I went into greater excess of apparel than I had freedom to do, even before I became acquainted with Friends. In this condition I continued till my husband came, and then began the trial of my faith.

Before he reached me, he heard I was turned Quaker; at which he stamped, and said, "I had rather have heard she was dead, well as I love her; for, if it be so, all my comfort is gone." He then came to me; it was after an absence of four months; I got up and said to him, "My dear, I am glad to see thee." At this, he flew into a great range, exclaiming, "The devil thee, thee, thee, don't thee me." I endeavoured, by every mild means, to pacify him; and, at length, got him fit to speak to my relations. As soon after this as we were alone, he said to me, "And so I see your Quaker relations have made you one;" I replied, that they had not, which was true, I never told them how it was with me. He said he would not stay amongst them; and, having found a place to his mind, hired, and

came directly back to fetch me, walking, in one afternoon, thirty miles to keep me from meeting the next day, which was first day. He took me, after resting this day, to the place where he had hired, and to lodgings he had engaged at the house of a churchwarden. This man was a bitter enemy of Friends, and did all he could to irritate my husband against them.

Though I did not appear like a Friend, they all believed me to be one. When my husband and he used to be making their diversions and reviling, I sat in silence, though now and then an involuntary sigh broke from me; at which he would say, "There, did not I tell you your wife was a Quaker, and she will become a preacher." On such an occasion as this, my husband once came up to me, in a great rage, and shaking his hand over me, said, "You had better be hanged in that day." I was seized with horror, and again plunged into despair, which continued nearly three months. I was afraid that, by denying the Lord, the heavens would be shut against me. I walked much alone in the woods, and there, where no eye saw, nor ear heard me, lamented my miserable condition. Often have I wandered, from morning till night, without food. I was brought so low that my life became a burden to me; and the devil seemed to vaunt, that though the sins of my youth were forgiven me, yet now I had committed an unpardonable sin, and hell would inevitably be my portion, and my torments would be greater than if I had hanged myself at first.

In the night, when under this painful distress of mind, I could not sleep, if my husband perceived me weeping, he would revile me for it. At length, when he and his friend thought themselves too weak to overset me, he went to the priest at Chester, to inquire what he could do with me. This man knew I was a member of the Church, for I had shown him my certificate. His advice was, to take me out of Pennsylvania, and settle in some place where there were no Quakers. My husband replied, he did not care where we went, if he could but restore me to my natural liveliness of temper. As for me, I had no resolution to oppose their proposals, nor much cared where I went. I seemed to have nothing to hope for. I daily expected to be made a victim of divine wrath, and was possessed with the idea that this would be by thunder . . .

GLOSSARY

Church: Church of England

churchwarden: minor official in a Church of England parish

enemy of mankind: Satan

first day: Sunday; Quakers did not use traditional names for weekdays or months, which they regarded as tainted by paganism.

Friend: used by a Quaker to refer to another Quaker

George Fox: founder of Quakerism

papist: derogatory term for Roman Catholic

Trent-town: Trenton, in what is now New Jersey

Document Analysis

This excerpt from Elizabeth Ashbridge's autobiography recounts part of the story of her conversion to Quakerism and the beginnings of her struggle with her husband Sullivan over her new faith, the main subject of the work. Her conversion was not merely spiritual but social, cultural, and personal as well. It required Ashbridge, like other Quaker converts, to break with the society in which she had grown up and adopt new lifeways, extending to such fundamental aspects of the persona as speech and clothing. It also threatened her relationship with her non-Quaker husband, a volatile and angry man strongly opposed to Quakerism and intent on exerting his male authority over his wife. Her conversion was not the solution to the problems in her life but the opening of a new struggle in which she fought to establish her new religious identity in a community hostile to it. The story therefore is one of internal and external struggle, as Ashbridge tells how she grappled with her own hesitation and cowardice as well as the rules of her society and her husband's authority within her own family. Like other spiritual autobiographies, her account is based on a view of an explicitly providential view of life, ascribing to God the credit for the actions and events that draw Ashbridge closer to him and incorporating direct addresses to God through prayer into the narrative. Although the idea of a direct relationship between the individual and God, not mediated through a hierarchical church, is found in many branches of Christianity, including the Protestant tradition, it was particularly characteristic of Quakerism. Words, whether written or spoken, also play a central role in the spiritual narrative.

Although Quakers were no longer executed for their faith as they had been in seventeenth-century Puritan Boston, they still faced a great deal of hostility in the mid-eighteenth century. Quakers were widely despised for their distinctive ways such as their plain dress and their use of *thee* and *thou* rather than the formal second person pronoun *you* used to address social superiors. Quakers also refused to participate in the rites of social subordination such as removing hats in the presence of a superior; their refusal was considered an assault on the hierarchical relations on which early modern society depended.

On a deeper level, the Quaker religion was considered dubiously Christian (a feeling Ashbridge initially shared), and Quakers were tarred with the same brush as the radical sects of the English Civil War. Ashbridge had been brought up in the Church of England by her parents, remained formally affiliated with it via the certificate she was given to allow her into Anglican congregations during her travels, and would have been exposed to the Church's hostility to dissenters of all stripes. Earlier sections of the narrative discuss her quest for spiritual fulfillment, which the Church was unable to fill.

Ashbridge fully shared the anti-Quaker feelings common in other branches of Anglo-American Protestantism, referring to her dislike of Quakers while living in Ireland and her taunting of a "handmaid of the Lord," presumably a woman Quaker preacher or activist, in Boston. She asserts that she despised the Quakers even more than the Roman Catholics, a strong insult common among eighteenth-century Protestants. She believed wrongly that Quakers did not read the Bible or hold it sacred. (Her recounting of these anti-Quaker sentiments, however, may have been affected by the standard trope of spiritual autobiography of exaggerating one's own sinfulness and alienation from God before the moment of conversion in order to heighten the contrast between the old, sinful self and the new postconversion self.) She was surprised to hear that her relatives in Pennsylvania were Quakers.

Converting to Quakerism

Despite her initial shock, exposure to the Quaker community in Pennsylvania led to Ashbridge's conversion. However, she downplayed the role of social contact with Quakers in bringing her to Quakerism. As was common in conversion narratives, God is the chief actor, bringing Ashbridge to the true faith out of love and concern for her soul. The role of the written word, the book she reads at her relative's house in Pennsylvania and her intense response to it, is also important. This was another common theme in Protestant spiritual autobiographies and conversion narratives. Her initial disdain for Quakers is largely based on their verbal insufficiencies. She wonders when she picks up the Quaker book, "what can these people write about?" and suspects that they read little, including the Bible, outside of George Fox's *The Journal* (1694). Her discovery that Quakers read and wrote books did much to erode her resistance to conversion.

The spoken word also plays a central role in Ashbridge's conversion. A climactic experience in the document, after which her commitment to Quakerism becomes permanent, comes when she hears the preaching of a Quaker minister named William Hammans. (Quakers did not have a professional ministry per se as did Anglicans and Puritans, but some "Public Friends," male and female, were licensed by their local Quaker meetings to preach.) Prior to that, she had wished to attend a Church of England service, but the nearest church was too far away for this to be practical, and she accompanied her aunt and uncle to a Quaker meeting instead. The silence at the Quaker meeting did not initially impress her nor did the Friends in attendance,

and she fell asleep. Ashbridge reports that following the meeting, she was filled with "spiritual pride," and thought herself better than the Quakers. Several weeks after, however, at a Quaker meeting at her uncle's home, Hammans delivered a sermon that addressed the topic of baptism, which Ashbridge had recently disputed with her Quaker uncle. Quakers differed from other Christian denominations at the time in not practicing baptism with water, arguing that the only true baptism was the baptism of the spirit. This was a very important issue, and one reason why many did not consider Quakers to be true Christians. Water baptism was among the "shadows" that Quakers believed had faded with the coming of Christ.

Hammans discussed the very difficulties Ashbridge had with Quaker beliefs on baptism in a way that intellectually removed her doubts so appositely that at first she suspected her aunt and uncle of having prearranged the sermon topic with Hammans. When they denied this, she concluded that Hammans was "the messenger of God to me" and the sermon was a "divine revelation."

Throughout Ashbridge's conversion, language—written or spoken—is paramount; Quakerism fully shared and even extended Protestantism's traditional distrust of images. It is her interest in reading that causes her to pick up the book and take the first tentative steps towards Quakerism. (She points out that while in Ireland, she had neither read Quaker books nor attended meetings, thus cutting herself off from the word.) Ashbridge writes about being haunted by Satan's nighttime "insinuations" that her faith is weak because she has shown an interest in Quakerism and casts his attack in terms of "advancing several texts of scripture against [her]." When she then yields temporarily to these insinuations, she expresses her backsliding in terms of avoiding Quaker books. She is also concerned to establish that her relatives did not force her or even encourage her into Quakerism, including in her story of the first time she read a Quaker book the fact that her aunt discouraged her from reading it, thinking that she was opposed to Quakerism. When this issue comes up later in her conflict with Sullivan, she reasserts that her family had not made her a Quaker, and even claims that she had not told her relatives of her conversion. Credit must be given to God, not to any human agency.

Ashbridge's realization that Hammans was the bearer of a message from God was followed by her "open[ing her] heart to receive the truth," in effect accepting Quakerism. Having served his purpose, Hammans then disappears from the narrative rather than becoming a kind of spiritual teacher or exemplar, which would make him an intermediary between her and God. As in the case of the relatives, Ashbridge minimizes the role of individuals in her conversion. She viewed the conversion as a mutual act of love between her and God. She also considered it a contest between God and Satan for her soul, with Satan deceiving her into thinking he is "the right source," or God. The intense emotionalism of Ashbridge's conversion is manifested physically in tears and cries. The eighteenth century was an age of "sentiment" as expressed in novels such as Samuel Richardson's *Pamela*, the British classic of the sentimental genre, which was first published in America in 1740, around the time of Ashbridge's conversion. Tears and cries were considered signs of true, sincere emotion, not weakness.

After her conversion, Ashbridge remained constrained by society's prejudices against Quakers. Her conversion became known in the area despite her attempts to conceal it and invited the taunts of her non-Quaker neighbors and acquaintances. She attempted to avoid this hostility by concealing her new beliefs and her visits to the meeting house and dressing in a more luxurious fashion than that of Quaker women, even dressing more luxuriously than she had before the conversion. Her tactics were ineffective, however, as her identification as a Quaker remained widely known. Furthermore, her attempts at subterfuge and concealment created a crisis of conscience, as she feared that God would punish her for hiding the truth—many believed that the denial of what one knew to be true about God was the "unforgiveable sin."

Challenging patriarchal authority

The social stigma attached to Quakerism became a more serious problem on the return of Ashbridge's husband Sullivan, who had already heard of her conversion and quickly verified his suspicions through observing her behavior, such as her use of *thee* rather than *you*. Sullivan's role is particularly important since eighteenth-century households, including Quaker households, expected the husband to be the spiritual leader. Ashbridge's temporary separation from her husband during her trip to Pennsylvania may have facilitated her conversion. By converting to Quakerism, Ashbridge was challenging her husband's authority, and as a member of the Church of England, he undoubtedly held strong anti-Quaker sentiments.

Ashbridge's use of the Quaker *thee* for her husband rather than the *you* with which one addressed a social superior was a particularly egregious attack on Sullivan's leadership of the household and was essentially a rebellion against Sullivan's patriarchal authority. Sullivan also seems to have regarded Quakerism as changing Ashbridge into a different woman from the one he married, complaining about the loss of her "natural liveliness of temper" in favor of her new Quaker sobriety. Sullivan had initially been attracted to Ashbridge at a time in her life when she was frequently singing and dancing and even thinking of a theatrical career. However, since by the end of the narrative Sullivan himself may have become a Quaker and even suffered martyrdom for Quaker nonviolence, Ashbridge's emphasis of his hostility to Quakerism and resistance to her conversion could also be a literary device, rendering his final conversion more dramatic.

Ashbridge's struggle with Sullivan occupies a central place in the narrative as the "trial" of her newfound Quaker faith. Now that she had become a Quaker, it was dramatically important that she suffer for her religion, with religious suffering being an important part of many spiritual autobiographies. The mere malicious gossip of neighbors was insufficient to fill this space, but given the commonness of domestic violence and the lack of recourse a wife had against a violent or otherwise abusive husband, a struggle between a wife and husband was indeed a trial or test of faith. As a memoirist, Ashbridge was walking a narrow path in treating her relations with her husband. Since Quakers, like other colonists, believed in a wife's duty to submit to her husband, she had to be careful to show that any defiance was a result of her greater duty to God and not of putting her own will ahead of her husband's. In discussing her decision to visit her relatives in Pennsylvania, she claims that Sullivan "gave me liberty," acknowledging his authority in nonreligious decision making.

Sullivan's angry reaction to his wife's conversion is reminiscent of the reaction people have today when members of their family join fringe religious groups or "cults." The local Church of England minister or "priest," (a term always used in a negative sense in Ashbridge's *Account* , which is full of criticism of male authority figures in religion) suggests that Sullivan "deprogram" his wife by removing her from Quaker-dominated Pennsylvania, in effect isolating her from other Quakers. Pennsylvania, the geographical location of Ashbridge's conversion, functions in the narrative as a symbol of Quakerism, a place to which she journeys and from which her husband wishes to remove her. Sullivan relocated himself and Ashbridge to a house owned by an Anglican churchwarden and strong opponent of Quakerism, hoping in vain that immersing her in this anti-Quaker environment would change her beliefs. Isolation from the Quaker community was another test of Ashbridge's faith.

Quakerism was often associated with female rebellion against male authority, and "mad" Quaker women were frequent targets of anti-Quaker polemic and satire. From the founding of Quakerism in the 1650s, Quakers were among the few denominations that allowed women to preach. By choosing a public career over their domestic duties to their husbands and families and presuming to expound religious truth to men as well as women, Quaker women preachers, as Ashbridge later became, were challenging the dominant gender ideology of the patriarchal subordination of women to men, both within in the family and the Anglican church. This idea was at first shocking to Ashbridge as well as to her husband and friends, as can be seen from her dismay to learn that her aunt was a Quaker preacher.

Although social and domestic struggles move to the center stage, Ashbridge's spiritual struggles were by no means over. Doubts about one's own salvation, inspired by the devil, were part of a conversion story, and Ashbridge's story is no exception. Many of the symptoms she describes in the period when she and her husband were staying at the churchwarden's house might now be diagnosed as clinical depression, but Ashbridge and many other people in her own time interpreted them spiritually rather than medically. At the end of the excerpted passage, she is in a state of hopelessness that she and her contemporaries would identify as "despair" and classify as a sin against God. Fear over one's own salvation was a common experience in conversion narratives, and it was compounded in her case by the fear that by denying God—she does not specify what action she is referring to—she had committed an unforgivable sin and has doomed herself to hell. Her overcoming of despair, which occurs later in the narrative, was another sign that her faith had become deep and permanently rooted.

Essential Themes

Ashbridge became a widely admired and influential figure in the Quaker community on both sides of the Atlantic, partly on the strength of her autobiography, which circulated as a manuscript and is the earliest evidence of the text, as Ashbridge's original does not survive. Her account was not printed, however, until nearly two decades after her death and was accompanied by a statement from her surviving third husband, Aaron Ashbridge, describing her later career and death. It was frequently reprinted in the nineteenth century, although it was never as influential as John Woolman's *Journal*, another Quaker text published posthumously in 1774. (Woolman shared many acquaintances with Ashbridge and may have been familiar with her work when preparing his own autobiographical writings, although his situation was very different, both as a man and as someone born into Quakerism rather than a convert like Ashbridge.) Ashbridge's account also entered the Quaker canon by being included in an influential mid-nineteenth century collection of standard Quaker writings, *The Friends' Library*. *Some Account of the Fore Part of the Life of Elizabeth Ashbridge* would become a touchstone for Quakers, particularly for Quaker women, in the nineteenth and early twentieth centuries.

The influence of Ashbridge's *Account* on American culture was initially limited because it was little known outside the Quaker community. However, Quaker women like Ashbridge had a more diffuse impact on nineteenth-century thought about women, particularly as Quakers began to think of themselves less as a people apart and interacted more freely with the larger society around them. The image of the Quaker woman of the colonial era boldly confronting male authority contributed to nineteenth-century American feminism, and assertive, though meek, Quaker women frequently appeared in period novels aimed at social reform, such as Harriet Beecher Stowe's *Uncle Tom's Cabin*. When Ashbridge occupied a public role as a Quaker minister, Quaker women were generally more active in the public sphere than were women from other Christian traditions. Quaker women were leaders in a variety of nineteenth-century movements for social reforms such as abolition and suffrage. Four out of the five women who planned the 1848 Seneca Falls meeting that began the women's suffrage movement in America were Quakers. In recent decades there has been a revival of interest in Ashbridge and her book, an interest that is inspired by feminism and the growing interest in women's lives and documents.

William E. Burns, PhD

Bibliography

Andrews, William L., ed., et al. *Journeys in New Worlds: Early American Women's Narratives*. Madison: U of Wisconsin P, 1990. Print.

Levenduski, Christine M. *Peculiar Power: A Quaker Woman Preacher in Eighteenth-Century America*. Washington, DC: Smithsonian Inst. P, 1996. Print.

Additional Reading

Bacon, Margaret Hope, ed. *Wilt Thou Go on My Errand?: Journals of Three 18th Century Quaker Women Ministers: Susanna Morris, 1682–1755; Elizabeth Hudson, 1722–1783; Ann Moore, 1710–1783*. Wallingford, PA: Pendle, 1994. Print.

Imbarrato, Susan Clair. *Declarations of Independency in Eighteenth-Century American Autobiography*. Knoxville: U of Tennessee P, 1998. Print.

Larson, Rebecca. *Daughters of Light: Quaker Women Preaching and Prophesying in the Colonies and Abroad, 1700–1775*. New York: Knopf, 1999. Print.

Shea, Daniel B. *Spiritual Autobiography in Early America*. Madison: U of Wisconsin P, 1988. Print.

Smolenski, John. *Friends and Strangers: The Making of a Creole Culture in Colonial Pennsylvania*. Philadelphia: U of Pennsylvania P, 2010. Print.

LESSON PLAN: Elizabeth Ashbridge's Struggle Within Herself

Students analyze excerpts from Ashbridge's account of her internal and external religious struggles and their implications in new roles for women in colonial America.

Learning Objectives

Read Ashbridge's narrative imaginatively; describe the diversity of religion in colonial communities; evaluate the importance of Quakerism in the evolution of women's roles; compare the experiences of Elizabeth Ashbridge and Jane Hoskens.

Materials: Elizabeth Ashbridge, *A Stranger in a Strange Land: Some Account of the Fore Part of the Life of Elizabeth Ashbridge* (1774); Jane Hoskens, *The Life and Spiritual Sufferings of That Faithful Servant of Christ Jane Hoskens, a Public Preacher among the People Called Quakers* (1771).

Overview Questions

What themes recur through the entire passage? In what ways does Ashbridge wrestle with her changing beliefs? How can Quakerism be understood as an early step to women's equality? What characteristics do Jane Hoskens's accounts of her Quakerism share with Ashbridge's?

Step 1: Comprehension Questions

What personal struggles does Ashbridge reveal in her narrative about her? How do they intertwine?

▶ **Activity:** Select a student to read the opening paragraph. Discuss how the paragraph establishes Ashbridge's goals, tone, and personality. On duplicated copies of the excerpt, have students highlight sentences in which Ashbridge details her self-doubts.

Step 2: Context Questions

How does Quakerism differ from Ashbridge's original faith, Anglicanism? How does she come to accept Quakerism?

▶ **Activity:** Direct a student to prepare a brief summary of the differences between the Anglican and Quaker faiths. On their copies of the excerpt, have students highlight sentences that describe Ashbridge's acceptance of Quakerism. Have students discuss her reasons.

Step 3: Context Questions

What limitations does Ashbridge face as a woman in the mid-eighteenth century? How does her conversion to Quakerism alter her self-perception?

▶ **Activity:** Have students read aloud passages reflecting Ashbridge's relationship with her husband. Discuss why this may have been typical in the era. Have students read passages that underscore the status of women within Quakerism and how others reacted to it.

Step 4: Historical Connections Questions

How does Jane Hoskens's struggle over her right and responsibility to preach compare to Ashbridge's? Seen from our contemporary eyes, which woman more fully embraces the opportunity and challenge to preach?

▶ **Activity:** Have students read copies of Hoskens's account and highlight sentences that suggest her doubts and eventual self-assurances. Have students compare the passage to Ashbridge's struggles. Discuss how the opportunity to preach alters both women's self-perceptions.

Step 5: Response Paper

Word length and additional requirements set by Instructor. Students answer the research question in the Overview Questions. Students state a thesis and use as evidence passages from the primary source documents.

Supplemental Historical Documents

HISTORICAL DOCUMENT

A Discourse Concerning the Currencies of the British Plantations in America

Date: 1739
Author: Douglass, William
Genre: essay; report

The many Schemes at present upon the Anvil in Boston, for emitting enormous Quantities of Paper Currencies; are the Occasion of this Discourse. The Writer does not vainly pretend to dictate to Government, or prescribe to Trade; but with a sincere Regard to the publick Good, has taken some Pains, to collect, digest, and set in a proper Light, several Facts and Political Experiences especially relating to Paper Currencies; which tho' plain in themselves, are not obvious to every Body. If any Expressions should sound harsh, they are not to be understood as a Reflection upon this Province in general: It was always my Opinion, That the Province of the Massachusetts-Bay, is by far the most vigorous and promising Plant (with proper Cultivation) of all the British Plantations; in the best of Countries at Times, bad Administrations, and private evil Men of Influence have prevailed. The Author is not a transient Person, who from Humour or Caprice, or other Views may expose the Province; but is by Inclination induced, and by Interest obliged to study the Good of the Country.

All Commerce naturally is a *Truck Trade*, exchanging Commodities which we can spare (or their Value) for Goods we are in want of. *Silver it self is a Merchandize*, and being the least variable of all others, is by general Consent made the *Medium of Trade*. If a Country can be supposed to have no Dealings but within it self; the Legislature or tacit Consent of the People, may appoint or receive any Currency at Pleasure: But a trading Country must have regard to the universal commercial Medium, which is Silver; or cheat, and trade to a Disadvantage: It is true, that in some Countries of Europe *Billon* (a base mixture of Metals) is used for small Change, but not as a Medium of Trade.

Every Country or Society have their own peculiar Regulations, which may be called their *Municipal*, or By-Laws in Trade: but the universal trading Part of the World, as one tacit Confederacy have fallen into some *general Rules*, which by Custom of Merchants are become as Fundamental: One of these is a *Silver Medium of Trade*, that all Contracts (Specialties excepted) are understood to be payable in this Medium, being always of the same fixed Value, or easily adjusted by the *Par*, and accidental small Differences of Exchange from one Country to another.

There can therefore be no other proper *Medium* of Trade, but Silver, or Bills of Exchange and Notes of Hand payable in Silver at certain *U'sos* or Periods, which by a currant Discount are reducible to Silver ready Money, at any Time. The Debitor Party (I am ashamed to mention it) being the prevailing Party in all our Depreciating-Paper-Money Colonies, do wickedly endeavour to delude the unthinking Multitude, by perswading them, that all Endeavours of the Governour, or Proposals and Schemes of private Societies, to introduce a Silver Medium, or a Credit upon a Silver Bottom, to prevent the honest and industrious Creditor from being defrauded; are Impositions upon the Liberty and Property of the People.

Depreciating the Value of *nummary Denominations*, to defraud the Creditors of the Publick and of private Persons; by Proclamations of Sovereigns, by Recoinages, and by a late Contrivance of a depreciating Paper-Credit-Currency; were never practised but in notoriously bad Administrations.

All over *Europe* for many Ages preceeding the 14th Century, the *nummary* Pound, and the *Ponderal* or Pound Weight of Silver were the same: but in some following Ages in bad Administrations the Values of nummary Denominations were gradually reduced; as in *England* to 4 oz. Silver value (upon all Occasions I use the nearest round Numbers) one third of its original Value; in *Holland* the Pound *Ulams* (6 Guilders) to 2 oz. Silver being only one sixth of its original Value. A general Stop has been put to those notorious publick Frauds ever since Trade began to flourish; the civil Governments becoming more polite, found it their Interest in Affairs of a *Medium* of Trade, to be advised by the more knowing and experienced Traders: Thus, since the Reign of *Edward* VI. *in England*, the Shilling Denomination hath lost only 2 gr. Silver. We have two or three Instances of late in *Europe*, that have deviated from that *Maxim* of a fixed Value of Silver in Trade; these were in arbitrary Governments, under most arbitrary Administrations. 1. *France* by *Recoinages* from A. 1689, to the wise Administration of *Cardinal Fluery*, was obliged to defraud the Subject, to maintain unjust Wars and Rapines upon its Neighbours,

and lessen'd the Value of nummary Denominations from a *Mark* of Silver at 27 *Livres* to 80 *Livres*. 2. *The King of Spain* A. 1688 lowered his Denominations 25 *per Cent*. A heavy Piece of *Eight* formerly 8 *Ryals* Plate, passed for 10 *Ryals* currant. 3. *Sweden* under the Administration of Baron *Gortz*.

In all Sovereignties in *Europe* where *Paper-Money* was introduced, great Inconveniencies happened; upon canceling this Paper Medium all those Inconveniencies did vanish. 1. In *Sweden*, *Baron Gortz*, by imposing *Government Notes* (and *Munt tokyns*) reduced the People to extreme Misery (this was one of the principal Crimes alledged against him when he suffered capital Punishment) but these being called in, and the *Coin* settled upon the same Foundation as it was before *Charles* XIIth Accession, *Sweden* flourished as formerly. 2. The late *Regent of France*, by the Advice of Mr. *Law*, did form a Project A. 1720, and by his arbitrary Power, endeavoured to put it on Execution; to defraud State Creditors and others, by banishing of Silver Currency, and by substituting a *Paper Credit*: the Effect was, the greatest Confusion, and almost utter Subversion of their Trade and Business: The *Remedy* was (Mr. *Law* having sneak'd off, became a *Profugus*, and at last died obscurely) after a few Months the Court of *France* were obliged to ordain, that there should be no other legal Tender but Silver-Coin; and Commerce was flourished in *France* more than ever. At present, under the wise Administration of Cardinal *Fleury* (who allows no Paper Currencies, nor Re-coinages, which had the same Effect in depreciating nummary Denominations in *France*, that frequent and large Emissions of Paper-Money have in our Colonies) their Trade, bids fair to outdo the Maritime Powers (as *Great Britain* and *Holland* are called) and has a much better Effect in advancing the Wealth and Glory of *France*, than the Romantick butcherly Schemes of Conquest over their Neighbours, under the Administrations of *Richelieu*, *Mazarine* and others, in the Reigns of *Lewis* XIII and XIV. 3. In *Great Britain* A. 1716, were current four and a half Millions of Pounds Sterling in *Exchequer Notes*, being the largest Quantity current at one Time: although they bore about half of legal Interest, and not equal to one third of the concomitant national Silver Currency; they laboured much in Circulation, and the Government to prevent their being depreciated, was obliged to give considerable *Premiums* to the *Bank* for cancelling some of them, and circulating the remainder.

It is not easily to be accounted for, how *England, France* and *Holland,* have tacitly allowed their several *American Colonies;* by *Laws* of their several Provinces, by *Chancerings* in their Courts of Judicature, and by *Custom;* to depreciate from Time to Time, the Value of their original Denominations, to defraud their Principals and Creditors in *Europe.* The *British Plantations* have not only varied, from Sterling, but have also very much varied from one another; to the great Confusion of Business, and Damage of the Merchant. This will appear plain by inserting at one View the State of the Currencies in the several British Plantations; whereof some are per *Exchange,* some in *Spanish Silver* Coin, and some in *Paper Money* called Colony or Province Bills of publick Credit.

Originally and for some Years following in all the *English American Colonies,* 5s. Denomination was equal to an English Crown Sterl. after some Time *Pieces of Eight,* being the general Currency of all foreign American Colonies, became also their Currency; and they remitted or gave Credit to the Merchants at Home (by Home is meant *Great Britain*) a Piece of Eight (value 4 s. 6d. Sterl.) For a Crown or 5 s. Sterl. *this was a Fraud of 11 per Cent.* In sundry of our Colonies were enacted Laws against passing of light Pieces of Eight; these Laws not being put in Execution, *heavy and light Pieces of Eight passed promiscuously;* and as it always happens, a bad Currency drove away the good Currency; heavy Pieces of Eight were ship'd off. This current Money growing daily lighter, a Difference was made between heavy Money which became Merchandize, and light Money in which they paid their Debts gradually from 10, 15, 20, to 25 per Cent. as at present in *Jamaica: this was another and continued Course of cheating their Creditors and Employers at Home.* From a Complaint of Merchants and others dealing to the Plantations; Q. *Anne* by Proclamation, and the Parliament of Great Britain, afterwards by the *Proclamation Act,* ordered, that after A. 1709, *A heavy Piece of Eight and other Pieces in Proportion to their Weight, in all our Colonies should pass not exceeding 6 s. Denomination.* This Act continues to be observed in none of our Colonies, excepting in *Bar-*

badoes, and *Bermudas. Virginia* Currency was formerly, and continues still better than what the Act directs. . . .

✳✳✳

MASSACHUSETTS-BAY: This being more especially the scene of our Discourse, we shall be more particular. At the first settling of the *New England* Colonies; their Medium was Sterling Coin at Sterling Value, and Barter; some Part of their Taxes was paid in Provisions and other Produce, called *Stock in the Treasury.* When they got into Trade a heavy piece of Eight passed at 5 s. A. 1652, *They proceeded to coin Silver Shillings, six Pences, and three Pences, at the Rate of 6s. to a heavy Piece of Eight;* Silver continued current at this Rate by sundry subsequent Acts of Assembly till A. 1705, by a Resolve of the General court Silver was to pass at 7s. per Oz. A. 1706 the Courts of Judicature chancered Silver to 8s. per Oz. in satisfying of Debts, being nearly after the Rate of 6s. a light Piece of Eight as then current. At this Rate Silver and Province Bills continued upon *Par* until A. 1714, the Assembly or Legislature fell into the Error of making from Time to Time large superfluous Sums of *Paper Money upon Loans,* and the Emissions for Charges of Government not cancellable for many Years, so that these *Publick Bills have been continually depreciating for these last 26 Years, and are now arrived to 29 s. per Oz. Silver*

Massachusetts-Bay was the Leader of Paper Currencies in our Colonies. Their first Emission was of £40,000 A. 1690 & 1691, to pay off the publick Debts incurr'd by that expensive, tho' unsuccessful, Expedition against *Canada;* of this Sum £10,000 was cancelled and burnt in *October* A. 1691: In the following Years no more new Emissions, but some Re-emissions of the remainder, and that only for the necessary Charges of Government, called in by Rates or Taxes within the year; the last Remission of these Bills was A. 1701, of £9,000 Bills all this Period continued at the Rate of 6s. a heavy Piece of Eight, and were called *Old Charter Bills.* A.1702 began new Emissions of Province Bills; but, as it ought to be in all wise Administrations, cancelled by Taxes of the same and next following Year, until A. 1704, the Rates for calling them in, were in Part postponed two Years; they began A. 1707 to postpone them in Part for three Years; A. 1709 for 4 Years; A. 1710 for 5 Years; A. 1711 for 6 Years; *A.* 1715 for 7 Years; *A.* 1721 for 12 Years; *A.* 1722 for 13 Years: *Thus unnaturally instead of providing for Posterity, they proceeded to involve them in Debt.* This long publick Credit and the enormous publick Loans, have depreciated our Province Bills to the small Value they bear at present; the Issues and cancellings of their Bills being for a long Series of years too tedious to be particularly and minutely inserted.

The Province of the *Massachusetts-Bay* besides the Emission & Re-emissions of the £40,000 old Charter Bills, have since *A.* 1702 emitted and re-emitted Bills of publick Credit, £1,132,500 upon Fund of *Taxes*, and £310,000 upon *Loans*, being in all near one and a half Million; whereof about £230,000 still outstanding, and if publick Faith be better kept will be gradually cancelled by *A.*1742. The ordinary Charges of Government may be about £40,000 *New England* Currency per Ann. *Exchange with Great Britain 450 per Cent. Advance*, or five and an half *New England* for one Sterl. . . .

LESSON PLAN: William Douglass Argues About Money

Students analyze excerpts from William Douglass's *Discourse* to understand his goals, the effectiveness of his arguments, and their impact on colonial economy.

Learning Objectives

Identify Douglass's central purpose and his argumentative techniques; appreciate the historical perspective Douglass offers on currencies; compare alternative theories to Douglass's; decide how and why Douglass might or might not agree with the views of Thomas Hutchinson.

Materials: William Douglass, *A Discourse Concerning the Currencies of the British Plantations in America* (1739); Thomas Hutchinson, *The History of the Colony and Province of Massachusetts-Bay* (1764–1828).

Overview Questions

What exactly was Douglass's goal in writing this pamphlet? What does Douglass accomplish in explaining European and colonial currency history? What arguments can be made against his viewpoint? How do Douglass's views on currency compare to Hutchinson's?

Step 1: Comprehension Questions

What currency position is Douglass arguing for? What first impressions do his attempts at persuasion make?

▶ **Activity:** Have students discuss Douglass's stated viewpoint. Select students to read aloud passages in which Douglass describes those people or governments that disagree with him or use polices he decries. Invite students to judge whether his tone and approach hurt his argument.

Step 2: Comprehension Questions

How does his tracing of monetary history help Douglass make his point? Given the argumentative nature of his pamphlet, how should his telling of this history be judged?

▶ **Activity:** Have students list examples of failed paper currency plans that Douglass cites. Discuss whether or these examples are solid arguments against nonsilver-backed paper currency use. Have students explain their reasoning.

Step 3: Context Questions

What arguments are there against Douglass's view? How can formal counterarguments be discovered from the text?

▶ **Activity:** Discuss with students why the currency strategies that Douglass derides were attempted. Ask students where they would turn to look for other points of view. Discuss how closely Douglass's preferences align with current United States currency practice.

Step 4: Historical Connections Questions

How does Thomas Hutchinson employ Douglass's ideas? In what ways would Douglass approve of Hutchinson's words?

▶ **Activity:** Have students review *The History of the Colony and Province of Massachusetts-Bay*. Instruct students to note similarities between Hutchinson's and Douglass's ideas. Ask students to note what Hutchinson says about Douglass. Instruct students to research why the men disagreed.

Step 5: Response Paper

Word length and additional requirements set by Instructor. Students answer the research question in the Overview Questions. Students state a thesis and use as evidence passages from the primary source documents.

DOCUMENTS ILLUSTRATIVE OF SLAVERY AND INDENTURED SERVITUDE

Although historically promoted as the land of opportunity, America in fact built its early economic success—from the seventeenth to the nineteenth centuries—on the backs of indentured servants and slaves. Indentured servitude was a common way for poor European immigrants in search of a better life to defray the cost of their transatlantic journey, by signing a contract binding them to a certain number of years of labor in the New World. The contract was typically entered into by the worker (or his or her parents) and the captain of the ship on which they traveled; the captain would then sell the contract to an employer, such as a farmer or shop owner, in America. Indentured servants were not paid cash, but, in addition to the ship voyage, received food, clothing, and housing from their masters.

In practice, indentured servants were largely at the mercy of their masters, and the institution is widely regarded as having been only a few steps up from slavery. While most indentured servants successfully fulfilled the terms of their contracts and went on to become independent farmers, wage laborers, or business owners, a large number also died on the long ocean voyage or from disease and poor working conditions in America before their contracts were up.

Slaves, on the other hand, had no contracts and almost no prospects for freedom. They were simply owned, like livestock. Overwhelmingly, the enslaved people put to work in America were Africans, who, because of their skin color and utterly foreign culture, were quickly reduced categorically to the status of slaves, first in the eyes of European Americans, and then formally, under the terms of the many slave laws passed in the late seventeenth and early eighteenth centuries. One such law passed in Virginia stipulated that "all servants imported and brought into the country, by sea or land, who were not Christians in their native country . . . shall be accounted and be slaves."

While slavery existed in all the early British colonies, the institution soon became critical to the economy of the southern colonies in particular, where intensive plantation agriculture came to rely on a large and ready supply of permanently unpaid labor. The divide pertaining to slavery between the Northern and Southern colonies, and then states, only widened over time. By the late eighteenth century there was an organized antislavery (or abolitionist) movement in the North, but before then only a small minority—including, notably, Quakers—spoke out against the practice.

Adam Groff, MA

■ The Virginia Slave Codes 1662-1705

Date: 1662–1705
Author: Virginia General Assembly
Genre: legislation; law

"All servants imported and brought into this country, by sea or land, who were not christians in their native country . . . shall be accounted and be slaves . . ."

Summary Overview

Although the earliest Africans in Virginia had a status comparable to that of European indentured servants, a series of legal, economic, and social changes increasingly pushed these Virginians into complete slavery. Written from the mid-seventeenth through early eighteenth century, Virginia's slave laws exemplify the slow but steady removal of rights from enslaved Africans in favor of more restrictive practices and harsh punishment that dehumanized and oppressed them. During the latter half of the seventeenth century, laws made it more difficult for enslaved Africans to obtain liberty and expanded the groups automatically considered enslaved. At the same time, new laws removed rights from black colonists, such as the right to marry English Virginians, the right to own property, and the right to own slaves themselves. Such changes broadened the divisions between white and black Virginians for centuries to come.

Defining Moment

Some of the first Africans in continental North America were in the English colony of Virginia. A Dutch ship captured a group of some twenty Africans from a Spanish ship and brought them to the English colony of Jamestown in 1619. Unlike later African arrivals, these colonial immigrants were treated an indentured servants rather than chattel slaves. Thus, early Africans had the chance to obtain their liberty after a set period of labor and possibly become wealthy landowners who relied on unfree labor themselves in order to acquire large holdings under Virginia's head-rights laws. Yet this early African population of Virginia was a minute one. Records indicate that fewer than twenty-five Africans lived in Virginia in 1625; by 1650, that number had risen to roughly three hundred. A decade later, that number had tripled. Yet this still represented a very small minority of the overall population, and Africans found their status lowered even as their numbers grew. In 1640, for example, a slaveholder successfully argued before the Virginia courts that his African indentured servant could be made to labor for life, a sign that the idea of lasting servitude had sway with the colonial government well before it was formalized in slave laws.

From this time onward, the move toward complete, lifelong slavery accelerated. During the 1640s, colonists purchased African servants as laborers for the duration of their lifetime, with the right to require any of those servants' children to themselves work as unfree laborers for life. Beginning in the early 1660s, the Virginia legislature passed laws that formalized this practice. Legislation accepted that servants of African descent, unlike European servants, were liable to labor throughout their lifetimes and thus could not have their terms of service extended in punishment for various infractions. Other laws established the condition of slavery as hereditary and limited the ways by which Africans could obtain the freedom so readily granted fewer than fifty years before. Over the next several decades, more and more laws restricted the rights of Africans. At the same time, the European indentured servants, alongside whom they had once labored, declined greatly in number as the growth of the colonies and improvements in the English labor market spread more thinly the people willing to exchange a long period of labor for a passage across the Atlantic. An enslaved black underclass oppressed by the colonial government thus emerged.

Author Biography

The Virginia General Assembly was the first elected legislative body in the North American colonies. The General Assembly had roots in the earliest years of colonial settlement, when the royal charter issued to the Virginia Company allowed for the creation of a small representative body to legislate for the colony under the auspices of the governor. This body evolved over the next few decades as the colony came under direct royal control, becoming a bicameral legislature perhaps best known for its lower house, the popularly elected House of Burgesses, in 1643. This group comprised two representatives, or burgesses, from each of Virginia's counties, and a handful of additional representatives from leading towns including Jamestown, Williamsburg, and Norfolk. By the end of the century, this had changed to include just one urban representative, from the colonial capital of Jamestown.

During the 1650s, the political authority of the House of Burgesses over the governor and upper house of the assembly grew. By the time of the passage of the first slave laws in the 1660s, the House of Burgesses was the dominant political force in Virginia. Because of an extended period during which no elections were held, the same burgesses served between 1661 and 1676, making the earlier collection of slave laws the work of one group of men. Although the overall power of the House of Burgesses had declined somewhat by 1705, the body remained an important legislative unit. Historians have suggested that it probably played a significant part in the revision of the colonial legal code that began in 1705 and included the creation of more slave laws.

Throughout its colonial existence, the Virginia General Assembly was largely made up of wealthy elites who sought to support the interests of their own social and economic class. After 1670, the right to vote for members of the House of Burgesses was limited to white adult male property holders. Many voters of this group were farmers with relatively small landholdings, but the representatives they chose were men of local power and influence. As a result of its composition, the House of Burgesses worked for the support of slavery as an integral force behind the colonial agricultural economy, which relied heavily on the production of tobacco as a cash crop.

HISTORICAL DOCUMENT

December 1662-ACT XII. Negro womens children to serve according to the condition of the mother.

WHEREAS some doubts have arrisen whether children got by any Englishman upon a negro woman should be slave or ffree, Be it therefore enacted and declared by this present grand assembly, that all children borne in this country shalbe held bond or free only according to the condition of the mother, And that if any christian shall committ ffornication with a negro man or woman, hee or shee soe offending shall pay double the ffines imposed by the former act.

✱✱✱

September 1667-ACT III. An act declaring that baptisme of slaves doth not exempt them from bondage.

WHEREAS some doubts have risen whether children that are slaves by birth, and by the charity and piety of their owners made pertakers of the blessed sacrament of baptisme, should by vertue of their baptisme be made ffree; It is enacted and declared by this grand assembly, and the authority thereof, that the conferring of baptisme doth not alter the condition of the person as to his bondage or ffreedome; that diverse masters, ffreed from this doubt, may more carefully endeavour the propagation of christianity by permitting children, though slaves, or those of greater growth if capable to be admitted to that sacrament.

October 1669-ACT I. An act about the casuall killing of slaves.

WHEREAS the only law in force for the punishment of refractory servants resisting their master, mistris or overseer cannot be inflicted upon negroes, nor the obstinacy of many of them by other then violent meanes supprest, Be it enacted and declared by this grand assembly, if any slave resist his master (or other by his masters order correcting him) and by the extremity of the correction should chance to die, that his death shall not be accompted ffelony, but the master (or that other person appointed by the master to punish him) be acquit from molestation, since it cannot be presumed that prepensed malice (which alone makes murther ffelony) should induce any man to destroy his owne estate.

October 1705-CHAP. XXII. An act declaring the Negro, Mulatto, and Indian slaves within this dominion, to be real estate.

I. FOR the better settling and preservation of estates within this dominion,

II. Be it enacted, by the governor, council and burgesses of this present general assembly, and it is hereby enacted by the authority of the same, That from and after the passing of this act, all negro, mulatto, and Indian slaves, in all courts of judicature, and other places, within this dominion, shall be held, taken, and adjudged, to be reat estate (and not chattels;) and shall descend unto the heirs and widows of persons departing this life, according to the manner and custom of land of inheritance, held in fee simple.

X. Provided, and be it enacted, That when any person dies intestate, leaving several children, in that case all the slaves of such person, (except the widow's dower, which is the be first set apart) shall be inventoried and appraised; and the value thereof shall be equally divided amongst all the said children; and the several proportions, according to such valuation and appraisement, shall be paid by the heir (to whom the said slaves shall descend, by virtue of this act) unto all and every the other said children. And thereupon, it shall and may be lawful for the said other children, and every of them, and their executors or administrators, as the case shall be, to commence and prosecute an action upon the case, at the common law, against such heir, his heirs, executors and administrators, for the recovery of their said several proportions, respectively.

XI. And be it further enacted by the authority aforesaid, That if any widow, seised of any such slave or slaves, as aforesaid, as of the dower of her husband, shall send, or voluntarily permit to be sent out of this colony and dominion, such slave or slaves, or any of their increase, without the lawful consent of him or her in reversion, such widow shall forfeit all and every such slave or slaves, and all other the dower which she holds of the endowment of her husband's estate, unto the person or persons that shall have the reversion thereof; any law, usage or custom to the contrary notwithstanding. And if any widow, seized as aforesaid, shall be married to an husband, who shall send, or voluntary permit to be sent out of this colony and dominion, any such slave or slaves, or any of their increase, without the consent of him or her in reversion; in such case, it shall be lawful for him or her in reversion, to enter into, possess and enjoy all the estate which such husband holdeth, in right of his wife's dower, for and during the life of the said husband.

October 1705-CHAP. XLIX. An act concerning Servants and Slaves.

IV. And also be it enacted, by the authority aforesaid, and it is hereby enacted, That all servants imported and brought into this country, by sea or land, who were not christians in their native country, (except Turks and Moors in amity with her majesty, and others that can make due proof their being free in England, or any other christian country, before they were shipped, in order to transportation hither (shall be accounted and be slaves, and as such be here bought and sold notwithstanding a conversion to christianity afterwards.

V. And be it enacted, by the authority aforesaid, and it is hereby enacted, That if any person or persons shall hereafter import into this colony, and here sell as a slave, any person or persons that shall have been a freeman in any christian country, island, or plantation, such importer and seller as aforesaid, shall forfeit and pay, to the party from who the said freeman shall recover his freedom, double the sum for which the said freeman was sold. To be recovered, in any court of record within this colony, according to the course of the common law, wherein the defendant shall not be admitted to plead in bar, any act or statute for limitation of actions.

VI. Provided always, That a slave's being in England, shall not be sufficient to discharge him of his slavery, without other proof of his being manumitted there.

XI. And for a further christian care and usage of all christian servants, Be it also enacted, by the authority aforesaid, and it is hereby enacted, That no negros, mulattos, or Indians, although christians, or Jews, Moors, Mahometans, or other infidels, shall, at any time, purchase any christian servant, nor any other, except of their own complexion, or such as are declared slaves by this act: And if any negro, mulatto, or Indian, Jew, Moor, Mahometan, or other infidel, or such as are declared slaves by this act, shall, notwithstanding, purchase any christian white servant, the said servant shall, ipso facto, become free and acquit from any service then due, and shall be so held, deemed, and taken: And if any person, having such christian servant, shall intermarry with any such negro, mulatto, or Indian, Jew, Moor, Mahometan, or other infidel, every christian white servant of every such person so intermarrying, shall, ipso facto, become free and acquit from any service then due to such master or mistress so intermarrying, as aforesaid.

XV. And also be it enacted, by the authority aforesaid, and it is hereby enacted, That no person whatsoever shall, buy, sell, or receive of, to, or from, any servant, or slave, any coin or commodity whatsoever, without the leave, licence, or consent of the master or owner of the said servant, or slave: And if any person shall, contrary hereunto, without the leave or licence aforesaid, deal with any servant, or slave, he or she so offending, shall be imprisoned one calender month, without bail or main-prize; and then, also continue in prison, until he or she shall find good security, in the sum of ten pounds current money of Virginia, for the good behaviour for one year following; wherein, a second offence shall be a breach of the bond; and moreover shall forfeit and pay four times the value of the things so bought, sold, or received, to the master or owner of such servant, or slave: To be recovered, with costs, by action upon the case, in any court of record in this her majesty's colony and dominion, wherein no essoin, protection, or wager of law, or other than one imparlance, shall be allowed.

XVI. Provided always, and be it enacted, That when any person or persons convict for dealing with a servant, or slave, contrary to this act, shall not immediately give good and sufficient security for his or her good behaviour, as aforesaid: then in such case, the court shall order thirty-nine lashes, well laid on, upon the bare back of such offender, at the common whipping-post of the county, and the said offender to be thence discharged of giving such bond and security.

XVIII. And if any woman servant shall have a bastard child by a negro, or mulatto, over and above the years service due to her master or owner, she shall immediately, upon the expiration of her time to her then present master or owner, pay down to the church-wardens of the parish wherein such child shall be born, for the use of the said parish, fifteen pounds current money of Virginia, or be by them sold for five years, to the use aforesaid: And if a free christian white woman shall have such bastard child, by a negro, or mulatto, for every such offence, she shall, within one month after her delivery of such bastard child, pay to the church-wardens for the time being, of the parish wherein such child shall be born, for the use of the said parish fifteen pounds current money of Virginia, or be by them sold for five years to the use aforesaid: And in both the said cases, the church-wardens shall bind the said child to be a servant, until it shall be of thirty one years of age.

XIX. And for a further prevention of that abominable mixture and spurious issue, which hereafter may increase in this her majesty's colony and dominion, as well by English, and other white men and women intermarrying with negroes or mulattos, as by their unlawful coition with them, Be it enacted, by the authority aforesaid, and it is hereby enacted, That whatsoever English, or other white man or woman, being free, shall intermarry with a negro or mulatto man or woman, bond or free, shall, by judgment of the county court, be committed to prison, and there remain, during the space of six months, without bail or mainprize; and shall forfeit and pay ten pounds current money of Virginia, to the use of the parish, as aforesaid.

XX. And be it further enacted, That no minister of the church of England, or other minister, or person whatsoever, within this colony and dominion, shall hereafter wittingly presume to marry a white man with a negro or mulatto woman; or to marry a white woman with a negro or mulatto man, upon pain of forfeiting and paying, for every such marriage the sum of ten thousand pounds of tobacco; one half to our sovereign lady the Queen, her heirs and successors, for and towards the support of the government, and the contingent charges thereof; and the other half to the informer; To be recovered, with costs, by action of debt, bill, plaint, or information, in any court of record within this her majesty's colony and dominion, wherein no essoin, protection, or wager of law, shall be allowed.

XXIII. And for encouragement of all persons to take up runaways, Be it enacted, by the authority aforesaid, and it is hereby enacted, That for the taking up of every servant, or slave, if ten miles, or above, from the house or quarter where such servant, or slave was kept, there shall be allowed by the public, as a reward to the taker-up, two hundred pounds of tobacco; and if above five miles, and under ten, one hundred pounds of tobacco: Which said several rewards of two hundred, and one hundred pounds of tobacco, shall also be paid in the county where such taker-up shall reside, and shall be again levied by the public upon the master or ownmer of such runaway, for re-imbursement of the public, every justice of the peace before whom such runaway shall be brought, upon the taking up, shall mention the proper-name and sur-name of the taker-up, and the county of his or her residence, together with the time and place of taking up the said runaway; and shall also mention the name of the said runaway, and the proper-name and sur-name of the master or owner of such runaway, and the county of his or her residence, together with the distance of miles, in the said justice's judgment, from the place of taking up the said runaway, to the house or quarter where such runaway was kept.

GLOSSARY

accompted: accounted

essoin: exemption; excuse from appearing in court

fee simple: complete ownership and possession

imparlance: an extension of time to put in a response in pleading a case

Mahometans: Muslims

mainprize: the release of an accused person on the basis of surety from another

manumitted: freed from slavery

murther: murder

refractory: resisting control or authority

reversion: the right of succession or future possession

spurious: illegitimate

Document Analysis

The Virginia slave laws display the steady removal of civil rights and increasing racial divisions that marked the coalescence of colonial slavery during the late seventeenth and early eighteenth century. The colony of Virginia first formally recognized the institution of slavery in 1661, and soon after, began making laws that drew more and more Africans into slavery, rather than indentured servitude. This was the first sign of the dehumanization of slaves that characterized later slave legislation. The legislation reproduced here exemplifies both the measures taken that expanded slavery throughout Virginia and the changing ideas about race, class, and servitude that affected the colony during this time. By the time of the passage of the 1705 laws, for example, racial divisions had become something to emphasize and enforce through the prohibition of interracial marriage. These slave codes thus not only affirmed colonial custom regarding the lifelong bondage of enslaved Africans, but also created an entirely separate system of laws and punishments that affected that group. The legislature thus served the economic motives of the wealthy white planter elite.

The earliest piece of slave legislation passed in 1662 after the formal recognition of slavery. In the document from the Virginia General Assembly, the law states that children would inherit the condition of bondage or liberty directly from their mothers, regardless of the state of their fathers. Hence, a child born to an enslaved mother automatically entered into a lifetime of bondage. This law broke with traditional English inheritance practices, which strongly favored primogeniture—the passing of property and status to the eldest son or other closest male relative. Virginia's decision to pass on enslaved status through the maternal line was therefore a revolutionary one that clearly reflected the existence of illegitimate children fathered on enslaved African women by free English colonists. The law did try to stymie this practice by placing a heavy fine on white Virginians who procreated with an African colonist, either enslaved or free, outside of marriage. However, the decision to make slavery a heritable condition proved a momentous one that tied new generations to the institution and created a large pool of enslaved persons even after the formal abolition of the transatlantic slave trade some 150 years later.

As the legislature sought to make becoming a slave easier, it made ending one's term of bondage more difficult. Early European ideas about slavery forbade the ownership of one Christian by another; thus, Africans who converted to Christianity in their native countries were typically considered exempt from potential bondage, and even enslaved Africans who converted after their arrival in the Americas often gained liberty upon their baptism as Christians. Virginia ended this policy in 1667 by stating that baptism was no longer an automatic path to freedom to end "doubts" about whether the sacrament conferred manumission. This law served a dual purpose: limiting a path to freedom for enslaved persons that had only recently become legally tied to lifelong bondage and encouraging slave owners to seek to spread Christianity among their slaves. In doing so, the law reversed earlier justifications for slavery, which had pointed to the heathen religious practices of Africans and American Indians. The economic motive of slavery now trumped the earlier moral rationales.

The next slave code, enacted in 1669, promotes the idea of slaves not as humans, but as soulless property, in its removal of any potential punishment for "the casuall killing of slaves." Because slaves, unlike indentured servants, could not be threatened with measures such as the extension of bondage—and because the legislature believed that the natural "obstinacy" of enslaved African was so great—the assembly freed any master or overseer from all blame if an enslaved person was killed during the course of punishment for any type of resistance. The assembly justified this law by stating that no rational master would intentionally murder a slave because to do so would be to damage his own economic holdings; consequently, any such death was accidental and therefore not to be counted as murder. Under such reasoning, slaves were no more people than were any other economic plantation resource and thus not deserving of equal protection from violence or even death.

The transition of enslaved persons from person to property continued with the institution of several new laws as part of the overhaul of the Virginia legal code undertaken by the General Assembly from 1705 onward. Like other slave codes developed throughout the colonies, these laws assert their purpose as improving safety and order within the colony. In their October 1705, Chapter XXII ruling, Virginia lawmakers specifically state that their purpose in declaring enslaved persons to be real estate was the "better settling and preservation of estates." This statement clarifies the economic and organizational motives of the laws; although the social and cultural effects of slave laws were immense, they existed primarily to support the plantation agriculture system on which Virginia and other southern colonies relied.

The declaration of enslaved persons as real estate, rather than chattel, reinforced these agricultural connections. Section II of Chapter XXII declares all slaves to be real estate treated under the law as fixed property. This meant that slaves were passed "unto the heirs and widows" of deceased slaveholders in the same way as owned land rather than as a moveable possession, essentially tying people held in bondage to the physical plantations of their owners in much the same way that medieval serfs had been attached to the land owned by their manor's lord. By 1750, however, Virginia would revert to the usage of chattel slavery. In severing the ties that bound enslaved people to the land, enslaved families could be broken up through sales. Valuation as real estate, while dehumanizing, had actually been somewhat to the benefit of enslaved people, who could at least generally expect to remain on the same plantation.

The remaining sections of the October 1705 laws deal with various legal issues relating to the process of the inheritance of slaves that were considered real estate. Section X covers the distribution of enslaved persons to the children of a slave owner who died intestate, or without a will. Those enslaved persons who were promised to a widow as part of her husband's estate first went to her; any additional slaves were counted and given a value. The total value was then divided equally among all of the slaveholder's children, although the enslaved workers themselves passed to the deceased's primary heir. That heir was then required to pay each other beneficiary the amount due to him or her for the relevant proportion of the total value of the enslaved part of the estate.

Section XI addresses potential actions by a widow regarding the slaves she held as part of her inheritance after her husband's death. The legislation bans the widow from removing such enslaved persons from Virginia without the approval of the person who would take control of those slaves once the widow's claim expired. A widow who broke this law would lose all claim to her inheritance from her husband. The economic repercussions for a potential next husband to such a widow could also be severe. If a husband removed the enslaved persons from the colony, he faced action from the next claimant for all of the property that had come to the former widow through her previous husband's death. These strictures therefore sought to ensure that those held in bondage in Virginia stayed in the colony even after the original owner's death.

Other slave codes increased the number of people automatically considered enslaved, rather than indentured, upon arrival in Virginia. According to Chapter XLIX of the October 1705 codes, all people who came to Virginia as a "servant"—meaning an indentured servant with a fixed, limited term of service—were to "be accounted and be slaves" if they did not originate in Christian nation. Exceptions were granted for Muslims of the powerful Turkish Ottoman Empire or other nations that had friendly diplomatic relations with England, and for those few who could prove that they held freedom in England or any other Christian (that is, European) nation. Such persons forced into slavery in this manner could not attain freedom through baptism in an affirmation of the 1667 law barring manumission through conversion.

Simple presence in England was not enough to prove one's freedom; instead, a free person of African descent was required to produce manumission papers to attest to his or her liberty. This law finalized the importation of Africans as slaves rather than indentured servants, ensuring that the latter category remained reserved for white Christian Europeans. The law also made it possible for free individuals who could not prove their status to be forced into slavery. Tied to this, slaves were forbidden from serving as witnesses in court, making it impossible for a wrongfully enslaved person to speak in his or her own favor.

The Virginia General Assembly did establish punishment for those who sold free persons into slavery, however. If a slave was found to be legitimately free, the seller was forced to pay the purchaser "double the sum for which the said freeman was sold." The person sold in slavery received nothing. Again, an economic punishment for the dubious sale of property was inflicted, rather than an action that reflected the moral ramifications of the buying and selling of human beings. Even free blacks were considered of less importance than free whites.

Legislators also wished to reserve the owning of indentured servants and slaves to only white Christian Virginians. Although some early Africans in Virginia had achieved freedom from servitude and established themselves as slave-owning planters, the 1705 slave codes barred the purchase of white Christian indentured servants or any slaves by not only Africans and

American Indians, but also by Muslims or Jews. Any such European servant contracted by a master from these restricted groups immediately gained his or her freedom upon arrival in Virginia. Similarly, any white person with indentured servants who married a member of a restricted group immediately gave up his or her right to require servants to complete their contracts. Although outright interracial marriage between whites and blacks was barred entirely by the slave codes, this measure served as a disincentive for intermarriage of white Christian Europeans with members of other religious groups, thus further stratifying the racial and cultural divides among colonial society to the benefit of white Christian landowners.

Culturally, therefore, the Virginia legislature sought to strengthen the divisions between the races to prevent the intermingling of white and black in colonial society over time. Indentured servants were forcibly separated from enslaved workers, despite being of similar economic class. A European servant who gave birth to a child fathered by an enslaved African faced either the prospect of paying a sizable fine to the clergy of the parish in which the child was born at the end of her term of indenture or of being returned to servitude for five years to pay this debt. A free white woman who gave birth to such a baby was sold into servitude unless she was able to pay the sum required. Mulatto, or mixed-race children, born to indentured or free white women did not, in contrast to earlier law, automatically assume the status of their mothers; instead, they were placed in indentured servitude until their thirty-first birthdays. White men, in contrast, faced no such prohibition, allowing them to engage in sexual relations with enslaved Africans that resulted into the birth of numerous enslaved children.

Colonial cultural aversions to the mixing of races resulted in other slave codes that emphasized the separation of races. In Section XIX of the 1705 codes, the intermarriage of African and European colonists is outlawed, with the reasoning that it was necessary to "[prevent] . . . that abominable mixture and spurious issue." To many English Virginians, the idea of intermingling was morally abhorrent, a further reflection of the low opinion of Africans in society. No white colonist was permitted to marry a black one, whether enslaved or free. Offenders were required to serve six months in prison, without the possibility of early release, and pay a fine. To help ensure that this stricture was observed, the Virginia General Assembly prohibited clergy members from performing marriages between white and black Virginians. The fine for a transgressing minister was a steep one: ten thousand pounds of tobacco. Yet only half of this fine went to the government. The other half rewarded the person who informed on the minister for performing the marriage, giving the average Virginian a substantial incentive to police his or her neighbors. Such measures encouraged the support of the colony's numerous small farmers who did not have a substantial economic stake in the furtherance of slavery, by making these farmers potential stakeholders in the institution.

Other laws worked to keep the economic relationship between whites and blacks one of ownership and servitude rather than one of mutual benefit. Section XV of the slave codes barred the act of trade between free colonists and either indentured or enslaved workers. The language of the code implies that punishment for this act was severe. The free party was forced to serve a prison sentence and provide a monetary bond against the repetition of such an act in the near future. Repeat offenders faced increasingly steep penalties paid directly to the owner or master of the servant or slave. Those who could not pay the required fine instead faced the threat of a public whipping of "thirty-nine lashes." Such measures kept skilled servants or slaves extremely economically depressed and unable to sell their own handiwork to earn money, limiting their abilities to successfully escape from their plantations or gather the materials needed to mount a serious insurrection.

Virginia legislators also sought to increase the support and participation of non-slaveholders by setting rewards for the recovery of fugitive slaves. Runaway slaves captured fewer than ten miles from their home plantation carried a reward of one hundred pounds of tobacco; those captured at greater distances were worth rewards of two hundred pounds of tobacco. Thus, as with the act of informing on illegal interracial marriages, the act of pursuing another's fugitive slave carried personal rewards for non-slaveholders. In section XXIII of the 1705 codes, slave owners are encouraged to monitor their own plantations to ensure that potential fugitives could not escape, as the owners were the ones liable for the payment of any reward. This law reiterated tenets set forth in earlier slave laws and remained in effect well into the nineteenth century. Records indicate that individual Virginians claimed cash rewards under this 1705 law as late as the 1840s.

Other measures of the 1705 slave codes followed similarly harsh lines to ensure the dominance of the wealthy white planter elite over the economically vital black underclass. For example, runaway slaves faced the prospect of facial branding, and those who resisted capture could be legally killed by their pursuers. Slaves faced severe physical punishment or automatic execution for infractions such as theft, violence, or even assembly, if that meeting was believed to be in support of a rebellion. Such measures laid the groundwork for the years of oppression that followed.

Essential Themes

Virginia's slave codes were not the first in colonial British North America, but they did prove highly formative for the colony and, later, the state of Virginia. Contemporary historians remain interested in the transition from indentured to enslaved labor in colonial Virginia, and the study of the era's slave laws provides a window on that evolution. The passage of the slave codes sealed the status of imported Africans and their descendents as lifelong slaves rather than as contracted indentured servants with a set term of service, firmly establishing the split between free—or potentially free—European labor and forced African labor. Prior to the mid-seventeenth century, Virginia relied much more heavily on European indentured labor than on imported African work. The slave laws of the latter seventeenth century exemplify the shift toward the use of enslaved labor. By eliminating paths to freedom and assuring the continuation of slavery from generation to generation, planters of European descent—a group that often overlapped with colonial legislators—guaranteed themselves a lasting pool of unpaid workers that in turn allowed their agricultural holdings to attain profitability.

The laws passed in the early eighteenth century served to establish and reinforce cultural divisions between European and African colonists. By dehumanizing African workers through restrictive laws that denied them the same rights as Europeans and punished them harshly for efforts to resist the system, colonial legislators encouraged colonists to embrace the perceived superiority of white Christian Europeans over others. Laws like the Virginia slave codes thus helped ally white indentured servants—who might otherwise have joined social and economic forces with enslaved black laborers—with the slaveholding class along purely racial lines. The focus on slaves as real estate property rather than independent humans further supported this racial divide and carved out a purely economic niche for these colonial workers. Laws required subservience by enslaved workers to their masters and forbade slaves from standing up for their rights at the price of their lives.

Many of the laws passed as part of the 1705 codes remained in force until the abolition of slavery following the American Civil War, and the social and cultural systems that they created endured even beyond that time. As late as the early twentieth century, for example, Virginia passed laws barring the intermarriage of white and nonwhite residents; the 1967 Supreme Court decision that eventually overturned all such laws around the nation stemmed from a challenge to the prohibition of interracial marriage in Virginia. Thus, the prejudices of the Virginia General Assembly in the early eighteenth century informed the civil rights battles fought by Virginians more than 250 years later.

Vanessa E. Vaughn, MA

Bibliography

Berlin, Ira. *Many Thousands Gone: The First Two Centuries of Slavery in North America*. Cambridge: Harvard UP, 1998 Print.

Eltis, David. *The Rise of African Slavery in the Americas*. New York: Cambridge UP, 2000. Print.

Gottlieb, Matt. "House of Burgesses." *Encyclopedia Virginia*. Ed. Brendan Wolfe. Virginia Foundation for the Humanities, 10 Feb. 2012. Web. 14 June 2012.

Hadden, Sally. *Slave Patrols: Law and Violence in Virginia and the Carolinas*. Cambridge: Harvard UP, 2001. Print.

Mintz, Steven. "Virginia Slave Laws." *Digital History*. Digital History, 6 June 2012. Web. 14 June 2012.

Morgan, Edmund S. *American Slavery, American Freedom*. New York: Norton, 1975. Print.

Reiss, Oscar. *Blacks in Colonial America*. Jefferson: McFarland, 1997. Print.

Schwarz, Philip J. *Slave Laws in Virginia*. Athens: U of Georgia P, 1996. Print.

"Slavery and Indentured Servants." *Law Library of Congress*. Library of Congress, n.d. Web. 14 June 2012.

Wood, Betty. *Slavery in Colonial America, 1619–1776*. Lanham: Rowman, 2005. Print.

Additional Reading

Addison, Kenneth N. *"We Hold These Truths to be Self-Evident": An Interdisciplinary Analysis of the Roots of Racism and Slavery in America*. Lanham: UP of America, 2009. Print.

Davis, David Brion. *Slavery in the Colonial Chesapeake*. Williamsburg: Colonial Williamsburg Foundation, 1986. Print.

Finkelman, Paul, ed. *Slavery and the Law*. Lanham: Rowman, 2002. Print.

Hening, William Waller. *The Statutes at Large; Being a Collection of All the Laws of Virginia, from the First Session of the Legislature, in the Year 1619*. New York: Bartow, 1823. Print.

Wood, Peter. *Strange New Land: Africans in Colonial America*. New York: Oxford UP, 2003. Print.

LESSON PLAN: **Slavery and Indentured Servitude in Colonial Virginia**

Students analyze different slave acts that were enacted in colonial Virginia and a letter written by an indentured servant to understand the colonial government's motives, beliefs, and interests.

Learning Objectives

Compare and contrast the characteristics of indentured servitude and chattel slavery; evaluate the rights of and lack of rights granted to indentured servants and enslaved people; analyze the causes and effects of limitations imposed on indentured servants and enslaved people; consider multiple perspectives on labor in colonial Virginia.

Materials: Virginia General Assembly, The Virginia Slave Codes 1662-1705 (1662–1705); Richard Frethorne, "Letter to His Parents" (1623).

Overview Questions

How were indentured servitude and slavery similar and different? What rights were guaranteed to both, if any? What restrictions were imposed on indentured servants and enslaved people? Why? What caused the government to enact slave laws? What effects did the laws have? How do multiple perspectives on labor and rights reveal a better understanding of the colonial government's motives, beliefs, and interests?

Step 1: Comprehension Questions

How were indentured servitude and slavery similar and different? How was each role defined?

▶ **Activity:** Have students form small groups and read aloud key passages in both selections. Ask students to underline the similarities between the passages and circle the differences.

Step 2: Comprehension Questions

What rights were guaranteed to indentured servants and enslaved people, if any? What restrictions were imposed upon them? Why?

▶ **Activity:** Ask students to create a list of the rights of indentured servants and enslaved people as well as the restrictions imposed upon them. Next, have students write in their journals an explanation for why these rights and restrictions existed.

Step 3: Context Questions

What caused the colonial government to enact slave laws? What effects did the laws have on indentured servants and enslaved people, as well as society itself?

▶ **Activity:** Discuss with students why the Virginia government enacted the slave laws and the context in which they were created. Have students work in small groups to discuss the social, political, and economic effects of the laws on colonial society.

Step 4: Exploration Questions

How do multiple perspectives on labor and rights reveal a better understanding of the colonial government's motives, beliefs, and interests?

▶ **Activity:** Ask students to create an outline for an essay on the motives, beliefs, and interests of the colonial government to impose restrictions and enact laws that affected indentured servants and enslaved people. Invite volunteers to share their outlines with the class.

Step 5: Response Paper

Word length and additional requirements set by Instructor. Students answer the research question in the Overview Questions. Students state a thesis and use as evidence passages from the primary source document as well as support from supplemental materials assigned in the lesson.

The Selling of Joseph: A Memorial

Date: June 24, 1700
Author: Sewall, Samuel
Genre: essay

> *"These* Ethiopians, *as black as they are;*
> *seeing they are the Sons and Daughters of the*
> *First* Adam, *the Brethren and Sister of the Last*
> *ADAM, and the Offspring of GOD; They ought to*
> *be treated with Respect agreeable."*

Summary Overview

The Selling of Joseph: A Memorial was one of the earliest antislavery essays published in America. Written by Samuel Sewall in 1700, decades before the antislavery movement of the late eighteenth and nineteenth centuries, this essay was an important early component in the development of antislavery writing and sentiments. *The Selling of Joseph* offers readers an opportunity to analyze Sewall's arguments against slavery. Sewall crafted an attack on slavery based primarily on verses from the Bible, as well as pragmatic arguments drawn from contemporary affairs. These lines of argument both foreshadow and present a counterpoint to later antislavery writing. *The Selling of Joseph* is also a window into the racial prejudices and cultural biases of Sewall and many of his contemporaries and thus demonstrates the fraught relationship between antislavery and racism. The tract provides a reminder that slavery was not restricted to the southern colonies, but existed in all thirteen original colonies.

Defining Moment

The Selling of Joseph was a response by Samuel Sewall to an injustice. In 1700, Adam, the African slave of John Saffin, enlisted the aid of a white lawyer to petition the courts for his freedom. Saffin hired Adam out to a tenant farmer for seven years and, as a reward for Adam's obedience, promised Adam his freedom. When seven years had passed, Saffin claimed that Adam was shiftless and lazy and denied Adam his freedom, thus causing Adam to resort to legal channels. Most historians agree that Adam was on Sewall's mind as he wrote *The Selling of Joseph* and that this fact accounts for Sewall's frequent repetition of the name "Adam," including his reference to "the last Adam."

Sewall's anger does not fully explain why he wrote *The Selling of Joseph*. The climate of fear in Massachusetts Bay played a critical role. In 1692, these fears resulted in the Salem witch trials, where twenty people were executed for witchcraft. Historians have offered various reasons to explain the trials: jealousy among members of different factions, fears of attack by American Indians, fears about devils and spirits, and ergot poisoning. Whatever the reason (likely a combination of these factors), Sewall, like many of his contemporaries, felt himself under siege. Fears of devils may seem incomprehensible to modern readers, but American Indians were a very real presence. As the colonists and Indians fought many bloody skirmishes, it is hardly surprising that fears of outsiders would run deep, that Puritans would conceptualize attacks from outsiders as attacks by the forces of the devil, and that the increasing numbers of slaves in Massachusetts would alarm people.

Finally, the context of slavery in Massachusetts is an important component of this story. The existence of slavery in New England may come as a surprise to many students, but slavery did exist outside of the southern colonies. While the number of African slaves in Massachusetts was never as high as the number of slaves in the southern colonies, slaves were nevertheless numerous; the highest estimate of the slaves in Massachusetts was two thousand in a population of forty thousand white colonists. This is not surprising because the colonists needed a supply of cheap labor and they easily justified the enslavement of Africans to themselves on biblical grounds.

Author Biography

Samuel Sewall was born in the village of Bishop Stoke, in Hampshire, England, on March 28, 1652. In 1661, Sewall and his family crossed the Atlantic and settled in Newbury in Massachusetts Bay Colony. Beginning in 1667, Sewall attended Harvard, earning both a bachelor's and a master's degree. During his time at Harvard, Sewall met Hannah Hull, the daughter of an affluent Boston merchant John Hull, whom he married in 1676. After Hannah's death in 1717, Sewall married Abigail Tilley in 1719, but she died about seven months later. In 1722, Sewall married Mary Gibbs, his third and final wife. Although Sewall did not have children with Abigail or Mary, he had fourteen children with Hannah, of whom only six lived past childhood and only three survived their father.

Sewall, a tremendously important figure, was best known for his role in the Salem witchcraft trials. In 1692, Sewall was appointed a member of the Court of Oyer and Terminer to hear the cases of alleged witches. Until its dissolution in 1693, the court sent twenty people to their deaths. In 1697, Sewall publicly repented his actions. The fact that Sewall was the only judge to do so gained him both a measure of fame, especially in later centuries, and a measure of notoriety, particularly among the other judges who never publicly apologized. In addition to his participation in the Court of Oyer and Terminer, Sewall was elected to the Massachusetts General Court and served as a member of the Superior Court of Judicature, on the Provisional Council, and as a probate judge. Sewall was, in other words, deeply involved in the legislative and judicial branches of Massachusetts Bay. Sewall also published a variety of works, including *Phaenomena quondam Apolcalyptica* (1697), a reading of on the biblical book of Revelation, and *Talitha Cumi; or, An Invitation to Women to Look After Their Inheritance in the Heavenly Mansion* (1711), which argues that the bodies of both women and men are resurrected in Heaven. A devout Puritan, Sewall was accepted as a member of the Third (South) Church of Boston in 1677. Sewall died in his house on January 1, 1730.

HISTORICAL DOCUMENT

For as much as Liberty *is in real value next unto* Life: None *ought to part with it themselves, or deprive others of it, but upon most mature Consideration.*

The Numerousness of Slaves at this day in the Province, and the Uneasiness of them under their Slavery, hath put many upon thinking whether the Foundation of it be firmly and well laid; so as to sustain the Vast Weight that is built upon it. It is most certain that all Men, as they are the Sons of *Adam,* are Coheirs; and have equal Right unto Liberty, and all other outward Comforts of Life. GOD *hath given the Earth* [with all its Commodities] *unto the Sons of Adam, Psal.* 115.16. *And hath made of One Blood, all Nations of Men, for to dwell on all the face of the Earth, and hath determined the Times before appointed, and the*

bounds of their habitation: That they should seek the Lord. Forasmuch then as we are the Offspring of GOD &c. Act 17.26, 27, 29. Now although the Title given by the last ADAM, doth infinitely better Mens Estates, respecting GOD and themselves; and grants them a most beneficial and inviolable Lease under the Broad Seal of Heaven, who were before only Tenants at Will: Yet through the Indulgence of GOD to our First Parents after the Fall, the outward Estate of all and every of their Children, remains the same, as to one another. So that Originally, and Naturally, there is no such thing as Slavery. *Joseph* was rightfully no more a Slave to his Brethren, than they were to him: and they had no more Authority to *Sell* him, than they had to *Slay* him. And if *they* had nothing to do to Sell him; the *Ishmaelites* bargaining with them, and paying down Twenty pieces of Silver, could not make a Title. Neither could *Potiphar* have any better Interest in him than the Ishmaelites had. Gen. 37. 20, 27, 28. For he that shall in this case plead Alteration of Property, seems to have forfeited a great part of his own claim to Humanity. There is no proportion between Twenty Pieces of Silver, and LIBERTY. The Commodity it self is the Claimer. If Arabian Gold be imported in any quantities, most are afraid to meddle with it, though they might have it at easy rates; lest if it should have been wrongfully taken from the Owners, it should kindle a fire to the Consumption of their whole estate. 'Tis pity there should be more Caution used in buying a Horse, or a little lifeless dust; than there is in purchasing Men and Women: Whenas they are the Offspring of GOD, and their Liberty is,

-- *Auro pretiosior Omni.*

And seeing GOD hath said, He that Stealeth a Man and Selleth him, or if he be found in his hand, he shall surely be put to Death. Exod. 21.16. This Law being of Everlasting Equity, wherein Man Stealing is ranked amongst the most atrocious of Capital Crimes: What louder Cry can there be made of the Celebrated Warning,

Caveat Emptor!

And all things considered, it would conduce more to the Welfare of the Province, to have White Servants for a Term of Years, than to have Slaves for Life. Few can endure to hear of a Negro's being made free; and indeed they can seldom use their freedom well; yet their continual aspiring after their forbidden Liberty, renders them Unwilling Servants. And there is such a disparity in their Conditions, Colour & Hair, that they can never embody with us, and grow up into orderly Families, to the Peopling of the Land: but still remain in our Body Politick as a kind of extravasat Blood. As many Negro men as there are among us, so many empty places there are in our Train Bands, and the places taken up of Men that might make Husbands for our Daughters. And the Sons and Daughters of *New England* would become more like *Jacob*, and *Rachel*, if this Slavery were thrust quite out of doors. Moreover it is too well known what Temptations Masters are under, to connive at the Fornication of their Slaves; lest they should be obliged to find them Wives, or pay their Fines. It seems to be practically pleaded that they might be Lawless; 'tis thought much of, that the Law should have Satisfaction for their Thefts, and other Immoralities; by which means, *Holiness to the Lord*, is more rarely engraven upon this sort of Servitude. It is likewise most lamentable to think, how in taking Negros out of *Africa*, and selling of them here, That which GOD ha's joyned together men do boldly rend asunder; Men from their Country, Husbands from their Wives, Parents from their Children. How horrible is the Uncleanness, Mortality, if not Murder, that the Ships are guilty of that bring great Crouds of these miserable Men, and Women. Methinks, when we are bemoaning the barbarous Usage of our Friends and Kinsfolk in *Africa*: it might not be unseasonable to enquire whether we are not culpable in forcing the *Africans* to become Slaves amongst our selves. And it may be a question whether all the Benefit received by Negro Slaves, will balance the Accompt of Cash laid out upon them; and for the Redemption of our own enslaved Friends out of Africa. Besides all the Persons and Estates that have perished there.

Obj. 1. *These Blackamores are of the Posterity of* Cham, *and therefore are under the Curse of Slavery.* Gen. 9. 25, 26, 27.

Answ. Of all Offices, one would not begg this; *viz.* Uncall'd for, to be an Executioner of the Vindictive Wrath of God; the extent and duration of which is to us uncertain. If this ever was a Commission; How do we know but that it is long since out of Date? Many have found it to their Cost, that a Prophetical Denunciation of Judgment against a Person or People, would not warrant them to inflict that evil. If it would, *Hazael* might justify himself in all he did against his Master, and the *Israelites*, from 2 *Kings* 8.10, 12.

But it is possible that by cursory reading, this Text may have been mistaken. For *Canaan* is the Person Cursed three times over, without the mentioning of *Cham*. Good Expositors suppose the Curse entaild on him, and that this Prophesie was accomplished in the Extirpation of the *Canaanites*, and in the Servitude of the *Gibeonites*. *Vide Pareum.* Whereas the Blackmores are not descended of

Canaan, but of *Cush.* Psal. 68.31. *Princes shall come out of Egypt* [Mizraim] *Ethiopia* [Cush] *shall soon stretch out her hands unto God.* Under which Names, all *Africa* may be comprehended; and their Promised Conversion ought to be prayed for. *Jer.* 13. 23. *Can the Ethiopian change his skin?* This shews that Black Men are the Posterity of *Cush:* who time out of mind have been distinguished by their Colour. And for want of the true, Ovid assigns a fabulous cause of it.

> *Sanguine tum credunt in corpora summa vocato*
> *Aethiopum populous nigrum traxisse colorem.*
> Metamorph. lib. 2.

Obj. 2. *The* Nigers *are brought out of a Pagan Country, into places where the Gospel is Preached.*

Answ. Evil must not be done, that good may come of it. The extraordinary and comprehensive Benefit accruing to the Church of God, and to *Joseph* personally, did not rectify his brethrens Sale of him.

Obj. 3. *The* Africans *have Wars with one another: our Ships bring lawful Captives taken in those Wars.*

Answ. For ought is known, their Wars are much such as were between *Jacob's* Sons and their brother *Joseph.* If they be between Town and Town; Provincial, or National: Every War is upon one side Unjust. An Unlawful War can't make lawful Captives. And by Receiving, we are in danger to promote, and partake in their Barbarous Cruelties. I am sure, if some Gentlemen should go down to the *Brewsters* to take the Air, and Fish: And a stronger party from Hull should Surprise them, and Sell them for Slaves to a Ship outward bound: they would think themselves unjustly dealt with; both by Sellers and Buyers. And yet 'tis to be feared, we have no other kind of Title to our Nigers. *Therefore all things whatsoever ye would that men should do to you, do ye even so to them: for this is the Law and the Prophets.* Matt. 7.12.

Obj. 4. Abraham *had servants bought with his Money, and born in his House.*

Answ. Until the Circumstances of *Abraham's* purchase be recorded, no Argument can be drawn from it. In the mean time, Charity obliges us to conclude, that He knew it was lawful and good

It is Observable that the *Israelites* were strictly forbidden the buying, or selling one another for Slaves. *Levit.* 25. 39, 46. *Jer.* 34. 8--22. And GOD gaged His Blessing in lieu of any loss they might conceipt they suffered thereby. *Deut.* 15. 18. And since the partition Wall is broken down, inordinate Self love should likewise be demolished. GOD expects that Christians should be of a more Ingenuous and benign frame of spirit. Christians should carry it to all the World, as the *Israelites* were to carry it one towards another. And for men obstinately to persist in holding their Neighbours and Brethren under the Rigor of perpetual Bondage, seems to be no proper way of gaining Assurance that God ha's given them Spiritual Freedom. Our Blessed Saviour ha's altered the Measures of the Ancient Love-Song, and set it to a most Excellent New Tune, which all ought to be ambitious of Learning. *Matt.* 5. 43, 44. *John* 13. 34. These *Ethiopians,* as black as they are; seeing they are the Sons and Daughters of the First *Adam,* the Brethren and Sister of the Last ADAM, and the Offspring of GOD; They ought to be treated with Respect agreeable.

Servitus perfecta voluntaria, inter Christianum & Christianum, ex parte servi patientis saepe est licita quia est necessaria; sed ex parte domini agentis, & procurando & exercendo, vix potest esse licita; quia non convenit regulae illi generali: Quaecunque volueritis ut faciant vobis homines, ita & vos facite eis. Matt. 7. 12.

Perfecta servitus poenae, non potest jure locum habere, nisi ex delicto gravi quod ultimum supplicium aliquo modo meretur; quia Libertas ex naturali aestimatione proxime accedit ad vitam ipsam, & eidem a multis praeferri solet.

Ames. Cas. Consc. Lib. 5. Cap. 23. Thes. 2, 3.

BOSTON of the Massachusets; Printed by Bartholomew Green, and John Allen, June 24, 1700.

GLOSSARY

Abraham: Jewish patriarch and grandfather of Jacob

auro pretiosior omni: Latin meaning "more precious than gold"

Blackamores: Africans

caveat emptor: Latin meaning "let the buyer beware"

First Parents: Adam and Eve

Potiphar: Egyptian who purchased Joseph from the Ishmaelites

train bands: militia

Document Analysis

The Selling of Joseph: A Memorial was one of the earliest antislavery documents published in America. Sewall's central message was captured in his opening statement, "For as much as Liberty is in real value next unto Life: None ought to part with it themselves, or deprive others of it." This document deserves careful and meticulous attention not simply because it was one of the first antislavery tracts, but because of the opportunities it offers for study and analysis. For one, in less than two thousand words, Sewall succinctly presents many different antislavery arguments. Most of Sewall's arguments are based on biblical verse. Sewall does not limit himself to one section of the Bible, but rather draws lessons from both the Old and New Testaments to make his points. Sewall's essay also highlights the relationship between antislavery and racism in New England and the rest of the colonies in 1700. Finally, Sewall's arguments are critical because they anticipate both the rhetoric of later opponents and proponents of slavery. While one should not draw a straight line from Sewall to famed abolitionist William Lloyd Garrison (1805–79), both Sewall and Garrison were part of a tradition of antislavery discourse.

Antislavery and Racism in *The Selling of Joseph*

Sewall's various concerns—the increasing number of African slaves in Massachusetts, the particular case of Adam, the enslavement of white Europeans by Barbary pirates in Africa and the Mediterranean, and more

generally the climate of fear—prodded him to write an essay excoriating slavery and slavers. Estimates of the number of slaves in Massachusetts during this period vary between five hundred and two thousand slaves in a colony with a total population of about forty thousand people. Accepting the highest estimate, slaves constituted about 5 percent of the population. This point is vital because while Sewall spoke of the weight of the system and the fears of slave insurrections, white men and women clearly outnumbered slaves by a lopsided majority in Massachusetts. Sewall begins his essay by asserting that black and white people are of one blood and therefore equal. To reinforce his point, Sewall quotes from the books of Psalms and Acts. All people are descended from the First Parents, Adams and Eve, Sewall proclaims, and thus share common ancestors. Furthermore, Sewall believed that God gave everyone a similar inheritance, another proof of the equality of all people, which meant that there is not and can never be such a thing as slavery. Notably, unlike the Spaniards in the early years of the conquest of the New World, Sewall never doubted the humanity of the slaves, nor did he think, as did many proponents of the theory of polygenesis in the nineteenth century, that black people were a separate species.

Sewall uses biblical figures and verses to lend weight to his arguments. Appropriately, in *The Selling of Joseph*, Sewall draws on the biblical figure of Joseph. Although Joseph arrived in Egypt as a slave, the book of Genesis recounts that he was favored by God and therefore rose to a position of power, which enabled him to save his family and all of Egypt from starvation during a prolonged famine. Sewall uses this story to frame his essay because he saw the selling of Joseph as both an awful crime (brothers selling their brother into slavery) and as a way to level a sharp critique against slave traders. Joseph's brothers had neither the right to slay nor to sell him, and their actions violated God's laws, as do the actions of slavers today, Sewall argues. Sewall skillfully utilizes Bible verses to demonstrate that God judged man stealers (kidnappers) harshly; that under Mosaic law, slavers were to be put to death; that the Israelites were strictly prohibited from buying or selling one another as slaves; and that slavery was reckoned the most atrocious crime known to man. Like many other antislavery voices, Sewall ignores the proslavery verses of the Bible, most notably the sentences in the Pauline epistles enjoining slaves to obey their masters. The tendency to ignore verses was reciprocated by the apologists of slavery who either ignored or denigrated the verses Sewall cites. Thus, the Bible was cited by both proponents and opponents of slavery to buttress their arguments.

In place of African slaves, who were held in bondage for a lifetime, Sewall advocates for the use of white indentured servants. In making this argument, Sewall draws on an important precedent. The first Africans were brought to British North America in 1619, but for many decades thereafter, white indentured servants outnumbered them. Even in sugar producing colonies such as Barbados, more white servants were imported than slaves. In 1700, white indentured servants were still coming to the New World, but African slaves, particularly in the southern colonies, were imported in greater numbers. Sewall's reasons for opposing African slavery are instructive. For one, Sewall explains that the prejudice of slave owners worsens the lot of the slave. Slave owners are opposed to freeing their slaves, Sewall asserts, and this opposition causes them to make the lives of their slaves harder and nastier than necessary. Sewall also correctly observes that slaves are not content with their lot in life. This point may seem exceedingly obvious, but the rhetoric of the proslavery apologists hinged on descriptions of happy, contended, simple, and loyal slaves. Sewall's writing is marked by his own racial and cultural prejudices, but significantly, Sewall did not regard slaves as less than human, as a different species from white people, or as happy and contented.

If Sewall makes some impressive statements about the equality of all men, some of the material in this section speaks to Sewall's own prejudices and biases. For one, Sewall comments on the physical differences between white and black people (phenotype and hair) and makes a vague comment about the conditions of Africans. Sewall contends that Africans and whites cannot mix either in a physical or political sense. He asserts that Africans are inferior and childlike, though he never explicitly uses that word. Africans, in Sewall's eyes, were not capable of producing orderly families. In this framing, black slaves represent anarchy to white people's order and barbarism to white people's civilization. According to Sewall, slaves cannot spread out across the land and will thus remain a group within the colony, certainly not a part of the political body. Sewall deliberately uses the word *extravasat* (extravasate), an anatomical term meaning "not contained within a particular vessel." Africans are therefore in but not of the colony and cannot, in Sewall's formulation, exist inside it because they are not orderly. Sewall's use of the word "condition," his list of the differences between white and black people, and his negative appraisal of Africans might seem a bit surprising from a man who previously spoke about how all people are children of God and how everyone is equal. On the other hand, most people in the seventeenth century believed society to be hierarchical (a view not limited to Puritans), which may explain some of the limitations in this essay. Perhaps the surprise should not be that Sewall had strong anti-African cultural biases, but rather that he formulated an essay advancing antislavery ideas.

Sewall's critique of Africans jumps quickly from one idea to the next. After his discussion of disorder, Sewall complains that the large presence of Africans in Massachusetts means that there were empty places in militia bands. The result, of course, is that these places have to be filled by white men who could have married white women and, following the example of Jacob and Rachel, produced children, but now they will not. Sewall's charge here is odd because New England had a high birthrate (consider Sewall's fourteen children)! Furthermore, Sewall misremembers the biblical story of Jacob, Rachel, and Leah. Both Rachel and Leah offered Jacob their maids to bear children and Jacob had children with both of his wives and both of their maids. Sewall's misremembering aside, he crafts here an argument contending that the presence of slavery literally retards the growth of white families and white people in general, but also has the same effect on black families and black people in general. Slave owners, Sewall contends, ignore lewd behavior among slaves. Instead of finding wives for male slaves, Sewall writes that slave owners allow slaves to fornicate at random and thus commit both a sin and a crime. Though he does not make the connection explicit, this may be why Sewall found black slaves incapable of making orderly families.

From these complaints about slaves, Sewall turns to a series of more general complaints about slavery. For one, Sewall laments the fact that the law colludes in man stealing. Second, Sewall returns to the theme of disorderly families. How terrible it is, Sewall writes, that men break the bonds God has established between people and their native lands, husbands and wives, parents and children. Sewall mentions, although not with the detail of Olaudah Equiano, the horrors of the Middle Passage from Africa to America: "How horrible is the Uncleanness, Mortality, if not Murder, that the Ships are guilty of that bring great Crouds of these miserable Men, and Women." Sewall ends by drawing on white fears about white slavery and argues that white people no longer have the luxury of decrying Barbary slavery—the capture and enslavement of white Europeans by Barbary pirates in Africa and the Mediterranean—because white people are so involved with the African slave trade and slavery. Sewall's vivid language merits quoting: "It may be a question whether all the Benefit received by Negro Slaves, will balance the Accompt of Cash laid out upon them; and for the Redemption of our own enslaved Friends out of Africa." Sewall had negotiated the release of a man held captive by Barbary pirates, so he knew whereof he spoke.

Raising and Refuting Proslavery Dogma

Thus far, *The Selling of Joseph* has advanced the central idea that slavery was wicked and wrong. Sewall next uses a different rhetorical strategy: he brings up four objections that a proslavery interlocutor would raise and refutes them. The first objection concerns the curse of Cham (Ham). The book of Genesis states that, after the Great Flood, Noah's son Ham angered Noah by "looking upon his nakedness," an offense whose meaning remains subject to scholarly debate. Noah then cursed Canaan (who is identified either Ham's son or Noah's son, depending on the passage) and declared that the descendants of Canaan would be the slaves of the descendants of Noah's other sons. Many white people assumed Africans were the descendants of Ham

and Canaan and thus were their slaves, by biblical mandate. Sewall answers this assumption by stating that it is not the duty of man to be the executor of God's wrath because one cannot be certain of the extent and duration of the said wrath. Furthermore, Sewall indicates that the curse of Ham might not be accurate because, he asserts, Africans did not descend from Ham and Canaan, but from Cush and Ethiopia. Sewall cites biblical verses, as well as Ovid, an ancient authority, thus drawing on biblical and classical precedents to buttress his point.

Sewall's second objection anticipates the "schoolhouse of civilization" rhetoric, which held that Africans were uncivilized and benefited from being introduced to America. The objection states that Africans were brought from a pagan country to a Christian land and therefore slavery was justified. Sewall questions how one can justify evil on the basis that some good might come out of it. Despite this statement, Sewall himself agrees that it was beneficial for pagan Africans to be exposed to Christianity. On the other hand, using again the example of Joseph, Sewall avers that, regardless of the benefit of the action, nothing could justify the sale of Joseph by his brothers and, by extension, nothing could rectify the enslavement of Africans by white people.

Sewall's third objection revolves around the idea that, because Africans make war against each other, any slaves brought to the New World were lawful captives. Every war, Sewall contends, is unjust and unjust wars cannot produce lawful captives. He makes a compelling argument by asking his reader to consider a fictional example: Suppose a group of fishermen were overpowered and sold by a stronger group. Would they not object strenuously? Then why do people participate in the buying and selling of human beings? Critically, Sewall allows his own prejudices to influence his ideas when he states that "And by Receiving, we are in danger to promote, and partake in their Barbarous Cruelties." His reference to barbarism is problematic. Sewall's argument constructs a dichotomy between African barbarism and white civilization and suggests that participation in the slave trade imperils and threatens white civilization. Throughout this section, Sewall frequently cites the Golden Rule: Do unto others as you would have others do unto you. Sewall's fourth objection concerns the presence of purchased servants in Abraham's house. Sewall's answer to this objection is the essay's weakest. Sewall does not dispute the purchase, he writes, because Genesis 17:27 states that Abraham did, in fact, own slaves he had purchased. Sewall therefore assumes that Abraham's actions were lawful and good.

If Sewall's answer to the fourth objection does not strengthen the essay, his final lines provide a tight conclusion. Sewall draws together both the Old and New Testament lines of argument and recalls Jesus and the Golden Rule to talk about treatment of slaves. Sewall indulges in a rare flight of fancy and allows his language to stray toward the ornate, writing, "Our Blessed Saviour has altered the Measures of the Ancient Love-Song, and set it to a most Excellent New Tune, which all ought to be ambitious of Learning." In essence, Sewall contends that white people needed to become better Christians and treat Africans with the respect that they deserve as fellow children of God. Sewall also makes a pragmatic argument intended to appeal to a wide swath of Puritan society and the common uncertainty of one's status among the Elect (those the Puritans believed were predestined for eternal salvation). Sewall asks if enslaving one's fellow men seems likely to give assurance of one's salvation. Sewall offers a sharp critique of all levels of society and does not single out a particular faction (i.e., slave traders, as did many later proslavery apologists), but rather indicts everyone and renders everyone equally culpable.

Essential Themes

In 1701, John Saffin issued *A Brief and Candid Answer to a late Printed Sheet Entitled the Selling of Joseph*, a venomous reply to Sewall's pamphlet. Saffin's response attacks Sewall with many of the same arguments that later proslavery apologists employed: namely, that slavery was defended by the Bible, citing verses to support this argument. Saffin takes exception with Sewall's assertion that all men are descended from Adam and therefore equal, and he claims that this statement, if true, would upset order and natural hierarchies. Saffin attacks Sewall's arguments by stating that there is an important difference between enslaving one's own people and enslaving heathen and that the Bible does not preclude the enslavement of heathen Africans. Most contemporaries judged that Saffin had gotten the better of Sewall in the argument, and Saffin's points were more broadly accepted than Sewall's because Saffin's reply tapped into two pervasive ideas: the hierarchical nature of society and slavery as part of the natural order.

The differences between Sewall and later antislavery writers are instructive. Whereas the Bible's defense of slavery offered by Saffin was parroted by proslavery ideologues, the Bible's attack against slavery as seen by Sewall was often overlooked in favor of discussions of higher law, sentimentality, and free-soilism. *The Selling of Joseph* proved that one could make a case for slavery being precluded on the basis of biblical verse, just as one could make a case for slavery being allowed, again based on the Bible.

In addition, *The Selling of Joseph* raises questions about the complicated relationship between antislavery and racism. Just because Sewall was horrified by slavery did not mean that he was a racial egalitarian. Indeed, Sewall had definitive ideas about the inequalities between white and black people. This is a particularly important theme because there is often the temptation to assume that antislavery rhetoric, especially that of the nineteenth century, signaled a deeper commitment to equality. This, however, is simply not the case. Racism often went hand in hand with antislavery, particularly because many people felt that slavery harmed the free white population and opposed slavery on these, and not humanitarian, grounds. Although Sewall was slightly different in that sense because he believed that black and white people descended from Adam and Eve and therefore shared a common inheritance as human beings, he still did not believe people of different racial backgrounds were equals. This document thus foreshadowed tensions in the antislavery movement that flowered in the next century and a half, as well as the problems of slavery, race, liberty, and equality, fundamental issues that played no small part in the coming of the Civil War and the crisis of the American republic.

Evan C. Rothera, MA

Bibliography

Allegro, James J. "'Increasing and Strengthening the Country': Law, Politics, and the Antislavery Movement in Early-Eighteenth-Century Massachusetts Bay." *New England Quarterly* 75.1 (2002): 5–23. Print.

Boyer, Paul, and Stephen Nissbaum. *Salem Possessed: The Social Origins of Witchcraft*. Cambridge: Harvard UP, 1974. Print.

Butcher, Philip, ed. *The Minority Presence in American Literature, 1600–1900*. Vol. 1. Washington: Howard UP, 1977. Print.

Cantor, Milton. "The Image of the Negro in Colonial Literature." *New England Quarterly* 36.4 (1963): 452–77. Print.

Chamberlain, Nathan Henry. *Samuel Sewall and the World He Lived In.* 2nd ed. Boston: De Wolfe, 1898. Print.

Ewell, John Lewis. "Judge Samuel Sewall (1652–1730), A Typical Massachusetts Puritan." *Papers of the American Society of Church History* 7 (1895): 25–54. Print.

Francis, Richard. *Judge Sewall's Apology: The Salem Witch Trials and the Forming of an American Conscience.* New York: Harper, 2005. Print.

Greene, Lorenzo. *The Negro in Colonial New England, 1620–1776.* New York: Columbia UP, 1942. Print.

Hall, David D. "The Mental World of Samuel Sewall." *Proceedings of the Massachusetts Historical Society* 3rd ser. 92 (1980): 21–44. Print.

Husband, Julie. *Antislavery Discourse and Nineteenth-Century American Literature: Incendiary Pictures.* New York: Palgrave, 2010. Print.

Kaplan, Sidney. *American Studies in Black and White: Selected Essays, 1949–1989.* Ed. Allan D. Austin. Amherst: U of Massachusetts P, 1991. Print.

Karlsen, Carol F. *The Devil in the Shape of a Woman: Witchcraft in Colonial New England.* 1987. New York. Norton, 1998. Print.

LaPlante, Eve. *Salem Witch Judge: The Life and Repentance of Samuel Sewall.* New York: Harper, 2007. Print.

Norton, Mary Beth. *In the Devil's Snare: The Salem Witchcraft Crisis of 1692.* New York: Vintage, 2003. Print.

"October Meeting, 1863." *Proceedings of the Massachusetts Historical Society* 7 (1863–64): 152–68. Print.

Peterson, Mark A. "*The Selling of Joseph*: Bostonians, Antislavery, and the Protestant International, 1689–1733." *Massachusetts Historical Review* 4 (2002): 1–22. Print.

Sewall, Samuel. *The Diary of Samuel Sewall, 1674–1729.* Ed. M. Halsey Thomas. Vol. 2. New York: Farrar, 1973. Print.

---. *The Selling of Joseph: A Memorial.* Ed. Sidney Kaplan. Amherst: U of Massachusetts P, 1969. Print.

Towner, Lawrence W. "'A Fondness for Freedom': Servant Protest in Puritan Society." *William and Mary Quarterly* 3rd ser. 19.2 (1962): 201–19. Print.

---. "The Sewall-Saffin Dialogue on Slavery." *William and Mary Quarterly* 3rd ser. 21.1 (1964): 40–52. Print.

Turner, Lorenzo Dow. "The Anti-Slavery Movement Prior to the Abolition of the African Slave-Trade (1641–1808)." *Journal of Negro History* 14.4 (1929): 373–402. Print.

Von Frank, Albert J. "John Saffin: Slavery and Racism in Colonial Massachusetts." *Early American Literature* 29.3 (1994): 254–72. Print.

Winslow, Ola Elizabeth. *Samuel Sewall of Boston.* New York: Macmillan, 1964. Print.

Additional Reading

Brown, Christopher Leslie. *Moral Capital: Foundations of British Abolitionism.* Chapel Hill: U of North Carolina P, 2006. Print.

Goodman, Paul. *Of One Blood: Abolitionism and the Origins of Racial Equality.* Berkeley: U of California P, 2000. Print.

Hoffer, Williamjames Hull. *The Caning of Charles Sumner: Honor, Idealism, and the Origins of the Civil War.* Baltimore: Johns Hopkins UP, 2010. Print.

Litwack, Leon F. *North of Slavery: The Negro in the Free States, 1790–1860.* Chicago. U of Chicago P, 1965. Print.

Manegold, C. S. *Ten Hills Farm: The Forgotten History of Slavery in the North.* Princeton: Princeton UP, 2009. Print.

Morgan, Edmund S. *The Puritan Family: Religion & Domestic Relations in Seventeenth-Century New England.* 1944. Westport: Greenwood, 1980. Print.

Newman, Richard S. *The Transformation of American Abolitionism: Fighting Slavery in the Early Republic.* Chapel Hill: U of North Carolina P, 2002. Print.

Schwartz, Stuart B., ed. *Tropical Babylons: Sugar and the Making of the Atlantic World: 1450–1680.* Chapel Hill: U of North Carolina P, 2004. Print.

Stewart, James Brewer. *Holy Warriors: The Abolitionists and American Slavery.* 1976. New York: Hill, 1997. Print.

Tise, Larry E. *Proslavery: A History of the Defense of Slavery in America, 1701–1840.* Athens: U of Georgia P, 1987. Print.

LESSON PLAN: Two Views on Slavery

Students analyze two different viewpoints on slavery in colonial America.

Learning Objectives

Analyze overt and passive resistance to slavery; consider multiple perspectives on slavery in America; analyze the evidence used and references made by the authors to support their points of view; analyze the causes and effects of both points of view and assess their impact on the abolitionist and pro-slavery movements.

Materials: Samuel Sewall, *The Selling of Joseph, A Memorial* (1700); John Saffin, *A Brief Candid Answer to a Late Printed Sheet, Entitled, The Selling of Joseph* (1701).

Overview Questions

How do the selections express resistance to or support of slavery in America? What perspectives do they present on the issue of slavery? What evidence do they use to support their points of view? What references do they make? Why did Sewall and Saffin make these arguments? What impact did they have on the abolitionist movement and the pro-slavery movement?

Step 1: Comprehension Questions

How do the selections express resistance to or support of slavery in America? What is the overall purpose of the selections?

▶ **Activity:** Select students to read key passages in both selections. Have students underline or highlight examples of resistance to or support of slavery in America and then write a paragraph to explain the purpose of each selection.

Step 2: Comprehension Questions

What perspectives do Sewall and Saffin present on the issue of slavery? How are they different?

▶ **Activity:** Ask students to work in pairs to draw a T-chart to compare both perspectives. Discuss the examples that students have listed as a class. In the discussion, have students consider the tone of each selection.

Step 3: Context Questions

What evidence do the authors use to support their points of view? What references do they make?

▶ **Activity:** Have students locate and circle the references and supporting evidence that both writers use. Ask students to write an analysis of their findings in their journals, evaluating whether the evidence presented supports each writer's assertion.

Step 4: Exploration Questions

Why did Sewall and Saffin make these arguments? What impact do you think they had on the abolitionist movement and the pro-slavery movement?

▶ **Activity:** Ask students to consider the effect of these selections on beliefs related to slavery in America. Have students work in pairs or in small groups to prepare a brief oral presentation in which they make an inference about how these arguments will have long-term effects on ideas about slavery in America.

Step 5: Response Paper

Word length and additional requirements set by Instructor. Students answer the research question in the Overview Questions. Students state a thesis and use as evidence passages from the primary source document as well as support from supplemental materials assigned in the lesson.

Documents Illustrative of the History of the Slave Trade to America

Date: 1671–1760
Author: Donnan, Elizabeth (ed.)
Genre: law; petition; letter; report

"Every such Negroe ... Is are and be and shall att all tymes hereafter be adjudged Reputed deemed and taken to be and Remayne in Servitude and Bondage ..."

—An Act for the Encourageing the Importation of Negros and Slaves into this Province, 1671

"There have been already Imported since the 1st of November upwards of 2000 Negroes, and there are some Ships that are still expected from Africa with more ..."

—Governor James Glen's letter to the Board of Trade, 1754

Summary Overview

Slavery is part of the history of all the original lands occupied by European colonists in the Americas. These excerpts, collected and published by historian Elizabeth Donnan in the twentieth century, trace the growth and institutionalization of slavery and the slave trade in British North America during the colonial era. Labor shortages and the need for large numbers of workers to make the frail economies of these early colonies a success contributed to colonial measures to encourage and shelter the transatlantic slave trade, particularly in the more agricultural southern colonies. In time, the slave trade became a major commercial endeavor, and enslaved Africans outnumbered free white colonists in places such as South Carolina. Yet this economic dependence on slave labor carried great consequences, especially for those forcibly enslaved and transported across the Middle Passage. Disease and ill treatment killed many even before arrival in the Americas, and legal protection upon arrival was essentially nonexistent.

Defining Moment

Slavery was a part of European settlement of the Americas from the beginning. After Spanish enslavement of native peoples and European diseases led to rapid, massive depopulation, Europeans began importing enslaved workers from West Africa to staff the growing numbers of sugar, rice, and indigo plantations in the New World. West Africa, which had its own cultural tradition of bondage, offered ease of transport, a network of slavers, and a population familiar with the agricultural techniques needed to grow American cash crops. Thus began the triangular trade of raw materials, finished goods, and enslaved humans that linked the Americas, Europe, and Africa.

Imports of enslaved Africans into the Caribbean began as early as the sixteenth century, and the practice may have spread to the nascent English colonies in North America as early as 1619, when African workers began arriving to labor on Virginia's tobacco plantations. During its earliest years, slavery in North America existed alongside the somewhat more dominant system of indentured servitude, in which white European workers committed themselves to a master for a period of several years in exchange for their passage to the New World. By 1650, for example, records show just four hundred Africans among Virginia's population of about nineteen thousand; a notable subsection of these Africans were free, and some were even property owners. Within about a decade, however, colonial governments began passing laws that encouraged the dominance of slavery, such as the elimination of the requirement for manumission (freeing) of slaves who converted to Christianity. At the same time, economic changes in England made the prospect of indentured servitude less enticing for poor European workers. Slavery began a period of sharp ascendency.

In total, an estimated ten million to fifteen million enslaved Africans were shipped from their native lands to the Americas between the sixteenth and nineteenth century. English slave traders took on an increased role after 1672 when the Royal African Company was founded, and the number of slaves arriving in British North America on British slave ships grew by nearly tenfold during the first half of the eighteenth century. Although slavery was first formally recognized in the North American colonies in Massachusetts, the agricultural South became the primary hub of slavery on the continent. Slaves often reached the American South after a stopover in the Caribbean, making for a total sea voyage of some sixty to ninety days on cramped, disease-ridden vessels. As many as two million Africans died along the Middle Passage. The US government eventually outlawed the importation of slaves in 1808.

Author Biography

Between the late seventeenth and late eighteenth century, the slave trade in the British North America became a formalized and highly profitable activity. This shift is reflected in the authorship of the documents ex-

cerpted in this essay. The earliest document, authored by the Colony of Maryland, reflects the types of laws passed that transformed former African "servants" with a fair prospect of liberty into true black "slaves." Before long, the English slave trade had increased, and colonists such as James Frisby began to link their economic well-being closely with the transatlantic slave trade. As the rate of imports increased, the overall number of African slaves in the colonies rose greatly. The letters of the governor and Council of South Carolina to their English government overseers show this transition and indicate the economic motives of and benefits for those who relied on slavery. The extent of the slave trade in colonial life may be seen in the numerous anonymous sales notices and news items of the 1730s. Sales took place with obvious regularity and involved a notable quantity of enslaved workers. The quickened pace of the Middle Passage trade led to widely acknowledged illness, death, and burials at sea of those forced to make the journey. The courts also continued to discuss and test the nature of slavery, as seen in the depositions regarding the legal status of one African later in the century.

The excerpts reprinted here were first collected and published in the early 1930s as part of historian Elizabeth Donnan's four-volume *Documents Illustrative of the History of the Slave Trade to America*, which presents documents that were originally drafted between the 1440s and 1808. Donnan, a professor of economics and sociology at Wellesley College, gathered the documents on the behalf of the Division of Historical Research of the Carnegie Institute in Washington, DC. To do this, she drew upon formal government records such as those of the Royal African Company and the Colonial Office as well as pertinent legal, commercial, and personal documents. Although these records existed prior to Donnan's efforts, her work brought together a wealth of information focused on the slave trade for deeper historical study; the information contained within presented largely the ideas and viewpoints of the European and American slave traders, governments, and others profiting from the slave trade, not those of the Africans whom it so directly affected. Donnan's works, despite their limitations, remain a standard source for firsthand records and accounts of the trade as practiced, and modern historians continue to recognize Donnan as the most knowledgeable scholar of the transatlantic slave trade of her time.

The slave deck of the ship "Wildfire," brought into Key West on April 30, 1860. (Library of Congress)

HISTORICAL DOCUMENT

An Act for the Encourageing the Importation of Negros and Slaves into this Province

April 19, 1671.

Whereas Severall of the good people of this Province have been discouraged to import into or purchase within this Province any Negroes or other Slaves and such as have Imported or purchased any such Negroes or Slaves have to the great displeasure of Almighty God and the prejudice of the Soules of those poore people Neglected to instruct them in the Christian faith or to Endure or permitt them to Receive the holy Sacrament of Babtisme for the Remission of their Sinns upon a mistake and ungrounded apprehension that by becomeing Christians they and the Issues of their bodies are actually manumitted and made free and discharged from their Servitude and bondage be itt declared and Enacted by his Lordship the Lord and Proprietary of this Province by and with the advice and consent of the upper and lower houses of this present Generall Assembly and by the Authority of the same That where any Negro or Negroes Slave or Slaves being in Servitude or bondage is are or shall become Christian or Christians and hath or have Received or shall att any time Receive the Holy Sacrament of Babtizme before or after his her or their Importacion into this Province the same is not nor shall or ought the same be denyed adjudged Construed or taken to be or to amount unto a manumicion or freeing Inlarging or discharging any such Negroe or Negroes Slave or Slaves or any his or their Issue or Issues from his her their or any of their Servitude or Servitudes Bondage or bondages Butt that Notwithstanding any such Act or thing Acts or things And Notwithstanding any such becoming Christian or Christians or Receiveing the Sacrament of Babtizme Every such Negroe and Negroes slave and slaves and all and every the Issue and Issues of every such Negroe and Negroes Slave and Slaves Is are and be and shall att all tymes hereafter be adjudged Reputed deemed and taken to be and Remayne in Servitude and Bondage and subject to the same Servitude and Bondage to all intents and purposes as if hee shee they every or any

of them was or were in and Subject unto before such his her or their Becomeing Christian or Christians or Receiveing of the Sacrament of Baptizme any opinion or other matter or thing to the Countrary in any wise Notwithstanding.

✱✱✱

Petition of James Frisby 1700.

May 6, 1700.

The Peticion of James Frisby Esqre. being read in the house wherein he prays an allowance for the import of Twenty Six Negroes that arrived in Captn. Thornbury and dyed before sale of them was here read.

And Putt to the Vote whether the Peticion shalbe rejected or not. Carried in the Affirmative.

✱✱✱

Case of the *Edward*, 1760.

J. Ross to James Weems.

Annapolis, 22d September 1760.

Sir, It having been this Day represented to the Governor and Council, that a Negroe called Capt. Gray and three or four more of the Negroes who were lately imported into Patuxent River in the Brigantine *Edward* of which one John Cousins is Master have declared that they are not Slaves but Freemen, that the Negroe called Capt. Gray in particular is the son of a person of some Consequence and Power on the African Coast, and that the said Cousins treacherously stole and brought them away. I am Ordered by his Excellency and their Honours to communicate to you the Information that hath been given them and moreover to Desire that on the Receipt hereof you will send for, and examine the Surgeon Mates and Boatswain of the said Vessell and Endeavour to discover whether Capt. Cousins hath committed the Crime whereof he is accused, and if you shall either by the Evidence of those Persons or any others be inclined to think that the Master is guilty, you will be pleased to have him apprehended immediately and delivered into the Custody of the Sheriff of Calvert County, and to give that Sheriff Orders to deliver him over to the Sheriff of this County, so that he may be brought without Delay before his Excellency and the Council to be dealt with as to them shall seem meet. If you see Cause for having him apprehended you will be pleased to send hither all the Persons that shall be able to give Evidence against him, and whether you Cause him to be apprehended and brought hither or not, you are desired to return to me the Depositions or Examinations that shall be by you taken on this Occasion. . . .

Deposition of Elias Glover

The Deposition of Elias Glover Chief Mate of the aforesaid Brigantine being Sworn on the holy Evangels of Almighty God Deposeth and saith, that as to the Negroe called Capt. Gray he was taken in a Theft on board the aforesaid Brigantine and for that detained, that he afterwards was principally concerned in cutting the Cable and endangering the Loss of the Vessel; that as to the negroe called Capt. Buck, and the eleven other Negroes they were brought on board the Vessel by the Traders, and there left as Pledges, but that to his knowledge there was as much Goods given for them as for the other Slaves, that they had been on board of the Vessel for seven or eight Weeks before the Vessel Sailed, and that the Traders never offered to redeem them and further saith not.

September 27th, 1760, Sworn to before James Weems.

Deposition of Eneas Loughrig

The Deposition of Eneas Loughrig Aged about twenty-one years who being duely sworn on the holy Evangels of Almighty God Deposeth and saith that he is a Saylor on board of the Brigantine *Edward* John Cousins Commander and that he sailed from Liverpool along with the said Capt. Cousins before the Mast on a Voyage to the Coast of Guinea to purchase Slaves, that during their Trade on that Coast Capt. Cousins made a Purchase of several Slaves and that he this Deponent believes and never heard to the Contrary but hat all the negroes brought in by Captain Cousins were Slaves;

unless a negroe who calls himself Capt. Gray should be Free whose particular Circumstances are as follows, he Gray was a Servant to a Freeman upon the Coast of Guinea and that he used to be employed by his Master to go in a Cannoo to carry Slaves on Board of Trading Vessels and as a Plavvrer (Palaverer) that he carried some on board of the Brigantine *Edward* whilst he was in that Vessell he stole a Scarlet Jacket from Capt. Cousins who never permitted him (Gray) to go on Shore afterwards, but offered to return him if he could get another Slave for him which was refused by those to whom the Offer was made, they said he was a scandal to his Country and they would not give a slave of four feet high for him, and this Deponent has heard that it was usual to punish Thieves after than [that] manner in that Country.

Sworn to this 25 Day of Septemr. 1760 before me. Geo.: Steuart.

✳✳✳

Governor and Council of South Carolina to the Board of Trade, 1709

September 17, 1709.
The number of the inhabitants in this province of all sorts are computed to be 9580 souls, of which there are 1360 freemen, 900 free women, 60 white servant men, 60 white servant women, 1700 white free children, 1800 negro men slaves, 1100 negro women slaves, 500 Indian men slaves, 600 Indian women slaves, 1200 negro children slaves and 300 Indian children slaves . . . negro men slaves [are increased in the last five years] by importation 300, negro women slaves 200 . . . negro children 600. . . .

Wee are also often furnished with negros from the American Islands, chiefly from Barbados and Jamaica. . . . And the inhabitants by a yearly addition of slaves are made the more capable of improving the produce of the Colony. Notwithstanding 'tis our opinion that the value of one [our?] import is greater (if we include negros with the commodities that are consumed here) then our export by which means it comes to pass that wee are very near drained of all our silver and gold coine, nor is there any remedy to prevent this. . . .

N. Johnson Tho. Broughton Robt. Gibbes Geo. Smith Richd. Beresford

✳✳✳

Notices of Sales, 1732

July 15, 1732.
To be sold, On Wednesday next, the 19th Instant, by Benjamin Godin and John Guerard, a Parcel of Gold Coast Slaves, lately imported from Barbadoes, for Rice, or Currency on Credit till January next.

Sept. 30, 1732.
To be Sold on Thursday next, being the 5th of October, by George Austin, for ready Money, a Choice Parcel of Negroes, lately imported in the Ship *Edward*, to be seen on board the said Ship at Eliott's Wharff.

Dec. 6, 1732.
To be sold by Benjamin Godin and John Guerard, on Thursday the 21st Instant, a Parcel of Negroes, imported directly from Gambia in the Ship *Molley* Galley, Capt. John Carruthers.

News Items Relating to Slave Trade, 1738

May 4, 1738.
Several of the Negroes imported in the Ship *London* Frigate, which arrived here the 13th April last, have been since discovered to have the small Pox, there are few of them in Town but more in the Country and several were sent on board again, the ship having been ordered to fall down to the Fort to perform Quarentine.

June 1, 1738.
On the 25th May last, two of the Sailors late on board the *London* Frigate, John Pickett Commander, appear'd

before Maurice Lewis Esq., Judge of his Majesty's Court of Vice Admiralty, and made Oath, That they were on board said Vessel from her first setting out from England to her Arrival in Africa, and from thence to her Arrival at Charleston, and that during that time no Persons whatsoever were thrown over board, except about 14 Slaves, who died, as they believ'd of Fevers and Fluxes, and that, to the best of their Knowledge, no Person on board said Ship was taken ill of or discovered any symptoms of the Small-pox during the Voyage, nor till after the Day of Sale of the Negroes. N. B. The principal Depositions may be seen in the Records of the said Court of Vice-Admiralty.

✳✳✳

Governor James Glen to the Board of Trade, 1754

August 26, 1754.
There have been already Imported since the 1st of November upwards of 2000 Negroes, and there are some Ships that are still expected from Africa with more, they have all been readily sold and at great Prices, the men for 250, 260, and 270 Pounds Currency and the Women for 200, the Boys and Girls for little less; Some years agoe the usual prices were 170 or 180 pounds for the best picked men to be paid in Rice the following Crop, but they are now all purchased for ready money or with bonds bearing Interest, which are really as good as ready money, for I know of few or no Planters whose Credit is suspected. As Negroes are sold at higher Prices here than in any part of the King's Dominions we have them sent from Barbadoes, the Leeward Islands, Jamaica, Virginia and New York, this I think is a plain proof that this Province is in a flourishing condition, for these Importations are not to supply the place of Negroes worn out with hard work or lost by Mortallity which is the case in our Islands where were it not for an annual accretion they could not keep up their stock, but our number encreases even without such yearly supply. I presume tis Indigo that puts all in such high Spirits. . . .

GLOSSARY

fluxes: influenza

hither: here

issue: children

King's Dominions: lands under the control of the British monarchy

manumicion (manumission): the freeing of an enslaved person

prays: asks for

Patuxent River: Maryland river flowing into the Chesapeake Bay

saith: says

Document Analysis

The size, scope, and nature of the transatlantic slave trade changed greatly in British North America between the early seventeenth century and the mid-eighteenth century. In general, slavery and the slave trade became increasingly important to agricultural colonial economies and thus supported by colonial governments even as slavery grew more and more oppressive for the individuals forced to labor under the institution. The excerpts presented here offer an opportunity to trace this change over time and to determine some of the effects of these changes on white slave-owning society and black enslaved society alike. They also present a chance for analysis of the views of white authorities—African voices are essentially absent—on some of the moral, legal, and economic ramifications of the slave trade.

The first excerpt reproduced from *Documents Illustrative of the History of the Slave Trade to America* exemplifies the new laws passed in the latter half of the seventeenth century that contributed to the transformation of black servants with a status similar to that of white indentured servants to true, racially defined slaves. The earliest African laborers imported into the Americas reflected traditional English ideas about slavery, which was considered morally acceptable when the enslaved were non-Christians. Thus, enslaved Africans could and did gain their freedom by converting to Christianity. By the mid-seventeenth century, however, the Church of England had begun to embrace the idea that Christians could, in fact, enslave other Christians in a system of lifelong bondage. This idea was influential even among American populations that were not affiliated with the Anglican Church. Both the Quakers—who later led the religious opposition to slavery in the New World—and the Puritans accepted the righteousness of the institution and took part in slaveholding and slave trading.

This doctrinal shift, accompanied by a general social acceptance of slavery by English citizens in Europe and the Americas, was closely followed by legal changes in the colonies. In 1671, the Colony of Maryland passed an "Act to encourage the Importation of Negroes" that freed potential slaveholders from the responsibility of giving an enslaved person his or her liberty upon conversion to Christianity. The purpose of the law was quite baldly stated—"encourageing the Importation of Negros and Slaves into this Province"—although, interestingly, its division of racial Africans and slaves shows that the two groups had not yet become synonymous. Barely a decade after this act was written, however, the terms "Negro" and "slave" had indeed become interchangeable. The need for such a law was also clearly noted. Maryland colonists who had imported slaves had neglected to convert these people to Christianity, much "to the great displeasure of Almighty God" and to the perceived detriment to the immortal souls of the slaves who continued to engage in their native religious practices; other colonists had been reluctant to import slaves at all, presumably because of their concern that this type of religious instruction would liberate their slaves. To encourage the conversion of slaves to Christianity and to soothe the consciences of those who had opted out of the slave trade over the issue, the colony declared that the belief that conversion granted a slave liberty was a "mistake and ungrounded apprehension." The act then affirmed in strong terms that becoming a Christian was assuredly not a path to automatic manumission, displaying a clear break from earlier moral ideas limiting slavery only to non-Christians. The act also affirmed that slavery was an inheritable condition, noting that the children of enslaved people were also "deemed . . . in Servitude and Bondage" regardless of their own status as Christian or non-Christian.

The colony was also called on in business affairs relating to the slave trade. In 1700, one James Frisby of Maryland petitioned the colony for a financial allowance after twenty-six African slaves he imported for the purpose of the slave trade died during the course of their voyage. This relatively low number of imported slaves was common of the border colonies of Maryland and Virginia; groups of enslaved workers tended to arrive in fairly small groups from the Caribbean rather than in shiploads directly from Africa, as was common in slave-trading hubs such as South Carolina. Although the colony refused Frisby's request, the matter went unresolved for some time. Donnan noted additional records that showed two London merchants claimed that Frisby had cheated them of £2,700—just over £100 per head—by not paying for the failed delivery. Nor was Frisby's case an isolated incident. Donnan pointed out that a Peregrine Browne made a similar petition the following year to equally negative results.

Slave owners and slave traders were not the only ones engaged in legal disputes over slavery, however; sometimes enslaved Africans themselves brought their cases before colonial courts. In 1760, for example, Maryland records indicate that an enslaved Guinean named Captain Gray filed a complaint that he had been wrongfully taken into bondage because he was a free man in his native land. According to Gray's complaint, John Cousins, the captain of the slave ship *Edward* had "treacherously"—and illegally—stolen him and forced him into slavery. Typically, the crew of slave ships received enslaved Africans from African slavers, who themselves kidnapped and forced people, often from the interior lands, into slavery. In this instance, however, Gray claimed that he had been placed into bondage without the proper process. The governor of Maryland ordered the taking of depositions from "all the Persons that shall be able to give Evidence against [Cousins]," showing that the government was at least willing to make an effort to consider Gray's allegations.

The depositions that follow detail the events surrounding Gray's enslavement. A crew member of the *Edward*, Elias Glover, explained that Gray had been caught stealing aboard the ship and later tried to sabotage it, and the other complainants had been brought onboard the slave ship by African traders as usual. Glover noted that the Africans other than Gray had been paid for in the usual manner and that they had remained onboard the *Edward* for nearly two months before the ship departed for the Americas without any effort by the African slave traders to fetch them back. This extended wait was in no way unusual. Slave traders docked in harbors along the West African coast sometimes for months as African slavers brought them a slow supply of bodies to fill the hulls; for example, the ship which reputedly transported the slave-narrative author Olaudah Equiano to the New World lingered just off shore for eight months. Thus Glover's testimony showed nothing unusual about slave trading practices except, perhaps, in the case of the reportedly thieving Gray.

Another crew member, Eneas Loughrig, provided more detail. He stated that the ship had sailed from Liverpool, the leading English slave port of the era, to the coast of Guinea to acquire its human cargo. Loughrig believed that all of the Africans that they had onboard their ship had been legally purchased per usual but offered an explanation for Gray's claim. Gray, apparently, had worked for a free African along the Guinea coast as a courier of enslaved persons from shore to slave ship; during their long stays along the African coast, slave ships docked a short distance out in the ocean, forcing slave traders to ferry their captives from shore to ship on each transaction. Gray performed this duty and, while onboard the *Edward*, he stole a coat belonging to Cousins and was caught. Cousins refused to let the thief return to shore but offered him liberty in exchange for another slave, presumably free of charge, from his employer. Gray's employer, however, refused to bargain with Cousins, calling Gray "a scandal to his Country" and declaring that "they would not give a slave of four feet high for him." Loughrig further observed that he believed it was the practice of Guineans to punish thieves with enslavement. The court ultimately dismissed Gray's claims against Cousins as groundless, however, thus showing that one's status as free or enslaved in the Old World was not a precondition for one's status in the New World.

Further south, colonial North America was heavily reliant on slave labor to support its economy—so much so that enslaved populations sometimes outnumbered free populations. For example, this was true for much of South Carolina's early history. In 1709, the government and council of South Carolina wrote a report to their English government overseers detailing the present population of the colony. According to the authors, South Carolina was home to 9,580 people. Within this total population, the authors further broke out the colony's residents roughly by age, race, free or unfree status, and gender. The total free population of all ages and races was just 3,960—barely over 40 percent of the colony's citizenry. White indentured servants made up a very small minority of the remaining unfree population. The enslaved black population, at 4,100 persons, outnumbered the combined free and indentured white population by a bare margin. An additional 1,400 American Indian slaves rounded out the population. The authors noted that the enslaved population was growing rapidly, with 1,100 new black slaves arriving on South Carolina's shores in the preceding five years alone. The high number of annual arrivals, nearly one-quarter of the total enslaved population, thus suggests either an extremely high death rate among the colonial enslaved population or a miscalculation of some type. Otherwise, the enslaved population would presumably have been much larger as the slave trade had been growing South Carolina's population for nearly a century by this time.

South Carolina's colonial leadership seems to found this situation something of a mixed blessing. The authors hailed the influx of enslaved laborers for making its free population "the more capable of improving the produce of the Colony." Yet the authors also noted that the costs of purchasing this great number of slaves were a significant financial drain on colonial coffers, complaining, "The value of [our] imports is greater . . . than our export." As a result, despite the increase in production made possible by a great deal of enslaved labor, the colony still made little profit. Unmentioned here but certainly a concern of colonial South Carolinians was the possibility of massive slave revolts. Because the enslaved population so greatly outnumbered the free population, whites worried that blacks would eventually rise up and murder them to win their own liberty.

Nevertheless, the slave trade continued to grow. During the 1730s, for example, some seventeen thousand slaves were imported in Charleston, South Carolina, alone. The vast majority of these slaves originated in Africa, sometimes arriving by way of a British Caribbean island. In 1732, a South Carolina newspaper began printing notices of arriving slaves for sale, allowing more accurate tabulations to be made of the frequency and number of such importations. The first of the notices reproduced here notes that slaves were to be sold not for cash, but in exchange for rice or credit until after the harvest, an indication that planters then lacked the ready cash needed to finance such purchases. The system also shows that the slave trade was a profitable enough venture that at least some slave traders were able to extend a lengthy period of credit to their customers and that they expected the colony's planters to be successful enough that the risk of such a loan was minimal. Yet not all slave merchants were willing to offer such an arrangement. The second notice—printed after the harvest season was underway—calls for "ready money" purchases only. The regular arrival of ships indicates a steady demand for enslaved labor even outside of the traditional agricultural season.

Slave ships carried more than just enslaved humans; they also brought infectious diseases that could devastate both enslaved and free populations after arrival in the New World. From the early eighteenth century, a quarantine system was used off the coast of South Carolina to ensure that imported African slaves did not carry dreaded contagious illnesses with them. Sometimes, though, disease slipped through, as shown in the first news item reprinted here. Quarantine systems grew more sophisticated in time, requiring slavers to send potentially infected slaves to a special sick house or keep them onboard ship, where they could be isolated from the rest of the population. By the 1710s, enslaved arrivals were not permitted to come ashore for a period of several days if their ship had been found to carry infectious disease.

Indeed, most slave ships were incubators of illness. Cramped quarters, nonexistent medical care, and cruel treatment were an environment ripe for deadly diseases to spread from person to person. Slaves were often chained together during the Middle Passage and kept in a small cargo hold with little movement and less fresh air. Sometimes, living slaves remained chained to deceased ones, forced to lie or sit in pools of blood, excrement, or spittle. The crew of the *London*, however, argued that in this case the smallpox infection that afflicted the slaves who had traveled on it had not been evident while onboard ship. This claim seems more than a little questionable, however, as the acknowledgement that fourteen slaves had died from "Fever and Fluxes" and been thrown overboard certainly indicates that disease was rampant on the vessel. The early symptoms of smallpox include fever and other less visible concerns, so the crew may simply have failed to identify these as indications of smallpox without the telltale skin lesions.

Buoyed by commercial profitability and moral indifference, the slave trade thrived as the eighteenth century progressed. Writing in 1754, the governor of South Carolina, James Glen, informed the English government that more than two thousand Africans had been imported into South Carolina between November 1753 and the following August alone; this figure was nearly double that of the number of imported slaves in a five-year span quoted by the governor and council just fifty years previously. The growing value of enslaved workers in South Carolina was also evident in the rising prices of newly arrived slaves. At the same time, the extent to which those workers supported the South Carolinian economy may be inferred from the fact that earlier in the century, as Glen notes, planters paid for slaves with a promise of rice—one of South Carolina's leading cash crops—to be delivered at a future time. By 1754, however, Glen writes that planters had cash on hand or interest-bearing bonds to use for their transactions and that he knew of "few or no Planters whose Credit is suspected."

Glen observes that South Carolina's buyers paid the highest prices for enslaved workers and thus received a steady supply from a variety of willing sellers. He took this as "a plain proof" of the colony's financial success, a sharp contrast to the concerns expressed by colonial leaders in the early eighteenth century about the financial drain upon the colony caused by the constant importation of slaves. Glen also favorably compares the conditions that enslaved workers faced in South Carolina to those of the Caribbean islands, where, as he rightly notes, mortality rates from overwork or harsh treatment were extremely high. Laws passed in the wake of the Stono Rebellion (1740) had sought to limit some of the harsh treatment of South Carolina slaves by their masters by outlawing workdays in excess of fifteen hours and barring work on Sundays, for example. Along with the physical differences in the labor required to raise Caribbean sugar and South Carolina rice and indigo, these measures helped ensure that slaves at least remained alive. Doing this also helped slave owners renew their supply of workers naturally through childbirth, a process that would become vital to the perpetuation of slavery in the following century after the eventual ban of the slave trade.

Essential Themes

The growth and influence of slavery and the slave trade proved one of the most defining—and divisive—issues in American life with ramifications that continue to shape US society today. The ready availability of unpaid slave labor allowed the South to develop economics that depended heavily on manual force to produce profitable agricultural crops even as economies in the northern and Mid-Atlantic colonies grew economic systems more centered on paid labor of free workers. By the time of the American Revolution, for example, the population of South Carolina consisted of more than 60 percent enslaved black workers. In comparison, the colony of Virginia—also a major cash crop–growing region—had an enslaved population just over 40 percent of its total, and both Massachusetts and Pennsylvania had a negligible enslaved population, measuring 2 percent of their total numbers. These differences contributed to the creation of vastly different economic, social, and cultural systems in the colonial regions that carried significant political ramifications. One of the primary challenges facing the framers of the US Constitution in 1787 involved the determination of how to measure the enslaved population for the purposes of representation, as southern delegates scrambled to ensure that their relatively small free white populations would wield sufficient power in the new Congress to safeguard the continuation of slavery. Mere discussion of the slave trade issue was banned for twenty years' time due to the controversy it automatically carried. The roots of these issues reached to the seventeenth century and the rise of slave importations to British North America.

Even after the slave trade was legally ended in 1808, its effects shaped the nation. The millions of slaves transported across the Atlantic generated children themselves born into slavery, allowing the institution to persist in British colonies and the United States for generations after the slave trade itself ended. Regional disputes over the spread of slavery dominated US politics during the first half of the nineteenth century, only to worsen as what had begun as fringe voices against slavery during the era of the slave trade grew into a vocal abolitionist movement that began to speak for an ever-larger minority of Americans. The Civil War—a conflict fought over slavery—was the single bloodiest war to affect the nation. Ideas about African Americans formed during the era of slavery and the slave trade shaped public policy for decades to come. Indeed, the myth of the Confederacy drew on the same notions of the moral righteousness of slavery that had encouraged English colonial governments to expand the institution centuries before. Later, the restrictive Jim Crow laws of the post–Civil War South hearkened back to the statutes stripping black colonial residents of their limited freedoms during the seventeenth and eighteenth centuries. Not until the publication of works such as Donnan's *Documents Illustrative of the History of the Slave Trade to America* allowed historians to conduct research needed to challenge traditional notions of the "peculiar institution" could revisionist history of America's long involvement with slavery truly begin.

Vanessa E. Vaughn, MA

Bibliography

"The African Slave Trade and the Middle Passage." *Africans in America*. WGBH Educational Foundation, 1999. Web. 25 May 2012.

Berlin, Ira. *Many Thousands Gone: The First Two Centuries of Slavery in North America*. Cambridge: Harvard UP, 1998. Print.

Deyle, Steven. *Carry Me Back: The Domestic Slave Trade in American Life*. New York: Oxford UP, 2005. Print.

Donnan, Elizabeth, ed. *Documents Illustrative of the History of the Slave Trade to America*. 4 vols. Washington: Carnegie Inst. of Washington, 1930–1935. Print.

Eltis, David. *The Rise of African Slavery in the Americas*. New York: Cambridge UP, 2000. Print.

"From Indentured Servitude to Racial Slavery." *Africans in America*. WGBH Educational Foundation, 1999. Web. 25 May 2012.

Reiss, Oscar. *Blacks in Colonial America*. Jefferson: McFarland, 1997. Print.

Thomas, Hugh. *The Slave Trade: The Story of the Atlantic Slave Trade, 1440–1870*. New York: Simon, 1997. Print.

Wood, Betty. *Slavery in Colonial America, 1619–1776*. Lanham: Rowman, 2005. Print.

Additional Reading

Addison, Kenneth N. *"We Hold These Truths to be Self-Evident": An Interdisciplinary Analysis of the Roots of Racism and Slavery in America*. Lanham: UP of America, 2009. Print.

Bailey, Anne C. *African Voices of the Atlantic Slave Trade: Beyond the Silence and Shame*. Boston: Beacon, 2005. Print.

Gould, Philip. *Barbaric Traffic: Commerce and Antislavery in the 18th Century Atlantic World*. Cambridge: Harvard UP, 2003. Print.

Rediker, Marcus. *The Slave Ship: A Human History*. New York: Penguin, 2008. Print.

Wood, Peter. *Strange New Land: Africans in Colonial America*. New York: Oxford UP, 2003. Print.

LESSON PLAN: **The Slave Trade to America**

Students analyze documents, records, and a map of the slave trade to America to understand multiple perspectives on its growth and development.

Learning Objectives

Appreciate historical perspectives on the slave trade that are illustrated in the documents; draw upon historical data from the slave trade in maps; utilize visual and mathematical data in order to clarify the growth and development of slavery; identify the central question on the justification of slavery in the documents.

Materials: Elizabeth Donnan, *Documents Illustrative of the History of the Slave Trade to America (1930)*; Robert Sayer, "Atlantic or Western Ocean" (1815).

Overview Questions

How were perspectives on the issue of slavery different among the European colonists and the Africans? How does the data shown in the map illustrate or support the information presented in the documents? How does the mathematical data in the documents elaborate upon the importance of slavery in America? What arguments and issues do the documents raise about the slave trade to America?

Step 1: Comprehension Questions

How were perspectives on the issue of slavery different among the European colonists and the Africans? What viewpoints do they express about freedom?

▶ **Activity:** Have students select key documents that reveal different perspectives, grouping them together. Ask students to write one paragraph to compare and contrast the multiple perspectives that are presented.

Step 2: Comprehension Questions

How does the data shown in the map illustrate or support the information presented in the documents? What geographic information is shown that helps to clarify perspectives on the slave trade?

▶ **Activity:** Enlarge the map so that students are able to see more detail. Ask students to identify any places that are mentioned in the documents that are on the map and add any new ones.

Step 3: Context Questions

How does the mathematical data in the documents elaborate upon the importance of slavery in America? What does the data indicate?

▶ **Activity:** Have students work in small groups to examine the data provided in the documents. Ask students to make graphs and plot the data. Next, hold a class discussion on what the data reveals about slavery in America.

Step 4: Exploration Questions

Based on the information in these documents, was slavery justified? What arguments and issues do the documents raise about the slave trade to America?

▶ **Activity:** Have students write a brief summary of the arguments and issues raised in the documents. Point out that they should select key excerpts from the documents to use as evidence.

Step 5: Response Paper

Word length and additional requirements set by Instructor. Students answer the research question in the Overview Questions. Students state a thesis and use as evidence passages from the primary source document as well as support from supplemental materials assigned in the lesson.

■ A Narrative of the Life and Adventures of Venture, a Native of Africa

Date: 1798
Author Name: Smith, Venture
Genre: autobiography; memoir

> *"All of us were then put into the castle, and kept for market. On a certain time I and other prisoners were put on board a canoe, under our master, and rowed away to a vessel belonging to Rhode-Island."*

Summary Overview

Born in West Africa and sold into North American slavery, Venture Smith became an unusual African American success story as an adult by buying his freedom, earning a great deal of money, and establishing himself as a respected member of his Connecticut community. Before these adult accomplishments, however, came the dramatic events of Smith's childhood that led to his enslavement and transport across the Atlantic Ocean. His early years as the eldest son of an African tribal leader were interrupted by the invasion of a competing tribe. This conflict led to the death of Smith's father and the transport of the young boy several hundred miles to a slave trade hub on the Atlantic coast. During his journey, Smith was captured with the rest of his party on two separate occasions. Despite the change of captors, his ultimate destination remained the same: sale to white slave traders. The details of Smith's early life and capture are recounted in his autobiography, *A Narrative of the Life and Adventures of Venture, a Native of Africa.*

Defining Moment

The slave trade had been a part of the Americas almost from the time of European arrival in the early 1500s. Spanish plantation owners had first enslaved indigenous peoples to work on the large sugar plantations that sprang up around the Caribbean. As bondage and disease decimated native populations, Europeans turned to West Africa as a source of bonded labor. West Africans had a tradition of enslaving captives from rival ethnic groups, although African slavery was not as brutal an institution as American slavery became; slave traders there expanded their operations to service European demand, and the trans-Atlantic journey known as the Middle Passage was born.

The process of enslaving Africans was a simple yet devastating one. European or American slave traders docked a ship near one of the slave trading centers along the West African coast. Several weeks or even months generally passed as the crew purchased captive Africans from local traders who delivered these charges to the slave ship. Enslaved captives were held in prisons known as slave castles along the coast, or, if they had been sold to a crew, onboard ship while awaiting their dispatch to the New World. Once a ship's cargo hold was packed with men, women, and children, the voyage began. Prisoners were usually chained together and held in miserable circumstances. Forbidden to walk above deck and thrust into highly unsanitary holds, many enslaved Africans died before even reaching their destination, which during this time period was usually the British-held island of Barbados. There, surviving slaves were auctioned off. Many joined the ranks of Caribbean sugar laborers, hard labor that gave arriving slaves a life expectancy as short as seven years.

Unsold slaves were transported north for possible sale to North American colonies.

Although slavery was concentrated in the Caribbean and South American coast during the sixteenth century, it spread northward to British North America as settlers established new colonies there. At first, colonists preferred the usage of indentured servants—white Europeans who agreed to serve a term of labor in exchange for passage to the New World—but over time the demand for cheap labor outstripped the supply of indentured servants. By the time of Smith's arrival in the Americas in the 1730s, enslaved African labor had become vital to the agricultural economies of colonies such as Virginia and South Carolina. Slavery was practiced throughout the colonies, including the northeastern region where Smith was taken by Rhode Island–based slave traders. This increased demand eventually led slave traders to bypass the Caribbean altogether and deliver enslaved Africans directly to North America.

Author Biography

Born in West Africa in about 1729, the African American businessman Venture Smith began life as Broteer Furro. Smith was the eldest son of a tribal leader and spent his early years somewhere in inland West Africa; historians continue to debate the precise location and nature of Smith's ethnic group. During the mid-1730s, however, what was most likely interethnic conflict led to the murder of Smith's father and the capture of most of his people for sale as slaves. Smith was sold to an American slave trade crew and taken to British North America.

Renamed Venture by his American owner, the young Smith spent several years working on the estate of Robertson (sometimes called Robinson) Mumford in coastal New York. Enslaved workers in the northern colonies engaged in a greater variety of tasks than their southern counterparts, who performed agricultural labor more or less exclusively. Smith thus developed diverse skills that would serve him well in adulthood. In his early twenties, Smith married a fellow slave, Meg, and began a family. This family was split up, however, after Smith was sold to Stonington, Connecticut, estate owner Thomas Stanton in late 1754. Not long after, Stanton purchased Smith's family and brought them to Connecticut as well. After a dispute with Stanton in the late 1750s, Smith was again sold, this time to Hempstead Miner. By this time, Smith was determined to earn enough money to purchase his freedom—although Stanton had destroyed a promissory note for a substantial sum belonging to him. Smith changed hands again soon after, joining the household of Colonel Oliver Smith. Under this master, Smith undertook massive efforts to earn enough money to secure his freedom. He cut hundreds of cords of wood, fished, farmed, and employed his considerable brawn to the cause of liberty. In 1765, he successfully purchased his own freedom.

After purchasing his freedom, Smith continued to work and save. Over the next several years, he bought the liberty of his family and some other, unrelated enslaved Africans in Connecticut. He also built up a successful maritime trading business, and later, purchased a large tract of land in East Haddam, Connecticut. His personal strength garnered Smith a great deal of regional renown, which was only reinforced by the 1798 publication of his memoirs. Smith died in 1805, but his memory endured in Connecticut thanks to local folk tales of a man whom historians later dubbed a black Paul Bunyan.

HISTORICAL DOCUMENT

I WAS born at Dukandarra, in Guinea, about the year 1729. My father's name was Saungm Furro, Prince of the Tribe of Dukandarra. My father had three wives. Polygamy was not uncommon in that country, especially among the rich, as every man was allowed to keep as many wives as he could maintain. By his first wife he had three children. The eldest of them was myself, named by my father, Broteer. The other two were named Cundazo and Soozaduka. My father had two children by his second wife, and one by his third. I descended from a very large, tall and stout race of beings, much larger than the generality of people in other parts of the globe, being commonly considerable above six feet in height, and every way well proportioned. . . .

The land for a great way on each side is flat and level, hedged in by a considerable rise of the country at a great distance from it. It scarce ever rains there, yet the land is fertile; great dews fall in the night which refresh the soil. About the latter end of June or first of July, the river begins to rise, and gradually increases until it has inundated the country for a great distance, to the height of seven or eight feet. This brings on a slime which enriches the land surprisingly. When the river has subsided, the natives begin to sow and plant, and the vegetation is exceeding rapid. Near this rich river my guardian's land lay. He possessed, I cannot exactly tell how much, yet this I am certain of respecting it, that he owned an immense tract. He possessed likewise a great many cattle and goats. During my stay with him I was kindly used, and with as much tenderness, for what I saw, as his only son, although I was an entire stranger to him, remote from friends and relations. The principal occupations of the inhabitants there, were the cultivation of the soil and the care of their flocks. They were a people pretty similar in every respect to that of mine, except in their persons, which were not so tall and stout. They appeared to be very kind and friendly. I will now return to my departure from that place.

My father sent a man and horse after me. After settling with my guardian for keeping me, he took me away and went for home. It was then about one year since my mother brought me here. Nothing remarkable occured to us on our journey until we arrived safe home.

I found then that the difference between my parents had been made up previous to their sending for me. On my return, I was received both by my father and mother with great joy and affection, and was once more restored to my paternal dwelling in peace and happiness. I was then about six years old.

Not more than six weeks had passed after my return, before a message was brought by an inhabitant of the place where I lived the preceding year to my father, that that place had been invaded by a numerous army, from a nation not far distant, furnished with musical instruments, and all kinds of arms then in use; that they were instigated by some white nation who equipped and sent them to subdue and possess the country; that his nation had made no preparation for war, having been for a long time in profound peace that they could not defend themselves against such a formidable train of invaders, and must therefore necessarily evacuate their lands to the fierce enemy, and fly to the protection of some chief; and that if he would permit them they should come under his rule and protection when they had to retreat from their own possessions. He was a kind and merciful prince, and therefore consented to these proposals.

He had scarcely returned to his nation with the message, before the whole of his people were obliged to retreat from their country, and come to my father's dominions.

He gave them every privilege and all the protection his government could afford. But they had not been there longer than four days before news came to them that the invaders had laid waste their country, and were coming speedily to destroy them in my father's territories. This affrighted them, and therefore they immediately pushed off to the southward, into the unknown countries there, and were never more heard of.

Two days after their retreat, the report turned out to be but too true. A detachment from the enemy came to my father and informed him, that the whole army was encamped not far out of his dominions, and would invade the territory and deprive his people of their liberties and rights, if he did not comply with the following terms. These were to pay them a large sum of money, three hundred fat cattle, and a great number of goats, sheep, asses, &c.

My father told the messenger he would comply rather than that his subjects should be deprived of their rights and privileges, which he was not then in circumstances to defend from so sudden an invasion. Upon turning out those articles, the enemy pledged their faith and honor that they would not attack him. On these he relied and therefore thought it unnecessary to be on his guard against the enemy. But their pledges of faith and honor proved no better than those of other unprincipled hostile nations; for a few days after a certain relation of the king came and informed him, that the enemy who sent terms of accommodation to him and received tribute to their satisfaction, yet meditated an attack upon his subjects by surprise, and that probably they would commence their attack in less than one day, and concluded with advising him, as he was not prepared for war, to order a speedy retreat of his family and subjects. He complied with this advice.

The same night which was fixed upon to retreat, my father and his family set off about break of day. The king and his two younger wives went in one company, and my mother and her children in another. We left our dwellings in succession, and my father's company went on first. We directed our course for a large shrub plain, some distance off, where we intended to conceal ourselves from the approaching enemy, until we could refresh and rest ourselves a little. But we presently found that our retreat was not secure. For having struck up a little fire for the purpose of cooking victuals, the enemy who happened to be encamped a little distance off, had sent out a scouting party who discovered us by the smoke of the fire, just as we were extinguishing it, and about to eat. As soon as we had finished eating, my father discovered the party, and immediately began to discharge arrows at them. This was what I first saw, and it alarmed both me and the women, who being unable to make any resistance, immediately betook ourselves to the tall thick reeds not far off, and left the old king to fight alone. For some time I beheld him from the reeds defending himself with great courage and firmness, till at last he was obliged to surrender himself into their hands.

They then came to us in the reeds, and the very first salute I had from them was a violent blow on the head with the fore part of a gun, and at the same time a grasp round the neck. I then had a rope put about my neck, as had all the women in the thicket with me, and were immediately led to my father, who was likewise pinioned and haltered for leading. In this condition we were all led to the camp. The women and myself being pretty submissive, had tolerable treatment from the enemy, while my father was closely interrogated respecting his money which they knew he must have. But as he gave them no account of it, he was instantly cut and pounded on his body with great inhumanity, that he might be induced by the torture he suffered to make the discovery. All this availed not in the least to make him give up his money, but he despised all the tortures which they inflicted, until the continued exercise and increase of torment, obliged him to sink and expire.

He thus died without informing his enemies of the place where his money lay. I saw him while he was thus tortured to death. The shocking scene is to this day fresh in my mind, and I have often been overcome while thinking on it. He was a man of remarkable stature. I should judge as much as six feet and six or seven inches high, two feet across his shoulders, and every way well proportioned. He was a man of remarkable strength and resolution, affable, kind and gentle, ruling with equity and moderation.

The army of the enemy was large, I should suppose consisting of about six thousand men. Their leader was called Baukurre. After destroying the old prince, they decamped and immediately marched towards the sea, lying to the west, taking with them myself and the women prisoners. In the march a scouting party was detached from the main army. To the leader of this party I was made waiter, having to carry his gun, &c. As we were a scouting we came across a herd of fat cattle, consisting of about thirty in number. These we set upon, and immediately wrested from their keepers, and afterwards converted them into food for the army. The enemy had remarkable success in destroying the country wherever they went. For as far as they had penetrated, they laid the habitations waste and captured the people. The distance they had now brought me was about four hundred miles. All the march I had very hard tasks imposed on me, which I must perform on pain of punishment. I was obliged to carry on my head a large flat stone used for grinding our corn, weighing as I should suppose, as much as 25 pounds; besides victuals, mat and cooking utensils. Though I was pretty large and stout of my age, yet these burthens were very grievous to me, being only about six years and an half old.

We were then come to a place called Malagasco. When we entered the place we could not see the least appearance of either houses or inhabitants, but upon stricter search found, that instead of houses above ground they had dens in the sides of hillocks, contiguous to ponds and streams of water. In these we perceived they had all hid themselves, as I suppose they usually did upon such occasions. In order to compel them to surrender, the enemy contrived to smoke them out with faggots. These they put to the entrance of the caves and set them on fire. While they were engaged in this business, to their great surprise some of them were desperately wounded with arrows which fell from above on them. This mystery they soon found out. They perceived that the enemy discharged these arrows through holes on the top of the dens directly into the air. Their weight brought them back, point downwards on their enemies heads, whilst they were smoking the inhabitants out. The points of their arrows were poisoned, but their enemy had an antidote for it, which they instantly applied to the wounded part. The smoke at last obliged the people to give themselves up. They came out of their caves, first spatting the palms of their hands together, and immediately after extended their arms, crossed at their wrists, ready to be bound and pinioned. I should judge that the dens above mentioned were extended about eight feet horizontally into the earth, six feet in height and as many wide. They were arched over head and lined with earth, which was of the clay kind, and made the surface of their walls firm and smooth.

The invaders then pinioned the prisoners of all ages and sexes indiscriminately, took their flocks and all their effects, and moved on their way towards the sea. On the march the prisoners were treated with clemency, on account of their being submissive and humble. Having come to the next tribe, the enemy laid siege and immediately took men, women, children, flocks, and all their valuable effects. They then went on to the next district which was contiguous to the sea, called in Africa, Anamaboo. The enemies provisions were then almost spent, as well as their strength. The inhabitants knowing what conduct they had pursued, and what were their present intentions, improved the favorable opportunity, attacked them, and took enemy, prisoners; flocks and all their effects. I was then taken a second time. All of us were then put into the castle, and kept for market. On a certain time I and other prisoners were put on board a canoe, under our master, and rowed away to a vessel belonging to Rhode-Island, commanded by capt. Collingwood, and the mate Thomas Mumford. While we were going to the vessel, our master told us all to appear to the best possible advantage for sale. I was bought on board by one Robertson Mumford, steward of said vessel, for four gallons of rum, and a piece of calico, and called VENTURE, on account of his having purchased me with his own private venture. Thus I came by my name. All the slaves that were bought for that vessel's cargo, were two hundred and sixty.

GLOSSARY

affrighted: frightened

burthens: burdens

dominions: lands over which one has authority or ownership

faggots: small bundles of sticks

instigated: urged; provoked

inundated: flooded

mate: naval officer directly under the captain

pinioned: tied up

tribute: payment of goods or money to a dominant power

victuals: food

Document Analysis

Published in installments in a newspaper in New London, Connecticut, in 1798, Venture Smith's *A Narrative of the Life and Adventures of Venture, a Native of Africa* was one of the earliest slave narratives published in the young United States. The illiterate Smith orally recounted his autobiography to a white transcriber, Connecticut schoolteacher and abolitionist Elisha Niles, when the former slave was approaching the end of what had been a full life—one that took him from a boyhood in Africa to a young adulthood enslaved in British North America and, finally, to middle and later years as a prosperous African American entrepreneur in the United States. The opening chapters of Smith's *Narrative* discuss his experiences as a relatively privileged boy in West Africa who was captured and sold into slavery by fellow Africans, a common method by which free Africans were transformed into enslaved New World laborers.

Set within the greater historical context of the West African world, Smith's personal journey from freedom to bondage exemplifies the experiences of the estimated ten to twelve million Africans who were sold into slavery between the fifteenth and nineteenth centuries. Like the vast majority of other enslaved Africans, Smith was kidnapped by local slave traders who sent him on a forced march covering hundreds of miles. He traveled from his inland home to the coastal region where European slave traders had established commercial forts or docked cargo ships offshore, at which they exchanged European and American manufactured goods for live human beings. Unlike most other enslaved Africans, Smith was later able to attain liberty and personal success. Yet the beginnings of his journey were not uncommon.

Life in West Africa

Smith recounts that he was born at a place called Dukandarra in the West African region of Guinea in about 1729. Guinea was a large and somewhat undefined area that contained several smaller kingdoms and a number of diverse ethnic groups. It spanned roughly the peninsular area stretching from the Atlantic Ocean in the west, the Sahara Desert in the north, and the Gulf of Guinea in the south. Because of the size of this region and the absence of further specific details from Smith, modern scholars are uncertain of the precise location of Dukandarra; some have suggested that Dukandarra might have been one of the Mossi states of what is now Burkina Faso and Ghana.

The narrator does, however, provide ethnographic details of his Dukandarra tribe. The people were, like the adult Smith, of large stature and "commonly considerable above six feet in height." His father, Saungm Furro, was a leader of the people, and Smith unapologetically notes that he had three wives. "Polygamy was not uncommon in that country" among the wealthy and powerful, Smith explains. Although the practice was widely condemned by white European colonists as proof of African moral turpitude, Smith's brief description of the practice does not support that contention. In contrast, Smith's unnamed mother seems to have expected a fair amount of say in the management of the household, as Smith observes that she became very angry when his father took a third wife—not because he did so, but because he did not first consult her over the matter.

This dispute led to a rift between Smith's parents that, although not reprinted in this excerpt, directly affected later events. Angry with her husband, Smith's mother took him and his two younger siblings far distant from their home. Smith recalls that the party left essentially unprepared, and that his mother foraged for food as they spent some five days traveling over barren desert to reach lands suitable for sustaining human life. Smith describes the land as "flat and level," and fertile despite the overall lack of rainfall thanks to nightly dewfall and annual flooding from a nearby river. There, Smith's mother left the boy with an unnamed wealthy farmer. This farmer put the young Smith to work tending his livestock, but the narrator remembers that he was "kindly used" and treated by his guardian as a son. The practice of sending young tribal nobles to other African elders for work and training in preparation for later leadership was a common one; scholars have suggested that this was Smith's mother's goal in leaving the boy with this guardian. Smith also gained valuable lessons in how to tend animals, a job which he would undertake as a slave in later life. After about a year, Smith's father sent someone with a horse to collect the boy and return him to his homeland.

Back at home, Smith recalls that he was delighted to discover that his parents had reconciled in his absence, for both "received . . . [him] with great joy and affection." Smith estimates his age at six years old at this time. Modern historians, however, question the narrator's recollection of his age, given the clarity of his memory of the land and the events that occurred at that time. Historical documents that support Smith's remembrances of his later voyage into slavery suggest that he was at least two years older.

Soon after his return, Smith's life was caught in the upheaval of the slave trade. News reached his father that the region where Smith had been apprenticed had been invaded by a group of Africans who "were instigated by some white nation who equipped and sent them to subdue and possess the country," presumably to capture individuals to force into bonded labor. Having enjoyed a long period of peace and thus being completely unprepared for war, these peoples sought refuge with Smith's tribe, who agreed to host them. Smith's father worked to protect the displaced peoples, but news that the invaders had followed them forced the initial group to again flee south.

Because of the uncertainty surrounding the location of Dukandarra, historians have been unable to agree on the identity of the force that captured and enslaved Smith's people. Some historians have pointed to the ongoing intertribal Akyem warfare that was rooted in the struggle for power between the Dutch and the Danish. Others have associated the attacks with the efforts of the Bambara kingdom of Segu to take over the Gangara region under the auspices of the French. Nevertheless, Smith was doubly a victim of European influence in Africa—first as a captive of ethnic conflict spurred by European involvement, and again as a victim of the slave trade.

When the invading force arrived in Dukandarra, they demanded a huge quantity of money and livestock in exchange for allowing Smith's tribe to remain at liberty. Smith's father paid the ransom "rather than that his subjects should be deprived of their rights and privileges," being aware that any captives would be sold into slavery. Despite accepting the bribe, the invaders planned to attack anyway—an action that Smith found particularly dishonest and detestable.

Smith's father gathered his people and fled. Luck was not on their side, however, and the smoke from their cooking fire alerted the invaders of their location. Smith's father fought back against the enemy party, but could not hold them off and was forced to surrender. The enemy party then captured the remainder of the group and took them to their own camp. There, the invaders tortured Smith's father to find out where the tribe had concealed its riches. He refused to reveal the location and died as a result. The young Smith witnessed the scene and was so struck by that it was "to

this day fresh in my mind, and I have often been overcome while thinking on it."

Capture and Enslavement
With his father murdered and his home in shambles, Smith was held captive by an army of men he estimated to be six thousand strong. With this group, the women and children were forced to march across inland West Africa toward the ocean, where they would be sold to European and American slavers. Smith himself was charged with waiting on his captors and forced to cart supplies for the traveling party. His burdens were food and cooking implements, including a twenty-five-pound grinding stone, which he carried on his head. The sheer size and weight of these tools again suggests that Smith underestimated his age on the journey, as a six year old—even one unusually tall and large for his size—seems unlikely to have been physically able to manage such a large load.

Smith also recalls the devastation that the party inflicted upon the countryside that they passed through. The party stole and slaughtered livestock to feed themselves, destroyed villages and captured their people, and generally "laid . . . waste" to the region. Thus, the tolls of slavery on Africa were greater than depopulation and personal suffering. They also included the devastation of the actual land itself, making it more difficult for those who escaped the net of the slave trade to thrive in the damaged countryside. The capture of Malagasco—another exact location that Smith mentions, lost to time and translation—exemplifies the damage wrought by the invaders. The villagers had hidden in dugouts near water sources, from which the enemy party smoked them out. Even though the villagers fought back with poisoned arrows, the invaders eventually forced the people from their secure dens and took them captive.

With this new group added, Smith's party continued en route to the coast. Their captors, Smith recalls, treated them well because of "their being submissive and humble"—most likely following orders and not attempting escape—even as the captors continued to raid tribes on the way to the Atlantic coast. Consequently, the prisoners' numbers had further swelled by the time they reached the district of Anamaboo, a center of the slave trade. Their arrival there was not without drama. Smith reports that the people of the region, "knowing what conduct [his captors] had pursued" and realizing that captors and captives were at the nadir of their strength after the long journey, attacked and captured

the entire party. Scholars have suggested that this attack was one typical of a West African practice known
as *panyarring,* in which one party could attack and seize
the goods of another as compensation for an unpaid
debt. In this way, Smith was transferred among Africans for a final time before being held in a slave castle
somewhere in the Anamaboo region.

From this fort, Smith and some of his companions
were rowed out to a slave trade vessel docked nearby.
Although the early slave trade had been dominated by
Dutch middlemen, by the 1730s England and American slave ships had become a growing force in the market. The ship to which Smith was taken was based in
the American colony of Rhode Island. Historical evidence suggests that the ship was the *Charming Susanna,* a Rhode Island vessel that arrived in West African
waters to conduct the slave trade during May or June of
1739. This documentary evidence contradicts some of
Smith's recollections. He places his age at this time at
about eight, although his estimated birth year of 1729
would have made him ten. Records also indicate that
the ship carried a human cargo of about ninety as opposed to the 260 that Smith asserts.

On board the vessel, Smith was sold to the ship's
steward, Robertson—called Robinson in other historical records—Mumford for a bargain price of "four gallons of rum, and a piece of calico." A fully grown male
slave, in contrast, was typically valued at the price of one
hundred gallons of rum. Smith's new owner renamed
the former Broteer Furro "Venture" in recognition of
his status as a private business endeavor. Renaming enslaved Africans was standard practice among European
slave owners. Regardless of the new first name chosen,
slaves almost never received or retained a surname, in a
move meant to break them from their heritage and deny
them full adult status. After leaving Africa, Smith himself did not carry a surname again until his mid-thirties,
when the owner who freed him allowed Smith to take
his own name.

The remaining two-thirds of Smith's *Narrative* discusses his life after leaving Africa. He crossed the notorious Middle Passage but was, unlike the wide majority
of his shipmates, spared the Caribbean sugar plantations to instead become one of the just 233 slaves imported into New York from Africa during the 1730s.
There, he took part in the mixed economy typical of the
region, using the herding skills that he had garnered
during his boyhood to tend livestock and relying on his
size and strength to develop a near-legendary working

prowess. In time, Smith successfully saved enough
money earned from labors outside of his regular duties
to purchase his freedom and become a successful entrepreneur in the late colonial and early republican era.

Smith did not forget his African heritage, however;
his two sons, for example, bore names that reflected
African tradition. Smith was silent on the nature of
his religious beliefs and practices, making it possible
that he continued to follow traditional African spiritual
practices throughout his life rather than converting, as
many enslaved Africans did, to Christianity after arrival in the Americas. Smith's ties to the Africa of his
early years therefore seem to have remained a part of
his identity throughout his adult life. In this way, Smith
represents a true African American—a man of Africa
who came, through his economic successes, to exemplify the American rags to riches story and display the
ideals of personal liberty that informed the early American psyche.

Essential Themes
At the time of the publication of the Smith's autobiography in 1798, the United States had already begun
dealing with the question of slavery that would drag the
nation into civil war less than sixty-five years later. The
protection of slavery had been a source of significant
debate during the writing of the United States Constitution some ten years previously. Some political and
social leaders questioned whether a nation founded on
the ideals of universal liberty could justify its stance
when many of its residents existed in a state incompati-
ble with those principles. In northern states where slavery was not viewed as an economic necessity—including Smith's own adopted home of Connecticut—plans
were already underway at the time of the *Narrative*'s
publication to enact emancipation.

The respect afforded to Smith's moral character and
business savvy made him a natural voice to promote
the growing emancipation movement, and his memoirs served as fuel both for his own personal legacy and
for the larger anti-slavery movement. Narratives such
as Smith's, along with changing social ideas about the
institution of slavery both in the United States and
abroad, helped bring about a United States ban on the
overseas slave trade in 1807, less than a decade after
the publication of Smith's autobiography. The short-
term effect of slave narratives in persuading Americans
that those of African descent were not inherently inferior is thus apparent.

Smith's autobiography has also had enduring historical value as not only an autobiography of an unusually successive African American man of the era, but also as a record of the process of enslavement as it took place within West Africa. Although some of the narrative's details are unclear, such as Smith's precise place of origin and what tribe captured him, the information relating to his purchase, transport, and freedom has been corroborated by independent historical evidence. This measure of support gives credence to Smith's overall narrative, and the truthfulness of his story remains generally unquestioned.

Thus the *Narrative* stands as an important primary source on the situations that led to Africans being drawn into slavery, as Smith was. It is not clear whether Olaudah Equiano, the author of the leading contemporary slave narrative, was actually a native of Africa or, as some records seem to indicate, the American colonies. Later slave narratives, such as that of Frederick Douglass, cannot address this issue as their authors were typically born in America. Historians have continued to study Smith's life and times, with excavations of his Connecticut property helping to fill in some of the details lacking in the author's own memoirs.

Vanessa E. Vaughn, MA

Bibliography

"The African Slave Trade and the Middle Passage." *WGBH Educational Foundation*. Public Broadcasting Service (PBS), 2012. Web. 25 July 2012.

Andrews, William L. *To Tell a Free Story: The First Century of Afro-American Autobiography, 1760–1865*. Urbana: U of Illinois P, 1986. Print.

Berlin, Ira. *Many Thousands Gone: The First Two Centuries of Slavery in North America*. Cambridge: Harvard UP, 1998. Print.

Desrochers, Robert E. Jr. "'Not Fade Away': The Narrative of Venture Smith, an African American in the Early Republic." *Journal of American History* 84.1 (1997): 40–66. Print.

Saint, Chandler B., and George A. Krimsky. *Making Freedom: The Extraordinary Life of Venture Smith*. Middletown: Wesleyan UP, 2009. Print.

Smith, Venture. *A Narrative of the Life and Adventures of Venture, a Native of Africa, but Resident above Sixty Years in the United States of America, Related by Himself*. 1798. Ed. Selden, Henry M. 1896. *Documenting the American South*. U of North Carolina at Chapel Hill, 2004. Web. 25 July 2012.

Stewart, James Brewer, ed. *Venture Smith and the Business of Slavery and Freedom*. Amherst: U of Massachusetts P, 2010. Print.

Wood, Betty. *Slavery in Colonial America, 1619–1776*. Lanham: Rowman, 2005. Print.

Additional Reading

Bontemps, Arna, ed. *Five Black Lives: The Autobiographies of Venture Smith, James Mars, William Grimes, the Rev. G. W. Offley, and James L. Smith*. Middletown: Wesleyan UP, 1987. Print.

Gould, Philip. "'Remarkable Liberty': Language and Identity in Eighteenth-Century Black Autobiography." *Genius in Bondage: Literature of the Early Black Atlantic*. Ed. Vincent Carretta and Philip Gould. Lexington: UP of Kentucky, 2001. 116–29. Print.

Kaplan, Sidney, and Emma Nogrady Kaplan. *The Black Presence in the Era of the American Revolution*. Amherst: U of Massachusetts P, 1989. Print.

Lovejoy, Paul E. "The African Background of Venture Smith." Ed. James Brewer Stewart. *Venture Smith and the Business of Slavery and Freedom*. Amherst: U of Massachusetts P, 2010. 35–55. Print.

Waldstreicher, David. "The Vexed Story of Human Commodification Told by Benjamin Franklin and Venture Smith." *Journal of the Early Republic* 24.2 (2004): 268–78. Print.

LESSON PLAN: **Venture Smith, an Unexpected Voice**

Students analyze excerpts from Venture Smith's account of his life and use their observations to challenge assumptions about enslaved African Americans.

Learning Objectives

Identify the central purpose of Smith's narrative; formulate historical questions about the writing of the narrative; interrogate historical data to assess the contribution of enslaved and free Africans to colonial America; consider Elisha Niles's perspective on Venture Smith.

Materials: Venture Smith, *A Narrative of the Life and Adventures of Venture, A Native of Africa* (1798); Elisha Niles, preface to *A Narrative of the Life and Adventures of Venture* (1798).

Overview Questions

What did Smith hope to achieve in telling his life story? How might the authorship of Smith's narrative affect its content? How does Smith's narrative challenge perceived views of slaves and slave owners? In a different context, what success might Smith have had?

Step 1: Comprehension Questions

What was Smith's likely goal in dictating his narrative? What was Elisha Niles's likely purpose in writing down Smith's words?

▶ **Activity:** Have students speculate on why Smith chose to tell his story. Have students choose and read passages that demonstrate Smith felt he had a meaningful story to tell. Ask students to determine how many other narratives there are from African American contemporaries of Smith.

Step 2: Context Questions

How does Elisha Niles's involvement in the creation of this document affect how you read it? Why is this narrative considered a primary document?

▶ **Activity:** Discuss whether any assumptions can be made about Niles's influence on the narrative. Instruct students to list statements in the excerpt that can have the potential for verification in other primary sources. Discuss what kinds of sources those could be. Discuss why this is a primary document.

Step 3: Context Questions

How do Smith's actions and achievements align with what you would expect of enslaved African Americans in the eighteenth century? What actions and achievements did you not expect?

▶ **Activity:** Have students read aloud passages that are consistent with their expectations of the treatment and life of a slave in colonial America. Have students list events in Smith's life that run counter to stereotyped expectations.

Step 4: Historical Connections Questions

Why does Elisha Niles say that Smith may equal a Franklin or Washington in a state of nature? What qualities in Smith's narrative might prove or disprove that?

▶ **Activity:** Have students read Niles's preface and then put into literal terms Niles's assessment of Smith. Challenge students to identify common characteristics of Franklin and Washington. Invite debate about whether or not Niles's assessment could be true.

Step 5: Response Paper

Word length and additional requirements set by Instructor. Students answer the research question in the Overview Questions. Students state a thesis and use as evidence passages from the primary source documents.

Letter from Governor Bull to the Royal Council Regarding the Stono Rebellion, October 1739

Date: October 5, 1739
Author: Bull, William
Genre: letter

"[O]n the Ninth of September last at night a Great number of Negroes arose in rebellion, broke open a store where they got arms killed twenty one White Persons and were marching in a daring manner out of the Province."

Summary Overview

South Carolina Lieutenant Governor William Bull's letter to the British Royal Council stands as the only surviving eyewitness account of the events surrounding the 1739 Stono Rebellion, the largest slave uprising in the British North American colonies. The revolt failed to win freedom for its participants and resulted in the deaths of more than sixty people—mostly enslaved Africans. It fed white colonial fears about the possibility of significant violent resistance by the people they kept as chattel. Modern historians agree that the scope of the Stono Rebellion itself paled in comparison to the long-term effects on white and black Americans alike.

Bull's status as a firsthand witness was accidental. Traveling back to Charles Town in the South Carolina colony (now Charleston),he and a small group of companions encountered the rebels on the road. Several weeks later, Bull recounted his group's flight, told of later efforts to crush the rebellion, and suggested further military steps to prevent similar rebellions.

Defining Moment

When the Stono Rebellion took place in late 1739, it marked the height of a period of growing tensions between South Carolina's white slave-owning minority and enslaved black population. Black slaves—many forcibly imported from Africa, others born into slavery in the Americas—had long outnumbered white colonists in the Carolinas; by 1740, estimates placed the black population at just over 39,000, nearly double the roughly 20,000 white South Carolinians. Although slaves formally lacked even basic civil rights during the early eighteenth century, their numbers and the level of skill required of both agricultural and crafts laborers in this pre-industrial era meant that, in practice, slaves were often able to assemble, move from plantation to plantation at will, and exercise some autonomy over their work.

This racial imbalance in the population, along with other issues, contributed to concerns among white colonists that the enslaved population, on which their agricultural economy was greatly dependent, could mount an effective rebellion to achieve liberty. During the two decades preceding the Stono Rebellion, many slaves took matters into their own hands by running away, some successful and others not. The intended destination for a fair portion of these runaways was St. Augustine, Florida, then under the control of the Spanish. From the late seventeenth century, the Spanish city had officially offered freedom to any English slave who managed to escape there; in reality, this freedom was not always granted, and slaves were returned to their colonial masters. By 1733, however, tensions between Spain and Great Britain were building, and such cooperation ceased. The Spanish king issued a declaration assuring escaped slaves liberty in Florida. As word spread northward, white fears of black desertion grew.

Several events closely preceded the Stono Rebellion. Disease sickened and killed many residents of Charleston during the late summer. The Security Act, a law requiring white colonists to carry arms to church on Sundays, had been announced that August. Finally, news of the looming War of Jenkins's Ear between Britain and Spain reached South Carolina. Historians have identified all of these as likely contributing factors to the uprising on September 9.

It was on this day in 1739 that a group of slaves marched down the road leading to St. Augustine, Florida, chanting the world *liberty* and holding banners that read the same message. Their journey had begun at the Stono River, about twenty miles from Charlestown. They recruited others as they moved south, bringing their number to about one hundred. The local militia dispersed the group as they rested. Some were killed in the ensuing clash. Others were hunted down and arrested, only to be hanged later.

Nearly a month after the uprising began, Bull penned a letter to his superiors at the British Royal Council detailing the revolt, its aftermath, and his suggestions for preventing such uprisings in the future. Yet even after Bull's letter crossed the Atlantic, white concerns over black rebellions remained high. These concerns were not entirely unfounded; some participants in the revolt, including one of its ringleaders, had not been caught; and other, smaller rebellions sprung up over the next several months.

Author Biography

A native of South Carolina, William Bull was born in April of 1683 to Colonel Stephen Bull, a Welsh immigrant who had been one of the colony's first settlers in about 1670; his mother's name is lost to history. After arriving in South Carolina, the elder Bull had served in the colonial government and helped select the site of Charleston as he built a fortune in land speculation and rice production on his plantation, Ashley Hall.

Like his father, Bull became a large-scale planter and a land surveyor. In 1706, he won his first election to the colonial assembly, serving in that body off and on over the next ten to fifteen years; sources differ on the exact dates of his time in the legislature. By this time, Bull had married Mary Quintyne, the daughter of a South Carolina landowner. The couple went on to have five children. Bull's sons, Stephen and William, were also active in colonial government. The latter served as governor for several years in the period preceding the American Revolution.

Bull also served as a militia captain during the bloody Yamassee War of 1715 and 1716, which pitted a collection of regional American Indian groups against white South Carolinian colonists. In this role, Bull took part in the 1716 Convention of Tugaloo, which resulted in amity between the colonists and Cherokee for several years. Later in his career, Bull acted as one of the colony's Indian commissioners. After the Yamassee War, Bull served on the council of the Lords Proprietors in 1719, and, after the changeover from proprietary to royal colony, on the new royal council from 1720 to 1737.

Because of Bull's experience with American Indians and his skill as a surveyor, he was selected to assist James Oglethorpe in establishing the colony of Georgia in 1733, contributing particularly to the foundation of the coastal town of Savannah. In 1737, Bull became the acting governor of South Carolina after the incumbent died in office. It was in this capacity that Bull had a role in the Stono affair. By the time his tenure ended in 1744, Bull had also seen the colony through a yellow fever epidemic, a fire that greatly damaged Charles Town, conflict with the Spanish to the south, and a period of relative peace with local American Indians. Bull closed out his public career as the Anglican commissioner of Prince William parish near Sheldon, South Carolina. He died on March 21, 1755, in Sheldon.

HISTORICAL DOCUMENT

5th Octob. 1739
My Lord,

By the Tartar Pink I am Honoured with His Majesty's Commands under His Royal Sign Manual and also with your Graces letter further Signifying His Majesty's Pleasure. I shall always endeavour in the best manner to answer his Majesty's gracious Intentions by pursuing these Orders in every particular and by a Proclamation have made known the same.

I had the Hounour some time ago to lay before your Grace, some account of our affairs in regard to the desertion of our Negroes who are encouraged to it by a certain Proclamation published by the King of Spain's Order at St. Augustine, declaring freedom to all Negroes who should Desert hither from the British Colonies; since which several parties have deserted and are there openly received and protected; many attempts of others have been discovered and prevented notwithstanding which on the Ninth of September last at night a Great number of Negroes arose in rebellion, broke open a store where they got arms killed twenty one White Persons and were marching in a daring manner out of the Province killing all they met and burning the Houses on the Road through which they passed, returning in any way from the Southward with four Gentlemen, I met these Rebels at Eleven o'clock in the forenoon so that I fortunately discerned the danger time enough to avoid it and to give notice to the Militia who on the Occasion behaved with so much expedition and bravery as by four o'clock the same day to come up with them, and killed and took so many as put a stop to any further mischief at that time. Forty four of the Rebels have been killed & executed, some few yet remain concealed in the Woods and expecting the same fate seem desperate. If such an attempt was made in a time of Peace and Tranquility what might be expected if an Enemy should appear upon our Frontier with a design to invade us? Which we have great reason to expect upon the first Notice of a Rupture, being so fully informed by several hands of the great preparations that were made some time ago at the Havana which according to an account I lately received lye ready waiting only for orders to put that Design in Execution, I have pursuant to His

Majesty's Orders given notice thereof to ye Commander of His Majesty's Ships.

It was the opinion of his Majesty's council with several other Gentlemen, that one of the most effectual means that could be used at present, to prevent such desertion of Our Negroes is to encourage some Indians by a suitable reward to pursue and if possible to bring back the deserters, and while the Indians are thus employed they would be in the way ready to intercept others that might attempt to follow, and I have sent for the Chicasaws living at New Windsor and the Catabaw Indians for that purpose.

From the Governor of New York I have advice that about the 10th of July an army consisting of Two hundred French and Five hundred Indians, was marched from Mount Real and was to be Enforced by other French and Indians on their March, that they were designed against some Indians situated near a Branch of the Missicipi River, in amity with His majesty's Subjects and have a trade with the People of Georgia and Virginia. I imagine that the design of this army is against the Chickasaws who are a small but brave People living near the Missicipi River who have already twice withstood and defeated the French about three years ago. I have therefore sent to those Indians to give them notice of the dangers I apprehended to be coming on them. I have been informed that the French have a Design to cut off the Chickesaws entirely, and to reduce and subdue the Chactaws, if they should succeed in these attempts it would discourage the Indians in Amity with us from withstanding or opposing them in any attempt of the like nature.

The French have for a long time wanted an opportunity to get an Interest among the Cherokees and build a Fort there. As this army which the French now have on its March from Montreal will come down a branch of the Missicipi River which runs near the Cherokees, they will probably endeavor to get the consent of those People to build a Fort there which may enable them to have a Considerable Influence in that Nation as they have already among the Upper Creeks by their Fort at the Albamas.

I apprehend that the Limits of the Charter granted by His late Majesty King Charles the Second to the Lords Proprietors of Carolina, since surrendered to His present Majesty, includes the Cherokees and your Grace best knows whether that is not a sufficient objection against the French's taking possession of the Land by a Fort within the Limits thereof doubtless the French will endeavour by all means to accomplish this as soon as possible, as it will be such a Considerable step towards their grand design of Surrounding the British Colonies. As their success in these designs might interrupt the Security of His Majesty's Subjects in case of a War I thought it

my duty to acquaint your Grace therewith I am with the greatest Respect

My Lord
Your Graces
Most Obedient and
Most humble Servant
William Bull.

GLOSSARY

charter: a document laying out the legal rights and limitations upon the settlement of a colony

desertion: the act of running away

hither: to this place

Missicipi River: Mississippi River

Tartar Pink: the name of the ship bringing the King's letter

Document Analysis

William Bull's letter to the British Royal Council remains the sole and thus by default most important surviving eyewitness account of the 1739 Stono Rebellion. This uprising rocked South Carolina and reshaped race relations in the southeastern colonies for decades to come. Although this letter is supplemented by contemporary accounts written by people living in the region who experienced the events tangentially, the overall scarcity of primary sources—including a complete lack of representation of the enslaved rebels themselves—means that the historian must carefully consider both what Bull does and does not say in order to gain a fuller understanding of this event and its ramifications. Bull's words and objective tone suggest a certain finality to the incident that presumably served to place him in a positive light but did not always reflect reality. Indeed, Bull's brevity of description belies the scope of the rebellion that actually took place.

Considerable time passed between the dramatic events of the Stono uprising on September 9 and the composition of Bull's letter on October 5. This letter had the dual purpose of informing the authorities who ultimately controlled the colony of the dramatic events that

had taken place and, presumably, of placing Bull's own involvement in the affair in the best possible light. Some historians have speculated that this latter goal kept Bull from providing a fuller report of the matter. The drive to protect his reputation as an effective governor able to keep peace within the colony may also have deterred Bull from discussing the true extent to which the rebels remained at large at the time of the letter's composition. It has been noted that Bull had the time to perform his own investigation of the uprising by questioning planters and slaves and to consider the place of Stono in a larger colonial context. Yet the letter does not suggest that Bull did this, preferring—as might be expected—to serve his own interests by emphasizing mostly in his letter that the affair had been dealt with.

To open his discussion of the Stono uprising, Bull points a firm finger at Spain and the Spanish king's promise of freedom to any slave who escaped from the English colonies to Spanish Florida. Before the growing conflicts between Spain and England, Spain had habitually returned escaped slaves form Spanish Florida to the English colonies. However, once England had declared war on Spain, Spanish Florida became a safe haven for fugitive slaves.

By May of 1739, the declaration had incited enough slaves to attempt escape that the English colonial government considered it a problem; a successful escape effort by a small group of slaves who had worked as cattle hunters and thus were especially familiar with the land caused great concern among slaveholders that April. Two runaways from the group were captured and publicly punished—one whipped and the other executed—but colonial authorities felt that stronger measures were needed to keep other slaves from attempting similar escapes.

Fears of slave insurrections and desertions grew among white South Carolinians through 1739. Bull had written to the Crown that the minority white colonists were afraid that the black majority population would rise up and overthrow them, and believed that the colonial government would be unable to withstand a concerted effort to achieve that end. Based on Bull's comment that "several parties have deserted…[and] many attempts of others have been discovered and prevented," were very real. The Spanish decision to grant freedom to British slaves bolstered by stories of successful escapes made liberty for those enslaved persons living within a reasonable distance of the border a real possibility. Bull thus connects the Stono Rebellion to the ongoing issue of slave desertions to St. Augustine, in Spanish Florida.

Next, Bull succinctly sums up the outbreak of the rebellion on September 9 by stating that the participants "broke open a store where they got arms killed twenty one White Persons and were marching in a daring manner out of the Province killing all they met and burning the Houses of the Road through which they passed," but this short description fails in several respects. A rebellion of the size and scope of the Stono Rebellion seems unlikely to have been conceived and executed on the spot, implying that the rebels saw September 9 as an auspicious time to launch their uprising.

Unlike Bull—who placed the blame exclusively on the attraction of St. Augustine and freedom without consideration for the reason why the event happened precisely when it did—historians have suggested several possible factors contributing to the outbreak of the rebellion on September 9. Among these causes is the Spanish decision to assure liberty to escaped slaves, which had contributed to runaway attempts for several months previously. In addition, however, historians have pointed to potential factors closer to home. In August, word had spread of the Security Act, requiring white men to carry weapons with them to Sunday church services. The period when white masters attended church had long afforded slaves an opportunity to gather unsupervised, and—as the Stono uprising broke out during a time when planters were at church—it is possible that its organizers hoped to improve their chances of success by making their attempt before the law became effective later in September. Late summer also brought a deadly outbreak of yellow fever to Charleston, and illness interfered with the city's day-to-day business, closing schools and newspapers and even greatly delaying a meeting of the colonial legislature. Finally, news of the recent declaration of war between Britain and Spain had reached the colony the week preceding the outbreak, possibly serving as an immediate incentive to set plans for the escape attempt in motion as the rebels believed Spanish Florida would certainly welcome their group.

Bull's account does cover the essential facts of the beginning of the rebellion, but leaves out some illuminating details found in other contemporary sources that were almost certainly known to the lieutenant governor. An account of the rebellion written by an unknown author in Georgia at about the same time offers an interesting comparison. Bull's letter generalizes the group of rebels at the outset as "a Great Number," while the Georgia account numbers the participants more specifically as twenty. This account also provides the name of the group's leader, Jemmy; still other reports give it as Cato, but most historians agree that the former name is more accurate. According to the Georgia report, the twenty rebels had to overcome just two men at the weapons shop in order to collect the arms and gunpowder kept there. Bull's letter, however, does not point out this great imbalance between black rebels and white shopkeepers; perhaps the lieutenant governor saw this detail as unimportant, or perhaps he believed leaving the specifics out allowed the reader to imagine a large and more powerful force of rebels more obviously unable to be easily put down by colonial forces.

The Georgia account also notes the rebels did not, in fact, kill every white person they encountered, in contrast to Bull's assertion that the group killed "all they met." Instead, the Georgia author specifically comments that the rebels bypassed the tavern belonging to a Mr. Wallace, because he treated his slaves well. This suggests that the white observers killed by the rebels were in large part the opposite, although the group murdered family members and passers-by alike. As the rebels passed from place to place, the group grew; some slaves joined willingly, but others had to be coerced so that none remained to sound the alarm. The trail of destruction traveled along the Pons Pons Road, which connected South Carolina with the rebels' presumed destination of St. Augustine.

Bull himself enters the story at this point, coincidentally riding along the Pons Pons Road toward Charleston from Granville County, where a court session had taken place. He notes that at about eleven in the morning his group encountered the Stono rebels, whose numbers had grown to an estimated sixty participants by this time. Armed with stolen weapons, beating on drums in what historians have associated with traditional African military practices, and bearing a military-style standard, the group must certainly have been intimidating. Bull and his companions quickly grasped the significance of what they saw coming up the road toward them, and by virtue of their relative speed on horseback—in contrast to that of the slave band on foot—managed to escape unharmed.

Presumably surprised and perhaps terrified by the shouting, drumming group coming toward them—the very type of insurrection that the white South Carolinians feared—Bull and his companions, as he put it, "discerned the danger time enough to avoid it;" in other words, they fled the scene as quickly as they could. Although Bull strongly implies that he was the person who alerted the militia of the situation and directed it to the rebels, this seems unsupported by fact. Another member of Bull's party was the one who performed this duty; Bull himself, despite his previous military experience and his duty under his colonial post as the commanding officer of the militia, does not seem to have directly engaged the rebels. The possibility of being perceived as a coward—or even worse, a man unable to meet the responsibility of his job—may have led Bull to retell the events of the afternoon, although very briefly. He may have hoped that the king would fail to notice the absence of details or even assume that his personal modesty prevented him from speaking too highly of his deeds.

Even without the leadership of their formal commanding officer, however, the militia did its job effectively. By late afternoon, the rebels had covered several miles on the Pons Pons Road and decided to stop for a rest. The group made no secret of their location, perhaps hoping to attract more slaves looking to escape to freedom and thus bolster their numbers, which by then may have approached one hundred. About five hours after Bull and his party first encountered the rebels, a colonial force estimated to be as high as one hundred strong took the relaxing escapees by surprise at their camp. Other contemporary sources assert that the slaves mounted a respectable defense, firing their arms twice but achieving little against the stronger militia. However, Bull, who does not seem to have been directly involved, is silent on this count. One solid volley from the militia decimated the rebel group, and the white colonists moved in quickly to surround and neutralize much of the remaining body. Bull notes that forty-four rebels were either killed in the fighting or executed soon afterward, acknowledging in more general terms that some of the participants in the uprising had escaped the militia.

Bull plays down these rebellious holdouts, noting simply that "some few yet remain concealed . . . and expecting the same fate seem desperate." As might be expected from someone trying to assure his superior that he has the situation well in hand, Bull does not mention, as the Georgia account does, that as many as twenty rebels remained unaccounted for in early October. By late in the month, however, most had been found and executed. Bull also does not mention the aura of fear that must have pervaded the area around Stono. One month after Bull's letter was written, several planters and their families living in the region packed up and moved in with friends and relatives outside of the area due to lingering fears about the possible actions of the rebels who still remained at large.

Next, Bull outlines the plan that colonial leaders decided to take to prevent further attempts at escape. Explaining that the colonial council in conference with other advisers had determined that the "most effectual means" to this end was "to encourage some Indians by a suitable reward" to find and neutralize any remaining rebels and to forestall any other slaves who might try to follow in their footsteps, Bull was echoing a policy that had already come into use in the colony. Some months earlier, South Carolina had approved substantial bounties for escaped slaves captured in neighboring Georgia, which at that time had no slave population of its own. Under this policy, adult male slaves fetched £40, adult female slaves £25, and children £10; an adult scalp containing both ears was valued at £20. Extending rewards for captured slaves was thus not an innovative practice, but a proven one.

The remainder of Bull's letter deals with other matters of colonial concern, particularly the growing tensions between the British colonists and the French and their American Indian allies. Fifteen years later, these tensions would lead to the beginning of the French and Indian War, which allowed the British to assert their preeminence among European powers seeking to control the North American continent; the conflict also contributed greatly to the institution of several economic measures that the American colonists objected to, leading in turn to the American Revolution. Although these matters had little direct connection to the Stono Rebellion, the juxtaposition of the two topics highlights the competing pressures facing Southern colonists. On the one hand, they feared a large-scale slave rebellion from within that could destabilize their delicate political, social, and economic system. On the other hand, they lived with the very real possibility of external violence from competing European nations or from the American Indians that the English had displaced. South Carolinians who, like Bull, had lived through the Yamassee War, which rivals the better-known King Philip's War in the North in terms of bloodshed, were likely to be the especially aware of that latter danger.

Thus it is perhaps not surprising that Bull attributed less importance to the Stono Rebellion than modern scholars, who can see its significance among the long string of conflicts over slavery, first in the colonies and then in the newly formed and expanding United States. Efforts by slaves to escape to Spanish Florida were relatively common by the time of Stono, and Bull—who had no way of knowing that the Stono Rebellion would go down in history as the largest slave insurrection on mainland North American during the colonial era— may have seen this rebellion as just another attempt in this vein. To Bull, historians have noted, the most important aspect of the uprising was not that it had happened, but that it was over. The varied demands of governing and the fact that Bull had certainly failed in his essential duty to keep order in the colony may have made the Stono Rebellion one that the lieutenant governor was happy to treat as succinctly as possible before redirecting royal attention to other ongoing matters.

Essential Themes

Although the Stono Rebellion failed to secure the freedom of its participants and resulted in what was actually relatively limited loss of life and property among white colonists—the yellow fever epidemic that had struck Charleston in the weeks before resulted in much greater death toll than the Stono Rebellion did—it is nearly impossible to overstate the importance of the rebellion in shaping racial patterns in South Carolina over the next century. In the short-term, white colonists worked to find and execute the estimated thirty participants who had escaped the militia's attack. Militia members and hired American Indians sought fugitives over the next few weeks, but some rebels remained at large for months or even years. A series of apparently justified rumors of additional revolts swept the colony in late 1739 and into 1740. One reputed rebellion involved as many as two hundred slaves who planned to invade Charles Town to seize weapons. The Stono Rebellion may have failed, but its mere existence raised worries that one might succeed.

The uprising also confirmed white fears of black plans to desert the colony. Indeed, Bull focuses on this topic repeatedly throughout his letter. White colonial leaders soon set about discussing ways to ensure the obedience of the enslaved population in earnest. As a result of these efforts, the legislature passed the 1740 Slave Code, which had the express purpose of "the better ordering and governing of negroes and other slaves in this province." Among the code's provisions were strong bans on the abilities of slaves to assemble, to learn to read and write English, to grow their own food, and to travel from place to place unescorted. The code also laid out harsh punishments for infractions of these laws, and provided financial incentives for blacks to inform on their fellow slaves. Historians generally agree that these measures so greatly weakened slaves' abilities to agitate for their freedom that even the outbreak of the American Revolution with its sweeping cries for liberty failed to provide sufficient grounds for abolition. Instead, South Carolina's black population remained largely enslaved until the end of the Civil War more than 125 years after the Stono Rebellion.

The lack of other true primary sources on the Stono Rebellion has given Bull's short account great historical significance. Other contemporary sources provide stories about the events that are more informative, but secondhand at best. Thus Bull's perspective on the rebellion, informed by his status as a white, slave-owning planter and his probable desire to justify his own actions, has become the main one passed through history. In order to consider the full picture of the uprising,

Bull's looming concerns of protecting the white colonists' safety and interests must be balanced by a historical awareness of the motivations that surely influenced the rebels, who openly sought liberty.

Vanessa E. Vaughn, MA

Bibliography

Bull, Kinloch. "William Bull." *American National Biography Online*. American Biography Online, n.d. Web. 3 May 2012.

"The Bull Family of South Carolina." *South Carolina Historical and Genealogical Magazine* 1.1 (1900): 76–90. Print.

Coker, Michael. *Charleston Curiosities: Stories of the Tragic, Heroic, and Bizarre*. Charleston: History, 2008. Print.

Hoffer, Peter Charles. *Cry Liberty: The Great Stono River Slave Rebellion of 1739*. New York: OUP, 2010. Print.

Horton, James Oliver and Lois E. Horton. *Slavery and the Making of America*. New York: OUP, 2005. Print.

Smith, Mark M. *Stono: Documenting and Interpreting a Southern Slave Revolt*. Columbia: U of South Carolina P, 2005. Print.

Wood, Peter H. Black *Majority: Negroes in Colonial South Carolina from 1670 through the Stono Rebellion*. New York: Norton, 1974. Print.

Additional Reading

Meroney, Geraldine M. *Inseparable Loyalty: A Biography of William Bull*. Norcross: Harrison, 1991. Print.

LESSON PLAN: **Governor Bull Reacts to Rebellion**

Students analyze Governor Bull's letter and then research the causes and effects of the Stono Rebellion.

Learning Objectives

Reconstruct the literal meaning of the letter; analyze the causes of the Stono Rebellion; consider William Bull's perspective; analyze the effects of the rebellion.

Materials: William Bull, "Letter from Governor Bull to the Royal Council Regarding the Stono Rebellion" (October 1739); William Bull, "Report Re. Stono Rebellion Slave-Catchers" (November 1739); South Carolina General Assembly, Slave Code of South Carolina (May 1740): Sections XLV, XXXIII, XXXVI, XXXVII, and XXXVIII.

Overview Questions

What does Bull describe in his letter? What were the potential causes of the Stono Rebellion? Were Bull's fears and reactions reasonable in the context of his times? How do the "Report Re. Stono Rebellion Slave-Catchers" and the Code of South Carolina demonstrate the effects of the rebellion?

Step 1: Comprehension Questions

Who is Bull addressing and why? What does he hope to accomplish by sending his message?

▶ **Activity:** Have students identify who Bull is and to whom he is writing. Ask students to summarize his view of the rebellion's cause and his solutions to avoid future revolts. Discuss whether his recounting of his role in suppressing the rebellion is self-serving or merely factual.

Step 2: Context Questions

What historical events does Bull not mention that may have contributed to rebellion? What common sense causes does he ignore?

▶ **Activity:** Have a student restate the causes that Bull cites. Direct students to use secondary sources to research and identify other factors in fomenting both the revolt and its specific timing. Discuss how enslavement itself was a cause.

Step 3: Context Questions

What does Bull appear to fear the most in the aftermath of the rebellion? Why are his fears and the fears of other South Carolinians rational?

▶ **Activity:** Have a student review the actions that Bull suggests. Discuss why this makes sense from his and white colonialists' perspectives. Have students hypothesize about other possible reactions of ordinary South Carolinians to the rebellion.

Step 4: Exploration Questions

What is the purpose of the "Report Re. Stono Rebellion Slave-Catchers"? How is the 1740 Slave Code retaliation for the rebellion?

▶ **Activity:** Have students summarize the report and who benefits from it. Have students create a list of limitations put on enslaved African Americans and slaveholders in the slave code. Direct students to summarize how these documents are a direct result of the rebellion.

Step 5: Response Paper

Word length and additional requirements set by Instructor. Students answer the research question in the Overview Questions. Students state a thesis and use as evidence passages from the primary source document as well as support from supplemental materials assigned in the lesson.

■ Slave Code of South Carolina

Date: May 1740
Author: South Carolina General Assembly
Genre: legislation

"so that the slave may be kept in due subjection and obedience, and the owners and other persons having the care and government of slaves may be restrained from exercising too great rigour and cruelty over them, and that the public peace and order ... may be preserved"

Summary Overview

Written by provincial governor William Bull and the colonial legislature in the wake of the Stono Rebellion of 1739—the largest slave rebellion in the continental English colonies—the Slave Code of South Carolina sought to formally establish laws that both restricted the ability of enslaved persons from organizing such an uprising again and, to a lesser extent, sought to tamp down on the excesses that encouraged them to do so. The laws nevertheless heavily favored the rights of slaveholders over those of slaves, helping cement the lack of basic civil and legal privileges afforded slaves for the duration of the institution by transforming certain colonial customs regarding the ownership and treatment of slaves into law. The Slave Code of 1740 intensified restrictions established under earlier colonial codes, effectively squashing attempts by wrongfully enslaved people to prove their freedom and even disallowing African cultural practices. It later served as a model for the slave code adopted in colonial Georgia.

Defining Moment

Slavery had been an accepted part of South Carolina culture since the colony's inception in the mid-seventeenth century. Before the establishment of the slave trade from Africa, English settlers enslaved the local American Indian people they encountered upon landing in the colony. The earliest enslaved Africans in South Carolina arrived as the property of white Caribbean planters, and before long the colony formally acknowledged the institution. Over the next several decades, the enslaved black population grew and the already limited legal rights of slaves declined. The expansion of the slave trade accelerated the rise in the number of South Carolina's slaves in comparison to the growth of the white population so greatly that by the early eighteenth century enslaved blacks outnumbered free whites in the colony; by the time of the writing of the 1740 Slave Code, the black population was nearly double that of the white population. During this same period, colonial customs changed the status of the enslaved black laborers from a condition similar to medieval serfdom to that of hereditary chattel slavery.

Unsurprisingly, this oppression of the majority by the minority resulted in fear among white South Carolinians that the enslaved population would rise up against them. These fears were, to a certain degree, justified. Individual slaves sought freedom by running away from their masters, with some hoping to find liberty in nearby Spanish Florida after 1733. In September 1739, several dozen slaves escaped their plantations to mount the Stono Rebellion, the largest such uprising on the continent of North America. The chance crossing of the paths of colonial governor William Bull and the rebels soon led to the suppression of the uprising by the colonial militia, but the violence and early success of the revolt further terrified already nervous white colonists.

South Carolina's legislature acted quickly in the wake of the Stono Rebellion. Two months later, a special committee began leading a discussion of possible efforts to prevent another similar revolt. In the spring of 1740, legislation aimed at ensuring the safety of the colony's white residents—at the expense of the limited freedoms of its black population—began to flow from the General Assembly. Chief among these efforts was a new slave code that built upon the provisions of the colony's 1712 slave code. The new slave code sought to eliminate the freedoms that had allowed the Stono rebels to plot their revolt while also preventing slave owners from engaging in gross abuse by limiting legal work hours, requiring the provision of adequate food and shelter, and punishing obvious abuse.

Author Biography

The writing of the Slave Code of 1740 was undertaken by the leading colonial political authorities, Royal Governor William Bull, and the General Assembly. A second-generation South Carolinian, Bull had himself sporadically served in the colonial assembly since first winning election in 1706 while still in his early twenties. He was considered something of an expert on American Indian affairs, but had acted as colonial governor only since 1737. From the beginning, his term was plagued with difficulties. Along with the constant specter of slave revolts fire, disease, and regional tensions threatened South Carolina's safety during the late 1730s. Bull's handling of the Stono Rebellion had been effective, but not until after the rebels had killed a handful of white colonists and briefly terrorized the countryside. As governor, Bull was charged with maintaining order in the colony; in that respect, he had clearly failed. Assuring his royal overseers in England that measures had been taken to prevent another such rebellion was surely among his main concerns, as the letter he wrote to the authorities concerning the matter emphasized that the rebellion was ended and any rebels-at-large were being rapidly dealt with. Discouraging another incident of the type from happening again followed naturally on this course of action.

South Carolina's General Assembly shared this goal. Created during South Carolina's period as a proprietary colony, the assembly handled internal legislative duties and was composed of elected members. Qualifications for election were economically stringent, however, with members required to hold more than five hundred acres of land along with at least ten slaves; legislators also had to be part of the Anglican Church. The franchise itself was limited to white, Christian men who owned a substantial amount of property. The colonial elite thus made up the legislative body. The interests of this group as a class favored the institution of slavery, on which their agricultural success and personal financial gain largely rested. Yet the members also acknowledged that the continuation of slavery in an atmosphere less conducive to rebellion carried some restrictions on the actions of slaveholders. They thus were willing to write laws that had the potential to directly limit some actions and potentially cost themselves and others of their social class significant sums of money in order to ensure the security of the colony as a whole.

HISTORICAL DOCUMENT

AN ACT FOR THE BETTER ORDERING AND GOV-ERNING NEGROES AND OTHER SLAVES IN THIS PROVINCE

WHEREAS, in his Majesty's plantations in America, slavery has been introduced and allowed, and the people commonly called Negroes, Indians, mulattoes and musti-zoes, have been deemed absolute slaves, and the subjects of property in the hands of the particular persons, the extent of whose power over such slaves ought to be settled and limited by positive laws, so that the slave may be kept in due subjection and obedience, and the owners and other persons having the care and government of slaves may be restrained from exercising too great rigour and cruelty over them, and that the public peace and order of this Province may be preserved: We pray your most sacred Majesty that it may be enacted,

I. *And be it enacted*, by the honorable William Bull, Esquire, Lieutenant Governor and Commander-in-chief, by and with the advice and consent of his Majesty's honorable Council, and the Commons House of Assembly of this Province, and by the authority of the same, That all Negroes and Indians, (free Indians in amity with this government, and degrees, mulattoes, and mustizoes, who are now free, excepted,) mulattoes or mustizoes who now are, or shall hereafter be, in this Province, and all their issue and offspring, born or to be born, shall be, and they are hereby declared to be, and remain forever hereafter, absolute slaves, and shall follow the condition of the mother, and shall be deemed, held, taken, reputed and adjudged in law, to be chattels personal, in the hands of their owners and possessors, and their executors, administrators, and assigns, to all intents, constructions and purposes whatsoever; provided always, that if any Negro, Indian, mulatto or mustizo, shall claim his or her freedom, it shall and may be lawful for such Negro, Indian, mulatto or mustizo, or any person or persons whatsoever, on his or her behalf, to apply to the justices of his Majesty's court of common pleas, by petition or motion, either during the sitting of the said court, or before any of the justices of the same court, at any time in the vacation; and by the said court, or any of the justices thereof, shall, and they are hereby

fully impowered to, admit any person so applying to be guardian for any Negro, Indian, mulatto or mustizo, claiming his, her or their freedom; and such guardians shall be enabled, entitled and capable in law, to bring an action of trespass in the nature of ravishment of ward, against any person who shall claim property in, or who shall be in possession of, any such Negro, Indian, mulatto or mustizo; and the defendant shall and may plead the general issue on such action brought, and the special matter may and shall be given in evidence, and upon a general of special verdict found, judgment shall be given according to the very right of the cause, without having any regard to any defect in the proceedings, either in form or substance; and if judgment shall be given for the plaintiff, a special entry shall be made, declaring that the ward of the plaintiff is free, and the jury shall assess damages which the plaintiff's ward hath sustained, and the court shall give judgment and award execution, against the defendant for such damage, with full costs of suit; but in case judgment shall be given for the defendant, the said court is hereby fully impowered to inflict such corporal punishment, not extending to life or limb, on the ward of the plaintiff, as they, in their discretion, shall think fit; provided always, that in any action or suit to be brought in pursuance of the direction of this Act, the burthen of the proof shall lay on the plaintiff, and it shall be always presumed that every Negro, Indian, mulatto, and mustizo, is a slave, unless the contrary can be made appear, the Indians in amity with this government excepted, in which case the burthen of the proof shall lye on the defendant; provided also, that nothing in this Act shall be construed to hinder or restrain any other court of law or equity in this Province, from determining the property of slaves, or their right to freedom, which now have cognizance or jurisdiction of the same, when the same shall happen to come in judgment before such courts, or any of them always taking this Act for their direction therein.

✳✳✳

VI. *Provided always, and be it further enacted* by the authority aforesaid, That if any Negro or other slave, who shall be employed in the lawful business or service of his master, owner, overseer, or other person having charge of such slave, shall be beaten, bruised, maimed or disabled by any person or persons not having sufficient cause or lawful authority for so doing, (of which cause the justices of the peace, respectively, may judge,) every person and persons so offending, shall, for every such offence, forfeit and pay the sum of forty shillings, current money, over and besides the damages hereinafter mentioned, to the use of the poor of that parish in which such offence shall be committed: And if such slave or slaves shall be maimed or disabled by such beating, from performing his or her work, such person and persons so offending, shall also forfeit and pay to the owner or owners of such slaves, the sum of fifteen shillings, current money, per diem, for every day of his lost time, and also the charge of the cure of such slave; and if the said damages, in whole, shall not exceed the sum of twenty pounds, current money, the same shall , upon lawful proof thereof made, be recoverable before any one of his Majesty's justices of the peace, in the same way and manner as debts are recoverable by the Act for the trial of small and mean causes; and such justices before whom the same shall be recovered, shall have power to commit the offender or offenders to goal, if he, se or they shall produce no goods of which the said penalty and damages may be levied, there to remain without bail, until such penalty and damages shall be paid; any law, statute, usage or custom, to the contrary notwithstanding.

***

XXII. *And be it further enacted* by the authority aforesaid, That if any person in this Province shall, on the Lord's day, commonly called Sunday, employ any slave in any work or labour, (works of absolute necessity and the necessary occasions of the family one excepted,) every person in such case offending, shall forfeit the sum of five pounds, current money, for every slave they shall so work or labour.

***

XXIV. *And be it further enacted* by the authority aforesaid, That if any slave shall presume to strike any white person, such slave, upon trial and conviction before the justice or justices and freeholders, aforesaid, according

to the directions of this Act, shall, for the first and second offence, suffer such punishment as the said justice and freeholders, or such of them as are empowered to try such offence, shall in their discretion, think fit, not extending to life or limb; and for the third offence, shall suffer death. But in case any such slave shall grievously wound, maim or bruise any white person, though it by only the first offence, such slave shall suffer death. Provided always, that such striking, wounding, maiming or bruising, not be done by the command, and in the defense of, the person or property of the owner or other person having the care and government of such slave, in which case the slave shall be wholly excused, and the owner or other person having the care and government of such slave shall be answerable, as far as by law he ought.

XXV. *And be it further enacted* by the authority aforesaid, That it shall and may be lawful for every person in this Province, to take, apprehend and secure any runaway or fugitive slave, and they are hereby directed and required to send such slave to the master or other person having the care or government of such slave, if the person taking up or securing such slave knows, or can, without difficulty, be informed, to whom such slave shall belong; but if not known or discovered, then such slave shall be sent, carried or delivered into the custody of the warden of the work-house in Charlestown; and the master or other person who has the care or government of such slave, shall pay for the taking up of such slave, whether by a free person or slave, the sum of twenty shillings, current money; and the warden of the work-house, upon receipt of every fugitive or runaway slave, is hereby directed and required to keep such slave in safe custody until such slave shall be lawfully discharged, and shall, as soon as conveniently it may be, publish, in the weekly gazette, such slave, with the best descriptions he shall be able to give, first carefully viewing and examining such slave, naked to the waist, for any mark or brand, which he shall also publish to the intent the owner or other person who shall have the care and charge of such slave, may come to the knowledge that such slave is in custody. And if such slave shall make escape through the negligence of the warden of the work-house, and cannot be taken within three months, the said warden of the work-house shall answer to the owner for the value of such slave, or the damage which the owner shall sustain by reason of such escape, as the cause shall happen.

***

XXXVI. And for that as it is absolutely necessary to the safety of this Province, that all due care be taken to restrain the wanderings and meetings of Negroes and other slaves, at all times, and more especially on Saturday nights, Sundays, and other holidays, and their using and carrying wooden swords, and other mischievous and dangerous weapons, or using or keeping of drums, horns, or other loud instruments, which may call together or give sign or notice to one another of their wicked designs and purposes; and that all masters, overseers and others may be enjoined, diligently and carefully to prevent the same, Be it enacted by the authority aforesaid, That it shall be lawful for all masters, overseers and other persons whosoever, to apprehend and take up any Negro or other slave that shall be found out of the plantation of his or their master or owner, at any time, especially on Saturday nights, Sundays or other holiday, not being on lawful business, and with a letter from their master, or a ticket, or not having a white person with them; and the said Negro or other slave or slaves, met or found out of the plantation of his or their master or mistress, though with a letter or ticket, if he or they be armed with such offensive weapons aforesaid, him or them to disarm, take up and whip: And whatsoever master, owner or overseer shall permit or suffer his or their Negro or other slave or slaves, at any time hereafter, to beat drums, blow horns, or use any other loud instruments or whosoever shall suffer and countenance any public meeting or feastings of strange Negroes or slaves in their plantations, shall forfeit ten pounds, current money, for every such offence, upon conviction or proof as aforesaid; provided , an information or other suit be commenced within one month after forfeiture thereof for the same.

GLOSSARY

chattels: property

cognizance: awareness or understanding

corporal punishment: physical or bodily punishment

mulatto: a person of mixed European and African heritage

mustizo: a person of mixed European and Native American heritage; also written *mestizo*

per diem: by the day

ravishment of ward: a legal term describing the kidnapping or sexual trespass of a young or otherwise dependent person

shilling: An English unit of money used in the colonies; equal to twelve pence

ward: a person under the protection of a guardian; often, but not necessarily, under the age of adulthood

Document Analysis

Written in the wake of the Stono Rebellion, South Carolina's slave code of 1740 reflected the concerns that the ruling white slaveholding elite held about the prospect of another uprising. The slave code made laws affecting both slaves and slave owners, but was written for a white colonial audience; this is obvious both from the overall tone of the piece and from a provision barring white slave owners from teaching their slaves to read and write, ensuring that no enslaved person could read the code. Thus the slave code informs slave owners of the rules binding the institution, and, often, of the punishments for various infractions. The 1740 slave code built upon the laws set out in earlier codes, most recently in 1712. Legislators had been debating revisions for several months. The Stono Rebellion encouraged them to speed the process considerably. The finalized code therefore reflected existing colonial practices while responding directly to the perceived causes of the recent uprising.

This goal is clear from the opening language of the document, which announces itself an "act for the better ordering and governing Negroes and other slaves" in South Carolina. Although the slave code was addressed to white slave owners and did contain statutes that applied solely to them, the main purpose of the document was to manage the behavior of enslaved people; the actions of the owners, who are not referenced in this title, were affected only as they were likely to affect the work of the colony's slaves. The introduction to the slave code then goes on to identify the groups typically considered slaves in the colony, and declares that it is the right of the colony to make laws ensuring that "the slave may be kept in due subjection and obedience" even as slaveholders must be "restrained from exercising too great rigour and cruelty." Finally, the preamble states a third goal: preserving "public peace and order," a direct nod to the breakdown of peace that took place during the Stono Rebellion. The remainder of the document serves to provide specific statutes that meet at least one of these three purposes.

The first statute set forth in the slave code formally affirms the custom of chattel slavery, or the holding of enslaved persons and their descendents outright as property. Early in its history, South Carolina had practiced freehold slavery, a variation of the institution that tied enslaved persons to the land rather than to a specific owner. Freehold slavery granted enslaved persons a slightly higher status, as slaveholders owned only a given slave's labor rather than the person himself. Over time, however, the practice of chattel slavery took the place of freehold slavery, and in 1740 the slave code affirmed that all presently enslaved people were legally considered "absolute slaves" who were "chattels personal" of their owners in perpetuity. This laid the groundwork not only for the legality of the restrictive statues that followed but also for the system of slavery that persisted in South Carolina until the Civil War.

At least in theory, however, people taken as slaves who were in fact free had a legal recourse to avoid being pulled into chattel slavery. The slave code established a procedure through which people asserting themselves as free could have their day in court. However, this system was not one conducive to even a truly free person seeking legal liberty. According to the slave code, a wrongfully enslaved person first had to find a separate "guardian" to apply for freedom on his or her behalf. This guardian then had the right to file a legal claim against the person who had allegedly taken the enslaved person wrongfully into service. The slave code placed the burden of proof with the plaintiff, assuming always that any African or American Indian, other than those native peoples "in amity" with the colonial government, were in fact rightfully slaves. If the court found in favor of the plaintiff, the enslaved person was free and granted a financial award for damages; no other repercussions were placed upon the transgressor. If the court found in favor of the defendant, however, the enslaved claimant legally suffered any form of physical punishment that the court deemed fit, short of removing a limb or causing death.

In practice, these restrictions made it extremely difficult for a wrongfully enslaved person to seek justice. The enslaved person could not file his or her own claim with the courts, and so was immediately faced with the challenge of finding someone else willing to undertake the case. Proving one's own freedom in the face of the assumption of slavery was not an easy chore, especially in a time when formal record-keeping was minimal and support for slavery was high; an approximate modern equivalent would be the announcement that all persons accused of a crime were presumed guilty until proven otherwise. The threat of extreme physical violence if the court found against a claimant surely was intended as a deterrent against any but the very strongest of cases. Thus a free person seized as a slave was likely to remain a slave.

The authors of the slave code nevertheless wanted to protect enslaved Africans from the types of gross abuses that they believed had encouraged the outbreak of the Stono Rebellion. Although laws fining white colonists for murdering slaves already existed in South Carolina thanks to the provisions of the 1712 slave code, the revisions enacted in 1740 made them much more stringent. Section VI of the slave code levied a fine of forty shillings on any person who, without good cause, injured—but did not kill—an enslaved person engaged in his or her duties or performing any other legal action. The penalty for injuring the slave so greatly that he or she was rendered unable to perform his or her regular work placed an additional burden of fifteen shillings per lost work day on the offender along with the actual costs of the medical care for the injured party. Assuming the maximum amount of damages was equal to or less than twenty pounds—a substantial sum in a time when the average selling price for an enslaved person in nearby Virginia ranged from twenty-eight to thirty-five pounds—any justice of the peace could hear the matter and order the offender to jail in the event that he could not pay. Thus the slave code suggests that in the minds of its authors the damage done to injured slaves was not punishable on the grounds of either moral concerns or civil liberty violations, but rather on economic ones; the value of slaves purely as laborers rather than humans is apparent in the decision to imprison only those offenders who could not provide sufficient monetary recompense not to the actual injured person, but to the slaveholder whose plantation went partially untended due to the lack of a worker.

The wording of the statute left much interpretation available to the courts, which determined, for example, whether the offending party had suitable cause for inflicting injury. The law also left colonists free to engage in violence against enslaved persons who were not "employed in the lawful business or service" of their owners, freeing any white colonist of legal blame for physically punishing a slave who broke any of the other numerous statutes limiting their behavior as laid out in the slave code.

In stark contrast, enslaved persons who engaged in violence against white owners or colonists faced much graver consequences than a simple fine or even the threat of jail time. From the outset, the bar of offending behavior was set lower and the level of required punishment much higher. While a person engaging in violence against an African slave had to cause enough damage that the victim was considered "beaten, bruised, maimed or disabled," a slave needed only to "strike any white person" to draw the ire of the slave code upon him or herself. Offenders were granted the right to a trial, although proving one's own innocence would have been severely hampered by the social and legal restrictions of the day; other portions of the code, for example, required a trial that could result in the death penalty to take place within three days of the slave's entry into custody. Upon conviction, first- and second-time offenders were subject to any form of punishment deemed appropriate by the courts short of the removal of a limb or execution. Third-time offenders, however, were executed. This le-

gal imbalance meant that a slave who merely slapped a white overseer could potentially face death as a result.

The repercussions for a slave who managed to "grievously wound, maim or bruise any white person" were even more severe. Even first-time offenders faced the death penalty for their actions. Thus, a white person who beat a black slave so severely that the injured party was unable to work faced only a financial punishment, while a slave who inflicted a bruise on a white colonist faced certain death. The higher colonial value of white safety and security is apparent in such a divide.

Exceptions to the law existed, but essentially served to protect white slaveholders rather than black slaves. Slaves were exempted from punishment if the violence in question was undertaken on the order of the slaveholder or master, or to protect that person from violence. In such an instance, the white colonist ordering or benefiting from the attack was liable under the law rather than the slave. As the laws affecting white colonists were not as harsh as those affecting African slaves, the penalties for the initiator of the attack may be assumed to be less than those than the slave would have suffered if he had undertaken the action of his own accord—another clear breach of the concept of equality under the law. Yet the exception allowed white slaveholders to rely on their slaves to take physical risks to protect their owners' safety. Worth noting, too, is that the slave code grants no exemptions for slaves who undertake violence in their own self-defense. Thus, a slave who fought back an attack from a while colonist faced the same legal repercussions as one who engaged in an entirely unprovoked attack.

The next section of the slave code establishes South Carolinian law regarding runaway slaves. Earlier legislation had sought to deter slaves from running away and to punish white colonists who encouraged slaves to desert their posts, presumably to illegally work for these new masters. But the events of the 1730s encouraged the act of running away more so than in the past. Until 1733, South Carolina shared a border with Spanish Florida because the colony of Georgia did not yet divide the two. Even after Georgia was established as a colony, only a small strip of land separated South Carolina from Spanish Florida, which from 1734 promised liberty to any fugitive slaves who entered the territory. Rumors of successful runaway attempts presumably attracted slaves to try to win liberty for themselves in that way, and numerous slaves tried to escape do Spanish Florida during that time. Additionally, Florida was the probable destination of the Stono rebels, making tight provisions against running away essential to the slave code's overall goal of enhancing the safety and security of the white slave-holding populace.

The post-Stono slave code thus enacted several measures to deter potential runaways. The law formally enabled "every person in the Province" to act as a fugitive slave catcher and required that person to return the runaway to his or her owner or overseer. If the owner was not known and could not be readily discovered, the slave was instead sent to Charleston. There, he or she—although the majority of runaways were men—was held at a workhouse. The warden was then required to regularly publish a description of all runaway slaves held so that owners or overseers had the opportunity to locate their missing property. These advertisements appeared regularly in the colonial newspaper, and serve as one of the best primary sources for modern historians to learn about the act of running away during this period. Upon identifying the fugitive, the owner paid a reward of twenty shillings to reclaim the runaway. Yet being held in the workhouse was no guarantee that a slave dedicated to winning his freedom would not run away again. This prospect must have been very real, for the law requires the warden to compensate the slaveholder for either the value of the slave or the costs entailed by his flight should a slave manage to escape again and elude capture for at least three months.

Among the restrictions placed by the slave code on slave owners were those affecting working days and hours. Section XXII, for example, barred slave owners from requiring enslaved persons to work on Sundays; an exception was granted for "works of absolute necessity and the necessary operations of the family," meaning that the law limited ongoing agricultural labor as opposed to work done by domestic slaves who performed duties such as meal preparation. A later section barred slave owners from requiring slaves to work in excess of fifteen hours in any given day during the agricultural season and fourteen hours per day during the off season. These strictures were made to prevent the gross abuse of slaves by requiring them to work around the clock or without a sufficient rest period. The authors of the slave code hoped that such restrictions would provide living conditions that were less likely to incite enslaved persons from running away or rebelling against their masters. To encourage compliance, the code levied fines on slave owners who required their slaves to work in violation of these rules.

Some aspects of the slave code sought to limit the abilities of enslaved persons to travel, assemble, or even engage in simple cultural practices; these restrictions stemmed largely from the perceived beginnings of the Stono Rebellion. Section XXXVI of the slave code, for example, bars slaves from traveling on their own, particularly during times when they were unlikely to be working—Saturday nights, Sundays, and holidays. The authors of the slave code believed that this freedom of movement allowed enslaved persons to meet and plan uprisings or other measures that could threaten the stability of the colony. The statute also outlaws the keeping of weapons—a fairly obvious measure to deter armed rebellion—along with the playing of drums or other instruments that "may call together or give sign" of an impending uprising. The Stono rebels had marched to the beat of drums, creating a distinct connection between the prospect of slave rebellion and that instrument in the colonial mind. The punishment for such an infraction once again reflected the divisions established throughout the code: enslaved Africans suffered physical harm, while white colonists faced economic penalties.

Other sections of the code mandated various measures for both slave and slaveholder. Travel by enslaved persons, though generally barred, was allowed if the traveler carried a standardized pass or ticket granting permission from the owner. To prevent slaves from writing their own tickets or communicating secretly, they were forbidden to learn to read or write. Strictures also required slaveholders to provide a basic standard of living for their slaves, including providing adequate shelter, food, and clothing. These diverse measures all served to meet the same purpose: keeping slaves well under the thumb of their masters and unwilling or unable to rise up against the institution of slavery as individuals or in a mass rebellion.

Essential Themes

The slave code instituted by South Carolina in 1740 influenced not only that colony and, later, state, but also other slave-holding colonies and states in the nascent United States in a variety of ways. The concept of chattel slavery did not initiate in South Carolina—the colony itself drew on the practices of other English slaveholding territories such as Barbados—but its formalization in the colony was an important step in the spread of the institution throughout the southeastern United States. The influence of the system of chattel slavery around the nation proved immense. Granting one person the legal right to entirely own another person became a moral issue that drove the nineteenth-century abolition movement and, eventually, set the stage for the American Civil War. On a broader scale, the laws set forth in the slave code were closely followed by the colony of Georgia, which was first formed from land taken from Carolina during the 1730s. Although slavery was initially barred in Georgia, the colony allowed the institution after 1750. The practices of and attitudes about slavery in Georgia largely came to mirror those of its geographic parent.

The attitudes of South Carolinians towards slaves are apparent in the statutes of the slave code. In addition to deeming enslaved persons property and stripping them of the few civil liberties that they had retained to that point, the slave code also focused heavily on slaves as an economic resource, in sharp opposition to the definition of white colonists as humans whose safety did not carry a readily a defined price. White colonists who injured slaves paid the costs associated with their lost economic value or reduced labor; slaves who injured white colonists paid with their lives. The acceptance of enslaved Africans as economic instruments is evident in these distinctions, and indeed this view of slaves endured in South Carolina. Although colonists in places such as Virginia saw the institution of slavery as a problematic economic necessity that would eventually end in the United States, South Carolinians saw no such disconnect. Local support for slavery was so great in South Carolina that the colony demanded concessions on the issue from Northern politicians as a condition for its participation in the American Revolution just thirty-five years after the writing of the slave code. The value of slaves as economic resources later contributed to South Carolina's willingness to secede from the United States; even after the Civil War ended, former slaves became sharecroppers with civil rights that were restricted through state law, a continuance of the government-sponsored classification of black Americans as lower human beings suitable only for labor.

Vanessa E. Vaughn, MA

Bibliography

Bull, Kinloch. "William Bull." *American National Biography.* Oxford UP. n.d. Web. 17 May 2012.

Eltis, David. *The Rise of African Slavery in the Americas.* New York: Cambridge UP, 2000. Print.

"Transcription of 1740 Slave Code." *Teaching American History in South Carolina.* Teaching American History in South Carolina Project, 2009. Web. 7 May 2012

Tyer, Charlie B. and Richard D. Young. "The South Carolina Legislature." *The South Carolina Governance Project.* Center for Governmental Services, Institute for Public Service and Policy Research, University of South Carolina. n.d. Web. 17 May 2012

Wood, Peter H. *Black Majority: Negroes in South Carolina from 1670 through the Stono Rebellion.* New York: Norton, 1974. Print.

Additional Reading

Berlin, Ira. *Many Thousands Gone: The First Two Centuries of Slavery in North America.* Cambridge, MA: Harvard UP, 1998. Print.

Hoffer, Peter Charles. *Cry Liberty: The Great Stono River Slave Rebellion of 1739.* New York: OUP, 2010. Print.

Reiss, Oscar. *Blacks in Colonial America.* Jefferson, NC: McFarland, 1997. Print.

Smith, Mark M. *Stono: Documenting and Interpreting a Southern Slave Revolt.* Columbia, SC: U of South Carolina P, 2005. Print.

Thomas, Hugh. *The Slave Trade.* New York: Simon, 1997. Print.

Wood, Betty. *Slavery in Colonial America: 1619–1776.* Lanham, MD: Rowman, 2005. Print.

LESSON PLAN: South Carolina Slavery Laws

Students analyze the Slave Code of South Carolina and its practical effect on slaves and slaveholders.

Learning Objectives

Reconstruct the literal meaning of the slave code sections; identify the central purpose and cause of the slave code's enactment; consider the values of the authors of the code in the context of their times; read Venture Smith's narrative and Eliza Lucas's letters imaginatively in the context of slave code realities.

Materials: South Carolina General Assembly, Slave Code of South Carolina (May 1740): Sections I, VI, XXIV, XXV, XXII, and XXXVI; Eliza Lucas, *Letters on Plantation Life* (1739–1762); Venture Smith, *A Narrative of the Life and Adventures of Venture, a Native of Africa* (1798).

Overview Questions

What are the main points of each of the slave code's cited sections? Why was the code revised in 1740? How does it value enslaved people, and what does this suggest about slave owners in South Carolina? How would the code affect specific individuals?

Step 1: Comprehension Questions

How does the Slave Code of South Carolina define slaves? What specific limitations are put on slaves? What specific limitations are put on slave owners?

▶ **Activity:** Have a student read the section defining a slave. Discuss the breadth of the definition. Instruct students to write summaries of each section and cite limitations the code puts on slaves and slave owners.

Step 2: Comprehension Questions

What events caused the South Carolina legislature to revise the colony's slave code? How did those events shape the revision?

▶ **Activity:** Have students review the Stono Rebellion (also called Cato's Rebellion), including its causes and specific chronology. Challenge students to match sections of the slave code to the causes of the rebellion.

Step 3: Context Questions

Why are the slaves generally treated harshly in the code? Why are there also provisions to protect them? Why are there provisions to punish slave owners under some circumstances?

▶ **Activity:** Challenge students to find passages that suggest slaves are considered anything more than property. Have students discuss why the code has warnings and fines for slave owners. Discuss the varied reasons why it seems somewhat protective of slaves.

Step 4: Exploration Questions

If Venture Smith had lived in South Carolina, how would the slave code have altered his life? How was Eliza Lucas affected by the code?

▶ **Activity:** Have students review Smith's narrative and Lucas's letters. Discuss how Smith would have fared if he was enslaved in South Carolina. Discuss how Lucas probably benefited from the slave code. Direct students to use these two historical figures to contrast how the code affected slaves and slave owners.

Step 5: Response Paper

Word length and additional requirements set by Instructor. Students answer the research question in the Overview Questions. Students state a thesis and use as evidence passages from the primary source document as well as support from supplemental materials assigned in the lesson.

■ Benjamin Franklin on Reverend George Whitefield

Date: 1788
Author: Franklin, Benjamin
Genre: memoir; essay

"It was wonderful to see the Change soon made in the Manners of our Inhabitants; . . . it seem'd as if all the World were growing Religious. . . .

And methinks my Testimony in his Favour ought to have the more Weight, as we had no religious Connection."

Summary Overview

In this document, Benjamin Franklin writes about some of the public events that occurred during his friendship with Reverend George Whitefield, who was one of the principal traveling evangelists of the religious revival known as the First Great Awakening. Although focusing on Whitefield, this passage also gives information regarding Franklin's approach to life. Franklin documents the manner in which Whitefield is able to bring people around to his way of thinking, sharing these events both to demonstrate the importance of Whitefield and to clarify Whitefield's intrinsic honesty. The fact that Franklin and Whitefield have strongly differing ideas about religion is contrasted with their ability to remain friends and to cooperate in other areas. In addition, the common religious experiences described in this passage helped build the emerging American culture that challenged the colonial rule of Great Britain.

Defining Moment

The 1700s were a time of great change in the American colonies. Benjamin Franklin witnessed these changes not just as an observer but as a participant. This memoir is taken from the section of Franklin's *Autobiography* that was written in 1788. Franklin had started writing

his autobiography some seventeen years earlier, seeking to inform people regarding some of the events of his life. Initially, it was written for his son, but the latter sections were written after he and his son split over their views concerning American Revolution, and thus these were directed toward a more general audience. The section in which this passage appears deals with Franklin's desire to instill personal values, including morality and a strong work ethic, in his readers.

Just prior to this passage Franklin discusses how his work as a printer advanced his cause, especially through the publication of *Poor Richard's Almanac*. He also discusses advances made through the various civic organizations with which he was associated, many of which he had started. George Whitefield entered the picture as an accomplished preacher who had many of the same ideals as Franklin. Whitefield saw these ideals as the result of a strong, personal Christian faith. While Franklin agreed that they were an integral aspect of religion, he suggested that, perhaps more importantly, they were also a necessary part of an enlightened society. Thus, Franklin's emphasis on the change in the people who accepted Whitefield's message was not focused on personal salvation, but rather on the utilitarian benefits of living a virtuous and moral life. Franklin's lack of religious response to Whitefield's view of personal salvation is why Franklin says they have no "religious connection."

Against the background of Franklin's writings, something greater was occurring in the colonies: An American culture was flourishing, one that would give the colonies the ability to unite in their grievances against the British government. The Great Awakening was giving new life to religion in the colonies as it was transformed from the traditional forms brought from the Old World. Denominational differences were not as strong, with people from a variety of churches gathering to experience the preaching of well-known evangelists.

Author Biography

Benjamin Franklin was born in Boston, Massachusetts, on January 17, 1706. His father, Josiah, had emigrated from England, while his mother, Abiah, had been born in Massachusetts. Ben was the fourteenth of seventeen children. Raised in a Puritan home, his parents encouraged Franklin to enter the ministry, but his inclinations, as well as his limited formal education, took him in a different direction. Leaving school at age ten, Franklin worked in family businesses for the next seven years. During this time he developed a strong understanding of the need for personal moral development and social outreach, and began to try to influence others through articles on the subject. The five years he worked as a printer gave him the skills and business experience he needed to become a success.

In 1728, he and a partner set up a printing business in Philadelphia. Initially through the *Pennsylvania Gazette* and then through the successful *Poor Richard's Almanac* in 1733, Franklin began to advocate moral development, especially through many adages that would later become very popular. During this time he took Deborah Read as his common-law wife and they had two children, with Franklin previously having had a son. In the 1740s, Franklin sold his printing business to spend his time on social, scientific, and political endeavors.

His social contributions to life in Philadelphia included the first hospital in the colonies, and what became the public library, the fire department, and the University of Pennsylvania. Franklin had wide range of scientific interests, but he principally worked in the field of physics. Electricity is the best-known area of his research, but he also worked in the areas of thermodynamics and sound, as well as the philosophical foundations of science and life in general. Through his research, Franklin invented many devices to make life more comfortable.

Politically, Franklin represented Pennsylvania, and later many of the colonies, to the British government. He played an important role in the repeal of the Stamp Act, which had enraged the colonies. Franklin represented Pennsylvania to the Second Continental Congress and served on the committee that drew up the Declaration of Independence. During the Revolutionary War he was the ambassador to France, playing a vital role in securing French support for the new nation. He negotiated the Treaty of Paris, which formally ended the Revolutionary War. Later, he served as a member of the Constitutional Convention and as president (now the office of governor) of Pennsylvania.

HISTORICAL DOCUMENT

In 1739 arrived among us from Ireland the Reverend Mr. Whitefield, who had made himself remarkable there as an itinerant Preacher. He was at first permitted to preach in some of our Churches; but the Clergy, taking a Dislike to him, soon refus'd him their Pulpits, and he was oblig'd to preach in the Fields. The Multitudes of all Sects and Denominations that attended his Sermons were enormous, and it was [a] matter of Speculation to me, who was one of the Number, to observe the extraordinary Influence of his Oratory on his Hearers, and how much they admir'd & respected him, notwithstanding his common Abuse of them, by assuring them they were naturally half Beasts and half Devils. It was wonderful to see the Change soon made in the Manners of our Inhabitants; from being thoughtless or indifferent about Religion, it seem'd as if all the World were growing Religious, so that one could not walk thro' the Town in an Evening without Hearing Psalms sung in different Families of every Street.

And it being found inconvenient to assemble in the open Air, subject to its Inclemencies, the Building of a

House to meet in was no sooner propos'd, and Persons appointed to receive Contributions, but sufficient Sums were soon receiv'd to procure the Ground and erect the Building, which was 100 feet long & 70 broad, about the Size of Westminster Hall; and the Work was carried on with such Spirit as to be finished in a much shorter time than could have been expected. Both House and Ground were vested in Trustees, expressly for the Use of any Preacher of any religious Persuasion who might desire to say something to the People of Philadelphia, the Design [purpose] in building not being to accommodate any particular Sect, but the Inhabitants in general, so that even if the Mufti of Constantinople were to send a Missionary to preach Mahometanism [Islam] to us, he would find a Pulpit at his Service.

Mr. Whitefield, in leaving us, went preaching all the Way thro' the Colonies to Georgia. The Settlement of that Province had lately been begun, but instead of being made with hardy industrious Husbandmen [farmers] accustomed to Labour the only People fit for such an Enterprise it was with Families of broken Shopkeepers and other insolvent Debtors, many of indolent & idle habits, taken out of the Gaols [jails], who being set down in the Woods, unqualified for clearing Land, & unable to endure the Hardships of a new Settlement, perished in Numbers, leaving many helpless Children unprovided for. The Sight of their miserable Situation inspir'd the benevolent Heart of Mr. Whitefield with the Idea of building an Orphan House there, in which they might be supported and educated. Returning northward, he preach'd up this Charity, & made large Collections;—for his eloquence had a wonderful Power over the Hearts & Purses of his Hearers, of which I myself was an Instance.

I did not disapprove of the Design [plan], but as Georgia was then destitute of Materials & Workmen, and it was propos'd to send them from Philadelphia at a great Expense, I thought it would have been better to have built the House here [Philadelphia] and brought the Children to it. This I advis'd, but he was resolute in his first Project, rejected my Counsel, and I thereupon refus'd to contribute. I happened soon after to attend one of his Sermons, in the Course of which I perceived he intended to finish with a Collection, & I silently resolved he should get nothing from me. I had in my Pocket a Handful of Copper Money, three or four silver Dollars, and five Pis-

toles [Spanish coins] in Gold. As he proceeded I began to soften, and concluded to give the Coppers. Another Stroke of his Oratory made me asham'd of that, and determin'd me to give the Silver; and he finish'd so admirably that I empty'd my pocket wholly into the Collector's Dish, Gold and all. At this Sermon there was also one of our Club, who being of my Sentiments respecting the Building in Georgia, and suspecting a Collection might be intended, had by Precaution emptied his Pockets before he came from home. Towards the Conclusion of the Discourse, however, he felt a strong Desire to give, and apply'd to a Neighbour who stood near him to borrow some Money for the Purpose. The Application was unfortunately to perhaps the only Man in the Company [audience] who had the firmness not to be affected by the Preacher. His Answer was, "At any other time, Friend Hopkinson, I would lend to thee freely; but not now, for thee seems to be out of thy right Senses."

Some of Mr. Whitefield's Enemies affected to suppose that he would apply these Collections to his own private Emolument [profit], but I, who was intimately acquainted with him (being employ'd in printing his Sermons and Journals, &c.) never had the least Suspicion of his Integrity, but am to this day decidedly of Opinion that he was in all his Conduct a perfectly honest Man. And methinks my Testimony in his Favour ought to have the more Weight, as we had no religious Connection. He us'd, indeed, sometimes to pray for my Conversion, but never had the Satisfaction of believing that his Prayers were heard. Ours was a mere civil Friendship, sincere on both Sides, and lasted to his Death.

The following Instance will show something of the Terms on which we stood. Upon one of his Arrivals from England at Boston, he wrote to me that he should come soon to Philadelphia, but knew not where he could lodge when there, as he understood his old kind Host, Mr. Benezet, was remov'd to Germantown. My Answer was: "You know my House; if you can make shift with its scanty Accommodations, you will be most heartily welcome." He reply'd that, if I made that kind Offer for Christ's sake, I should not miss of a Reward. And I return'd, "Don't let me be mistaken; it was not for Christ's sake, but for your sake." One of our common Acquaintance jocosely remark'd that, knowing it to be the Custom of the Saints, when they receiv'd any favour, to shift the Burden of the

Obligation from off their own Shoulders and place it in Heaven, I had contriv'd to fix it on Earth.

The last time I saw Mr. Whitefield was in London, when he consulted me about his Orphan House Concern, and his Purpose of appropriating it to the Establishment of a College. He had a loud and clear Voice, and articulated his Words & Sentences so perfectly that he might be heard and understood at a great Distance, especially as his Auditories [listeners], however numerous, observ'd the most exact Silence. He preach'd one Evening from the Top of the Court House Steps, which are in the middle of Market Street, and on the West Side of Second Street which crosses it at right angles. Both Streets were fill'd with his Hearers to a considerable Distance. Being among the hindmost in Market Street, I had the Curiosity to learn how far he could be heard, by retiring backwards down the Street towards the River; and I found his Voice distinct till I came near Front Street, when some Noise in that Street obscur'd it. Imagining then a Semi-Circle, of which my Distance should be the Radius, and that it were fill'd with Auditors, to each of whom I allow'd two square feet, I computed that he might well be heard by more than Thirty Thousand. This reconcil'd me to the Newspaper Accounts of his having preach'd to 25,000 People in the Fields, and to the ancient Histories of Generals haranguing whole Armies, of which I had sometimes doubted.

By hearing him often, I came to distinguish easily between Sermons newly compos'd & those which he had often preach'd in the Course of his Travels. His Delivery of the latter was so improv'd by frequent Repetitions that every Accent, every Emphasis, every Modulation of Voice, was so perfectly well turn'd and well plac'd that, without being interested in the Subject, one could not help being pleas'd with the Discourse, a Pleasure of much the same kind with that receiv'd from an excellent Piece of Music. This is an Advantage itinerant Preachers have over those who are stationary, as the latter cannot well improve their Delivery of a Sermon by so many Rehearsals.

His Writing and Printing from time to time gave great Advantage to his Enemies. Unguarded Expressions and even erroneous Opinions delivered in Preaching, might have been afterwards explain'd or qualify'd by supposing others that might have accompany'd them, or they might have been deny'd; but litera scripta manet. Critics attack'd his Writings violently, and with so much Appearance of Reason as to diminish the Number of his Votaries [adherents] and prevent their Increase; so that I am of Opinion if he had never written anything he would have left behind him a much more numerous and important Sect, and his Reputation might in that case have been still growing, even after his Death; as there being nothing of his Writing on which to found a Censure and give him a lower Character [reputation], his Proselytes would be left at Liberty to feign for him as great a Variety of Excellencies [good features] as their enthusiastic Admiration might wish him to have possessed.

GLOSSARY

censure: criticism intended to diminish a person's influence

Grand Mufti of Constantinople: the highest Islamic religious official in what became the Ottoman Empire

itinerant preacher: an individual who traveled from place to place to proclaim his or her understanding of the Christian message

inclemencies: bad weather

jocosely: jokingly

litera scripta manet: a Latin phrase meaning "the written word endures"

oratory: public speaking, in this case a sermon

proselytes: people who convert to and follow a religious belief, in this case Whitefield's teachings regarding Christianity

psalms: hymns; both terms were used synonymously in the eighteenth century

Document Analysis

Benjamin Franklin's essay on the power of Reverend George Whitefield's preaching illustrates the changes that occurred during the Great Awakening. Whitefield was a British preacher who epitomized this religious revolution, which was taking place both in the British Isles and in the American colonies. Franklin was never a proponent of Whitefield's particular brand of religious enthusiasm. Yet in this essay it is evident that he was moved by the words of the reverend and identified with the social outreach advocated by Whitefield. The two men were friends for more than thirty years, despite their differences in interpretation of what would later be called the Great Awakening. The essay also demonstrates how individuals who are not in complete agreement can still share the same values and social goals. It also shows the manner in which Franklin tried to understand the world around him.

George Whitefield was an ordained minister in the Anglican Church. While at Oxford University, he helped found the Holy Club, whose members later became known as Methodists. Methodists emphasized Bible study, church attendance, spiritual exercises for personal growth, and outreach to the poor and those in prison. This included those in need in the colonies, especially the penal colony in Georgia. Early in the club's existence Whitefield and John Wesley, the founder of Methodism, were its leaders. Whitefield continued to lead the club when Wesley went to the Georgia colony to be its chaplain. During this period Whitefield was introduced to the idea of preaching in the open air, rather than only in church sanctuaries. When Wesley returned from Georgia in 1738, Whitefield went to replace him. Seeing the need for an orphanage, he returned to Britain after four months to raise the necessary funds. He returned to the American colonies in 1739 to secure the final funds and materials necessary for the orphanage and to carry the Christian message to the colonists. This is the journey described in the opening of the essay.

Whitefield represents the transformation of religion in the colonies. It would seem that he should have been welcomed into most of the Protestant churches in the colonies, the Anglican Church (Church of England) being the dominant sect in most of the colonies. In addition, Whitefield accepted Calvinist theology, as was the case for the Puritans. However, Whitefield's beliefs and methods differed from the traditional approaches of both the Anglican and Puritan churches.

As Franklin put it, Whitefield's preaching was based on his belief that prior to accepting the Christian faith, people were "naturally half Beasts and half Devils." In addition, Whitefield did not exclusively invite members of the Anglican Church to his services; rather he encouraged everyone to attend. His message was one of personal responsibility and salvation and included the need to respond as an individual, not as part of a larger community. By moving outside the established order of the various churches, Whitefield challenged their authority. His teachings upset the religious leaders of colonial America. As a result, they "soon refus'd him their Pulpits, and he was obliged to preach in the Fields."

But Whitefield's ability to raise funds quickly and construct a nondenominational assembly house underscores the widespread support he received from the community at large. Through this action, and his successes, he demonstrated his ability to draw otherwise indifferent colonists to his flock. In the first paragraph, Franklin makes it clear how impressed he is by Whitefield's ability to move people toward religion. Despite his own tendency toward humanism, he welcomes the newfound religious fervor in the people he sees around him, illustrated by the hymns (psalms) he hears sung in private homes each evening. Franklin supported this change because he believed that religion provided a strong foundation for the moral virtues he advocated.

Reflection on Franklin's friendship with Whitefield demonstrates Franklin's scientific mind, as well as the many qualities that helped Franklin become a political and social leader later on. In all aspects of life, it seems as if Franklin wanted to understand everything. When Whitefield arrived in 1739, Franklin was intrigued by this new preacher. He listened to his sermons in an effort to understand how one person could have such a large impact upon so many. (Whitefield had been known to draw thousands of listeners to his outdoor sermons.)

Generally, Franklin saw the Great Awakening and Whitefield's arrival as positive events, because he was a strong advocate of personal virtue and morality, traits that the followers of the new religious movement valued as well. Franklin's writings usually ignored most Christian doctrine, even though he considered himself a Christian and was interested in the teachings of the various religious leaders of the time. In 1726 Franklin developed a list of thirteen virtues that he wanted to develop within himself and thought desirable in others. He recalls in this memoir how he was pleased with people accepting the personal challenges put to them by Whitefield.

Boston, the northernmost major port in the colonies, was an unusual point of arrival for Whitefield, considering his intent to reach the southernmost colony of Georgia. However, he did this so that he could preach in each colony along his journey. With the coming of the Great Awakening, there was a great demand for preachers who focused on personal salvation. Prior to the rise of Whitefield, and American preachers such as Jonathan Edwards, churches and pastors were mainly concerned with doctrinal theology. This was the result of the proliferation of denominations during the preceding two centuries and the constant disputes regarding various points of doctrine. Thus individuals who attended most church services prior to the Great Awakening would hear a long theological treatise each Sunday. Although some local pastors played a role in the Great Awakening, as a traveling preacher and evangelist, Whitefield was able to reach many more people than did local church pastors. Although challenged by traditional religious leaders, Whitefield was welcomed by many of the laypeople, who responded to his message.

The dramatic need for an orphanage in Georgia came about because of its establishment as a penal colony. Certain English citizens convicted of a crime were given the choice to serve an extended jail sentence in England, or go to Georgia and to start a new life in America. Many of those who chose the latter did not come equipped with the skills to survive in the primitive colonial frontier. In addition, the preparations settlers normally made before moving to the colonies were not possible for those who were transported to Georgia. Of the original 144 colonists, about two-thirds survived. Many children were left alone after their parents perished.

Whitefield's power as an orator is apparent in Franklin's response to the collection being taken for the orphanage. Although Franklin approved of the project, he initially only intended to support it financially if it was located in Philadelphia. However, Whitefield was such an eloquent and powerful speaker that Franklin was persuaded by steps to empty "my pocket wholly into the Collector's Dish, Gold and all." The power of Whitefield's proclamation and his ability to get most individuals to respond was almost unheard of at that time.

It is clear that Franklin had some differences with Whitefield regarding the orphanage. Franklin desired that the orphans be brought to Philadelphia, while Whitefield wanted to help them in Georgia. With regard to religion, Franklin wrote that Whitefield "us'd, indeed, sometimes to pray for my Conversion, but never had the Satisfaction of believing that his Prayers were heard." And so it was on a number of issues that there was disagreement. While Whitefield's motives were always driven by his Christian faith, Franklin's were guided by his scientific and analytical perceptions of the world around him.

Franklin's analytical mind and scientific interests are reflected in his calculation of how many people at one time might be able to hear Whitefield preach. Happening upon Whitefield preaching at the London court house, Franklin went down the street until the noise of the city drowned out Whitefield. Calculating the area of a semicircle with a radius of the distance from Franklin to Whitefield, and assuming the number of square feet occupied by a single listener, Franklin estimated the number of people potentially within earshot of Whitefield at more than thirty thousand.

He also examined the development of Whitefield's oratorical skills through an examination of what today would be called his "stock sermons": "His Delivery of the latter was so improv'd by frequent Repetitions that every Accent, every Emphasis, every Modulation of Voice, was so perfectly well turn'd and well plac'd that, without being interested in the Subject, one could not help being pleas'd with the Discourse, a Pleasure of much the same kind with that receive'd from an excellent Piece of Music." Thus, Franklin's inquiring mind sought to understand the physical as well as the theological dynamics of Whitefield's preaching.

Franklin used his professional and business skills to assist Whitefield's ministry, as he had been "employ'd in printing his Sermons and Journals, &c." Decades later, Franklin analyzed the result of Whitefield's publications and believed them to have had a negative impact upon people's views of Whitefield. In contrast to the spoken word, in an era prior to audio recordings, the written word was lasting. It was there for people to read, examine, and contemplate. Thus, Franklin believed that Whitefield's opponents successfully used his printed sermons and writings against him in various disputes, causing him to lose popularity over time, whereas Franklin thought if Whitefield had concentrated on preaching rather than publishing, "his Reputation might in that case have been still growing, even after his Death."

Throughout this essay, it is clear that individualism was growing in this period. Although most colonists personally made the decision to emigrate to America, they came to the New World as a part of a group. Rules and regulations for each colony were established by those organizing the groups. Decisions about social welfare projects were made within the small leadership circle of the colony, or by the royal governor. The leaders of the established churches (synonymous with the political leadership in some colonies) took care of other tasks. However, Franklin's account of Whitefield's ministry shows new approaches to social problems. Whitefield felt free to preach in any location, regardless of what the colonial religious leaders had to say. In order to facilitate the free expression of ideas by Whitefield and others, the people of Philadelphia constructed a nondenominational meeting hall. Having seen the need for an orphanage, which the colonial leaders were unable or unwilling to meet, Whitefield traveled to Britain and throughout the colonies to raise the funds needed for the project. He did this not by appealing to groups that might be interested; rather he went directly to the individual American colonists for support. He published tracts to challenge individuals to accept his understanding of the Christian faith. He also went into all types of places to appeal directly to the individual to make a personal decision regarding faith.

Through all these actions, it can be seen that the individual was becoming the foundation for social action. While there were still leaders in the various economic, social, and political organizations, individuals could no longer be taken for granted. This growth in the degree of personal choice became very important in the colonies. The freedom to have differing views on religion was an important step.

In Franklin's writings about Whitefield, it is possible to learn a great deal about both men, as well as about conditions in the colonies. The strength of these two leaders and their ability to work with other people demonstrated the strength that would be needed in the coming decades as colonists struggled to secure their desired political and economic goals. Throughout his life, Franklin sought to assist in worthwhile civic projects. Thus, when Whitefield needed a place to stay in Philadelphia while carrying on his ministry, Franklin offered the use of his home. When Whitefield accepted this offer and spoke in theological terms of its value for the Christian mission, Franklin replied that that was not the motivation behind his hospitality: "Don't let

me be mistaken, it was not for Christ's sake, but for your sake." His offer of housing illustrates the common-sense approach he took to most things in his life.

Because of the Great Awakening and projects such as the orphanage, the separate colonies had begun to have a common vision for their future. They began to see that it was not only possible, but beneficial, to reach across boundaries and assist each other. The fact that people in all the colonies were being exposed to this new form of Christian preaching illustrates that a common culture and experience was developing all along the Atlantic coast. A unified America was emerging from the various colonial enterprises.

Essential Themes

Although some of the American colonies were founded on a basis of religious toleration, most did not guarantee religious freedom for all people. Colonies generally had an established church with the expectation that all colonists would be members of that denomination. In the 1730s, new energy was felt by many inside and outside the various colonial churches. The Great Awakening began to demand that individuals respond to the call to demonstrate their faith; it transformed the various Protestant churches into American entities. Rather than maintaining the status quo, the churches began to revitalize society. With the disestablishment of the colonial churches in the upcoming decades, the churches that participated in the spirit of the Great Awakening were the churches that grew into the leading civic organizations of American society. The acceptance of a renewed emphasis on individual faith and salvation became the norm within many denominations. The effect of this emphasis is a major source of the difference between American and European branches of some denominations.

Social outreach, including personal responsibility to underwrite these activities, came to the forefront. The individual working with others, and yet still independent, to achieve desired ends was the manner in which American society developed. Both the personal examples of Franklin and Whitefield, as well as the projects described in the memoir, demonstrate how individuals can successfully work together. Individuals such as Franklin and Whitefield could use their skills to make major contributions and to assist others to see the possibilities of cooperation. Individuals in the crowds that Whitefield addressed, or who read what Franklin printed, understood that through uniting for a common purpose, they also could have a major effect on other's lives.

As Franklin reflected on a few points in his relationship with George Whitefield, he brought forward several aspects of life in the middle of the eighteenth century. The most obvious aspect is the religious revival that occurred and shaped many facets of colonial life. The Great Awakening not only brought a lively version of the Christian faith into many homes, it also started to unify the culture. Although regionalism continued to exist, this step toward an American culture and identity was a factor in the ability of the various colonies to co-operate politically. The willingness of many in the colonies to help those in need in the new colony of Georgia illustrates this growing unity.

Donald A. Watt, PhD

Bibliography

Cragg, G. R. *The Church and the Age of Reason 1648–1789*. Baltimore: Penguin, 1990. Print.

Drexler, Kenneth, Susan Garfinkel, Mark F. Hall, and Jurretta Jordan Heckscher. "Finding Franklin: A Resource Guide." *Library of Congress*. Library of Congress, Feb. 2006. Web. 27 Feb. 2012.

Stout, Harry S. *The Divine Dramatist: George Whitefield and the Rise of Modern Evangelicalism*. Ed. Mark A. Noll and Nathan O. Hatch. Grand Rapids: Eerdmans, 1991. Print.

Additional Reading

"Benjamin Franklin." *PBS*. Twin Cities Public Television, 2002. Web. 27 Feb. 2012

Brands, H. W. *The First American: the Life and Times of Benjamin Franklin*. New York: Anchor, 2002. Print.

Isaacson, Walter. *Benjamin Franklin: An American Life*. New York: Simon, 2004. Print.

Kidd, Thomas S. *The Great Awakening: A Brief History with Documents*. New York: Bedford, 2008. Print.

Mansfield, Stephen. *Forgotten Founding Father: The Heroic Legacy of George Whitefield*. Nashville: Turner, 2001. Print.

Whitefield, George. *The Revived Puritan: The Spirituality of George Whitefield*. Ed. Michael A. G. Haykin. Dundas, Ontario: Joshua Press, 2000. Print. Classics of Reformed Spirituality

---. *Sermons of George Whitefield*. Ed. Leo Gattis. Peabody, MA: Hendrickson, 2009. Print.

LESSON PLAN: **Witnessing the Great Awakening**

Students analyze Benjamin Franklin's comments on Reverend George Whitefield and use them in conjunction with Jonathan Edwards's observations to create a full picture of Whitefield.

Learning Objectives

Identify Franklin's humanism and values; appreciate the historical perspective of Franklin's views on Whitefield; explain the influence of Great Awakening ideas on colonial society; compare and contrast comments of Franklin and Jonathan Edwards about Whitefield and the Great Awakening.

Materials: Benjamin Franklin, *The Private Life of the Late Benjamin Franklin* (1793), Excerpt: "On Reverend George Whitefield"; Jonathan Edwards, "On the Great Awakening" (1743).

Overview Questions

What do Franklin's observations about Whitefield reveal about Franklin? How do Franklin's observations about Whitefield humanize the preacher? What effects of the Great Awakening does Franklin bear witness to? How does Franklin's view on Whitefield compare with Jonathan Edwards's view?

Step 1: Comprehension Questions

What is Franklin's attitude toward Whitefield? What character traits in Franklin emerge as he talks about Whitefield?

▶ **Activity:** Choose students to read aloud passages that reveal Franklin's differences of opinions with Whitefield. Have students characterize the passages' tone and what it implies about Franklin. Have students also select passages that show Franklin's unique methods of inquiry.

Step 2: Comprehension Questions

What do Franklin's eyewitness accounts reveal about Whitefield's talents and influence? Why do Franklin's opinions matter?

▶ **Activity:** Have students list details Franklin supplies about Whitefield, his sermons, and his influence. Discuss why this contemporary view is essential to historians and our understanding of Whitefield's power. Ask why the fact that Franklin provides the view increases its value.

Step 3: Context Questions

What does Franklin say about the Great Awakening and its effects? How does his view help inform us about the reach of the Great Awakening?

▶ **Activity:** Have a student read the first paragraph aloud. Discuss why the views expressed here might be surprising in the context of our modern assumptions about Franklin. Have students identify other passages that suggest the impact of the Great Awakening.

Step 4: Exploration Questions

Why would you expect Franklin's views on Whitefield and the Great Awakening to differ from Jonathan Edwards's? What portrait emerges of Whitefield based on the observations of both Franklin and Edwards?

▶ **Activity:** Have students review Edwards's "On the Great Awakening." Discuss his description of the movement and how his words are influenced by his role in it. Instruct students to compare and contrast Franklin and Edward on Whitefield and then use the information from both to create a character sketch of the man.

Step 5: Response Paper

Word length and additional requirements set by Instructor. Students answer the research question in the Overview Questions. Students state a thesis and use as evidence passages from the primary source document as well as support from supplemental materials assigned in the lesson.

■ The Present State of Virginia

Date: 1724
Author: Jones, Hugh
Genre: report

*"But to me it seems to be more Prudence and Charity
for our own Poor and Vagabonds to be there imployed
and provided for, than for us to maintain and use
such great Numbers of Africans."*

Summary Overview

The Present State of Virginia was a short book written
to inform British people of conditions in Virginia and
the surrounding region. It covers the colony's population, geography, economy, and political and religious
institutions. Like many works on the colonies, its purposes were largely promotional, encouraging interest
in and immigration to Britain's possessions in North
America by painting a rosy picture of colonial life. It
was one of a group of texts on the colonies produced
in the era, and its author, Hugh Jones, even suggested
that it be read along with Robert Beverly's *History and
Present State of Virginia*. The book is not merely descriptive, however, but contains suggestions by Jones
on how Virginia and British relations with the colony
could be improved.

Defining Moment

The Present State of Virginia reflects the formation of
colonial Virginia's tobacco plantation economy based
on African slavery. Tidewater Virginia had ceased to
be a frontier zone with the final marginalization of the
American Indian communities of the area, and the
increased security following the War of the Spanish
Succession had led to an era of peace and prosperity that was attracting notice in Britain as well as Virginia itself. Indentured servitude, an important tool
for labor recruitment in the seventeenth century, was
diminishing in importance, although it still existed.

There were relatively few white servants in Virginia
or the southern colonies compared to the northern
ones, as enslaved Africans filled more and more of the
need for both skilled and unskilled labor. The society
of colonial Virginia, based on dominance by the owners of large plantations and country houses coexisting
with smaller landowners, was also formed by this time.
However, Virginia planters were concerned about the
large numbers of African and African-descended slaves
in the colony, and there had been an insurrection scare
in September 1722. Most opposition to slavery at the
time was rooted in these pragmatic concerns, rather
than being motivated by opposition to the slaves' lack
of freedom or a humanitarian desire to improve their
condition.

Jones's career also reflects the growing interest and
presence of the Church of England in the southern
colonies, where it was the dominant religious institution. In Virginia, the Church of England was the established church and ran the College of William and
Mary, the only institution of higher education in the
southern colonies and the second oldest (after Harvard) in the British North American colonies.

The Present State of Virginia was also designed
to attract British interest in Virginia at a time when
many, following the collapse of the South Sea Bubble
in 1720, were suspicious of colonial schemes. At the
time when Jones was writing, British elites were concerned with the large number of poor people, vagrants,

and criminals in Britain itself. One solution was the large-scale relocation of British convicts to the American colonies, a process that began with the passage of the Transportation Act in 1718 and would continue until the American Revolution. The colonies were becoming one possible solution to the large numbers of poor people in Britain itself.

Author Biography

Hugh Jones was born around 1691 in Hereford County, England, close to the Welsh border. His name indicates Welsh ancestry. He matriculated at the University of Oxford and became a clergyman in the Church of England. Throughout his career, he remained a loyal supporter of the established order in church and state. Jones planned to emigrate to the colonies, and the bishop of London, John Robinson, recommended him to fill the professorship of mathematics and natural philosophy at the College of William and Mary. He arrived in Virginia in 1716 and filled the professorship from 1717 to 1721, when he returned to England. Williamsburg, the location of the college, was also the capital of the colony following the abandonment of Jamestown, and Jones was connected to Virginia's colonial landholding political and economic elite as a clergyman affiliated with local churches and as chaplain to the House of Burgesses, Virginia's legislative body. He became involved in Virginia politics as an ally of Lieutenant Governor Alexander Spotswood in Spotswood's many quarrels with Reverend James Blair, then the president of William and Mary and the commissary of the bishop of London, the administrative head of the Church of England in the American colonies.

In England, Jones published *The Present State of Virginia* and a short guide to English grammar, *An Accidence to the English Tongue*, in 1724. That year, he again journeyed to Virginia, where he became a parish minister. Blair, still his enemy, assigned him to a notoriously difficult parish. After a quarrel with the vestry (administrative committee of parishioners), he migrated north to Maryland, where he had a successful career in the church. Jones served as the representative of Lord Baltimore, the proprietor of Maryland, to the Pennsylvania-Maryland commission for determining the border of Delaware. The meeting ended in failure, and Jones was charged with trying to extend the territory of Maryland because it would increase the size of his parish. In addition to *The Present State of Virginia*, his best-known book, he published works on standards of measurement and calendar reform. He died in Maryland in 1760.

HISTORICAL DOCUMENT

The *Negroes* live in small Cottages called *Quarters*, in about six in a *Gang*, under the Direction of an *Overseer* or *Bailiff*; who takes Care that they *tend* such Land as the Owner allots and orders, upon which they raise *Hogs* and *Cattle*, and plant *Indian Corn* (or *Maize*) and Tobacco for the Use of their Master; out of which the *Overseer* has a Dividend (or Share) in Proportion to the Number of *Hands* including himself; this with several Privileges is his Salary, and is an ample Recompence for his Pains, and Encouragement of his industrious Care, as to the Labour, Health, and Provision of the *Negroes*.

The *Negroes* are very numerous, some Gentlemen having Hundreds of them of all Sorts, to whom they bring great Profit; for the Sake of which they are obliged to keep them well, and not over-work, starve, or famish them, besides other Inducements to favour them; which is done in a *great Degree*, to such especially that are laborious, careful, and honest; tho' indeed some Masters, careless of their own Interest or Reputation, are too cruel and negligent.

The *Negroes* are not only encreased by fresh Supplies from *Africa* and the *West India* Islands, but also are very prolifick among themselves; and they that are born there talk *good English*, and affect our Language, Habits, and Customs; and tho' they be naturally of a barbarous and cruel Temper, yet are they kept under by severe Discipline upon Occasion, and by good Laws are prevented from running away, injuring the *English*, or neglecting their Business.

Their Work (or Chimerical hard Slavery) is not very laborious; their greatest Hardship consisting in that they and their Posterity are not at their own Liberty or Disposal, but are the Property of their Owners; and when they are free, they know not how to provide so well for themselves generally; neither did they live so plentifully nor (many of them) so easily in their own Country, where they are made Slaves to one another, or taken Captive by their Enemies.

The Children belong to the Master of the Woman that bears them; and such as are born of a *Negroe* and an *European* are called *Molattoes*; but such as are born of an *Indian* and *Negroe* are called *Mustees*.

Their Work is to take Care of the *Stock*, and plant *Corn*, *Tobacco*, *Fruits*, &c. which is not harder than *Thrashing*, *Hedging*, or *Ditching*; besides, tho' they are out in the violent Heat, wherein they delight, yet in wet or cold Weather there is little Occasion for their working in the Fields, in which few will let them be abroad, lest by this means they might get sick or die, which would prove a great Loss to their Owners, a good *Negroe* being sometimes worth three (nay four) Score Pounds Sterling, if he be a Tradesman; so that upon this (if upon no other Account) they are obliged not to overwork them, but to cloath and feed them sufficiently, and take Care of their Health.

Several of them are taught to be *Sawyers*, *Carpenters*, *Smiths*, *Coopers*, &c. and though for the most Part they be none of the aptest or nicest; yet they are by Nature cut out for hard Labour and Fatigue, and will perform tolerably well; though they fall much short of an *Indian*, that has learn'd and seen the same Things; and *those* Negroes make the best Servants, that have been *Slaves* in their *own Country*; for they that have been *Kings* and *great Men* there are generally lazy, haughty, and obstinate; whereas the others are sharper, better humoured, and more laborious.

The *Languages* of the *new Negroes* are various harsh *Jargons*, and their *Religions* and *Customs* such as are best described by Mr. *Bosman* in his Book intitled (I think) *A Description of the Coasts of Africa*.

The *Virginia* Planters readily learn to become good *Mechanicks* in Building, wherein most are capable of directing their Servants and Slaves.

***

The Country is yearly supplied with vast Quantities of Goods from *Great Britain*, chiefly from *London*, *Bristol*, *Liverpool*, *Whitehaven*, and from *Scotland*.

The Ships that transport these Things often call at *Ireland* to victual, and bring over frequently white Servants, which are of three Kinds. 1. Such as come upon certain Wages by Agreement for a certain Time. 2. Such as come bound by Indenture, commonly call'd *Kids*, who are usually to serve four or five Years; and 3. those Convicts or Felons that are transported, whose Room they had much rather have than their Company; for abundance of them do great Mischiefs, commit Robbery and Murder, and spoil Servants, that were before very good: But they frequently there meet with the End they deserved at Home, though indeed some of them prove indifferent good. Their being sent thither to work as Slaves for Punishment, is but a mere Notion, for few of them ever lived so well and so easy before, especially if they are good for any thing. These are to serve seven, and sometimes fourteen Years, and they and Servants by Indentures have an Allowance of Corn and Cloaths, when they are out of their Time, that they may be therewith supported, till they can be provided with Services, or otherwise settled. With these three Sorts of Servants are they supplied from *England*, *Wales*, *Scotland*, and *Ireland*, among which they that have a Mind to it, may serve their Time with Ease and Satisfaction to themselves and their Masters, especially if they fall into good Hands.

Except the last Sort, for the most Part who are loose Villains, made tame by *Wild*, and then enslaved by his *Forward Namesake*: To prevent too great a Stock of which Servants and Negroes many Attempts and Laws have been in vain made.

These if they forsake their Roguery together with the other Kids of the later *Jonathan*, when they are free, may work Day-Labour, or else rent a small Plantation for a Trifle almost; or else turn Overseers, if they are expert, industrious, and careful, or follow their Trade, if they have been brought up to any; especially Smiths, Carpenters, Taylors, Sawyers, Coopers, Bricklayers, &c. The Plenty of the Country, and the good Wages given to Work-Folks occasion very few Poor, who are supported by the Parish, being such as are lame, sick, or decrepit through Age, Distempers, Accidents, or some Infirmities; for where there is a numerous Family of poor Children the Vestry takes Care to bind them out Apprentices, till they are able to maintain themselves by their own Labour; by which Means they are never tormented with Vagrant, and Vagabond Beggars, there being a Reward for taking up Run-aways, that are at a small Distance from their Home; if they are not known, or are without a Pass from their Master, and can give no good Account of themselves, especially Negroes.

✳✳✳

It is a monkish Opinion too prevalent with many still, that there is no good Living without the Bounds of their own Cloyster. And Abundance of *English* entertain the *Chinese* Notion, that they are all Fools and Beggars that live in any Country but theirs. This home Fondness has been very prejudicial to the common Sort of *English*, and has in a great Measure retarded the Plantations from being stock'd with such Inhabitants as are skilful, industrious, and laborious.

For these Reasons, such Persons of Sense and Resolution as have entered into Projects for Improvements in the Plantations (who have evinced us, that all Schemes are not Bubbles) have been obliged for the generality to make Use of the worst and vilest of Mankind, for the Execution of the noblest and most useful Undertakings; tho' indeed continually several People of Sense, Vertue, and Fortune, entertaining tolerable good Notions of these Affairs, have embarked themselves and Families in such laudable and useful Designs: But for the generality, the Servants and inferior Sort of People, who have either been sent over to *Virginia*, or have transported themselves thither, have been, and are, the poorest, idlest, and worst of Mankind, the *Refuse of Great Britain* and *Ireland*, and the *Outcast of the People*.

These Servants are but an insignificant Number, when compared with the vast Shoals of *Negroes* who are imployed as Slaves there to do the hardest and most Part of the Work; the most laborious of which is the felling of Trees and the like, to which kind of Slavery (if it must be so called) our Wood-Cutters in England are exposed; only with this Difference, that the *Negroes* eat wholsomer Bread and better Pork with more Plenty and Ease; and when they are Sick, their Owners Interest and Purse are deeply engaged in their Recovery, who likewise are obliged to take all the Care imaginable of the Children of their Slaves for their own great Profit; so that the *Negroes*, though they work moderately, yet live plentifully, have no Families to provide for, no Danger of Beggary, no Care for *the Morrow*.

But to me it seems to be more Prudence and Charity for our own Poor and Vagabonds to be there imployed and provided for, than for us to maintain and use such great Numbers of *Africans*. If we can do better without them certainly we should forbear importing so many (though this may interfere with the Interest of some), since it would advance the Good of the Publick; and that we may be without them is plain, since we have Rogues and Idlers enough of our own to do the same Work, to which if they were compelled by mild Methods, it would ease the Publick of a great deal of Charge, Trouble, and Loss, and would highly tend to the Advancement of the temporal and spiritual Happiness of our *Poor*, and be very instrumental in the Suppression of Theft and Villany, and for the Reformation of the most Profligate. Thousands of poor, honest, unfortunate People of all Trades and Occupations might be there imployed for the Support of themselves and Interest of Trade, that can find neither Work nor Maintenance for themselves and Families at Home; and such as had rather stroll or steal here, might be confined by mild Force to moderate Labour there, sufficient to support themselves, and benefit their Imployers.

GLOSSARY

chimerical: imaginary

cloyster (cloister): monastery

cooper: barrel-maker

Indian corn: maize corn

Negroes: African and African-descended people

new Negroes: slaves recently arrived from Africa

sawyer: lumber worker

stock: livestock

West India Islands: Caribbean colonies

Document Analysis

These passages from *The Present State of Virginia* deal with labor relations, specifically slavery and indentured servitude, primarily in an agricultural context as was suited to Virginia's agrarian economy. Anxious to paint Virginia in as pleasant a light as possible, Jones minimizes the hardships and oppressions suffered by slaves, painting a picture of slavery as an institution that both provided a good life to the slaves and profitable estates to the masters. His praise of slavery accompanies a poor estimate of the mental and emotional capacities of African and African-descended people. However, Jones's principal ideological goal was not the defense of slavery, which as an institution was not under serious attack at the time, but the encouragement of the immigration of the British poor to the colony, whether voluntarily as free or indentured servants or under coercion, as in the case of convicts. For this reason, he also shows the conditions of white servants as in a very positive way, both during their indentures and afterward, and claims that the colonies offer opportunities to poor British and Irish people.

Jones's portrait of Virginia was designed to attract English interest and support at a time when many were suspicious of colonial ventures. His parenthetical remark that not all schemes are bubbles is a reference to the South Sea Bubble, a financial crash based on the stock of the South Sea Company that had wiped out many British investors in 1720. Jones claims that Virginia is a going concern, not another potential disaster, and points out that the slave-worked tobacco plantations of Virginia are highly profitable. Like other promoters who wanted to emphasize the economic value of the colonies to Britain, Jones wrote of the great mass of commodities shipped every year from British ports to Virginia, establishing prosperous colonies as valuable markets for British exports. Excluding rival exporters from the British colonies had been a goal since the seventeenth century.

Jones presents some aspects of Virginia culture in a way that would be familiar to British readers, for example, referring to the landowners as "gentlemen," the same term used for members of the landowning class in Britain. However, although the abolitionist movement had not begun by 1724, slavery and the plantation system was still a major challenge in presenting Virginia to British readers. Part of the reason was the simple issue of unfamiliarity. Britain was not populated by the large numbers of African-descended people characteristic of the southern British colonies, and British agriculture was organized on a far different basis than Virginia plantation agriculture. Although some literature of the time, such as Aphra Behn's popular novel, *Oroonoko* (1688), presented slavery as a cruel institution, Jones portrays slavery as practiced in Virginia as a humane institution. One reason for this, he claims, is that African and African-descended people (whom he refers to most often as "Negroes") are particularly well adapted to the physical conditions of Virginia tobacco plantations. He minimizes the burdens slaves face in their work, which he describes as "not very laborious." The intense heat characteristic of the Virginia summer he identifies as something the slaves actually enjoy. He also asserts that during the cool, damp times of the season, presumably less congenial to people originating in tropical Africa, their owners protect them from heavy work. The frequent use of the whip and other forms of physical punishment on plantations goes unmentioned.

Of course, slavery was not merely hard physical labor, but also the deprivation of freedom, an important value for Jones's British readers, who saw Britain as a country enjoying a freedom unique in the world and frequently referred to those living under foreign despotic regimes as "slaves." Although Jones recognizes that the slaves complained of their lack of freedom, he immediately adds that they do not know what to do with themselves when free. He also points out that many slaves were already slaves in Africa and are thus accustomed to the condition.

A major part of Jones's praise of slavery consists of favorably contrasting the lot of slaves with that of free workers in terms of material rewards. Jones claims that although both slaves in Virginia and free people in England work as woodcutters, the slaves are better fed. Jones also argues that the slaves were better off in America than they were in Africa, pointing out that many would have been slaves in Africa as well.

Although Jones's idyllic portrait of slavery has little to do with the harsh exploitation that was the lot of the typical slave, it is somewhat more accurate in depicting Virginia tobacco slavery than it would be in describing other forms of agricultural slavery, such as the sugar slavery of the Caribbean and the rice slavery of South Carolina, which were far more physically debilitating. In these areas, slaves lived shorter lives and reproduced at a much lower rate than in Virginia. By contrast, Jones describes the Virginia slave population as "prolifick," and such was the reproductive rate on tobacco plantations that Virginia planters were much less dependent on slave importations to maintain their work forces than were planters in South Carolina and the Caribbean colonies, although the expansion of the Virginia colony did lead to large-scale slave importation.

Although Jones emphasizes the carefree life, good working conditions, and plentiful food allegedly available to Virginia slaves, he does not sentimentalize slavery as based on the benevolence of the master, but rather explains that its beneficial nature is rooted in the master's economic interest. Since slaves were an important economic asset to their owners, it was in the owner's interest to maintain the slaves' health and even to care for slave children, who would grow up to be valuable economic assets in the future. (Jones does not touch on the fate of slaves who grew too old or too sick to work and lost their economic value to their master.) Cruel and careless masters were actually harming their own economic interests, as well as their reputations. The same economic incentives extended to overseers, whose compensation was based on a proportion of the slaves' production. (The sexual exploitation of enslaved women by masters and overseers alike, an important part of the culture of slavery, goes unmentioned, save for a brief reference to mulattoes.)

Jones did little research into the history and lifeways of the slaves themselves, nor were his opinions of the overall benevolence of the system apparently based on conversations with slaves. Jones distinguishes between the slaves born in Virginia, who had adopted, however superficially, the English language and English lifeways, and those recently arrived from Africa. Since a larger proportion of Virginia slaves were American-born, the process of acculturation that Jones observes was more advanced in Virginia (and the other Chesapeake and northern colonies) than it was in colonies farther south. His description of African languages as "various harsh *Jargons*" is virtually meaningless and reflects a profound cultural arrogance; for African customs, he simply refers his readers to another book. Clearly, he did not regard the African cultural background of the slaves as of significant value, but he did not consider the assimilation of the slaves into English customs as altogether good either. He states that the slaves "affect" the culture of the English, suggesting that they do not wholeheartedly adopt it and that their adoption of English customs is an affectation. Curiously, for a clergyman, he says little of slave religion.

At the time, the Church of England that dominated religious life in Virginia was not greatly concerned with converting the slaves, nor did many plantation owners encourage it, although this would change later. There is some evidence that later in his career, as a parish clergyman in Maryland, Jones worked hard to spread Christianity among the slave population. He also distinguishes the African slaves who had been slaves in Africa and are resigned to their lot in Virginia as well from those leaders in African society who had been enslaved by their enemies and have not accepted their enslavement, even in America. These latter figures were not presented as tragic, like the title character of Oroonoko would be in European literature, but as comic—"haughty" and "lazy."

Jones's discussion of the nature of the slaves themselves is basically negative. According to him, Africans have an inherently "barbarous and cruel" nature that is only restrained by keeping them under a strict discipline. He clearly thought little of the mental capacities of African-descended people as well. Jones portrays African and African-descended slaves as best suited for hard physical labor and less able to perform skilled labor such as artisanal work. Although he does recognize that slaves trained as artisans are the most valuable slaves, he adds that they are not suited for this work, as could be seen in the relatively poor quality of what they produce. According to Jones, African-descended people are not only inferior in intellectual capacity to whites, but to American Indians as well; the good "Mechanicks" are the plantation owners themselves, and the slaves only perform well under their direction. The difficulties former slaves face in dealing with their new freedom is presented as further evidence that they are not truly worthy of it.

What keeps Jones from fully endorsing the slave society of early eighteenth-century Virginia, ironically, is his positive valuation of the lives of enslaved workers. In effect, he argues that work in Virginia is too good for Africans and that the support given the African population should instead go to the British poor. Like many of his contemporaries, Jones believed that there was not enough work for the poor in Britain itself and that relocating them to Virginia would provide them work to support themselves while enabling Virginia to fill its labor needs without importing Africans. (He does not specify what would happen to the African-descended people already in Virginia if his plan were adopted.) Jones recognizes that this would interfere with the business of slave traders but dismisses this consideration as unimportant. (Slave traders as a class were not highly regarded in colonial society, and elsewhere in *The Present State of Virginia*, Jones suggests that they should go into other professions.)

Jones sees the solution to Virginia's labor problem, therefore, as ultimately solvable by encouraging white immigration. The wish to encourage immigration was one he shared with many other writers on the colonies going back to the earliest days of colonization. Jones focuses principally on the immigration of the lower classes who would become workers in America rather than those already doing well in Britain, who would be much harder to persuade, due in part to cultural prejudices. Most English people, Jones asserts, view England as the best country in the world and are reluctant to leave it for another, no matter how bad their circumstances. (Although Jones mentions Scottish, Irish, and Welsh as well as English people in the context of immigration, he ascribes this stay-at-home prejudice solely to the English.) By default, the majority of immigrants were considered the refuse of English society.

Jones views a mass migration of poor British whites to the colonies as the solution for many social problems, including unemployment and petty crime. Although he does not advocate the enslavement of the poor, he does allow for a coercive element in dealing with the criminal classes, in line with the Transportation Act of 1718.

In discussing the fate of white convicts shipped to America, Jones adopts basically the same line that he does with slaves, claiming that convicts live better as servants, with more "Ease and Satisfaction" in Virginia, than they did as either convicts or free people in their home countries. Regarding the contributions made by servants, Jones is most skeptical of those of convicts, many of whom, he claims, would simply renew their lives of crime in a new setting, exert a bad influence on other servants, and ultimately face the same fate—hanging—that they had avoided in Britain itself. However, Jones does not believe that this is true of all transported convicts, nor do problems with individual convicts cause him to question the entire project of convict transportation. He does point to efforts to regulate the number of convict laborers and slaves in Virginia but adds that these efforts have been ineffective.

Jones refers to two Jonathans in dealing with the subject of convict labor. Jonathan Wild was the mas-

ter criminal of early eighteenth-century London, and before his hanging, he controlled hundreds of thieves and other offenders. "His *Forward Namesake*" was the tobacco and slave merchant Jonathan Forward, who contracted with the British government to transport convict laborers across the Atlantic after the passage of the Transportation Act. The fact that the government turned to a slave merchant to transport convicts and that Forward won the contract based on being able to ship the convicts for the lowest amount of money per head indicates a connection between the brutalities of the established African slave trade and those of the new convict trade. It also suggests that shipping British workers across the Atlantic was perceived as an economic alternative for slave traders as well as for employers in Virginia. Jones explicitly refers to convict laborers as "enslaved." Although skeptical of the possibility of reformation in most cases, Jones places convict labor in the context of the need of the American colonies for labor rather than in that of punishment, since he maintains that work in Virginia is relatively easy.

While he believes that African laborers are best suited for hard, unskilled physical work in the hot Virginia sun and not well suited to becoming free workers, Jones emphasizes the diversity of economic options available for white immigrants once they have finished their indenture: In addition to laborers, white immigrants could become overseers, tenant farmers, or artisans. Jones lists a range of occupations that could be followed in Virginia. He maintains that any able-bodied person should be able to support himself. (Jones did not explicitly distinguish between male and female emigrants here, but most of the professions he lists were male professions, and males outnumbered females among emigrants. The principal economic advantage for female emigrants was the ease of finding a husband in a predominantly male society as compared to staying at home.)

Jones endorses the regulation of the movement of laborers, white and black, within Virginia by means of a pass system, where workers who were found away from their place of employment would be required to produce a written pass from their employer or owner. This system prevented the growth of an unregulated, mobile, "vagrant" population, which, like other English social reformers going back to the sixteenth century, Jones sees as a major problem in England itself. Virginia offered the possibility of a far more regulated society, through slavery, indentured servitude, convict labor, and the pass system.

Essential Themes

Although Jones's book itself was not reprinted until 1865, when it was an antiquarian curiosity, its themes would have a long history. Numerous writers on Virginia and other southern colonies would deal with similar issues of slavery and free labor.

Although *The Present State of Virginia* was not produced as part of the debate on slavery that would start later in the eighteenth century, it introduces several key themes that would underlie later proslavery polemics. Jones's glowing picture of life under slavery as carefree would contribute to the image of the slave as fundamentally contented and irresponsible. Jones's favorable comparison of a slave's life to that of a free worker would be a staple of slavery apologias and anti-abolitionist literature into the Civil War, as would his argument that slaves were better off in America than they had been in Africa. Jones's assumptions about the inferior capacity of Africans would be more explicit in subsequent proslavery writings, explained in both scientific and religious terms. Although Jones's fundamentally economic analysis of the master's motives for treating slaves well would not disappear, it would be partially supplanted by one that emphasized the patriarchal benevolence of the slave owner and his role in spreading Christianity to the enslaved population.

Jones's hope to replace slavery with the mass immigration of the English poor proved in vain. Although the high wages and relative class mobility of the American colonies attracted English immigrants, the poor mostly went to the northern colonies where land was cheaper. There was also substantial white immigration from other parts of Europe, particularly Germany, which Jones discusses in another part of the book, but again, most of those immigrants went north. The economic success of slavery continued to discourage mass white immigration to the south, as white craftspeople could not compete with cheaper slave artisans. Convict transportation to the Americas, which aroused resentment among colonists, would end with the American Revolution. (Jones had denied that a revolt on the part of the colonies was possible, claiming that they would find it impossible to cooperate with each other.) The idea of solving Britain's social problems with the poor by encouraging settlement, however, would remain popular in British elite circles into the twentieth century. It underlay James Oglethorpe's later colonizing venture in Georgia (which initially excluded slavery) and, after the loss of the thirteen colonies, Britain would launch the largest convict resettlement program in history in Australia.

The idea of a multitiered labor system, with immigration from Europe encouraged as an alternative to hiring blacks, however, would have a long history in independent America.

William E. Burns, PhD

Bibliography

Jones, Hugh. *The Present State of Virginia, from Whence Is Inferred a Short View of Maryland and North Carolina*. Ed. Richard L. Morton. Chapel Hill: U of North Carolina P, 1956. Print.

Morton, Richard L. "The Reverend Hugh Jones: Lord Baltimore's Mathematician." *William and Mary Quarterly* 3rd ser. 7.1 (1950): 107–15. Print.

Additional Reading

Bell, James B. *The Imperial Origins of the King's Church in Early America, 1607–1783*. New York: Palgrave, 2004. Print.

Davis, Richard Beale. *Intellectual Life in the Colonial South, 1583–1763*. Knoxville: U of Tennessee P, 1978. Print.

Ekirch, A. Roger. *Bound for America: The Transportation of British Convicts to the Colonies, 1718–1775*. Oxford: Clarendon, 1990. Print.

Morgan, Edmund S. *American Slavery, American Freedom: The Ordeal of Colonial Virginia*. New York: Norton, 2003. Print.

Parent, Anthony S., Jr. *Foul Means: The Formation of a Slave Society in Virginia, 1660–1740*. Chapel Hill: U of North Carolina P, 2003. Print.

LESSON PLAN: Hugh Jones Describes Labor in Virginia

Students analyze Hugh Jones's *The Present State of Virginia* and investigate his conclusions.

Learning Objectives

Identify the author and purpose of this document; evaluate a contemporary minister's view of slavery and indentured servitude; investigate views on a new source of non-slave labor; compare and contrast Jones's description of slave life with that offered by Venture Smith.

Materials: Hugh Jones, *The Present State of Virginia* (1724); Venture Smith, *A Narrative of the Life and Adventures of Venture, A Native of Africa* (1798).

Overview Questions

What were Jones's goals in writing his report? How does Jones describe and judge differing types of labor in Virginia? Why does Jones encourage the employment of poor Europeans in places of enslaved Africans? How does Jones's description of slavery coincide with or differ from Venture Smith's?

Step 1: Comprehension Questions

What is Jones's background and how might it affect his point of view? What does he attempt to accomplish in his report?

▶ **Activity:** Choose a student to report basic biographical information about Jones. Discuss how Jones's perspective as an Englishman might be different from an American view. Have students identify passages that directly or indirectly suggest Jones's purposes in writing.

Step 2: Comprehension Questions

How does Jones judge slavery and the work of enslaved peoples? How does he compare slavery to forms of non-slave labor?

▶ **Activity:** Have students create charts to visually breakdown the four types of laborers Jones observes. The chart should describe who comprises each group, why its members are in America, and Jones's judgments about each group and the quality of work they produce.

Step 3: Context Questions

What arguments does Jones offer for an alternative supply of labor? What motivates his suggestion?

▶ **Activity:** Have read aloud and then paraphrase passages in which Jones suggests a new source of labor. Discuss what his suggestion implies about his attitude toward the use of enslaved African peoples. Challenge students to gauge the potential historical impact of a fully implemented version of his plan.

Step 4: Exploration Questions

Is the plantation environment that Jones describes consistent with impressions that Venture Smith provides? What issues would Smith take with Jones's descriptions?

▶ **Activity:** Have students review Smith's narrative. Have students read aloud passages from it that describe the kind of world that Smith survived and left. Discuss whether or not Smith's life debunks some of Jones's conclusions, keeping in mind agricultural differences between the northern and southern colonies. Challenge students to use the two documents to describe the early stages in the growth of African American culture.

Step 5: Response Paper

Word length and additional requirements set by Instructor. Students answer the research question in the Overview Questions. Students state a thesis and use as evidence passages from the primary source document as well as support from supplemental materials assigned in the lesson.

SUPPLEMENTAL HISTORICAL DOCUMENTS

DOCUMENTS ON INDENTURED SERVITUDE: RICHARD FRETHHORNE'S LETTER AND JOHN HAMMOND'S *LEAH AND RACHEL*

DATE: 1623; 1656
AUTHOR: Frethorne, Richard; Hammond, John
GENRE: letter; memoir

LOVING AND KIND FATHER AND MOTHER: My most humble duty remembered to you, hoping in god of your good health, as I myself am at the making hereof. This is to let you understand that I you child am in a most heavy case by reason of the country, [which] is such that it causeth much sic kness, [such] as the scurvy and the bloody flux and diverse other diseases, which maketh the body very poor and weak. And when we are sick there is nothing to comfort us; for since I came out of the ship I never ate anything but peas, and loblollie (that is, water gruel). As for deer or venison I never saw any since I came into this land. There is indeed some fowl, but we are not allowed to go and get it, but must work hard both early and late for a mess of water gruel and a mouthful of bread and beef. A mouthful of bread for a penny loaf must serve for four men which is most pitiful. [You would be grieved] if you did know as much as I [do], when people cry out day and night—Oh! That they were in England without their limbs—and would not care to lose any limb to be in England again, yea, though they beg from door to door. For we live in fear of the enemy every hour, yet we have had a combat with them É and we took two alive and made slaves of them. But it was by policy, for we are in great danger; for our plantation is very weak by reason of the death and sickness of our company. For we came but twenty for the merchants, and they are half dead just; and we look every hour when two more should go. Yet there came some four other men yet to live with us, of which there is but one alive; and our Lieutenant is dead, and [also] his father and his brother. And there was some five or six of the last year's twenty, of which there is but three left, so that we are fain to get other men to plant with us; and yet we are but 32 to fight against 3000 if they should come. And the nighest help that we have is ten mile of us, and when the rogues overcame this place [the] last [time] they slew 80 persons. How then shall we do, for we lie even in their teeth? They may e asily take us, but [for the fact] that God is merciful and can save with few as well as with many, as he showed to Gilead. And like Gilead's soldiers, if they lapped water, we drink water which is but weak.

And I have nothing to comfort me, nor is there nothing to be gotten here but sickness and death, except that one had money to lay out in some things for profit. But I have nothing at all—no, not a shirt to my back but two rags (2), nor clothes but one poor suit, nor but one pair of shoes, but one pair of stockings, but one cap, [and] but two bands [collars]. My cloak is stolen by one of my fellows, and to his dying hour [he] would not tell me what he did with it; but some of my fellows saw him have butter and beef out of a ship, which my cloak, I doubt [not], paid for. So that I have not a penny, nor a penny worth, to help me too either spice or sugar or strong waters, without the which one cannot live here. For as strong beer in England doth fatten and strengthen them, so water here doth wash and weaken these here only keeps life and soul together. But I am not half [of] a quarter so strong as I was in England, and all is for want of victuals; for I do protest unto you that I have eaten more in [one] day at home than I have allowed me here for a week. You have given more than my day's allowance to a beggar at the door; and if Mr. Jackson had not relieved me, I should be in a poor case. But he like a father and she like a loving mother doth still help me.

For when we go to Jamestown (that is 10 miles of us) there lie all the ships that come to land, and there they must deliver their goods. And when we went up to town [we would go], as it may be, on Monday at noon, and come there by night, [and] then load the next day by noon, and go home in the afternoon, and unload, and then away again in the night, and [we would] be up about midnight. Then if it rained or blowed never so hard, we must lie in the boat on the water and have nothing but a little bread. For when we go into the boat we[would] have a loaf allowed to two men, and it is all [we would get] if we stayed there two days, which is hard; and [we] must lie all that while in the boat. But that Goodman Jackson pitied me and made me a cabin to lie in always when I [would] come up, and he would give me some poor jacks [fish] [to take] home with me, which comforted me more than peas or water gruel. Oh, they be very godly folks, and love me very well, and will do anything for me. And he much marvelle d that you would send me a servant to the Company; he saith I had been better knocked on the head. And indeed so I find it now, to my great grief and misery; and [I] saith that if you love me you will redeem me suddenly, for which I do entreat and beg. And if you cannot get the merchants to redeem me for some little money, then for God's sake get a gathering or entreat some good folks to lay out some little sum of money in meal and cheese and butter and beef. Any eating meat will yield great profit. Oil and vinegar is very good; but, father, there is great loss in leaking. But for God's sake send beef and cheese and butter, or the more of one sort and none of another. But if you send cheese, it must be very old cheese; and at the cheesemonger's you may buy very good cheese for twopence farthing or halfpenny, that will be liked very well. But if you send cheese, you must have a care how you pack it in barrels; and you must put cooper's chips between every cheese, or else the heat of the hold will rot them. And look whatsoever you send me—be in never so much—look, what[ever] I make of it, I will deal truly with you. I will send it over and beg the profit to redeem me; and if I die before it come, I have entreated Goodman Jackson to send you the worth of it, who hath promised he will. If you send, you must direct your letters to Goodman Jackson, at Jamestown, a gunsmith. (You must set down his freight, because there be more of his name there.) Good father, do not forget me, but have mercy and pity my miserable case. I know if you did but see me, you would weep to see me; for I have but one suit. (But [though] it is a strange one, it is very well guarded.) Wherefore, for God's sake, pity me. I pray you to remember my love to all my friends and kindred. I hope all my brothers and sisters are in good health, and as for my part I have set down my resolution that certainly will be; that is, that the answer of this letter will be life or death to me. Therefore, good father, send as soon as you can; and if you send me any thing let this be the mark.

ROT
Richard Frethhorne, Martin's Hundred

✳✳✳

It is the glory of every Nation to enlarge themselves, to encourage their own foreign attempts, and to be able to be able to have their own, within their territories, as many several commodities as they can attain to, that so others may rather be beholding to them, than they to others. . . . But alas, we Englishmen . . . do not only fail in this, but vilify, scandalize and cry down such parts of the unknown world, as have been found out, settled and made flourishing, by the charge, hazard, and diligence of their own brethren, as if because removed from us, we either account them people of another world or enemies.

This is too truly made good in the odious and cruel slanders cast on those two famous Countries of Virginia and Mary-land, whereby those Countries, not only are many times at a stand, but are in danger to moulder away, and come in time to nothing. . . .

The Country [Virginia] is reported to be an unhealthy place, a nest of Rogues, whores, dissolute and rooking persons; a place of intolerable labour, bad usage and hard Diet, &c. To Answer these several calumnies, I shall first shew what it was? Next, what it is?

At the first settling and many years after, it deserved most of those aspersions (nor were they aspersions but truths). . . . The usual allowance for servants is (besides their charge of passage defrayed) at their expiration, a year's provision of corn, double apparel, tools necessary, and land according to the custom of the Country, which is an old delusion, for there is no land customarily due to the servant, but to the Master, and therefore that servant is unwise that will not dash out that custom in his covenant and make that due of land absolutely his own, which although at the present, not of so great consequences; yet in few years will be of much worth. . . .

When ye go aboard, expect the Ship somewhat troubled and in a hurlyburly, until ye clear the lands end; and that the Ship is rummaged, and things put to rights, which many times discourages the Passengers, and makes them wish the Voyage unattempted: but this is but for a short season, and washes off when at Sea, where the time is pleasantly passed away, though not with such choice plenty as the shore affords.

But when ye arrive and are settled, ye will find a strange alteration, an abused Country giving the lie to your own approbations to those that have calumniated it.

. . . The labour servants are put to, is not so hard nor of such continuance as Husbandmen, nor Handicraftmen are kept at in England, I said little or nothing is done in winter time, none ever work before sun rising nor after sun set, in the summer they rest, sleep or exercise themselves give hours in the heat of the day, Saturdays afternoon is always their own, the old Holidays are observed and the Sabbath spent in good exercises.

The women are not (as is reported) put into the ground to work, but occupy such domestic employments and housewifery as in England, that is dressing victuals, right up the house, milking, employed about dairies, washing, sewing, &c. and both men and women have times of recreations, as much or more than in any part of the world besides, yet some wenches that are nastily, beastly and not fit to be so employed are put into the ground, for reason tells us, they must not at charge be transported then maintained for nothing, but those that prove so awkward are rather burthensome than servants desirable or useful. . . . Those Servants that will be industrious may in their time of service gain a competent estate before their Freedoms, which is usually done by many, and they gain esteem and assistance that appear so industrious: There is no Master almost but will allow his Servant a parcel of clear ground to cut some Tobacco in for himself, which he may husband at those many idle times he hath allowed him and not prejudice, but rejoice his Master to see it, which in time of Shipping he may lay out for commodities, and in Summer sell them again with advantage and get a Pig or two, which any body almost will give him, and his Master suffer him to keep them with his own, which will be no charge to his Master, and with one years increase of them may purchase a Cow Calf or two, and by that time he is for himself; he may have Cattle, Hogs and Tobacco of his own, and come to live gallantly; but this must be gained (as I have said) by Industry and affability, not by sloth nor churlish behavior. . . .

LESSON PLAN: **Slavery and Indentured Servitude in Colonial Virginia**

Students analyze different slave acts that were enacted in colonial Virginia and a letter written by an indentured servant to understand the colonial government's motives, beliefs, and interests.

Learning Objectives

Compare and contrast the characteristics of indentured servitude and chattel slavery; evaluate the rights of and lack of rights granted to indentured servants and enslaved people; analyze the causes and effects of limitations imposed on indentured servants and enslaved people; consider multiple perspectives on labor in colonial Virginia.

Materials: Virginia General Assembly, The Virginia Slave Codes 1662-1705 (1662–1705); Richard Frethorne, "Letter to His Parents" (1623).

Overview Questions

How were indentured servitude and slavery similar and different? What rights were guaranteed to both, if any? What restrictions were imposed on indentured servants and enslaved people? Why? What caused the government to enact slave laws? What effects did the laws have? How do multiple perspectives on labor and rights reveal a better understanding of the colonial government's motives, beliefs, and interests?

Step 1: Comprehension Questions

How were indentured servitude and slavery similar and different? How was each role defined?

▶ **Activity:** Have students form small groups and read aloud key passages in both selections. Ask students to underline the similarities between the passages and circle the differences.

Step 2: Comprehension Questions

What rights were guaranteed to indentured servants and enslaved people, if any? What restrictions were imposed upon them? Why?

▶ **Activity:** Ask students to create a list of the rights of indentured servants and enslaved people as well as the restrictions imposed upon them. Next, have students write in their journals an explanation for why these rights and restrictions existed.

Step 3: Context Questions

What caused the colonial government to enact slave laws? What effects did the laws have on indentured servants and enslaved people, as well as society itself?

▶ **Activity:** Discuss with students why the Virginia government enacted the slave laws and the

context in which they were created. Have students work in small groups to discuss the social, political, and economic effects of the laws on colonial society.

Step 4: Exploration Questions

How do multiple perspectives on labor and rights reveal a better understanding of the colonial government's motives, beliefs, and interests?

▶ **Activity:** Ask students to create an outline for an essay on the motives, beliefs, and interests of the colonial government to impose restrictions and enact laws that affected indentured servants and enslaved people. Invite volunteers to share their outlines with the class.

Step 5: Response Paper

Word length and additional requirements set by Instructor. Students answer the research question in the Overview Questions. Students state a thesis and use as evidence passages from the primary source document as well as support from supplemental materials assigned in the lesson.

AN EXHORTATION AND CAUTION TO FRIENDS CONCERNING BUYING OR KEEPING OF NEGROES

DATE: August 13, 1693
AUTHOR: Keith, George
GENRE: essay

Some Reasons and Causes of our being against keeping of Negroes for Term of Life.

First, Because it is contrary to the Principles and Practice of the Christian Quakers to buy Prize or stollen Goods, which we bore a faithful Testimony against in our Native Country; and therefore it is our Duty to come forth in a Testimony against stollen Slaves, it being accounted a far greater Crime under *Moses's* Law than the stealing of Goods: for such were only to restore four fold, *but he that stealeth a Man and selleth him, if he be found in his hand, he shall surely be put to Death, Exod.* 21. 16. Therefore as we are not to buy stollen Goods, (but if at unawares it should happen through Ignorance, we are to restore them to the Owners, and seek our Remedy of the Thief) no more are we to buy stollen Slaves; neither should such as have them keep them and their Posterity in perpetual Bondage and Slavery, as is usually done, to the great scandal of the *Christian Profession.*

Secondly, Because Christ commanded, saying, *All things whatsoever ye would that men should do unto you, do ye even so to them.* Therefore as we and our Children would not be kept in perpetual Bondage and Slavery against our Consent, neither should we keep them in perpetual Bondage and Slavery against their Consent, it being such intollerable Punishment to their Bodies and Minds, that none but notorious Criminal Offendors deserve the same. But these have done us no harm; therefore how inhumane is it in us so grievously to oppress them and their Children from one Generation to another.

Thirdly, Because the Lord hath commanded, saying, *Thou shalt not deliver unto his Master the Servant that is escaped from his Master unto thee, he shall dwell with thee, even amongst you in that place which he shall chuse in one of thy Gates, where it liketh him best; thou shalt*

oppress him, Deut. 23. 15. 16. By which it appeareth, that those which are at Liberty and freed from their Bondage, should not by us be delivered into Bondage again, neither by us should they be oppressed, but being escaped from his Master, should have the liberty to dwell amongst us, where it liketh him best. Therefore, if God extend such Mercy under the legal Ministration and Dispensation to poor Servants, he doth and will extend much more of his Grace and Mercy to them under the clear Gospel Ministration; so that instead of punishing them and their Posterity with cruel Bondage and perpetual Slavery, he will cause the Everlasting Gospel to be preached effectually to all Nations, to them as well as others; *And the Lord will extend Peace to his People tike a River, and the Glory of the Gentiles like a flowing Stream; And it shall come to pass, saith the Lord, that I will gather all Nations and Tongues, and they shall come and see my Glory, and I will set a sign among them, and I will send those that escape of them unto the Nations, to* Tarshish, Pull *and* Lud *that draw the Bow to* Tuball *and* Javan, *to the* Isles *afar off that have not heard my Fame, neither have seen my Glory, and they shall declare my Glory among the Gentiles, Isa.* 66. 12–18.

Fourthly, Because the Lord hath commanded, saying, *Thou shalt not oppress an hired Servant that is poor and needy, whether he be of thy .Brethren, or of the Strangers that are in thy Land within thy Gates, least he cry against thee unto the Lord, and it be sin unto thee; Thou shalt neither vex a stranger nor oppress him, for ye were strangers in the Land of Egypt, Deut.* 24. 14, 15. *Exod.* 12. 21. But what greater Oppression can there be inflicted upon our Fellow Creatures, than is inflicted on the poor Negroes! they being brought from their own Country against their Wills, some of them being stollen, others taken for payment of Debt owing by their Parents, and others taken Captive in War, and sold to Merchants, who bring them to the American Plantations, and sell them for Bond Slaves to them that will give most for them; the Husband from the Wife, and the Children from the Parents; and many that buy them do exceedingly afflict them and oppress them, not only by continual hard Labour, but by cruel Whippings, and other cruel Punishments, and by short allowance of Food, some Planters in *Barbadoes* and *Jamaica*, 'tis said, keeping one hundred of them, and some more, and some less, and giving them hardly any thing more than they raise on a little piece of Ground appointed them, on which they work for themselves the seventh days of the Week in the after-noon, and on the first days, to raise their own Provisions, to wit, Corn and Potatoes, and other Roots, &c. the remainder of their time being spent in their Masters service; which doubtless is far worse usage than is practised by the *Turks* and *Moors* upon their Slaves. Which tends to the great Reproach of the *Christian Profession*; therefore it would be better for all such as fall short of the Practice of those *Infidels*, to refuse the name of a Christian, that those *Heathen* and *Infidels* may not be provoked to blaspheme against the blessed Name of Christ, by reason of the unparallel'd Cruelty of these cruel and hard hearted pretended Christians: Surely the Lord doth behold their Oppressions & Afflictions, and will further visit for the same by his righteous and just Judgments, except they break off their sins by Repentance, and their Iniquity by shewing Mercy to these poor afflicted, tormented miserable Slaves!

Fifthly, Because Slaves and Souls of Men are some of the *Merchandize of Babylon* by which the Merchants of the Earth are made Rich; but those Riches which they have heaped together, through the cruel Oppression of these miserable Creatures, will be a means to draw Gods Judgments upon them; therefore, *Brethren*, let us hearken to the Voice of the Lord, who saith, *Come out of* Babylon, *my People, that ye be not partakers of her Sins, and that ye receive not her Plagues; for her Sins have reached unto Heaven, and God hath remembered her iniquities; for he that leads into Captivity shall go into Captivity, Rev.* 18. 4, 5. & 13. 10.

Given forth by our Monthly Meeting in Philadelphia, *the 13th day of the 8th Moneth, 1693. and recommended to all our Friends and Brethren, who are one with us in our Testimony for the Lord Jesus Christ, and to all others professing Christianity.*

THE END.

LESSON PLAN: Resistance to Slavery

Students analyze excerpts from two pamphlets that call for resistance to slavery to understand their influence in the development of the abolitionist movement.

Learning Objectives

Analyze overt and passive resistance to enslavement; consider multiple perspectives and analyze the evidence used to support the authors' points of view; analyze the causes and effects of resistance to slavery; draw comparisons across regions to define the early development of the abolitionist movement.

Materials: George Keith, *An Exhortation and Caution to Friends Concerning Buying or Keeping of Negroes (1693)*; Samuel Sewall, *The Selling of Joseph: A Memorial (1700)*.

Overview Questions

How do the selections express resistance to slavery? What evidence do they use to support their points of view? How are their points of view similar and different? What motivated Keith and Sewall to speak out against slavery? How do the arguments that Keith and Sewell make help to drive the development of the early abolitionist movement?

Step 1: Comprehension Questions

How do the selections express resistance to slavery? What points do they make?

▶ **Activity:** Select students to read key passages in both selections. Discuss the five points that Keith makes as well as the points that Sewall uses.

Step 2: Comprehension Questions

What evidence do Keith and Sewall use to support their points of view? What references do they make? How are their points of view similar and different?

▶ **Activity:** Ask students to work in pairs and highlight the words that each author uses to support his points. Have students look at the format and language in each. Ask students to write a summary of the similarities and differences between the pamphlets.

Step 3: Context Questions

What motivated Keith and Sewall to speak out against slavery? What prompted them to make an appeal for their cause?

▶ **Activity:** Discuss with students the social, political, economic, and importance of slavery in colonial America. Ask students to write three

reasons why Keith and Sewall spoke out against slavery.

Step 4: Exploration Questions

How do the arguments that Keith and Sewell make help to drive the development of the early abolitionist movement? Why are their arguments important to the greater cause?

▶ **Activity:** Provide an opportunity for small groups of students to research and choose at least two later primary sources that were written in support of the abolition of slavery. Next, have students prepare an oral presentation in which they make comparisons between the earlier and later documents, noting similar evidence, influences, and the development of the argument against slavery.

Step 5: Response Paper

Word length and additional requirements set by Instructor. Students answer the research question in the Overview Questions. Students state a thesis and use as evidence passages from the primary source document as well as support from supplemental materials assigned in the lesson.

APPENDIXES

Chronological List

Historical Timeline

NORTH AMERICA		THE WORLD
Leif Ericson lands in North America, c. 1000	1000	The First Crusade begins, 1096
Iroquois Constitution, c. 1200	1200	Magna Carta, 1215 The Inquisition begins under Pope Gregory IX, 1231
Mandan migrate from the Ohio Valley, 1250	1300	The beginning of the Renaissance in Italy, c. 1325
Journal of the First Voyage of Columbus, Christopher Columbus, 1492	1400	Joan of Arc is burned at the stake as a witch, 1431
St. Augustine, Florida is established by the Spanish; it is the first town established by Europeans in the US, 1565 Sir Walter Raleigh founds North Carolina, the first English colony in North America, 1587 Virginia Dare, the first English child born in America, is born, 1587.	1500	Hernando Cortes conquers Mexico, 1519 Ferdinand Magellan reaches the Pacific, 1521 The English defeat the Spanish Armada, 1588
The first African slaves are brought to Jamestown, 1619 The House of Burgesses, the first representative assembly in America, meets for the first time, 1619 The Mayflower lands in Cape Cod, 1620 *The Articles of Confederation of Plymouth Plantation*, William Bradford, 1621 Peter Minuit buys Manhattan from Indians, 1626	1600	*Don Quixote*, the first modern novel, is published, 1605 Shakespeare publishes his sonnets, 1609 Galileo observes the moons of Jupiter, 1610 The Thirty Years' War begins, 1618 The first English newspaper, *Corante*, appears, 1621
Boston is founded by Massachusetts colonists led by John Winthrop, 1630 North America's first university is founded at Cambridge in the Massachusetts Bay Colony, and Limitation of Government, John Cotton, 1639 *A Key into the Language of America*, Roger Williams, 1643	1625	End of the Thirty Years' War, German population cut in half, 1648 Charles I is put on trial for fighting a war against Parliament and is beheaded, 1649
Rhode Island enacts the first law in the colonies declaring slavery illegal, 1652 *The Virginia Slave Laws*, Act I, III, XII, with chapters XXII, XLIX, 1662	1650	Parliament establishes the first of many Navigation Acts to preserve international trade for English ships, 1651 The Great Plague kills 75,000 people in London, 1665

NORTH AMERICA		THE WORLD
King Philip's War, 1675-1676 Pennsylvania is founded as William Penn, a Quaker, receives a royal charter with a large land grant from King Charles II, 1681 *The Salem Witch Trials: The Case against John and Elizabeth Proctor*, 1692	1675	Ole Roemer, while working with Cassini in Paris, calculates the speed of light with an error of 25 percent, 1676 Isaac Newton publishes *Principia Mathematica*, showing gravity is constant in all physical systems, 1687
The Boston News Letter becomes the first newspaper in America, 1704 French Colonists found New Orleans, 1718	1700	The War of Spanish Succession begins, 1701 Thomas Newcomen creates a piston steam engine, beginning the Industrial Revolution, 1710 Fahrenheit perfects the mercury thermometer, 1714
In Defense of John Zenger and the Press, Andrew Hamilton, 1733 Zenger is acquitted of libel in New York, establishing freedom of the press, 1735 *Sinners in the Hands of an Angry God / On the Great Awakening*, Jonathan Edwards, 1741, 1743	1725	The War of Jenkin's Ear begins, 1739 British overcome Scots under Stuart Pretender Prince Charles at Culloden Moor; it is the last battle fought on British land, 1746
Ben Franklin invents the lightning rod, 1752; also creates the first American political cartoon, the chopped-up snake with the caption "Join or Die," urging the unity of the colonies, 1754	1750	Publication of the *Encyclopédie* begins in France, the "bible" of the Enlightenment, 1751 The first physical map of France is made by Jean Etienne Guettard, 1751

Web Resources

www.americanjourneys.org

Chronicles American exploration through over 18,000 pages of firsthand accounts of North American exploration. Visitors can read through the views of various historical figures from America's lively and momentous past.

docsouth.unc.edu

A digital publishing project that reflects the southern perspective of American history and culture. It offers a wide collection of titles that students, teachers, and researchers of all levels can utilize.

teachinghistory.org

A project funded by the US Department of Education that aims to assist teachers of all levels to augment their efforts in teaching American history. It strives to amplify student achievement through improving the knowledge of teachers.

www.ushistory.org/us

Contains an outline that details the entire record of American history. This resource offers historical insight and stories that demonstrate what truly an American truly is from a historical perspective.

teachingamericanhistory.org

Allows visitors to learn more about American history through original source documents detailing the broad spectrum of American history. The site contains document libraries, audio lectures, lesson plans, and more.

www.history.com/topics/american-history

Tells the story of America through topics of interest such as the Declaration of Independence, major wars, and notable Americans.

www.loc.gov/topics/americanhistory.php

Covers the various eras and ages of American history in detail, including resources such as readings, interactive activities, multimedia, and more.

www.si.edu/encyclopedia_si/nmah/timeline.htm

Details the course of American history chronologically. Important dates and significant events link to other pages within the Smithsonian site that offer more details.

www.smithsonianeducation.org

An online resource for educators, families, and students offering lesson plans, interactive activities, and more.

edsitement.neh.gov

An online resource for teachers, students, and parents seeking to further their understanding of the humanities. This site offers lesson plan searches, student resources, and interactive activities.

www.digitalhistory.uh.edu

Offers an online history textbook, Hypertext History, which chronicles the story of America, along with interactive timelines. This online source also contains handouts, lesson plans, e-lectures, movies, games, biographies, glossaries, maps, music, and much more.

www.earlyamerica.com

Includes a wealth of articles, images, and other archival material that helps visitors to see and understand the beginning years of what would become the United States of America.

havefunwithhistory.com

An online, interactive resource for students, teachers, and anybody who has an interest in American history.

library.thinkquest.org/28936/history.htm

Provides a detailed history of the early stages of the American endeavor. Also contains detailed readings on specific events, people, and on the original thirteen colonies themselves.

www.history.org

Offers an array of resources for visitors, including information on people, places, and culture. There are also resources for teachers including e-newsletters and electronic field trips.

www.gilderlehrman.org

Offers many options in relation to the history of America. The History by Era section provides detailed explanations of specific time periods while the primary sources present firsthand accounts from a historical perspective.

www.gilderlehrman.org/history-by-era/americas-1620

Provides an interactive timeline of the early events and accounts of what is now called America. The timeline stretches from human migration in 70,000 BCE all the way to the Mayflower Compact of 1620.

www.nps.gov/jame/index.htm

Presents a wealth of knowledge related to Jamestown. The online exploration allows visitors to view the history and culture, as well as sort through the online resources for teachers as well as students.

www.masshist.org

Home to millions of rare and distinctive documents that are crucial to the course of American history, many of them being irreplaceable national treasures. Online collections, exclusive publications, and teacher resources are included.

historymatters.gmu.edu

An online resource from George Mason University that provides links, teaching materials, primary documents, and guides for evaluating historical records.

www.loc.gov/teachers/classroommaterials/themes/colonial-america

Includes resources and materials for teachers, including lesson plans, primary sources, activities, and collections. Also available for teachers is the opportunity for professional development through self-directed modules as well as the professional development builder.

Bibliography

"The African Slave Trade and the Middle Passage." *Africans in America*. WGBH Educational Foundation, 1999. Web. 25 May 2012.

"AJ-107 Document Page: Background." *American Journeys*. Wisconsin Hist. Soc., 2011. Web. 6 Feb. 2012.

Alexander, James. *A Brief Narrative of the Case and Trial of John Peter Zenger*. Ed. Stanley N. Katz. Cambridge: Belknap, 1963. Print.

Allegro, James J. "'Increasing and Strengthening the Country': Law, Politics, and the Antislavery Movement in Early-Eighteenth-Century Massachusetts Bay." *New England Quarterly* 75.1 (2002): 5–23. Print.

Alvarez, Kate. "Ann Putnam, Jr." *Salem Witch Trials: Documentary Archive and Transcription Project*. University of Virginia, 2002. Web. 1 Jan. 2012.

"Americapedia: Massachusetts Body of Liberties (1641)." *Bill of Rights Institute*. Bill of Rights Institute, 2010. Web. 30 May 2012.

Anderson, Robert Charles. "Pilgrim Village Families Sketch: Edward Winslow." *American Ancestors: New England Historic Genealogical Society*. n.d. Web. 11 Apr. 2012.

Anderson, Virginia DeJohn. "King Philip's Herds: Indians, Colonists, and the Problem of Livestock in Early New England." *William and Mary Quarterly* 51.4 (1994): 601–24. Print.

Andrews, William L. *To Tell a Free Story: The First Century of Afro-American Autobiography, 1760–1865*. Urbana: U of Illinois P, 1986. Print.

Andrews, William L., ed., et al. *Journeys in New Worlds: Early American Women's Narratives*. Madison: U of Wisconsin P, 1990. Print.

Arch, Stephen Carl. "The Glorious Revolution and the Rhetoric of Puritan History." *Early American History* 27.1 (1992): 61–74. Print.

Arsić, Branka. "Mary Rowlandson and the Phenomenology of Patient Suffering." *Common Knowledge* 16.2 (2010): 247–75. Print.

"Background on *Journal of the First Voyage of Columbus*." *American Journeys*. Wisconsin Historical Society, 2011. Web. 4 June 2012.

Badertscher, Eric. "Christopher Columbus." *Christopher Columbus* (2009): 1–3. *History Reference Center*. Web. 4 June 2012.

Bakeless, John. *The Eyes of Discovery: A Pageant of North America as Seen by the First Explorers*. New York: Lippincott, 1950. Print.

Balkun, Mary McAleer. "Sarah Kemble Knight and the Construction of the American Self." *Women's Studies* 28.1 (1998): 7–27. Print.

Bangs, Jeremy Dupertuis. *Indian Deeds: Land Transactions in Plymouth Colony, 1620–1691*. Boston: New England Historic Genealogical Society, 2002. Print.

---. Jeremy Dupertuis. *Strangers and Pilgrims, Travelers and Sojourners: Leiden and the Foundations of Plymouth Plantation*. Plymouth, MA: General Society of Mayflower Descendants, 2009. Print.

Barbour, Philip L. *The Three Worlds of Captain John Smith*. Boston: Houghton, 1974. Print.

Barreiro, Jose, and Carol Cornelius. *Knowledge of the Elders: The Iroquois Condolence Cane Tradition*. Ithaca: Akwekon, 1991. Print.

Bassett, John Spencer. "The Historians, 1607–1783: Thomas Hutchinson". *The Cambridge History of English and American Literature in 18 Volumes*. Bartleby.com, 2000. Web. 29 May 2012.

Baylies, Francis. *An Historical Memoir of the Colony of New Plymouth*. Vol. 2. Boston: Hilliard, 1830. Print.

Beaver, R. Pierce. "Methods in American Missions to the Indians in the Seventeenth and Eighteenth Centuries: Calvinist Models for Protestant Foreign Missions." *Journal of Presbyterian History* 47.2 (1969): 124–48. Print.

---. "Protestant Churches and the Indians." *Handbook of North American Indians*. Ed. William C. Sturtevant and Wilcomb E. Washburn. Vol. 4. Washington: Smithsonian, 1988. 430–58. Print.

Berkovitch, Sacvan. "New England's Errand Reappraised." *New Directions in American Intellectual History,* ed. John Hingham and Paul Conkin. Baltimore: Johns Hopkins UP. 1979. Print.

--- ed. *Typology and Early American Literature*. Amherst: U of Massachusetts P, 1972. Print.

Berkhofer, Robert F. *Salvation and the Savage: An Analysis of Protestant Missions and American Indian Response, 1787–1862*. New York: Atheneum, 1972. Print.

Berlin, Ira. *Many Thousands Gone: The First Two Centuries of Slavery in North America*. Cambridge: Harvard UP, 1998 Print.

Beverley, Robert. *The History and Present State of Virginia*. Ed. Louis B. Wright. Charlottesville: UP of Virginia, 1947. Print.

"Biography: Cotton Mather." *The Mather Project*. Georgia State University, 2011. Web. 14 June 2012.

Blackstone, Kenneth E. "The Salem Witch Trials: A Case Review." *Blackstone Polygraph*. Blackstone Polygraph, 2009. PDF file.

Boas, Ralph, and Louise Boas. *Cotton Mather: Keeper of the Puritan Conscience*. New York: Harper, 1928. Print.

Bolus, Malvina, ed. *People and Pelts: Selected Papers of the Second North American Fur Trade Conference*. Winnipeg: Peguis, 1972. Print.

Bowden, Henry Warner. *American Indians and Christian Missions: Studies in Cultural Conflict*. Chicago: U of Chicago P, 1981. Print.

Boyer, Paul, and Stephen Nissbaum. *Salem Possessed: The Social Origins of Witchcraft*. Cambridge: Harvard UP, 1974. Print.

Bradford, William. *Bradford's History of Plymouth Plantation: 1606–1646*. Ed. William T. Davis. New York: Scribner's, 2005. Print.

---. *Bradford's History of the Plymouth Settlement, 1608–1650*. Ed. Harold Paget. New York: McBride, 1909. Print.

Breen, Louise A. *Transgressing the Bounds: Subversive Enterprises Among the Puritan Elite in Massachusetts, 1630–1692*. New York: Oxford UP, 2001. Print.

Breitweiser, Mitchell Robert. *Cotton Mather and Benjamin Franklin: The Price of Representative Personality*. Cambridge: Cambridge UP, 1984. Print.

Bremer, Francis J. *John Winthrop: America's Forgotten Founding Father*. New York: Oxford UP, 2003. Print.

---. *The Puritan Experiment: New England Society from Bradford to Edwards*. New York: St. Martin's, 1995. Print.

Brians, Paul. "The Enlightenment." *The Enlightenment*. Washington State University, 18 May 2000. Web. 30 May 2012.

Briceland, Alan Vance. *Westward from Virginia: The Exploration of the Virginia-Carolina Frontier, 1650–1710*. Charlottesville: UP of Virginia, 1987. Print.

Bridenbaugh, Carl. *Jamestown, 1544–1699*. New York: Oxford UP, 1980. Print.

Brimacombe, Peter. *All the Queen's Men: The World of Elizabeth I*. New York: St. Martin's, 2000. Print.

"The Bull Family of South Carolina." *South Carolina Historical and Genealogical Magazine* 1.1 (1900): 76–90. Print.

Bull, Kinloch. "William Bull." *American National Biography Online*. American Biography Online, n.d. Web. 3 May 2012.

Buranelli, Vincent. *The King & the Quaker: A Study of William Penn and James II*. Philadelphia: U of Pennsylvania P, 1962. Print.

---. *The Trial of John Peter Zenger*. Westport: Greenwood, 1975. Print.

Burg, B. R. "Dudley, Joseph 1647–1720." *Oxford Dictionary of National Biography* (2010): 1. *Biography Reference Center*. Web. 30 May 2012.

Burgan, Michael. *John Winthrop: Colonial Governor of Massachusetts*. Minneapolis: Compass Point, 2006. Print.

Burnham, Michelle. "Inflation: Thomas Morton and Trading-Post Pastoral." *Folded Selves: Colonial New England Writing in the World System*. Hanover: Dartmouth College P, 2007. 72–94. Print.

---. "Land, Labor, and Colonial Economics in Thomas Morton's *New English Canaan*." *Early American Literature* 41.3 (2006): 405–28. Print.

Bush, Sargent, Jr. "The Journal of Madam Knight." Introduction. *Journeys in New Worlds, Early American Women's Narratives*. Ed. William L. Andrews, Sargent Bush Jr., Annette Kolodny, Amy Schrager Lang, and Daniel B. Shea. Madison: U. of Wisconsin P, 1990. 69–83. Print.

Butcher, Philip, ed. *The Minority Presence in American Literature, 1600–1900*. Vol. 1. Washington: Howard UP, 1977. Print.

Byrd, William. *Prose Works: Narratives of a Colonial Virginian*. Ed. Louis B. Wright. Cambridge: Belknap, 1966. Print.

Campbell, Donna M. "Puritanism in New England." *Literary Movements*. Dept. of English, Washington State University, 21 Mar. 2010. Web. 29 May 2012.

Campeau, Lucien. "Roman Catholic Missions in New France." *Handbook of North American Indians*. Ed. William Sturtevant and Wilcomb E. Washburn. Vol. 4. Washington: Smithsonian Institution, 1988. 464–71. Print.

Cantor, Milton. "The Image of the Negro in Colonial Literature." *New England Quarterly* 36.4 (1963): 452–77. Print.

Carroll, Meghan, and Jenny Stone. "Mercy Lewis." *Salem Witch Trials: Documentary Archive and Transcription Project*. University of Virginia, 2002. Web. 1 Jan. 2012.

Castañeda, Pedro de. "Account of the expedition to Cibola which took place in the year 1540, in which all those settlements, their ceremonies and customs, are described." *The Journey of Coronado, 1540–42.* Ed. and trans. George Parker Winship. New York: Barnes, 1904. xxix–148. Print.

Castro, Daniel. *Another Face of Empire: Bartolomé de Las Casas, Indigenous Rights, and Ecclesiastical Imperialism.* Durham: Duke UP, 2007. Print.

Cave, Alfred A. "Who Killed John Stone? A Note on the Origins of the Pequot War." *William and Mary Quarterly* 3rd ser. 49.3 (1992): 509–21. Print.

Chamberlain, Nathan Henry. *Samuel Sewall and the World He Lived In.* 2nd ed. Boston: De Wolfe, 1898. Print.

Champagne, Duane. *Native America: Portrait of the Peoples.* Detroit: Visible Ink, 1994. Print.

Chaney, Charles L. *The Birth of Missions in America.* South Pasadena: William Carey Lib., 1976. Print.

Church, Thomas, and Benjamin Church. *The Entertaining History of Philip's War, Which Began in the Month of June, 1675; As Also of Expeditions More Lately Made Against the Common Enemy, and Indian Rebels, in the Eastern Parts of New-England: With Some Account of the Divine Providence Towards Col. Benjamin Church.* 2nd ed. Newport, RI: Solomon Southwick, 1772. Print.

Clark, Ronald W. *Benjamin Franklin: A Biography.* New York: Barnes and Noble, 2004. Print.

Cohen, Matt. "Morton's Maypole and the Indians: Publishing in Early New England." *Book History* 5 (2002): 1–18. Print.

Coker, Michael. *Charleston Curiosities: Stories of the Tragic, Heroic, and Bizarre.* Charleston: History, 2008. Print.

Colacurcio, Michael J. "A Costly Canaan: Morton and the Margins of American Literature." *Godly Letters: The Literature of the American Puritans.* South Bend: Notre Dame UP, 2006. 3–33. Print.

"Colonial Settlement, 1600s–1763: Establishing the Georgia Colony, 1732–1750." *Lib. of Congress.* US Lib. of Congress, n.d. Web. 25 May 2012.

Cotton, John. "Discourse about Civil Government in a New Plantation Whose Design is Religion." 1658. Shropshire, Engl.: Quinta. 2011. Print.

"Cotton Mather." *Salem Witchcraft Trials 1692.* University of Missouri—Kansas City School of Law, n.d. Web. 14 June 2012.

Cragg, G. R. *The Church and the Age of Reason 1648–1789.* Baltimore: Penguin, 1990. Print.

Cushman, Robert. *The Sin and Danger of Self-Love Described, in a Sermon Preached at Plymouth, in New England, 1621.* Boston: 1846. Print.

Danforth, Samuel. "A Brief Recognition of New-England's Errand into the Wilderness: An Online Electronic Text Edition." Ed. Paul Royster. *DigitalCommons@ University of Nebraska-Lincoln.* Libraries at University of Nebraska-Lincoln. 2006. Web. 18 May 2012.

Davenant, Charles. *An Essay upon the Government of the English Plantations on the Continent of America.* New York: Arno, 1972. Print.

Davis, David Brion. *The Problem with Slavery in Western Culture.* Oxford: Oxford UP, 1988. Print.

"Declaration and Resolves of the First Continental Congress." *Colonial Williamsburg Foundation.* Colonial Williamsburg Foundation, 2012. Web. 30 May 2012.

Deloria, Vine, Jr., and Clifford M. Lytle. *American Indians, American Justice.* Austin: U of Texas P, 1983. Print.

Desrochers, Robert E. Jr. "'Not Fade Away': The Narrative of Venture Smith, an African American in the Early Republic." *Journal of American History* 84.1 (1997): 40–66. Print.

Deyle, Steven. *Carry Me Back: The Domestic Slave Trade in American Life.* New York: Oxford UP, 2005. Print.

Dignan, Brendan. "Governor, Sir William Phips." *Salem Witch Trials: Documentary Archive and Transcription Project.* University of Virginia, 2012. Web. 3 Jan. 2012.

Documenting the American South. University Library of the University of North Carolina at Chapel Hill, 2004. Web. 1 June 2012.

Donegan, Kathleen. "'As Dying, Yet Behold We Live': Catastrophe and Interiority in Bradford's *Of Plymouth Plantation.*" *Early American Literature* 37.1 (2002): 9–37. Print.

Donnan, Elizabeth, ed. *Documents Illustrative of the History of the Slave Trade to America.* 4 vols. Washington: Carnegie Inst. of Washington, 1930–1935. Print.

Drake, James D. *King Philip's War: Civil War in New England 1675–1676.* Amherst: U of Massachusetts P, 1999. Print.

Drexler, Kenneth, Susan Garfinkel, Mark F. Hall, and Jurretta Jordan Heckscher. "Finding Franklin: A Resource Guide." *Library of Congress.* Library of Congress, Feb. 2006. Web. 27 Feb. 2012.

Dudley, Joseph. "English Liberties and Deference." *Digital History*. Steven Mintz, 2011. Web. 9 May 2012.

Dunn, Mary Maples. *William Penn: Politics and Conscience*. Princeton: Princeton UP, 1967. Print.

Easton, John. "A Relacion of the Indyan Warre." *Narratives of the Indian Wars, 1675–1699*. Ed. Charles Henry Lincoln. New York: Scribner's, 1913. 2–17. Print.

Eccles, W. J. *France in America*. New York: Harper, 1972. Print.

Eisenstadt, Peter, and Laura-Eve Moss. *The Encyclopedia of New York State*. Syracuse: Syracuse UP, 2005. Print.

Eliot, Charles W. "The Massachusetts Body of Liberties (1641)." *American Historical Documents, 1000–1904*. New York: Collier, 1909–14. Print. Harvard Classics 43.

"Elisha Williams." *Yale U Library*. Yale University, 14 Feb. 2008. Web. 7 June 2012.

Eltis, David. *The Rise of African Slavery in the Americas*. New York: Cambridge UP, 2000. Print.

Engel, Katherine Carté. "Mittelberger, Gottlieb." *Encyclopedia of American History*. Ed. Gary B. Nash and Billy G. Smith. Vol. 2. New York: Facts on File, 2010. 239. Print.

Ewell, John Lewis. "Judge Samuel Sewall (1652–1730), A Typical Massachusetts Puritan." *Papers of the American Society of Church History* 7 (1895): 25–54. Print.

Ewers, John C. *Indian Life on the Upper Missouri*. Norman: U of Oklahoma P, 1968. Print.

Fausz, J. Frederick. "An 'Abundance of Blood Shed on Both Sides': England's First Indian War, 1609–1614." *Virginia Magazine of History and Biography* 98.1 (1990): 3–56. Print.

Fenton, William N. *The Great Law and the Longhouse: A Political History of the Iroquois Confederacy*. Norman: U of Oklahoma, 2010. Print.

Ferguson, Henry. "Sir Edmund Andros." *Essays in American History*. Port Washington: Kennikat, 1969. 111–51. Print.

Field, Jonathan B. "The Antinomian Controversy Did Not Take Place." *Early American Studies* 6.2 (2008): 448–463. Print.

Finkelman, Paul. Introduction. *Brief Narrative of the Case and Tryal of John Peter Zenger*. Boston: Bedford/St. Martin's, 2010. Print.

"First Continental Congress: Proceedings of the First Continental Congress." *US History*. Independence Hall Association, 2011. Web. 30 May 2012.

Flint, Richard, and Shirley Cushing Flint, eds. *The Coronado Expedition From the Distance of 460 Years*. Albuquerque: U of New Mexico P, 2003. Print.

Fogelman, Aaron. "From Slaves, Convicts, and Servants to Free Passengers: The Transformation of Immigration in the Era of the American Revolution." *Journal of American History* 85.1 (1998): 43–76. Print.

Folsom, Franklin. *Indian Uprising on the Rio Grande: The Pueblo Revolt of 1680*. Albuquerque: U of New Mexico P, 1996. Rpt. of *Red Power on the Rio Grande: The Native American Revolution of 1680*. 1973. Print.

Fox, Robert, ed. *Thomas Harriot: An Elizabethan Man of Science*. Aldershot: Ashgate, 2000. Print.

Francis, Richard. *Judge Sewall's Apology: The Salem Witch Trials and the Forming of an American Conscience*. New York: Harper, 2005. Print.

Franklin, Benjamin. *Franklin: Writings*. Ed. Joseph A. L. Lemay. New York: Literary Classics, 1996. Print.

French, B. F. *Historical Collections of Louisiana and Florida*. New York: Mason, 1875. Print.

"From Indentured Servitude to Racial Slavery." *Africans in America*. WGBH Educational Foundation, 1999. Web. 25 May 2012.

Fryer, Darcy R. "The Mind of Eliza Pinckney: An Eighteenth-Century Woman's Construction of Herself." *South Carolina Historical Magazine* 99.3 (1998): 215–37. Print.

Fuller, Mary C. *Voyages in Print: English Travel to America, 1576–1624*. Cambridge: Cambridge UP, 1995. Print.

Furer, Howard. *New York: A Chronological and Documentary History, 1524–1970*. Dobbs Ferry, NY: Oceana, 1974. Print.

Gallagher, Carole S. *Christopher Columbus and the Discovery of the New World*. Philadelphia: Chelsea, 2000. Print.

Gaustad, Edwin S. *A Documentary History of Religion in America*. Grand Rapids: Eerdmans, 1982. Print.

"George Wyllys: Governor of the Colony of Connecticut 1642." *Connecticut State Library*. Connecticut State Library, Apr. 1999. Web. 14 Dec. 2011.

Gibson, Matthew, ed. *Encyclopedia Virginia*. Virginia Foundation for the Humanities, 2001. Web. 1 June 2012.

Glover, Lorri, and Daniel Blake Smith. *The Shipwreck That Saved Jamestown*. New York: Holt, 2008. Print.

Goodman, Jennifer Robin. "The Captain's Self-Portrait: John Smith as Chivalric Biographer." *Virginia*

Magazine of History and Biography 89.1 (1981): 27–38. Print.

Goodrick, Alfred Thomas Scrope. "Introduction." *Edward Randolph; Including His Letters and Official Papers from the New England, Middle, and Southern Colonies in America, and the West Indies.* Boston: Prince Society, 1909. 1–67. Print.

Gottlieb, Matt. "House of Burgesses." *Encyclopedia Virginia.* Ed. Brendan Wolfe. Virginia Foundation for the Humanities, 10 Feb. 2012. Web. 14 June 2012.

Greene, David L. "New Light on Mary Rowlandson." *Early American Literature* 20.1 (1985): 24–38. Print.

Greene, Lorenzo. *The Negro in Colonial New England, 1620–1776.* New York: Columbia UP, 1942. Print.

Grinde, Donald A., Jr., and Bruce E. Johansen. *Exemplar of Liberty: Native America and the Evolution of Democracy.* Los Angeles: UCLA American Indian Studies Center, 1991. Print.

Groulx, Lionel. *Roland-Michel Barrin De La Galissonière, 1693–1756.* Toronto: U of Toronto P, 1971. Print.

Gura, Philip F. "Thoreau and John Josselyn." *New England Quarterly* 48.4 (1975): 505–18. Print.

Hackett, Charles Wilson. Introduction. *Revolt of the Pueblo Indians of New Mexico and Otermín's Attempted Reconquest, 1680–1682.* 2 vols. Albuquerque: U of New Mexico P, 1942. Print.

Hadden, Sally. *Slave Patrols: Law and Violence in Virginia and the Carolinas.* Cambridge: Harvard UP, 2001. Print.

Haffenden, Philip S. *New England in the English Nation, 1689–1713.* London: Clarendon, 1974. Print.

Hall, David D. "The Mental World of Samuel Sewall." *Proceedings of the Massachusetts Historical Society* 3rd ser. 92 (1980): 21–44. Print.

Hall, Michael G. *Edward Randolph and the American Colonies, 1676–1703.* Chapel Hill: U of North Carolina P, 1960. Print.

Harriot, Thomas. *A Brief and True Report of the New Found Land of Virginia.* Ann Arbor: Edwards Bros., 1931. Print.

Hatch, Charles E., Jr. *The First Seventeen Years: Virginia, 1607–1624.* Charlottesville: UP of Virginia, 1957. Print.

Hayes, Kevin J. "Defining the Ideal Colonist: John Smith's Revisions from *A True Relations* to the *Proceedings* to the Third Book of the *General History.*" *Virginia Magazine of History and Biography* 99.2 (1991): 123–44. Print.

Heath, William. "Thomas Morton: From Merry Old England to New England." *Journal of American Studies* 41.1 (2007): 135–68. Print.

Heimert, Alan, and Andrew Delbanco, eds. *The Puritans in America: A Narrative Anthology.* Cambridge: Harvard UP, 1985. Print.

Heinsohn, Robert Jennings. "Pilgrims and Puritans in 17th Century New England." *Sail 1620.* Society of Mayflower Descendants in the Commonwealth of Pennsylvania, 2012. Web. 30 May 2012.

Hernandez, Bonar Ludwig. "The Las Casas-Sepulveda Controversy: 1550–1551." *Ex Post Facto* 10.1 (2001): 95–104. Print.

Heyrman, Christine Leigh. "The First Great Awakening." *National Humanities Center.* Dept. of History, University of Delaware, 2008. Web. 29 May 2012.

"History of the Office of Coroner." *Indiana Coroner's Manual.* Purdue University, n.d. Web. 29 May 2012.

Hochstrasser, Julie. *Still Life and Trade in the Dutch Golden Age.* New Haven: Yale UP, 2007. Print.

Hoffer, Peter Charles. *Cry Liberty: The Great Stono River Slave Rebellion of 1739.* New York: OUP, 2010. Print.

Horn, James. *A Kingdom Strange: The Brief and Tragic History of the Lost Colony of Roanoke.* New York: Basic, 2010. Print.

Horton, James Oliver and Lois E. Horton. *Slavery and the Making of America.* New York: OUP, 2005. Print.

Huetteman, Susan. "Roger Williams (1603–1683): First Author and Founder of Rhode Island." *NCTE American Collection.* National Council of Teachers of English and ExxonMobil Masterpiece Theatre, n.d. Web. 24 May 2012.

Hume, Ivor Noël. *The Virginia Adventure: Roanoke to James Towne: An Archaeological and Historical Odyssey.* New York: Knopf, 1994. Print.

Husband, Julie. *Antislavery Discourse and Nineteenth-Century American Literature: Incendiary Pictures.* New York: Palgrave, 2010. Print.

Hutchinson, Thomas. "Massachusetts-Bay: A Colony of Loyal Britons? The Governor's View: 1760–63." *The History of the Province of Massachusetts Bay, From 1749–74, Comprising a Detailed Narrative of the Origin and Early Stages of the American Revolution.* Ed. John Hutchinson. *National Humanities Center.* Dept. of History, University of Delaware, 2009. Web. 29 May 2012.

Jackson, Kenneth, and David Dunbar. *Empire City: New York Through the Centuries.* New York: Columbia UP, 2002. Print.

Jacobs, Jaap. *New Netherland: A Dutch Colony in Seventeenth-Century America.* Boston: Brill, 2005. Print.

James, Ellen Mosen. "Decoding the Zenger Trial: Andrew Hamilton's 'Fraudful Dexterity' with Language." *The Law in America, 1607–1861.* Ed. William Pencak and Wythe Holt, Jr. New York: New York Historical Soc., 1989. 1–27. Print.

Jennings, Francis. *The Invasion of America: Indians, Colonialism, and the Cant of Conquest.* Chapel Hill: U of North Carolina P, 1975. Print.

Johansen, Bruce E. *Forgotten Founders: Benjamin Franklin, the Iroquois, and the Rationale for the American Revolution.* Ipswich: Gambit, 1982. Print.

"John Carver." *MayflowerHistory.com.* MayflowerHistory.com, 1994–2012. Web. 29 May 2012.

"John Proctor." *Famous American Trials: Salem Witchcraft Trials, 1692.* University of Missouri–Kansas City School of Law, n.d. Web. 1 Jan. 2012.

"John Proctor, of the Salem Witch Trials." House of Proctor Genealogy. House of Genealogy, 1945. Web. 2 Jan. 2012.

"John Winthrop: First Governor of Massachusetts, 1588–1629." *Boston History and Architecture.* iBoston.org, 2008. Web. 14 Dec. 2011.

"Jonathan Edwards: On the Great Awakening" *Who We Are: The Story of America's Constitution.* National Humanities Institute, 1998. Web 30 Apr. 2012.

Jones, Hugh. *The Present State of Virginia, from Whence Is Inferred a Short View of Maryland and North Carolina.* Ed. Richard L. Morton. Chapel Hill: U of North Carolina P, 1956. Print.

Kaplan, Sidney. *American Studies in Black and White: Selected Essays, 1949–1989.* Ed. Allan D. Austin. Amherst: U of Massachusetts P, 1991. Print.

Karlsen, Carol F. *The Devil in the Shape of a Woman: Witchcraft in Colonial New England.* 1987. New York. Norton, 1998. Print.

Kawashima, Yasu. "Jurisdiction of the Colonial Courts over the Indians in Massachusetts, 1689–1763." *New England Quarterly* 42.4 (1969): 532–50. Print.

Keen, Benjamin. *Essays in the Intellectual History of Colonial Latin America.* Boulder: Westview, 1998. Print.

Kelso, Dorothy Honiss. "William Bradford." *Pilgrim Hall Museum.* Pilgrim Hall Museum, 18 May 2005. Web. 4 June 2012.

Kennedy, J. H. *Jesuit and Savage in New France.* New Haven: Yale UP, 1950. Print.

Kizer, Kay. "Puritans." *University of Notre Dame.* University of Notre Dame, n.d. Web. 10 Apr. 2012.

Knaut, Andrew L. *The Pueblo Revolt of 1680: Conquest and Resistance in Seventeenth-Century New Mexico.* Norman: U of Oklahoma P, 1995. Print.

Knight, Sarah Kemble. *The Private Journal of a Journey from Boston to New York in the Year 1704.* Ed. William L. Learned. Albany: Little, 1865. Print.

Knoppers, Laura L. *Puritanism and Its Discontents.* Newark: U of Delaware P, 2003. Print.

Kohnova, Marie J. "The Moravians and Their Missionaries: A Problem in Americanization." *The Mississippi Valley Historical Review* 19.3 (1932): 348–61. Print.

Kolchin, Peter. *Unfree Labor: American Slavery and Russian Serfdom.* Cambridge: Belknap, 1987. Print.

Kupperman, Karen Ordahl. "English Perceptions of Treachery, 1583–1640: The Case of the American 'Savages.'" *Historical Journal* 20.2 (1977): 263–87. Print.

Lang, Amy S. *Prophetic Woman: Anne Hutchinson and the Problem of Dissent in the Literature of New England.* Berkeley: U of California P, 1987. Print.

LaPlante, Eve. *American Jezebel: The Uncommon Life of Anne Hutchinson, the Woman Who Defied the Puritans.* San Francisco: Harper, 2004. Print.

---. *Salem Witch Judge: The Life and Repentance of Samuel Sewall.* New York: Harper, 2007. Print.

Laut, Agnes C. *Pathfinders of the West, Being the Thrilling Story of the Adventures of the Men Who Discovered the Great Northwest: Radisson, La Vérendrye, Lewis and Clark.* New York: Grosset, 1904. Print.

Lawson, John. *A New Voyage to Carolina.* Ed. Hugh Talmage Lefler. Chapel Hill: U of North Carolina P, 1967. Print.

Leach, Douglas Edward. *Flintlock and Tomahawk: New England in King Philip's War.* New York: Macmillan, 1958. Print.

---. "The 'Whens' of Mary Rowlandson's Captivity." *New England Quarterly* 34.3 (1961): 352–63. Print.

Learned, Marion Dexter, and Samuel W. Pennypacker. *The Life of Francis Daniel Pastorius, the Founder of Germantown.* Philadelphia: Campbell, 1908. Print.

Lemay, Joseph A. L. *The Life of Benjamin Franklin.* 3 vols. Philadelphia: U of Pennsylvania P, 2006–09. Print.

Lepore, Jill. *The Name of War: King Philip's War and the Origins of American Identity.* New York: Knopf, 1998. Print.

Levenduski, Christine M. *Peculiar Power: A Quaker Woman Preacher in Eighteenth-Century America.* Washington, DC: Smithsonian Inst. P, 1996. Print.

Levy, Babette May. *Cotton Mather*. Boston: Hall, 1979. Print.

Lewis, Theodore B. "Royal Government in New Hampshire and the Revocation of the Charter of the Massachusetts Bay Colony, 1679–1683." *Historical New Hampshire* 25.4 (1970): 2–45. Print.

Liebman, Matthew. *Revolt: An Archaeological History of Pueblo Resistance and Revitalization in Seventeenth Century New Mexico*. Tucson: U of Arizona P, 2012. Print.

Linder, Douglas. "Cotton Mather." *Famous American Trials: Salem Witchcraft Trials, 1692*. University of Missouri–Kansas City School of Law, n.d. Web. 1 Jan. 2012.

Lippy, Charles H., Robert Choquette, and Stafford Poole. *Christianity Comes to the Americas: 1492–1776*. New York: Paragon, 1992. Print.

Locke, John. *An Essay Concerning Human Understanding*. Ed. R. S. Woodhouse. New York: Penguin, 1997. Print.

---. *John Locke's Two Treatises of Government: New Interpretations*. Ed. Edward J. Harpham. Lawrence: UP of Kansas, 1992. Print.

---. *Political Writings of John Locke*. Ed. David Wootton. Indianapolis: Hackett, 2003. Print.

Lockwood, James. "Man Mortal: God Everlasting, and the Sure, Unfailing Refuge and Felicity of His Faithful People, in All Generations." New Haven, CT: Parker, 1756.

Logan, Lisa. "Mary Rowlandson's Captivity and the 'Place' of the Woman Subject." *Early American Literature* 28.3 (1993): 255–77. Print.

Loskiel, George Henry. *History of the Missions of the United Brethren among the Indians of North America*. Trans. Christian Ignatius LaTrobe. London: Brethren's Soc. for the Furtherance of the Gospel, 1794. Print.

Lovejoy, David S. "Plain Englishmen at Plymouth." *New England Quarterly* 63.2 (1990): 232–248. Print.

---. *Religious Enthusiasm in the New World: Heresy to Revolution*. Cambridge, MA: Harvard UP, 1985. Print.

Lustig, Mary Lou. *The Imperial Executive in America: Sir Edmund Andros, 1637–1714*. Madison: Fairleigh Dickinson UP, 2002. Print.

MacDonald, William, ed. *Select Charters and Other Documents: Illustrative of American History 1606–1775*. 1899. Whitefish: Kessinger, 2010. Print.

Marambaud, Pierre. *William Byrd of Westover, 1674–1744*. Charlottesville: UP of Virginia, 1971. Print.

Martinez, Fernando Rey. "The Religious Character of the American Constitution: Puritanism and Constitutionalism in the United States." *Kansas Journal of Law and Public Policy* Spring 2003. Web. 29 May 2012.

Mason, Louis Bond. *The Life and Times of Major John Mason of Connecticut, 1600–1672*. New York: Putnam, 1935. Print.

Mason, Otis T. *Traps of the American Indians*. Washington: GPO, 1901. Print.

"Massachusetts Body of Liberties." *Massachusetts Executive Office for Administration and Finance*. Commonwealth of Massachusetts, 2012. Web. 30 May 2012.

Mather, Cotton. *Magnalia Christi Americana, or, The Ecclesiastical History of New England from Its First Planting, in the Year 1620, unto the Year of Our Lord 1698*. Ed. Thomas Robbins. Hartford: Andrus, 1853. Print.

---. *Selected Letters*. Comp. Kenneth Silverman. Baton Rouge: Louisiana State UP, 1971. Print.

McCartney, Martha. "Sir Thomas Gates (d. 1622)." *Encyclopedia Virginia*. Ed. Brendan Wolfe. Virginia Foundation for the Humanities, 4 Apr. 2012 .Web. 2 June 2012.

McConaghy, Mary D., Michael Silberman, and Irina Kalashnikova. "Introduction: From Franklin's Vision to Academy to University of Pennsylvania." *University Archives and Records Center*. University of Pennsylvania University Archives and Records Center, 2004. Web. 20 June 2012.

McLynn, Frank. *1759: The Year Britain Became Master of the World*. New York: Atlantic Monthly, 2004. Print.

McMillan, Alan D., and Eldon Yellowhorn. *First Peoples in Canada*. Toronto: Douglas, 2009. Print.

Meyers, Albert Cook, ed. *Narratives of Early Pennsylvania, West New Jersey and Delaware, 1630–1707*. New York: Scribner's, 1912. Print.

Michaelsen, Scott. "Narrative and Class in a Culture of Consumption: The Significance of Stories in Sarah Kemble Knight's *Journal*." *College Literature* 21.2 (1994): 33–46. Print.

Middleton, Richard, and Anne Lombard. *Colonial America: A History to 1763*. 4th ed. Malden: Wiley-Blackwell, 2011. Print.

Miller, Lee. *Solving the Mystery of the Lost Colony of Roanoke*. New York: Arcade, 2001. Print.

Miller, Perry, and Thomas H. Johnson, eds. *The Puri-

tans: A Sourcebook of Their Writings. Mineola: Dover, 2001. Print.

Mintz, Steven. "Virginia Slave Laws." *Digital History.* Digital History, 6 June 2012. Web. 14 June 2012.

Mittelberger, Gottlieb. *Journey to Pennsylvania.* Ed. Oscar Handlin and John Clive. Cambridge: Belknap, 1969. Print.

Morgan, Edmund S. *American Slavery, American Freedom.* New York: Norton, 1975. Print.

Morison, Samuel Eliot. *The European Discovery of America: The Northern Voyages, AD 500–1600.* Vol. 1. New York: Oxford UP, 1971. Print.

Morton, Richard L. "The Reverend Hugh Jones: Lord Baltimore's Mathematician." *William and Mary Quarterly* 3rd ser. 7.1 (1950): 107–15. Print.

Nabokov, Peter, ed. *Native American Testimony: A Chronicle of Indian-White Relations from Prophecy to the Present, 1492–1992.* New York: Penguin, 1992. Print.

"Nathaniel Ward, 1578–1652." *Duhaime.org.* Lloyd Duhaime, 2 June 2009. Web. 30 May 2012.

"New England Confederation." *Columbia Electronic Encyclopedia,* 6th ed. 11 Nov. 2011: n.pag. *Academic Search Complete.* Web. 12 Dec. 2011.

"New France circa 1740." *The Atlas of Canada.* Natural Resources Canada, 14 Mar. 2003. Web. 1 June 2012.

The New Georgia Encyclopedia. Georgia Humanities Council and the University of Georgia Press, 2012. Web. 25 May 2012.

New Haven Colony Historical Society. *Papers of the New Haven Colony Historical Society.* New York: Oxford UP, 1865. Print.

Norton, Mary Beth. *In the Devil's Snare: The Salem Witchcraft Crisis of 1692.* New York: Vintage, 2003. Print.

Oberg, Michael Leroy. *Dominion and Civility: English Imperialism and Native America, 1585–1685.* Ithaca: Cornell UP, 1999. Print.

"October Meeting, 1863." *Proceedings of the Massachusetts Historical Society* 7 (1863–64): 152–68. Print.

Olson, Alison. "The Zenger Case Revisited: Satire, Sedition and Political Debate in Eighteenth Century America." *Early American Literature* 35.3 (2000): 223–45. Print.

Olson, Julius E., and Edward G. Bourne, eds. "Journal of the First Voyage of Columbus." *The Northmen, Columbus, and Cabot, 985–1503.* New York: Scribner's, 1906. 89–258. Print.

"Origins and History of the Jury." *VermontJudiciary.org.*

VermontJudiciary.org, n.d. Web. 29 May 2012.

"Our History." *Moravian Church of North America.* Moravian Church of North America, 2012. Web. 16 May 2012.

Parkman, Francis. *A Half Century of Conflict.* 1894. New York: AMS, 1969. Print.

---. *The Jesuits in North America in the Seventeenth Century.* 1867. Charleston: Bibliobazaar, 2011. Print.

Parrington, Vernon Louis. "Stirrings of Liberalism: John Wise, Village Democrat." *Main Currents in American Thought: The Colonial Mind, 1620–1800.* Vol. 1. 1927. Norman: U of Oklahoma P, 1987. Print.

Parrish, Susan Scott. *American Curiosity: Cultures of Natural History in the British Atlantic World.* Chapel Hill: U of North Carolina P, 2006. Print.

Payne, Samuel B., Jr. "The Iroquois League, the Articles of Confederation, and the Constitution." *The William and Mary Quarterly* 53.3 (1996): 605–20. Print.

Penn, William. "England's Present Interest Considered, with Honour to the Prince, and Safety to the People (1675)." *Online Library of Liberty.* Online Library of Liberty, 2012. Web. 7 June 2012.

Pennington, Kenneth. *Popes, Canonists, and Texts 1150–1550.* Aldershot: Variorum, 1993. Print.

Peterson, Mark A. "*The Selling of Joseph*: Bostonians, Antislavery, and the Protestant International, 1689–1733." *Massachusetts Historical Review* 4 (2002): 1–22. Print.

Philbrick, Nathaniel. *Mayflower: A Story of Courage, Community, and War.* New York: Penguin, 2006. Print.

"The Pilgrims." *History.com.* A&E Television Networks, 1996–2012. Web. 29 May 2012.

"Pilgrims and Puritans: Background." *The Capitol Project.* University of Virginia, n.d. Web. 29 May 2012.

"Pilgrim Patents: The 1621 Second Peirce Patent and the 1630 Bradford Patent." *Pilgrim Hall Museum.* Pilgrim Hall Museum, 18 May 2005. Web. 4 June 2012.

Pinckney, Eliza Lucas. *The Letterbook of Eliza Lucas Pinckney.* Ed. Elise Pinckney and Marvin R. Zahniser. Columbia: U of South Carolina P, 1997. Print.

Plane, Ann Marie. "Putting a Face on Colonization: Factionalism and Gender Politics in the Life History of Awashunkes, the 'Squaw Sachem' of Saconet." *Northeastern Indian Lives, 1632–1816.* Ed. Robert Steven Grumet. Amherst: U of Massachusetts P, 1996. 140–165. Print.

Pole, J. R. *Political Representation in England and the Origins of the American Republic*. London: Macmillan, 1966. Print.

Ponce, Pedro. "The Pueblo Revolt of 1680." *Humanities* 23.6 (2002): 20–24. Print.

Pratt, Richard H. "The Advantages of Mingling Indians with Whites." *National Conference on Social Welfare Proceedings (1874–1982): Official Proceedings of the Annual Meeting, 1892*. 46–59. Graduate Library University of Michigan Preservation Office, 24 Sept. 2002. Web. 14 Aug. 2012.

Proctor-Smith, George. *Religion and Trade in New Netherland: Dutch Origins and American Development*. Ithaca: Cornell UP, 2010. Print.

"Pufendorf's Moral and Political Philosophy." *Stanford Encyclopedia of Philosophy*. Stanford Department of Philosophy, 2010. Web. 15 Apr. 2012.

Pulsipher, Jenny Hale. *Subjects unto the Same King: Indians, English, and the Contest for Authority in Colonial New England*. Philadelphia: U of Pennsylvania P, 2005. Print.

"Puritanism." *History.com*. The History Channel. 2012. Web. 18 May 2012.

Putnam, William Lowell. *John Peter Zenger and the Fundamental Freedom*. Jefferson: McFarland, 1997. Print.

Randolph, Edward. "An Answer to Several Heads of Enquiry Concerning the Present State of New-England." *Hutchinson Papers*. Vol. 2. Albany: Prince Society, 1865. 210–51. Print.

Ranlet, Philip. "Another Look at the Causes of King Philip's War." *New England Quarterly* 61.1 (1988): 79–100. Print.

---. "Joseph Dudley." *American National Biography* (2010): 1. *Biography Reference Center*. Web. 30 May 2012.

Read, David. *New World, Known World: Shaping Knowledge in Early Anglo-American Writing*. Columbia: U of Missouri P, 2005. Print.

Read, David. "Silent Partners: Historical Representation in William Bradford's *Of Plymouth Plantation*." *Early America* 33.3 (1998): 291–314. Print.

Reeds, Karen. "Don't Eat, Don't Touch: Roanoke Colonists, Natural Knowledge, and Dangerous Plants of North America" *European Visions: American Voices*. Trustees of the British Museum, n.d. Web. 10 Apr. 2012.

Reiss, Oscar. *Blacks in Colonial America*. Jefferson: McFarland, 1997. Print.

Rice, Gene. "The Alleged Curse on Ham." *American Bible Society Bible Resource Center*. American Bible Society, 2011. Web. 7 June 2012.

Richter, Daniel K. *The Ordeal of the Longhouse: The Peoples of the Iroquois League in the Era of European Colonization*. Chapel Hill: U of North Carolina P, 1992. Print.

Richter, Daniel K., and James H. Merrell. *Beyond the Covenant Chain: The Iroquois and Their Neighbors in Indian North America, 1600–1800*. Rev. ed. University Park: Pennsylvania State UP, 2003. Print.

Riley, Carroll. *The Kachina and the Cross: Indians and Spaniards in the Southwest*. Salt Lake City: U of Utah P, 1999. Print.

Roberts, David. *The Pueblo Revolt: The Secret Rebellion that Drove the Spaniards out of the Southwest*. New York: Simon, 2004. Print.

"Roger Williams." *Freedom: A History of Us*. PBS, 2002. Web. 15 May 2012.

"Roger Williams." *Roger Williams National Memorial*. National Park Service, 2012. Web. 15 May 2012.

Round, Philip H. *By Nature and by Custom Cursed: Transatlantic Civil Discourse and New England Cultural Production, 1620–1660*. Hanover: UP of New England, 1999. Print.

Rountree, Helen C. *Pocahontas's People: The Powhatan Indians of Virginia through Four Centuries*. Norman: U of Oklahoma P, 1996. Print.

Royster, Paul, ed. "The Negro Christianized. An Essay to Excite and Assist that Good Work, the Instruction of Negro-Servants in Christianity (1706)." *Libraries at University of Nebraska–Lincoln*. University of Nebraska Lincoln, n.d. Web. 7 June 2012.

Rozwenc, Edwin C. "Captain John Smith's Image of America." *William & Mary Quarterly* 3rd ser. 16.1 (1959): 27–36. Print.

Rutherford, Livingston. *John Peter Zenger: His Press, His Trial*. New York: Chelsea, 1981. Print.

Saint, Chandler B., and George A. Krimsky. *Making Freedom: The Extraordinary Life of Venture Smith*. Middletown: Wesleyan UP, 2009. Print.

Salem Witch Trials: The World beyond the Hysteria. Discovery Education, 2012. Web. 1 Jan. 2012.

Salisbury, Neal. "Introduction: Mary Rowlandson and Her Removes." *The Sovereignty and Goodness of God: With Related Documents*. Ed. Neal Salisbury. Boston: Bedford, 1997. Print.

Sando, Joe, and Herman Agoyo. *Po'pay: Leader of the First American Revolution*. Santa Fe, NM: Clear Light, 2004.

Sandoz, Ellis, ed. Political Sermons of the American Founding Era, 1730–1805. Indianapolis, IN: Liberty Fund 1998. Print.

"The Santa Maria." Columbus Santa Maria, Inc., 2012. Web. 21 Mar. 2012.

Saum, Lewis O. The Fur Trader and the Indian. Seattle: U of Washington P, 1965. Print.

Schaaf, Gregory, and Chief Jake Swamp. The US Constitution and the Great Law of Peace: A Comparison of Two Founding Documents. Santa Fe: CIAC P, 2004. Print.

Schaaf, Gregory. "From the Great Law of Peace to the Constitution of the United States: A Revision of America's Democratic Roots." American Indian Law Review 14.2 (1988/89): 323–31. Print.

Schmidt, Gary D. William Bradford: Plymouth's Faithful Pilgrim. Grand Rapids: Eerdmans, 1999. Print.

Schwarz, Philip J. Slave Laws in Virginia. Athens: U of Georgia P, 1996. Print.

Sewall, Samuel. The Diary of Samuel Sewall, 1674–1729. Ed. M. Halsey Thomas. Vol. 2. New York: Farrar, 1973. Print.

---. The Selling of Joseph: A Memorial. Ed. Sidney Kaplan. Amherst: U of Massachusetts P, 1969. Print.

Shea, Daniel B. "'Our Professed Old Adversary': Thomas Morton and the Naming of New England." Early American Literature 23.1 (1988): 52–69. Print.

Shirley, John W. Thomas Harriot: A Biography. Oxford: Clarendon, 1983. Print.

Shorto, Russell. The Island at the Center of the World: The Epic Story of Dutch Manhattan and the Forgotten Colony That Shaped America. New York: Vintage, 2004. Print.

Silverberg, Robert. The Pueblo Revolt. New York: Weybright, 1970. Print.

Silverman, Kenneth. The Life and Times of Cotton Mather. New York: Welcome Rain, 2001. Print.

"Slavery and Indentured Servants." Law Library of Congress. Library of Congress, n.d. Web. 14 June 2012.

"Slaves in New England." Medford Historical Society. Medford Historical Society, n.d. Web. 7 June 2012.

Slotkin, Richard, and James K. Folsom, eds. So Dreadfull a Judgment: Puritan Responses to King Philip's War, 1676–1677. Middletown, CT: Wesleyan UP, 1978. Print.

Smith, Abbot Emerson. Colonists in Bondage: White Servitude and Convict Labor in America, 1607–1776. Chapel Hill: U of North Carolina P, 1947. Print.

Smith, Bradford. Bradford of Plymouth. Philadelphia: Lippincott, 1951. Print.

Smith, John. The Complete Works of Captain John Smith (1580–1631). Ed. Philip L. Barbour. 3 vols. Chapel Hill: U of North Carolina P, 1986. Print.

---. Writings with Other Narratives of Roanoke, Jamestown, and the First English Settlement of America. Ed. James P. P. Horn. New York: Lib. of America, 2007. Print.

Smith, Mark M. Stono: Documenting and Interpreting a Southern Slave Revolt. Columbia: U of South Carolina P, 2005. Print.

Smith, Venture. A Narrative of the Life and Adventures of Venture, a Native of Africa, but Resident above Sixty Years in the United States of America, Related by Himself. 1798. Ed. Selden, Henry M. 1896. Documenting the American South. U of North Carolina at Chapel Hill, 2004. Web. 25 July 2012.

Smolinski, Reiner, ed. "Sinners in the Hands of an Angry God" Electronic Texts in American Studies. Digital Commons @ University of Nebraska, 1998. Web 30 Apr. 2012.

Soderlund, Jean R., ed. William Penn and the Founding of Pennsylvania: A Documentary History. Philadelphia: U of Pennsylvania P, 1983. Print.

St. Jean, Wendy B. "Inventing Guardianship: The Mohegan Indians and Their 'Protectors.'" New England Quarterly 72.3 (1999): 362–87. Print.

Starna, William A. "The Diplomatic Career of Canasatego." Friends and Enemies in Penn's Woods: Indians, Colonists, and the Racial Construction of Pennsylvania. Ed. William A. Pencak and Daniel K. Richter. University Park: Pennsylvania State UP, 2004. 144–66. Print.

Stearns, Raymond Phineas. Science in the British Colonies of America. Urbana: U of Illinois P, 1970. Print.

Steele, Ian K. "Origins of Boston's Revolutionary Declaration of 18 April 1689." New England Quarterly 62.1 (1989): 75–81. Print.

Stein, Stephen J, ed. Jonathan Edwards's Writings: Text, Context, Interpretation. Bloomington: Indiana UP, 1996. Print.

Stern, Julia. "To Relish and to Spew Disgust as Cultural Critique in 'The Journal of Madam Knight.'" Legacy: A Journey of American Women Writers 14 (1997): 1–12. Print.

Stewart, James Brewer, ed. Venture Smith and the Business of Slavery and Freedom. Amherst: U of Massachusetts P, 2010. Print.

Stick, David. *Roanoke Island: The Beginnings of English America*. Chapel Hill: U of North Carolina P, 1983. Print.

Stiles, T. J., ed. *In Their Own Words: The Colonizers—Early European Settlers and the Shaping of North America*. New York: Perigee, 1998. Print.

Stout, Harry S. *The Divine Dramatist: George White-field and the Rise of Modern Evangelicalism*. Ed. Mark A. Noll and Nathan O. Hatch. Grand Rapids: Eerdmans, 1991. Print.

Strachey, William. "A True Reportory." *Virtual Jamestown*. Virginia Center for Digital History, University of Virginia, 2000. Web. 2 June 2012.

Sullivan, Francis. *Indian Freedom: The Cause of Barto-lome de Las Casas, 1484–1566; A Reader*. Lanham: Rowman, 1995. Print.

Taillemite, Etienne. «Barrin de la Galissonière, Roland-Michel, Marquis de La Galissonière.» *Dictionary of Canadian Biography Online*. University of Toronto/Université Laval, n.d. Web. 31 May 2012.

Taylor, Larissa Juliet, and Frank N. Magill, eds. "William Penn." *Great Lives from History: The Seventeenth Century, 1601–1700*. Vol. 2. Pasadena: Salem. 2006. Print.

Taylor-True, Victoria. "Tribal Names." *Erie Moundbuild-ers*. Erie Indian Moundbuilders Tribal Nation, 2006. Web. 17 May 2012.

Thomas, Hugh. *Rivers of Gold: The Rise of the Spanish Empire from Columbus to Magellan*. New York: Random, 2003. Print.

---. *The Slave Trade: The Story of the Atlantic Slave Trade, 1440–1870*. New York: Simon, 1997. Print.

Thompson, Augustus C. *Moravian Missions: Twelve Lectures*. New York: Scribner's, 1882. Print.

Towner, Lawrence W. "'A Fondness for Freedom': Servant Protest in Puritan Society." *William and Mary Quarterly* 3rd ser. 19.2 (1962): 201–19. Print.

---. "The Sewall-Saffin Dialogue on Slavery." *William and Mary Quarterly* 3rd ser. 21.1 (1964): 40–52. Print.

"Transcription of 1740 Slave Code." *Teaching American History in South Carolina*. Teaching American History in South Carolina Project, 2009. Web. 7 May 2012

Trent, William P., and Benjamin W. Wells, eds. "John Wise." *Colonial Prose and Poetry*. New York: Crowell, 1903. Print.

---. "John Josselyn." *Colonial Prose and Poetry: The Beginnings of Americanism, 1650–1710*. New York: Crowell, 1901. Print.

Trigger, Bruce G. *Natives and Newcomers: Canada's "Heroic Age" Reconsidered*. Kingston: McGill-Queen's UP, 1985. Print.

---. *The Huron: Farmers of the North*. New York: Harcourt, 1990. Print.

Turner, Lorenzo Dow. "The Anti-Slavery Movement Prior to the Abolition of the African Slave-Trade (1641–1808)." *Journal of Negro History* 14.4 (1929): 373–402. Print.

Tyer, Charlie B. and Richard D. Young. "The South Carolina Legislature." *The South Carolina Governance Project*. Center for Governmental Services, Institute for Public Service and Policy Research, University of South Carolina. n.d. Web. 17 May 2012

van der Donck, Adriaen. *A Description of New Netherland*. Lincoln: U of Nebraska P, 2008. Print.

Vaughan, Alden T. "Pequots and Puritans: The Causes of the War of 1637." *William and Mary Quarterly* 3rd ser. 21.2 (1964): 256–69. Print.

"The Vision of William Penn." *ExplorePAhistory.com*. WITF, 2011. Web. 30 May 2012.

Von Frank, Albert J. "John Saffin: Slavery and Racism in Colonial Massachusetts." *Early American Literature* 29.3 (1994): 254–72. Print.

Wakelyn, Jon L., ed. *America's Founding Charters: Primary Documents of Colonial and Revolutionary Era Governance*. Vol. 1. Westport, CT: Greenwood, 2006. Print.

Waldman, Carl. *Atlas of the North American Indian*. 3rd ed. New York: Facts on File, 2009. Print.

Walton, R. "Pilgrim History". *RichmondAncestry.org*. RichmondAncestry.org, n.d. Web. 29 May 2012.

Ward & Trent, et al. "The Puritan Divines, 1620–1720." *The Cambridge History of English and American Literature in 18 Volumes*. Bartleby.com, 2000. Web. 29 May 2012.

Weber, David, et al. *What Caused the Pueblo Revolt of 1680?* Boston: Bedford/St Martin's, 1999. Print.

Weir, Robert M. *Colonial South Carolina: A History*. Millwood: KTO, 1983. Print.

Wheeler, Robert C. *A Toast to the Fur Trade: A Picture Essay on its Material Culture*. St. Paul: Wheeler Productions, 1985. Print.

White, J. T., ed. The National Cyclopedia of American Biography, Vol. 1. New York: White, 1892–1984. Print.

"William Bradford." *MayflowerHistory.com*. MayflowerHistory.com, 1994–2012. Web. 29 May 2012.

Willison, George F. *Saints and Strangers*. New York: Reynal, 1983. Print.

Winship, George Parker, ed. and trans. *The Journey of Coronado, 1540–42: From the City of Mexico to the Grand Canyon of the Colorado and the Buffalo Plains of Texas, Kansas and Nebraska*. New York: Barnes, 1904. Print.

Winslow, Ola Elizabeth. *Samuel Sewall of Boston*. New York: Macmillan, 1964. Print.

Winslow, William Copley. *Governor Edward Winslow: His Part and Place in Plymouth Colony*. New York, 1896. Print.

Wolf, Edward C. "Music in Old Zion, Philadelphia, 1750–1850." *Musical Quarterly*. 58.4 (1972): 622–52. Print.

Wood, Andrew. *Summary of John Winthrop's "Model of Christian Charity."* Communications Department, San Jose State University, n.d. Web. 25 May 2012.

Wood, Betty. *Slavery in Colonial America, 1619–1776*. Lanham: Rowman, 2005. Print.

Wood, Peter H. Black *Majority: Negroes in Colonial South Carolina from 1670 through the Stono Rebellion*. New York: Norton, 1974. Print.

Young, Alexander, ed. *Chronicles of the Pilgrim Fathers of the Colony of Plymouth from 1602–1625*. New York: Da Capo, 1971. Print.

INDEX